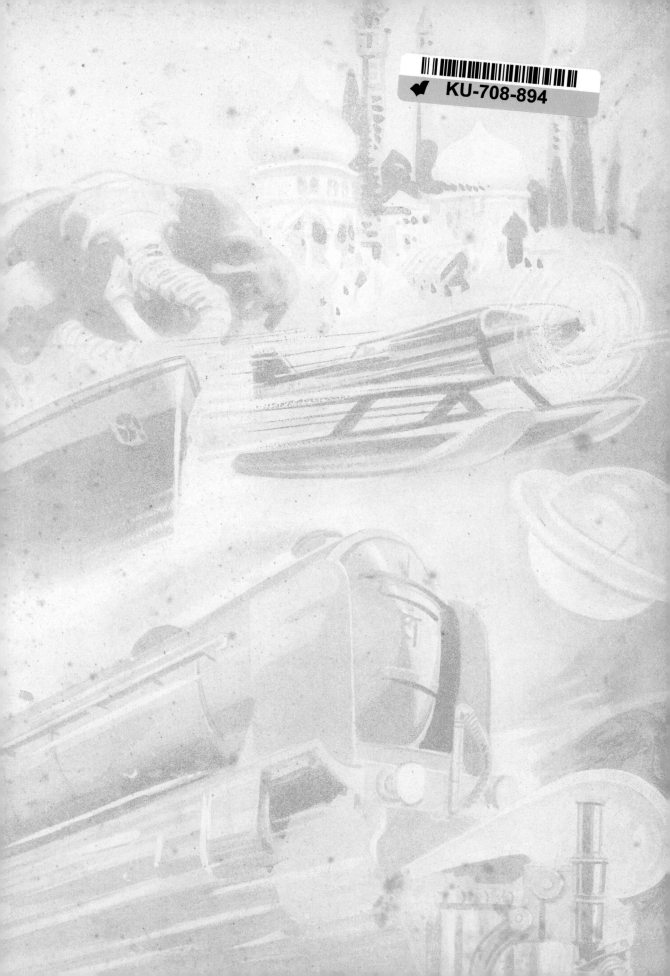

THE WONDERLAND OF KNOWLEDGE

Here are a number of characters celebrated in literature. They are Dick Turpin, Robin Hood, Aladdin, Don Quixote, Sancho Panza, Long John Silver, D'Artagnan, the Pied Piper, Shylock, Rip Van Winkle, King Arthur, a Viking, Cinderella, Robinson Crusoe, Mary Queen of Scots, Gulliver, Little Lord Fauntleroy, Oliver Twist, Ali Baba, Peter Pan, a Goblin, Mr. Pickwick, Rob Roy, Uncle Tom, the Mad Hatter and Alice.

THE WONDERLAND OF KNOWLEDGE

AN
UP·TO·DATE
ILLUSTRATED
ENCYCLOPAEDIA

Edited by
ERNEST OGAN

VOLUME II

ODHAMS PRESS LIMITED, LONG ACRE, LONDON.

Copyright in all countries
subscribing to the Berne Convention.

Printed and Bound in Great Britain by the
Greycaine Book Manufacturing Co., Ltd., Watford, Herts.

CONTENTS OF VOLUME II

THE STORY OF THE WEATHER

THE ROMANCE OF EXPLORATION

THE STORY OF THE NATIONS

GREAT NAMES IN ENGLISH LITERATURE

CONTENTS OF VOLUME II

CONTENTS OF VOLUME II

GREAT NAMES IN GREEK LITERATURE

COLOUR PLATES IN THIS VOLUME
(The page number is that which the plate faces)

SPECIAL COLOUR SUPPLEMENTS

KEY TO PRONUNCIATION

To help readers to pronounce difficult technical words and proper names appearing in "The Wonderland of Knowledge," the following phonetic system, or scheme of pronunciation, is adopted. It is framed on simple but adequate lines, and no attempt has been made to cover the complicated method required to give the more delicate distinctions of the science of vocal sounds.

ā as in māte
å as in senåte
â as in hâir
ă as in hăt
ä as in fäther
ch as in chest
ē as in ēve
ė as in rėlate
ě as in běnd
ē as in hēr
g as in go
ī as in bīte
ĭ as in ĭnn
j as in join
K the guttural sound of ch, as in the German *ach*, or the Scottish *loch*

N indicates the French nasal sound, as in *bon*
ō as in bōne
ŏ as in Christŏpher
ô as in lôrd
ŏ as in hŏt
oi as in toil
o͞o as in so͞on
o͝o as in bo͝ok
ou as in shout
s as in so
sh as in ship
th as in thumb
th as in thus
ū as in cūre
û as in fûr
ŭ as in bŭt

ü a sound formed by pronouncing ē with the lips in the position for oo, as in the German *über* and the French *une*
z as in maze
zh as in azure
' an indication that a vowel sound is elided or cut off, as in apple (ăp″l)
An accent (′) follows a syllable receiving stress, and a heavy accent (′) the principal syllable when more than one is stressed

How the WEATHER Makes HISTORY

We Have Learned the Way to Outwit the Climate, Although We Should Never Have Become Civilized Without Its Whims

WHY are some people black and others white? Why do some live mainly on fish, others on fruit, and others on flesh and cereals? Why do some build towering cities while others are satisfied with scattered huts? There are a good many different answers to all these questions, but the general idea is that the weather is a ruling factor, either now or in past ages. Or perhaps it would be better to say because of the climate, for "climate" means all the changes of weather a given place may have.

We are all used to having our own affairs affected by the weather. Often rain has upset our plans for a picnic. Some of us may have broken a bone on an icy road—and we have all heard of houses struck by lightning or of men lost in a blizzard. Listen to people talking, and you will learn how much they think about the weather.

But it is not only your plans and mine that are disturbed in this way. The weather has upset the lives of whole nations. It has altered the map; it has made history. And without the changes it has brought about, you and I would not be living where we live to-day.

Nor should we look as we look or act as we act. For it has even given us our colour! In lands where the heat is intense and the sun beats mercilessly down twelve months in the year, even the fairest skins grow tanned. And after long centuries the whole race turns dark. It takes on a lasting coat of tan that protects it against sunburn. So natives of regions that lie along the Equator are dusky brown or black, while the

Photo by Tourist Information Office, The Hague

These happy little Dutch girls are enjoying the sea-breezes on the dunes of Walcharen Island. It is the wind which forms these miniature hills or mounds of sand, and if grass or some other vegetation does not hold them fast, the wind will gradually move them on again, possibly some nine or ten feet every year.

races that live farther north have skins that are fairer.

Their features are different, too; for example, they have large noses to warm the cold air which they breathe, before it reaches

Nature has been **very** kind to this happy-go-lucky mother of the tropics. Can you imagine her living, just as she is, in London or New York?

their lungs. Negroes have short snubby noses, because they breathe warm air.

Often, too, it was the weather that sent their forefathers into the land in the first place. For ever since man has been on the earth he has been driven about by dry weather or flood or frost. Whatever disturbed his supply of food has sent him wandering. Sometimes a whole tribe, roused by hunger or thirst, have snatched up their arms and gone forth to murder and rob, and in this way a war has been caused by the weather. And sometimes the hungering peoples have settled peaceably in new lands or with other nations. The races have

To her children of the temperate zone Nature is a firm but kindly parent—the best kind to possess. So there men lead busy, interesting, comfortable lives, and civilization flourishes. Food is not too easy to obtain—and not too difficult.

mingled together and new races have been the result—and all on account of the weather.

We do not need to look far to see what the weather can do to civilizations. In the jungles of Central America are the ruins of Maya cities more than two thousand years old; and buried in the sands of the Gobi Desert are the ruins of other dead cities that once had a throbbing life. Often it was the weather that killed them. In many cases, at least, it was some great and lasting change in rainfall or temperature that drove the people away from their homes and changed their busy towns into crumbling, silent ruins, like bleaching skeletons.

When the sun-loving Spaniards and Portuguese discovered the

To her Eskimo children Nature is a very stern mother indeed. This Eskimo woman will have to sit in the cold for hours, waiting to catch a meal of fish through a hole in the ice.

New World they were able to settle in the tropical regions and thrive there, because they found a climate more or less like their own at home. The English, who were accustomed to cooler air and shorter summers, were able to weather the winters of New England.

It was the skilful fingers of the wind that carved these beautiful curves and masses. But few people ever see them, for here in Death Valley, California, U.S.A., the climate is as hot and dry as any in the world. So the place is a desert, with little or no rain and with a heat that day after day may climb to 120° F.

Let us jump off a little way into space and look at the earth through a telescope. We shall see at once that some parts of the earth are swarming with people, while other regions have not a single inhabitant; and it will be easy to guess that the places where the people live are those that have the climate that is best for man. But, strangely enough, they will not always be the places where living is easiest—or where the climate is most comfortable.

Children of the Frozen Wastes

Mother Nature seems to have arranged that we should thrive best when we have to work for a living. So climate has a great deal to do with character. Admittedly, we need a certain amount of comfort. Neither men nor animals can live long in the midst of the blizzards that rage at the North and South Poles. And even outside the Arctic Circle the Eskimo has quite a task to keep himself alive.

Wrapped in heavy furs, he takes his spear and crawls out of his hut of snow to hunt for his food. He goes down to the frozen shore, climbs into his canoe, and paddles about all day among the ice floes looking for fish or seal. Fish, blubber—huge masses of fat, mostly from whales—and the flesh of a few Arctic animals are his only food. It is easy to see that he will have little time or inclination to build himself railways and factories, libraries, theatres, and schools.

In deserts, too, life may make men self-reliant, but does not give them a chance to develop a high level of culture. Even though the shifting soil may be rich, there is so little moisture that scarcely anything will grow. Only two animals can cross a wide desert— man and the camel. The camel is built by Nature to do so, and man has learned how; but the hardy Bedouin, whose wild, roving life takes him from watercourse to watercourse, is not likely to turn his thoughts to fine music, science or architecture as he rides on the back of his camel.

Pampered Darlings of Mother Earth

Neither can the man for whom Nature does too much. In the hot forests along the Amazon are tribes who do not need to till the soil to get their food. They are the pampered darlings of our great Mother Earth. The land around them is rich, and there is plenty of rain and warmth to make things grow all the year round. They do not need warm clothing, or any shelter other than the thick foliage above their heads. As one writer humorously puts it, "the natives lie flat on their backs and the bananas drop into their mouths." So, like

One glance at these three homes will tell you in what section of the globe each one is to be found. The Eskimo makes his hut out of ice and snow because it is the only building material he has—and, luckily for him, it is excellent for keeping out the cold. But we know what would happen to such a house when spring came along if it were built in Southern Canada. There, fortunately, the people have plenty of wood and stone with which to build houses, and because they are visited by a temperate sun, they can fill their walls with windows and doors, and live on spacious verandas. The Zulus in Africa find it much too hot for very heavy labour. So they put up a hasty shelter against sun and rain, and build it of grass or leaves, or whatever comes to hand. They do not intend to hand it down to their children.

all spoiled children, they cannot do anything for themselves. Since they do not need to work or plan for a living, they never have learned how to work or plan for anything else. Their civilization is no higher than that of the Eskimo. They are still savages because of their climate.

So it is in the temperate zones, between the ice-bound poles and the blazing tropics, that we find men at their best. There the earth will grow all the varied foods we need to make us strong, but we must work to raise them. For there is a season when plants cease to grow; so we must spend the summer storing up food for the rest of

the year. And we must build warm houses to shelter ourselves against the winter's cold. In other words, man must constantly use his wits to keep himself comfortable—and it is only by using his wits that he can develop them and so become capable of building up a great civilization.

The weather may even have helped in the origin of man himself. Before the Great Ice Age, when ice sheets spread across most of England, the record of the rocks tells us that there were hardly any mountains, and for millions of years the weather was far more genial than it is now. The seasons came and went without disturbance, light breezes blew, and

showers were frequent. Storms were infrequent, and there was hardly any snow or ice. Long ago the lords of the earth were gigantic cold-blooded reptiles, and the mammals—the ancestors of the dog, horse and man—were few and weak.

Then the earth's surface was forced into great folds which formed ridges of mighty

SENTINELS OF SNOW AND ICE THAT GUARD THE WAY TO THE NORTH POLE

This is a scene from an Arctic land, and it shows the kind of scenery to be found there all the year round. There are similar scenes everywhere near the Poles. The winds that blow over the ice make our weather colder; they bring us the clear, bracing days that act as a tonic. And in other ways those ice-fields affect the lives of civilized men. For from time to time, with thunderous roar, a giant mass will break away and, as an iceberg, go sailing down into warmer waters, perhaps to crash against some gallant ship and sink it.

mountains, and depths into which the oceans receded. The free movement of the water over the earth was hindered, and the polar regions grew colder, much as a radiator grows colder when the pipe leading to it is partly blocked. Snow and ice formed, and the weather grew more stormy. And lightning began to play all about the earth's body, till now there are nearly two thousand thunderstorms flashing somewhere at any moment in the day.

How Changes in the Weather Have Prevented Man from Becoming Lazy

It was not until things became disturbed that man appeared. One wonders if he could have grown into the talented animal he is without this exciting variety in the state of the atmosphere. He might have been much like the natives of the tropics about whom we have just read—too lazy to do anything but eat and sleep. As it is, he is always busy shutting out the cold or getting in his food or providing clothes for his back. Day by day he attends to his own requirements and those dependent on him, playing his particular part in the life going on around him. And when he has time enough left over, he will fill it with diverting sports and arts, in order to use up the energy he is now accustomed to spending.

So he will tell stories and paint pictures and play sweet music; he will invent hard games and delve into all branches of knowledge; he will swim the seas and climb the mountains and fly to the ends of the earth. And all this will be, to a great extent, due to the influence of the weather.

(CONTINUED ON PAGE 537)

Photo by Rischgitz

Cortes is riding victorious over the battlefield of Otumba, where his Spanish soldiers have finally conquered the brave Aztecs, the remarkable Indian people who had ruled Mexico for more than three hundred years.

The MAN Who MASTERED MEXICO

Even if You Hate and Despise Him for His Cruelty, You Must Admire Hernando Cortes for His Courage and Resource

IN THIS century of enlightenment, when, with the passing of each day, we become more and more convinced of the soundness underlying the ideal of Freedom, many of the stories of the discoveries of new lands and the conquests of their people are certain to strike us as being tales of needless cruelty and oppression. We must remember, however, to judge the old explorers not by the methods they adopted, but by the great work they did in putting new places on the map and bringing new treasures to the storehouse of knowledge. Here we tell the story of Hernando Cortes (kôr'tĕz), the man who mastered Mexico.

Cortes was born in Spain in 1485, about seven years before the discovery of the New World, where he was destined to meet with much adventure. He was only nineteen when he set out to make his fortune there. At San Domingo, and later in Cuba, he became rich and had his share of adventure among the Indians. But it was not until fifteen years later (in 1518), that he was sent on the great expedition that was to make him famous—the exploration and conquest of the recently discovered land of Mexico.

Cortes set out on his trip with ten ships, some six hundred men, eighteen horses and a few cannon. The horses were as new and strange as the cannon in the land to which he was going. The Indians were astonished and terrified at the sight of both; and as for the men who rode on the horses and fired the deadly cannon, the Indians could only think they must be some new kind of gods. And they were going to learn a great deal about such gods in the next few months.

Cortes Ordered to Return

Cortes landed at the Tabasco River, a little south of the peninsula we now call Yucatan. In the meantime, the governor of Cuba, from whom Cortes had received his instructions, regretted his decision and ordered the return of the expedition. But

Cortes was not the man to relinquish such a glorious opportunity, and confident of the loyalty of his soldiers, he turned a deaf ear to the governor's command. With his strange and mighty weapons he easily overcame the large tribes of natives and made them promise to be good Spanish subjects. Then he sailed on up the coast.

Determined to Conquer

Whenever Cortes found it possible to make friends with the natives and secure their help, he did so. But when it was necessary to shoot them down, or scare them into helping him, he did not scruple to do that. He had come to conquer the wonderful new country and he meant to do so at all costs.

He made a second landing where Vera Cruz now stands, and laid the foundations of that town. The Indians he discovered in this region were not altogether uncivilized, for they were very different from the tribes that inhabited the interior of North America. They lived in villages, and even in large cities. They planted gardens and orchards, wove cloth out of cotton, and built houses and great temples out of stone. And though these Indians had been conquered some time before by the fierce Aztecs, and were now ruled by them, they were still a strong and warlike race.

From them Cortes came to hear of the great Aztec chief Montezuma (mŏn'tē-zōō'-mȧ), who lived amid his fabulous riches in the island city of Tenochtitlan (Mexico), 160 miles away. In fact, Montezuma sent him some very rich gifts in the hope that he would go away and leave the country in

Here are some descendants of the people whom Cortes so cruelly conquered. They had progressed in the arts and in government far beyond the tribes of North America. They could write, and weave cotton and build in stone.

peace. But that was the wrong way in which to persuade Cortes to depart. It only excited a desire in him to see Montezuma and his wonderful city, and to obtain the rest of the riches.

With a few hundred of his own men and as many Indians as he could persuade or force to accompany him, he now set out for the city of the great Aztec chief. On the way he craftily persuaded the tribes he met to rebel against their Aztec rulers and to join with the forces of Spain. Finally he came to the mountain pass from which he could look down on the fertile valley in which nestled the beautiful city he was seeking. Some days later, clad in armour and plumed helmet, and accompanied by a few chosen officers, he rode ahead of his men across the long, broad causeway that led through the lake to Tenochtitlan. All around him thronged the wondering Aztecs, curious to see the bearded visitors. What a sight it must have been to look upon the first men from the other side of the world!

But the Aztecs knew nothing of the other side of the world, or of other men like these. They still took them, not for men, but for gods come down from heaven. So Montezuma received them with due honour at his great palace and loaded them with rich presents. But Cortes was determined to possess himself of the wealth of Montezuma, and when the head of one of the Spanish soldiers was brought to the Aztec chief, Cortes conceived the bold idea of holding Montezuma responsible for the outrage and taking him captive. He even brought him in irons to witness the burning alive of the actual culprit before the imperial palace.

At length Montezuma was induced to swear allegiance to Cortes and to the king of Spain, and to supply the Spaniards with all the rich gifts they demanded.

Cortes now received the news that a new general had been sent over from Cuba to take command. Leaving a few soldiers to guard Montezuma, he hurried back to Vera Cruz. By judiciously bribing them, he persuaded the new general's troops to desert their leader, captured the general himself and all his supplies, and took him back to Tenochtitlan. There Cortes found that the Aztecs had risen against the garrison he had left in charge and were holding it in siege. He managed to rejoin the garrison, and several days of severe fighting followed. Montezuma was wounded and soon after died. But Cortes, realizing that he was greatly outnumbered by the enraged natives, decided that he must escape if he was to avoid death, and so he planned to steal out with his men by night.

Photo by J. Ruiz Vernacci

CORTES DECIDES UPON A BOLD ACTION

Here the fearless Hernando Cortes is shown giving an order which he hopes will result in his becoming governor of Mexico. He has all along been under the command of Velasquez, governor of Cuba, but has come to conquer Mexico against Velasquez's orders, though he sailed in the governor's ships. Now that he sees the country within his grasp, he has decided on a bold move. He will send the best ship back to Spain loaded with gifts given him by Montezuma, the Aztec king. It will carry to the Spanish ruler news of Cortes's great deeds and a request for his appointment as governor of Mexico. And Velasquez's other ships he will burn. That will make him for ever independent of the governor of Cuba. So he gives the order to burn the ships— and the artist has shown him at the moment of that daring command. His own followers at once elected him as their commander-in-chief.

It is not easy to steal away from Indians, however. A slight noise told them what was happening, and a fierce battle ensued on the causeway. It is known in Spanish history as the "Dreadful Night." Less than half the Spaniards managed to get away, and many of these were wounded before they escaped. The Aztecs pursued them—these people they had regarded as gods such a little while before. But the Spaniards had far greater experience of fighting a pitched battle than the Aztecs; and once they had lured the enemy into the open the conflict was soon over. Cortes was the victor, and the Spanish power was planted in Mexico, to persist for many years to come. The following year Cortes returned and captured the city of Tenochtitlan.

When he arrived back in Spain he was received with the highest honours. The king showered rewards on him, and made him governor and captain-general over all Mexico, or New Spain. But when Cortes returned to rule the land and bring it into closer union with Spain he was beset by many difficulties. His iron rule led to the natives rebelling against their new masters, and although the revolt was effectually quelled by Cortes, he had later to contend against the court of Spain, which had become jealous of his power.

Cortes Becomes a Marquis

To set his affairs in order, he once more returned to his native land and was received with great favour by the king, who made him a marquis, but on his arrival back in Mexico he found that his administrative powers had been greatly reduced. Ten years later, with his health impaired, he returned again to Spain, but on this occasion his reception was in sad contrast with the glory of his previous homecomings.

Cortes died in 1547, having spent his last few years in grim solitude, embittered by the ingratitude of a king and country for whom he had striven so hard and done so much.

When Cortes landed in Mexico this strange old granary was already in use. Visitors to Chihuahua may still see it standing in front of an ancient cliff dwelling.

Photo by Mexican Railway

Surrounded by Spaniards and Indians, Hernando de Soto is gazing for the first time on the vast waters of the Mississippi. In the bed of this great river its discoverer was destined to find his last long resting-place.

The MAN Who FOUND the MISSISSIPPI

Seeking a Mythical El Dorado the Adventurous Hernando de Soto Discovered Instead the "Mighty Father of Waters"

THE news had travelled far and wide through Spain and Portugal that the great captain, Hernando de Soto (dā sō'tō) was about to lead an expedition into Florida. And was not Hernando de Soto one of the richest adventurers of Spain, who had come home from Peru laden with treasure and would doubtless know how to lead his followers to still greater treasure? And had not the explorer de Vaca sworn that Florida, that wide land found by Ponce de Leon but still unexplored, was "the richest country yet discovered"? No wonder that from all parts of Spain, and even from Portugal, eager adventurers came thronging to Seville, where De Soto lived in princely state.

This magnificent De Soto had been poor enough once. Born about 1496, at eighteen he had gone to the Isthmus of Darien, in the fabulous New World, to seek his fortune with nothing more than his sword and shield. He had soon risen to the command of a troop of horse, and gaining in years and experience as soldier and explorer, he had risen in favour with the governor.

At the Isthmus, De Soto met the great explorer and soldier Pizarro. Later, when Pizarro had gone to South America to plunder the riches of Peru, De Soto was sent to him with reinforcements and supplies, and took an important part in the capture of Cuzco (kōōs'kō), the capital. Pizarro rewarded him with a generous share of the immense treasure wrung from the unhappy ruler of that country. So, with his fame and his hundred thousand pesos of gold—somewhere about £60,000 in English money—De Soto returned to Spain and married the daughter of his old friend the governor of Darien.

But De Soto had enjoyed his taste of glory and wealth so much that he could not be satisfied until he had acquired more. He wanted to surpass the conquests and plunderings of Pizarro himself, and of Cortes, the conqueror of Mexico. So when news came of fabulous riches to be gained and an empire to be won in that mysterious land lying a few days' sail north of Cuba, he persuaded

including iron collars and chains for the Indians he expected to seize as slaves.

Two weeks later the expedition landed at what we know as Tampa Bay, on the west coast of the Florida peninsula. A camp was pitched and exploring parties sent out. They returned with reports of hostile natives, thick forests and treacherous swamps. But De Soto never doubted that farther from the

De Soto's desire for wealth and fame led him farther and farther into lands no white man had ever seen.

Here he is shown, with his gallant company, on the shore of what is now known as Tampa Bay, in Florida, U.S.A.

the king to grant him the governorship of that island, and gracious permission to conquer and settle Florida at his own expense. It was for this expedition that daring adventurers were flocking to him from all over Spain. Choosing the best of them, he set out one spring day in 1538, to the salutes of booming cannon and the gay farewell of flying flags.

Preparing for a Wonderful Journey

The new governor of Cuba spent his first year on the island in careful preparation before he finally set sail for this marvellous Florida—a land in that day vaguely extending over the whole southern part of what is now the United States. For his conquest of the wilderness, De Soto had four ships, 620 men, more than a hundred horses, and a generous quantity of supplies of all sorts—

coasts there were rich cities to be plundered. So, sending some of his ships back to Cuba for more supplies, he set out on the march that was to last for three long years.

Slowly the little army pushed its way into the heart of the country. There was continual fighting, for De Soto was cruel and faithless in his treatment of the Indians. At length, having found nothing but hardships, the Spaniards turned back to the coast and passed the winter near Apalachee Bay. By spring, still full of hope, they were again on their way.

That year their march took them across what is now Georgia. Their hopes soared high, for they obtained a large quantity of pearls from a river tribe. Food was plentiful, too. They pressed on across the Blue Mountains practically to Tennessee, and then turned into what is now Alabama.

Here, at Mavilla, near the present city of Mobile, they were fiercely attacked. De Soto himself and more than a hundred of his men were wounded, and much of the baggage, including the pearls, was burned. Then De Soto heard that his ships were off the coast, only six days' march away. But he was too proud to let it be known that he had not found the expected treasure, and accordingly sent no word.

The dauntless adventurers spent the second winter in a wretched Indian village on the Yazoo River, in what is now Mississippi. And there the worst disaster so far befell them. There had been constant trouble with the neighbouring Indians, the Chickasaws; and one day the Indians descended on the hated invaders, setting fire to the huts and destroying a great deal of what supplies remained to them after the fight at Mavilla. Eleven Spaniards were killed, and most of the survivors lost everything—even their clothes. Fifty horses were burned, and several hundred pigs, which were to have supplied meat to the explorers. But De Soto and his men fashioned clothes out of the skins of wild animals, closed up their ranks, and struggled on to the north-west.

First Sight of the " Great River "

Then on May 8, '1541, they saw the "Great River." "The River was almost half a league broad," one of them later wrote. "If a man stood still on the other side, it could not be discerned whether he were a man or no." The current was deep and strong, and "trees and timber" were continually floating down stream on its muddy waters. De Soto and his followers were the first white men ever to gaze on the broad reaches of the Mississippi.

The explorers spent a month building barges on which to cross the river. Once on the other side, they started again on their westward march. Surely the golden land they had come so far to find lay just beyond. So they struggled westward across Arkansas, braving the perils of forests and wild beasts and hunger and Indians. They even met the roving Indians of the plains, and heard tales of the shaggy buffalo that roamed the country to the west. The Indians said that farther on they might find guides to lead them to "the other side."

But it was of no avail. If the fabled treasure lay "just beyond," it was always receding from them. Supplies were very low, and they had been gone a long time. At last they turned south-east again. The third winter was spent in a snowy and miserable Indian village on the Wichita. It was a gloomy company that, with milder weather, followed the stream back to the Great River. They had lost half their number, the Indians were becoming bolder, and men and horses were weakened by the terrible hardships. In his discouragement the great leader fell ill.

De Soto's Last Farewell

He knew he was going to die. His fortune spent, his hopes of treasure destroyed, his companions in misfortune muttering that it was he who had caused all their useless misery—what had he to live for now? So he bade them all farewell, and on May 21, 1542, on the banks of the mighty river he had discovered, he died. In fear of the hostile Indians, his followers wrapped his body in mantles, weighted it with sand, and carried it secretly to the Mississippi. Taking it in a canoe, they lowered it "into the middest of the river."

After numerous adventures, the remnants of De Soto's once hopeful band reached the Spanish settlements at last. It was more than a year since they had left their valiant leader in his lonely grave beneath the waters of the mighty stream he had discovered.

Photo by Chauffourier

Just a few miles to the north-west of Rome was the city of Veii, a stronghold of the Etruscans. These warlike people, according to the Roman historian Livy, felt that Rome, the little city on the Tiber, should be subdued, for under the leadership of Romulus it was promising to become a source of trouble to the Etruscan lords.

But the Etruscans did not then know how valorous and strong the despised Romans had become. The people of Veii were defeated in the battle which you see represented above. They were forced by the victors to surrender a part of their possessions and were also made to sign a truce which would last for a hundred years.

EARLY RIVALS *of the* ROMANS

Strong and Warlike, Sea-loving and Artistic, the Etruscans are Still Such a Mystery That We Cannot Be Sure of What Race They Were, or What Language They Spoke

WHO were the mysterious people we call the Etruscans (ē-trŭs′kăn)—the people who held Italy in their power for several hundreds of years, who were among the legendary kings of Rome, and from whom were borrowed so many customs which survived even through the days of the Roman empire? The answer is that nobody knows exactly who they were, where they came from, or when they arrived in Italy. They left no history of their own to tell us of their deeds, and even had they done so, we could not understand it, for their language is just as mysterious as are the people themselves.

Even the histories of Rome do not tell us much about them, for the Romans were ashamed of the fact that a foreign people had conquered them. Whenever they could they belittled the Etruscans, although we know that Etruscan civilization must have been far more advanced than that of early Rome. Most people seem to agree that the Etruscans were an Oriental race from the coasts of Asia Minor, a seafaring people who made their living as pirates. No one knows why they left their homes to sail to an unknown land far across the Mediterranean; but we do know that, perhaps as early as the tenth century B.C., but more probably at the end of the ninth century, these hardy pirates began to invade Italy.

525

Little by little they conquered the primitive peoples who lived there and established themselves in that portion of Italy known as Etruria (ē-trōō'rĭ-ȧ).

Every Etruscan city had its own way of living and its own government. The Etruscans were never banded together under one king. Yet, unlike the tumultuous Greek cities, the Etruscan cities did not spend their time fighting one another. Each city fought its own foreign enemies and settled its own quarrels, but even after hundreds of years there was friendly relationship between them.

Instead of killing or driving away the native peoples in Italy, whom they conquered, the Etruscans always put them to work. The natives could do the ploughing and harvesting, the building and fortifying. While the Etruscan soldiers spent their own time in fighting and in defending their conquests, they were satisfied to perform the respective tasks that were allotted to them, doing useful and important work as farmers, cooks, carpenters and in the many necessary routine occupations.

A DELICATE EXAMPLE OF ETRUSCAN ART

This charming little safety-pin was once worn by some Etruscan maid more than 2,600 years ago. It is one of the most beautiful pieces of gold work the Etruscans ever executed—and they were famous for their jewellery. The body of the mule and the clasp of the pin are ornamented with a network of tiny grains of gold. Since this photograph is about twice the size of the actual pin, you can imagine how tiny these golden grains are; yet, if you look at them through a microscope, you will find that every grain, or granule, is set upon a pedestal of its own. No one knows how such delicate work as this was done. Modern craftsmen have made every effort to imitate it, but, in comparison, their work is crude.

Yet we must not suppose that the Etruscans forgot the sea over which they had come. We know that they traded with Greece and Egypt, and kept up a splendid fleet of ships. With these swift and many-oared vessels the Etruscans often engaged in battle with the ships of Greece or Carthage (kär'thăj), the thriving city which the Phoenicians had planted on the African coast. In the western Mediterranean the Etruscan ships were seldom beaten. Nor did they try to sail to other countries for further conquests; they were content with conquering the islands of Sardinia and Corsica.

Among the native tribes dwelling near the Etruscans were the Latins, who lived in Latium (lā'shĭ-ŭm) across the River Tiber, a few miles from the Etruscan city of Veii (vē'yī). These Latins traded with the Etruscans at a place where a bridge had been built across the Tiber. Ships could come up the river to this market-place; and when a ship arrived the Latin traders would hurry down to the river with oxen and grain and hides to exchange for iron weapons and tools and other goods.

This little Latin town, or trading-station, was called Rome, and, since it was so near to the Etruscan territory, it was only to be expected that sooner or later the Etruscan soldiers would attack it. The Latins were a strong and vigorous race, but they were no match for the Etruscans. Rome fell, and for more than a hundred years its Latin population was ruled by a line of Etruscan kings. Not only Rome, but the whole of Northern Italy and the western coast down as far as Naples, came under Etruscan rule.

Perhaps, if their only enemies had been the natives of Italy, the Etruscans might have extended their power still further. But two other countries, Greece and Carthage, fought the Etruscans continually. The Greeks wanted to establish colonies of their own in Italy and Sicily, and the Carthaginians, who wished to trade freely, looked upon the Etruscan seamen as pirates.

Many a fierce sea battle was fought between the Etruscans and these two rival

TWO MAIDS OF ANCIENT ETRURIA PAY A VISIT TO THE POTTERY SHOP

These two Etruscan maidens are out shopping and have stepped into the pottery dealer's shop to see what he has for sale. They are inspecting some black glazed ware and other pottery made by their own people. And here, too, are many fine vases from Greece and the Greek islands. Some of these Greek vases are large and imposing; others are graceful, fragile little things. All of them are gaily painted with designs of plants, animals, or people which—even in the tiniest of the vases—are done with so much imagination and attention to detail that we are as charmed and delighted with them to-day as the two maidens must have been.

nations. At last, in 474 B.C., the Greeks of Syracuse (sĭr′ȧ-kūs), in Sicily, sent forth an immense fleet and succeeded in destroying the Etruscan ships in the battle of Cumae (kū′mē). A little while before this, about 509 B.C., Rome had been able to free herself from Etruscan rule.

From this time on, the power of the Etruscans was broken. They were soon attacked on the north by the Gauls, who were pouring down into Italy from the other side of the Alps. The Etruscan cities would not join together to fight against the other tribes of Italy, and little by little the Etruscans and their civilization were absorbed into the growing power of Rome.

The Etruscans spoke a language which the Greeks, who knew many tongues, declared was like none other in the whole world. For writing they used an alphabet like that of the Greeks, so that we know something of the sounds they used, even though we do not always know what those sounds meant.

The Etruscan language has been a great puzzle to scholars. We know a few words, but even yet no one can read an Etruscan inscrip-

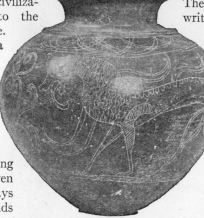

This vase was made by the Etruscans at the time when they were trying to copy Eastern designs. The strange animal which is cut into the black, glazed surface of this vase is a near relative of those monsters which the Babylonians and Assyrians were so fond of using as decorations.

tion perfectly. Discoveries like those of Professor Trombetti in 1928 have helped towards unlocking this strange speech, but the problem is very difficult. There are only a few Etruscan writings on which to work, and we have scarcely any translations of these into Latin or any other known language. So the deciphering of Etruscan inscriptions is one of the great puzzles that scholars have yet to solve.

It is from their tombs that we learn most of what we know of the Etruscans, for this strange race, like the Egyptians, believed that after death the souls of the dead continued to live much the same sort of life that people lived on earth. They built elaborate tombs to serve as

FIGURES CARVED IN RELIEF ON THE SIDE OF A COFFIN

From very early times we find the Etruscans placing the remains of their dead in burial urns. Some of these urns were made to look like the houses in which the people had lived; others were simply crude jars which had, perhaps, a portrait bust of the dead person serving as a lid. As the artists became more skilful they made elaborate coffins, called sarcophagi, which were not only decorated with reliefs round the sides, but had portrait figures of the dead reclining on the lid, as though at a banquet. It was possibly from the truth-loving Etruscans that the Romans got their interest in lifelike portraiture. Above is a lively scene carved in relief on the side of an Etruscan sarcophagus (sär-kŏf′ǎ-gŭs′). The action of the figures is perfect.

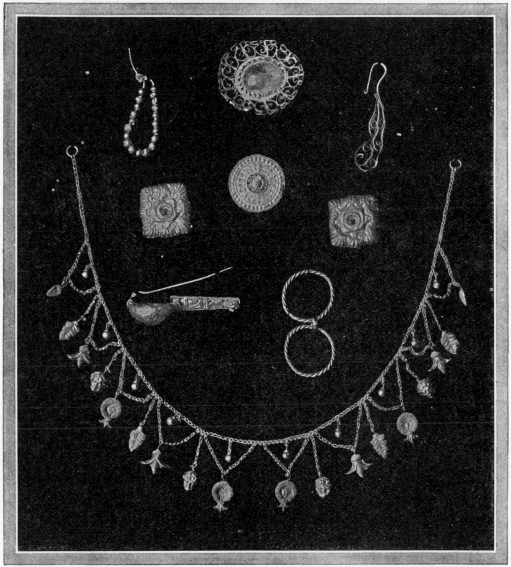

Photo by Alinari

These objects of gold, which were made by the Etruscans, will give you an idea of how clever their craftsmen were. A necklace such as the one above probably graced the throat of some high-born lady of Etruria, who may also have worn the ear-rings and pin. The other ornaments were originally sewn upon garments.

dwelling-places for the dead, and filled them with works of art, pottery, armour, and jewellery. The walls of these tombs were covered with fascinating paintings: some of religious and mythological scenes, and others, by far the most interesting, of scenes from the daily life of the Etruscans. These tombs are found in some of the Etruscan cities that have been unearthed.

What a prosperous, luxury-loving people they were! At their banquets they were shown reclining on long couches, and waited on by slaves who filled their goblets with wine and entertained them by playing on the flute and lyre. Some of the artists who painted these scenes, have even included the chickens that stalked in and out among the table legs, to peck up the crumbs.

We cannot always be sure how much of the Etruscan way of doing things was borrowed from other peoples, although they themselves were fine craftsmen, and brought with them to Italy a knowledge of art, which they developed. We do not always know whether some of the works of art found on Etruscan soil were made by the Etruscans themselves, or imported from some other country, or made by foreign workmen hired by the wealthy lords of Etruria. For the Etruscans were great traders, and were fond of imitating styles.

Their Love of Beautiful Things

Towards the close of the eighth and through the seventh century B.C. we find the Etruscans using designs from Asia and Egypt. They liked beautiful things, and imported a mass of Oriental objects, among which were carved ivory figurines, gold and silver bowls, and all sorts of articles traded by the energetic Phoenicians. Some of the things the Phoenicians made were in imitation of Egyptian styles, and were carved with hieroglyphics which had no meaning at all, but were used merely to impress.

Through the sixth and fifth centuries B.C. the Etruscans traded briskly with Greece, and were imitating the Greeks. Some of the finest Greek pottery we have to-day was preserved in Etruscan tombs; for Greek potters and other craftsmen found a ready market in Etruria, and it is more than probable that many of the sculptures and tomb paintings were made by Greek work-

men who had made their homes in Italy. In architecture and sculpture, however, the Etruscans remained generally independent, especially in statuary. They were the first people in Italy to use stone for building; their use of the arch, seen in the famous gate of Perugia, which they may have learned how to make from the Phoenicians, was a device adopted by the Romans, who saw the value of such a useful thing.

Unlike the Greeks, however, the Etruscans built their temples on high platforms, for they believed that the home of their gods should tower above their own dwellings. Later Romans also, copying the Etruscans, built their temples on platforms. When the Romans built their great circular mausoleums, such as the tombs of Augustus and Hadrian, they were probably modelling them on the burial mounds of the Etruscans, which the Etruscans had borrowed from Asia Minor.

Rome Learns Another Art

But it was not only in architecture that Etruscan influence was felt. Tradition has it that the gladiatorial tournaments, which became so popular in Rome, were introduced by this entertainment-loving people. And certainly it was from the Etruscans that the Romans learned the art of augury—that deep lore by which a priest was supposed to foretell the future by examining an animal's inside. In fact, everything in their public life the Romans owed to the Etruscans.

Photo by Alinari

This house of the dead resembles a house of the living. Many of the rock-cut tombs of the Etruscans were made to look like real houses, with roof beams carved on the ceiling and a square basin cut in the centre of the room to catch the raindrops from an imaginary opening in the roof. The room above is decorated with reliefs of weapons, kitchen utensils, mirrors, and jewellery to make its dead occupants feel quite at home.

In this humble cottage Robert Burns, Scotland's greatest poet, first saw the light of day. Later, he described his life there in the beautiful poetry of "The Cottar's Saturday Night." In the oval is a portrait of the poet.

Photo by National Portrait Gallery

The PLOUGH-BOY POET of SCOTLAND

Robert Burns Sang as He Worked in the Fields, and His Lyrics are Now Enshrined in the Heart of a Nation

(CONTINUED FROM PAGE 511)

THERE is a story that a visitor who called on the Burns family one day found them at dinner, each one with a spoon for his oatmeal and a book by his plate. The oatmeal was often all they had to eat, for they were desperately poor. But they were Scottish, and so they were readers; and whether or not the rest of them made it a practice to have a book at hand with their porridge, certainly young Robert did. For he was plainly the genius of the family.

Even so, little did his parents and the other people of the neighbourhood ever dream he was going to write the sweetest songs in all Britain, the poetry that every Scot always carries in his heart wherever he may wander and whatever he may do.

Robert Burns was born at Alloway, near Ayr, on January 25, 1759. He went to school only in such spare time as he had, for he had to do hard work on the farm. But he did all the reading he could in odd hours, and above all he read the great poets, Scottish and English. Behind the plough he carried a little book of poems in his pocket, taking it out to read a few lines when he could, and reciting the poems to himself as the plough cut through the hard soil.

How Robert Burns First Came to Write Poems

Then poems of his own came into his mind. Many an hour behind the plough he would muse over his little songs as they came to him, many an evening he would think over them, put them in shape, and write them down. He had little thought of ever being famous. He was just singing to himself because he could not help it.

Then his father died, and he had to work harder than ever. But the farm did not pay; there was never enough money, and in his hardships the young singer fell into dissolute ways. He had several unhappy love affairs, which often nearly broke his heart while they left their record in the beautiful poems that he wrote about them. Yet all

531

the while he kept writing his matchless little songs—such as the one to the field-mouse whose warm nest his plough had wrecked just as the cold winter was coming on.

At last, however, growing weary of the continued check to his ambitions, he decided to emigrate. To this end he accepted a position as book-keeper to a slave estate in Jamaica; but Fate had other plans in store for him, for, with the publication of his first volume of poems at Kilmarnock in 1786, fame suddenly descended upon him, and the passage abroad was cancelled. Invited to Edinburgh, he was received into the most exclusive literary circles.

However, he was still all but penniless. He would leave the garret in which he had to live, astonish and delight the great people of the city at some brilliant gathering, and then steal back through the night to the dismal garret again. It was not a life worthy of the man, but it was his little period of glory.

When it was over he went back to farming. He married his Jean Armour, of whom we hear so much in his songs. But life was always hard for them.

One farm after another failed. He obtained very little money from his poems, and it was always difficult to make a comfortable living. To add to his many troubles, he began to lose his friends. The poor health he had suffered since he worked so hard as a boy could not bear the strain, and he met an untimely death on July 21, 1796.

But his name lives on in glory. With all his faults, he is beloved not only by his fellow countrymen but all the world over. He was a blithe and kindly spirit, a great Nature lover, and a good friend to lowly man. We have only to read his fine poem called "A Man's a Man for a' that" in order to realize that he fully understood the true worth of the commoner; and his war-songs, such as "Scots wha hae wi' Wallace Bled," bear witness to his great love of liberty. There are no other songs sweeter than his, more tender, or more appealing. His lyrics must be sung or spoken by a Scot, in the true accent, for the full beauty of them to be realized, but even then the uninitiated will lose a lot by not understanding the meaning of many words in the dialect.

Probably Burns's deepest love was for his Highland Mary, with whom he is here shown. To her he wrote some of his tenderest verses. "To Mary in Heaven" and "Highland Mary." But the romance had an unhappy end, which he sorrowfully describes in the closing lines of the last-named poem:

Oh pale, pale now, those rosy lips,
  I aft hae kiss'd sae fondly!
And closed for aye the sparkling glance,
  That dwelt on me sae kindly!
And mouldering now in silent dust
  That heart that lo'ed me dearly!
But still within my bosom's core,
  Shall live my Highland Mary.

The strange, other-worldly character of Blake's genius is well shown in this picture in which he portrays the meeting between David and Goliath. To Blake it was a matter of no concern that his David was clad in the flowing draperies of a Greek shepherd while another figure was encased in a complete suit of medieval armour.

A POET *of* STRANGE VISIONS

The Childlike William Blake Lived in a Mystical Inner World in Which His Beautiful Thoughts and Dreams were More Real to Him than All Other Things

WILLIAM BLAKE was one of the happiest men who ever lived. He started to sing when he was a mere boy, and he was literally singing when he died.

It was not that life treated him very well. He did not fit at all well into the picture of the England of his time—if, indeed, he would have fitted into any picture in any place or time—hardly any one realized his genius or understood him, with the result that he was all his life neglected and poor. But, except for sudden black moods of despair which soon passed away, he did not greatly care.

For he had his art, and he had his visions. Even as a child, he had seen angels leaning down from the clouds.

When he looked at the sun, it seemed to him to be a mighty, singing host. He talked familiarly with the shade of Milton. He drew portraits of sitters whom no one else could see. His later poems, he said, were dictated to him by "the Immortals." Many people thought him mad. But he lived in a world of his own creation, so he cared little about what people said.

This vision-seeing artist and poet was born

in London in 1757, a very unlikely place and time for a seer of visions to be born. Yet it looked for a while as though he might get a foothold in the ordinary world. His father, a prosperous hosier, encouraged the boy's desire to become an artist, and gave him money to buy fine prints and casts from which to draw.

At fourteen William was apprenticed to an engraver, for whom he worked for seven years. During the last five of these years he went regularly to draw pictures of old monuments in churches, especially those in Westminster Abbey. He came to love the Gothic art he found in these churches, and he continued to love it all his life, although its laws were very different from those laid down by the teachers in the art schools of his own day.

He Wins a High Honour and Struggles Fiercely Against Drab Poverty

After drawing all day long, Blake would go home and work on pictures and poems of his own. In due time he exhibited his pictures in the Royal Academy, and was thought to be mildly promising. About the same time he met the Rev. Henry Mathew and John Flaxman, the sculptor, and in 1783 they helped him to publish a book of poems. It was called "Poetical Sketches," and is partly in the style of the poets of Shakespeare's day. But the poems did not attract much attention.

By this time, Blake was already deep in the struggle with poverty and neglect which lasted most of his life. He had married in 1782, and his wife bravely upheld him in all he did, learning to draw and paint well enough to be able to help him in his work.

Meanwhile Blake's poetry and engraving became more and more "different" from other people's, and he paid less and less attention to what people might say of it. He became a printer, and started to turn out books which he had not only written but illustrated and printed himself. Often the poems and the pictures are but two halves of the same idea, and you can understand and enjoy them much better together than apart. For, being a seer of visions, Blake wrote about all kinds of things—from clods of earth to clouds in the sky—as if he saw

their souls in human form; and so he draws them that way, as you may see for yourself if you look at the pictures in any of his books.

The Happy Songs of Innocence and the Sadder Songs of Experience

The loveliest of Blake's poems are found in the companion books called "Songs of Innocence" and "Songs of Experience." The "Songs of Innocence" tell of happy childhood; they are about the little lamb, and the baby whose very name was Joy, and the merriment of spring, and the laughter of children at play. The "Songs of Experience" are sadder, but just as beautiful. There is one about the weary sunflower, "that countest the steps of the sun," and another about the terrible beauty of a tiger

. . . burning bright
In the forests of the night.

This is, perhaps, the best known poem of all.

As he grew older, Blake saw more and more visions. They burned in his brain like the tiger's beauty, and he worked out a whole elaborate religion around them. He imagined a set of new gods and goddesses who have as exciting and varied a story as that of the gods and goddesses of the old Greeks. He wrote about these strange beings, who had strange names like Ahania and Los and Urizen, in a long series of poems called "Prophetic Books."

They are written in strange and beautiful rhythms. Most people do not even pretend to understand all of them; yet, even so, the books are packed with thought, and can be read to-day with much less bewilderment than when they were written. For Blake was far ahead of his time.

Fine Pictures Painted in Colours and Fine Pictures Painted in Words

Not many men have been worthy of fame as both artist and poet. Blake is one of the few. Besides the drawings that go with his poems, he did other water-colours and engravings. Possibly the most famous series is a set of engravings illustrating a poem by Robert Blair called "The Grave." There is another fine set to illustrate the Book of Job.

Blake even invented a method of what he called "colour printing," which he said had been revealed to him by the spirit of a dead brother. In these books both the text of the poem and the illustrations have been etched on copper, printed in colour, and afterwards retouched by hand. They are rare and beautiful volumes, valued now as they never were when William Blake was alive.

When he was an old man, Blake drew round him a devoted band of followers, who were known as "the Ancients." But though he was by no means unappreciated when he died in 1827, it was not till our own day that the world in general realized that he was a very great artist and a greater poet

GENTLE, PITIABLE COWPER

When He was Ill He Suffered from a Terrible Delusion, but when He was Well He Wrote Beautiful Poems

THIS is the sad story of a very gentle poet. William Cowper's mother died when he was only six years old, and his stern father sent him off to school. There the shy little boy was very unhappy. One of the big boys bullied him so brutally that he hardly dared to look his tormentor in the face. He knew the tyrant better by his shoe buckles than by his face, as he tells us many a year later; but "May God pardon him," he adds, "and may we meet in glory!"

Soon, however, young Cowper was sent to another school—Westminster—where he was far happier. When he left there, he began to study law in London. He had come of a good family, and was expected to carve out a career as a public man.

William Cowper, a writer of poems and hymns that are familiar to most of us.

He served a three years' apprenticeship to a solicitor in London, but he was not greatly interested in his studies, and in a letter to a friend he admitted as much. Nevertheless, at the end of his apprenticeship, he occupied chambers in the Inner Temple, and continued in a half-hearted manner to study the law with a view to becoming a barrister. He spent a good deal of his time writing little essays and poems for a "Nonsense Club" to which he belonged, and in "giggling and making giggle" with his pretty cousins. With one of these, Theodora, he fell deeply in love. He describes her as being "remarkably elegant,

and her understanding more than ordinarily good." But he was destined never to marry her, because of a great shadow that was soon to fall upon his life.

It was during the early part of his legal studies, which extended over a period of about eleven years, that the first signs of the approaching shadow became noticeable. He suffered from depressed spirits, and, as he himself put it: "I was upon the rack, lying down in horror and rising in despair." His sensitive mind was becoming unbalanced.

On concluding his studies, the malady began to show itself in a very definite form; and the crisis which finally robbed him of his reason came about in this way. Cowper's grandfather was possessed of considerable influence, and it was his intention to secure for his grandson a clerkship in the House of Lords. Therefore, when several vacancies occurred, Cowper's name was put forward, but his acceptance of the post required that he should appear before the bar of the House. Such, however, was Cowper's timidity, that the prospect of having to undergo a public examination filled him with the greatest terror and apprehension— and the struggle and worry of preparing for his ordeal proved too much for him.

Several times he attempted suicide, and his friends were compelled to have him placed in a mental institution. There he was cured, at least for the time being; but insanity came upon him again and again during his life, and in the end it settled down upon him permanently.

And yet he became a great and very lovable poet. After his first illness, he left

a fairly long life—for he had been born in 1731, and lived to 1800. The unhappy part is a very different story, and a terrible one. For in his periods of insanity, he believed that he was a lost soul for all eternity.

It was to keep Cowper from brooding on this terrible delusion that kindly women friends persuaded him, at the age of fifty, to write verses. He cared nothing about fame; he simply wrote to free his mind from torment. Yet he wrote much poetry of charm and merit. He wrote many hymns, such as "God moves in a mysterious way" and "There is a fountain filled with blood." He wrote the tenderest poems about the mother whom he could hardly remember, and the lovable Mrs. Unwin, "My Mary."

Cowper also wrote the rollicking ballad of "John Gilpin," of which he was ashamed because it was so light-hearted. He translated Homer, and above all, he wrote a long and beautiful poem called "The Task," which treats of the beauty of nature and the joy of rural life and simple pursuits; and his fine ballad "On the Loss of the Royal George" will be remembered for all time. Then the shadows closed about him, and he wrote no more.

Here we see John Gilpin, the prosperous linen-draper of Paternoster Row, London, as he is depicted by William Cowper in his celebrated poem.

the world and all its ways behind him, and went away to live a very quiet life in the country. Here he lived in great peace with his friends the Unwins, whose deep religious faith was a great comfort to him. He worked in the garden, took long rambling walks, and read comforting religious books; and kept pet hares about which he wrote.

In this way he passed the happier part of

Cowper had brought a new spirit into English verse. So much of the poetry written previously had been artificial in the feeling it expressed; Cowper introduced the "human element"; and his verses also show his great love of nature and animal life.

(CONTINUED ON PAGE 584)

Here is an Eskimo fishing for seal. It may well be noon, but no sun is to be seen, for the chances are that there is no sun in the sky. Only in the summer does he ever see the sun—and if you will look at the picture up in the corner you will see why that is. The earth is there shown with its North Pole tipped towards the sun—in constant daylight. The South Pole, you will observe, is having its long spell of darkness.

Do You GET Your SHARE of SUNLIGHT?

A Few Hours of Sunshine Every Day Make All the Difference between Life and Death

(CONTINUED FROM PAGE 517)

HAVE you ever seen a potato that had sprouted in the dark? Its sickly shoots are pallid instead of a healthy green, and the unhappy plant soon dies. It cannot live without sunlight. And it is much the same with men. There is a very good reason why we like sunny weather. We may think, perhaps, that it is only because the sunshine makes us gay and the whole world beautiful. But under it all lies the fact that sunlight keeps us well and makes us vigorous. Without it plants die, as a rule; and the human race would die, too, if it had to live in the dark. We owe our very life to the sun.

What can it be in sunlight that is necessary to life, and how does it exert its beneficent influence? To answer these questions we must first split a sunbeam into its various parts. Sunlight seems to be simply white, but really a ray of it contains all the colours of the rainbow, beautifully blended. Each one of the seven colours—violet, indigo, blue, green, yellow, orange, and red—may be sifted out from its fellows if the sunlight is passed through a prism (prĭz'm). This is a triangular solid of glass that casts the light in a series of coloured bands very much like the rainbow. It can do this because each colour travels in waves of a different length from all the rest; and when a sunbeam passes through the prism, each separate ray is bent by the glass according to the length of its wave. So we have all the colours spread out in a row before us. You may see them yourself if you hold a glass pendant from a chandelier between the sun and a sheet of white paper. A coloured object reflects only the waves of its own colour, and so it is these "visible" waves that make the world so gay and glad to look upon.

Why Our Skin Tans and Freckles

But while we see seven colours, there really are many more rays that the eye cannot see at all. These lie at each end of the rainbow—beyond the red and the violet. It is those on the end next to the violet—we call them the "ultra-violet rays"—that have so much to do with health.

They have a powerful effect on the colour of the skin, too. We have all been burned or have got a coat of tan from their action during the summer. For the skin, in order to keep from being blistered, protects itself with tiny particles of brown colouring matter that keep out the rays. Those particles are what make tan and freckles. In the same way, races that live in the tropics, where the sun's rays are most powerful, are born brown or black as a protection from the burning light.

Lately we have found out that many diseases may be treated by ultra-violet rays; so many hospitals now have electrical sun-ray wards. And since the magical light cannot pass easily through ordinary window glass, the windows of many sun parlours are filled with a special glass through which the ultra-violet rays come freely.

Counting the Hours of Sunshine

Sunshine is so important that the meteorologist keeps a daily record of the number of hours that we have. He has found that in the British Isles less than half the daylight hours are sunny. But men can be well and strong on quite a little sunshine. In certain parts of Northern Scotland the sturdy inhabitants see the sun for only about

UNDER THE HEALTH-GIVING CARE OF DR. SUNLIGHT

One might not suspect it, but all the patients shown here are taking their medicine, which consists of a dose of sunlight. In Miami, Florida, U.S.A., where this hospital is situated, the sun is always high and warm, so its health-giving rays are used there in the treatment of all kinds of diseases. Such diseases the little Maori boy up in the corner is not likely to suffer from. He lives in New Zealand, and basks in the sun all day long. In the picture he is seen bathing in one of the hot pools provided by Nature.

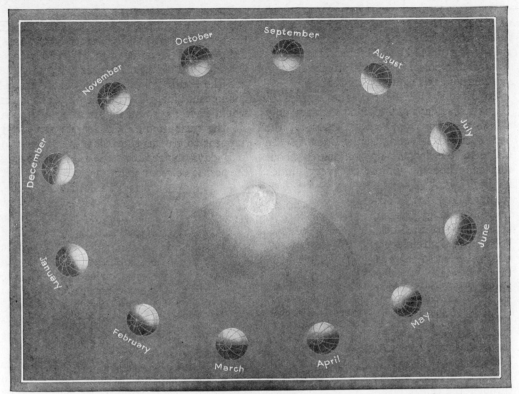

THE ETERNAL MARCH OF MOTHER EARTH AROUND THE GLOWING SUN

Here are twelve pictures of the earth in its yearly march round the sun. You will notice that, no matter on which side of the sun the earth may be, its axis—or a line running through the earth from pole to pole—is always tilted in the same direction for anyone looking down at the solar system. Let us suppose you live in London, Paris, or New York. You would be living in the Northern Hemisphere—or that half of the globe which is north of the Equator. It is the half that the picture shows; for the pole that we see in the picture is the North Pole. Now, you will see, if you look closely, that during the winter months the North Pole is tipped away from the sun and is in shadow. The result is that the whole of the Northern Hemisphere, whirling round on its axis every day, is getting less sunlight than the Southern Hemisphere during those months, and so we are having our winter. But during the summer months the North Pole is tilted towards the sun, instead of away from it, and is in full sunlight. So the whole of the Northern Hemisphere is then getting more sunlight than the Southern Hemisphere, and London, Paris, and New York are having their summer. In spring and autumn the two hemispheres have days and nights of the same length—but when we in the north are having our autumn, the Southern Hemisphere is having its spring.

two-ninths of the total number of daylight hours, or for an average of only about two and three-quarter hours a day.

Where the Sun Goes to When the Darkness of Night Descends Upon Us

The sun does not shine on all parts of the earth equally, as it might if the world were a great flat plain spread out directly beneath it. Because the earth is round, certain parts of it receive the sun's rays directly—they come from straight overhead—but elsewhere the curve of the earth brings the surface slantingly under the beams. And one-half of the planet is always turned away from the sun entirely—it is in darkness; though luckily the earth turns round, so that all parts get the light once in twenty-four hours.

If you look at the diagram on page 540 you will see that between the circles round the earth near the Equator the sun's rays strike the ground almost vertically; that is, they come almost straight down. In this zone—or belt—the day and night are each about twelve hours long at all times of the year. The longest day and the longest night last only a little over thirteen hours.

Between this zone and the poles the day varies greatly in length. It may last only a few minutes or it may be as much as six months long; and while one pole is having six months of day, the other is having six months of night. The nearer one goes towards the poles, the longer are the days in summer and the nights in winter.

So Entebbe (ĕn-tĕb′bē), the capital of Uganda, has days and nights that vary only a few minutes from twelve hours all the year round; it is very near the Equator. In Calcutta the longest day measures about fourteen hours. Bordeaux, very much farther north, has a summer day that is sixteen hours long; London, nearly seventeen; Stockholm, more than eighteen; and Iceland, about twenty-two. At the North Pole the summer day lasts six months.

All this will be easy to understand if you try the following experiment. Take a small globe, or thrust a long pencil through the centre of an orange. Then darken the room and hold the globe in front of a strong light, as the boy holds it in the picture—a torch-light will do. Tip the globe a little, so that the top, or North Pole, will point away from the torch just enough to keep the light from shining on it. You will notice that the South Pole, at the other end of the globe, is in the light. Now turn the globe slowly on its axis—that is to say, twirl the pencil. You will see that spinning the globe does not have anything to do with the amount of light that reaches the North Pole. It remains in darkness, just as the South Pole remains in light. In other words, the South Pole keeps having day and the North Pole keeps having night, though on the Equator, day and night follow each other in any one spot as often as the globe is turned all the way round.

HOW THE SUN SHINES ON THE GLOBE

The Equator and that part of the globe which lies directly north or south of it always get more sunlight than the parts near the poles. The tilt of the earth's axis sometimes brings one pole into the sunlight and sometimes the other, but it is nevertheless true that the middle part of the globe is in the sun all the time, and gets its rays much more directly than the lands farther north and south. On this little map you can see by the shading how much sunlight any part of the globe gets in the course of a year. If you lived in Central Africa you would get all there was to be had, for you would be at the Equator, where the sun's rays are more nearly direct than anywhere else in the world. But as you travelled north or south, you would find that they grew less strong.

But this does not explain why days should be of different lengths at different times of the year. If you continued to turn the globe in the position in which it is now, the North Pole would never see the light and the South Pole would be bathed in unending sunshine, while all the places between would have days and nights of fixed length all the year round. So let us see what happens to give us short days in winter and long days in summer. Without changing the position of your globe, trace with a pencil, as you twirl the globe, the edge of the shadow all the way round it. You will find that the part of the globe south of the Equator is getting a good deal more light than the northern half. The southern half is having its summer, and the days there are longer than the nights.

But the earth does something more than spin. It also circles round the sun once a year. You may see what happens during this long journey if you walk slowly round the light, always keeping the globe tilted at just the same angle, and the axis—or pencil—pointing in the same direction. If you are walking round a marked circle, the South Pole was pointing inside the circle when you started. When you are a quarter of the way round the room, the South Pole points directly at the circle, and begins to grow dark and the North Pole to grow light; and you will notice that the part of the globe north of the Equator now gets as much light as the southern part. It is now spring above the Equator and autumn below it, and the days and nights everywhere on the globe are of equal length.

We have a name that we give to this

moment when the sun is directly over the Equator and the days and nights are of equal length. We call it the equinox (ē'kwĭnŏks), from two Latin words meaning "night of equal length." There are two equinoxes in a year—the spring equinox about March 21, and the autumn equinox about September 21.

When you have circled half-way round the light and are opposite your starting-point, you will be in the same position as the boy in the second illustration. The North Pole of your globe now leans towards the sun and is constantly in the light; it is having its six months of day. But the South Pole is now in continual darkness; it is having its six-months'-long night.

Now compare the line on the globe where the shadow ends with the line you drew when on the other side of the room. You will see that the two lines fall in quite different places. More light now strikes the upper part of the globe than the lower part. The days will be longer north of the Equator than south of it, and the northern part of the earth will be having its summer.

So you see it is the tipping of the axis of

the earth towards or away from the sun that makes the days grow longer or shorter and causes the seasons. If the earth were not tilted in this way, we should have the same temperature all the year round, and our days would never change in length. And the sun would always rise and set at just the same point on the horizon.

We who live to-day know that it is the change in the tilt of the earth towards the sun that causes the seasons. But in ancient times, before men knew that the earth travels round the sun, they naturally thought it was the sun that travelled to and fro in the sky. It seemed to them to start in the south-east in December and rise each day a little farther north and mount a little higher in the heavens. When the longest day of the year was reached, on June 21, it had climbed to its highest point in the sky. People always celebrated that day. Then it turned and went south again—and we call the moment before it turns the solstice (sŏl'stĭs), a term derived from two Latin words meaning sun standing still."

The line on the

WHY WE HAVE WINTER AND SUMMER

Here is the sun—represented by the boy holding the torch—and the earth, which is revolving round and round the sun. In picture number 1 the North Pole is tipped away from the sun; the Northern Hemisphere is having its winter and the North Pole itself is having its six months of night. But in picture numbr 2 the earth has got round to the other side of the sun; so now the North Pole is no longer tipped away from the light. It is having its six months of day, and the Northern Hemisphere is having its summer. The dotted line in the second picture shows where the shadow fell when the North Pole was tipped away from the sun. The earth always stays in the same position with relation to the stars, but its slant in relation to the sun changes —and gives us our seasons. Of course, the earth is all the while spinning, even while it revolves round the sun. It is the spinning that gives us our day and night, for it takes twenty-four hours for our globe to turn completely round, and during that time any given spot has part of the time been turned towards the light and part of the time away from the light.

earth which at this time has the sun directly overhead has been named from a Greek word that means "to turn"—we call it a "tropic" (trŏp'ĭk). There are two of them—one which forms the northern boundary of the belt where the sun's rays fall almost vertically, and the other which forms the southern boundary. When the northern half of the globe has its longest day —or summer solstice—the sun is directly overhead along the line on the earth that we call the Tropic of Cancer (kăn'sĕr); and when it has its shortest day—or winter solstice— the sun is directly above the Tropic of Capricorn (kăp'rĭ-kôrn), south of the Equator.

How the Tropics Got Their Names

One wonders why those imaginary lines should bear such curious names. The story is an interesting one. If the stars could be seen in the daytime and you were to look beyond the sun on June 21, our longest day, you would see a group of stars behind it that the ancients used to call the Crab—for "cancer" is the Latin for "crab." On reaching this point in the sky, the sun seemed to retrace its path and start south again, therefore the line of the earth which

is directly under the sun at this time was named after the group of stars in which it seemed to turn round; it was called the Tropic—or turning point—of Cancer.

It is the Sun that Makes the Weather

In the same way, if you could look beyond the sun on the shortest day, December 21, you would see it against a group of stars that the ancients called the Goat—the Latin word is "capricornus." This group was probably so named because there was a myth that the young sun god had once been nursed by a goat. So the line on the earth which has the sun directly overhead when it turns north again was named after the group of stars in which it appears to face about—the Tropic of Capricorn.

It is the amount of sunlight we get that really governs our annual march of weather. The "swing" of the sun from north to south in the heavens gives us the snows of winter and the flowers and fruit of summer. It gives us our long summer twilights and the early sunsets of December. To the tropics it brings the wet and dry seasons; to the poles six months of day and night. It marshals the endless pageant of the seasons.

(CONTINUED ON PAGE 577)

Perhaps it will be your good fortune some day to see a total eclipse of the sun, and then you will learn, in a startling way, how much the sun has to do with the temperature. For though it is hidden but a few moments, as the moon swings across its face, a strange darkness and chill immediately settle over the earth.

It is hard to say whether the mice chose this knoll for a meeting-place because of its charming scenery or because it gave no cover to their enemy the cat. Certainly their discussion has filled them with a noble spirit, and they have just thought of a plan which could save them all, to the last whisker—if only it were a practicable one.

TANSY *and* BOBBLES *on* FABLE ISLAND

The Mice Hold an Important Council, and the Little Ant Makes Up His Mind that One Good Turn Deserves Another

(CONTINUED FROM PAGE 458)

BOBBLES and Tansy had already learned what a council of the frogs meant, and one evening they stepped right into a council of the mice. So they remained invisible and sat down to listen.

It appeared that the mice were in great danger from a cat who often lay in wait to pounce upon them.

The council decided that something must be done about it, and the members talked and argued and squabbled as to which of them had the best scheme.

But at last a young mouse, refusing to be silenced by the chairman, came forward and declared that he had the best scheme. It was nothing less than to hang a bell round the cat's neck, so that they would all hear her coming, and have good time to escape.

This was such a new and brilliant idea that the mice clapped delightedly, and when the chairman put the scheme to the vote, all the members held up their paws with the exception of one old mouse.

The Old Mouse Discovers a Flaw in the Scheme of the Young Mouse

After the scheme had been carried amid much applause, the old mouse asked to be allowed to say a word.

"This scheme," he said, "is an excellent one, and I am proud to think that my young friend over there has thought of it. It does credit to his intelligence."

At that the young mouse bowed and blushed with pride.

"There appears to me to be but one

small trouble in carrying out the plan. Which mouse among you is going to put the bell round the cat's neck? I propose, Mr. Chairman, that we now select that mouse."

But all of a sudden there was a great scurrying. The mighty council scattered through the grass, and only the old mouse remained.

"Booh!" said Bobbles. "You are wise, Mr. Mouse. It's one thing to propose, and another thing to carry out."

"Oh! Oh!" cried Tansy. "There's the cat!" And the old mouse fled for his life.

But now the air was filled with the sound of loud talking.

A farmer's sons were quarrelling as to which was to mend the hedge, which to drain the field, and which to carry off the stones.

When it seemed as if they might come to blows, the farmer came along, carrying with him three sticks tied together.

"My sons," he said, "when you have done quarrelling, I should be glad if you would break this bundle of sticks for me."

Each of the sons tried, but in vain.

Then the farmer untied the sticks, and gave one to each of his sons.

This is an agreeable-looking fellow, but a donkey for all that, as you will discover when you read the sad story of his fatal obstinacy.

"Now try," he said.

So the sons tried, and each broke his stick quite easily.

"You see, my sons," said the farmer, "that if you are like separate sticks, anyone can break you, but if you join together, you will be strong. The land will prosper and you need have no fear of enemies."

Then the fairies darted out, and promised that if only the sons would shake hands, they would fly right off to the sun, the rain, and the wind, and ask them to join in bringing the very best weather for the farm.

One day Tansy and Bobbles were feeling rather idle, and not very pleased with themselves.

Mother Fairy had asked if they would bring her some very red thyme from the high rocks.

Now it was a hot day, and a tiring climb to the high rocks; and though the fairies had not been so unkind as to refuse, their looks had made Mother Fairy say rather sadly, "If your going about finding out the meaning of things makes you unwilling to do a small kindness for your own mother, I shall have to talk seriously to your father."

And now, as they idled, just below the spot where the climb to the high rocks began, they were attracted by a tremendous buzzing of bees.

"Another council," said Tansy.

"No! Look, it's a court," said Bobbles. "There's Judge Wasp and his officers."

So it was. And it appeared, as the case proceeded, that the drones and the working bees were disputing with one another as to which of them owned the honeycomb that was in the hollow trunk of the oak tree.

The drones insisted that it was theirs; and the other bees, defending, pleaded that it was theirs.

"Before I give my decision," said the judge at last, "I propose that two hives shall be procured. The working bees shall fill one with honey, and the drones the other. Whichever party makes honey that matches the honey in the oak will prove itself the rightful owner."

The workers joyfully agreed to this test, but the drones began to buzz and grumble.

The Verdict of Judge Wasp

"Ah!" announced Judge Wasp, "I can now see clearly that the honey in the oak tree was made by the workers; so to them it shall belong." And he smiled, wisely.

The foolish miller could not make up his mind whether he or his son, or both of them, should ride on the donkey. At length he came to the conclusion that it would be best to carry the animal. They are debating how to do it.

As the court broke up, Tansy and Bobbles looked at each other, and their faces were scarlet.

"We're rather like the drones, because we're too lazy to get mother the thyme from the high rocks," said Bobbles.

"That's just what I was thinking," said Tansy, who really felt very ashamed.

The Wilful Donkey Who Thought He Knew Better than His Master

Off they ran, not minding at all how steep the rocks were. But just in front of them they noticed a donkey trotting along, far too close to the precipice that ran by the side of the path.

"Come back! Come back!" shouted the driver, "or you'll fall over the precipice!"

"Not I! Not I!" called back the donkey; and he trotted on, nearer and nearer.

Then the master ran up at a great pace and seized the donkey by the tail.

"Come back, you stupid beast!" he cried, pulling with all his might.

But the donkey also pulled with all his might; and as a donkey is stronger than a man, it looked as if he might pull the man over the precipice.

"Very well," said the master; "have your wilful way and take what your obstinacy brings you."

Then he loosened his hold on the donkey's tail, and the donkey went flying over the precipice and was dashed to pieces.

The fairies went on soberly enough and gathered great bunches of very red thyme to take to the fairy bower for their mother.

"It is lovely—just what I wanted!" cried Mother Fairy; and she kissed them both.

"And you won't talk seriously to father, and stop us from finding out the meaning of things?" asked Tansy, anxiously.

"Not so long as you find out when you are wrong, and honestly try to do right," said Mother Fairy with a sweet smile.

If You Try to Please Everyone You End by Pleasing No One

Some gay young boys were dancing merrily along the road as Bobbles and Tansy, full of eagerness and curiosity, set forth on their next day's adventure.

A miller and his son were also on the road, going to the fair in the town to sell their donkey.

"Do look," mocked one of the boys, "at those two silly fellows trudging along by the donkey, when they might ride on his back."

When they had passed, the miller gave a gruff laugh. "We certainly are fools. Get up, my son." And he gave his son a lift on to the donkey's back.

A little later the fairies noticed some men walking slowly together, arguing and disputing and nodding their heads and gesticulating with their hands.

"There!" cried one triumphantly. "Proof of what I've been saying! The young care nothing for the old in these evil days. Look at that youngster riding in comfort while his father tramps along in the dust."

When they had passed, the miller said, "I must have been a fool. Get down, son, and I will ride."

But now there came some women and children along the road, and an old woman cried out, "How shameful of that man to ride himself and let his poor son struggle along to keep up with him."

So when they had passed, the miller saw there was nothing for it but to take his son up beside him.

They were about to cross the bridge to the town when some townsmen came along.

"It's clear enough," said one of them, "that that donkey isn't yours or you wouldn't be breaking its back by riding it!"

Then the miller wondered what he could do now.

So he and his son got off the donkey's back, found a pole in the hedge, and tying the donkey's legs to the pole, they mounted it across their shoulders and carried the donkey, upside-down, between them.

This sight made Tansy and Bobbles and all the people laugh and laugh. As the donkey was very uncomfortable, it began

Why is he crying? Because he is very greedy, and so cannot get his hand out of the jar.

to plunge and kick; and while they were crossing the bridge it broke loose, fell into the river, and then scrambled out and made for the wild moor.

"Good! Good!" cried Tansy, clapping her hands. "How silly that man was."

"Father says that by trying to please everyone, you please no one," said Bobbles. "Let's fly to the wild moor."

So off they flew. Presently they came upon a hound chasing a hare. But the hare was too cunning for the hound, and by dodging this way and that he escaped.

"Well," said a goatherd to the hound, "I should have thought that you were too clever to lose a hare."

"You forget," said the hound, as he lay down panting, "that I was only running for my dinner, while the hare was running for his life."

"What in the world is that boy trying to do?" exclaimed Tansy.

A boy was sitting on the ground with a pitcher between his legs. He had thrust his hand down the mouth of the pitcher and was trying in vain to pull it out.

"Booh!" cried the fairies. "What's the matter?"

"I can't get my hand out," and the boy burst into tears. "I put it in to get out the nuts and figs."

"You've seized too many in your hand," said Bobbles merrily. "Stop crying and let go some of the fruit from that greedy hand."

It was a burning hot day, and all over the wild moor there was no shelter from the scorching sun that shone down pitilessly.

Those Who Foolishly Dispute a Trifle May End by Losing the Whole

But Bobbles and Tansy didn't mind the sun a bit; neither did the butterflies with whom they were romping, and neither did the grasshoppers who always made them so welcome.

But presently there came toiling over the turf a donkey with a youth sitting on his back and the driver walking along at his side.

"Oh, dear!" sighed the youth, "I really can't endure this heat another moment," and he flung himself from the saddle. "I'm going to lie down and have a nap under the donkey's shadow."

"No, no!" cried the driver; "it is I who have the right to sleep under the shadow."

"Well," exclaimed the youth, "whoever heard of such an idea! Wasn't it I who hired the donkey?"

"True enough," said the driver; "you hired the donkey, but you didn't hire his shadow."

"But——" began the youth.

But Bobbles and Tansy were clapping their hands with mischievous joy; for while the youth and the driver were disputing, the donkey was kicking up his heels and galloping away.

Now the fairies had brought with them a basket of delicious fruit which Mother Fairy had given them. So they flew off to an entrancing pool, shaded with willows and edged with ferns and beautiful marsh flowers.

As they ate they noticed an ant taking a drink from the pool. But, alas, he toppled over and would have been drowned had it not been for a kindly dove who was sitting on a branch overhanging the pool. She saw the ant's trouble, and plucking a leaf she dropped it beside him. He climbed up on to it, and then Bobbles waded into the pool, and brought the leaf and ant ashore.

"Hush!" said Tansy under her breath, as she turned towards the brushwood behind them. "There's a fowler with his net, coming to snare the birds."

It was true enough. The fowler had a net at the end of a pole, and as he crept forward it was clear that he had his eye on the dove.

It might be hard to understand how so small a thing as an ant could save the life of a dove. Yet that is just what is about to happen here.

But just as Bobbles and Tansy were thinking that they must warn the dove, the ant noticed the danger and bit the fowler's foot. The nip was so sharp and startling that the man dropped the net. This warned the dove and, with a cry of thankfulness, she flew off in safety.

"So that's all right," said Tansy.

They were just going to run off when they noticed a blind man making his way slowly along the path to the pool.

"We'll help him," said Tansy.

So Tansy and Bobbles each took a hand of the blind man and said, "We're fairies. We'll lead you to a pleasant seat, and give you some fruit."

"There's a pool here, and you mustn't fall in," said Bobbles.

The blind man thanked them, and enjoyed the fruit, and told them that if they put any animal into his hand, he could tell them what it was.

Bobbles winked at Tansy, and darted off to a wolf's den close by and asked the mother wolf to lend him a cub, which he promised faithfully to return.

The mother wolf could trust Bobbles; so she lent him the cub, and he placed it in the blind man's hands.

"Can you tell me what this animal is?" he asked.

While the blind man felt the cub all over, it struggled and gave little snarls.

"I don't know whether thy father is a wolf or a dog," said he, "but I know that I wouldn't trust thee among any flock of sheep!"

"Quite right," said Tansy. "Let me take the cub back." And off she ran with it.

"I'm afraid," sighed Tansy, as she looked down on a field where four bulls were feeding, "that that lion means mischief."

She had caught sight of a lion watching the bulls from behind a tree, and moving his tail angrily.

"He dare not hurt them," said Bobbles, "for the four bulls are the best of friends, and a match for any lion."

"I know," agreed Tansy. But she was still doubtful, for as the lion trotted off he looked very cunning indeed.

Although Beauty May Have Fair Leaves the Fruit May be Very Bitter

But the fairies soon forgot about the lion and the bulls, for they were attracted by the sight of a beautiful stag who was drinking in a clear pool, and turning his head from side to side in order the better to admire his reflection in the water.

"Dear, dear," he murmured to himself, little knowing that Bobbles and Tansy were close by, "I do wish my legs and feet were not so miserably thin. I wish they didn't disgrace my magnificent horns." And he moved his head as he watched the reflection of his horns in the water.

"Booh!" cried Bobbles. "Your legs are the best part of you."

"Booh!" cried Tansy. "Take care of yourself, I hear the **hunters** coming."

Away galloped the stag, on the light springy legs he had so despised. And the fairies flew after him, hoping he would escape.

But, alas, as he entered some brushwood his wonderful horns became entangled; and the more he tried to get loose the more hopeless he found it. The hunters, seizing their chance, caught up with him and killed him.

"Poor stag," grieved Tansy. "If he had not been so vain he would still have been alive."

"Yes," agreed Bubbles, thoughtfully; "his thin legs served him better than his beautiful antlers."

(CONTINUED ON PAGE 627)

If you had to guess, what would you say they were— wolf cubs or puppies? And if you were blind, would it not be even more difficult for you to guess?

This masterpiece of bronze is the work of Verrocchio, a famous Italian sculptor and painter of the fifteenth century. The bold rider is Bartolommeo Colleoni, a famous soldier of fortune who fought, now on one side now on another, in the glamorous but war-racked Italy of that day.

Photo by Alinari

BEAUTIFUL THOUGHTS *in* BRONZE

How the Ancient Secret of Mixing Tin with Copper Has Enabled the Sculptor to Portray in Metal Grace and Charm in Many Forms

STEEL is the metal of our day. We make the skeletons of great buildings out of it, most of our numerous machines, and sometimes even our railway coaches and our furniture. But the Age of Steel belongs only to the past two hundred years or so.

For thousands of years before men knew how to make steel, they used iron for nearly all their tools and for many of their utensils. And the Age of Iron was preceded by the Age of Bronze. Before men discovered how to use bronze for tools and weapons, they did not know how to work any metal at all, but only used the sharp edges of stones. Learning to use even stone tools was a mighty step forward, but the use of metal was a second advance as important as the

first. So one of the great landmarks in man's history was the discovery of the way to make bronze.

Bronze is not a pure metal, but an alloy (ă-loi′)—that is, a mixture of metals. It consists mostly of copper, but must also contain some tin; and sometimes it contains other metals, too, such as a little zinc. There may be anywhere from three to sixteen per cent. of tin in bronze, the hardness of the bronze varying with the amount of tin. Ten per cent. of tin is usually the best proportion.

Men have known for more than five thousand years that by adding tin to copper a better metal is obtained for weapons and tools. Copper itself was the first metal used in this way, for it is sometimes found in a

549

pure state; that is, it does not have to be smelted out of ore—a process that took men a long time to learn. Now "native," or unsmelted, copper often contains a little tin; such copper is yellow instead of tawny red. Observant men noticed that the yellow copper was stronger and better for making tools and weapons, and somehow discovered what it was that made it so. The next step was to put the tin in, if it was not there already—and in this way the Bronze Age began.

All this took place long before people began to record events in histories. In those dim past ages, so difficult for us to imagine, the knowledge of bronze seems to have come out of the East, from the Sumerians (sŭ-mēr′ĭ-ăn) who dwelt in the lower Tigris-Euphrates Valley. The Egyptians appear to have known of it about 3500 B.C., as did also the people who lived in the island of Crete. It was the Cretans who passed it on to the rest of Europe.

This strange and ancient civilization in Crete has disappeared so completely that it is hard for us to realize that it ever existed. Yet its cities rose and its kings grew rich from about 3400 B.C. until about 1100 B.C.—something like twenty-three centuries, or as long as from the present time back to the days of Alexander the Great. They were a race of seafaring merchants, living in fine homes and noble palaces adorned with paintings and sculpture and

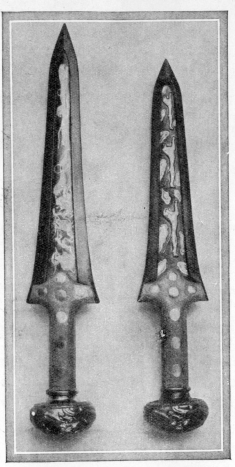

BRONZE WEAPONS FROM MYCENAE

The beautiful daggers from Mycenae, two of which you see above, were made of bronze inlaid with gold of different colours, some red and some as white as silver. Lively hunting scenes and graceful plants gleam on the sturdy blades. On some are rows of animals galloping after one another at headlong speed. This galloping pose, which shows the animal flying through the air with feet off the ground, is often seen in the art of Crete and Mycenae; it was the way in which the artist indicated that the beasts were in motion.

furnished with rich decorations. They fashioned ornaments of gold and silver, and now and then a statuette of bronze. But, living in the Bronze Age, bronze was to them primarily a useful metal. Trinkets of bronze were suitable only for barter with the barbarians with whom they traded to the north. But bronze weapons were the Cretan's defence against his enemies, and with bronze tools he fashioned his ships, shaped stones for his palaces, carved his statues and vases out of semi-precious stones, and cut store-houses, treasuries, and tombs in the solid rock.

At Cnossus (nŏs′ŭs) and other places in Crete where cities once stood, we have dug up a wealth of things which those vanished craftsmen fashioned from bronze. So though all this craftsmanship was being exercised before history began to be written, we know that they could not only hammer bronze into the shapes they wanted, but could also cast it in moulds. Most marvellous of all, they could temper, or harden it, as we do steel. That art has been lost, and no modern scientist or engineer has ever been able to find out how it was done. But the Cretans made bronze daggers and bronze swords with blades a yard long, which must have been tempered. These weapons are often decorated with metal inlay, and adorned with silver rivets and with delicate spiral work,

BRONZES OF RARE BEAUTY FASHIONED BEFORE THE DAWN OF CHRISTIANITY

All these fascinating bronzes were fashioned before the birth of Christ. For three thousand years before the beginning of the Christian era men had known how to obtain bronze, and the discovery of the secret and its application in the making of implements of various kinds introduced what is known as the Bronze Age. No. 1 is a Greek lamp and lamp-stand. Nos. 2, 4, and 7 are Chinese vessels made in about 800 B.C., at the time of the ancient Chou dynasty, which ruled China for nearly a thousand years. No. 3 is an Etruscan mirror made in about 300 B.C., at a time when the craftsmen of Etruria were influenced by the Greeks. No. 5 is a Greek water-jar which was won as a prize in 475 B.C. by an athlete. No. 6 is an ancient Chinese wine cup of about 1000 B.C. The bronzes of this period were decorated with designs representing thunder-clouds, demons, and mythological animals. No. 8 is a Greek cauldron; No. 9, an Etruscan vase found in a tomb; No. 10, a lamp from Egypt.

or with pictures of war and the chase. The Egyptians, too, must have been able to temper bronze to make it hard, for during their Bronze Age they were able to carve in several kinds of stone that turn the edge of the steel tools we employ to-day.

The Cretans, as we have said, were merchants and seafarers. They carried on a brisk trade in the Aegean Sea, along the shores of Greece and Asia Minor, and among the Aegean islands. They brought to these peoples their knowledge of bronze, if only by means of the barter of bronze trinkets. As time went on, other civilizations sprang up in these lands and carried on the making of all kinds of things in bronze. You have heard how city after city rose and fell on the site of ancient Troy. In these old cities, before the time of Homer's story, the craft of working in bronze grew up; Homer's Troy was a bronze-making centre, too. And Homer's Greeks themselves were workers in bronze.

Now all these peoples, whether from Crete or Greece or the other Aegean lands, were great traders and colonists. And all of them made their tools and weapons out of bronze. But in order to make bronze, there must be a supply of copper and tin. There was plenty of copper in the rich mines of Cyprus (sī'prŭs); but tin was so rare in those regions that it was considered almost as precious as silver or gold. So, little by little, the bold traders ventured out across the uncharted waters and into the unknown lands of Northern and Western Europe, in search of tin.

Seeking for tin, they sailed the full length of the Mediterranean in their tiny boats, and opened mines in Spain and Portugal. Still seeking for tin, they ventured northward to distant Britain and the Scandinavian lands. They pressed north into Russia from the Black Sea. They made their way up the Danube, in order to barter for the tin of Bohemia.

Wherever they went they traded bronze wares to the natives, and so, little by little, the knowledge of bronze passed to the savage tribes of Central and Northern Europe. The native peoples began to discard their clumsy stone implements and make better ones of bronze. And when we dig up their swords and axes now, we observe that the earliest bronze work of the northern peoples was much finer than the earliest bronze work of the older peoples; for they were able to learn from the pioneers what it had taken the older peoples thousands of years to work out at great pains for themselves.

Thus, between about 2300 B.C. and about 1800 B.C. the Age of Bronze spread slowly over the whole of Europe. But it lasted much longer in the more remote places, where trade and civilization were slow to penetrate. It lingered longest of all, perhaps, in far-away Scandinavia and in the deep forests of Northern Germany. There iron, which was to succeed bronze as the most widely-used metal, may have been almost unknown as late as the fifth century B.C., during the most glorious days of the civilization of the Greeks.

Yet though the highest degree of civilization in those days was centred in the south, the northern peoples, in their Age of Bronze,

By courtesy of the British Museum

This is not a photograph of modern plumbing fixtures. The article represented is a bronze force-pump which was made by the ingenious Romans more than 1900 years ago.

Bronze objects like these were left at shrines as offerings to the gods. When people were sick, they offered a model of the part affected—like the leg and foot above—hoping that the god would use his power to make it well again.

These toilet articles inlaid with bronze belonged to a lady of imperial Rome—all but the rouge pot with its pretty cover. The other interesting objects are a brush, combs, a mirror, a hook and eye, and some finely carved bone pins.

By courtesy of the British Museum

A tea-strainer is a very modern article indeed, yet above you see an ancient strainer that looks like a tea-strainer—only it was made of bronze. The other articles are also kitchen utensils.

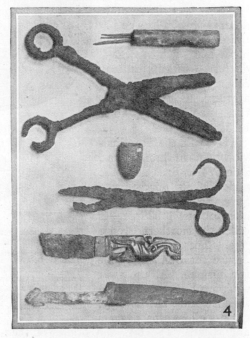

These scissors, knives and other articles are Roman, except the smaller scissors, which are Greek. At the top is a case of bronze needles, and in the centre of the picture you may see a thimble.

were by no means such barbarians as some people believe. They planted crops, and kept horses and sheep and cattle. They wove cloth and made pottery. They buried their dead with great care, surrounding them with fine ornaments, weapons, and utensils, as though equipping them for a life beyond the grave. This last practice has proved to be a fortunate one for us, since it is from these burial mounds that we are able to discover to what use bronze was put in those past ages.

By about 1600 B.C., Bohemia, a land rich in minerals, was the centre of a great bronze-working region. Soon bronze was being used in Hungary and throughout Germany. The art of bronze working passed down the Rhine and crossed to Britain, where it took firm hold and flourished. Thence it travelled north to Denmark and on into Scandinavia. In the latter country it was brought to a greater degree of perfection than by any other barbarian people.

The work the Scandinavians did in bronze was, indeed, so fine that the period of its flourishing—for a thousand years or so after about 1400 B.C.—is called the Northern Bronze Age. These people used bronze for everything one can imagine. All their war equipment was of bronze—shields and battle-axes, chain-mail, swords, daggers and spears. The bits and bridles of their horses were of bronze, and the harness was also decorated with it. Their razors, tweezers, and other toilet articles were made

By courtesy of the London Museum

These bronzes were found in Great Britain, and belong to far-off periods in English history. Just above is a viking axe-head wielded by one of the hardy northerners who invaded our shores. In the centre is a vessel used by the vikings for cooking. At the top is a brooch, the cherished possession of some early Saxon.

of bronze. Rings and bracelets, arm bands, chains, pendants, crowns for their kings, all were of bronze. They decorated the bronze articles with gold and silver. If they could not make an article entirely from bronze, they would decorate it with bronze. They hammered ornamental bronze nails into all sorts of wooden articles, from buckets to sword-sheaths. They shaped bronze into figures of men and beasts for decorating anything from a hairpin to a helmet. They moulded it and hammered it, inlaid it and engraved it. The designs included embossed knobs, or bosses, punched dots, and engraved lines arranged in triangles and circles and in the form of the swastika, a cross which has its four arms bent at right angles. The spirals are fascinatingly varied and interlaced.

Long after iron was discovered and the Age of Bronze was past, men continued to use bronze for weapons and armour, for household utensils, and for articles intended primarily for ornament. The Greeks in their most flourishing period were masters of bronze work. They used the fine metal particularly for making statues and statuettes to adorn their temples and the public places of their cities. Some of these statues were of gigantic size. Of the small ones, the statuettes, there were countless numbers. Later on, when Greece was overrun by enemies, these statues would be carried off for their beauty by the invaders, or melted down for the metal that was in them. In the first century A.D., the Roman

Photos by Alinari

TYPICAL EXAMPLES OF ETRUSCAN ART IN BRONZE

These Etruscan bronzes belong to the early period of Etruscan art. No. 1 is a candlestick. No. 2 is a handle, cleverly decorated with rams' heads. A hole was left for the rivet which joined the handle to the main body of a vase. No. 3 is a cauldron fastened to a complicated stand. The strange monsters that rear their fantastic heads from the sides of the cauldron are close relatives of animals from Western Asia; and when you read of the art of the Far East you will find that the early Chinese, too, put heads and craning necks on their bronzes. No. 4 is another handle. Notice the pointed caps the riders are wearing, for you will see them in Etruscan tomb paintings and on Hittite reliefs. Nos. 5, 6, and 7 were made of baked clay, but their sharp outlines and traceries imitate vases made of metal. The Etruscans displayed exceptional ability in the working of bronze, and their craftsmanship compared favourably with that of the Greeks, whose technique and design they followed faithfully. They were equally gifted in the casting of ornamental wares and statues.

555

emperor Vespasian ordered his soldiers to carry away more than three thousand statues from the city of Delphi alone—and ten years earlier the emperor Nero had taken five hundred from the same place. They were set up to adorn the streets and parks in the city of Rome.

During the days of the glory of Rome, thousands of Greek bronze workers carried on their trade in Italy. They made household utensils and statuettes of emperors and empresses, of famous generals and actors and athletes, and of the gods and goddesses and heroes of mythology More than twenty thousand such pieces have already been discovered in the ruins of Herculaneum (hẽr'kū-lā'nḗ-ŭm), a small Roman city buried by an eruption of Vesuvius in A.D. 79. From this you can conjecture as to how many there must have been in the great and fashionable city of Rome.

Among the people of Italy it was not the Romans who excelled in bronze work, but the Etruscans (ḗ-trŭs'kȧn). The Etruscans were a somewhat mysterious race who lived just north of the Tiber. They were conquered by the warlike Romans before Rome attained to the height of its power, but for centuries they continued to supply the people of Italy with all sorts of metal work, not the least of it in bronze. So numerous and so skilful were the Etruscan craftsmen that when the Roman general, Publius Scipio (pŭb'lĭ-ŭs sĭp'ĭ-ō), was once preparing an expedition against Carthage, Etruscan bronzeworkers in a single little town made him

By courtesy of the British Museum

This fine example of art in bronze is from the hand of some clever craftsman of Rome who lived in the late fourth, or early third, century before the birth of Christ. It represents Hercules taming the horses of Diomedes.

fifty thousand javelins and thirty thousand shields in fifteen days. And they had no machinery like we have to-day to aid them in their work.

The Etruscans also fashioned bronze articles less grim than war equipment. They were famous for their mirrors, which were not made of glass at all, but were actually plates of bronze, so highly polished that they served almost as well as glass does to-day. Not content with decorating the handles and backs of these elegant mirrors, they traced designs on the face of them also, although these were executed so delicately that the image was not distorted. Imagine looking at yourself through a graceful picture, possibly of happy children playing games in a garden.

The Etruscans could cast statues in bronze, too. The famous bronze wolf in the Capitol at Rome is of Etruscan workmanship. This celebrates the legendary wolf which is a sort of patroness of Rome because she cared for Romulus (rŏm'ū-lŭs) and Remus (rē'mŭs) when they were infants. Some sixteenth-century sculptor has added figures of the children crouching under the great wolf figure cast by the Etruscan artist.

Like most bronze statues and a great deal of other work in bronze, these figures are all hollow. The method of casting or moulding bronze into hollow shells was known to the Greeks, and other early workers seem to have understood it too. The same method is widely used to-day, and is now called by its French name, "cire perdue" (sēr pĕr-dü'), which means "lost wax."

This name describes the process perfectly.

THOUGHTS IN BRONZE THAT WILL BE TREASURED FOR EVER

In the old days when almost every painter or sculptor had received his early training as a metal-worker, the great artists of the time often put as much thought and care into the making of a decorative bronze object as they would have given to the fashioning of a great statue. And what beautiful things they produced! No 1 is a fifteenth-century Venetian lamp; No. 2, a door-knocker from Siena; No. 3, a Florentine incense-burner of the seventeenth century; Nos. 4 and 5, church ornaments of the eighteenth century; No. 6, a fourteenth-century reliquary; No. 7, Peter Vischer's "King Arthur"; No. 8, a door-knocker at Genoa, a specimen, perhaps, of Cellini's art; No. 9, a candlestick made by Cellini. All the keys shown here, of such amazingly intricate and delicate design, were made by clever Florentine and French artists who flourished in the seventeenth century.

First of all the sculptor moulds a clay image more or less like the statue he wishes to make. He coats this "core" with wax, and models the wax, with all the skill at his command, to look exactly as he desires the statue to look when finished. Then he daubs clay on it again until the whole figure seems to be only a shapeless block of earth. Through the top of the outer clay covering the bronze caster pierces a hole through which to pour the molten metal. He also pierces a few holes through the clay covering at the bottom to allow the melted wax to escape. Then he pours molten bronze into the mould. It melts the wax, which streams out at the bottom while the metal takes its place, filling every tiniest crease and crevice once filled by the wax that has been "lost," and thus reproducing exactly the artist's design. When the bronze has had time to cool and become firm, the outer crust is carefully removed and the clay core is punched out, as far as possible, through little openings cut in the metal shell for that purpose. These openings are

Photo by Alinari

A MASTERPIECE IN METAL

This beautiful bronze statue is the work of the famous Benvenuto Cellini, the master goldsmith. It represents Perseus just after the slaying of Medusa the Gorgon, and is the great artist's most celebrated work. Cellini had a difficult task casting it. First he had the misfortune to set his workshop on fire, and although a timely shower extinguished the flames, the exertion and excitement made him so ill that he was compelled to take to his bed. There, word was brought him that the bronze was caking, and not flowing into the mould. So he got up and threw into the mixture more than fifty pounds of pewter and two hundred pewter plates and dishes. Then the bronze began to flow, and when, two days later, the mould was broken away, the figure was found to be almost perfectly cast.

then soldered over or patched, the finished figure is smoothed with files and chisels, and there the statue stands—complete.

Now, as we have already intimated, iron had by this period been known for some considerable time. And during the Middle Ages, from about the fourth to the thirteenth century, the use of iron was rapidly spreading among the peoples of Europe, so that the Age of Bronze, after centuries of existing alongside the Age of Iron, was giving place to the Age of Iron at last. Weapons, tools, and other useful implements were increasingly being made of iron. Yet this was far from being an indication that bronze was no longer used at all. Even weapons were still sometimes made of bronze, and as late as the sixteenth century cannon were cast of this enduring metal; these cannon were often very beautifully decorated, just as armour and swords had always been.

But the chief use to which bronze was put during this period was for ornament. In the great castles of the barons and in the palaces of the kings there would be bronze screens and

Photo by Alinari

THE MARVELLOUS BAPTISTERY GATE BY LORENZO GHIBERTI

If you go to Florence you must not miss seeing what are probably the most beautiful gates in all the world, Lorenzo Ghiberti's bronze gates to the baptistery. The illustration shows his second and most famous gate.

lamps and other decorative furnishings. In the cathedrals, churches, and chapels in particular there would be a good deal of bronze. The tall branched candlesticks at the altar or before the shrines of the saints; the candelabra (kăn'dĕ-lā'brä) holding the dim light above the kneeling audience; the crucifix held aloft by the priest; and the swinging censer full of burning incense —these would be of bronze. The font at which the believer received baptism would be of beautifully decorated bronze, as were the great bells which rang to call him to worship. There might be bronze statuettes of the saints on the altar; the very altar itself might be made of bronze. Frequently the high altar was separated from the rest of the church by an elaborate and beautiful grille (grĭl), like an openwork fence, made of bronze.

How a Town of Flanders Gave Its Name to Examples of Bronze Work

Many cities became famous for the making of these magnificent objects. Dinant (dē-nôN'), a town in Flanders, came to be so well known for its bronze work that small bronze objects, wherever they were made, came to be called after it, "dinanderie" (dē-nôN'd'-rē').

When the Renaissance (rĕ-nā'säns), or intellectual "rebirth," swept over Europe, in the fourteenth, fifteenth, and sixteenth centuries, bringing with it a great wave of interest in ancient arts and learning, men began again to do more ambitious work in the casting of bronze. In particular in Italy, which was the source and centre of the Renaissance, glorious work was done. In Florence, Lorenzo Ghiberti (gĕ-bĕr'tē) made a pair of gates for the baptistery which the great Michelangelo (mī'kĕl-ăn'jĕ-lō), himself a master artist, knew intimately from childhood. Often he gazed on them as in a dream. "They are so beautiful," he said, "that they might fittingly stand at the gates of Paradise." Verrocchio (vä-rŏk'kyō) cast a huge bronze statue of Colleoni (kŏl'lā-ō'nē), which portrays that princely warrior of Venice astride his charger as though riding into battle. Cellini (chĕl-lē'nē), the world's master goldsmith, cast, also, some mighty works in bronze. Antonio Pisano (pē-sä'nō)

specialized in medals, coins, and tablets, and made an art of his craftsmanship.

One of the World's Most Famous Craftsmen Who Worked in Bronze

All these great men lived in Italy. But in other parts of Europe beautiful work was being done. In Nuremberg, "the Florence of the North," for instance, lived Peter Vischer (fĭsh'ẽr), one of the greatest bronze workers of all time. His most magnificent work was the tomb of Saint Sebaldus (sĕ-bawl'dŭs) for the church of that saint in Nuremberg. He is remembered best, however, for a statue of a knight in splendid armour, which stands in the cathedral at Innsbruck, Austria. The knight is supposed to be King Arthur.

Although those were the greatest days of the artist in bronze, the metal has never ceased to be used for statues and decorations. Practically all the great sculptors have at one time or another worked in bronze. In the seventeenth century the leadership in bronze work passed to France, where it remained for about two centuries. From Louis XIV down to Napoleon, the rulers of France encouraged fine work in bronze. They and their princes and favourites built many grand palaces, and employed the best artists and craftsmen to furnish them. Many of the most beautiful furnishings were of bronze.

Some of the Many Ingenious Ways in which Bronze has been Employed in Art

For a long time the work of these men constituted the model for the world. Styles have changed now, and it is not so much copied; but we admire it still. Besides casting and chiselling fine clocks and candelabra in bronze, they sometimes made similar articles in tin, or lead, or pewter, and then overlaid them with gilt to make them look like bronze. Or they would combine bronze with many-coloured marbles in handsome mantels, or fit exquisite porcelain vases with bronze handles.

Many of our best modern sculptors have used and are using bronze very extensively. The work of Rodin is an example. Probably no other material equals bronze for sculpture that is to be placed in the open air. Epstein in England, Carl Milles in Sweden, Bourdelle, Maillol and Charles Despiau in France and Paul Manship in America, are among the great masters of modern sculpture who often have their work cast in bronze.

A new use has been found for the metal in making parts of machinery. The modern chemist has discovered that a metal which is closely allied to bronze can be produced by mixing copper with other metals besides tin, and that these new bronze-like metals can be so made that they are nearly as strong as steel. They may be made soft or hard at will, and sometimes they have a wonderful richness and a colour which surpass anything of which the early masters of bronze work ever dreamed.

Yet perhaps the most beautiful colouring that bronze ever takes on is the exquisite green or greenish-blue which you will see on antique bronzes that had lain long-buried in the earth before we found them. This lovely colour, called the patina (păt′ĭ-nà), can be copied almost perfectly by artificial means— a fact which explains why it is so easy for dishonest people to "fake" antiques, in this way making a new statuette appear to be thousands of years old to any but the most expert eye.

On the other hand, when a piece of bronze lies too long buried, especially if there is much moisture in the soil, its surface will sometimes corrode (kŏ-rōd′). Then a thick crust will form over the original image, blurring or even destroying its outlines. Until a few years ago no one knew how to treat this crust. The best that could be done to "restore" the bronze was to chisel the crust off, or bathe it in strong acids, which injured the sound bronze within. But recently a much better process has been worked out.

Perhaps a statuette of some Egyptian goddess is so crusted and corroded that it looks lumpy and rough. It is treated, sometimes for months at a time, to an electric bath, and from this treatment it emerges smooth and fresh, every line and curve as perfect as it must have been when it was made long ago. This treatment by "electrolysis" (ĕ-lĕk-trŏl′ĭ-sĭs) has turned the materials in the crust back to metal. In this way we have restored many old bronzes.

THE SHRINE OF SAINT SEBALDUS

This model of the shrine of Saint Sebaldus is in the Metropolitan Museum of Art, New York. The original, made in bronze by Peter Vischer (1455-1529), is in Nuremberg, where the artist lived. It is one of the great works of art in bronze. If you ever see it you must look for the portrait of himself which the artist has introduced among its many figures. He depicts himself as a thick set, bearded man carrying his tools and wearing a leather apron.

If the brave La Salle had only been kindly as well as strong and determined, disaster might not have followed him so persistently. But he found it hard to get on with people. Though he could command, he could not persuade. So he came to an untimely end. In the picture above, the artist has chosen to show him at the most glorious moment in his career—when he claimed the Mississippi Valley for his king, Louis XIV.

LA SALLE'S GREAT GIFT *to His* KING

He Gave the Whole Mississippi Valley to Louis XIV, and Somewhere in Its Soil He Lies, Where He was Shot Down by His Own Men

THREE hundred years ago the city of Rouen, in France, was famous for its rich merchant families; and richest of them all were the Caveliers (kä-vē-lyā'). They lived like nobles. Some of them ranked high in the Church, and some were even courtiers in the household of Louis XIV, the Grand Monarch. One member of the family, however, was thought to be a ne'er-do-well. Yet this younger son, named René (rẽ-nā') Robert, but better known as Cavelier de La Salle, brought lasting glory to the family by winning for France the greatest of all her oversea possessions.

La Salle was born in Rouen (roō-óN') on November 22, 1643, but at the age of twenty-four he sailed for Montreal, where an older brother was in charge of a monastery. This part of the world was then known as New France, for it was not until later that the land was named Canada. For a trifling sum he bought a large tract of land near the Lachine Rapids, and at once began trading with the Indians. From them he heard of a great river which they said flowed westwards into the Pacific Ocean; and in 1669 he set out to discover it.

After two years he returned, and though he had lost all the maps he had made, it seems that he had travelled down the Ohio River to the point where Louisville now stands. Even more important, he had learned that

562

the big river of which the Indians had spoken was really the Mississippi, and he had heard, as had Joliet (zhō-lyā') the year before, that this river flows from the lakes of the north, southwards into a great sea.

This fact gave La Salle the one idea that was to lead him ever onward until the day of his death. Before he told anyone about it, however, he made a trip to Lake Huron, then down Lake Michigan to near where Chicago now stands, and on to the Illinois River. Learning from the Indians that this stream empties into the Mississippi, he returned to Montreal and laid his great plan before Count Frontenac (frŏN'tĕ-näk'), the governor of New France.

La Salle's scheme was to build a chain of forts along the upper St. Lawrence River, round the Great Lakes, and along the Ohio and the Mississippi. These, he knew, would give New France many trading posts; and he thought they would hold the western country against the Dutch, the English, and the Spaniards, all of whom were eager to possess the region. Frontenac agreed to the plan, and in 1673 La Salle set to work.

La Salle's Courageous Fight Against Many Misfortunes Ends Successfully

Until his death on March 19, 1687, La Salle carried on one expedition after another. Fate seemed to be against him from the first. His forts were besieged and destroyed. His ships were lost in storms. Powerful enemies in the New World and the Old plotted against him. His men played traitor, and often deserted him. But with a strength and courage beyond description, he refused to give up until he had voyaged to the mouth of the Mississippi and claimed for France all the lands drained by that great river and its tributaries. Proud of his country and of his king, Louis XIV, he named this vast territory of the Mississippi Valley after his sovereign—"Land of Louis," or Louisiana.

When La Salle again reached Montreal he found that his good friend Frontenac was no longer in power. In his stead was a mean-spirited, grasping governor, eager to rob the explorer of his glories and of any profits he might make from his great ventures. But La Salle was not so easily thrust aside. He went to the king in France, told him his story, and received from him the right to govern all the regions he had discovered. Soon he set sail again, intending to go by sea direct to the mouth of the great Mississippi River.

A Perilous Journey Through Trackless Wilds that Ended in Tragedy

Once again disaster dogged the sturdy man. Throughout the voyage there was discontent aboard the ships. The commander of the fleet missed the mouth of the Mississippi, and after voyaging about for days, anchored at Matagorda Bay, far to the west on the coast of Texas. In a short time he sailed away, thus leaving La Salle and his companions behind on that inhospitable shore.

Still undaunted, the plucky explorer set out with a few men through the thousands of miles of forest that lay between him and Quebec. He lost his way and wandered aimlessly about through plain and forest for several months. Every day the men grew more disheartened and more angry with their leader. At last, after a bitter quarrel, four of them ambushed him and treacherously shot him.

His ambition, his determined purpose, and his courage brought glorious fame to La Salle when he had completed the work of discovery done by his countrymen Marquette and Joliet, and by the Spaniard, Hernando de Soto. But his pride and stern nature made enemies for him all through his life, and finally brought him to an unmarked grave somewhere in the silent depths of the trackless forest.

A PIONEER VOYAGER to AUSTRALIA

The Important Discoveries of Captain Cook, Who Successfully Navigated the Arctic and Antarctic Seas and Added Vast and Valuable Tracts of Land to the British Empire

NO ONE guessed when James Cook came into the world in a little Yorkshire cottage on an October day in 1728 that he would become one of England's great explorers. Nor did his early years give promise of what was ahead, for he had only sufficient schooling to enable him to read and write and do the simplest sums in arithmetic. At twelve years of age he was apprenticed to a shopkeeper in a neighbouring fishing-town, but he soon gave up that occupation for the sea. At the age of twenty-seven he had become the mate of a vessel engaged in coastal trading.

Then he took an important step; he enlisted in the British Navy as an ordinary seaman. He was a welcome recruit, for not only was he a sturdy man, six feet in height, with keen brown eyes under his heavy brows, but he was an experienced sailor as well. Assigned to a man-of-war commanded by Captain Hugh Palliser, young Cook soon won the esteem of all the officers by his alert, intelligent way of carrying out an order. Four years later he was appointed sailing-master, or navigator, of a ship that was bound for America to assist General Wolfe in his activities at Quebec.

Photo by the Public Library, Melbourne

Before the days of Captain Cook men's ideas about the South Seas were so vague that no one was quite sure whether or not there was another continent to the south-east of Asia. To be sure, the Dutch had trading posts in Australia, but they knew scarcely anything about that vast island continent. Then in 1770 Captain Cook explored long stretches of the Australian shore and claimed the whole continent for England. This picture shows him landing at Botany Bay, not far from where Sydney, the capital of New South Wales, now stands.

There, when a brave, reliable man was needed to take soundings by night of the channel of the river in front of the French camp, Captain Palliser recommended Cook; and after barely escaping capture, he drew such an accurate chart that he was entrusted to make others. He came to be regarded as an able marine surveyor, and was employed for several years in charting along the coast from Newfoundland to Labrador. His leisure hours he devoted to study, mastering such books as he possessed and acquiring a good education.

It was now that there occurred the turning-point in his life. It was known that the planet Venus would pass across the sun in 1769, and that this important event could best be observed in the South Seas. So King George III ordered a ship, the "Endeavour," to be fitted out for carrying astronomers and other scientists to the Pacific island of Tahiti (tä-hē'tĭ). On Captain Palliser's advice, Cook was made a lieutenant and given command of the vessel.

Sailing from England in August, 1768, and rounding Cape Horn, the "Endeavour" reached Tahiti the following April. The islanders were friendly, although they were incurable thieves, like most of the South Sea natives. A camp was set up on shore for the astronomers, and there (June 3) they had an excellent view of the "transit of Venus." Soon afterwards the "Endeavour" sailed for New Zealand. There the natives proved to be so hostile that few landings were made; but several months were spent exploring and charting the coast before sailing to "New Holland," as Australia was then called.

Here the inhabitants were scattered and timid, and so the scientists were frequently able to go ashore, where they found many

Photo by National Portrait Gallery

Captain James Cook, who discovered Hawaii, claimed Australia and New Zealand for England, and explored the islands and coast-lines of the Pacific.

varieties of strange life—swarming millions of butterflies, fishes that hopped about on land, huge ants' nests in the trees, the curious kangaroos, and so many new plants that Lieutenant Cook named one place Botany Bay. They sailed northwards along the eastern coast of Australia; and since they had no charts to warn them of reefs and shallows, navigation became more and more dangerous. One night the ship struck a rocky shoal and was almost wrecked. The crew escaped this peril only to meet with others that threatened to send them to the bottom of the sea; but finally a sheltered cove was reached where the "Endeavour" could be repaired.

Many dangers still lay before them, but the cool courage and good sense of their commander overcame them in every instance. But a still greater danger was awaiting them at Batavia, in Java, when they arrived there four months later; for there the climate was such that during their two months' stay, while the "Endeavour" was being made seaworthy, all but ten of them fell ill; and before the vessel arrived back in England many had died.

Home again, in June, 1771, Cook found himself famous, and was quickly raised to the rank of captain. He made two more voyages. On the first of these he crossed the Antarctic Circle, only to be driven back by intense cold, thick fogs, and icebergs, which he called "floating rocks." This cruise lasted three years and covered sixty thousand miles.

On his return in 1775, Captain Cook was rewarded with higher rank and further honours, and he published a diary of the voyage. But he had been at home scarcely a year before he set out again—on July 12, 1776. This time he went in search of a

Photo by Rischgitz

THE END OF A VERY GALLANT EXPLORER

One night, after Captain Cook's return to the Hawaiian Islands, it was discovered that a ship's boat had been stolen by the natives. Early the following morning—February 14, 1779—Cook and a party of marines set out for the island to interview the native chief about the missing boat. The natives becoming hostile, the party was obliged to retreat, and the captain, the last to retire, was stabbed in the back as he turned to give an order.

northern passage from the Atlantic Ocean to the Pacific. This was to be his last voyage.

Following the eastern route, he again explored the Pacific, discovering the Hawaiian, or Sandwich Islands, before he sailed for the western coast of North America, where he examined every promising opening as he made his way north and passed through Bering Strait into the "Icy Sea," where he found his passage barred by an immense wall of ice rising twelve feet above the water and stretching to the horizon. On his second voyage he had crossed the Antarctic Circle; now he crossed the Arctic Circle.

He is Treated Like a King

In November (1778) he was back among the Sandwich Islands, and in the following January he discovered the island of Hawaii itself. The natives, seemingly a gentle, kindly people, made the strangers welcome. Thousands came from all over the island to see them, lining the shore, swimming round the ship, and crowding about it in canoes. The captain was received like a king.

Then one night a ship's boat was stolen, and Captain Cook landed with a small party to demand its return. At first everything went well; but the throng about him grew suddenly hostile, and within a few yards of safety and in sight of his panic-stricken men, he was struck down from behind.

So died, on February 14, 1779, one of the most gallant of explorers. He was devotedly loved by his men—and no wonder, for he saw that they had good food and fresh water, and he kept his ships clean, dry, and well aired. And what great discoveries he made, what lands and waters he charted on those long voyages! He left the map of the Southern Hemisphere much as it is to-day, filling in many a vague outline. Furthermore, he claimed Australia for England, and thus affected the lives of countless people.

The EXPLORER of the RIVER NIGER

A Man Whose Perseverance Nothing Could Daunt and Who Never Failed to Answer the Call of the Unknown

MUNGO PARK crowded into his short life of thirty-four years more adventure than most people experience in the course of three score years and ten. He was born into a world to whom the interior of Africa was an entirely unexplored region, abounding with unknown and awful terrors, but presenting to the brave and adventurous a land of rivers to be discovered and traced and mountain barriers to be conquered—a mystery to be solved.

Such a brave and adventurous man was Mungo Park, who was born on September 10, 1771, at Foulshiels, on the Yarrow. A brilliant student, especially of botany, his father intended him for the Church, but young Mungo's heart was set upon another and far different career, and he went up to the university of Edinburgh, where he succeeded in taking his surgeon's diploma.

Mungo Park, the Scottish surgeon, who preferred the dangers of African exploration to the practise of medicine.

His training completed, he journeyed to London in search of employment, and was fortunate in securing an introduction to Sir Joseph Banks, who was then the president of the Royal Society, who obtained for the young doctor a position as assistant surgeon on board the "Worcester," a ship in the service of the East India Company. Park sailed for Sumatra (soo-mä'trä) in 1792, and while abroad collected valuable botanical data, together with a description of eight hitherto unknown Sumatran fishes.

He was absent for a year on this voyage, which increased his already strong desire for travel and adventure, and he looked only for a further opportunity of gratifying it.

This occurred very soon, when he heard that the African Association were contemplating an expedition to explore the river Niger (nī'jēr), and obtained, with the aid of Sir Joseph Banks, the leadership of the expedition.

For some time the Association had been attempting to ascertain the course of the Niger, the existence only of which was known, but the obstacles attending such an attempt—the danger from fever, wild animals and hostile natives, to mention but a few—had made the task a difficult one. Park, however, was undeterred by such dangers. Filled with enthusiasm for the adventure and the wonderful opportunities it offered, he studied hard to fit himself for it, and eventually set sail from England on May 22, 1795, reaching the mouth of the Gambia on June 21.

From thence he went up-river to Pisania (pĭ-zä'nyä), where he stayed for six months with the resident medical officer, Dr. Laidley, perfecting his knowledge of the native language and generally preparing for the journey before him.

In December he bade farewell to his host and started for the interior, under instruction to reach the Niger and examine its course; to visit the various native towns and villages on its banks; and, if possible, to discover its source and outlet. Park crossed the basin of the Senegal (sěn-ė-gawl') river and the arid wastes of Kaarta (kär'tä), meeting on the journey with the most obstinate and sometimes fierce opposition from the natives, by whom he was suspected and mistrusted.

At one time he was imprisoned for four torturing months by a Moorish chieftain, when he contrived to escape, and at last, after enduring three weeks of hardship and misery, reached Sego, where he saw, as he wrote later, "the long sought for majestic Niger, glittering to the morning sun, as broad as the Thames at Westminster, and flowing slowly *to the eastward.*"

Mungo Park Marches on, but is at Last Conquered by Great Exhaustion

He managed to follow its course downstream for more than seventy miles to Silla, but here he was forced by exhaustion and lack of supplies to turn back. It was, however, impossible for him to retrace his steps by way of Sego, owing to native opposition, and he accordingly took a more southerly route, keeping close to the river for 300 miles to Bamako (bä-mä′kō), where he decided that to proceed alone in his weakened condition would be fatal. For this reason he decided to join a slave caravan at Kamalia (kä-mä′-lyä), and returned to Pisania on June 10, 1797, where two days later his doctor friend greeted him as one risen from the dead. Six months later he was back in England.

To all intents and purposes Park now decided to settle down in his native land. In 1799 he published a book in which he told of his travels and the varied knowledge he had gained during them, which was accorded immediate success, and which, by reason of its wealth of incident and style, is still regarded as a classic of its kind. In August of the same year he married a Miss Anderson, daughter of a former tutor, and bought a practice at Peebles.

Tiring of Country Life, Mungo Park Seeks Brave Adventure Once Again

But Park was unable to accustom himself to the quiet and uneventful life of a country doctor, and in 1803 he gladly accepted a government offer to lead an expedition for the purpose of pursuing the course of the Niger as far as possible, and effecting some kind of relations with the natives dwelling on its banks.

During the delay which occurred before the actual start was made, he employed his time in learning Arabic and the use of astronomical instruments, and it was at this period that he became acquainted with Sir Walter Scott. The expedition finally sailed in January, 1805, and the start for the interior was made on April 27. The party, which included Park's brother-in-law Alexander Anderson, numbered forty-four Europeans, thirty-eight being recruited from a military station.

This second and final expedition of Park's was doomed to failure. Unfortunately, he made a tragic mistake at the outset in starting at the wrong period of the year, when the rainy season was approaching; and when at last he and his party reached the Niger, in August, after a terrible journey, only eleven Europeans remained of those who had set out so bravely and hopefully, the rest having been carried off by fever or dysentery. But disease was not the only peril that had to be faced. Native opposition was strong, and was eventually to prove the defeat of the intrepid explorers.

Why the Tragic End of a Gallant Explorer was Shrouded in Mystery

Having reached Bamako, they proceeded to Sago by canoe, and there they obtained permission from the local ruler to continue. The canoes were accordingly converted into a boat at Sansanding, and here Anderson died, to the great grief of Park, who nevertheless preserved his courage and fortitude and continued on his journey, the remnants of the expedition setting out from Sansanding in November on the last stage of the journey.

From that point, however, no news was received of the party. Although it was generally believed in England that they had perished, it was not until 1810 that government inquiry was made through Isaaco, Park's guide, who finally elicited from a slave —the sole survivor of the hapless expedition —that the boat had reached Boussa, where a native army attacked Park and his followers at a difficult point of navigation. The unhappy victims were forced to jump into the water, and were drowned, only this one slave escaping death. But Park had penetrated a thousand miles up the unknown river.

The Greeks were the first ancient people to experiment in self-government. Naturally, they had much to learn, but they were able to establish the most just and humane form of government that had ever been devised.

The RISE of GLORY in ANCIENT GREECE

Why the Barbarians Who Swept Down into That Land were Fitted to Become the Most Brilliant People in History

THE Greeks come first into the light of history as herdsmen following their flocks from pasture to pasture. They came from the north or north-east, about two thousand years before the beginning of the Christian era. They were not a single tribe, but many, and as these many tribes mingled with the Mediterranean peoples already there, the result was a very mixed race, a little like the mixture of nationalities in the United States to-day.

However, all these people resembled each other in certain things. They all spoke very much the same language, and they all had heads of much the same shape. Also, they all told much the same stories about their gods. These stories we call Greek myths (mĭth). One of these myths attempted to explain the origin of the Greeks, and why they

were called Hellenes (hĕl'ēn); for that is the name they always gave themselves.

How the Greeks were Divided into Many Countries and Colonies

Right at the beginning of our story, we ought to say that these Hellenes never joined to make a single nation. They never bound themselves together into one people as the French or the Germans are bound together to-day. Greece was not one country, it was many countries; and there were also many Greeks who did not live in Greece at all. For, outside Greece itself, the Greeks settled in little groups or colonies all over the Old World.

There were Greek cities in Egypt from the very beginning of Greek history. There were Greek colonies in what are now Turkey and Russia, and Greek colonies in Italy and Sicily. Western Asia Minor was nearly all Greek. All these colonies were "Hellas" to the Hellenes. For "Hellas" was the name they gave to their country.

Why Greece was Divided into Many Separate and Independent Districts

Even in Greece itself, where most of the Hellenes lived, there was no one nation with a single ruler at its head. There were not even good roads from one town to another. The country was split up into a large number of separate districts, each with its own government and its own habits. And if you look at the map of Greece on this page, you will soon discover the reason for this.

Greece is a very small country with a very long coast-line. While the area of Greece is a good deal less than that of Portugal, its coast-line is longer than that of Portugal and Spain together. A glance at the map will show you how the coast-line zigzags backwards and forwards to form a great many deep bays all round the shore of the country. In one place the seashore cuts back so far that it has nearly sliced off a large portion of the land, and this sliced-off part, which is almost an island, the Greeks called the Peloponnesus (pĕl'ŏ-pŏ-nē'sŭs).

And to the long coast of the mainland we must add that of many islands. There are hundreds of them near the shores of Greece, especially on the eastern side. And those

ANCIENT GREECE
- - - - Routes of Persian attacks by sea
— · — · — Route of Persian land forces.

Scale of Miles
0 10 20 30 40 50   100

This is a map of a rugged little land of sea-torn coasts and many isles—the land of Greece. The early Greeks thought that their country was placed at the centre of the earth, and that the point which exactly marked the centre was at Delphi. The names of some of the districts into which Ancient Greece was divided indicated by numbers are as follows: 1 Thessaly; 2 Acarnania; 3 Aetolia; 4 Aeniania; 5 Oetaea; 6 Doris; 7 Locris; 8 Phocis; 9 Boeotia; 10 Attica; 11 Euboea; 12 Achaea; 13 Elis; 14 Laconia; 15 Arcadia; 16 Argolis; 17 Messenia.

islands—Lesbos (lĕz'bŏs), Samos (sā'mŏs), Chios (kī'ŏs), and many another—were Hellas just as much as Greece itself was Hellas. They are so close together that we may take a good boat and wind our way in and out from one to another in no great length of time; and of all the trips we can take this is one of the most beautiful.

For out of the blue waters, in sunny Hellas, rise mountains sheer from the sea, and between the mountains are lovely valleys where grow olives, almonds, oranges and grapes. There are broad plains, too, where sheep and goats find pasture. But the mountain ridges cut the plains off from one another and divide the country up into many little coastal districts, each with its valley and plain and harbour. It was in those districts that the ancient Greeks erected their towns.

So now you can see why the Greeks were naturally divided from one another. It was because their country was divided. They also quarrelled a great deal among themselves; but the blame for their quarrels cannot all be laid upon the mountains that divided them. For the Greeks were a very lively people, and were as quick at quarrelling as they were at thinking. That did them a great deal of harm, as we shall see.

Into Hellas, which included not only Greece itself but all the other countries where the Greeks settled, there was more than one wave of immigration. The first immigrants called themselves Achaeans (ă-kē'ăn). They came into Greece with their horses and flocks, their wives and children, before 1500 B.C. Advancing slowly to the south, they fought and conquered the Mediterranean peoples, and settled in the towns which the natives had built. They made the conquered peoples learn to speak Greek, and forced them to do nearly all the work. The Achaeans loved to hunt and fight, and once they united to fight the Trojans, their cousins across the Aegean Sea.

Even shepherd peoples require a ruler—such a leader as Abraham had been. But when the Achaeans conquered Greece, each ruler began to call himself a king. And when they set out to conquer Troy, they made one king the leader of them all.

The Iliad (ĭl'ĭ-ăd) and the Odyssey (ŏd'ĭ-sĭ), two poems by Homer, tell us much about early Greek life under the kings. The king was no potentate on a throne, with a crown. His house or palace might be a little better than that of other men, but even so the pigs ran in and out of his front door. He might, indeed, boast of his skill at ploughing or building, for kings did such things in Greece about 1000 B.C.

Photo by Rischgitz

HECTOR'S PARTING FROM ANDROMACHE

One of the most touching scenes in Homer's tale of the Trojan war is the parting of Hector from his wife, Andromache (àn-drŏm'-ă-kē). Hector was the most illustrious of the Trojan heroes, and when he was killed by Achilles, his body was tied behind a chariot and dragged round the walls of Troy. Then the gods themselves stepped in to prevent further outrage, and see that he had the burial that he deserved.

When the Achaeans returned from Troy, ready to settle down and tell their grandchildren stories of the war, they were greatly disappointed. For a second wave of men from the north, called Dorians (dōr'ĭ-ăn), was pouring into Greece. These men had iron weapons, so the Achaeans, who had nothing better than bronze weapons, were forced to depart, and leave their families and goods behind them. There was no way to flee except by sea, and nowhere to go except to the islands of the Aegean, or beyond these to the coasts of Asia Minor. There they prospered and progressed so quickly that it took Greece two hundred years to catch up with them.

There was a great deal of fighting in Greece, but peace finally came to the country about 800 B.C. The Dorians conquered, or were given a share in, every city but one. That one was Athens; and it escaped partly because it was off the main line of Dorian advance and partly because the Athenians fought desperately with their backs to the sea.

LYCURGUS THE SPARTAN LAWGIVER

The early kings and statesmen of Greece are so confused with mythical gods and heroes, and so many fabulous tales are told about them, that it is hard to say where fancy ends and fact begins. No one knows if Lycurgus, the Spartan lawgiver, really existed, much less what he looked like, and therefore the painter of this picture has drawn upon his imagination in portraying him.

With peace came law and order, trade and the need for some way to write. The Greeks did not learn to write from the Cretans, as the Cretans themselves had learned from the Egyptians. It was not until about 800 B.C. that the Greeks learned how to write, and then they acquired the art from the Phoenicians (fē-nĭsh'ăn), who came to them as traders. After this it was no longer necessary for Greek towns to have a "rememberer," who would keep important matters in mind, since they could now keep their own records of all such things.

Hellas was a country of city-states. Each of these was made up of a city, town or village, with the farming or pasture country around it. Sometimes there would be two or even more villages to one district; but, unlike Egypt, Greece never produced a Menes who succeeded in making the districts all one. In the island of Crete alone there were more than fifty such districts.

Four districts were later united under one city. The first was Argos and the second was Sparta; these two took up a great part of the Peloponnesus. The third was Boeotia (bē-ō'shĭ-à), with its capital city Thebes (thēbz), and the fourth and most important of all was Attica, with Athens as its chief city. Sparta and Attica are the two most interesting Greek city-states.

In spite of all their quarrels and differences, there were certain things that helped to hold the Greeks together in fellowship. Two of these things were their common religion and the Olympic games.

We have said that all the Greeks had the same gods. All over the country they built beautiful temples to those gods, and at certain times of the year they held religious feasts or celebrations, perhaps in honour of Poseidon (pŏ-sī'dŏn), god of the sea, or to the glory of Diana, goddess of the hunt and of the pure, cold moon. To these celebrations would come Greeks from many districts, and they would all mingle as brothers about the temple of the god, their quarrels forgotten for the time.

The temple had to be supported and sup-

PRAYING TO APOLLO, ONE OF THE GREAT GODS OF OLYMPUS

Here is a scene in the temple of Apollo. From earliest times the people of Greece from far and wide came to Delphi to offer prayers and sacrifices to Apollo, and to consult the famous oracle. In this rugged gorge of Mount Parnassus, surrounded by steep cliffs, a shining little city of temples, treasuries, sacred monuments, and altars sprang up; for all the people of Greece took part in building it. The great temple of Apollo was rebuilt on several occasions throughout the centuries, but in each temple the room which held the chasm of the oracle always remained. Over this cleft there was placed a tripod, which was sacred to Apollo as the god of prophecy.

plied throughout the year as well as at feast times; and for this and other reasons there grew up here and there in Greece religious councils called Amphictyonies (ăm-fĭk'tĭ-ŏ-nĭ), whose members were drawn from several districts. These committees, or councils, naturally had an influence making for peace, and certain rules of peace were made by them. One was that no quarrelling or fighting should take place at the religious feasts. Another was that the water supply of a town that was being besieged should not be cut off. These rules applied only to members of the Amphictyony, but even so they represented a step towards harmony. The Amphictyony was the nearest thing the Greeks had to a parliament.

Games in Which the Finest Athletes of Greece Took Part

Perhaps the greatest force that helped to make all Greeks brothers was their love of manly games, like wrestling and running and throwing weights. At religious celebrations such games were often played in honour of the god, but the most splendid games were those held at Olympia (ŏ-lĭm'pĭ-ȧ), in the western part of the Peloponnesus. The first record of these games dates back to 776 B.C. and they were held every four years, this four-year period being called an Olympiad (ŏ-lĭm'pĭ-ăd). The Greeks counted time in Olympiads.

Young men from all over Hellas went into training and strove to become strong and skilful, so that they might win the prize in the Olympic games. It was only a crown of wild olive leaves; but this simple reward of victory was the highest honour a Greek might attain. To win it a young man had to keep clean and strong and live a healthy life; these games thus helped greatly in giving the Greeks their beautiful bodies. There has never been another people who loved beauty of face and form so much. During the games, also, Hellas must be at peace, and the games themselves were therefore a bond of brotherhood.

Near the centre of the map of Greece you will see the city of Delphi (dĕl'fĭ), the centre of Greece in more ways than one. Its great temple was sacred to Apollo (ȧ-pŏl'ō), god of the sun, and it was believed that the god himself actually came and talked to the priestess of his temple, and told her important things about human affairs.

This priestess was called a sibyl (sĭb'ĭl), and she sat on a three-legged stool over a fissure, or crack, in a great rock. Out of this crack often rushed great blasts of air. The Greeks believed that this air was the breath of the god, and that as the sibyl breathed in the air she might become inspired and so hear the words the god was saying with his breath.

The priestesses of Apollo at Delphi were very clever, for their words of wisdom and prophecy were often so good and true that no Greek ruler would do anything without first consulting the Delphic oracle (ŏr'-ȧ-k'l). As you may easily realize, this gave the Delphic sibyls great power and influence, which they maintained for many centuries. But they often made their messages very difficult to understand, and frequently their words might be taken in two ways. Then a king who saw only one meaning in the message might find out all too late that there was another; and the oracle would still be right, but greatly to the monarch's cost.

The Brave and Hardy Inhabitants of the Famous City of Sparta

Of the two most famous Greek cities, Athens and Sparta, we shall talk of Sparta first, because it was the one which first became famous. The district in which Sparta lay is named Laconia (lȧ-kō'nĭ-ȧ), and the Spartans themselves are often called by a very long name—Lacedaemonians (lăs'-ė-dė-mō'nĭ-ȧn).

The Spartans were of the Greek tribe known as Dorians. They were the ruling class of their district, and furnished all the soldiers, but they were not the only people in the district. Besides the Spartans themselves there were the free farmers, or perioeci (pĕr'ĭ-ē'sī), who lived on the land, and the helots (hĕl'ŏt), or serfs, who did the meanest and hardest work. Slaves existed all through Greece, and this is one of the worst faults in Greek civilization, but slavery existed all over the ancient world.

The Spartans were such a brave and hardy people that nowadays we speak of "Spartan courage," to mean the greatest power of endurance. And if you had asked a Spartan how his fellow citizens came to be so strong, he would have told you that it was because the Spartans lived by the wise laws of Lycurgus (lī-kŭr′gŭs).

To-day we are not quite sure that there ever was a Lycurgus, though we think it likely that the Spartans did have a king by this name—probably in the ninth century B.C.—who became a kind of god to them later on, as men told more and more marvellous stories about his wisdom. In Sparta most wise things were attributed to Lycurgus.

When a baby was born in Sparta it was inspected to see if it was a good size and well shaped. If it was crippled or too small, or defective in any other way, it was put out on the mountain side to perish. This cruel custom was instituted because the Spartans wanted only strong, healthy people to grow up. When Spartan boys were very young, they were taken away from their mothers and brought up in schools which were almost public nurseries. Their hair was cut short, they were given very few clothes, and their teachers trained them daily in athletic games and manly sports, as well as in other studies.

These children were taught always to endure and never to complain. There is a story of a Spartan boy who had to keep a fox hidden underneath his coat, and who never winced or gave a sign, though all the while the fox was gnawing at his flesh. Every Spartan boy was trained on that story. No wonder Sparta became a land of heroes.

The girls were not neglected; they were also trained to run and to play games. There was one race in which each girl carried a lighted candle, which must not be blown out by the wind.

The Spartans had to live in the plainest and simplest houses. They all ate together,

and of the plainest food—black broth, cheese, bread, figs and wine. A Spartan must never get drunk. Sometimes a teacher would make a helot drunk to show the boys what a disgusting thing drunkenness is. At the public tables Spartan boys learned about government and good habits.

The Spartans were remarkable for their money. It was made of iron, and was so heavy that a strong ox could carry only a little of it. We are told that Lycurgus made the money heavy so that no one would ever be fond of it, for he firmly believed that the love of money is the root of all evil.

This sculpture in relief was discovered in the ruins of the wall of Themistocles, in Athens, in 1922. It dates from about 500 years before the dawn of Christianity.

For five hundred years after his death the Spartans kept the rules of Lycurgus, and those rules made them one of the strongest and most remarkable people that have ever lived. They believed in action, not in talking; so much so that we derive our word "laconic" (lă-kŏn′ĭk), meaning "brief in speech," from these Laconians.

At first, as you have been told, the Greeks had kings, one in each little city-state. Later, the nobles, or the wealthy men, began to win control of the city-states, and government developed into an aristocracy.

Since they did not always like to be ruled by the nobles, who cared mostly for their own wealth and comfort, during the centuries from about 800 B.C. many of the common people in Greece packed up their goods and left for other countries, where they hoped for more freedom. In this way unwise government in Greece itself helped to disperse the Greeks throughout the Old World.

(CONTINUED ON PAGE 615)

You will never need to live in gloomy or unattractive surroundings if you will learn to use a paint-brush and stencil. And the sooner you begin to practise the better.

HOW TO MAKE A STENCIL

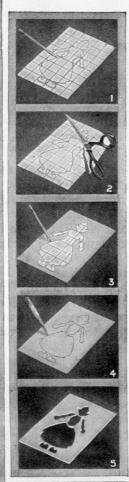

A rainy day can be made to go like the wind if you spend it stencilling. By following these directions you can decorate curtains, box lids, luncheon sets, furniture, and even your bedroom wall—and you need not be an artist to do it. First pick out a simple and attractive design, and draw it or trace it on a piece of thin tracing paper. If you feel that it is too large or too small, you can reduce or enlarge it by following the directions for drawing to scale which we have given elsewhere in these books. If you reduce or enlarge your design, you will have to rule your paper into squares, as shown in Fig. 1. Now cut your design out of the paper on which you have drawn or traced it (Fig. 2), and trace it on a stencil board (Fig. 3). This may be bought at a colourman's, but a piece of strong cardboard can be made to serve quite well. Your next step will be to cut the design out of the stencil board with a sharp, pointed knife (Fig. 4), but before doing so, decide carefully just where you are going to leave little strips of cardboard to serve as braces. For if you will look carefully at Fig. 8, you will see that there the whole design would fall apart and have to be traced all over again if it were not for the fact that at various points it is still attached to the rim of the pattern. The braces should never spoil the design, but should help to make it clearer whenever possible. When you have cut your design in the stencil board, smooth all its edges so that there will be no jagged points or loose fibres to make smudges when you put on the paint that you are now going to apply. Fig. 5 shows the simplest kind of stencil ready for use, and Fig. 6 shows how the paint is applied to it in order to leave the picture underneath it. In Fig. 7 the design has been painted and the stencil is being removed. All sorts of things about the house (Fig. 9) can be used to make designs, and the articles in Fig. 10 will come in handy, too. Practice, patience, and advice from your colourman will teach you how to apply the paint.

CAT AND THE FIDDLE

Hi! diddle diddle,
The cat and the fiddle,
The cow jumped over the moon;

The little dog laughed
To see such sport,
While the dish ran after the spoon.

HICKORY, DICKORY, DOCK

Hickory, Dickory, Dock,
The mouse ran up the clock,
The clock struck one,
The mouse ran down,
Hickory, Dickory, Dock.

TO MARKET, TO MARKET,
TO BUY A PIG

To market, to market, to buy a fat pig,
Home again, home again, Jiggety Jig.
To market, to market, to buy a fat hog,
Home again, home again, Jiggety Jog.

PETER, THE PUMPKIN EATER

Peter, Peter, pumpkin-eater,
Had a wife and couldn't keep her;
He put her in a pumpkin shell,
And there he kept her very well.

BYE, BABY BUNTING

Bye, Baby Bunting.
Daddy's gone a-hunting
To get a little rabbit skin
To wrap a Baby Bunting
in.

LITTLE JACK HORNER

Little Jack Horner sat in a corner
Eating a Christmas pie;
He put in his thumb, and he took out a
plum,
And said, "What a good boy am I!"

When you eat an orange on a snowy day, do you ever stop to picture the beautiful sunny grove where it blossomed and grew and ripened? Here is such a grove in California, U.S.A., with the oranges ready for gathering; and yet, in spite of the warmth there, snow caps the high peaks of the mountains only a few miles away.

SUMMER HEAT *and* WINTER COLD

How High and Low Temperatures are Distributed Over the Earth, and How We Manage to Measure Them

(CONTINUED FROM PAGE 542)

ALL the warmth on the surface of the earth comes from the sun, except a very little that filters out from the earth's hot interior. But, strangely enough, this does not mean that the nearer we get to the sun, the hotter we become. On the contrary, as we go up into the air we get colder and colder. Only a mile above the earth water would freeze on the hottest summer day; and aviators who have flown some eight miles up find the cold unbearable. Even on the surface of the earth high mountains are topped with snow throughout the seasons of the year.

It may appear strange, seeing that the sun gives us our heat, that we should get colder and colder as we get nearer to it. It is because the sun's hot rays warm the earth, but they give up very little heat to the air as they pass through it. The air gets its warmth from the earth; on a hot day you can see the air shimmering over a bare road. Warm air is lighter than cold air at the same level, and being light it rises. That is why a fire-balloon goes up. The shimmer over a hot road is caused by a number of thin threads of rising air waving about. Now, near the surface of the earth, the air is more closely pressed together than it is higher up; a room on the sea-shore holds more air than a room of the same size on top of a mountain. When the warm air rises, it spreads out, or expands, to fill a bigger space, and it is a curious fact that this spreading out makes it very much colder. The higher it goes the more it expands and the colder it gets. So the farther we go from Mother Earth the colder we become. High mountain peaks are always snow-clad.

Why it is Hotter and Brighter at the Equator Than at the Poles

The sun's heat comes to us in rays that are much like light rays, but with two great differences: our eyes can see the light rays but not the heat rays, while our bodies can feel the heat rays readily but the light rays scarcely at all. Both heat and light travel together, and they are both distributed over the earth in the same way, according as the earth is tilted under the rays of the sun.

Imagine that the sun's rays are divided into a number of beams, like the beams of the two torches in the picture. The beam which shines directly at the middle of the earth—the Equator—makes only a small spot of light; but the beam which shines slantingly towards the pole is spread over a large area and makes a large splash of light. Both beams are equally bright, but the one shining on the Equator is concentrated, and the other is spread out. Therefore the spot on the Equator is the more brightly lit. If the two torches sent out heat as well as light, like the sun, the spot at the Equator would be hotter as well as brighter than that near the pole.

You will have no trouble proving all this with a burning-glass. A common reading-glass will do. Throw the sun's rays directly on a sheet of white paper. Try to make the circle of light as small and as clear as you

WHY IT IS HOTTER AT THE EQUATOR THAN IN THE POLAR REGIONS

You can see for yourself that the torches are of the same size and give the same amount of light. But the rays from the one in the boy's left hand fall directly on the surface of the sphere and so light a much smaller area than those from the right-hand flashlight, whose rays fall slantingly and so spread over a much larger surface. That is exactly what happens to rays falling on the earth from the sun. Those reaching the part of the earth towards the poles are distributed over a considerably larger surface than those that strike the Equator, so they cannot heat the earth nearly as much. That is why the climate is so hot at the Equator.

Here are pictures of the earth at every season of the year. We start with the North Pole tipped away from the sun. It will be winter in the north.

When the earth has travelled a quarter of the way around the sun, spring has come. Birds begin to sing and buds to burst. The farmer sows his seed, and we make preparations for cricket and tennis. And when the earth has gone half-way round, as shown in the lower left-hand corner, we are having summer.

By autumn the earth has covered three-fourths of its circuit, and is on the home stretch back to its starting point in mid-winter. The lower right-hand corner shows you the point it has reached.

can. It will not take long to set the paper on fire, for you are directing the sunbeams straight at the paper.

Now turn the paper at an angle, so that the ray from the glass falls slantingly on it. You will see that the circle of light is spread out over a great deal more paper and that it takes much longer to start a flame. This is exactly what happens to sunbeams on the Equator, where they fall straight from overhead, their heat is great. But let them strike somewhere in Scotland, say at Edinburgh, and the same amount of heat that a square mile got on the Equator has to warm nearly one and a half square miles of Scottish soil. Naturally it cannot accomplish so much.

The same thing

pass through this layer easily, they lose a little heat in doing so, and the more air they pass through the more heat they lose. Now, if you were to thrust a red-hot poker straight through a sheet of ice, of course, the poker would be colder when you pulled it out; it would have given up some of its heat to the ice. But suppose, instead of thrusting the poker straight through the ice, you were to put it through slant-wise. It would have to pass through a good deal more ice than when it went straight through, and naturally it would be cooled still more.

The sun's rays which fall on the Equator at noon pass straight through the air, and are

Nothing has happened to the torch seen in the right-hand picture. It is only that its rays fall slantingly on the fence and so are spread over a big oval patch, instead of striking directly and being concentrated on a small surface as in the left-hand picture. The same thing happens when you do not direct the rays of a burning glass directly on to a paper; they are too weak to start a fire. And that is just what happens on our globe. At the Equator the sun's rays strike directly, and so seem very bright and hot. But, on account of the curve of the earth, they strike slantingly on most of the Northern Hemisphere; and the farther north one goes, the weaker they seem. You can see on this map how little sunlight Canada has in comparison with Northern Brazil.

happens when a given part of the earth—let us say the northern half of the globe—is tilted away from the sun. The rays that fall over a square mile in summer are now spread over a good deal more than a square mile. Naturally they do not heat the earth to anything like the same extent.

There is another reason why the Equator is hotter. The earth is surrounded by a great layer of air of a depth of some two hundred miles or more. Although the sun's rays

cooled very little. In the evening, when the sun is low, they fall slant-wise, and pass through more air, so they are cooler. Nearer the poles they always fall slant-wise, and so they are never quite so hot when they reach the earth as they are at noon on the Equator.

All this is what gives us our interesting variety of seasons, without which life would seem so much more monotonous. Whenever the globe north of the Equator is tilted towards the sun, so that it gets the rays from high up in the heavens during more than twelve hours of the day, the people there are having spring or summer. And whenever it is tilted away from the sun, the people—who see it low in the sky for only a few hours a day—are having autumn or winter.

As the nights grow longer and the days shorter, earth and air lose more heat than they get from the sun. So the air grows colder and colder and in some countries the ground freezes quite hard. In December winter begins. Streams and ponds put on a stout overcoat of ice and all green things

long time after the sun has faced about at the winter solstice and is climbing up the sky again. It is difficult to realize that on February 20 he is sending us just as much heat as on October 20. The difference in the temperatures of the air on those two days is due to the fact that when the earth has once cooled off it takes a long time to heat up again; and when it is thoroughly hot—as it is, say, in August—it takes a long time for it to cool off.

But as the sun mounts higher and higher in the sky, and smiles on the earth longer

SHARING THE SUN'S RAYS

As the earth travels round the sun it is sometimes tilted one way and sometimes another in relation to the sun. That means that sometimes one part of the earth and sometimes another receives the full force of the sun's rays. The picture at the left shows, in the shaded band, which is the hottest part of the earth when the North Pole is tilted away from the sun. The "heat belt" then lies well to the south. But, as the earth swings round the sun, the Northern Hemisphere comes in for its share of sunlight. Then the heat belt moves towards the north, as is shown at the right.

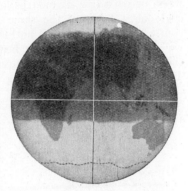

fall sound asleep. In England we do not often get intense cold, because we are surrounded by warm seas; but in Russia and Siberia, a long way from the sea, the cold is very severe. Sometimes, when the wind blows steadily from east or north-east, the cold air from Russia is blown across Europe to England, and we have a severe winter with ice on all the ponds and lakes.

Occasionally, but very rarely, the thermometer here falls below zero (on the Fahrenheit scale of temperature). In Canada and Siberia, however, the thermometer remains far below zero almost the whole of the winter. The coldest place in the world where men live permanently is a little village in northern Siberia called Verkhoyansk, where it has been as cold as 94° below zero.

Although in the winter in England people sometimes die from the effects of the cold weather, the biting wind also carries health and energy. It whisks away dust and smoke, blows the stale air out of all the corners, and sweeps everything clean.

As a matter of fact the cold lasts for a

and longer every day, its rays finally conquer Jack Frost. In March spring comes in, and before the end of the month days begin to get longer than nights. Now the sun gives the chilly earth more heat than the nights can steal away. Streams are breathing again, the snow has disappeared, and grass and flowers and trees awaken. At last, in June, summer comes in—to stay as long as the sun is high enough to keep the earth from cooling off.

As the sun's rays lessen in strength in September, autumn begins. Sometimes there is a short warm spell that we know as Indian summer, so named, some people say, from the fact that the Indians, who cared more for the hunt than for the drudgery of farming, left their crops to be gathered during those few last warm days

Why the Earth Never Gets Old

But autumn nights are usually sharp; and trees and flowers, finished with their labours for the year, drop their fruits and seeds and settle down again for their long sleep. And in shedding leaves and pods they give back to the soil part of the materials they have taken from it as nourishment during the growing season. So you see Mother Earth never becomes old and outworn.

You will remember we said that climates grow colder as one travels towards the poles. Let us see if the thermometer bears us out. In Cairo the average summer temperature is 81° F., in Rome 74° F., in Berlin 65° F., in Copenhagen 61° F., and in Stockholm 59° F. At the poles there are only two seasons, a warm one and a cold one. The warm one is a day six months long, and the cold one a night of the same length. Of course, the warm season is nothing like what we should call summer; for near the poles the ice never melts to any noticeable extent. The few people who defy King Winter and live all the year round amid ice and snow have little to eat besides fish and blubber.

The differences of climate have a very important effect upon human life. The growth of crops depends on the temperature of the air and of the soil, and the welfare of the people depends upon the growth of crops. The "growing season" is the time between the last severe frost in spring and the first one in autumn. On its length and warmth depend the kinds of crops that are raised. Few crops can thrive when the temperature remains below 42° F. for any length of time. In the Scilly Isles the growing season lasts almost all the year round, but over the greater part of Great Britain it covers eight or nine months. In Southern England it is long enough for a good crop of wheat; but not in Scotland, where oats are the chief crop.

(CONTINUED ON PAGE 625)

WHEN JACK FROST PAINTS A LANDSCAPE IN GLITTERING WHITE

This is what our grandparents would probably call "an old-fashioned winter," perhaps with the comment that winters no longer are what they used to be. There are even people who are convinced that the Gulf Stream is changing its course, and that by swinging eastwards it will give England a climate much like that of Labrador. But none of these speculations must be taken seriously. The meteorologist says that winters are much the same as they always have been. Our grandparents would appear to forget the warm winters and remember only the really cold ones. Nor should we think that a few mild seasons are proof that there never can be cold ones again.

(THE SOLUTIONS TO THESE PUZZLES WILL BE FOUND ON PAGE 600 OF THIS VOLUME)

THE CLOCK STRIKES SIX

No. 21

The clock in the old church tower has just struck six. Betty, who has an inquiring mind, remarked that it took exactly thirty seconds to strike six. Then she asked her brother how long it would take to strike twelve. Her brother's answer was wrong. Do you know the right one?

HOW SHALL WE LAY THESE PIPES?

No. 22

Here is a problem for the gas company. These three houses are putting in gas, to be piped from the containers D, E, F. The house at B must be connected with D, C with E, and F with A. Ordinarily the arrangements would give rise to no difficulties, but in this case there is a clause in the title deed which forbids laying one pipe across another, and owners of land round this plot refuse to allow the pipes on their land. How will the gas company lay the pipes?

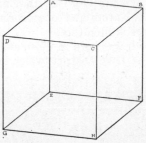

THE MAGIC CUBE

When you first glance at this cube the face GDCH appears to be at the front of the cube, with the top ABCD slanting up and to the right. But if you keep on looking, the cube will turn about. The face EABF will move to the front, and the top will slant down and to the left.

TO TEST YOUR EYE

Ask your friends where the top of a high hat would come if the hat were placed on the floor against the wall. Nearly everyone will guess the hat to be half again as high as it really is.

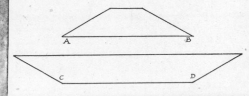

AN OPTICAL ILLUSION

Which is longer, the line AB or the line CD? Be sure to measure them after you decide.

The GREATEST of the NATURE POETS

William Wordsworth, Whose Love of the Peaceful Countryside Inspired Him to Write Poems of Exceptional Charm and Beauty, and Often He is Described as the Greatest of Our Poets since Milton

(CONTINUED FROM PAGE 536)

ONE lovely summer dawn, in the year 1788, a young student on vacation from Cambridge University was making his way home across the fields after a night of merrymaking. The morning rose, he tells us, "in memorable pomp," laughing over the sea and the mountains, the dewy meadows, and the labourers going forth to till the fields. And suddenly the young man was seized with a strange ecstasy, and knew that he must become "a dedicated spirit"; one who should celebrate the glory of Nature and of the simple men who live close to Nature's heart.

This was William Wordsworth, greatest of the poets of Nature and one of England's mighty names in literature.

Wordsworth was born in 1770, at Cockermouth, in the Lake District, which he loved so dearly all his life. As a boy he went to school at Hawkshead in the Esthwaite Valley in Lancashire. Already he loved Nature more than books, and in the stately poem called "The Prelude" he has given us many a vivid picture of himself as a boy—tramping the hills, rowing on the lake, skating at night between the ghostly mountains with the wind humming in his ears. In 1787 he went to Cambridge; but still it was in the vacations, when he could get close to Nature again, that he learned the most—as on that momentous morning when he knew what he must do in all his life to come.

Thrilled by the Majestic Alps and France's Stern Struggle for Freedom

On another of the long summer vacations (1791), Wordsworth took a walking tour

Amid such a quiet country scene as this, Wordsworth loved to wander; and the simple people he met, the children and farmers and shepherds, were those he liked best to put into his wonderfully descriptive poetry.

with a friend in France and Switzerland. He was thrilled by the grandeur of the Alps, and even more deeply thrilled at the first glorious excitement of the Revolution in France, which was overthrowing the tyrannous king and nobles and promising freedom and happiness to the people.

> Bliss was it in that dawn to be alive,
> But to be young was very heaven,

he has told us. The next year he was in France again for several months. He had become an enthusiastic democrat; in fact, if he had not been called home on business, he would very probably have stayed on in Paris — and lost his head by the guillotine at the outbreak of the Terror. On this trip, too, he fell passionately in love with a French girl, but for some reason, still not very clear, they did not marry.

Between these two trips, Wordsworth had taken his degree at Cambridge. Now he tried to make his home in London. His parents were dead, and he had so little money that it looked as if he ought to take up some profession; but he did not wish to do that. He had no liking for London, and was very unhappy. His heart was in France, not only with his Annette, but with the cause of liberty. But it was hard not to lose enthusiasm for the Revolution when news kept coming of more and more terrible violence and bloodshed—the Reign of Terror, as it is called.

As a crowning disappointment, his own country finally declared war on the struggling young French republic. The young man saw all his generous hopes, that the world was about to become a freer and happier place, tumbling in dismal ruin about his ears. He was in the depths of despair for the future of mankind.

William Wordsworth, who is often considered to be the greatest of the English poets since the time of Milton.

Then he fell heir to a small legacy, and went, with his beloved sister Dorothy, to set up a very simple home in the country. This was the turning point in Wordsworth's life. Wandering through the peaceful fields and talking with the country people, he forgot his despair and began to love life again and to remember his old worship of Nature and simple people. And at last, full of the wonder of his new happiness, he began to write great poetry.

Two dear friends joined with his love of Nature to inspire him. One of these was his sister Dorothy, a vivid and eager young woman, with the heart and eye of a poet and a great adoration for her brother William. Dorothy put down in her journals many a descriptive note or turn of phrase which William later made into poetry. The other friend was Samuel Taylor Coleridge, himself in the process of becoming a great poet, and as full of ideas about religion and philosophy as Wordsworth was of delight in skylarks and opening daisies. The three of them were accustomed to wander all day through the fields and woodlands, talking, talking, talking. Coleridge said they were "three people with only one soul."

It was in partnership with Coleridge that Wordsworth wrote the "Lyrical Ballads." This is one of the most famous books ever published, and from its appearance in 1798 scholars often date the triumph of the literary movement they call Romanticism. Coleridge's "Ancient Mariner" is included in the book, and that, as you know, is highly romantic.

Wordsworth did not go to the tropical seas for his romance, but found it lying all about him, in sunsets and waterfalls, and even in patient old men gathering leeches. In the most famous of the poems he contributed to this book—"Tintern Abbey"—he tells us how a beautiful landscape, once seen, can comfort and help us in memory,

The critics made great fun of "Lyrical Ballads," because it was written in much simpler language than most poetry of the time, and because they either did not understand or did not approve of what the poets were trying to do.

Treasures of the English Language

Wordsworth continued writing great poetry in his own way for many years, and dozens of his poems are among the treasures of the language. Such are the poems about Lucy, and the story of the shepherd Michael, and the poem about the daffodils that tossed their jocund heads "in sprightly dance," and the great ode on "Intimations of Immortality," in which he sings of childhood that comes "trailing clouds of glory . . . from God, who is our home." In this period, too, he wrote "The Prelude," the long verse-story of his own youth.

The tragedy is that the vision and the inspiration began to fade all too soon. Nearly all Wordsworth's greatest poetry was written by about 1807. After that he fell more and more into a habit of preaching in verse, and, though he still wrote once in a while a fine story poem or a magnificent sonnet, most of his later poetry is far from his best. The very time when his work was beginning to decline in quality was the time when other poets were catching up with his ideas and his verse began to be popular. When Southey died in 1843 Wordsworth became poet laureate.

That would never have happened if he had not long since given up the strong beliefs he had held at the time of his interest in the French Revolution. Indeed, he became very conservative in politics and religion. But he continued in a quiet way to worship Nature and to live close to her. When he was about thirty, he and his sister had gone to live at Grasmere, in the Lake District, and here he married and settled down in country retirement.

Coleridge lived near by for a time, and Southey for many years; these three are sometimes called the Lake Poets, because they all had homes in the Lake District. But it was Wordsworth who wrote of it in poems that have made it famous far beyond the borders of England. He died in 1850, famous and highly honoured.

In this beautiful cottage at Rydal Mount, in the Lake District, Wordsworth spent the latter part of his life, with his devoted wife and sister. To-day it is a literary shrine visited by thousands who love the poet's verse.

Samuel Taylor Coleridge, a seer of visions and dreamer of dreams, whose "Ancient Mariner" Swinburne described as the most wonderful poem of all.

Photo by National Portrait Gallery

DREAMER *and* POET, SAGE *and* SEER

The Most Brilliant Genius of His Great Day, Samuel Taylor Coleridge Traded Half His Glory for an Evil Habit

THE youngest of thirteen children, Samuel Taylor Coleridge was the genius of a family that has given us several famous men and some eccentric ones. His father was one of the eccentrics, but even before the age of four the boy had shown that he was going to be famous.

His first years were spent in beautiful Devon, where he first saw the light in 1772. But the father died when his son was nine, and Samuel was sent up to the famous charity school in London known as Christ's Hospital. Here he lived on lean fare at the table, and very fat fare in the library. For he not only read every book in sight, but he delved deep into the obscurer regions of Greek philosophy, where very few grown men could find their way. He also recited the poems he had begun to write. And he found a companion in a stammering boy at the school who was also to be a genius and

a friend for life. That was the little Charles Lamb.

Coleridge went to Cambridge University, but his fancy was too wild to let him stay in peace there. He ran off and enlisted in the cavalry, though he was totally unfitted for the life of a soldier. He became heartily tired of the army in a very short time and was glad when his friends discovered him and his discharge was obtained.

For a time he returned to Cambridge, but left there in 1794 without a degree. With his friend Southey, he conceived a great scheme for planting an ideal colony somewhere in America, where twelve men and twelve women should start a perfect life together. The scheme came to nothing, except that it led to Coleridge meeting a woman whom he married the following year.

To support his wife—a thing that Coleridge often failed to do—he had begun to give lectures and write poetry. And now he made friends with the great poet Wordsworth, and lived near him in Dorset. Wordsworth was the greatest poet of the age, and Coleridge was doubtless the most brilliant thinker; and the intimacy of the two is one of the famous stories in the history of literature. Together they planned and wrote a volume of poems called "Lyrical Ballads" (1798), the little book that is regarded as the beginning of what is called the Romantic Movement in English literature.

Coleridge the Poet Becomes Coleridge the Critic and Philosopher

Few books of poetry have ever been of more importance. It was in this volume that Coleridge gave us his "Ancient Mariner" —a poem of unearthly power and beauty— which, with his "Kubla Khan" and "Christabel," shows us the poet at his best.

Though he wrote many other poems, the great poetry of Coleridge was rather an episode in a brilliant and checkered life. In the main he now left poetry behind him, and gave himself up to criticism and philosophy. Already a famous thinker, he was now granted a modest annuity to free him from financial worry for the rest of his life, and to allow him to think and write. With this he went to spend a year of study in Germany, where the great new philosophers were waking up the world. Having made himself master of the German language, he came back to England and settled for a while in London writing both prose and verse for the "Morning Post." He also made a remarkable translation of Schiller's great tragedy of "Wallenstein." After this he went to live near Wordsworth again—this time in the north of England, in the Lake District. Here Southey also lived, and the three of them came to be known as the "Lake Poets."

About this time Coleridge began to suffer from the effects of a habit he had contracted some years earlier. During an illness he had started to take a drug to relieve his pain. It was opium, and before he was aware of the fact the habit was fixed on him for life. It dulled the keenest intellect of England in his day, and broke nearly all the promise his

genius had given. It robbed him of his health and spirits, killed his power as a poet, and blunted the edge of his thinking. It made him dream of vast works that he was never to write, or was only to write in fragments. It made him forget his duties and lose his wife and family and friends—all but the true and loyal Lamb. It brought him to despair.

For a while he sought relief in Malta, in the Mediterranean, but without success. Back in England again, he was dependent on the generous support of his friends. During this period he wrote very little, though he gave many lectures. Such was the influence of the drug habit, that sometimes he would not appear for the lectures and at other times would lecture on a subject different from the one he had announced. And yet there was many a flash of the old fire in his lectures. Even in the fragments that have been preserved, taken down in notes by members of his audience, there is a whole new body of literary criticism, on which many a critic has based his style

The "Damaged Archangel" Takes up His Powerful Pen Again

In his last years Coleridge made a great recovery. He was taken into the house of some kindly friends near London, and under their care he regained some of his old strength and power. If he never shook off the opium habit, he at least brought it under better control. A "damaged archangel" was what Lamb called him in these days. He began to write again, and during the last eighteen years, down to his death in 1834, he published several miscellaneous works, among them being "Aids to Reflection," his best-known work in prose, and his "Biographia Literaria," a minute examination of the nature of poetry and the principles of criticism.

An entirely new set of friends gathered round him—younger men of talent and genius who sat at his feet and drank in his words. Many of these men were already famous, many more were to be famous in their turn when he was gone. For some time after his death, as John Stuart Mill said, he had more influence on the thinking young men of England than any other man.

At Greta Hall, this spacious house at Keswick, near the beautiful lake of Derwentwater, the poet Southey spent the last forty years of his life. Here it was that he wrote his best poems and many of his finest works in prose.

The HISTORIAN'S POET

Besides Putting History into Fine Verse, Robert Southey Dreamed of Founding a Community That Should Be the Ideal One in Which to Live

ONE day in 1794 a friend brought another boy to Robert Southey's rooms at Oxford University. The stranger, whose name was Samuel Taylor Coleridge, soon became young Southey's dearest friend, and the two at once began to exchange ideas concerning a most exciting plan. A month or so later, at the little town of Bristol, where Southey had been born (in 1774), they met with a third youth named Robert Lovell, and worked out the scheme in detail. They were going to found an ideal community on the banks of the Susquehanna River, in America. They thought it ought not to be difficult to work out plans for a new way of living in a new country, and by a river with such a beautiful name. The young men's minds were not only full of new ideas about society, but were full of poetry, too.

They wanted to get married before they left for their "pantisocracy" (păn′tĭ-sŏk′-rȧ-sĭ), as they called it—meaning by that word that everyone should govern equally. Southey and Lovell had fallen in love with two sisters, Edith and Mary Fricker, and now they persuaded Coleridge to marry another of the Fricker sisters. So it looked as if everything was ready for the adventure.

Poems and a Play That Were Inspired by the French Revolution

Meanwhile, they were excitedly discussing the French Revolution, which was in progress across the Channel, and writing, together or separately, revolutionary poetry, such as a long poem on "Joan of Arc" and a play on the French Revolution—"The Fall of Robespierre" (rōb′spēr).

But the scheme for the pantisocracy had been Coleridge's idea in the first place, and it was not very long before Southey began to weaken. His aunt, with whom he had spent a good deal of his childhood, discovered the plan, and, being a testy and imperious woman, stopped his allowance and sent him from her house.

Things were not going very well with the Revolution in France, and Southey began to have doubts about the revolutionary ideas he had cherished. Then his uncle invited him to Lisbon, in Portugal, and he decided to go. So in November, 1795, he secretly married Edith Fricker, and sailed away, leaving her to await his return. Coleridge was furious, though later he forgave Southey. The pantisocracy scheme fell through, and America lost the chance of counting the poet-historian Southey and the poet-philosopher Coleridge among her early writers.

Southey Opens a Book of History and Finds Material for His Pen

This proved to be the end, not only of the plan to go to America, but of Southey's radical ideas, too. At Lisbon Southey started the first of his series of long poems telling stories of the legends and religions of different countries; and he began to study Portuguese history and life, a study which provided him with material for much of his prose. So when he returned to England (1797), his mind was centred on other things than American rivers or French ideas on the rights of man.

Besides, Robert Southey had a strong sense of duty, and he now decided that he ought to dedicate himself to providing for his wife and family. He published a volume of poems; made a serious, but unsuccessful, effort to study law; spent another year in Portugal and a short time in Ireland; and then, in 1803, installed himself in the big double house of Greta Hall in the Lake District, not far from where Wordsworth resided. Here he lived for the rest of his life, writing with heroic industry.

He had need to write industriously, for he had to provide for a growing family. To make matters worse, he had to bear the heavy burden of supporting the Coleridge family as well, since Coleridge was not in a position to do so himself. They occupied one half of Greta Hall, and the Southeys the other half. Since he had "to feed so many mouths out of one inkstand," as he whimsically put it, it is not strange that he was busy.

He wrote works of many different kinds. Though he is often called one of the "Lake Poets," because of his friendship with Coleridge and Wordsworth and his residence in the Lake District, his poems are really not in the least like theirs. He liked to write very long stories in verse, full of the romantic customs and superstitions of the peoples of different parts of the world. "Thalaba, the Destroyer" (thăl'ȧ-bȧ) is a tale of a mighty hero of Islam; "The Curse of Kehama" (kĕ-hä'mȧ) is full of the weird wonders of Hindu beliefs; part of "Madoc" (mā'dŏk) concerns the ancient Aztec rites in Mexico.

His tales have a resounding eloquence, and he tried experiments with new metres which sometimes remind one of modern free verse. Some of his smaller poems are now better remembered. Perhaps you know the one about "The Battle of Blenheim"? An old soldier has been telling a little boy about the battle, and the child wants to know "what good came of it at last?"

" Why that I cannot tell," said he,
" But 'twas a famous victory."

Most people now think that Southey wrote better in prose than in verse. His best prose books are histories and biographies. Coleridge called Southey's "Life of Wesley" "my favourite among favourite books." The "Life of Nelson," which is surely Southey's masterpiece, has been called "an immortal monument raised by genius to valour." Besides these and many other books, Southey wrote some ninety-five articles and reviews for the "Quarterly Review."

He Forgets His Learned Books and Tells the Story of " The Three Bears "

You will perhaps be surprised to know that this author of serious and very grown-up books is responsible, too, for the story of "The Three Bears." It appeared in "The Doctor," a huge seven-volume series of writings on anything and everything. This work Southey published without signing his name to it—and in it he included a picture showing the author with his back turned to the reader, a touch of humour that was typical of him.

Southey's old age was very sad. His wife lost her reason, and died in 1837. The old poet married again, but very soon his own mind began to weaken, and a few years afterwards, in 1843, he passed away.

(CONTINUED ON PAGE 633)

The AMAZING ADVENTURES of GULLIVER

Of All the Travellers to Imaginary Lands the Hero of Jonathan Swift is the Most Famous

THE places that the famous Dr. Lemuel Gulliver visited are as wildly impossible as fairyland, and Gulliver himself was born in the brain of Jonathan Swift. Yet Gulliver's travels are more famous than are those of many of the great travellers and explorers who have really lived. Who has not heard of Lilliput (lĭl'lĭ-pŭt), the land of tiny people?—or of Brobdingnag (brŏb'dĭng-năg), the land of giants? They are so familiar that we frequently describe little things as Lilliputian (lĭl'ĭ-pū'shăn) and big things as Brobdingnagian (brŏb'dĭng-năg'ĭ-ăn) and expect everybody to understand just what we mean.

Why do we still read and enjoy this book of imaginary travels published as long ago as 1726? Well, in the first and most important place, Swift possessed the gift of story-telling to a remarkable degree. He had a way of relating the most fantastic adventures so quietly that we are quite ready to believe they must actually have happened.

And what adventures they are! Besides those in Lilliput and Brobdingnag, which we are retelling here, there are others almost as famous. Gulliver visited Laputa (lȧ-pū'tȧ), a city on an island that flew in the air. He went to Balnibarbi, where the people were so obsessed with their own ideas and speculations that they had no time to notice what was going on about them. He discovered Glubbdubdrib, where ghosts waited at table, and Luggnagg, where he had to crawl on his stomach and lick the dust before the king. Last of all, he found the land of the

Photo by Rischgitz

GULLIVER'S AWAKENING IN THE LAND OF LILLIPUT

What a surprise it was for Gulliver when he awoke! He found that his arms and legs were bound with rope and that his hair was pegged to the ground. The ropes were barely thicker than threads, but there were so many of them that the poor fellow could scarcely move an inch. What had happened to him? Suddenly he felt something moving on his chest—something tiny and alive. It turned out to be a little man—he must be dreaming—a little man barely six inches high! Soon he was surrounded by an army of them.

Houyhnhnms (hwĭn'm), a noble and wise race of horses who were served by incredibly debased human creatures called Yahoos (yä'hoo).

Now, all these tales were written to show men how foolish they are at times, and accordingly Swift is not only a great story-teller but a great satirist. The Lilliputians act very much like men, but because they are tiny we can see how foolish their acts sometimes are; and in Brobdingnag the tables are turned, and human beings seem very little and foolish to the giants. But as we read the stories we can appreciate the satire or ignore it, just as we choose. For the adventures of Gulliver are intensely interesting in themselves, and always can be enjoyed just as a story.

The Surgeon's Apprentice Who Wanted to See the Great Wide World

Until the day when he first suffered shipwreck, Lemuel Gulliver had led a most uneventful and respectable life. His father owned a small estate in Nottinghamshire, and Lemuel went up to Cambridge at fourteen, remained there three years, and then apprenticed himself to a surgeon. The young man wanted to see the world, and so, as soon as he was qualified, he went to sea as a ship's surgeon. Even then nothing very strange happened to him for a long time.

At last, on one of his voyages, the ship was wrecked. Gulliver and his companions took to the little boat, but that, too, went down, and Gulliver was the only one to reach dry land.

He wandered inland, but came across neither houses nor people, and, being very tired he lay down on the soft close grass and fell sound asleep.

After a time he awoke; but what was his astonishment, when he attempted to get up and proceed on his way, to discover that he could not stir!

He tried to move his arms and legs, but they were fastened down tightly to the ground. He could not even turn his head, for his thick hair, which he wore long in the fashion of that day, was also somehow pegged down so that the least movement hurt him cruelly. And as he was lying on his back,

he could only stare at the blazing sun and blink his smarting eyes.

The most awkward part of it was that he did not understand what had happened to him. He could hear a confused noise going on all around him, but he could see no one. Then he felt something small and alive walking along his leg, and soon he managed to turn his eyes enough to see what it was. On his chest was a tiny man not more than six inches high! A crowd of others followed him, each carrying a tiny bow and arrow.

Gulliver gave so loud a roar that they all sprang back in fright. But they returned and shot their arrows at his hands and face. It was like having a shower of needles shot at him.

Gulliver had managed to wriggle his left hand free, but decided to lie quiet until night fell and then try to escape. It was the wisest thing he could have done. For when the little people understood that the "Man Mountain" meant them no harm, they were quite willing to be friends. One of them made him a long and friendly speech—of which he could not understand a word— and others cut the strings that fastened the left side of his head.

At a Single Meal the Man Mountain Eats Enough to Feed an Army

They even fed him when he made them understand by signs that he was hungry; and feeding a Man Mountain was no easy task! At the emperor's order whole joints of mutton, enormous quantities of bread and barrel after barrel of beer were hauled up his mountainous sides and put to his mouth. The mutton was beautifully cooked, but a joint was no bigger than a lark's wing, and Gulliver ate three of the loaves of bread at a mouthful. No wonder the little men who were feeding him shook all over with terror.

Meanwhile the emperor had ordered that an enormous trolley should be built to move the Man Mountain into one of the largest buildings in Lilliput. It took nine hundred men to raise him on the trolley, and fifteen hundred of the finest horses to draw it along. Gulliver lay at full length on the platform, still tightly bound. He slept soundly as he was rolled along, for the shrewd little people

GULLIVER ENTERTAINS A MOST DISTINGUISHED VISITOR

After Gulliver had been in Lilliput for a time, he learned the language of the country and so was able to talk with his strange little captors. Since they were so tiny, the Lilliputians had piping little voices, while to them Gulliver's voice sounded like a lion's roar. To make conversation easier he set them on a table in front of him. When the princess of Lilliput visited him in her smart little coach, he lifted her Highness up, coach, horses and all, and placed her on the table. Her attendants made themselves at home on the floor, and one of them, who was renowned for his bravery, explored the mysteries of Gulliver's hat, as you can see in the picture.

had put a sleeping draught in his beer; but suddenly one of the soldiers poked his pike up Gulliver's nostril—and the Man Mountain awoke, sneezing.

The big building which the Lilliputians had chosen to be Gulliver's home lay at some distance, according to Lilliputian measurements, and they could not reach it the first day. So Gulliver lay all night on the trolley, with five hundred little men as guards, some with torches and some with bows and arrows. The next day they continued on their way, and soon Gulliver found himself at the end of this strange journey.

His future home proved to be a temple— it was the only building large enough to hold the gigantic Gulliver. As it was, he could only just manage to lie at full length in it. The Lilliputians, however, decided to unbind him and let him sit outside and even walk a few paces—to the extent of the chains wound round one of his legs.

As you can very well imagine, Gulliver led a strange life in the temple. His bed was made of six hundred mattresses sewn together, and his daily supply of food consisted of six bullocks, forty sheep, and huge quantities of bread. It took three hundred tailors to make him a suit of clothes. All day long he was stared at by the curious Lilliputians. In fact, the little people flocked in such crowds to see the Man Mountain that villages were emptied and necessary work was stopped, and the emperor had to make strict regulations to keep the people from idling all their time away looking at Gulliver. The emperor himself came to visit his strange prisoner, and with him came the empress, the young princes, and the ladies and gentlemen of the court. Gulliver tried to speak to them in English, but they did not understand. Then he tried them with the scraps of Dutch, French, Spanish, and Italian that he had picked up in his travels; but it was of no use. Nor could he understand a word of what they said.

Finally, the court party retired, and the people crowded back about Gulliver in great excitement. One of the huge throng had the impertinence to shoot an arrow which narrowly missed one of Gulliver's eyes. This made the soldiers very angry and,

seizing six of the mob, they bound them, and marched them up to Gulliver. The crowd gasped and waited to see what terrible punishment the Man Mountain would mete out to his prisoners.

Gulliver put five of the frightened little men in his pocket, and holding up the sixth, he made a dreadful face at him. Then he took out his pocket knife and made as if he were going to chop off the poor little fellow's head. But instead he cut his bonds, set him down on the ground, and allowed him to run away. Then he took the other five out of his pocket, placed them on the ground, and let them run away, too.

The little people were delighted to find their giant so gentle and friendly, and the story made a great impression at court. The emperor ordered teachers to attend Gulliver, and he was soon learning the people's language. It was not until then that he learned that he was in Lilliput among the Lilliputians.

So Gulliver continued to live in the temple that was rather like a kennel, and the Lilliputians continued to crowd about him in curiosity and amazement. They could not wonder enough at his personal belongings. The ticking of his watch sounded to them like thunder; the powder from his snuff-box set them sneezing violently; and they were terrified indeed when he

The Lilliputians, all in their smartest uniforms, paraded before their king; and in honour of the occasion, the mighty Man Mountain, Gulliver, stood astride the marching column, like a triumphal arch. The tiny drum-beats of the marching host of Lilliputians sounded to him no louder than the patter of raindrops on a window-pane.

fired off his two pistols so that they might hear the thunderous report.

At length Gulliver was set free. Naturally, the emperor considered the matter carefully before he allowed such a huge giant to pass freely among his people, for Gulliver could probably have destroyed the whole nation if he had wished to. But when he had finally convinced them all that he was harmless and friendly, the emperor ordered his chain to be removed.

But he had to sign a solemn agreement and swear to keep it. Here are the things he had to promise:

He would never leave the country without permission.

He would never visit the capital city without leave, for when he came the inhabitants must have two hours' warning to keep indoors.

He would walk only on the principal roads, and would never walk or lie down in any meadow or field of corn.

He would walk carefully so as never to trample on horses, carriages or Lilliputians.

He would act as messenger to the emperor when his services were required.

He would act as an ally against the people of Blefuscu (blĕ-fŭs'kū)—with whom the Lilliputians had a great quarrel—and do his utmost to destroy their fleet, which was preparing an invasion of Lilliput.

He would help workmen lift great stones when needed.

In two months he should survey the circumference of Lilliput by pacing the coast.

Photo by Rischgitz

If the ticking of Gulliver's watch sounded like thunder to the people of Lilliput, how terrible must have been the roar of his pistols when he fired them! The report was violent enough to send the little people tumbling over each other in heaps.

For their part, the Lilliputians agreed to feed their new ally. They measured him carefully and decided that he was as big as 1,724 Lilliputians. So the emperor ordered that he should have enough food and drink for that number exactly.

At last the day came when Gulliver was allowed to visit the capital. He had to step very carefully over the houses and make sure that the flaps of his coat did not damage any of the roofs. He had to take special pains about these things because, although the people had been ordered to remain indoors, there nevertheless were stragglers on the streets and crowds of sightseers on the roofs. When he reached the palace, Gulliver was allowed to step over the wall into the emperor's garden, but he was much too big to enter the palace itself.

As Gulliver began to understand the language better, he learned more about this quarrel with Blefuscu, and he also discovered that all was not peace and happiness at home in Lilliput, any more than in England or any other country.

The troubles had begun because once, long ago, a royal prince had accidentally cut his finger while cracking an egg. From the most ancient times, Lilliputians had always cracked their eggs at the big end; but when the prince cut his finger in cracking one that way, the emperor had proclaimed, on pain of most horrible punishment, that everyone in Lilliput must break his egg thereafter at the small end.

The Secretary of State for Private Affairs himself explained the matter to Gulliver. This is what he said: "The people so highly resented this law that our histories tell us that there have been six rebellions raised on this account, wherein one emperor lost his life and another his crown. Eleven thousand people have, at different times, suffered death rather than submit to break their eggs at the smaller end."

Now, across the water there lay the island state of Blefuscu, and a great many of the rebellious Big-Endians had gone over to the emperor of Blefuscu for support. He had received them with open arms, and a violent war had been carried on for more than two years between the two nations. That is how it happened that at the time when Gulliver arrived in Lilliput the people were expecting a great invasion from Blefuscu.

Naturally, the Lilliputians expected their Man Mountain to give them some assistance. Gulliver would not use his mighty strength to attack the people of Blefuscu, who were no bigger than the Lilliputians; but he thought of a wonderful scheme to prevent the invasion and bring peace to the warring nations.

His scheme was no less than to capture, single-handed, the enemy fleet.

It was really very simple. Having provided himself with spectacles to protect his eyes from the arrows of the enemy, he waded or swam across the sea, and in half an hour had arrived where their navy lay proudly at anchor. The sailors were so terrified when they saw this Man Monster that they leaped out of their ships and swam to shore.

Gulliver had provided himself with iron hooks and a cable as thick as a pack-thread. He now proceeded to fasten a hook to the prow of each ship. Then he tied all the cords together at the end, grasped the cord, and began to pull. But the ships were anchored and he had to let go the cables and cut the vessels loose. All this time the soldiers of the enemy were firing at him with arrows, which stuck in his hands and face like so many needles. But Gulliver boldly continued with his work, and, picking up the cables again, started back to Lilliput—drawing fifty of the enemy's largest men-of-war after him.

Photo by Rischgitz

It was a great day for Lilliput when Gulliver came wading through the sea, dragging the whole fleet of Blefuscu behind him. You will notice that Gulliver is still wearing the spectacles which he had put on to protect his eyes from the arrows of the enemy.

The people of Blefuscu gave a great cry of grief and despair when they saw what he was doing.

Gulliver stopped a little way off and calmly picked the arrows out of his skin and rubbed the little wounds with ointment. Then, waiting until the tide had ebbed, he waded onward and brought the fleet safely to anchor at the royal port of Lilliput.

When they saw the fleet of Blefuscu advancing towards them so rapidly, the Lilliputians were seized with terror, for at first only Gulliver's head was visible above the water and they thought he must be

GULLIVER APPEALS TO HIS GIANT CAPTOR FOR MERCY

Poor little fellow! As he was struggling through the "forest" of wheat, Gulliver narrowly escaped a horrible death from a sickle. Luckily the giant farmer saw him just in time, and picked him up to have a look at him.

drowned and that the ships were approaching under command of the enemy captains. But as the channel grew shallower at each step, Gulliver heaved himself up out of the water—first his shoulders, then his waist, then his legs—so that all could see him plainly.

"Long live the most powerful emperor of Lilliput!" he cried.

Fear was turned into the wildest delight. The emperor received Gulliver with every mark of graciousness and gratitude, and created him a nardac, or grand duke, on the spot—the highest title of honour in all Lilliput.

Blefuscu at once sent an ambassador to sue for peace. But the emperor of Lilliput had become so proud and confident and vain that he refused terms and determined to reduce Blefuscu to a mere province of Lilliput.

But when he told Gulliver that he expected his help, Gulliver flatly refused.

"No, no," he cried; "I will never be an instrument for bringing a free and brave people into slavery!"

From that moment Gulliver's troubles

increased in Lilliput. He was accused of treason and threatened with starvation, and eventually had to flee to Blefuscu. He was thankful indeed when he found a boat from a wrecked ship, and could set sail for his native land. He had tucked some tiny sheep and cows in his pockets as curiosities, and found great amusement in displaying them on arriving safe and sound in London.

You might think that after all the strange things that had happened to him in Lilliput Gulliver would have been ready to settle down. But in two months he was off again, this time in a ship bound for Surat.

The Land of the Giants, where Grass Grows to a Height of Twenty Feet

He never reached Surat, however, for from this time on he was fated to have stranger and even stranger adventures. His ship ran into terrible storms in the southern seas and was blown off her course. Then a boy on the topmast sighted land, and, filled with thankfulness, a party went ashore to look for fresh water. Gulliver asked leave to accompany them on their expedition.

As the sailors wandered off on their search Gulliver examined the shore. He found it barren and rocky and not particularly interesting; so he went back slowly towards the creek at which the boat had put in.

You can imagine his amazement when he saw the sailors rowing off to the ship for dear life, with a huge giant stalking after them through the sea!

Gulliver did not wait to see what happened to those poor sailors. He was so terrified that he darted off towards some hilly ground to discover what sort of country it was in which he had been left stranded. To his astonishment he noticed that the grass was twenty feet high, and as he passed through a wheat field the grain rose on each side of him to the height of forty feet. Even when he came to a stile, he could not climb over it, for each step was six feet high.

"I must be in some land of giants!" thought Gulliver, fearfully.

This was indeed so. Instead of being a Man Mountain among tiny people, he was now himself a tiny person among giants.

He almost lost his life at the very outset of this new adventure. For a huge sickle swept through the grain, and he was saved only because, by a lucky accident, the farmer caught sight of him.

The giant farmer took Gulliver up between his finger and thumb, just as Gulliver had sometimes picked up a Lilliputian. Without intending it, he pinched so hard that Gulliver groaned and tears sprang to his eyes. Fortunately the giant seemed to understand, and loosened his hold.

There was great excitement at the farmhouse, you may be sure, when the farmer brought home this curious little mannikin. The farmer's wife screamed when she first saw Gulliver, for she thought he must be a toad or a spider. But when she saw he was really a human being, she became kind and tender.

At noon the giant family sat down to dinner—the farmer, his wife, their three children, and an old grandmother. The table was thirty feet high, and the dish of meat the servant brought in measured twenty-four feet in diameter. They set Gulliver on the table. He was naturally afraid of falling off, and kept as far as he could from the edge. But when the farmer's wife minced up some meat and crumbled some bread for him, as though he had been a pet kitten, Gulliver took his knife and fork from his pocket and started to eat.

The Farmer's Little Baby Nearly Writes "Finis" to the Adventures of Gulliver

The family watched him delightedly. They were charmed with the polite way he bowed to them. Once, when he stumbled over a crust, they were terrified lest he should be hurt, but he waved his hat gaily to show them that he was all right. Once the farmer's boy picked him up and nearly dropped him, once the baby got his head into her mouth, and certainly the monster cat glared at him horribly ; but he emerged from all these adventures safe and sound.

The next day Gulliver was put into the charge of the farmer's little daughter, whom he gave the name of Glumdalclitch (glŭm-dăl′klĭch). She was nine years old and forty feet high. She took the greatest delight in looking after Gulliver. The first thing she did was to make him a cradle to swing up out of reach of the rats—for they were bigger than mastiffs and Gulliver had had a most terrifying battle with them the first night. Then Glumdalclitch started to teach him the language of this strange land, which was called Brobdingnag.

All went well, until one day Glumdalclitch came to Gulliver in the greatest trouble. Her father, she said, had determined to make a fortune by taking his funny mannikin round the country as an exhibit. The poor child wept with grief and shame, for she was sure some mischief would befall Gulliver—some rude countryman would squeeze him to death or at the least break a leg or an arm

But there was no help for it, and the very next market day Gulliver was put into a box and carried off on horseback. The farmer himself rode the horse, and Glumdalclitch sat on a pillion behind.

Poor Gulliver! How he was shaken up on that horseback ride! The horse went forty feet at every step and trotted so high that the movement was

Photo by Rischgitz

In Brobdingnag, the land of the giants, Gulliver had a terrifying experience. Imagine wasps as big and as fierce as wolves! It was lucky for our hero that he possessed plenty of courage, and had his trusty sword by him when the terrible insects began to attack him.

like the rising and falling of a ship in a tempest. If Glumdalclitch had not thoughtfully put a quilt into the box the terrific jolting would have been unbearable.

Even so, for the next ten weeks Gulliver had a very bad time. It was extremely tiring to be exhibited to crowds of ridiculously large people, to whom he was supposed to show off all his "tricks." He was soon worn down to nothing but skin and bones.

In the end, his becoming so thin and worn was what saved him. The queen of Brobdingnag, hearing of him, offered to buy him from the farmer, and because the farmer thought his pet would surely die in a month or so, he was willing to sell. So Gulliver went to live at the court.

At the court it did not take him long to get well, for everyone was kind to him and he lived in the greatest luxury. Moreover, Glumdalclitch was engaged to be his attendant, and she eagerly supplied his every want.

The royal family made a great pet of Gulliver. His little table was placed on the great dining-table so that all the court could watch the amusing way in which he ate. Of course, their method of eating looked just as strange to Gulliver. He was rather horrified to observe that the queen took at one mouthful as much as a dozen English farmers could eat at one meal.

Gulliver was given a tank, too, as big as a lake; it was fitted with rowing and sailing boats which looked like dolls' toys to the Brobdingnagians but which were suited to Gulliver's size. He greatly amused the court by rowing and sailing before them, and the queen and her ladies enjoyed making storms for him with their fans.

Gulliver had one enemy—the court dwarf. He was only thirty feet high, but naturally that did not look so dwarfish to the Brobdingnagians since Gulliver's arrival, and the dwarf was jealous. One day, out of spite, he picked Gulliver up and dropped him into a bowl of cream, where he was nearly drowned. The queen was very angry indeed, and she commanded the dwarf first to drink up the whole of cream and then to go into exile.

Nor was that Gulliver's only narrow escape. Another time a monster monkey seized him, stuffed him full of the nasty food it produced from the pouches of its cheeks, and carried him off with it to the palace roof. It was only with the greatest difficulty that he was rescued.

Meanwhile Gulliver, with Glumdalclitch as a teacher, soon mastered the Brobdingnagian language, and he greatly enjoyed learning about the manners and customs of the country and trying to explain those of England. But all the time, in spite of everybody's kindness, he could not help being homesick. He longed to be among people of his own size again, and to walk about the streets and fields without being afraid that some great foot might accidentally tread him to death as if he were a frog.

Gulliver Sleeps, and is Caught Up Into the Sky by a Giant Bird

Gulliver had been two years in Brobdingnag, and now followed the court wherever it went, travelling in a wonderful box furnished with all he could possibly desire. Then one day he persuaded the boy who was carrying his box to set it down for a time on the seashore. The boy went off in search of sea-birds' eggs, and Gulliver fell comfortably asleep in the hammock slung from the roof of his box.

Suddenly he was awakened by a violent pull upon the ring which was fastened at the top of his box as a handle. He felt the box rise and spin through the air at tremendous speed. He called out, but calling produced no response, and as he looked from the window, he could see nothing but the clouds and the sky.

Finally, it occurred to him that there was a clapping of wings above him. Some giant eagle must be carrying his box—with him in it—high over land and sea. Then he knew that his danger was great indeed, for at any moment the bird might drop him on to the rocks or into the water.

And sure enough, all at once he felt the box falling at such a speed that he almost lost his breath. Then it struck with a terrible crash—louder, he said later, than the cataract of Niagara. For a moment all was darkness; then Gulliver felt his box rise, and he could see light through the top of the windows. He knew then that he must have fallen down into the sea.

Rescued From a Watery Grave

Now, there were staples fixed to the outside of the box, so that a servant, when riding on horseback, could buckle it to his belt. Presently, while Gulliver was groaning with anxiey, it seemed to him that something was tugging at these staples. At least there was a commotion that made the waves rise nearly to the top of his windows, leaving him almost in the dark. Suppose some ship had sighted this strange box of his and decided to grapple it and take it on board? Certainly the sailors would never guess that a miserable mortal was shut up inside it.

He would have to find some way to make them guess it. There was a sliding board in the roof, and he had already managed to push it back sufficiently to obtain a little fresh air. Now he fastened a handkerchief to a stick and pushed it up through the hole.

Nothing happened.

Yet it was by now quite clear that the box was being dragged through the water. At last it struck violently against something hard, which poor Gulliver thought might be a rock. Then he felt the box swing upwards, and he waved and shouted with all his might.

To his great delight he heard English voices speaking and calling to him.

The sailors released the poor prisoner, and Gulliver, almost crazed with happiness, stepped out on the deck of an English ship. He was taken to the captain's cabin, and there he told his story.

And so Gulliver returned once more safely home to his wife and daughter, although it was only to leave them again for fresh adventures in other marvellous lands.

ANSWERS TO PUZZLES
ON PAGE 583

21—The answer is 66 seconds. Between the first and sixth strokes there were five intervals of time, each interval of 6 seconds' duration. There were eleven intervals of 6 seconds each between the first and twelfth strokes.

22—

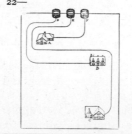

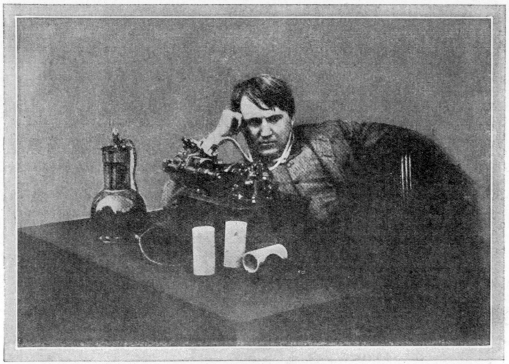

This is the famous inventor Thomas Alva Edison, looking very tired indeed. And no wonder! For he has just worked five days and nights with scarcely a break on the contrivance you see before him. And he has made it work at last. He has invented the phonograph, which will some day bring music to countless people.

How We MAKE a MACHINE TALK

The Gramophone Will Carry Our Voices Down through the Ages, Just as the Pen and the Printing Press Have Preserved the Words of Olden Times for Us

NOTHING dies away quicker than a sound. One moment we are hearing it, and the next it is gone for ever. And many a sweet singer in the years gone by has filled the air with music that vanished on the instant, never to be heard again.

What would we not give to hear the famous Jenny Lind sing "Annie Laurie" as she sang it seventy years ago? Or to listen to Mozart and Beethoven playing their own music! Or to hear Cicero declaiming one of his great speeches in the Roman senate-house! But these things we shall never hear. They are gone the way of all the sounds of long ago.

But future generations will be more fortunate. A hundred years from now, ten thousand years from now, they will be able to hear the great singers and orators of to-day as clearly as we can hear them now. They will have a vast collection of the words that have been sung and spoken through the ages, just as we have great collections, in our libraries, of the words that have been written. For we now have a machine that will catch the words we speak or sing and keep them for all time.

We cannot see a noise, but we can feel it—if it is violent enough. We have all felt explosions of the kind that make the windows rattle. What we feel is only a vibration, and it takes a loud one to be felt. But a machine has been made that will pick up the very lightest vibrations of a sound and write them down for us; and that machine will keep a record of anything we trust to it, even of our whispers.

The First Voice Signature

In 1857 an Englishman named Leon Scott grew curious about the way his voice shook and vibrated in his throat, and determined to get a kind of picture of what was going on. He took a piece of sheepskin and drew it tight over one end of a large tube, making a kind of drum. In the middle of the sheepskin he stuck a piece of bristle, with the free end resting on a sheet of sooty paper; and the sheet of paper was arranged to turn round slowly as he used it.

When he talked into the tube, the sheepskin vibrated and the bristle drew a wavy line on the sooty paper as it turned round. If he shouted, the bristle would make heavy scratches backwards and forwards, but if he spoke very low it moved barely enough to leave the lightest traces. When he had finished and had removed the paper, he had a kind of picture of all that he had said. The picture would not repeat what he had said, but at least it would show how loud and how fast he had been talking.

Leon Scott, who called his tracings the phonautograph, never got any further than this. He never found out how to make the picture repeat his words. But other men improved upon his first crude recording instrument, and finally Thomas Alva Edison produced a real talking-machine—the phonograph.

He it was who discovered how to bring back a voice out of the air and make it talk again long after it had ceased speaking. In place of the sooty paper he used a roll of tinfoil, and instead of the bristle he employed a sharp point of steel. He also used a thin diaphragm (dǐ'ȧ-frăm), or drum plate, of glass in place of the sheepskin, and a funnel instead of the round tube.

When he spoke into the funnel, the steel needle dug a long groove in the tinfoil— deep and rough if he spoke loudly, shallow and smooth when he used gentler tones.

Then Edison removed his tinfoil and started the needle again at the beginning of the groove it had just made. As it travelled through the groove once more, passing over the deep, rough places and the shallow, smoother ones, it made the glass diaphragm vibrate as it had vibrated with the voice in the first place. And then the sound issued from the funnel just as it had gone in, word for word. So the world had another wonder.

The Ingenious "Sound Writer"

That first talking-machine, made in 1877, is still to be seen in the Smithsonian Institution at Washington, U.S.A. It is a very simple affair; it cost only about £4 to make, and the tinfoil record was turned by hand with a crank. The machine was called a phonograph, from two Greek words meaning "sound writer."

The main trouble with the first machine was that the tinfoil was so soft as to wear out after it had been used seven or eight times. Edison might well have remedied the fault, but he was busy with a good many other inventions. So it was left to other men to perfect the machine and to bring it into popular use.

One of the chief of these was a German named Emile Berliner. He made a good many experiments at taking the record of the voice in wax and in copper, and at last gave us a disk such as we use in our records to-day. When he had perfected a durable disk from which as many copies as were wanted could be made, he was ready, in 1898, to put his machine on the market; and soon many a home had its "music box." It was called

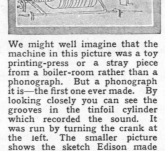

We might well imagine that the machine in this picture was a toy printing-press or a stray piece from a boiler-room rather than a phonograph. But a phonograph it is—the first one ever made. By looking closely you can see the grooves in the tinfoil cylinder which recorded the sound. It was run by turning the crank at the left. The smaller picture shows the sketch Edison made before he started to work out in detail his great idea.

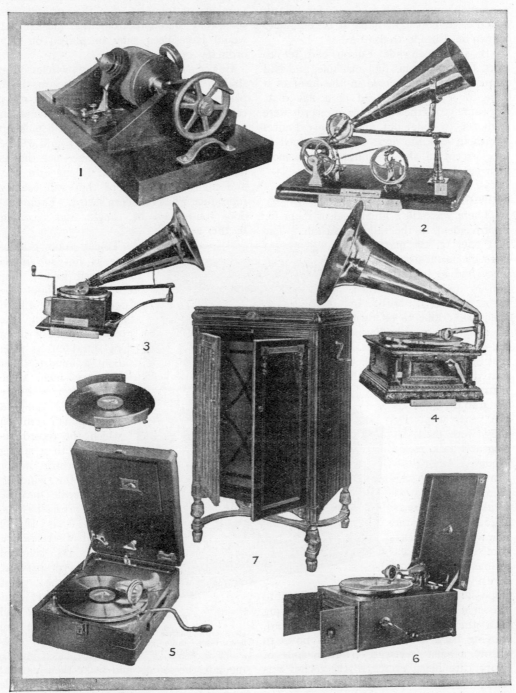

GRAMOPHONES OF YESTERDAY AND TO-DAY

Here are some old and new types of gramophones. Fig. 1. An Edison tinfoil experimental phonograph. Fig. 2. Machine invented by Emile Berliner in 1894. Fig. 3. The first commercial gramophone: His Master's Voice model of 1898. Fig. 4. H.M.V. Senior Monarch model, 1904. The last three illustrations are of more modern machines. Fig. 5. Portable model, showing detachable tray for carrying records. Fig. 6. First portable H.M.V. gramophone. Fig. 7. H.M.V. mahogany cabinet type, now replaced by the radio-gramophone.

a gramophone—which is Greek for "letter sound"—and by that name it is commonly known in Europe to-day.

In the meanwhile Edison had set to work to improve his first machine, and had perfected a record made in the form of a tube, or cylinder, instead of a flat disk. For some years the two kinds of records were sold side by side; but finally the cylinders vanished, and the disks alone remained in use—except in the machines that business men use for dictating letters.

Gramophones that were Turned by Hand.

There was still a great deal of room for improvement in the talking-machine. The first ones on the market were by no means perfect. They had to be turned by hand, and they talked through a big tin horn. In time they came to be turned by a spring, and the horn was hidden away in the box. The first machines, too, squeaked and grated so unpleasantly that many people would not listen to them; but as the years went by they were made to sing and talk melodiously. Among the many improvements, the greatest of all came as late as 1925. For then the new wonder of wireless came to the aid of the gramophone. Before then it had been impossible to sing a song naturally into the machine. The vocalist had to sing into the big horn to make the record, moving back a little on the loud notes to ensure against "blasting"; but in spite of every care being exercised, the record was always more or less strained and somewhat distorted.

An orchestra or band had to be crowded together before the horn; and frequently special instruments had to be called into service to make up for the inadequate number of players. So the record was somewhat different from the music that would have been sung or played on any ordinary occasion.

But since the coming of wireless the singers have sung and the orchestras have played before a microphone. Here they can perform just as they would before an audience. For the microphone will pick up all their lightest tones, and the sound will be carried through a vacuum tube—one that is emptied of air—before it is cut into wax and made into a record that will exactly reproduce what has been heard. Even outdoor music can be caught and recorded in this way.

To-day our gramophone is not so simple as it used to be. The record looks about the same—a flat disk of hard black wax with the groove indented in a long spiral on its face, about a hundred lines to every inch. The machinery is very much the same—a little platform on which the record revolves, with a spring or an electric motor to do the winding. The needle may be of various kinds, though it is usually a point of steel which should be changed with every playing, because the point wears blunt; but the sound box and the horn are all different, for electricity has come to regulate the sounds and make them natural and clear. That also was made possible by wireless.

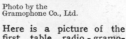

Photo by the Gramophone Co., Ltd.

Here is a picture of the first table radio-gramophone, H.M.V. model.

Down to 1911 the horn always appeared on the outside of the gramophone, which spoilt the appearance of the machine, however beautiful the cabinet might have been.

Not many of us could afford to hire a whole orchestra whenever we wanted to listen to a dance tune or a symphony. Not even our wireless set will always give us just what we want. But let an orchestra play our favourite piece to a gramophone, and the music is always ours.

In the foreground of the picture above you will notice the microphone, which is catching all the delicate tones and shadings of the music.

To the right is the recording gramophone, which is busily translating the sounds into bumps and hollows.

The fine modern gramophone on the left we have caught in the act of playing its miraculous music. If we could watch through a microscope as the steel needle travels over the record, it would look rather like the little picture in the inset below. Round and round the disk the needle follows the wavy grooves, which look to the naked eye like fine lines on the surface. The record is whirled by delicate clockwork, for the slightest irregularity of speed would spoil the tone. Whenever the needle hits any of the little bumps or hollows it passes the vibrations on to the sound-box, which turns them into sound. Thence the sound passes through the resonance-box, where it is "amplified," or made greater in volume. The little arrows in the picture show the course of the sound waves. We may imagine that they are the voice of the great Caruso, coming out to us in a pure and golden tone, just as if he were still alive and in the room in which we are sitting. The lower part of this gramophone consists of a cabinet for holding records. If we want to enjoy listening to them we must keep them in envelopes or portfolios where nothing can scratch them, and we must be careful never to play them with a worn-out needle.

So inventive genius was set to work to produce an internal horn, one that would be as satisfactory as the existing type, and yet would be hidden from view. This improvement was quickly effected, and further stages in the development of the gramophone began to receive the attention of the experts, who were constantly thinking out new ideas and experimenting with a view to arriving at the highest possible perfection.

The Wonderful Gramophone that Changes Its Records Automatically

A means of changing records automatically was devised, but it was not until some years later, when the mechanism had been considerably simplified, that a machine was produced that would play a record and then, by the simple action of pressing a button, could be made to discard it and begin another. A later invention, however, made it possible for a long series of records to be played without any human attention whatsoever.

Next came the pleated diaphragm, the invention of a Frenchman named Lumière. The diaphragm, mounted upright at right-angles to the record, was supported by a ring which was carried by an arm across the face of the disk, and a needle was fixed in a stylus which was connected by a long wooden bar through a bell-crank lever fastened to the centre of the diaphragm. The effect of this new type of diaphragm was to give a more natural reproduction of sound, by doing away with the hollow horn quality that had hitherto prevailed. It was another step towards perfection.

The Combined Gramophone and Wireless Appears on the Scene

By 1923 the first experimental single-dial combined wireless and gramophone had come into being, but its public appearance was delayed until a means of recording by an electrical process, which was then engaging the attention of experimenters, had been perfected a few years later. Later there came the electrical pick-up, by which records could be reproduced through the loudspeaker of a wireless set.

With a view to cheapening the cost of records, various experiments have been made, and these have resulted in disks being produced of cellulose or a cellulose compound, and of paper coated with a special lacquer. One company even manufactured a record on which three distinct tunes were recorded, but this was in the nature of a freakish experiment, although the record proved quite satisfactory.

Now let us see how records are made. After the recording has been done, the engraved wax is sent to the factory for the duplicating shells, or dies, to be made.

First the wax is coated with a special metallic preparation to form an attraction for the electro deposit. It is then put in the plating bath, and after a time a negative shell, or "master" matrix, is grown of the correct thickness. Records are pressed from the master and these are submitted to various tests, which, if satisfactory, prepare the way for the next stage. The master is again put in the plating bath, and a positive shell grown from it. This is known as the "mother," and from it any number of negative shells or "working matrices" can again be grown for the actual operation of pressing the records.

How the Voice of History is Preserved in the British Museum

The greatest care and accuracy must be employed in the carrying out of these intermediate processes. The "master," in particular, must not suffer any damage, and to ensure their safety all masters are stored in special fire-proof rooms. Matrices of certain records of historic interest are deposited at the British Museum, where future generations will be able to hear events that occurred many years before.

The raw materials are not very attractive, the principal ingredients being shellac and vegetable black. Of these, shellac, a resinous substance which comes from an East Indian insect, is the most expensive, and the method of grinding and mixing it with the other ingredients is what gives to a gramophone record its good surface and finish. The shellac is first graded in huge mills which automatically throw out any that contains impurities. It is essential that record

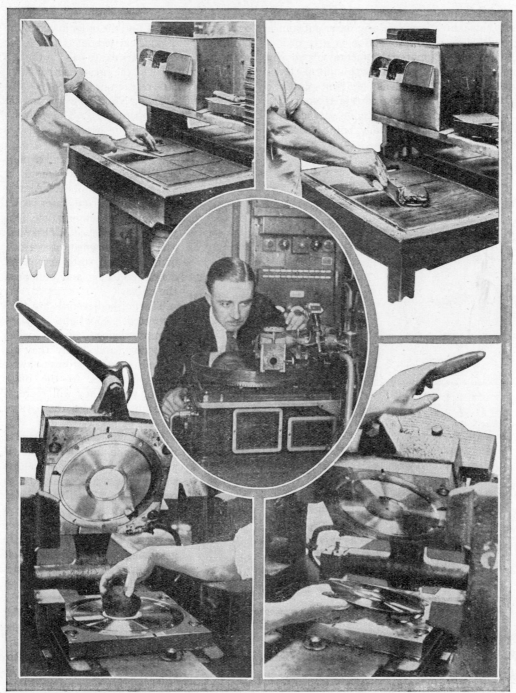

Photos by the Gramophone Co., Ltd.

HOW THE RECORDS ARE DUPLICATED

In the first of the upper pictures the "biscuit" is being placed on the hot slab. After it has been made sufficiently hot and plastic it is scraped off, as you see in the second picture, rolled into a ball and then—as shown at the bottom left-hand corner—placed in the centre of the press. Great pressure is applied, the disk is cooled, and when the press is opened the record appears as in the right-hand picture. In the oval is a recording machine.

material should be all of the same texture, as the slightest trace of any other substance would spoil the reproduction of a record.

The mixed material emerges from the rolling mill in large sheets of uniform thickness. This material is "thermo-plastic"; that is to say, above a certain temperature it becomes soft, but on cooling it hardens. Therefore it is rolled hot, but as soon as

Photo by the Gramophone Co., Ltd
This machine, which combines wireless and the gramophone, is known as the auto-radiogram. It is one of the latest models.

it has cooled down it is broken into "biscuits" of the same size and weight. Two of these biscuits are sufficient for a ten-inch record, three being used when a twelve-inch disk is required.

From the mixing factory the "biscuits" of record material are delivered to the press department, where they are converted into the familiar disks by semi-automatic presses.

The labels are affixed to each side of the record as it is pressed, and the order in which the pressing operation is carried out is as follows:

First the metal matrices are fixed in the top and bottom plates of the press. Label No. 1 is placed over the centre pin, face downwards on the lower matrix, No. 2 face upwards in the centre of the upper matrix. The requisite quantity of biscuit made hot and plastic is placed on top of Label No. 1. The press is closed, and a pressure of seventy tons or more per square inch is applied. Almost immediately a cold water jacket reduces the temperature, the record is hardened, and on the press being opened, it appears in its finished state except for a final polishing and buffing of the edges.

The finished records are then inspected, copyright royalty stamps being affixed when necessary, and finally they are passed on to the stores to await their summons to the outer world, where they will recreate in countless homes the joys of the art of music.

For a long time many lovers of music made fun of the gramophone. And they might well do so, for it was a poor and harsh contrivance. But the difficulty of the scratches and bumps was soon overcome; and now we have the sweetest music from great singers and orchestras that may never come within a thousand miles of our homes. Just as printing has scattered books far and wide over the world, the gramophone has carried the spoken word and music to the ends of the earth. Before we had wireless, the gramophone was so popular that a great singer might earn as much as £20,000 a year by recording.

And even since the advent of wireless the gramophone has continued to remain a popular form of entertainment. No other instrument in the wide world can hold and preserve a speech or song for all time.

FLAGS OF FOREIGN COUNTRIES

Flags of thirty foreign countries.   Other flags are shown in the colour plates facing pages 913 and 961.

The FIRST MEN to CROSS NORTH AMERICA

In Many Ways the Trip of Lewis and Clark over the Rocky Mountains to the Pacific was a More Daring Feat than Many of the Great Sea Voyages of the Explorers

IT WAS more than three hundred years after the discovery of North America that the trip across the Continent to the West Coast was made, a delay in exploration which was occasioned by the difficulties and dangers to be encountered, both in the form of jungles and hostile Indians.

In 1803 President Jefferson bought from Napoleon the vast territory of Louisiana, which at that time covered about half of the Mississippi Valley. He paid some two and a quarter million pounds for the land, additional sums for United States citizenship and interest bringing the total amount to nearly five and a half millions. This sounds a great deal of money, but actually it is no more than twopence an acre, for many parts of the land were merely tangled forest in which no white man's foot had ever trod.

For this reason it was considered necessary that an American expedition be made overland to the Pacific Ocean, and accordingly President Jefferson selected as leaders Meriwether Lewis and his friend William Clark.

Neither of these brave men could spell very well, and we quote here what they wrote in their journal when they had reached the end of their great pioneer trip. They had come "in view of the Ocian, this great Pacific Octean which we have been so long anxious to See. and the roreing or noise made by the waves brakeing on the rockey Shores . . . may be heard distictly."

Lewis was a captain in the army. He

LEWIS AND CLARK ARRIVE AT THE THREE FORKS

Far into the unknown wilderness, where no white man had ever penetrated before, Lewis and Clark have won their way until they stand at the Three Forks which they reached on July 27, 1805, where three small streams meet to form the Missouri. Not far beyond is the continental divide. And pointing the way onward, as she had been doing for many a difficult mile, stands Sacajawea, the gallant sixteen-year-old Indian girl, who knows the country half by instinct and half from childhood memories. With her baby strapped to her back she has come with her husband, a French-Canadian trapper, to visit the land of her own people and to show the way to the "kind white chiefs" who are so determined to cross the Shining Mountains to the Everywhere-Salt-Water. These "white chiefs" nearly always succeeded in making friends with the Indians they encountered.

LEWIS LOOKS OUT ON THE GREAT FALLS OF THE MISSOURI

One of the most thrilling moments of all his trip must have come to Captain Lewis when he first set eyes on the magnificent Great Falls of the Missouri, in what is now Montana. He and four others had gone ahead on foot, leaving Clark to bring the boats up the river. Here we see Lewis and one of his party resting and musing at the last of the five great cataracts. This awe-inspiring cataract has been named Black Eagle Falls, for Captain Lewis tells us of how he saw on a tiny island below it the nest of an eagle—"and a more inaccessible spot I believe she could not have found; for neither man nor beast dare pass those gulphs."

had been born near Charlottesville, Virginia, on August 18, 1774; Clark was also a captain, born near the same place four years earlier. They had long been friends. After serving in the army against the Indians, Clark had returned to his home, in Kentucky, and Lewis had been made private secretary to President Jefferson.

His service at Washington paved the way for Lewis's exploring trip. Since Jefferson had been interested in the great untravelled West even before he became president, he decided to send out an expedition into that region when he foresaw that the United States was likely to buy the territory. He appointed Lewis leader, and Lewis chose his friend Clark for a companion. Their instructions were to "go up the Missouri River to its source, to find out if possible the fountains of the Mississippi, cross the Stony Mountains, and, having found the nearest river flowing into the Pacific, go down it to the sea." Also, they were to find out all about the country, its Indian inhabitants, and the prospects of buying furs.

Here are the two men who first crossed North America from the Atlantic to the Pacific— William Clark above and Meriwether Lewis at the right.

No explorers ever set out with better trained men than those who started up the Missouri River on May 14, 1804. There were forty-three soldiers and woodsmen in the three stout boats. By the end of July they had reached the mouth of the Platte River, and on November 1 they pitched camp for the winter near an Indian village in what is now the state of South Dakota.

On April 8, 1805, they broke camp and again started westwards, though fourteen men were now sent back to St. Louis, according to the plan. The rest were accompanied from this point to the coast by a half-breed Indian and his wife and child. The woman, called Sacajawea, or "Bird Woman," served as guide and interpreter, for she had grown up in the country farther west.

From August 31 to September 22 the party crossed the Rocky Mountains and came to the place, in what is now southwestern Montana, where three streams unite to form the Missouri. Soon they crossed the Great Divide; and they rejoiced to find at last a tiny stream that was flowing westwards. They launched their canoes in this stream, the Clear Water River; passed on into the Snake River; and finally into a mighty rushing torrent that led them down to the Pacific Ocean. The mouth of this great river had been discovered from the Pacific in 1792 by Robert Gray, an American sea captain, who had named it the Columbia, after his ship.

Along the shore of the Pacific near this point the explorers built Fort Clatsop, which they named after "a nation of that name, who were our nearest neighbours," and went into camp for the winter. On March 23, 1806, they started back to the East. Guided by the friendly Indians, they made the trip back rapidly and fairly easily, and on September 23 they were again in St. Louis. In spite of floods and blizzards, wild animals and many hostile Indians, Lewis and Clark had travelled nearly nine thousand miles through pathless territory with the loss of only two members of the party—and had returned with a story of their expedition which read like a romance.

Honoured Posts for the Explorers

In 1807 Meriwether Lewis was made governor of the northern part of the Louisiana Territory, a post which he held until he died on October 11, 1809. William Clark lived until 1838. He had been territorial governor of Missouri from 1813 to 1820, and superintendent of Indian Affairs at St. Louis from 1822 until the day of his death.

SEEKING *the* NORTH-WEST PASSAGE

Sir John Franklin and His Gallant Companions Who "Forged the Last Link With Their Lives"

WHILE the Battle of Trafalgar raged, a young midshipman was in charge of the signalling on board the "Bellerophon" (bĕ-lēr′ŏ-fŏn). Although only eighteen, he had already experienced many adventures, and the great battle was but one more incident in an eventful career. When John Franklin was quite a young boy at Louth Grammar School, he had one day gone for a walk with a friend to the coast, and immediately there was born in him the desire to follow the sea as a career. His father, who intended him for the Church, scoffed at the notion, but finding the boy fixed in his resolution, placed him on a merchant ship plying between Hull and Lisbon, in the hope that the hardships of life on the sea would dispel once and for all his ambitions.

Instead of doing this, the voyage only increased the boy's longing to be a sailor, and eventually his father was forced to give in. And so it came about that on March 9, 1800, young Franklin joined the "Polyphemus" (pŏl-ĭ-fē′mŭs) as a midshipman. He was at this time not quite fourteen, having been born at Spilsby, in Lincolnshire, on April 16, 1786.

He immediately took to the life, and on April 2, 1801, received his baptism of fire at the Battle of Copenhagen. Just previous to this he had heard of an expedition which was to be fitted out for Australia and the South Seas. The idea captured his imagination, and a few weeks later he sailed on the "Investigator," commanded by his cousin, Captain Matthew Flinders. He soon became a great favourite on board, by reason of his enthusiasm and gaiety, while his skill in the use of astronomical and surveying

instruments proved most helpful. Always daring, and with a thirst for knowledge, these qualities were now directed into useful channels, and the boy not only gained sound experience but acquitted himself well.

And his courage was tested on that voyage. The "Investigator" developed signs of decay, and the crew were compelled to board the "Porpoise," which unfortunately struck a reef on the return voyage, and the men were stranded on a sandbank in danger of starvation. Captain Flinders eventually effected their rescue by making a solitary journey of several hundred miles in a small boat to secure help. But Franklin was yet to meet with adventure before he again saw England's shores, for at Canton he embarked on a homeward-bound vessel commanded by the famous Nathaniel Dance, and was concerned in a daring action with French men-o'-war which barred the ship's way. Undoubtedly the example of such men as Flinders and Dance left its impression on Franklin.

It was after his return from this expedition that he was appointed to the "Bellerophon" and took part in the action off Trafalgar. He was later transferred to the "Bedford," and during the attack on New Orleans, in the operations against America, he was slightly wounded.

But Franklin, who longed for a further opportunity for adventure, was delighted when government interest in exploration revived, and he was appointed to the command of the "Trent" under Captain Buchan (bŭk′ȧn) in the "Dorothea," with instructions to sail between Spitsbergen and Greenland, make a dash for the North Pole if conditions

Sir John Franklin, one of the best-loved of men and most gallant of explorers, who devoted his life to the service of his country in the remote places of the earth.

were favourable, and then attempt to reach Bering (bār'ing) Strait. Unfortunately, the "Dorothea" became considerably damaged by gales and pack ice, and, in spite of Franklin's earnestly expressed wish to continue alone, the "Trent" was forced to convoy her safely back to London.

Franklin Sets Forth on Another Expedition and Suffers Terrible Trials

This expedition, although immediately disappointing to Franklin, proved his worth. The government was impressed by his enthusiasm and powers of leadership, and he was placed in command of a further expedition to explore the coast of North America, of which all that was known were the mouths of the Coppermine and Mackenzie Rivers, the rest being shrouded in mystery.

On May 23, 1819, an expedition left England, Franklin being accompanied by two midshipmen—George Back and Robert Hood—and by Dr. John Richardson. In these four we have perhaps the most loyal and devoted companions in the history of exploration. Hudson's Bay was reached at the end of August and later the start was made across the continent, the party taking with them portable canoes especially built for the purpose.

Terrible sufferings were caused by cold, hunger and the persistent attacks of mosquitoes, but they yet accomplished a great deal, including the discovery of the River Hood, although the gallant young midshipman after whom it was named died on the expedition. This naming of the river was an example of Franklin's unselfishness. New lands, rivers, bays, or straits he named after his companions, rather than claim the honour for himself, and it was only through the agency of his loyal friend Dr. Richardson that some of the regions he discovered came to bear his name.

On Franklin's return to England, in 1822, honours awaited him. In 1823 he married his first wife, but the marriage was doomed to tragedy. In 1825 Franklin was again called upon to lead an expedition to the Polar regions, and, although his wife was dying, both he and she did what they felt to be their duty to England, and parted, although it was to mean a separation for ever. Favoured with good conditions, Franklin, who was again accompanied by Back and Richardson, accomplished the exploration of the Mackenzie River, and also located several bays and capes. The North American coastline was explored at last.

This time his return to England heralded a long period of rest from exploration. He

MOVING OVER THE WATERS OF LAKE PROSPEROUS

Seventeen Indian canoes accompanied Franklin's expedition when it was crossing Lake Prosperous, which you here see it doing, on May 30, 1820. Franklin reported that, although the shores of the lake were but scantily wooded, they were very picturesque.

married again in 1828, and was knighted the following year. Appointed to the command of the "Rainbow," where his popularity and the happiness of the officers and men under him became a byword in the navy, he saw considerable service in the Mediterranean. From 1836–43 he acted as lieutenant-governor of Tasmania, then known as Van Diemen's (văn-dē'mĕnz) Land, where he left behind him many memories of his wise and considerate administration.

Off on the Expedition from Which He was Fated Never to Return

In spite of his activity and usefulness, however, Franklin still longed to serve his country again in exploration, and when in 1845 the government decided to dispatch another expedition to complete the mapping of the coast of North America, and finally discover a north-west passage, Franklin, although then 59, was only too eager to go.

Because, apart from his age, he was the man most suited to lead such an attempt, he was placed in command of the expedition, which was fitted out as completely as was possible in those days, and composed of young and enthusiastic men eager to serve under the great commander.

They sailed on May 19 in the "Erebus" (ēr'ĕ-bŭs) and "Terror," were sighted by Europeans at the entrance to Lancaster Sound on July 26, and never seen again. As nothing was heard of them, anxiety in England became intense. Several relief expeditions were fitted out by the government, but it was Lady Franklin who, in 1857, finally organized the expedition, commanded by Captain McClintock, that was to learn their tragic fate.

McClintock, while himself clearing up a great deal of North American geography, discovered on King William's Land the last message of one of the officers of the ill-fated expedition, recounting their voyagings under orders among the islands off the coast of North America, the hemming in by ice of the ships, and the death of Franklin on June 11, 1847.

The survivors, who numbered just over a hundred, had started off on an attempt to reach supplies, but must have died on the way. It was, however, proved beyond a doubt that before Franklin died he had discovered the North-West Passage.

THE DAUNTLESS EXPLORERS REACH THE HILL RIVER

This is the type of scenery that Sir John Franklin saw during the early part of his journey in 1819. This picture, which was drawn by Midshipman Hood, shows the hill in Hill River, as seen from Morgan's Rocks.

The poet Homer tells the story of how Nausicaa (naw-sik´ā-ă), a Greek princess, was very fond of playing ball. One day she and her maidens went down to the river bank to play a game of ball. The game was interrupted, however, by the sudden appearance of a stranger whose sea-swept hair and unkempt beard frightened the maidens away. It was the shipwrecked hero Odysseus, or Ulysses, who had heard the laughter and shouts and had come to find out to what strange land the Fates had carried him. Nausicaa, braver than the rest—perhaps because she was a princess—waited to hear his story. Then she called her companions, and took Odysseus to the palace, where her father treated him kindly and gave him a ship to carry him home again.

GREECE *in* ARMS *Against* PERSIA

The Wars of These Two Lands May Perhaps Rank as the Most Important in History, Since They Settled the Question Whether the Main Current of Progress was to be European or Asiatic

(CONTINUED FROM PAGE 575)

NOWADAYS we think of a tyrant as a hard, cruel man who rules the people under him sternly and not very wisely. But before the people in Greece had learned to govern themselves, men called tyrants were helping to guide them to a much better life than any they had lived before. These tyrants, who ruled Greek cities throughout Hellas from Asia Minor to Italy and from Egypt to the Black Sea, were often very wise and considerate rulers.

The tyrants were really kings who had not been born as such, but had simply seized the power. To-day we should be more likely to call them dictators. The Greek tyrants did not have the royal glory of kings, and at any time they might lose their power and be killed or driven away; but while they held sway, they ruled their tiny domains like kings, and made laws and carried out reforms. The nobles and rich men did not often like the tyrants, for the nobles themselves wanted to rule. But the common people, who had been harshly treated by the nobles, supported the tyrants. In some cities, like Sparta, the people were not strong enough to sustain a tyrant. In other cities, like Corinth, the tyrant was driven out by the nobles. In still others, like Athens, the tyrant was driven out by the citizens, and a democracy (where the government is in the hands of the people) was set up.

Yet the tyrants did their best for the little Greek city-states, and some of them became famous. But no matter what the form of government—the rule of one man, the rule of the few, or the rule of the many—the Greeks began to make remarkable progress in every way. They grew less superstitious in religion. They busied themselves in making and selling pottery, cloth, and tools and weapons of bronze and iron. Their trade began to bring them riches with which they could build beautiful houses and temples, and strong walls round their cities.

This wealth which came into Greece did

But splendid buildings are improved by beautiful things inside them. What was a temple to the Greeks without a statue of the god in whose honour it was erected? The Greeks began by copying statues from Egyptian models. But they were such excellent artists that no sooner did they feel a chisel in their hands than they began to carve lifelike and beautiful figures such as Egypt had never dreamed of. Among the greatest

Greek potters took just as much care in making vases with beautiful shapes as they did in painting them with lively figures and delicate designs. To the left is a kylix (kī′lĭks) of the early sixth century B.C., painted with black figures on a light background. Below is a vase belonging to the middle of the fifth century, painted with red figures on a black ground.

not all go to the nobles or the people who were already rich. Much of it was acquired by common men, and these commoners became eager to have written laws which would protect their wealth. They felt that then the judges could not accept bribes so easily or be influenced so much by wealth or position. And their demands for laws were often granted, and written codes began to appear all over Hellas.

The rulers took great pride, too, in erecting splendid buildings. The old brick buildings did not satisfy them. Stone palaces were far handsomer, and stone temples would surely please the gods more. A new architecture—Greek —began to develop. The designs were at first copied from Egypt or Crete, but soon the Greeks added decorations of their own. They took the old Egyptian pillar, or column, and by designing different tops, or capitals, made the most beautiful columns ever seen. The majority of the Greek temples had these magnificent columns set all round them.

According to Greek mythology, Apollo invented the lyre, which you see above, and Pan the flute. The two gods had several heated arguments over which made the more beautiful music. A king named Midas, the same one whose touch turned everything to gold, agreed with Pan that the flute was the better. As a punishment, Apollo gave him a pair of ass's ears. Poor King Midas grew his hair long to hide them, but wherever he went the flowers and reeds would whisper softly, "King Midas has ass's ears!" The story is only a myth, but it shows what the beauty-loving Greeks thought of people who did not appreciate fine music—and it shows, too, that the lyre was their favourite instrument.

Greek sculptors were Phidias (fĭd′ĭ-ăs) and Praxiteles (prăk-sĭt′ē-lēz), both of whom lived after the Age of Tyrants had come to an end.

The Greeks loved paintings, too, and put them on walls, jars, dishes, and even pins and tiny ornaments. And they loved amusing pictures. They liked to draw a series of pictures something like the cartoons of to-day, with the words coming out of the mouths of the people who spoke them—and you do not need to know Greek to see the

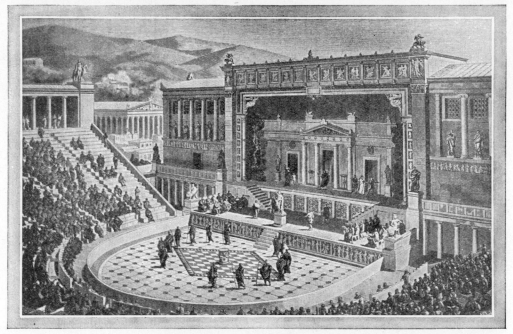

WHAT A THEATRE LOOKED LIKE IN THE DAYS OF ANCIENT GREECE

The theatre of Dionysus (dǐ'ŏ-nī'sŭs), at Athens, is now in ruins, but from the remains we may trace its growth from a circular threshing ground, or a ring where the people celebrated the harvest festival of the god of fertility, to the great theatre which by Roman times may have looked somewhat like the theatre shown above. The seats of the early Greek theatres were usually constructed on the sloping ground, and the roof was the sky.

humour of those pictures. In the same way they often made amusing statues.

The temples with their statues and paintings now encouraged another art—the art of music. What was a temple without feasts and processions? And what a procession without music and poetry? The flute and the lyre were perfected as musical instruments, and poems were written to be sung with musical accompaniment. Songs that were sung to the lyre were called lyrics (lǐr'ĭk).

The Greeks' Love of Song

But music and poetry were not confined to temple processions. The Greeks were always singing, and their poets could sing about anything—stories or ideas or scenes of nature, as well as religion. After a poet had composed his poem he would sing or recite it in public, and people would gather on the round, bowl-like slope of a hill to listen to the best singers. That is how the Greek theatre began. And it, too, developed in the time of the tyrants.

In the same way literature progressed as never before in the world's history. The Greeks made noble use of the Phoenician gift of an alphabet. Men wrote about everything, good and bad, in their experience, and often with a beauty of style and diction that has never been surpassed. All their extraordinary genius found its first expression in a period when the Greeks were doing a great deal in every form of work and play. They were farming, trading, fighting, and colonizing, gossiping, exercising, and entertaining—busy all the time and yet always looking round for more things to do.

You may wish to know the names of some of the famous men who did such wonders in awakening the soul of Hellas. The leaders of Athens are the most famous, of course, because Athens was the chief centre of Greek art.

How a Poem Recaptured an Island

First of all you should know about Solon (sō'lŏn). Solon was a noble, a business man, a warrior, a poet, a philosopher, and a statesman. One of his poems stirred the Athenians to recapture the island of Salamis (săl′ȧ-mĭs), at the mouth of their harbour, from some neighbours who had seized it. The people elected him archon (är′kŏn), or prime minister (594 B.C.), and after that he took things pretty much into his own hands.

Solon cancelled most of the debts that the men in the city owed to other men. He

Photo by Anderson

PYTHAGORAS AT WORK

Pythagoras, the greatest of all the early Greek scientists, will be remembered for all time because of the important discoveries which he made in mathematics and astronomy. He was the first to work out the theory that the earth is a globe, which, in company with the other planets, revolves round the sun.

and a new code of laws giving all men, except slaves, exactly the same rights in court. His laws, which were written down so that everyone might read and know them, made Solon famous as a lawgiver.

After Solon's death a real tyrant, Pisistratus (pī-sĭs′trȧ-tŭs), a rich nobleman, seized the governing power and ruled Athens for twelve years or so. As a tyrant Pisistratus was wise and good, and Athens grew richer than ever under his government. But when his two sons attempted to rule after his death, one was killed and the other driven away, for the Athenians wanted to rule themselves.

They soon adopted a device that made it harder for a tyrant to seize their state. We now call this ostracism (ŏs′trȧ-sĭz′m). If any man became too powerful or unpopular, the citizens could write his name on ostrakons, or pieces of pottery, and put them into the voting box or jar; and if a certain number were collected the man had to leave the country. A later story tells of one general, Aristides the Just (ăr′ĭs-tī′dēz), who was asked by an ignorant citizen—who did not know him— to write his own name on an ostrakon, and so help towards his own banishment. Aristides asked the man what there was against him, and the man answered that he really knew of nothing, but he was simply tired of hearing him called "the Just."

said that anyone who lost a lawsuit might appeal to a jury for a retrial. He made for his state a new constitution that gave the vote to poor people as well as to the rich,

While Athens was thriving under the rule of the tyrant Pisistratus, hundreds of other

618

Photo by Rischgitz

ARISTIDES HELPS TO BRING ABOUT HIS OWN BANISHMENT

Who would ever think that a little jar full of fragments of pottery might send a man away from his home for ten years? To protect themselves from tyrants, the citizens of Athens adopted a device which, in the end, did them just as much harm as good. When anyone felt that a certain man was becoming too powerful for the good of the state, he might write the man's name on an "ostrakon," or piece of pottery, and put it into a voting urn or jar. When a certain number of these were collected, the man was "ostracized," or banished, for a period of ten years. After that time he might return; all his property was given back to him, and he resumed his normal life as a citizen of Athens. To be ostracized meant no disgrace; but how sad it was for any man to be forced to leave the beautiful city in which were all his interests and pleasures and all his friends. The picture above shows Aristides the Just helping to bring about his own ostracism (see page 618). At the end of his ten years of banishment, Aristides returned to Athens and resumed his place of honour among its citizens. He helped to destroy the Persian fleet at the Battle of Salamis, and was later entrusted with the arrangements for forming an alliance between Athens and other states to take action against the Persians.

little states all over Hellas were also feeling the weight and the benefit of tyranny. Periander (pĕr'ĭ-ăn'dĕr) was tyrant at Corinth (kŏr'ĭnth), and made it one of the most beautiful cities of Greece. Dionysius (dī'ō-nĭsh'ĭ-ŭs), somewhat later (about 400 B.C.), was tyrant of Syracuse (sĭr-a̤-kūs), in Sicily, and established a powerful kingdom. Aristagoras (ăr'ĭs-tăg'ō-ra̤s) was tyrant (500 B.C.) of Miletus (mī-lē'tŭs), in Ionia, when that city was in its prime, and its wise men were more famous than those of Athens. And there were many other lesser tyrants in cities large and small.

How an Eclipse of the Sun Brought Great Fame to Thales of Miletus

It was in the Hellas of Asia Minor that the Greeks first earned their title of the most brilliant people in history. In Miletus lived Thales (thā'lēz), who, after studying some Babylonian books, is said to have predicted an eclipse of the sun in 585 B.C. When the sun was actually darkened at the time predicted, Thales naturally became very famous.

In the same city lived another Greek, Hecateus (hĕk'a̤-tē'ŭs), who wondered how big the world was and how the various countries were placed upon it. He travelled as far as he could in several directions, and (according to some accounts) made a map which described the Mediterranean Sea and the countries round or near it.

But the greatest of all early Greek scientists was Pythagoras (pĭ-thăg'ō-ra̤s), who was born on the island of Samos (sā'mŏs) but later lived at Crotona, in Italy. Pythagoras was a mathematician, who besides making a good many discoveries in mathematics, worked out the theory that the earth travels round the sun and not the sun round the earth. Because of his great discoveries his name will always be remembered.

The King of Persia Sets Out to Subdue the Troublesome Greeks

But the Greeks living in Asia Minor were to be the means of bringing war upon the whole Greek race. Cyrus, the Persian king, had fought and conquered the Ionian Greeks (546 B.C.) because they had helped Croesus (krē'sŭs), king of Lydia, against him. But after thirty or forty years the Ionian Greeks, helped by Athens, tried to revolt against the Persian rule, and the Persian king felt it was high time to subdue all Greece for daring to help his subjects to rebel against him.

If you will look at the map you will see that Europe and Asia almost meet across a narrow strip of water north-east of Greece. It was anciently called the Hellespont (hĕl'-ĕs-pŏnt), and is now known as the Dardanelles (där'da̤-nĕlz'). This narrow strip of water could easily be crossed by a bridge of boats, and Darius, who did not like sea fighting, thought the best doorway to Greece was through the Hellespont. In 492 B.C., therefore, he sent his armies over into Europe to sweep down on Greece.

The European country through which they had to pass was traversed by hills and mountains, with few farms and fertile valleys where food could be found for the army The Persian general, Mardonius (mär-dō'nĭ-ŭs), son-in-law of Darius, followed a road along the sea-coast, while a large fleet of boats sailed along the shore with supplies.

Miletus is Destroyed, and the Surrender of Athens and Sparta is Demanded

By travelling in this way the Persians might have reached Athens, in spite of the continual fighting with the hardy mountaineers whose country they were crossing. But one day a great storm arose, in which the supply fleet was destroyed. Far and wide the food ships were wrecked, and Mardonius was thus forced to stop, though he held all of the land north of the Aegean and had some allies in Northern Greece. And the Persians in Asia Minor succeeded in destroying Miletus, the home of so many illustrious Greek thinkers.

This defeat by wind and wave did not discourage Darius. He sent heralds to Athens and Sparta demanding "earth and water," which were the signs that a city had surrendered. The determined Greeks threw one herald into a pit and the other into a well, where they might find their own earth and water, for some of the Greeks were ready to fight for their liberty to the last man.

Within a year or two (in 490 B.C.) the second Persian army was ready to invade

LEONIDAS, KING OF SPARTA, WRITES HIS NAME ON THE ROLL OF FAME

There is a story that a Spartan mother said to her son, who was going forth to battle, ''Either come back with your shield or come back upon it''! For Greek shields were so large that they had to be thrown away when fleeing from the enemy, while the hero who gave his life in battle was carried home in state upon his shield.

To retreat or flee from the enemy was a terrible disgrace; so Leonidas, king of Sparta, and his tiny army of three hundred men who were left to defend the Pass of Thermopylae, would not desert their post when they were hemmed in by the huge Persian host. They fought with the greatest bravery, until all of them were killed.

Greece. This time the plan was to transport all the soldiers by ships direct to Attica. In this way the long march overland would be avoided, and in one short battle Athens might be crushed.

Six hundred ships carried the Persian army of some twenty thousand men. The passage was made safely, and the Persians burned the town of Eretria (ĕ-rē′trĭ-ả) and camped on the plain of Marathon, ready to march on Athens.

A Famous Athletic Feat

The Athenians were greatly alarmed. What was to be done? They sent to Sparta a swift runner, who covered the 150 miles in less than two days. But the Spartan leaders said their army could not march until the moon changed. There was nothing for tiny Athens to do but face the might of Persia alone. If they did not fight,

they would have to take back as tyrant the son of Pisistratus, for the Persians had brought him with them for that purpose.

A Clever Plan of Attack

But the Athenians preferred democracy, and fortunately they had elected as their general a soldier of great ability. His name was Miltiades (mĭl-tī′ả-dēz). He led his little army of ten thousand Greeks out upon the hills overlooking Marathon, and pitched his camp above the Persians. The Athenians could see the thousands of tents spread out beneath them, and the hundreds of ships in the bay. We can forgive them for feeling that the very gods were fighting against them. Their defeat seemed inevitable.

But victory is not always to the strong, and Miltiades told the Athenians to be brave. He had a plan which he thought might win the day. When the Persians began their march upon Athens, he proposed to swoop down upon their column from one side and try to destroy it.

The Persians, expecting such an attack, sent out archers to protect the marching soldiers. These archers were grouped in a mass, with only a few men on each wing. To trick them, therefore, Miltiades placed most of his men on the wings.

Darius Passes on His Way, but His Son Takes Up the Task of Vengeance

The plain of Marathon was now filled with tumult. The Greeks with their spears dashed forward; the Persian arrows darkened the air. At the first clash the Persian wings gave way before the charging Greeks. As the Persian centre advanced, their bowmen found themselves surrounded by the gallant Athenians, who wrought great havoc with their spears. In a very short time the Persian army was in complete disorder. The Persians threw down their bows and fled to their ships, leaving six thousand slain, while the Greeks lost only about two hundred men. Thus ended the second Persian invasion.

We can easily imagine how consumed with rage was Darius, the Persian king, when he heard of the Battle of Marathon. He swore he would be avenged if it cost him his kingdom, and he spent the following years preparing an army that no power on earth was expected to resist. Darius, however, was not destined to lead this army, for he died before it was ready; but his son Xerxes (zẽrk'sēz) took up the task of vengeance.

It was Xerxes' plan to attack the Greeks both by land and by sea. Two bridges were thrown across the Hellespont and an army of two hundred thousand men swarmed over them to annihilate every soldier on Greek soil. A fleet of a thousand ships followed this vast army along the shore. Moreover, the Persians were helped by the fact that they had many friends in Greece. There was so much jealousy among the city-states, and so much fear of Persia, that only about thirty of the cities were ready to fight for liberty.

Meanwhile, those of the Greeks who loved liberty had not been idle. Miltiades was dead; but Themistocles (thẽ-mĭs'tŏ-klēz),

the greatest statesman of all Greece, had succeeded him. Themistocles saw that Athens must be defended by means of ships, since she could never hope to muster a force as large as the Persian army. He therefore persuaded the Athenians to build about 180 ships, and he succeeded in getting the other cities to agree to his plan. Even Sparta was aroused and sent soldiers.

As the gigantic Persian host advanced from the Hellespont to enter Greece (480 B.C.), their road lay at one place through a narrow pass between mountains, called the Pass of Thermopylae (thĕr-mŏp'ĭ-lē). It was an excellent place to oppose their passage, for a few men could hold this defile against thousands. The Spartan king Leonidas (lē-ŏn'ĭ-dăs), with a small company of men, went accordingly to Thermopylae to hold the pass against all the Persian host.

When Xerxes and his army arrived at Thermopylae, they tried to force their way through, but Leonidas and his handful of men stood firm. There was no breaking the line of Grecian spears. For a whole day the Persians attacked, but in vain.

The Persian Army Sweeps On, and Beautiful Athens Goes Up in Flames

Finally a Greek peasant, one of those who did not object to Persian rule, led the Persian army over the mountains by another way. Now Leonidas and his brave men had enemies on both sides of them, and one by one they were cut down, fighting desperately to the very end—till the last man had fallen. They had fought what is surely the most famous fight in history. So for Leonidas and his three hundred men was written the epitaph: "Stranger, go tell the Spartans that we lie here in obedience to their orders."

While this brave and tragic battle was going on, the Greek ships were clashing with the Persian. Neither gained much advantage until a storm sprang up and wrecked two hundred or more of the Persian fleet. The skilful Greek sailors were not wrecked, but they returned to Athens, mooring their boats in the Bay of Salamis (săl'á-mĭs).

Nothing could stop the Persian army once it had passed Thermopylae. It swept down upon Attica from the north like a great

Photo by Rischgitz

THE RETURN OF THE GREEKS FROM THE BATTLE OF SALAMIS

The battle of Salamis, fought between the Greeks and the Persians in 480 B.C., is one of the most famous naval encounters in the history of the world. The Persian ships were clumsy to manage, and the light galleys of the Greeks created fearful havoc among them. Here we see the return of the Greeks, who are being welcomed as heroes.

storm. The Athenians deserted their city and took refuge in the islands of the bay. Looking back they could see the smoke and flames from beautiful Athens, which was totally destroyed by Xerxes.

The Greeks, in their ships, were bitterly disheartened. The Spartans, whose fleet was with them, wanted to retreat, and some of their vessels did withdraw. But Themistocles sent a message to Xerxes to say that his fleet was coming out of the bay. To prevent this the Persian ruler ordered his own fleet to attack the Greeks.

Now, the waters near Attica were very narrow because of the many islands, and the Persians, not being skilful sailors, found it very hard to steer their clumsy boats clear of the shores and of one another. When the swift, light Greek galleys came crashing down upon them, wild disorder reigned.

All day the Greeks fought, and when darkness fell, the Persian fleet was shattered beyond repair. Thus ended the Battle of Salamis (480 B.C.), one of the greatest naval encounters of all time.

Themistocles now had an opportunity of cutting off the supplies of Xerxes at the Hellespont, where they were carried across from Asia into Europe. But the other Greeks would not support him, and the chance was lost. The Persian king fled hastily back into Asia, leaving Mardonius with fifty thousand men to spend the winter in Thessaly (thĕs'á-lĭ).

The following year (479 B.C.) the Persians made their last effort to conquer Greece. An army of thirty thousand Greeks met Mardonius at Plataea (plă-tē'á), and in a terrific battle the Greek spear again triumphed over the Persian bow. The broken Persian army retreated finally into Asia.

After years of exhausting strife the Athenians were now free to turn their thoughts once more to the great works of peace.

(CONTINUED ON PAGE 651)

THE TUG OF WAR
No. 23

Each one of the boys in the picture above is exerting a force of a hundred pounds. What is the strain at the centre of the rope?

THE EXPLORERS
No. 24

Two boys wish to explore the wilds of a small island four yards square which is situated in the centre of a pond twenty feet square. With two planks measuring only eight yards in length they construct an ingenious bridge across the pond to the island. Yet the planks are not tied, nailed, or otherwise fastened together. How is it done?

If to-day is the to-morrow of yesterday, is to-day the yesterday of to-morrow?

(THE SOLUTIONS TO THESE PUZZLES WILL BE FOUND ON PAGE 807 OF THIS VOLUME)

HOW LONG IS A HORSE'S HEAD?
No. 26

What would be your guess as to the length in inches of the average horse's head?

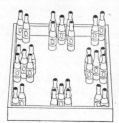

THE CLEVER THIEF
No. 25

A man once had a servant who used to help herself to the ginger ale with great regularity. Determined to set a trap to catch her, he arranged the twenty-eight bottles he had on hand as shown in the diagram above. He knew he could tell if they were disturbed, for he had put nine on each side of the bin. But the servant saw his plan. So the next time she helped herself to four bottles, she rearranged the remainder so that there were still nine on each side. And later, when she took four more bottles, she again rearranged the remaining bottles so that there were still nine on each side. How did she place them each time?

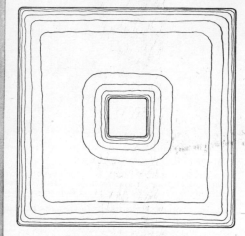

FUN WITH FIGURES

Think of a number, for example......... 7
Multiply it by 3.......................... 21
Add 2.................................... 23
Multiply by 3............................ 69
Add 2 more than the number thought of... 9
                                         ――
                                         78

The number of tens in the last answer gives the number thought of—7.

WILL THERE BE AN ACCIDENT?

Can the motor-cars below pass safely if they keep going straight ahead? Prove your guess with a ruler.

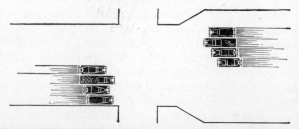

Nature often dresses the countryside like this in winter months. But exactly how cold it is no icicle or snow-drift can tell us; to "measure" the cold we must consult the useful little instrument known as a thermometer.

MEASURING *the* WEATHER

The Thermometer Settles All Our Arguments about the Temperature and Tells Us Just How Hot or Cold We Ought to Feel

(CONTINUED FROM PAGE 582)

IN OLDEN times men had no reliable method of telling how hot or cold a day was. There must have been endless disputes on the subject when one person thought the heat was intense and another felt quite comfortable. To-day we do not have to rely on our feelings. An impartial little instrument—the thermometer—tells us just how warm or how cold we have a right to feel.

It is hardly in human nature not to take satisfaction in being able to say, on some hot July afternoon, "It is ninety in the shade according to my thermometer!" And somehow we like to read in the paper that the temperature has been the lowest for forty years. It is foolish, perhaps, but people are like that. The worse the weather is, the more they like to boast about it. So they watch the thermometer from day to day and are happy if they find that it was colder round about their house than anywhere else in the district in which they reside.

The first thermometer was made more than three hundred years ago by the famous Italian scientist, Galileo (găl'ĭ-lē'ō). He had found out that nearly all substances, whether gases, liquids, or solids, fill more space when they are heated. That is, they expand. He noticed, too, that when he heated liquid in a glass, both the glass and the liquid expanded; but the liquid expanded more than the glass. So he made a thermometer by using a closed glass tube partly filled with air and partly with liquid. Later he filled it with alcohol—coloured red—the advantage of alcohol being that it will not freeze until it drops to about 170° below zero Fahrenheit. A thermometer that freezes easily is useless in very cold weather.

Nowadays alcohol is used in all thermometers meant to register very low temperatures, and mercury (mĕr'kū-rĭ), or quicksilver—a heavy, silvery fluid—in most of the others. For exceptionally high temperatures thermometers are made of metal.

For scientific experiments at high temperatures, electrical thermometers are also used. There are two kinds. One makes use of the fact that when two different kinds of metal are joined together, an electrical current will be set up if the temperature is changed at the point where they meet. The second kind relies on the fact that certain metals offer a great deal more resistance to an electrical current if they are heated.

In all thermometers a scale for reading changes in temperature is

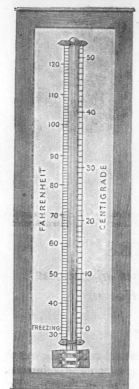

This thermometer has the centigrade scale on the right and the Fahrenheit on the left. On a centigrade thermometer the freezing-point is marked zero and the boiling-point 100—and the distance between the two is marked off into a hundred degrees. But on the Fahrenheit thermometer the freezing-point is marked 32 and the boiling-point 212; and the distance between these points is marked off into 180 degrees.

marked alongside the glass tube on a strip of metal, wood, or on the glass tube itself.

There are different kinds of scales for reading temperature. Scientists and the people of most European countries use what is called the centigrade (sĕn'tĭ-grād) thermometer. On it the space between the freezing-point and the boiling-point is divided into a hundred parts—or degrees. Indeed, it is from that fact that the thermometer takes its name—for "centum" is the Latin for "hundred" and "gradus" the Latin for "degree." The freezing-point

on a centigrade thermometer is marked zero and the boiling-point 100.

Another scale, first laid out about 1714 by a German scientist named Gabriel Fahrenheit (fä'rĕn-hīt), has for its zero the temperature of a mixture of equal parts of snow and salt. For the other end of his scale Fahrenheit took the temperature of the human body; and he divided the space between into ninety-six degrees. As it works out on our present Fahrenheit thermometer, the freezing-point is at 32° and the boiling-point at 212°—with 180°

Our common thermometers are made in different ways, but the principle on which they are made is very simple. First a long tube with a bulb on the end is partly filled with a liquid, such as mercury. The end of the tube is then closed. Next, two points are marked off on the wooden or metal scale to which the tube is attached. One of these is the point the top of the liquid will reach at a temperature of 212° Fahrenheit, or the boiling-point of pure water at sea level. That temperature is easy to find, for as soon as water begins to boil it has reached 212°. The other point to be marked on the scale is the level of the top of the liquid at the freezing-point of pure water at sea-level, or 32° Fahrenheit. It is the temperature at which a cake of ice begins to melt. Once these two points have been found, it is quite a simple matter to divide the distance between them into the correct number of degrees.

between the two, instead of 100°, as on a centigrade thermometer.

Other scales were formerly in use, such as that invented by Réaumur, in which the freezing-point is zero and the boiling point 80°, but these have now been given up. A new scale often employed in scientific work is called the absolute. In this the zero is 273° C. below freezing-point, because this is the greatest degree of cold which can exist.

(CONTINUED ON PAGE 646)

These foolish animals are destined to become a meal for the lions before the day is out—and all because, in spite of a lifetime of close friendship, they were quite willing to believe evil reports about one another.

TANSY and BOBBLES on FABLE ISLAND

The Story of the Donkey Who Would Learn to Sing and of the Stork Who Kept Bad Company

(CONTINUED FROM PAGE 548)

ONE evening, as the fairies were returning home by the field, they heard a tremendous bellowing. The bulls were engaged in a fierce quarrel.

Tansy had been right, for the lion had been spreading false stories about the bulls among the animals, and of course the animals had been delighted to tell the bulls. Instead of remembering their years of friendship, the bulls believed the reports against one another, and now they were bellowing and arguing, and might soon have been attacking each other with their horns, had not one of them suggested that they should separate and go and eat in different fields.

This was just what the lion wanted, and as he watched from behind a high rock he was delighted to see one bull go to the north field, one to the south, one to the east, and the other to the west.

"I know something dreadful will happen to-night," said Tansy.

And so, indeed, it did. When Tansy and Bobbles persuaded Father Fairy to come out with them in the moonlight, they found that the lion had killed all four bulls and was now returning with his friends to carry off the carcases.

"If only," said Father Fairy, "they had been wise enough to refuse to believe evil against one another, and had remained friendly companions, they would still have been safe in their pleasant field."

Never Believe a Boaster

In the centre of the king's garden there was a beautiful statue which the fairies greatly admired. It was of a mighty man strangling a lion.

Now, one day as they were walking in the wood, they heard a man and a lion having a heated argument as to which of them was the stronger.

"Booh!" said Bobbles.

"Booh!" said Tansy.

"Excuse our interruption," said Bobbles,

627

merrily, "but it may save time if you both go to the king's garden and see the statue, which shows that the man is the stronger."

"Pooh!" exclaimed the lion, amiably, "that won't settle it. Remember, my dear fairies, that the sculptor of that statue was a man."

"What difference does that make?" asked Tansy.

"All the difference," replied the lion. "If the sculptor had been a lion, you would have seen twenty men prostrate under the paw of one lion."

"You're both boasters; I shan't believe either of you," said Tansy. "Come on, Bobbles, we'll leave them alone."

Poor Donkey ! He is Always Wrong

So Bobbles followed her and presently the fairies stopped at the sight of a donkey lying under a tree, evidently on the point of death.

"Why are you so ill?" asked Bobbles, stooping over him.

"All in the cause of music," moaned the donkey.

"Music?" asked Tansy, astonished.

"Music!" repeated the donkey. "I heard the grasshoppers chirping such beautiful music that I asked them to tell me their secret. They informed me that they lived on nothing but dew; so I have been doing the same for a week. I fear not only that I am dying of it, but that my voice is as hoarse as ever."

"Oh, you foolish, foolish donkey!" cried Tansy. "Don't you know by this time that what is food for one may be poison for another?"

"Cheer up!" said Bobbles; and in a few minutes the fairies had brought some sweet grass, some thistles and a bundle of carrots.

"Now take your fill and forget all about the grasshoppers," said Tansy.

The Conceited Gnat

As the donkey ate his meal, a bull came strolling along to stand under the shade and swish the flies off his back with his long tail.

But it happened that a gnat had perched on his horn; and the fairies were amazed to hear the gnat pipe out in a conceited tone, "Sir Bull, if my weight on your horn causes you any distress, I shall remove it at once."

"Your weight on my horn?" answered the bull, tossing his head. "As I didn't notice when you sat down, I shan't notice when you get up."

"You have a tremendous amount of conceit in a very small body!" mocked Bobbles, as the gnat, flying off the bull's horn, perched near him and gazed proudly around.

"The smaller the head, the bigger the conceit," said the bull thoughtfully, as he walked away.

The poor donkey's soul was full of music, but his head was empty of sense. Even then he was better off than the little gnat, who, having neither sense nor soul, was a very conceited fellow indeed, as the bull could tell you if he desired.

If only the graceful deer could exchange his horns for a little imagination, he could wear that pretty dappled hide for a long time yet. But he is sure things will continue to be just as they always have been.

"Dear, dear!" said the donkey "I would not have believed that fresh carrots could work such wonders," and he rose and stood rather trembling on his legs.

"It wasn't just the carrots; it was being sensible again," said Tansy. "What would you think if we filled ourselves with the wrong food—raw fish, slugs, hay, thistles—so as to be birds, or horses, or donkeys!"

"I've a headache still," said the donkey. "Let me think that over."

Danger Lurks on Every Side

Tansy and Bobbles were enjoying themselves down by the sands when they noticed a deer nibbling grass near the shore.

"He has only one eye," said Tansy, "and he told me he always keeps that eye towards the land, so that he may look out for the hunters."

But even as Tansy spoke, some sailors from a boat, seeing the deer, shot an arrow at him and pierced his heart.

The fairies rushed up to the deer just in time to hear his dying moans.

"Alas, the danger came from the side whence I least expected it," he murmured.

Bobbles and Tansy flew off, for as they couldn't help the poor deer, they didn't want to watch the sailors take him away.

We Must Practise What We Preach

Alighting on the sands again, they rounded a cliff and came to a beautiful cove, where the sand was all gold and silver; and there—surprise of surprises!—they found Father Fairy and Mother Fairy enjoying the sunset.

They rushed up to their parents, sat down, and as they let the sand sift through their fingers, they begged Father Fairy to tell them a story.

"Do look at that old crab," said Mother Fairy. "I think she's trying to teach the young crab to walk straight."

The mother crab was scolding the young crab for walking sideways; and they heard the young crab say, "But, mother, you walk sideways yourself, and so must I! Show me a better way and I'll follow."

"Oh, mother!" cried Tansy, "you don't teach us to walk sideways. Show us how to dance!"

So Mother Fairy danced, and indeed she danced more beautifully than anyone in all the world; and Tansy watched, and tried to dance as Mother Fairy danced. Tansy danced almost as charmingly as her mother, but not quite.

When they were tired of this, Father Fairy told them a story.

Father Fairy Tells a Story

"Once upon a time," said he, "the arms and the legs and the head hatched a plot against the stomach. They whispered together that they did all the work while the stomach did none.

"The legs said that they walked to get the food, the arms said they laboured for it, the mouth said that it received the food. The teeth said that they chewed it.

"So they agreed not to do any more work, so as to prove to the stomach how helpless he was without them.

"Now the stomach had heard what they said, but pretended to take no notice.

"And it came to pass that after a couple of days of idleness, the legs found they were growing very weak, the arms found they couldn't lift, the mouth was growing dry, the teeth were tired of doing nothing, and it was clear that the whole body was wasting away.

"Then the legs, the hands, and the head began whispering again, still thinking that the stomach didn't hear them. But he did.

"The legs struggled to get some food, the hands struggled to lift it to the mouth, the mouth struggled to receive it, and the teeth struggled to chew it up into tiny pieces.

"And lo, the body revived, and became strong and hearty again. As for the stomach, he smiled to himself, but never said a single word.

"You see," said Father Fairy, "no part of anything is of use unless it works happily with all the other parts."

"And," added Mother Fairy, "a family is a poor sort of family unless all the members work together for the happiness of each other."

Why We Say "The Lion's Share"

"Hee-haw!" brayed the donkey, proudly. "I've just been out with the fox and the lion. We've been hunting. Look at all the spoil on my back! We are just going to divide it."

"Let's go and see how they divide it," said Tansy.

"I think I know which will get the biggest share," said Bobbles; and he wagged his head knowingly.

So they hurried after the donkey and reached an opening in the wood.

The lion and the fox were there; and the lion asked the donkey, very graciously, to divide the spoil.

The donkey was consumed with pride at such an invitation, and he promptly laid out the spoil, as near as he could guess, in three equal parts.

"I have now divided it as equally as I can," he said, making a bow to the lion and the fox, "and I hope you will each take your choice and make a very good meal."

Have you ever heard of "the lion's share"? And do you think the lion feels as if he had it?

"Equal!" exclaimed the lion. "Away with your impudence! Have you forgotten that I am the lion?"

"But we all went hunting together," ventured the donkey.

At that the lion set upon the donkey and tore him to pieces.

"Didn't I tell you?" whispered Bobbles.

"Now," said the lion to the fox, "will you divide the spoil?"

"Certainly, your Majesty," said the fox. He was determined not to get himself into trouble, so he laid out almost all the spoil for the lion and only one little morsel for himself.

"Ha, ha!" said the lion, looking very much pleased. "Who taught you how to make such a just division?"

"I wanted no other lesson, your Majesty," said the fox, "than to see yonder donkey lying there! Pray take the lion's share!" and seizing his morsel the fox hurried off, thankful to escape with his life.

"Booh!" said the fairies, as they followed the fox.

"You saw all that?" asked the fox. "It serves me right for having gone hunting with a lion. However, it was better to be made wise by the donkey's misfortune than my own." And off he cantered.

Something Worth Remembering

"Let's go and see what that farmer is doing," suggested Bobbles.

So they ran off across a field, and found the farmer examining the nets he had set to catch the cranes that came after his newly sown grain.

To his surprise he had found a stork; and the stork was protesting against the certain fate he saw in the farmer's eye.

"I am quite innocent, good farmer," he pleaded. "I am no crane. I never eat corn. I am a good son to my parents, and a good brother to my sisters, and . . ."

"That may all be quite true," interrupted the farmer. "But I've caught you in my nets, with your companions, the cranes; and he who goes with evil companions must

How long do you think you could lie quite still while a bear was sniffing round about your ears?

share their fate." And forthwith the farmer slew the stork.

"What's the meaning of that?" asked Tansy of Bobbles.

"It means that it's no use to pretend you are good when you keep bad company."

Then Tansy's eyes twinkled, and she laughed.

"That's why it's no use for me to try to be good when I keep company with you, Bobbles!" And away she flew; but Bobbles chased her till he caught her.

The Travellers and the Bear

"Those two men seem to be very good friends," remarked Tansy, pointing along the path in front.

"Perhaps they are, and perhaps they aren't," said Bobbles, cautiously. "Hello! Here's the test."

For a great bear was striding along the road towards the men.

One man forgot all about his friend and darted up into a tree for safety. The other man, finding himself deserted, didn't know for the moment what to do. But, like a flying arrow, Bobbles came to him and whispered, "Lie down on the ground. Pretend you're dead."

The man had no idea where the voice came from, but he lay down and pretended to be dead.

It was a terrible moment for him when the great bear sniffed about and growled. But he held his breath gallantly, and the bear, deciding that the man must be dead, and not caring to take away a stale meal for the family, trotted off.

The man in the tree came down very cautiously and looked round to make sure the bear had really gone.

"What secret was the bear whispering to you?" he asked with a laugh.

"Indeed," said the other man sternly, "he was telling me to beware of making friends with a man who, when danger came, refused to share it."

By now the men had come to a place where the roads divided; so one man went to the right and the other to the left.

Tansy was now looking at a crow which had flown up into a high tree with a large piece of cheese in her beak.

And Bobbles was pointing to a fox that came padding along with a merry grin on his face.

"I do believe the fox wants the crow's cheese," said Bobbles.

"Hush!" exclaimed Tansy.

It was quite true. The fairies watched the fox as he came under the tree and gazed up at the crow admiringly.

"My lovely crow," he cried, "the beauty of the island! Thy strength is greater than that of the eagle, thy flight more graceful than that of the swallow, thy colour more entrancing than that of the peacock. But alas, alas, that with all these charms Nature has refused to grant thee a voice!"

The crow was listening, and her black eyes sparkled with joy at the fox's flattery.

But his last words nettled her. What could he mean by hinting that she had no voice?

"Caw! Caw!" she cried.

Down dropped the cheese; and the fox ran off with it, laughing at his own success.

"Booh!" said Bobbles. "Why did you listen to that flattering fellow? He only wanted to rob you of your cheese."

Tansy Scolds the Ungrateful Men

The fairies did not wish to leave the wood, because it was so very warm, and as they passed a plane tree they noticed two travellers resting in its shade.

Imagine their surprise when they heard one of them say, "What an ugly, useless tree a plane is."

"Indeed!" exclaimed the tree, indignantly. "At the very moment that you are enjoying my shade, which I give you freely, you insult me and cry out that I am useless."

"Booh!" said Tansy, and the astonished travellers leaped up.

"Depart!" she cried, standing before them as though she were a young queen. "Beware lest I ever see you sheltering under a plane tree again."

So the men hurried off, and Bobbles and Tansy laughed heartily and danced round and round the plane tree to do it honour.

(CONTINUED ON PAGE 743)

Photo by National Portrait Gallery

Out of his earnings as a writer Sir Walter Scott built this fine house, Abbotsford ; and it stands to-day just as when he lived there. The merry, kindly face in the oval is that of the great author of historical romances.

The WIZARD of the NORTH

Sir Walter Scott, the First Author to Weave Thrilling Tales Around the People in History Books

(CONTINUED FROM PAGE 590)

YEARS ago an old lady in Edinburgh used to charm her grandson with heroic tales about his own forefathers. They had been Lowlanders, warlike people who lived along the Scottish border and hated both the English to the south of them and the Highlanders to the north. To this day their children tell of their brave deeds in song and legend, and repeat the very stories that made little Walter Scott (1771–1832) so proud to have been born of such a gallant race.

He, too, was destined to honour the land of his birth. The days of fighting were long since past; and the lad could hardly have engaged in combat anyway, for an infantile disease had left him lame. But he was of daring spirit, and as he scoured the country on his Shetland pony, he won the respect of all the boys in their sports. Besides, he could already thrill them with

delight or horror at the tales he made up as he went along.

When he grew up he became a lawyer, for in his day the law was one of the few callings that a gentleman could follow. But he was a remarkably hard worker, and so he found plenty of time for the life and studies that he really loved. On horseback he explored the wildest parts of Scotland, stopping at peasants' huts for food and rest. We can imagine how welcome his stories made him.

But all the time he was listening to the songs that these simple people and their ancestors had sung for centuries, though the songs had never been published. It was Scott who wrote them down and published them in his "Minstrelsy of the Scottish Border" (1802).

But he did not stop here. During the next few years he published a number of fine poems of his own—just as thrilling to read to-day as they were a century ago. In

"The Lay of the Last Minstrel" (1805), he tried his hand at imitating the ballads he had heard in his country rambles, and even included one of his own ancestors in the tale. It was so well received that he made up his mind to devote the greater part of his life to writing. "Marmion" (1808) followed, a tragic story ending in the defeat of the Scots on Flodden Field. Then the romantic poem of "The Lady of the Lake" (1810) sent tourists flocking to the Scottish lakes and mountains for a sight of the wild scenery it describes. But, soon after this, Scott gave up poetry and turned to telling stories in prose — and in this there is scarcely any one to surpass him.

All this time he had nursed another great desire. He wanted to own a great estate where he might entertain friends in lordly fashion. He was happily married, and the income from his books was so large that his family had every comfort. So he bought an estate on the River Tweed, which he called Abbotsford, and spent a large part of his earnings on beautifying it. Here guests were always welcome, and here they might ride and fish and hunt with their genial host.

The mansion was full of pets, especially dogs, which Scott loved dearly; and, most interesting of all, the rooms were stored with relics of Scotland's history. We can visit the place to-day, for it is now a museum; and among countless other treasures we may still see the sword of Montrose, the purse and pistols of Rob Roy, the drinking cup of Robert Burns, the seal and cross of tragic Mary Queen of Scots. Even a doorway from the ruined Melrose Abbey has been built into the old house.

In all his splendour, Scott was far from

Photo by National Portrait Gallery

Sir Walter Scott in his library at Abbotsford, with his favourite dog beside him. It was in this room that there flowed from his pen so many of the brilliant novels upon which the world hung breathless.

idle. In secret he began to write the "Waverley Novels." There are some thirty of them in all, and among them many of the world's best romances. The first one, "Waverley" (1814), gave its name to the whole series. To read the list is like calling a roll of old friends—"Guy Mannering" (1815), with its tales of the gipsy, wild Meg Merrilies; "Rob Roy" (1818), the great outlaw whom boys always love; "The Heart of Midlothian" (1818), with the story of Jeanie Deans, the heroic Scots lass who walks all the way to London to plead for the life of a sister accused of murder. And then there is "Ivanhoe" (1820), an exciting tale of castles and knights when Robin Hood lived in Sherwood; and the dazzling picture in "Kenilworth" (1821) of Queen Elizabeth and her lover, the earl of Leicester; and for those who love stories of France, the adventures of "Quentin Durward" (1823). The books are the first real historical novels that were ever written.

For his own reasons Scott kept the authorship of the novels secret for many years, and so the delighted public called the writer the "Great Unknown" and the "Wizard of the North"—so amazing was the rapidity with which the books appeared. Printers could hardly cope with the demand for each new story. When the truth finally came out, the king conferred on Scott the title of baronet.

Writing Hard to Meet a Heavy Burden of Indebtedness

But now a sad misfortune fell upon Sir Walter. Through no fault of his own, the publishing house in which he had invested his money failed. He might have taken refuge in bankruptcy and so escaped from his debts. But that was not Sir Walter's idea of honour. Instead, he took upon himself the enormous burden of paying the £130,000—a sum of much greater value then than it would be to-day. In spite of the fact that he was now in constant pain, he wrote in such feverish haste that in six years he had actually paid back half of the money. Few of the feats of authors have been so able or so noble.

It was too much, however, even for his stout heart. His health broke from the strain, and he could do no more. When it was learned that his doctor ordered a sea voyage, the government sent him a ship to cruise the Mediterranean. But it was all of no use, and finally he was carried back to his beloved Abbotsford to die.

Shortly before the end he called his son-in-law to him and said, "Lockhart, I may have but a minute to speak to you. My dear, be a good man—be virtuous—be religious—be a good man. Nothing else will give you any comfort when you come to lie here." Asked if Sophie and Anne, his daughters, should be sent for, he replied, "No, don't disturb them. I know they were up all night. God bless you all. I have unsettled no man's faith, I have corrupted no man's principles." They were his last words.

The GENTLEST NAME in ENGLISH LETTERS

A Brother and Sister Who Mastered Their Own Misfortune and Found Happiness by Making Others Happy

THE hum and buzz of London were always dear to Charles Lamb. He liked the people, the lighted shops, the bookstalls, the theatres—even the dirt and noise of the great city, where he lived nearly all his life.

Here, in 1775, he had been born in the Inner Temple. The windows of his parents' home looked out upon the quiet green of that ancient law school. The little boy loved it's great old buildings and the fountain by which he played. He also adored his elder sister Mary, who watched over him and mothered him until he was seven. Then, as his parents were poor, they were thankful to place their son in the good free school near by.

It was called Christ's Hospital—or sometimes "The Blue-Coat School" from the

Photos by
National Portrait Gallery

Charles and Mary Lamb, the gentle brother and sister who will long live together in the hearts of all who love a good tale well told and a valiant life well lived.

colour of the pupils' uniforms. The timid, stammering child with a gentle disposition easily won the other boys' affection. Among them was a young genius named Samuel Taylor Coleridge, who could already speak with the "tongue of angels." Little Charles Lamb looked up in admiration to his older playmate, and between the two began a friendship that lasted all their lives and grew ever closer in later years when both were famous writers.

At sixteen Lamb entered the office of a great business firm, the South Sea House. Then he changed to a desk in the East India House, where he remained nearly all his life. His great pleasures were reading and writing and going to plays. He was the bosom friend of most of the great authors of his day, and of many other men; for the manly, merry Charles Lamb was about the best friend any man could have.

One of the fine tales of Charles and Mary Lamb is their story of Shakespeare's "Othello." Our picture shows the noble Moor relating his wonderful and exciting adventures to Desdemona and Brabantio, her father.

When he was only twenty-one a terrible calamity befell the family. His sister Mary, worn out with nursing her invalid mother, went violently insane and stabbed her parent to the heart. The fit passed, but the poor young woman had to be placed in an asylum. There she would have remained except for her devoted brother. After their father's death he obtained her release by giving his word that he would watch over her all his life.

While he lived he guarded her with the tenderest affection. Only at those times when signs of the old illness returned were brother and sister separated. Then Mary would retire to a quiet place until her health was restored. When she was well, they were about the happiest people in the world. Thus for nearly forty years they lived for each other, until the death of Charles in 1834.

Together Charles and Mary wrote the "Tales from Shakespeare" (1807) for boys and girls who are still too young to understand all that the great poet has to say.

These tales are by far the best ever written about Shakespeare's plays, and are just as suitable for men and women as for children.

The greatest work, however, was done by Charles alone in the famous "Essays of Elia" (1820)—those sparkling, whimsical, moving, and humorous essays that are almost without a rival. The "Dissertation on Roast Pig" is the most amusing and probably the best-known of them; the essay on "Dream Children" is the tenderest and the most beautiful.

But the most purely delightful of all Lamb's writings are the thousands of letters that have come down to us just as he wrote them to his famous friends. They are full of charming humour and tender sentiment. The best are the ones he wrote to a friend named Thomas Manning, a man of a mathematical turn of mind, who spent some twelve years in China and India. For some reason he was able to bring out the most amusing vein in his gifted friend, and the letters are a fine record of the friendship.

A METEOR *in* ENGLISH POETRY

Lord Byron, Who Expressed the Spirit of Revolt against Tyranny, and was the Greatest Creative Poet of His Age

WHAT do people mean when they talk about a "Byronic person" or a "Byronic pose" or a "Byronic way of doing one's hair"? Here is the story of a man in whom the whole world was so interested—for his poetry and his personality—that even now, more than a century after his death, people are still forming an adjective from his name.

George Gordon, the sixth Lord Byron, was born in London in 1788. He spent his first ten years with his mother at Aberdeen. Then, when his great-uncle died and he became Lord Byron and a peer of the realm, he moved to the beautiful, half-ruined ancestral seat at Newstead Abbey, near Nottingham. He received a good education, first at the grammar school at Aberdeen, and later at Harrow and Cambridge.

That sounds as though he ought to have had a happy childhood and a fortunate prospect. But it was not so. Byron's father was a wild and unscrupulous man, who had squandered his wife's fortune, and his mother was a foolish, moody creature, who at one moment would spoil her son with flattering affection and the next would fly into a rage and say all manner of cruel things to him. He said that she even taunted him about his lameness; for he had been born with a club foot, and everything the doctors tried to do for it only made it worse.

Even Newstead Abbey was as much of a worry to Byron as it was a joy, and he was always in financial difficulties. So Byron's childhood was very unhappy, and practically all he got from his noble family was a bad heritage and a highly sensitive pride.

By the time he was twenty-one, Byron was already playing the world-weary lord as an accustomed part. There is a story that he gathered his friends together at Newstead

Photo by Robert Arnot

Being the romantic man he was, the poet Byron could hardly fail to be inspired to eloquence by the majestic beauty of scenery of Lake Geneva. Meanwhile his audience, as romantic as he, listen in rapt attention.

Abbey to masquerade in the robes of the ancient monks who had once lived there, and to drink wine out of skulls. He had already published two volumes of cynical poems, which had been savagely attacked by the "Edinburgh Review." The young man replied by a clever and stinging satire called "English bards and Scotch Reviewers," the title, of course, being due to the fact that the "Edinburgh Review" was a Scottish publication. In 1809 he took his seat in the House of Lords, where later he distinguished himself, with a brilliant speech. Later in the year, with a friend, he set off for a two-year trip on the Continent.

When he returned to England in 1811, it was "without a hope and almost without a desire." And in truth he had good cause to be somewhat troubled. His mother and several of his friends had died in his absence, and he was in need of money. But in 1812 he was persuaded to publish two cantos of a poem called "Childe Harold's Pilgrimage," which he had written while he was abroad. So it happened that, as he later put it, he woke up one morning to find himself famous.

"Childe Harold" has been followed by a series of melodramatic tales of the East—tales of Turkish harems and noble pirates and heroic lovers. The heroes were all handsome and proud and burdened with some secret guilt. They were all a good

deal like Byron himself—or at least like the dramatic and romantic picture he had created of himself in his own mind.

Byron married in 1815, choosing, incredibly, an admirable young woman who was so different from him that it was impossible for them to be happy together. In 1816, not much more than a year after the marriage, his wife separated from him. Byron's fine friends turned their backs on him, and he left England in disgrace and anger — never to return.

Feeling more than ever like one of his own heroes —proud and alone, victim of injustice and gnawing remorse —Byron went to Switzerland and then to Italy. He began to write much better poetry, for his own feelings were deeper, and, as we have said, his poetry is really all about himself. In Switzerland he climbed the Alps, revelling in their grand and awe-inspiring beauty; and he wrote about them and his own suffering in the magnificent dramatic poem called "Manfred."

He wrote two more cantos for "Childe Harold," much finer than the first two. They are full of splendid and eloquent descriptions of what he had seen in Switzerland and Italy—such as the famous passage

Photo by National Portrait Gallery

BYRON AND HIS PRISONER OF CHILLON

In the inset is a portrait of George Gordon, the sixth Lord Byron. It is not the face of a man who was insincere, but rather of one who could never forget to act the rôle in which he pictured himself. Byron was a man of generous impulses, and his enthusiasm in the cause of liberty was altogether genuine. One of its finest expressions is in the poem of " The Prisoner of Chillon," which tells the moving story of the man who was a prisoner in the castle of Chillon. Of that grim dungeon Byron wrote:

Chillon! thy prison is a holy place
And thy sad floor an altar, for 'twas trod,
Until his very steps have left a trace
Worn as if thy cold pavement were a sod,
By Bonivard! May none those marks efface!
For they appeal from tyranny to God.

about the Colosseum at Rome, with its picture of the gladiator "butchered to make a Roman holiday." Another of the great poems of this time is "The Prisoner of Chillon"—that moving story of a man who suffered for his love of liberty.

In Italy Byron lived for a time in Venice, and then settled down—comparatively speaking—in Pisa and other places. He saw something of the poet Shelley, and was interested with him and Leigh Hunt in the plan for an English paper to be published in Italy. Shelley has left us an amusing picture of Byron's strange establishment, with its astonishing pets, ranging from a wolf to a peacock.

All this time, of course, Byron continued to write. Though he saw with grief and defiance that his popularity was not so great as it had been, he must have been secretly pleased to know that whether they approved of him or not, people still talked about him. Shelley spoke of Byron's fame as "bent over his living head like Heaven."

A Poem, Hundreds of Pages Long, full of Satire, Romance, and Adventure

In his later poems Byron was returning to the mood of "English Bards and Scotch Reviewers," and was writing magnificent satire. "Don Juan" is hundreds of pages long—it comprises nineteen lengthy cantos —and yet it is not finished. Byron said half jokingly that he supposed it would run to a hundred cantos. It has very little plot, and its not being finished scarcely matters. The delight of it lies in the way it roves from one thing to another, mixing romantic love stories with sarcastic remarks about love, fantastic adventures with biting lines about war, and anything, in fact, with anything else. It is Byron's greatest work.

But in the midst of it he decided to go to Greece and help the Greeks in their struggle for independence from the Turks. He had always fancied himself a man of action, imagining that writing poetry was hardly worthy of a peer. And he was a genuine lover of liberty.

Death Prevents Byron from Helping the Greeks to Gain Their Freedom

While at Missolonghi (mĭs'ō-lŏng'gē) Byron planned to raise a brigade of troops at his own expense with the object of making an attack on Lepanto. The project, however, proved a failure, the troops that he enlisted being disorderly and quite unreliable. This was an intense disappointment to the poet, and it led to his becoming ill from epilepsy. He was advised to leave Missolonghi for a more healthy spot, but refused to do so; and after making further efforts in the cause of the Greeks, he again fell ill, and died on April 19, 1824. It was a splendidly dramatic death, coming in the midst of a generous attempt to help a down-trodden people. His remains were brought back to England, and after lying in state for a time in London, were laid to rest near his seat at Newstead Abbey.

England was full of "Byronism" when Byron died; and no one of her other poets has ever been so honoured abroad in his own lifetime. Even now, when styles have changed, when his eloquence seems at times a little flashy and his self-pity not in very good taste, he is still counted among the great poets, if not among the greatest.

For some seven hundred years this famous castle of Chillon has stood, as we see it to-day, at the eastern end of Lake Geneva, in Switzerland.

Here François Bonivard, the hero of Byron's great poem of "The Prisoner of Chillon," was imprisoned in a dungeon for six long years.

"*An* ANGEL *with* WINGS *of* LIGHT"

So a Great Critic has Called the Poet Shelley, to Whom His Dreams were More Real than the World around Him

PERCY BYSSHE SHELLEY was miserable at his school; he was expelled from his college; he was practically driven out of England—for deep down in his nature there was something that would not let him live like the other people in the world. Even before he went to school, Shelley found it difficult to live happily with his conservative family on their beautiful estate at Field Place, near Horsham, where he was born on August 4, 1792.

In his school he was far more unhappy; he strongly objected to the idea of "fagging," and the other boys simply set him down as queer beyond excuse, and proceeded to torment him for it. They called him the "mad Shelley" and the "atheist Shelley"—and you may imagine in what manner they treated him.

Then at Oxford he angered the authorities. He had published two strange novels as a student, and a little essay about atheism (disbelief in a God). So his tutors sent him down from college as a dangerous person, and then his wealthy father disowned him and set him adrift without a penny.

Mary Wollstonecraft Shelley, the poet's second wife and herself a distinguished writer. She was the daughter of William Godwin, a man who wielded a powerful pen on behalf of liberal ideas in the England of his day. Mrs. Shelley's best-known work, the novel "Frankenstein," was published when its author was only twenty-one. It is still read and has been dramatized. It is the story of a man so deeply learned that he was able to create a kind of monster which possessed many of the faculties of a human being. But the fearful creature was entirely without moral nature; and the history of its career is both thrilling and tragic.

In London he managed to exist for a time by borrowing a little money from his sisters who had an allowance. Then he married Harriet Westbrook, the sixteen-year-old daughter of a retired hotel keeper, in a fit of chivalry because she was persecuted. With his wife he went off to Ireland, where he hoped to help the people who were struggling to free themselves from tyranny. In his high, shrill voice he lectured to them; in his moving and brilliant prose style he wrote little pamphlets for them. He and Harriet used to throw the pamphlets out of the window to them as they passed in the street. Later, in Wales, he used to send the pamphlets up in balloons, or to sea in bottles, hoping they would be washed up on the Irish shore.

Then he and Harriet began to have misunderstandings; quarrelled frequently and soon drifted apart. Finally Shelley left her for good, and eloped with Mary Godwin, a young girl of talent who was later to write the novel about "Frankenstein." Further trouble was soon to befall the poet. Harriet drowned herself in the Serpentine, a little later, and

IRON HORSES *of the* WORLD

Here is an unusual view of a railway train. It is a London and North Eastern express speeding across the majestic Forth Bridge, in Scotland, on its journey from London to Edinburgh. The photograph was taken from a position at the top of the centre span, 204 feet above the rails and 361 feet above the level of the sea.

All trains do not run on surface rails. The train shown in the upper picture, for example, would find the ordinary method of progress impossible. It is an "express" on the Mont Blanc Railway, in Switzerland. Below are seen the "Flying Scotsman" and the "Edinburgh Express" just steaming out of the London terminus.

LOCOMOTIVES OF OTHER LANDS

Photo (top) by Swiss Federal Railways

Snow often obstructs the permanent way of the St. Gotthard line in Switzerland, and the rotary snow-plough in the top picture has to clear the track. The luxury coach train in the centre is the famous "Blue Comet" of the Central Railroad of New Jersey. At the bottom is a giant locomotive of the South Africa Railways.

SOME NEW IDEAS IN RAILWAY TRAINS

Photo by Associated Equipment Company

The strange affair at the top is a railplane car which was tried out in Glasgow. It is designed for a speed of one hundred miles an hour and is driven by means of air-screws. The stream-lined railcar is the newest type of passenger train adopted by the Great Western Railway. Driven by an oil engine, it can travel at sixty miles an hour.

BEAUTIFUL
BRITAIN

Photo by G.W. Rly.

In the quiet peace of our countryside we may find many cottages as beautiful as this one, but none, perhaps, quite so famous.   It is a place of pilgrimage for all lovers of Shakespeare, for it was here that the great poet came as a youth to woo Anne Hathaway.   The cottage is situated in Shottery, just outside Stratford-on-Avon.

THE GRANDEUR OF MIGHTY SCOTLAND

Photos by L.M.S. Rly.

At the top is a typical example of the wild but beautiful scenery to be found in Scotland. It is a view of the Three Sisters at Glencoe. Below is Edinburgh, the capital of Scotland, showing Castle Hill, on the left, and the National Gallery, in the centre. The streets of this ancient city are paved with historical and literary romance.

THE BEAUTY OF LAKE AND COAST

Photos by L.M.S. Rly.

The lakes of Killarney, in Ireland, the Emerald Isle, are famed throughout the world for their glorious beauty. The top picture is a view of one of these lakes—Lough Leane. Below is the rugged coastline seen at Amlwch, in Anglesey, North Wales. The walls of Britain are strong and forbidding, but they are wonderfully beautiful.

STILL WATERS AND A PEACEFUL COVE

Photos by L.M.S. Rly. and G.W. Rly.

The Lake District of England has thousands of enchanting pictures to spread before the eyes of the Nature lover. At the top is Coniston Lake, as seen from Beacon Crags. The picture below is of Mullion Cove, in Cornwall—a grand and very beautiful piece of coastline that has been the subject of many an artist's brush.

though it was not because Shelley had deserted her, it was a terrible blow to him. Then by an order of the court Harriet's children were taken from him, the court declaring that he was not a fit person to bring them up.

In 1818, following an illness that suggested the presence of consumption, Shelley and his family departed for Italy, where he lived in mingled joy and sorrow until he was drowned, while sailing in a little boat which capsized during a storm, on July 8, 1822.

of the world around him. Often he could not remember whether he had had his dinner or not; once at least he could not tell his own children from another person's.

These stories indicate that he was living in the land of dreams. In that land he was a gentle, kindly spirit—childlike or womanly in the deep love he felt for beauty and good in the abstract—and in that land he was also a fierce warrior fighting to right the wrongs with which the human race was burdened.

In this house lived Percy Bysshe Shelley, the famous English poet whose portrait is shown below. It was he to whom a great critic referred as a "beautiful but ineffectual angel beating his luminous wings in the void in vain."

Photo by National Portrait Gallery

Mystery still surrounds the unfortunate and sad ending to a young life of such promise. It is recorded that a rumour, which has, however, never been confirmed, had got abroad that a companion of Shelley's on the return voyage to Lerici was in possession of a sum of money. Shortly after they had started on their journey a tempest suddenly arose. It raged for less than thirty minutes, and when it had abated their little schooner had disappeared. Examination of the empty craft, which was found later, created suspicion that it had been run down either by accident or intentionally. When the bodies of Shelley and his companion, Williams, were recovered they were burned, in accordance with Greek custom, and the poet's ashes were buried in the new Protestant Cemetery in Rome. Shelley had lived only thirty tortured years, but in that time he had written more great poetry than almost any other man of the same age.

Shelley was no creature of this earth. His glorious dreams were more real to him than were the sticks and stones, the houses and the people, and the other material things

Nearly all of his poetry is an outcry for freedom. "Queen Mab" was the first long poem in this vein, and it was followed by "Alastor" and "The Revolt of Islam." Later came "Epipsychidion," (ĕp'ĭ-sĭ-kĭd'ĭ-ŏn) and "Adonais" (ăd'-ō-nā'ĭs), a beautiful poem on the death of Keats. There are many other long poems and several poetic dramas, of which the most powerful and beautiful are the tragedy of the "Cenci" (chĕn'chē) and rainbow-hued "Prometheus Unbound."

But possibly Shelley is still better known for his shorter pieces, of transcendent beauty, like the "Skylark," the "Cloud," and the magnificent "Ode to the West Wind,"

The REALM of GOLD in POETRY

You Will Find It in the Work of John Keats, Who Might Be Called the Most Poetical of All the Poets

MOST people are just starting a career when they are twenty-five. Here is a young man who died at that age and yet is now famous, a century later, as one of our greatest poets. It is John Keats.

Keats was born in 1795, in a London livery stable, the first child of the head ostler and his young wife, the daughter of the stable-man. Some of his critics in later years seemed unable to forget his humble origin, and referred to him as one of a group of "Cockney poets." Keats was never anything but poor, and money troubles dogged him to the end.

Although he could not afford to go to a university, the young man had a good education, so far as it went. At eight he was sent to a well-known school at Enfield. Although he was the smallest boy there, "Johnny" Keats did not lack courage, and was always ready for a fight, no matter how big the other boy might be. One of his friends later said that he was "like a pet prizefighter," admired for his "terrier courage."

He was also a generous and high-minded lad, and everyone was fond of him, pupils and teachers alike. Above all, he found a cherished friend in Charles Cowden Clarke, son of the head-master. Clarke was a fine boy who was to bring a great influence to bear on the poet.

It was Clarke who told him about the beautiful fairyland of poetry he would find in Spenser and the other great poets. Later, in his famous sonnet, Keats wrote:

> Much have I travelled in the realms of gold,
> And many goodly states and kingdoms seen.

His "realms of gold" were in the land of books; and it was while he was a friend of Clarke's at Enfield that he began to travel in them. Throughout his all too short life he never gave up that high adventure.

With his friends, his fights, and his golden poetry, Keats spent a normal, happy childhood. His father had died soon after John entered school, but when he was on holiday he could stay with his grandmother. He dearly loved his mother, his two younger brothers, and his little sister Fanny.

But when he was only fourteen, the mother fell very ill with tuberculosis. For days John was her nurse, letting no one else do anything for her, but after a short time she died. A few years later John was to nurse his brother Tom through his last struggles with the same terrible disease. And eventually he died of it himself.

After his mother's death (1810) Keats had to leave school and work for a surgeon at Edmonton. He was none too happy there, and after two or three years went to London to continue his surgical studies. All this time he was finding more and more joy in his reading and in the sweet, imaginative verses that he had already begun to write.

It was while working in a chemist's shop that the young poet Keats invented the famous phrase "a thing of beauty is a joy for ever." It has now passed into the language, and is quoted wherever the English tongue is spoken.

In London the eager young poet fell in with a group of friends who were very deeply interested in literature and new ideas. The moving spirit of the group was Leigh Hunt, himself a poet and essayist, and the editor of a well-known paper, the "Examiner." Keats began to contribute to Hunt's paper, and finally gave up all idea of being a surgeon. He decided to devote himself to the composition of poetry.

Keats Establishes Himself in the World of Poets and Poetry

For a time he was very happy. At last he was in his right sphere, and he was full of courage and confidence. It was a joy to move among kindred spirits to talk of art and reform, to write sonnets in competition with Hunt and Shelley, at Hunt's hospitable little cottage on Hampstead Heath. The ostler's son, by right of his superb gifts, had come into his own. He had made a place for himself among the choicest spirits of his age, and was able to move among them as an equal. The young man's brain was full of excitement and ferment, and on the horizon, as he said, he saw "huge cloudy symbols of a high romance."

He published a volume of poems in 1817, but it found no favour with the critics. The poet, however, was not discouraged—he was already full of plans for a greater work. He went to the Isle of Wight, seeking solitude for his writing. There he tramped the hills, drinking in their loveliness, or sat pondering by the sea. He was working on "Endymion" (ĕn-dĭm′ĭ-ŏn), a long poetic tale of the Moon and her earthly lover, a poem full of richly beautiful passages.

Poems of Great Merit and Charm That Earned Only Violent Criticism

The next year, when he published "Endymion," a storm of abuse broke in earnest about Keats' head. But he himself had already seen what was wrong with the poem, and had set about correcting it. Within the next two years he wrote most of his greatest poetry—the heroic story of the fall of "Hyperion" (hī-pēr′ĭ-ŏn), the sun god; the

The famous artist Sir John Everett Millais has left us this excellent specimen of his art to illustrate Keats' poem of "The Pot of Basil." If you have read the poem you will have no trouble in recognizing the lovers Lorenzo and Isabella in the two figures who are seated to the right. The other faces, also, are well worth careful study.

tale of "Lamia" (lā'mĭ-å), who was sometimes a serpent and sometimes a lovely lady; the romantic story of the lovers who fled on "The Eve of St. Agnes"; the sonnets of love and death, and the great odes "To a Nightingale," "To Autumn," and "On a Grecian Urn." No one has written lines laden with a richer music. No one has loved more truly the beautiful things of the earth, and expressed his love more fitly. Yet the more he wrote, the more savage the attacks upon him became. The abuse hurt him, but he continued to write, saying, "This is mere matter of the moment. I think I shall be among the English poets after my death." And he was right.

Photo by National Portrait Gallery

John Keats, a poet of such rare talent that, had he lived longer, he might well have rivalled Shakespeare as a master of phrase.

Meanwhile, misfortune was piling on misfortune to bring that time "after my death" all too near. One brother emigrated to America; the other brother died. Money troubles rose up. He had fallen desperately in love, and was too poor to marry. Most fatal of all, he had taken a walking trip with a friend in Northern England and in Scotland, and had returned home ill of the disease that had already carried off both his mother and his brother. For more than a year he fought it off, writing meanwhile his greatest poems. Then one cold night he rode home to Hampstead from London on the outside of a bus. The next day he knew that he was doomed.

This was early in 1820. Later in the year his friends persuaded him to go to Italy, hoping that the mild Italian air would bring him healing. But he continued to sicken, and a little more than a year from the time when he was taken ill he died. If you go to Rome to-day you may see his grave, near Shelley's, in the Protestant Cemetery. On it are words suggested by Keats himself: "Here lies one whose name was writ in water." But the name of John Keats is written in gold in the annals of the rich spirits of the world. If he had lived only another ten or twenty years—who knows what he might have achieved in the realms of poetry!

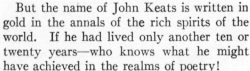

The "ENGLISH OPIUM EATER"

In This Famous Book, and in Many Others, Thomas De Quincey Gave Us Some Beautiful Prose

SOMETIMES you would have thought that the frail little man named Thomas De Quincey really lived in the world of strange dreams and unearthly imaginings which he could describe so well. He was so learned that he had been able to write and even speak Greek ever since he was fifteen. Yet he had no idea in his head about business, and was once known to go about frantically trying to borrow a few shillings while he had in his pocket a fifty-pound note which he did not know how to cash.

He could not bear to throw away manuscripts or papers. At the time of his death he was paying rent on six different lodgings in Edinburgh; for he would work in a room until he was completely snowed under by papers— and then he would calmly lock the door and move on to another place. Yet no one could be more charming in conversation than he, and no one more tender and courteous.

De Quincey had been talented and somewhat queer all his life. Born in Manchester, in 1785, he was only sixteen when he ran away from school—because, as he explained, his masters could teach him nothing more. He went to his mother's house in Wales and was given a weekly allowance, so that he might continue his studies in the country. But, in these out-of-the-way villages, "suffering grievously for want of books," he again became discontented. Then he drifted to London, and lived on practically nothing at all, until at last he was reconciled with his family, who were well-to-do, and was sent to Oxford.

Later, in 1809, he settled at Grasmere, in the Lake District, in Dove Cottage, made famous by the fact that William and Dorothy Wordsworth had lived there before him. Not only Wordsworth, but the other "Lake Poets," Coleridge and Southey, were his friends. When he was about twenty-three, a bank in which his money was deposited failed, and he had to return to London, to see if he could make his living by writing.

Few persons have written such magical prose as this gentle little dreamer of dreams, Thomas De Quincey.

of this powerful drug—dreams filled sometimes with heavenly loveliness, but oftener, alas, with terrors and nightmares—monstrous crocodiles, tropical jungle-horrors, a horrible feeling that he had lived through whole centuries in a single night. The essence of all these dream terrors is in the sketch called "Dream Fugue," which is the most famous description of a dream in the English language.

In fact, of all the huge mass of writing which De Quincey produced in London and later in Edinburgh, where he lived from 1828 to his death in 1859, the pieces best remembered are those in which he tells us either about dreams or about dream-like memories.

He wrote some fine criticism and even tried his hand at a novel. But what we read now of his is the "Confessions";

It was in London that he made his literary reputation. He wrote for the "London Magazine" a series of papers called "Confessions of an English Opium Eater," which is still the most famous of his writings. Ever since his days at Oxford, De Quincey had been in the habit of taking opium to deaden pain from which he was never quite free.

In this book he tells of the fantastic dreams he had dreamed under the influence the "Suspiria de Profundis"—especially the essay in it called "Levana and Our Ladies of Sorrow," which is as mournfully lovely as its name; and the series called "The English Mail Coach," which ends with the "Dream Fugue" already mentioned.

It is pleasing to know that De Quincey's later years were spent in comparative ease in the midst of his family. He was very fond of music and young people, and his fame as a host brought him many visitors, who were fascinated by his conversation.

(CONTINUED ON PAGE 699)

The feathery blanket that has tucked in this little Canadian cabin fell from out of the air. Yet before it began to descend, there was not a flake of it to be seen. Where, then, did all those tons of white flakes come from?

An OCEAN of AIR

It is from the Atmosphere, an Invisible Fluid Surrounding the Earth, that We Obtain Our Weather

(CONTINUED FROM PAGE 626)

ONE of the most amazing things in the world is air. It is all round us. We breathe it, we walk in it, we fly in it; it is spread all through our bodies—in all the tiny crevices—and the weight of thousands of pounds of it bears down upon us every instant of our lives. And yet we cannot see it, smell it, or feel its weight! If it were not for certain things it does we should not know that it was there at all. We see the tossing trees, and feel an invisible something that buffets us about, and we say it is the wind.

It is out of this magical blanket, resting on us so softly, that all our weather comes. Under the tireless action of the sun, all the amazing varieties of hot and cold and moist and dry weather, of breeze and calm and

tempest, are created. The air and its moisture are like the steam in a mighty engine which manufactures weather in twenty-four-hour shifts, and the sun is the furnace that heats the boiler. But so many are the various forces in the engine that the weather of no two years is ever exactly alike. That is what makes the subject so interesting to anyone who will take a little pains to find out about it.

We do not know just how high up the air reaches; probably from two to four hundred miles, though some put it as high as six hundred. Of course, there is no definite limit; the air just fades away to nothing. As soon as we start upward, it gets colder and thinner. If we were setting out on a winter trip to the moon, we should find that when we had risen to about three miles the air would be down to zero Fahrenheit, and a good deal thinner than on the earth; and at six or seven miles it would be so thin that we could not live in it unless we took with us a supply of oxygen. Seven or eight miles up the temperature would be about seventy-five degrees below zero Fahrenheit, for it drops about fifteen degrees for every mile we rise.

But here there would come a change. We should find ourselves in the second of

HOW A SHOWER OF RAIN IS CAUSED

Here is a recipe for making a shower. Take one good strong sun and place it over an ocean. At once its heat will set to work turning the water into vapour—or, as we say, evaporating it. The rising vapour is shown by the white column in the left-hand picture. Now you can watch your water vapour condense in tiny drops, though actually you would not be able to see it. Keep on pushing the water vapour higher and higher up into the sky. At last it will get so cold that it cannot all stay in the air as vapour—part of it will condense. You will have an active rain cloud, which will soon begin to drop its moisture as it drifts in over the land. Showers are made under differing circumstances, but it is always the same principle at work.

the great layers of atmosphere. It is called the stratosphere (strā'tŏ-sfēr). We know very little about it, for it is only in the last year or two that men have been there to see what it is like; but little balloons carrying instruments have been sent high up into it— as far as twenty-three and a half miles— and on coming down again have told some very interesting tales. Among other things they have reported that the temperature there remains at about seventy-

five degrees below zero all through the stratosphere, and that the air some twenty-five miles above the ground is probably only about one three-thousandth as dense as at sea level. Here are no moisture, clouds, or storms—no "weather" in our sense of the word.

What the Air is Like More Than Twenty-five Miles Up

Of the air at still higher altitudes almost nothing is known. It is so thin that it almost forms a vacuum (văk'ū-ŭm); in fact, there is scarcely any air at all. Yet we know that air is there, for meteors take fire from rubbing through it on their swift flight to earth. And thin as it is, there is enough of it to carry heavy charges of electricity, for the "northern" lights, which are really an electrical display, mount high into this upper zone. It is very probable that the temperature of this topmost layer may be much warmer than that of the stratosphere —warmer, perhaps, than at the surface of the earth.

Of what is it that the earth's invisible blanket is made? What can it be that weighs so much and yet cannot be felt?

The air is a mixture of certain substances that we call gases, and gases are the lightest and thinnest forms of matter. If you separated any hundred cubic feet of air into its various parts, you would get seventy-eight cubic feet of a gas called nitrogen (nī′trṓ-jĕn) and twenty-one of oxygen (ŏk′sĭ-jĕn). The one cubic foot that would be left would be made up of what are called the inert gases and certain other substances—water vapour, carbon dioxide (dī-ŏk′sīd) and ozone. Although these last form so small a part of the air, neither plants nor animals could live without them.

If you find it hard to believe that the air contains moisture—tiny particles of water that we call water vapour—watch a jug of ice-cold water that has been brought into the room on a hot day, when the air seems quite dry with the heat. In less time than it takes to tell, the jug will be covered with fine beads of water. These have not come from inside the jug, for none of the water can possibly leak through it. They have all come out of the air.

The water vapour in the normal air cannot be seen, but outdoor air is hardly ever without it. It is drawn up from the sea, from lakes and rivers and brooks, and from our breath Wherever moisture is found, it is being taken up into the air. If you hang up a damp cloth it will soon get dry; the water in it has turned into vapour, or "evaporated."

But at some time or another the water will all return to earth in the form of rain or hail or snow or dew. For every drop of moisture that the earth gives to the air it gets back again. The air merely serves to distribute the water over the surface of the earth. If it did not do so, nothing but the ocean would be wet, and every inch of land in the world would be desert. It is

If you find it hard to believe that the air is full of dust, just darken the room and look at the ray of light coming in through the keyhole. It will be full of tiny dancing particles. Now moisture, when it condenses, always forms into tiny drops round one or more of these little particles, or on some other nucleus. In our picture it is condensing on a jug of water—and so the jug appears to sweat. But none of the water came from inside the jug: it was all present in the air.

only by means of the air that the water drawn up out of the ocean is sprinkled over the land—thus forming the streams and rivers that carry it down to the sea again.

Carbon dioxide is even more mysterious than water vapour. It forms only three ten-thousandths of the air, and yet without that tiny fraction of it none of the plants could live. On this they build up their bodies. And if all the plants should die, what would become of man and all the other animals!

Carbon dioxide comes from combustion, and from the breath of animals; it pours out of volcanoes; yet all the fires and all the animals in the world do not seem greatly to increase its quantity. For the plants are always at work during the hours of daylight, breathing in the gas through pores in their leaves.

Ozone is still more mysterious. Not a great deal is known about it, except that it is a very powerful and active form of oxygen. There is only a very little of it in the air, though sometimes a sharp thunderstorm will set free enough for one to be able to smell it. Some people say it reminds them of a faint smell of horse-radish; others think it more like ammonia or burning sulphur.

There is still one other substance that helps to make the atmosphere—the humble and ever-present dust. Surely this is the last thing that one would ever believe to be beautiful or useful! But there is a great deal of dust in the air besides the kind that has to be cleaned off tables and chairs—there is a soft, floating dust so fine that we cannot see it. And if it were not for this unseen powder we should never have bright sunsets. For

Ether of space probably about 300 miles.

Atmosphere probably ends at 300 miles.

Meteor probably becomes visible at 75 miles and generally disperses at about 50 miles.

Highest balloon carrying instruments 23⅔ miles.

Highest passenger balloon, approximately 12 miles.

Stratosphere at Equator above 11 miles, at Poles above 3¾ miles.

Highest aeroplane 43,815 feet.

Highest kite 4 miles, 837 yards.

Highest clouds about 5½ miles.

Lightning 3000 to 7500 feet.

Rain clouds 1400 feet to 2½ miles.

WHAT WOULD WE DISCOVER IF WE COULD ASCEND THREE HUNDRED MILES INTO SPACE?

If we could build a column three hundred miles high and could climb to the top of it, we should probably discover some very interesting things on the way up. This column illustrates the relative heights which have already been reached by aeroplanes and balloons, and also gives one an idea of the conditions one might expect at the various stages. Above three hundred miles the atmosphere probably gives place to the ether of space.

the gorgeous colours of the sunset are made by the rays of the sun as they tint the particles floating in the air. Dust even helps rain to form, for we are going to find out a little later that every drop of rain forms on a nucleus, such as a tiny core of floating dust.

What is It That Makes the Sky Appear Blue to Us?

Even our skies would be less blue without the dust. For the tiny particles in the air, the dust and moisture and atoms of gas, are what keep us from seeing the sky as it really is—a vault of inky black with sun and stars scattered over it. That is what the sky would look like from the moon, where there is no atmosphere; but on the earth the air spreads all the rays of light that are constantly passing through it and screens off all but the blue ones. This is what gives us the azure dome of a summer's day.

Dust is always in the air, even in the high thin air above the clouds. If you let a tiny ray of sunlight into a dark room, you can see its shining path like a thin streak of grey light. What you are really seeing is the reflection of the sunlight on millions and millions of tiny particles of dust always floating in the air—little fragments of ash and unburned fuel that have risen in the form of smoke. They come from millions of chimneys and from outdoor fires.

Wherever anything burns, it must give off fine particles of dust in smoke. It is dust in the air that makes those long, slanting rays that sometimes lead, like shining paths, from the earth up to the sunset. People used to say that the sun was "drawing water." We know now that the sunbeams, piercing through a rift in the clouds, are reflected by all the tiny particles in the air, just as when they find their way into a dark room through a narrow slit in the blind.

But long before there were chimneys, long before man had a fire, there were gentle summer rains and beautiful sunsets. Where did dust come from then? It came from fuming volcanoes and from burning meteors, those pieces of metal and rock that, plunging through the sky, get caught in our atmosphere and are burned by the heat they make in rushing through it. Even now more dust may be shot into the air by volcanoes than from all the chimneys and fires in the world. For a volcano sometimes sends a cloud of dust as high as twenty miles, where it may hang for months and then be slowly wafted all the way round the world.

How Dust May Make Summer Seem More Like Winter

Sometimes the dust is so thick and is spread so widely that it changes for a time the whole climate of the lands from which it shuts off the warmth of the sun. They turn cold even in summer. In 1816, after great volcanic eruptions in other parts of the world, the temperature was so low even in the warmest months that this was known as "the year without a summer."

Of all the substances in the air, water vapour and dust affect the weather most. But before we can find out why this is so, we must make the acquaintance of those rude but jolly weather carriers—the winds.

(CONTINUED ON PAGE 695)

Strange things take place in the air, such as the formation of whirling funnels like this one.

As long as Athens chose wise and patriotic men to govern her, the city prospered, and with prosperity there came art and learning which paved the way for civilization in every country of the Western World.

The BRIGHTEST PAGE of HISTORY

In the Days of Pericles Athens Rose to a Glory Probably Higher than any Other City Has Ever Known

(CONTINUED FROM PAGE 623)

THIS is the story of the greatest days in ancient Greece. The happy end of the Persian Wars left Athens easily the foremost state in the country. The city had been destroyed, it is true; but the houses and other buildings sprang up again from the blackened ruins, and ordinary life began once more.

Themistocles (thĕ-mĭs′tŏ-klēz), who was by then the most powerful man in Athens, decided to put a wall round the rebuilt city, in order to make it more difficult for enemies to capture. The Spartans did not like this plan at all, because there was no wall round Sparta; and since Sparta had a great army she forbade Themistocles to build his wall.

Themistocles journeyed to Sparta to discuss the matter, and while he was gone the Athenians worked as hard as they could, and before long they sent word to Themistocles that the wall was finished. The Spartans were very angry, but there was

nothing they could do about it. No Spartan army could hope to conquer Athens now, nor could any other Greek state.

Besides making Athens a strongly fortified city, Themistocles had made Piraeus a harbour and fortress, which placed the city in the forefront of the trading centres of Greece. Moreover, Athens had emerged from the Persian War with the finest navy in the Mediterranean. Themistocles wanted to maintain it, for he knew it would protect Attica, but the Athenians could not agree with him. By now they were tired of being commanded as by Themistocles, so they ostracized (ŏs′trȧ-sīz) him, that is to say they banished him from society, and he fled to Persia, where he remained until his death.

The Jealous Spartans

Left to new leaders, the Athenians tried to make friends with Sparta, but that hard and sullen military city wanted no friendship with Athens. The Spartans were very jealous, and did not like to see Athens growing in riches and population and power. Athens was now the leader of a league of small cities, and she kept a treasury full of money to be used in case Persia should attack again. Sparta was also the head of a league, but she was not so rich and powerful.

The citizens of Athens were so angry at being rebuffed by Sparta that they overthrew the Athenian nobles who had been trying to keep the peace between the two cities. At the same time the citizens seized a great deal of power for themselves, and the city became a real democracy.

Anyone in Athens, except the slaves and the poorest labourers, might be elected archon (är'kŏn), or governor. The people took away the privileges of a council of elders, who were all nobles, and by drawing lots formed a council of five hundred citizens to carry on the government. They selected, also by lot, six thousand citizens to serve on juries, and these were paid, so that no one was too poor to spare the time for the work. In groups of from fifty-one to five hundred and one, these public jurors tried all cases. By 460 B.C., twenty years after the Battle of Salamis, the Greeks had learned to govern themselves democratically.

There was only one post they could not fill with an ordinary citizen chosen by lot. The head of the army—the military protector of Athens—could not be lightly chosen, for in his hands rested the defence of hearth and home. Thus, the only officers who were elected, and not chosen by lot, were the generals. There were ten of these, one from each of ten districts.

Here is the head of the great Pericles, who ruled Athens in its golden days. Although he was a dignified, stately man, he did not escape the attention of the wits of his day, who made fun of his dome-shaped head which, they said, looked like an egg! On that account he is said always to have worn a helmet, as you see him depicted above.

Before the end of the fifth century B.C., soon after the overthrow of the old nobles, a new leader arose from the noble class. This was Pericles (pĕr'ĭ-klēz), who was young, handsome, progressive, and an excellent orator. The common people of Athens soon learned to love him, for he was both wise and liberal. Every year for thirty years and more, Pericles was elected one of the leaders of Athens.

He was not a remarkable soldier, like Miltiades, or a great statesman, like Themistocles. Yet, while he was its leader, Athens became so renowned through his government, that the period of his leadership is called after him—the Age of Pericles.

What was it that made these few short years so wonderful? It was partly that Athens became the head of an empire, and the most wealthy of the Greek cities. What really made those years the most remarkable of any period of equal length in history was the development of art and literature to a state of perfection such as the world had never seen. While Pericles ruled, noble temples were built, statues carved, plays written and acted that to this day have scarcely been equalled. The Age of Pericles is the most glorious of ancient history, if not of all history. It is a Golden Age, an age in which the minds of men awoke to the greatest genius. Many a scholar has said that he would rather have lived in the Age of Pericles than at any other period since the world began.

When Pericles ruled Athens it was well protected against enemies from land or sea. Walls four miles long connected the city and its port town Piraeus, so that the

SACRED TO THE GODS OF ANCIENT GREECE

This is a reconstruction of the sacred city of Olympia, the scene of the Olympic games. In the centre is the great temple of Zeus, in which was placed Phidias's gold and ivory statue of that god which was considered one of the seven wonders of the ancient world. Here also was the Heraeum (hē-rē'ŭm), in honour of Hera, perhaps the oldest temple in the whole of Greece, since it was built not later than the seventh century B.C. It was originally built entirely of wood; and indeed the upper part must always have been of wood, for the columns which supported it were quite widely spaced and would not have been strong enough to support stone. As each wooden column decayed, it was replaced by one of stone; and because they were made at different times, each stone pier is a little different from the next, and shows the development of the Doric column. A famous traveller in Greece in the first century A.D. found one of the original oak columns still standing.

Athenians could always reach their ships and could not be starved by a land siege. The Athenian navy feared nothing afloat and was able to bring in food and supplies, no matter what wars were going on.

And above all, the treasury of Athens was overflowing with wealth. There was money enough to pay the soldiers and supply them with food over a long period of time. There was wealth enough to build new ships and to keep the old ones in repair. There were funds for all the needs of the state.

The rest of Greece was not nearly so well off as Athens, which had become rich through trade, as had the earlier cities of Egypt and Phoenicia. Athens sent her pottery jars and vases from one end of the old world to the other and received money for them; while the other states of Greece had nothing much to ship away, and besides were not so skilled in the ways of trade as were the Athenians. Athens could export furniture, tools, cloth, and much besides, while Sparta exported nothing at all.

The only other Greek city that knew how to carry on a foreign trade was Corinth (kŏr'ĭnth); and the Athenians were jealous of Corinth's trade and even hoped to destroy the city so that they could have all the commerce to themselves. Except for Corinth, no Greek city could compare in riches with glittering Athens.

Quarrels between Athens and Sparta were nothing new in Greek history, but as soon as Pericles became ruler, a serious conflict occurred between the two sister states. It is known as the First Peloponnesian (pĕl'ŏ-pŏ-nē'shăn) War, and, with intervals of peace, it lasted fifteen years. This struggle between Greek and Greek illustrates well the inability of the Greeks to join together and oppose a solid front to their enemies.

The Stupid War that Ended in a Truce of Thirty Years

Neither side won anything, though Athens obtained her wish in ruining Corinth. Again and again the Spartan army laid waste the fields of Attica, while the farmers sought safety behind the walls of Athens. But all that happened was that the crops were destroyed, and the farmers found themselves much poorer than before. Even the Greeks themselves finally saw the stupidity of the war, and at long last a thirty years' peace was signed, to give each state time to rest and regain its strength.

Athens did another foolish thing during this war with Sparta. Egypt had revolted against Persian rule, and Athens sent her entire navy, two hundred ships, to help Egypt. Every ship was lost to the Persians, and for a time Athens found herself with no navy at all.

From all this it may seem that Pericles, whatever his other gifts, was not a man to be trusted with the management of the Athenian army. Yet he held office continuously for many years. Perhaps there was no one better to put in his place. Certainly he retained the love of the common people, and that was not an easy thing to do.

Nor could even these ruinous wars make Athens poor. Her foreign trade poured riches into her treasury faster than wars could drain it out. Ships from all over the world came to the Piraeus (pī-rē'ŭs). Though many vessels were wrecked by storms or scuttled by pirates, the ships that arrived safely might bring back double the value of the goods that were lost.

Athens was no longer a little country town full of half-wild, uneducated peasants. Foreigners had settled in Attica, and if we add to these the slaves and citizens, we have a city-state that would not be very large for a modern city, but for those times was of great size. Almost all the Athenian citizens could read and write, too, which was not the case in Sparta or other Greek cities.

Foolishness Walks in the Streets which Surround the House of Wisdom

The Athenian houses were built of brick and set close round a hill called the Acropolis (ă-krŏp'ŏ-lĭs), where Athene, goddess of wisdom and special protector of Athens, was worshipped. Between the houses ran narrow alleys, unpaved and full of dirt, for everybody threw their rubbish into the streets, which were never cleaned. There were no windows in the houses, except a few on the

THE MAJESTIC SPLENDOUR OF THE PARTHENON
This is a reconstruction of the Parthenon, the most perfect Doric temple ever built. No wonder the Athenians were proud of it, for it combined a beautiful simplicity of line with great richness of detail. Its painted sculptures stood out even under the strong sun of Greece, and its marble grew honey-toned with age.

second floor. All the rooms were built round a courtyard in the centre of the house, and here people spent most of their time, since the weather in Athens was always very mild.

Housekeeping was easy in the Athenian home. The floors were merely clay and gravel pressed together, and they were never swept. There was no window glass, there were no chimneys, no fireplaces; even the wealthiest citizens lived in houses bare as barns with rooms little better than dens. But in those uncomfortable houses the Athenians placed most beautiful furniture, statues, vases, and other ornaments that would be priceless to-day.

It seems strange that people who made so many beautiful things did not make their own houses beautiful, too. But the truth is that really good homes come very late in the history of man. For man had built the most beautiful temples for his gods long before he made many places that were fit for himself to live in. Then, too, the Greeks spent a great deal of their time out of doors. Houses were used mainly for shelter from rain and for the few cold weeks of winter. Almost all the work was done in the open air. Business was carried on in the market-place. The household duties, cooking, weaving, sewing, spinning, were done in the courtyards. Even teaching was carried on under the trees or the open sky.

THE GODDESS OF WISDOM

The gold and ivory statue of Athene which stood in the centre of the great temple of the Parthenon was destroyed; but from the descriptions of ancient writers, from reproductions of it on coins, and from inferior copies of it by later sculptors, we can get some idea of what it looked like. It must have been a wonderful sight on the festival day of the goddess, for the temple was so placed that in the morning the light from the rising sun streamed through the eastern door and fell directly on the gleaming statue.

There were two kinds of schools in Athens. One was for the younger boys and the other for the older boys and young men. The boys had to learn to read and write and play the lyre, a kind of harp. They had to learn singing, too, because the Greeks loved music. But they did not study many of the subjects that we do to-day. There was a little history, but that mostly consisted of memorizing long historical poems.

The Athenian girls were even less afflicted with lessons. They did not learn anything at all except cooking and housework, and these they learned at home. The Athenians did not think it necessary for girls to know much, since they only became housewives and were not allowed to take part in government or public affairs.

In spite of the lack of schools for girls, however, some Greek women did become famous for their learning and artistic talents. Aspasia (ăs-pā'shĭ-à), a friend of Pericles, was not only beautiful but very intelligent. A little earlier than the Age of Pericles, Sappho (săf'ō) wrote undying lyric poetry; but Greek women of high education such as these were very exceptional.

The Academy and the Lyceum

The strangest schools of all were those for the older boys and the men. Outside Athens there were two athletics fields with plenty of shady trees and benches round them. One was called the Academy and the other the Lyceum (lī-sē'ŭm). Here teachers and lecturers used to give instruction to anyone who wished to learn. The most famous of these teachers were called Sophists (sŏf'ĭst), from a word meaning "wise"; and many of the Sophists were indeed very wise men. They taught mathematics and astronomy and geography and similar subjects, but chiefly they taught the art of making speeches. This was a very important thing for any Athenian to master if he wanted to hold an influential position among his fellow citizens.

Ideas that Shocked Athenians

The Sophists began to teach in this way during the Age of Pericles. The older Athenians had little respect for them, because they showed small regard for Zeus (zūs) and Hera (hē'rå) and the other gods; they did not believe the old myths. This was so shocking to religious people that the Sophists were often ostracized if they spoke out boldly. The younger men were not so much afraid of new ideas; they read the books the Sophists wrote and enjoyed the lectures, and laughed at the old-fashioned myths about the pagan gods.

How the Athenian Spent His Day

The Athenian citizen led an easy-going life. Most of the work was done by slaves, and people who had a little money had scarcely anything to do. The women stayed at home, but the men would go off to the athletics field in the morning and exercise at running, leaping, wrestling, and throwing the discus. In the hot afternoons they would idle about the market-place or in barbers' shops or taverns. At night they would go to dinner with their friends, and eat and drink to a late hour.

The only time these citizens led a hard life was when Athens was at war. Then they had to serve in the garrison or on

THE WISE AND BEAUTIFUL ASPASIA HOLDS COURT

Aspasia, the beautiful friend of Pericles, was born in one of the Greek cities of Asia Minor. She was an intelligent and gifted woman, and, unlike most of the women of her time, she was well educated. She settled down in Athens and became friends with its most learned men, who are said to have flocked to her little court to discuss philosophy, art, politics, and any subject which happened to be of interest at the moment.

board a ship, and they often endured terrible experiences.

But easy lives did not mean idle minds. The Athenian mind was awaking gloriously to knowledge and culture. A few wise men took the lead and taught the masses. They achieved marvels of knowledge. The astronomer Meton (mē'tŏn), without any telescopes or other instruments such as we have to-day, calculated the year's length to within half an hour of its actual time. Herodotus (hĕ-rŏd'ō-tŭs) wrote a world-famous history of the Persian War. Sophocles (sŏf'ō-klēz) and Euripides (ū-rĭp'ĭ-dēz) wrote famous plays about the heroic legends of the past. Hippocrates (hĭ-pŏk'rȧ-tēz), the great physician, was beginning to cure disease by medicine instead of merely trying to scare the devils out of sick people, as many a doctor before him had attempted to do.

In gratitude for the prosperity of their city, the Athenians set aside a large sum of money for building magnificent temples on the Acropolis. Ictinus (ĭk-tī'nŭs), a renowned architect, and Phidias (fĭd'ĭ-ȧs), perhaps the greatest sculptor of history, with dozens of other gifted artists, built and ornamented a temple called the Parthenon (pär'thē-nŏn), one of the glories of art of all time, at which, in its broken and ruined state, we marvel even now.

These two Greek maidens are admiring a statue of Cupid. That tiny but extremely powerful little god was a great favourite with the sculptors of Hellenistic and Roman times, in whose work he was frequently to be seen.

Many people think that the Age of Pericles in Athens was the best and noblest period of all history. It was the ideas in the minds of the Athenian citizens that made the time glorious. Except for the gentle guidance of Pericles, the citizens governed themselves. They ruled themselves and also a little empire of subject states, guarded by their fleet of ships. These same ships brought them not only wealth but new ideas from all over the old world. And their ideas were embodied in books, plays, poems, statues, pictures, and buildings such as the world had never seen, and may possibly never see again.

For though the Athenians had no printing presses, they did have books. These books were simply long strips of papyrus (pȧ-pī'rŭs), sometimes about two hundred feet long, rolled into a tube. As the reader went through the book he would roll up one end of it and unroll the other. Such book rolls were in use in many countries, and we may still see some of them in museums. In those books were written the poems of Homer and all the other great works of Greek writers. And there were also text-books on every subject—even books on cooking.

In the thirty years of Pericles's rule, Athens progressed from a vigorous, growing town to a great and flourishing city. She became supreme among the Greek states except perhaps for Sparta. Indeed, Athens completely conquered many of the smaller Greek states and ruled them as her empire, forcing them to pay tribute to her.

Nearly the Whole of Greece Unites to Teach Haughty Athens a Lesson

Although Athens and Sparta had concluded a thirty years' peace at the end of their war, it was soon broken and war renewed. This time (431 B.C.) nearly the whole of Greece joined in league against Athens; at the head were Sparta, Corinth, and Thebes (thēbz). All the Greeks felt it was time to cripple the pride of their haughty sister city. This was the Second Peloponnesian War.

Although the Athenians were rich and had many ships, they did not have enough soldiers to meet the combined armies of Greece on land. They remained behind their city walls and did what they could by sea raids. But plague began to fight on Sparta's side. In the crowded city with its dirty streets and mean houses, sickness soon broke out, and one Athenian in every three died of it.

Finding themselves in such a perilous situation, the Athenians were quick to lay the blame for all their troubles on the man whom they had elected to guide them. They accused Pericles of having brought down the anger of the gods. They declared he was a friend of the Sophists, who did not believe in the old religion, and that this was why Athens was afflicted with the plague.

Pericles Dies of the Plague, and Athens Does Another Foolish Thing

The Athenians attacked first the friends of Pericles, and then Pericles himself. They deprived him of all power. But they found no one capable of leading them, and after trying vainly to carry on the war without him they reinstated him. Pericles, however, was not to save Athens, for shortly after his return to power, he fell a victim to the plague and died (429 B.C.).

With the death of Pericles the fortunes of the Athenian state began to decline. Poor management and weak leadership made things go from bad to worse. The war with Sparta dragged to an end after ten years of weary struggle, but no sooner was peace declared than Athens made the fatal mistake of starting the Third Peloponnesian War, just because a young Athenian general named Alcibiades (ăl'sĭ-bī'à-dēz) wished to make a name for himself. He made a name indeed, but not for bravery or wisdom.

Alcibiades led a great fleet of Athenian ships against Syracuse (sĭr'à-kūs), in Sicily but just before he began the attack he was called back to Athens to be tried in court for not believing in the gods. Instead of returning to Athens, he deserted to Sparta, and for several years he fought on Sparta's side. Meanwhile the Athenian fleet which went to Sicily was completely destroyed, and all the soldiers were killed or sold into slavery.

The Mighty Power of Athens Crumbles Into Dust and is Lost for Ever

Still Athens remained mistress of the sea, and could bring in supplies from Asia to continue the war. Indeed, for a time Athens seemed to hold the upper hand, and the turncoat Alcibiades came back from Sparta and was once more chosen as their leader by the fickle Athenians. But he soon lost a battle and fell out of favour again.

The final ruin of Athens came when she lost her ships, and this happened in a truly ridiculous manner. The Peloponnesian ships were at anchor in a harbour of the Hellespont, and every day the Athenian ships would parade up and down before this harbour, trying to induce their enemies to come out and fight. At night the Athenian ships would return to their base, where the boats were left unguarded on the shore while all the sailors and soldiers were enjoying themselves.

One night the Spartan commander Lysander (lī-săn'dĕr) entered the Athenian base and sailed away with their boats. Then he blockaded the city; and that was the end of Athens. Unable to obtain food supplies, the city was starved into surrender, in 404 B.C. Under the terms of peace the walls of Athens were torn down, her ships were made over to Sparta, her colonies and other possessions were taken away, and her military glory was lost for ever.

(CONTINUED ON PAGE 687)

It is easy to tell who is the great artist seated surveying his work. No one but Michelangelo could have fashioned the giant figure of Moses you see on the left, or the slaves straining at their bonds on either side of their gifted creator. Pope Julius II, the sculptor's patron, is seen entering through the door on the right

The WONDERFUL WORK of the CARVER

With the Aid of a Sharp Knife an Expert in the Art of Carving Can Transform a Block of Shapeless Wood into a Thing of Most Delicate Beauty and Design

LEAVE a boy alone with a jack-knife and a stick of wood, and it will not be long before he has taken the first step in the art of carving. In this way, long ages ago, our primitive ancestors taught themselves to carve.

They did not have jack-knives, of course, and if they carved on sticks, the wood has rotted away and is no longer to be seen. But even in the time before men understood the use of metals, in the Old Stone Age, they knew how to carve. Some unknown artist took a sharp piece of stone and scratched a picture on the rock wall of the cave in which he lived. From this it was only a step to scratching lines and pictures on the bone of some animal killed in the chase, or on a drinking-horn made from the antler of a

reindeer or the tusk of a mammoth. Then someone tried making the figure of a woman or the head of an animal from the bone or horn, cutting it out, as we say, "in the round."

A great many of these antique carvings have been found in Europe, especially in Southern France, and they tell us much about the men of those old days. Most of them, naturally, are somewhat crude, but some of the carvers of the Old Stone Age were really artists.

Since art and science developed among different peoples at different times, we do not have to go back to the cave-men of Europe for all our primitive carvings. The Eskimos in Alaska, for instance, were decorating their snow goggles and harpoons with fine carving a thousand years and more ago, and are doing so still. They carve in ivory, using the tusks of walrus and even of mammoths buried for ages in the snow. The Alaska Indians, too, are famous for their carving in wood. Among their carvings are mammoth totem-poles. A totem-pole is a fetish (fĕt'ish), or sacred object, and is carved all over with monstrous and fantastic heads of men and beasts, each one with its separate meaning in the history and religion of the tribe.

Perhaps even more famous for their wood carving are the negro tribes of the Congo and other places in Africa, and the inhabitants of some of the islands of the South Seas. The African tribes make queer wooden images of their gods, with immense heads and tiny bodies, perhaps as they suppose their ancestors used to look long ago.

They also make huge wooden spoons with handles shaped like the head of a giraffe or a gazelle, and use them for spoon, fork, knife, cup, and plate, all in one. They carve their wooden shields and war clubs and the shafts of their spears. But the most fascinating things they carve are fantastic and hideous wooden masks to be worn by medicine-men and by the performers in religious dances. Many American Indians make such grotesque wooden masks, too.

This totem-pole from Alaska is carved with raven-demons and is painted with bright colours as startling as the carved figures themselves.

Some people think that all this primitive carving—that is, carving by simple and uncivilized people—is crude and ugly. But others like it because it is vigorous and alive, and sometimes even beautiful in its own way. Many "modernist" artists have lately been trying to copy it and to make it even more vigorous.

But before we start talking about the many different kinds of carving done by civilized peoples, we had better be certain that we know what carving is. The chief difficulty is that carving is easily confused with sculpture, for the maker of statues carves things, too. As a matter of fact, it is sometimes very difficult to say whether a thing is carving or sculpture.

But usually we can tell by asking this question: Did the artist carve this thing to be looked at for itself alone, or did he carve it as a decoration for something else? If he did the first, he has produced sculpture; if the second, carving. Thus the famous statue of Venus of Milo (mī'lō), in the Louvre (l'ōōvr), is sculpture — it is a complete work of art in itself. But the beautiful carved panelling in some fine room, or the tiny carved figure hung from a watch-chain, is carving; for the panelling decorates the room and the watch-charm decorates the chain—or, if you prefer it, the man. It is true that statues are usually larger than carvings—for mere size sometimes seems to lend dignity to a thing, and makes it look as if it were done for itself alone.

The primitive carving which we have just mentioned is carried out mostly in wood, or

These outlandish masks might well be the product of some hideous nightmare. At the top is a cow-face mask from Tibet. Anything less gentle or less cow-like it would be difficult to imagine. In the centre is a Bellacoola Indian mask from the northern Pacific coast. Below is a fringed mask from Africa. False faces like these are worn in certain primitive religious ceremonies.

in ivory or other bone. But there are many other materials suitable for the carver—leather, glass, certain stones such as quartz and jade, metals, precious and semi-precious stones. Each of these materials has to be treated differently, and much of the skill of the carver depends on his understanding of the particular material in which he is working.

If he is working in wood or leather, for example, the grain often decides what design he may use. If his material is shell or some multi-coloured stone such as agate, he must try to blend the natural colouring skilfully with his work. If he is working on precious stones, he has to know how to cut extremely tiny figures in the very hard surface—and you know how valuable these gems are and how sad it would be to put a single line in wrongly.

Yet the tools used in carving are very simple, and have not changed to any great extent through the ages. The Chinese and Japanese, who are famous carvers, use to-day the same simple tools their forefathers used. The Chinese are great carvers in ivory. It is supposed that in ancient times there were in China many elephants whose tusks furnished the Chinese with plenty of ivory for carving. Even now, when they have to obtain their ivory from abroad, they carry on the old art. They make all sorts of things — brush-holders and pendants and smoking implements and cages for birds and singing crickets. You would hardly believe what very small figures and delicate lines they can make.

Imagine, for instance, a tiny ivory model of a palace, all fitted out with little figures and trees and plants so fragile-looking that it seems as if a breath would break them.

Most fascinating of all Chinese ivories, perhaps, are the concentric (kŏn-sĕn'trĭk) spheres, or, to call them by their more amusing names, the "puzzle balls" or

Nos. 1 and 2 are sketches of a bison and a reindeer, scratched on stone by those astonishing ancestors of ours, the cave-men. Not wishing to leave his drawing incomplete, the artist who drew the reindeer continued the legs of the animal round the side of the stone.

No. 4 is the "Sheikh el Beled," a wooden statue of the fifth dynasty of the Old Kingdom. It seems remarkable that such ancient wood should be so well preserved, but you must remember that Egypt has a very dry climate. The "Sheikh el Beled" was not a royal personage, and, indeed, there is nothing very aristocratic about his plump, powerful body. But he is a very dignified, forceful figure.

No. 5 is a carved cylinder seal. When rolled over soft clay or plaster it leaves its impression. No. 6 is an impression made by a seal like the one shown at 5. It is inscribed with the name of Khashkhamer, viceroy of the city of Ish-kun-Sin, and an address to Ur-Engur, king of Ur, about 2300 B.C. The scene represents Ur-Engur as Khashkhamer being led into the presence of Sin, the moon god.

No. 3 is an Assyrian relief showing King Ashur-nasir-pal about to drink from a bowl of wine. His attendant is thoughtfully keeping the flies away with a special kind of fan.

No. 7. This is a statue in stone of Ashur-nasir-pal, king of Assyria, who is also shown at 3. He reigned from 885 to 860 B.C.

Photos by Alinari

To the left is the great column of Trajan, which stands in his forum at Rome. To the right is a part of the relief showing how the elaborately executed carvings wind themselves like a ribbon round the stone column.

"devil's work balls." In a solid piece of ivory the craftsman first makes several holes through the centre. This is known as "pierced work." He then, by means of special tools, divides the piece of ivory into several different balls, one within the other, and after carving the outside one with flowers or figures, he revolves the ball inside and carves it through the holes, and within that ball he carves another—and so on, till sometimes he has as many as ten, each moving freely inside the preceding one. No wonder these contrivances are called "devil's work"! Yet many of these wonderful balls are being made in Canton to this day.

The Chinese are famous, too, for their work in lacquer (lăk'ĕr) and in fine stones, like soapstone, rock crystal, and especially jade. Lacquer is a sort of varnish, with which they cover wooden objects, such as boxes, to a thickness of from one-fourth to one-half of an inch. Then they cut the design in the lacquer coating. Soapstone is soft and highly coloured; rock crystal is hard, nearly transparent, and veined with delicate colour; jade is a semi-precious stone in the loveliest of soft greens. From all these materials, the Chinese carve little figures and vases and other "objects of art" which are eagerly bought by people from Europe and America as well as by the Chinese themselves. The Chinese think that there is nothing in the world more precious than finely-carved jade.

The pagodas of China were built to fit in with the surrounding landscape. Some people believe that their jutting roofs, placed one above the other, may have been inspired by the spreading branches of a tree. The "Porcelain Pagoda" below, which was exquisite with carving, stood at Nanking, and was known as the "Reward of Kindness." It was built by a fifteenth century emperor in honour of his mother. The walls were covered with white porcelain, and all the overhanging eaves were covered with green porcelain tiles. A golden ball decorated the very top, and from every angle of the eaves hung little bells that tinkled with a fairy-like music in the breeze. This most famous of all pagodas was destroyed in the middle of the nineteenth century.

Both the Chinese and the Japanese do wood carving, too. The Chinese like to carve elaborate patterns all over the beams of a ceiling or the pillars and doors of a house. The designs are often full of meaning—the lotus, for instance, is one of the eight symbols of Buddha (boōd'á), the great religious teacher; and the peach, in their religion, stands for the tree of life. The Japanese like to keep their houses very simple, and so do not have decorated ceilings, or other heavy carvings. But they do sometimes use beautiful pierced-work carving in the oblong ventilating panels set over the screens between their rooms. These have the same graceful designs of birds and flowers that you see in Japanese prints. The Japanese make wooden masks, too, to be used in solemn plays.

But they are better known for little things, made of ivory and similar materials. When you read, in our story of tea, about the custom of tea drinking in Japan, it will interest you to know that the cover of the ceremonial teapot is nearly always made out of carved ivory.

Photos by Alinari and Anderson

Ever since the days of ancient Egypt it has been the custom of architects to decorate their buildings—temples, churches and palaces—with beautiful carvings. Here are some of them, from famous buildings of all ages. No. 1 is a Byzantine capital from the basilica of San Vitale in Ravenna; No. 2, egg and dart border from the Erectheum, Athens; No. 3, capital from the church of San Giovanni, Ravello; No. 4, Ionic capital; No. 5, column in St. Peter's, Rome, once thought to have come from Solomon's Temple; Nos. 6 and 8, fifth century French columns; No. 7, Corinthian capital; No. 9, Egyptian palm-leaf capital and shaft; No. 10, Roman architectural frieze; No. 11, thirteenth century capital; No. 12, section of the entablature and capital from the temple of Castor in Rome; No. 13, twelfth century capital from the basilica of the church of Saint Mark in Venice.

In the past, the best Japanese carving was to be found in the fittings for swords; for every Japanese nobleman used to wear a fine sword, of which he was very proud. The handle and the guard of the sword were both finely carved. The work might be executed in wood, ivory, bone, mother-of-pearl, shark-skin, horn or metal, or in several of these materials combined. Most exquisite of all was the metal work, for the Japanese used to know how to colour many metals very brilliantly, although it is a lost art now. These many-coloured metals were carved into landscapes, scenes of everyday life, animals, flowers and many other designs.

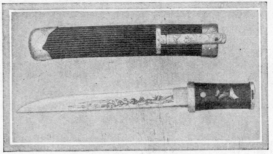

This short sword, with its delicately carved blade and sheath, is the product of Japanese workmanship.

No one but a nobleman was allowed to wear a sword, but that did not prevent the rest of the people, when they could afford it, from possessing fine carving. They decorated especially their smoking outfits. The crowning glory of the outfit was the "netsuke" (nĕt'sŏo-kā). This was a little figure or decorated knob from which the tobacco-box, pipe and pipe fittings, and pipe-case were all suspended by heavy silken cords drawn through the broad sash worn about the man's waist. The netsuke has gone out of fashion now, but many very clever and beautiful ones are still to be seen.

But it is time we were starting home from the Far

Charming carved lacquer boxes like these are to be found in shops all over the world, but they all come from Japan. Elsewhere in this work you may read with what infinite pains the lacquer is made.

East, to see what our own ancestors knew about carving. We may stop on the way for a hurried visit to one of the ancient rock temples of India; there we may see carved shrines and many strange, carved gods, which tell us that long ago the people of India understood carving. We may pause for another flying visit in Persia, where marvellous work has been done in inlaying wood with ivory—for that, too, is a form of carving. Here in the Near East, in Mesopotamia (Iraq), were some of the oldest of the civilizations that have influenced our own. And there men have known how to carve gems—precious and semi-precious stones—since somewhere around the year 400 B.C.

The Egyptians learned this art early, too, and it was they who began the practice of shaping their gems like beetles—scarabs (skăr'ăb) such gems are called. But the Egyptians are better remembered for their work in wood and stone. They were the first people to decorate their furniture with carving; about that you may read in our story of furniture, where you will also find a great deal of information concerning the carved furniture of other peoples. The Egyptians made great images of their kings in wood, and hewed monstrous beasts, like the sphinxes (sfĭngks), out of stone. They carved

From China and Japan come more entrancing carvings than one could count. The few shown on this page can give only a slight idea of their delicacy.

Fig. 2—A Chinese artist made this lovely vase out of a block of soft green jade. The creatures that are clinging to its sides are dragons.

Fig. 1—This delicate design, which represents a harnessed elephant, is carved in lacquer.

Fig. 3—From Japan comes this spirited horse carved upon a surface of gleaming lacquer.

Fig. 4—These odd little ivory figures, so complete in every detail, were carved in Japan.

Fig. 5—Flowers of jade. They seem almost to be growing in their charming enamel pots; and although they are made of stone, we can imagine we smell their perfume.

Fig. 6—This active little fellow comes from Japan, where he was carved from a piece of ivory.

Fig. 7—An ivory screen like this is expressive of the fondness of the Chinese for simple outlines and low relief.

Fig. 8—This is the Chinese war god who, carved of ivory, sits impassively upon his ivory throne. Below him is the tortoise, symbol of the north.

Fig. 9—To the Chinese artist who carved this ivory screen, a few clusters of grapes were as objects of the rarest beauty.

numerous pictures and inscriptions on their tombs and temples in what we call relief —that is, with the figures cut only partly away from the background.

The Minoans (mǐ-nō'ăn), who lived in Crete and colonized the shores of the Aegean Sea centuries before the beginning of Greek history, made many beautiful things in ivory, and delighted in the carving of gems. And the Greeks themselves, in the period of their great glory, were fine artists at carving, as at all other arts. No one has ever produced finer sculpture than they, and perhaps we might claim some of the great statues for carving, since they were sometimes made of wood covered with gold and carved ivory. The famous statue of Athena in the Parthenon

This Egyptian wood-carving represents Hathor, the cow-goddess. She is always easy to recognize; for even if she is not shown in the form of a cow, there is always something to identify her. Either she has cow's horns sprouting from her head, or else she has cow's ears, as she is shown in the picture.

(pär'thĕ-nŏn), a temple at Athens, was made in the fifth century B.C., and was accounted one of the seven wonders of the world. The figure was of wood, but the hair, the features, and the gorgeous garments were made of carved plates of ivory and gold.

But if you say that this sort of thing is really sculpture, we will turn to the marvels of Greek gems. No one before or since has done more exquisite carving in precious and semi-precious stones. Most of the gems were cut in intaglio (ĭn-täl'yō); that is, the design is cut into the stone instead of being made to stand out from it in relief. Such a gem could then be used as a seal; when it was pressed on soft wax, the wax received the imprint of the design, which

Photo by India State Rly.

About 350 miles south of Calcutta stands Puri, where, according to Hindu mythology, lies the hub of the universe. Above is its temple of Jagannath, the "Lord of the Universe," which was built in the twelfth century. Here a high tower, gleaming like an opal, rises above a number of shrines decorated with elaborate carvings.

Here are some exquisite specimens of ivory and gem carving. They belong to various periods ranging from the beginning of the Middle Ages to about two hundred years ago. No. 1 is a fifth century ivory jar from Syria, carved with figures of the Apostles; No. 2, a fifteenth century Italian reliquary shrine, with delicate Gothic carvings; No. 3, an ivory handle of the fourteenth century, made in France; No. 4, "Descent from the Cross," an Austrian ivory carving of the seventeenth century; No. 5, a French cameo of the eighteenth century, set in gold as a pendant; No. 6, a tenth century Byzantine ivory plaque; Nos. 7 and 9, carved gems of Greek workmanship; No. 8, an ivory box made in France in the fourteenth century and carved with scenes from a romance.

stood up on it in relief. When you look at any of these gems now in a museum, you will notice that they are frequently set in cases between you and the light, so that the delicate and lovely little pictures may be more easily seen.

The gems will be round or beetle-shaped, and the pictures will either be of gods and goddesses, or, more frequently, of the quiet doings of every day, such as a scene of women spinning. The Greeks wore these lovely jewels— amethysts, emeralds, agates, rubies, sapphires, beryls, garnets, sardonyx, topaz, lapis lazuli (lăp′ĭs lă z′ū-lī)— hung about their necks, sometimes as charms against serpents or scorpions or the "evil eye," or in signet rings. Athletes wore engraved gems as talismans to bring them victory in the games, and love-smitten youths wore them to win or keep their sweethearts' affection.

Gem carving travelled to Rome from Greece, along with the other arts. In the days during which Rome was passing from a republic to an empire, the collecting of gems was a very fashionable pursuit indeed. Julius Caesar gave six great collections to a temple in Rome, just as to-day wealthy men present books and paintings to libraries and museums. It is said that Mark Antony on one occasion exiled a certain senator because he would not give up an engraved gem on which Antony had set his heart.

Some of these Roman gems were very large and elaborate. The Romans admired large brooches decorated with portrait heads. They liked battle scenes and stories carved on slabs of semi-precious stone several inches across and fitted together to form jewel caskets or trinket-boxes. They made shallow drinking-cups adorned inside and out with similar scenes.

By this time the gem carvers had discovered how to make cameos. A cameo (kăm′ē-ō) is a gem carved in relief out of some hard substance —a shell or a semi-precious stone— which has layers of different colours.

Some of the most beautiful carvings in the world belonged to the France of the Middle Ages and the Renaissance. To the left is a fifteenth century French choir stall. Below is the figure of a saint from the cathedral at Chartres.

The clever carver will make use of the colours in his design. For instance, a stone with layers of white and golden brown will be cut so that there is a white figure standing out against a background of brown. Sometimes the carver is very skilled at making use of every colour in his material. One sixteenth century Frenchman, for example, carved a crucifixion scene in such a way as to make the flecks of red jasper in the greenish quartz he was working look like drops of blood from the Saviour's wounds.

But since the time of the Romans there has been comparatively little carving in gems.

Although some of the carvings illustrated here are of great antiquity, they cannot be numbered among the earliest examples of the art, since the history of carving dates back as far as the Palaeolithic period, or earlier Stone Age. Nos. 1 and 3 are Egyptian birds of many-coloured inlays, made about 500 B.C. to decorate a wooden shrine; No. 2, a tube carved in the shape of a palm column—it once held the kohl, or black paint, with which the Egyptians used to "make up" their eyes; No. 4, a seventeenth century ivory cup carved with little cupids; No. 5, a German twelfth century horn; No. 6, a Saxon eighteenth century hunting sword; No. 7, a Byzantine ninth century casket; No. 8, an Egyptian statuette of wood made about 1500 B.C.; No. 9, a Syrian tenth century writing-case carved in ivory; No. 10, an eighteenth century Turkish chest carved in wood and inlaid with mother-of-pearl; No. 11, a Byzantine tenth century carving in ivory of the Madonna and Child.

In the early Middle Ages, especially from the fifth to the eighth centuries, the best carving was done in ivory. Most of it was for use in the churches—covers for Mass books, altar furnishings, candlesticks, and ornamental screens to be set on the back of the altar. Scenes from the Bible and the lives of the saints were delicately carved in relief. Later in the Middle Ages there was more ivory in the homes of the people—mirrors and combs, writing tables, and wall-tablets, decorated perhaps with scenes from the romances.

In these later centuries, from the twelfth to the fifteenth, the wood-carvers were in their glory. In all the cathedrals and old churches of Europe you may see to this day the marvels that they wrought.

Marvellous Designs as Delicate as Lace-Work Carved Out of Solid Wood

There are pews and screens and altars, pulpits with great carved hoods over them, ceremonial chairs for visiting bishops, elaborate "stalls" for the choir—all carved with endless loving labour into exquisite designs of pierced work and relief, with here and there a figure in the round. Often the design is as delicate as lace-work.

As time passed, a good deal of wood carving was done for other buildings besides the churches. In fine houses, ceiling beams and staircases and the wall panelling of rooms came to be covered with carving. In the fifteenth and sixteenth centuries, when the Middle Ages had faded into the intellectual awakening that we call the Renaissance (rĕ-nā'sȧns), or "rebirth," the Italians took the lead, as the French had done during the later Middle Ages. They liked to work in rare and precious woods, instead of in the oak used in more northern lands. Great artists, like Michelangelo (mī'kĕl-ăn'jĕ-lō) and Raphael (răf'ȧ-ĕl), designed for them. Since the seventeenth century, wood carving has been largely for furniture, and you may read about it in our story of furniture. But doors and panels, cornices and mouldings, are not really furniture, and they gave the wood carvers much to do in fine houses for a long time. In France, in the eighteenth century, there was a fashion for bronze and gilt decorations on furniture

and in things like chandeliers, andirons, and balusters; and these were carved by a special process called "ciselure" (sēz'lür).

The most famous of all wood carvers—for we do not know the names of the medieval artists—was the Englishman Grinling Gibbons. He worked with his friend Sir Christopher Wren, the celebrated architect, who was building St. Paul's Cathedral and many other fine churches in London. Gibbons liked to carve immense bunches of fruits and flowers in very high relief—that is, with the wood so cut away from around and behind them that they sometimes look as though they were done in the round. In many places in England to-day, you may see splendid panels and ceilings and balustrades of his, the finest work of all being the choir loft at St. Paul's. Since the day of Gibbons there have been at least two famous wood carvers in England—George Hepplewhite and Thomas Sheraton (shĕr'ȧ-tŏn)—both of them furniture makers.

Why the Art of Carving in Wood and Other Materials Seems to be Dying Out

There are other kinds of carving which we have not yet mentioned. From the days of the Romans onwards, for instance, carvers have now and again liked to work in wax. Lifelike portraits can be carved in high relief in coloured wax on a base of wood. The Moors and other people have carved in leather, and have used their work to cover chests and chairs and other pieces of furniture, or have hung it as panels on walls or doors. With grindstones and diamond drills, craftsmen can carve in glass. The famous Portland Vase in the British Museum is a fine example of Roman work of this kind.

Our furniture and buildings are usually much simpler in design in these days than used to be the fashion, and that is one reason why there is not so much carving done now. But the chief reason is that we have machinery, which has made carving, like most kinds of hand-work, seem unnecessary and expensive. Yet hand carving is still done. And we must never forget that before you can make an article with a machine you must have a model, and that the model will almost certainly be made by hand.

These paintings of children are among the most famous in the world. From left to right they are "The Age of Innocence," by Sir Joshua Reynolds; "Boy with Rabbit," by Sir Henry Raeburn; "The Blue Boy," by Thomas Gainsborough; and "The Red Boy," by Sir Thomas Lawrence. "The Blue Boy" and a painting by Reynolds—"Mrs. Siddons as the Tragic Muse"—were sold in 1921 for £200,000.

ACROSS AUSTRALIA'S TRACKLESS WASTES

Few Men Have Displayed Greater Tenacity and Determination in the Interests of Discovery than that Intrepid Explorer Edward John Eyre

WHEN he found it absolutely impossible to continue with the attempt upon which he had set out, he did not retrace his steps, but, sending back the companions whom he refused to lead into unknown dangers, journeyed on by himself in a different direction, thereby earning the distinction of linking up the south and west of a practically unexplored continent.

The man to achieve this was Edward John Eyre, who was born on August 5, 1815, at Hornsea, near Hull. It was at first his intention to join the army, but, disappointed at his inability to obtain his commission, he set out for Australia in 1833, where he went in for cattle breeding on the Lower Murray River.

Here the idea of exploration took hold of his mind. In the course of his work he had often to lead his cattle across many miles of practically unknown and barren country, and this made him wish for longer and more daring journeys. In 1839 he discovered the great Lake Torrens, and soon after, when it was proposed to organize an expedition to explore the interior of Northern Australia, he was appointed its leader and himself bore a large part of the expense, so great was his desire to explore.

Eyre, who was then not twenty-five, left Adelaide on June 20, 1840, accompanied by Edward Scott, four other white men, two native boys, and with a large number of horses and sheep. All the party were young and high spirited, but their courage was to stand a very severe test, in the form of one of the worst evils man the explorer has to

Edward John Eyre, the Englishman who, though enduring great suffering and privation, crossed a thousand miles of desert to trace a route across Australia.

endure—shortage of water. The interior of the continent appeared, as they progressed, to consist of limitless and arid desert, and very little water indeed could be obtained there. On and on plodded the explorers, suffering more and more from a terrible thirst. They encountered scarcely any human beings, and the few natives they did come across fled at once, scared of the white men.

One day, at the point of collapse from thirst, the party managed to get into touch with some natives, and were able to make them understand that they wanted water. The natives offered to guide them to where it could be found, and, seeing at last a respite from their sufferings, the explorers followed them eagerly. One can well imagine their dismay when the natives led them to the sea. These savages probably thought that any white men wandering in that desolate region must have come by sea and wished to be guided back to the coast.

They were fortunate enough to find a spring, but this incident greatly impressed Eyre, who realized the absolute impossibility of their penetrating farther into the interior. It was at this point that the essential courage of the man became apparent. Seeing that he must perforce abandon his original intention, he decided to attempt to find an overland route between Southern and Western Australia. He refused, however, to subject his companions to the same dangers; regretfully, but firmly, he sent the white men back to Adelaide, keeping with him only his overseer, Baxter—whose loyalty would not allow him to return in spite of the perils Eyre pointed out to him—the two natives they had brought with them, and a young native named Wylie, who had joined them on the march.

Remarkable Determination and Courage of Young Edward Eyre

That Eyre knew perfectly well what lay before him is amply expressed in his own words. "The journey before us would of necessity be a long and harassing one—one of unceasing toil, privation and anxiety," but he was determined "never to return unsuccessful, but either to accomplish the object in view or perish in the attempt." Such was the amazing daring of a young man of twenty-five.

A year later, in July, 1841, when all hope had been abandoned, and Eyre was reckoned among the other brave men who had given their lives in the cause of exploration, there staggered into Albany two men —Eyre and Wylie. These two had traversed the unknown desert lands around the Great Australian Bight and had at last reached the west coast of Australia.

The story of the enterprise is a memorable one. Their misfortunes as well as the terrible thirst which assailed them included the murder of Baxter by two of the natives, who decamped with a large amount of the food, returning once by stealth to try and persuade Wylie to go with

When it seemed as though only death awaited him and his leader, the young native Wylie refused to think of his own safety. He survived to share the honours due to loyalty and courage.

them. But the boy refused, thereby remaining with Eyre to share the horrors of exhaustion by hunger and thirst, but also his hard-won success.

The sufferings of the two explorers were now rapidly intensified. They began to feel bitterly the theft of their food supply, while their burning thirst was only partially relieved by the juice squeezed from the roots of a gum-tree, or by dew laboriously collected with a sponge.

Once only had they received help—from the captain of a French whaler—but how these two managed to endure such hardship and privation on what must have seemed an endless journey to King George's Sound is a mystery of human achievement. Eyre not only accomplished his object, but showed what courage and endurance could do.

On Eyre's return to England in 1845, his "Expeditions into Central Australia" was published, and met with well-merited success. Its author afterwards held a succession of administrative posts in the colonies, being appointed lieutenant-governor of New Zealand, and, in turn, governor of St. Vincent, Antigua (än-tĕ′gwä) and Jamaica. From the last-named place he was recalled to England in 1865 to answer certain charges of cruelty in dealing with a native rebellion, and, though acquitted, was not restored to his governorship. He was awarded a pension by the government. He died on the last day of November, 1901.

The TRAGIC STORY of BURKE and WILLS

Without Knowledge of the Bush and Its Dangers and Lacking Experience of Exploration, These Two Brave Men Crossed the Southern Continent but Gave Their Lives in the Great Achievement

THE name of Robert O'Hara Burke is one of the most tragic in the annals of exploration, and he will always be remembered as a sacrifice to Australia. Misfortune dogged him everywhere, but before he met his sad fate he had fulfilled his mission, and had crossed the continent from south to north, a feat which no man had accomplished before him.

Burke, as his name implies, was an Irishman. Born in 1820 in County Galway, he early developed a love of adventure, and entered Woolwich Academy as a cadet, passing thence to Belgium, where he continued his studies. For a while he served with success in the Austrian army, but returned in 1848 to Ireland, where he joined the Irish Constabulary. In 1853 Burke, to whose adventurous spirit the hazards of life in the little-known antipodes made a strong appeal, decided to leave Ireland and emigrate to Tasmania. Later, however, he crossed to the mainland of Australia and became a police inspector at Melbourne.

Shortly afterwards he was appointed a magistrate, but on the outbreak of the Crimean War, he returned home in order to join up, only to arrive too late for active service. Back again in Australia, he was appointed to lead an exploring expedition across the continent from south to north. The fact that Burke, inexperienced as he was, should be chosen for such a position of responsibility, showed well the confidence that was placed in him, and he justified it not only by

William John Wills, the distinguished scientist, who gave his life heroically after he and his companions had successfully made their way across the great Southern Continent.

studying hard to fit himself for the work, but even by eventually giving his life in the effort.

Full of hope and confidence, Burke left Melbourne on August 20, 1860, accompanied by ten Europeans, a sepoy and two natives. But almost at the outset he encountered difficulties when internal dissension became apparent, and Burke's second in command rebelled from his authority and, together with another member—a German doctor—resigned from the expedition. His place, however, was filled by one who was to prove himself the most loyal and devoted of colleagues —William John Wills, the scientific observer of the party, and a man already eminent in his work.

After a while, however, Burke found himself obliged to send back a detachment of his party to bring up additional camels and supplies. He himself, with the remaining members, reached Cooper's Creek, in Queensland, on November 11, and there established a base camp. Impatient of waiting for the rest of the expedition, which, it afterwards transpired, did not start until late in the following January, Burke resolved to proceed, and accordingly he himself, accompanied by Wills and two others—King and Gray—with six camels and a horse, advanced towards the north, leaving an assistant named Brahe (brä'hě), together with the remainder of the men, in charge of the bulk of the supplies at Cooper's Creek, where they were to await the return of Burke and the advance party.

At first the four explorers passed through green country with abundance of bird life, where there was sufficient water for their needs. But before long all this was changed. Rain began to fall heavily, and the condition of the ground made the journey difficult for the camels, who had constantly to be rescued from morasses.

Seeing that the constant delays were becoming dangerous, Burke decided to push on ahead with Wills, and on February 9, 1861, the two at last reached the coast near the mouth of the Flinders River. Having successfully accomplished their object, Burke and Wills joined forces with their two comrades and commenced the return journey.

It was obvious at this point that they must reach Cooper's Creek and their depôt there as soon as possible, as their provisions were running short and delay meant the danger of

With Wills sinking fast, Burke and King decided to leave camp in a final effort to obtain help. Here you see the three gallant explorers as they bade each other what proved to be a last farewell.

starvation. But henceforth tragedy attended them everywhere. The incessant rain rendered their progress increasingly slow and extremely difficult; the continual rescuing of the camels from morasses taxed their strength more and more in their starved condition; and on April 16 Gray died, exhausted and worn out. Delaying a day to bury him, the others struggled on. But when at length

the three staggered up to Cooper's Creek on April 21, they found the depôt deserted and none to give them the much needed succour.

A message cut on a tree directing them to a few provisions left there revealed the fact that the others had been gone only a few hours, but Burke realized that, exhausted as they were, they could never hope to overtake them. The best they could attempt was to make for Mount Hopeless, the nearest haunt of civilization.

Burke and King Set Out to Find Help for the Dying Wills

But their agonies were merely prolonged. One of their two remaining camels was lost in a morass, and finally despairing of progressing further, they camped near a creek; here Burke buried his diaries and journals, hoping they would be found at some period. For a few days they were kept alive by food given them by some friendly tribesmen, but these suddenly left them. Rapidly growing weaker from starvation, the three explorers subsisted for a time on a kind of native grain discovered by King. On June 29, Burke and King, knowing Wills to be dying, set out in search of native help for him.

In the meantime, Brahe, on reaching Melbourne, had explained how he had waited on, suffering from illness and attacks by the natives until at last, deciding that Burke and his companions were dead or had returned by another route, he had left Cooper's Creek. On September 15 a relief expedition came upon King, very emaciated and weak, in the care of natives. Both Burke and Wills, however, had died at the end of June.

So tragically perished three gallant men, who had cheerfully and faithfully sacrificed their lives in the great cause of exploration and discovery.

A MIDSUMMER NIGHT'S DREAM

How Oberon, the King of the Fairies, Entrusted the Mischievous Puck to Administer a Love Potion, and the Strange Consequences that Follow His Mistake in Carrying Out the Mission

THE scenes in "A Midsummer Night's Dream" are laid in or near Athens; and many of the characters have Greek-sounding names. But the flowers and birds in the woodlands of which Shakespeare speaks, remind one more of the English countryside than they do of Greece. And the names of some of the more amusing characters are far more English than Greek.

But when you come to think of it, this is just as it should be; for it is supposed to be a dream play; and very often, when we are dreaming, places and people get all mixed up. It is one of the most delightful fairy plays ever written. So, as we are going to tell the story of the play, we may as well begin in the usual way.

Once upon a time there lived in Athens an important man named Egeus, who wished his daughter Hermia to marry a young nobleman called Demetrius. But she would not do as her father wished, because she was in love with another young man called Lysander. When Hermia's father spoke to her about it she told him that not only did she not love Demetrius, but that Demetrius himself had at one time been in love with her friend Helena, and Helena certainly loved him. Hermia's father insisted, however;

Photo by Rischgitz

Puck, the mischievous little sprite who delighted in teasing mortals, was Oberon's favourite messenger. In this picture you see him in the fairy wood, presiding over the magic revels being held by moonlight.

and, according to the law, Athenian fathers could order their daughters to marry anyone their fathers chose for them.

Egeus went to Theseus, the duke of Athens, who was also the chief magistrate, and asked him to compel Hermia to marry Demetrius. The duke ordered Hermia to do as her father told her, or be punished according to the dictates of the law.

"How is that?" she asks. And he tells her:

"Either to die the death, or to abjure
For ever the society of men."

Which meant that she was to be put to death, or imprisoned for her whole life.

He was very sorry to have to say this to her, especially as he himself was going to be married and the people were preparing for the festivities.

Poor Hermia, who was in great distress, hurried off to Lysander and told him all that had happened. Lysander also was terribly distressed and did not know what to do. Suddenly an idea struck him. He had an aunt living some distance away from Athens, where the laws were different, and if he could get Hermia to his aunt's house, she would be safe. So he told her to steal away from her father's house that night, and meet him in a wood not far from the town, when he would take her to his aunt's house and marry her at once.

Unfortunately she confided all this to her friend Helena, who went and told it to Demetrius. He, being at this time in love with Hermia, of course determined to try and prevent her from escaping.

Now, in the wood, the fairies, with Oberon their king and Titania their queen, were holding high revels.

The king and queen had had a dispute about a little boy, and in consequence had kept apart from each other. On that very night they happened to meet and again began quarrelling:

OBERON:
Why should Titania cross her Oberon?
I do but beg a little changeling boy,
To be my henchman.

TITANIA:
Set your heart at rest;
The fairy land buys not the child of me.
His mother was a votaress of my order:

And, in the spiced Indian air, by night,
Full often hath she gossip'd by my side,
And sat with me on Neptune's yellow sands,
Marking the embarked traders on the flood;
And for her sake I do rear up her boy,
And for her sake I will not part with him.

OBERON:
How long within this wood intend you stay?

TITANIA:
Perchance, till after Theseus' wedding-day.
If you will patiently dance in our round,
And see our moonlight revels, go with us;
If not, shun me, and I will spare your haunts.

OBERON:
Give me that boy, and I will go with thee.

TITANIA:
Not for thy fairy kingdom.—Fairies, away!
We shall chide downright, if I longer stay.
(*Exit Titania with her train.*)

OBERON:
Well, go thy way: thou shalt not from this grove
Till I torment thee for this injury.

Photo by Rischgitz

From the painting by Sir Edwin Landseer

TITANIA, UNDER THE MAGIC SPELL, MAKES LOVE TO BOTTOM

Poor Titania! Oberon has dropped some of the magic juice on her eyelids while she lay asleep, and now on awakening she falls in love with the clown Bottom, who is foolishly adorned with the head of an ass.

Photo by Rischgitz   From the painting by Noel Paton

TITANIA AND OBERON WATCH THE AWAKENING OF THE MORTALS

The dream of a Midsummer Night ends happily. Oberon takes pity on his Titania and releases her from the spell; the lovers and friends likewise are reconciled; and a double wedding takes place. Here you see the fairy king and queen awaiting the awakening of the mortals who are so shortly to see the end of their troubles.

They parted, and Oberon sent for his favourite messenger, a knavish sprite called Puck, who loved doing all sorts of mischievous tricks. Oberon told Puck to fetch him a little western flower that maidens called love-in-idleness, but which we know as the pansy or heartsease.

And he told him:

> The juice of it on sleeping eyelids laid
> Will make a man or woman madly dote
> Upon the next live creature that it sees.
> Fetch me this herb; and be thou here again,
> Ere the leviathan can swim a league.

PUCK:
> I'll put a girdle round about the earth
> In forty minutes.

While Oberon was waiting for Puck to come back he saw Demetrius and Helena coming through the wood, and heard Demetrius speaking angrily to Helena for following him.

Then Puck returned with the flower.

OBERON:
> I pray thee, give it me.
> I know a bank whereon the wild thyme blows,
> Where ox-lips and the nodding violet grows
> Quite over-canopied with luscious woodbine,
> With sweet musk-roses and with eglantine:
> There sleeps Titania some time of the night,
> Lull'd in these flowers with dances and delight;
> And there the snake throws her enamell'd skin,
> Weed wide enough to wrap a fairy in:
> And with the juice of this I'll streak her eyes,
> And make her full of hateful fantasies.
> Take thou some of it, and seek through this
>   grove:
> A sweet Athenian lady is in love
> With a disdainful youth: anoint his eyes;
> But do it when the next thing he espies
> May be the lady. Thou shalt know the man
> By the Athenian garments he hath on.
> Effect it with some care, that he may prove
> More fond on her, than she upon her love:
> And look thou meet me ere the first cock crow.

PUCK:
> Fear not, my Lord, your servant shall do so.

By this time the fairies had sung Titania to sleep.

Oberon, carrying out his threat to torment her, came and dropped some of the love juice into her eyes saying:

> What thou seest when thou dost wake,
> Do it for thy true-love take.

This means, of course, that she would fall in love with the first creature she saw on awakening.

Hermia had in the meantime escaped from home and had met Lysander, who was waiting to take her to his aunt's house. But, as she was very tired, he persuaded her to rest until morning; and they both fell asleep in the wood. Here Puck found them and thought they were the pair that Oberon told him had been quarrelling. Feeling sure that when they awoke the first thing they would see would be one another, he poured some of the juice into Lysander's eyes. But, unfortunately, Helena came that way, and the first object Lysander saw was Helena. Owing to the purple juice, he at once fell in love with her, and ran after her, forgetting all about Hermia; but Helena, knowing that Lysander was Hermia's lover, was very angry.

The Weaver with an Ass's Head

Now, while all this is going on, a weaver, named Bottom, and his fellow workmen come to rehearse a play in honour of the duke's wedding near to the place where the fairy queen is sleeping; and mischievous Puck comes upon them. Bottom, having spoken his part in the play, goes off into the wood, and Puck, as a prank, changes the weaver's head into that of an ass. Titania is still asleep; but, by chance, Bottom with his ass's head walks by singing:

> The Ousel-cock, so black of hue,
> With orange-tawny bill,
> The throstle with his note so true,
> The wren with little quill.

This awakes Titania, and as Bottom is the first person she sees, and thinking him both handsome and clever, she immediately falls in love with him.

Bottom continues singing to show that he is not afraid; and this is what he sings:

> The finch, the sparrow, and the lark,
> The plain-song cuckoo gray,
> Whose note full many a man doth mark
> And dares not answer nay.

TITANIA:
> Thou art wise as thou art beautiful.

She orders her attendants, Pease-blossom, Cobweb, Moth and Mustard-seed to wait on him.

TITANIA:
> Be kind and courteous to this gentleman:
> Hop in his walks, and gambol in his eyes;
> Feed him with apricocks, and dewberries,
> With purple grapes, green figs, and mulberries.

After a while Titania tells the fairies to lead him to her bower, and there she falls asleep by his side.

Oberon, wondering if his queen is awake, espies Puck coming back.

PUCK:
> My mistress with a monster is in love.

(The monster being, of course, Bottom, with his ass's head, that Puck had magically given him.)

Then Oberon asks him:

> But hast thou yet latched the Athenian's eyes,
> With love juice, as I bid thee do?

PUCK:
> I took him sleeping—that is finished, too.

By this he means that he has poured the love juice into Lysander's eyes.

Then Demetrius, having awakened, comes following Hermia, who has also awakened and found that Lysander has disappeared. She asks Demetrius what has become of him; but he refuses to say. So she leaves him.

Demetrius then lies down again and goes to sleep.

Oberon tells Puck he has made a mistake, that Hermia was not the woman who had been quarrelling with Demetrius, so he must go and find Helena and bring her to Demetrius; he must also put the love juice into Lysander's eyes, and be sure that he sees Hermia when he awakes.

This difficult task Puck carries out by cleverly mimicking the various voices of the four lovers and so leading them through the wood which has by now become misty. They fall asleep, near one another, and later on when they awake Lysander falls in love again with Hermia, and Demetrius with Helena.

Oberon now goes and finds Titania lying beside the ass-headed weaver. Then Oberon says to Puck:

> . . . gentle Puck take this transformed scalp
> From off the head of this Athenian swain.

He then touches Titania's eyes with a herb saying:

> Now, my Titania; wake you, my sweet queen.

TITANIA:

> My Oberon! what visions have I seen!
> Methought I was enamour'd of an ass.

He taunts her for some while, and demands again the changeling child, and Titania, ashamed at being discovered by the king, consents to hand over the boy.

Oberon and Titania now being good friends again, Oberon tells his queen all about the mistake Puck had made with the lovers, so they go to see what has happened to them.

Demetrius Again Loves Helena

Now, at the dawn of day, Egeus, Hermia's father, comes with Theseus and Hippolyta to find his daughter. He threatens Lysander and Hermia with punishment for their behaviour; but to his surprise Demetrius says, he knows not how or why, but he has once more fallen in love with Helena. Of course, Oberon and Puck could have told him.

Theseus then tells the lovers that as all has turned out so well he will over-rule Egeus. They shall be married and there shall be great festivities for the three brides and grooms: Theseus and his bride, Lysander and Hermia, and Demetrius and Helena.

At these festivities Bottom, the weaver, and his friends give the performance of their play about Pyramus and Thisbe; and a very amusing play it is.

The revels, which are to last for a fortnight, continue far into the night. But the fairies keep up their own revels until the break of day.

Puck finishes the play by saying:

> If we shadows have offended,
> Think but this, and all is mended,
> That you have but slumber'd here,
> While these visions did appear.
> And this weak and idle theme,
> No more yielding but a dream,
> Gentles, do not reprehend:
> If you pardon, we will mend.
> And, as I'm an honest Puck,
> If we have unearned luck
> Now to 'scape the serpent's tongue,
> We will make amends ere long;
> Else the Puck a liar call:
> So, good night unto you all.
> Give me your hands, if we be friends,
> And Robin shall restore amends.

You can make yourself quite a nice little circus consisting of these animals cut out of thin wood and painted in bright colours. You have already learnt how to draw to scale (pages 26 to 31) so it will be quite simple for you to enlarge these figures and mount them on wheels for exhibition purposes—and it will not be hard to build cages for your menagerie, once you have it ready for the big parade. A tent can be made from any discarded linen. And if you are a neat worker, you may be able to sell your toys if you wish to do so.

DESTROYING A TERROR OF THE SEA-ROADS

With a tremendous roar the explosive will shatter this mountain of ice, and the fragments will float harmlessly away, to melt in warmer waters. This is one of the numerous friendly acts performed by explosives, for icebergs are a great menace to shipping and have sent to destruction many a fine monarch of the sea.

Our PERILOUS FRIENDS the EXPLOSIVES

How We Can Pack Enough Power into a Little Space to Blow Up a Mighty Mountain, and What Produces that Power

WHAT is it that happens when something explodes? Why will a stick of dynamite that is only about twice the size of a man's finger send a great stone flying through the air, or tear the strongest rock to pieces?

It is all because the dynamite contains a good deal of nitrogen (nĭ′trŏ-jĕn) in a very restless state. Nitrogen is not always restless and violent, but only when it finds itself in company it does not like. When it is perfectly free it is as harmless as anything in the world; indeed, it forms about four-fifths of the air we breathe. But when it is united with certain other substances, it is always ready to break loose with great violence if it finds the opportunity; and its best chance comes when it catches fire or meets with a shock of some kind. Then it gets free, and in an instant it changes back into gas.

But a gas, as we know, is very thin and light and takes up a great deal of space. So when the nitrogen in dynamite gets free it needs several thousand times more room than it had in the dynamite—and it needs the room immediately. So it annexes the space, no matter what is in its way, and then we have an explosion that rocks the entire neighbourhood.

That is all that occurs in an explosion. No matter what the substance may be—petrol vapour mixed with air, gunpowder, T.N.T.—the principle is always the same. Suddenly a gas has had an opportunity to get free into a much greater space; and if there is heat, too, it makes the gas need still more room, for heat makes gases expand. If we could take all the air in a room and compress it into a small tin that was likely to burst at the slightest shock, we should have something like a tin full of high explosive.

And yet these violent explosives are among the very best friends of man—so useful that we manufacture many thousands of tons every year. Think of the time it would take to excavate enough rock for a road or a railway line, a canal or a tunnel, if the only tools we possessed were a pick and shovel! Think of the labour we save in working a mine!

How Explosives Are Used to Save Lives on Land and on Sea

The uses of explosives are many and varied. Sometimes, when a fire gets out of control in a great city, the buildings in its path have to be blown up with dynamite, so that the fire will die down because it can find nothing more to burn. Sometimes, too, when a ship is caught in a storm at sea, oil is thrown far and wide by exploding dynamite and the waves are calmed. Or a rescuing ship may send out a lifeline by fastening it to a rocket that is fired across the ship in distress. If ice dams a river until it threatens to flood towns and cities when it breaks loose, a hole is often made in the ice by exploding dynamite, and through it the water can gradually flow away. Explosives are also employed in making fireworks and various kinds of signals.

The invention of explosives dates from far back in the past, in China. But it is possible that in their present form they were first made by Roger Bacon, an English friar who may be called the first great modern scientist. Somewhere about 1242 he seems to have accidentally discovered gunpowder, the first real explosive; for, hidden away as a puzzle in one of his books, is a formula he left us for making it. The guns for using it had still to be invented, but in the next century they began to appear.

For five hundred years gunpowder was the only explosive known. It is made of charcoal, sulphur, and saltpetre—and in saltpetre the uneasy nitrogen has been confined.

When the old cannons were fired, the gunpowder that exploded and gave the cannon-ball its impetus sent out a tremendous quantity of smoke and a great torrent of flame, for the sulphur and charcoal caught fire. The gas rushed out at the rate of a thousand feet a second—and yet gunpowder is one of the slow-burning explosives! Modern gunpowder, used mostly for blasting, explodes to fill a space a thousand or fifteen hundred times its original size.

It was not till 1846 that a new explosive was discovered. In that year an Italian chemist named Sobrero (sō-brā′rō) invented nitro-glycerine (nī′trō-glĭs′ĕr-ĭn), a heavy, oily liquid made by spraying glycerine into nitric and sulphuric acid. The nitrogen from the nitric acid is so restless that nitro-glycerine will sometimes explode without any apparent cause—and certainly without any warning. Yet it will burn quietly in the open air. But when it is confined, a shock or heat will explode it with terrific force.

It was not till 1867 that Alfred Nobel, a Swede—and the man who founded the famous Nobel prizes—found a way to make nitro-glycerine useful. He mixed with it an absorbent earth called kieselguhr (kē′z′l-gür), and then pressed the mixture into sticks. The result was dynamite—the most useful of all our explosives.

How Dynamite is Exploded by Means of Another Explosive

To explode dynamite we must strike it a hard blow. Then, with a tremendous bang, the nitrogen frees itself. The nitro-glycerine in the dynamite expands to ten thousand times its original volume. But dynamite does not burn as gunpowder does. It just "goes off"—or detonates (dē′tṓ-nāt). Nowadays other explosives besides nitro-glycerine are used in its making.

We do not explode dynamite by giving it a direct blow. The blow is dealt by still another explosive—a very powerful one indeed—called mercury fulminate (fŭl′mĭ-nāt). A tiny particle of this is put into a small copper cap and the cap is exploded from a safe distance. This in turn provides the shock that explodes the dynamite.

Just about the time that dynamite was invented, guncotton came into use; it had been discovered in 1845, but was not then stable or safe in use. This is a terrible explosive, though it is nothing but plain cotton soaked in nitric and sulphuric acids

and dried out. If we light the cotton it will simply burn away with a hissing sound; but if we strike it with a hammer, it will explode and the gas will rush away at the rate of three miles a second.

In 1875 Nobel introduced a form of dynamite especially useful for blasting away rocks, calling this "blasting gelatine." Many other substances are to-day used to render the nitro-glycerine safe, from sawdust and wood pulp to plaster of Paris or common chalk.

Trinitrotoluene (trī-nī'-tro-tol'ū-ēn), made from toluene, a coal-tar product, is a safe explosive. The toluene is added to nitric and sulphuric acids.

When combined with ammonium nitrate,

Here are three of the many ways in which explosives can be of great service to man. Huge boulders and even hills were blown away before the broad, well-levelled highway you see at the top could be built. In the centre is a view of the Panama Canal, which was completed in only ten years. With the aid of dynamite whole mountains were moved in the process. Below are men reclaiming waste land by blowing out wide ditches for irrigation purposes.

T.N.T. makes an explosive called amatol, which is very useful for blasting in coal mines, since it does not leave red-hot particles behind to set coal dust and gas on fire. Ammonium nitrate was first used with T.N.T. in 1914. Liquid carbon dioxide (dī-ŏk'sīd) is used for the same purpose, and a substance called ammonal is used for blasting in quarries. In 1899 liquid oxygen was used for blasting out the famous Simplon tunnel between Italy and Switzerland.

Other substances besides those that are commonly called explosives will explode. The dust in a coal mine can "blow up." Coal-gas, or the fumes from petrol, when mixed with air can be ignited and made to push out the piston of an internal combustion engine. The gas from a gas-stove will flash out with a bang. But all these things require air before the explosion can take place, for the flame that causes it must have a supply of oxygen to burn.

These are only a few of our terrible friends, the explosives. We may well stand in awe of them, and give them a wide berth; but we must be grateful to them, too, and glad that more of them are employed for peaceful work than for the hideous purposes of war.

Cut a piece of black paper to represent spilled ink. Lay it flat on a white table-cover and beside it place an upset dry ink-bottle. Whoever owns the table-cloth will be greatly shocked.

THE WARNING BENEATH THE EGG-SHELL

Mix an ounce of alum with half a pint of vinegar. Then with a fine brush, using the mixture as an ink, write a message—a joke, a prophecy, anything you like—on the shell of an egg. After the egg is boiled in water for about fifteen minutes, the writing will disappear, but your unsuspecting friend who removes the shell will find the message on the hard-boiled egg inside.

FUN WITH TRICKS

THE INVERTED TUMBLER

1. Fill a tumbler to the brim. 2. Hold a piece of paper over it and turn the tumbler upside down. 3. Take your hand off the paper and you will find that the paper stays in place—and so does the water.

THE WELL-BEHAVED MATCH

Secretly break off the tip of a match and press the jagged end firmly down on your finger. Everybody will think that you are very clever to be able to balance the match.

HERE, PENNY, PENNY, PENNY!

Did you know that pennies could walk? Place a penny on a table on which is a table-cover. Over it place an inverted glass set on two lead-pencils, as you see in the picture above. Now begin scratching towards you on the table-cloth just outside the glass, and the penny will come creeping out.

HOW TO MAKE WATER RUN UP HILL

Put a lighted candle about three inches long in a pan containing about an inch of water. Then place a glass over the candle, as you see in the picture above. The water in the glass will rise above the water-line of the pan. As long as it has oxygen the candle will burn, and as long as the candle burns the water will rise.

THE COIN AND THE HOLE

In a stout piece of paper, cut a circle with a diameter three-sixteenths of an inch less than the diameter of a penny. Ask anyone to pass a penny through the hole without touching the penny or tearing the paper. When he has given it up, fold the paper exactly across the centre of the hole. Ask someone to drop in the penny, and when it is resting just above the hole, bend the corners of the paper slightly upwards and the penny will fall through.

BLOOD WILL TELL!

Stand with your back to a table and tell someone to put a penny and a halfpenny anywhere on the table, and to raise one arm above the head and let the other arm hang down. Then say, "Place the upraised hand over the penny and the other over the halfpenny." You can always tell which is the penny hand and which the halfpenny hand, because the blood will be drained from the hand that was in the air, while the other will be as red as before. Naturally the longer you keep your man waiting with one hand up and one down, the more marked the difference in colour will be, and the easier it will be for you to guess.

Greece fought against herself and brought about her own destruction. In spite of the fact that they were of the same blood and religion, the Greek city-states, instead of uniting together to form one powerful country, wore themselves down by wars which led nowhere, since not one of the city-states was capable of ruling the rest.

The END of "the GLORY THAT WAS GREECE"

How the Splendid Cities Lost Their Freedom and Strength, and were Ruled by One Foreign Conqueror After Another Almost Down to Our Day

(CONTINUED FROM PAGE 658)

THERE was never a time when the famous Greek cities could manage to live in peace for very long. After Athens fell from power, there were sixty years of almost constant warfare between city and city. If the various cities could only have agreed to live in peace, they might have made Greece the greatest power in the world. But each district stood out for its own rights against all the others, and none would submit to leadership until it was forced to do so.

When Athens was conquered (404 B.C.), Sparta naturally became the leading state of Greece. Spartan soldiers now occupied every Greek city, and usually chose a few rich men or nobles of the city to govern it under their direction. This kind of government, by a few rich or powerful men, is called an oligarchy (ŏl'ĭ-gär'kĭ). In Athens

and in many other cities the oligarchs governed rather badly. They quarrelled among themselves, and too often they retained their power by means of murder and robbery. Indeed, the rule established by Sparta was worse than anything the Greeks had yet to suffer.

It is not surprising, therefore, that Greece became embroiled in another civil war within six or seven years after the fall of Athens. This we call the Corinthian War (395–387 B.C.), and from it Sparta and Persia emerged as victors. Although Athens gained a few victories on the sea, Sparta still kept her control of Greece, and the Persian king, who liked nothing better than to see the Greeks quarrelling among themselves, quietly seized control of the Greek states in Asia Minor.

After nine years of not altogether undisturbed peace the city of Thebes revolted against Sparta. Thebes was a small place of no very great importance, but she was fortunate in having a wonderful leader named Epaminondas (ĕ-păm'ĭ-nŏn'dăs), who was a very skilful general. By clever handling of the Theban forces, Epaminondas managed to defeat the Spartan army, and after about twenty-five years of tyranny the Spartans were now forced to retreat to their own territory.

Famous Men of Ancient Greece Who Will Live for Ever

Yet even this Theban victory was of little use to Greece. Epaminondas himself was killed, and the turbulent Greek cities fell back into their customary state of quarrelling and fighting, except for short intervals when everybody was exhausted and forced to take a rest from warfare.

Although the Athenians were so oppressed during these years of Spartan tyranny, we must not imagine that the culture which had developed under Pericles had disappeared.

Praxiteles (prăk-sĭt'ĕ-lēz), one of the greatest of Greek sculptors, flourished during this period. Socrates (sŏk'rȧ-tēz), one of the wisest thinkers among the Greeks, lived and taught in these troublous times. Socrates tried to show the Athenian citizens the value of judging between right and wrong, something they sadly needed to learn. But many of the Athenians failed to understand his teachings, and they finally accused him of disbelief in the gods and corrupting the youth of the c'ty, and put him to death. Plato (plā'tō), a pupil of Socrates, wrote many books to explain the ideas of Socrates, and was himself a great philosopher.

When Athens Needed a Leader to Show Her How to Govern

But although she had many men of genius, Athens still lacked men with the capacity for government. That is why she could

This is a restoration of the market-place of Sparta. There the people held their meetings, and there were grouped the most important public buildings, the temples, and many fine statues of marble and bronze.

not shake off her masters and regain her freedom. She had plenty of wise men but no great leader to show her how to govern herself. She may be likened to a very talented person who has never learned the virtue of self-control.

The constant fighting in Greece had made the Greek soldiers very good soldiers, and thousands of Greeks took up fighting as a profession, selling their services to whatever king needed help. We call such hired soldiers mercenaries (mẽr′sě-ná-rǐ), and Greek mercenaries were famous from Egypt, where the pharaohs had been employing them for centuries, to as far as Persia, where they had often proved of great use to a ruler who lacked native troops. Greek mercenaries frequently

This painting is called "The Wages of War." To the right you see the soldier saying good-bye to his wife before he goes off to the fields of battle, and in the centre is the returned warrior dying of his wounds. His weeping wife and child are seen on the left.

figured in many exciting adventures, of which none is more famous than that described in Xenophon's (zěn′ṓ-fǒn) book called the Anabasis (ă-năb′-ȧ-sǐs), which means "the going up."

The Famous Ten Thousand

Xenophon was one of an army of ten thousand Greeks hired by Cyrus, the Persian prince who wished to take the kingdom by force from his brother Artaxerxes (är′tăk-zûrk′sēz). About 400 B.C. Cyrus marched his soldiers all the way across Asia Minor to the Euphrates River, where they won a battle but unluckily lost their leader. At this point, when the Greek troops were wondering how to get home again, the Persian leader invited their officers to a conference, and then put them to death, thinking that the soldiers would then surrender. But the soldiers were far from helpless. They elected Xenophon, the young Athenian volunteer, as general, and under his wise and vigorous leadership they fought their way home.

The most vivid picture in the story comes at the moment when, after a five months' march, the weary, sea-loving Greeks at last raised the shout "Thalassa"—"The sea! the sea!"—when they came to the sparkling waters of the Euxine (ūk′sǐn), as the Black Sea was called in those days. Even then the troubles of the ten thousand were by no means ended, but under Xenophon's wise direction they succeeded at last in reaching the Hellespont.

To the north of Greece there was a wild and mountainous country called Macedon (măs′ě-dǒn), where lived a rough, warlike people related to the Greeks in language and ancestry, but by no means so highly civilized as their southern neighbours. Yet their king, Philip, who gained the throne in 360 B.C., had been educated in Greece and had studied war under no less a leader than Epaminondas of Thebes.

Philip of Macedon built up a great standing army of regular soldiers, who would always be on hand for any conquest on which he might set his heart. Then he made it his business to secure little tracts of territory here and there, and add them to his kingdom. The Greeks began to fear that Philip coveted Greece, as indeed he did. In Athens the famous orator Demosthenes (dě-mǒs′thě-nēz) made passionate speeches against Philip. The speeches came to be called "philippics" (fǐ-lǐp′ǐk), and to our own day any violent speech may bear the same name. But Athens did little to guard against the enemy from the north, because she had no general to match her great orator.

It was not until twenty-two years after Philip became king that he finally struck the fatal blow at Greece, when, in 338 B.C., he fought the battle of Chaeronea (kĕr'ŏ-nē'ȧ), after which Macedon definitely took the place of Sparta as the leader of Greece. Although the Greeks were now under foreign rule, it was no worse than the rule of Sparta, and, indeed, hardly so bad, for Macedon was a country a great deal more like Greece than was either Persia or Egypt.

Alexander Sets Fire to Thebes, but Spares the Home of a Famous Poet

Two years after Philip had mastered Greece he was assassinated, and his son Alexander became king—at the age of twenty. Some of the restless Greek cities saw in this change a splendid opportunity for a revolt, but Alexander showed them their mistake when he dashed down from the north and burned Thebes, leaving untouched only the temples and the home of Pindar, the famous Theban poet.

The fact that Alexander spared the house of a great poet showed him to be a Greek both in feeling and in culture. His tutor had been the Athenian Aristotle (ăr'ĭs-tŏt''l), a philosopher who is often said to have had the greatest mind of all men. Aristotle had taught Alexander a great deal of the Greek love of art and wisdom, and when the turbulent Greek states saw that Alexander meant to rule them firmly, and that he was a ruler worthy of them, they submitted with a good grace. Some of them even sent soldiers to serve in the Macedonian army.

On the slopes of several of the hills at Athens there are many chambers cut out of the solid rock. Some of these were tombs and some were dwelling-places of the early Athenians. The one you see in the picture above has traditionally been called "the prison of Socrates."

Alexander was planning nothing less than war upon the Persian empire, to end Persia's dominion over the Greek states. He wanted to be the champion of Greece by destroying the power of Persia for ever.

The army that Alexander led over the Hellespont was the most formidable that had ever been collected by any military genius. In the centre of the line of battle he massed a heavy body of men armed with long spears. Such a company of heavy soldiers was called a Macedonian phalanx (făl'ăngks). On either side of it were bodies of cavalry, whose business was to charge the enemy while the phalanx marched straight on against the centre of the opposing army.

The Persians had no troops which could stand against this fighting machine of horse and footmen. The Persian mercenaries frequently gave up fighting when they saw the battle going against them, and the native subjects of the Persians often would have followed suit, had they been allowed to do so. The fiery rush of Alexander's troops terrified them, until the conquerors soon became the conquered.

Alexander fought three great battles against the Persians, in every one of which he was brilliantly successful. He first (334 B.C.) won the battle of Granicus (grȧ-nĭ'kŭs), where he scattered the hosts of the mighty king Darius III. Then in the battle of Issus (ĭs'ŭs), a year later, he met King Darius himself, and, turning back the wings of the Persian army with his irresistible cavalry, he inflicted upon the Persians a terrible defeat. After that Darius tried to make peace; but against the advice of his counsellors Alexander decided to go on and conquer all Persia.

First pausing to overrun Egypt and add it to the list of his conquests, Alexander met Darius once more (331 B.C.) in the battle of Arbela (är-bē lȧ). The young Macedonian king had only about half as many soldiers as the Persian had under his command, but the genius of his generalship and the fury of his assault proved too much for the out-of-date military tactics of Darius. The "Great King" was beaten once again, and as he fled into the mountains he was murdered by his own bodyguard.

Here is Lorus, an Indian prince who fought bravely against Alexander but was finally forced to surrender. Alexander was so impressed by his nobility and independence that he gave him back his kingdom to rule.

Though in five short years of brilliant exploits, Alexander the Great had made himself master of most of the known world, he was not content with his conquests. He pushed on farther into Asia, across India, and even down the valley of the Indus River before he turned back. Wherever he went he left garrisons of Greek and Macedonian soldiers to hold the new lands for Macedon. These soldiers introduced Greek ideas and customs into the lands as far east as India, and left the beginning of Greek culture in strange, out-of-the-way places, where it endured for centuries afterwards.

When Alexander returned in triumph to Babylon, his success had been so extraordinary and his power so mighty that to many he must have seemed inspired by the Gods. How far the glory of his empire might have risen we cannot tell, for in 323 B.C., when he was only thirty-three years old, the young conqueror died.

How the Empire Was Divided Among Alexander's Generals

Three of Alexander's generals divided his vast domains among them. One, named Ptolemy (tŏl'ĕ-mĭ), took the whole of Northern Africa, making himself king and successor to the pharaohs of Egypt. He lived in the Greek city of Alexandria—named after his great master—which had been built by Alexander at the mouth of the Nile. Seleucus (sĕ-lū'kŭs), another general, held his sway from the Indian Ocean to the Mediterranean, and he and his descendants ruled as the successors to the Persian kings. Antigonus (ăn-tĭg'ŏ-nŭs), the third general, took Greece and Macedonia.

A New Seat of Learning is Established at Alexandria

Of these three empires that of Ptolemy became the most powerful. Alexandria succeeded Athens as the seat of learning and culture, and for several centuries the Ptolemies occupied the throne of Egypt. The descendants of Seleucus made Antioch their capital, and built up there a kingdom almost as great as that of Egypt, and one which lasted a long time.

As for Greece itself, the story is not very happy. The Greek states tried to revolt against their Macedonian governors, and

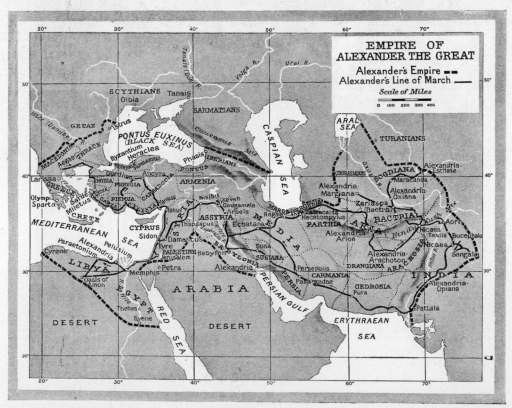

This is the far-flung empire of Alexander the Great, which brought East and West together. By planting colonies throughout his vast territory, Alexander had hoped to spread Greek culture over the entire world.

Photo by Rischgitz

This picture represents the destruction of Corinth by the Romans in 146 B.C. The wealthy city's many treasures and famous works of art were carried off by its conquerors, who left only a mass of smoking ruins behind them.

they also went on fighting one another, so that even stubborn Sparta finally grew weak from exhaustion. From the north the barbarians began to pour down into Greece, and many Greeks escaped to other countries, where they might find a brighter Hellas.

Greek Culture Becomes Supreme

With Greek generals and soldiers in every land, Greek merchants everywhere, and Greek teachers in every city, it is no wonder that we call the third century B.C. the Hellenistic (hĕl'ĕn-ĭs'tĭk) Age. Greek became the universal language learned by all business men as well as by all educated people. Greek culture was supreme in every land.

The centre of this Hellenistic culture was at Alexandria, in Egypt. This city was much grander and more luxurious than Athens had ever been. The houses, which were often of stone instead of brick, had floors inlaid with tile or with tiny pieces of coloured marble forming beautiful designs. On the plastered walls gay pictures were painted. Sanitation, too, was vastly improved, and Alexandria was much cleaner and healthier than other cities had been.

Throughout the Hellenistic Age in Alexandria the temples were no longer the only magnificent public buildings. The city had assembly halls, theatres, public baths, gymnasiums and libraries, all built by the city for the use of the citizens. There was a great lighthouse called the Pharos (fär'ŏs) at the entrance to the harbour, which is said to have been 500 feet high, and in the Royal Museum there was a vast library of books.

The House of Wisdom

The Royal Museum was a sort of university supported by the Ptolemies, where wise men from all over the world gathered to study the sciences and the arts. Here, too, students might read the many works of Aristotle, or study the geometry compiled by Euclid (ū'klĭd). Or they might investigate the strange new science mechanics discovered by Archimedes (är'kĭ-mē'dēz), with its levers and pulleys which would move great weights so easily as to allow a child to lift an elephant.

People were more open-minded now than

in the Age of Pericles. They did not fear the pagan gods so much, and the mass of them were far better educated. Boys could study mathematics and the sciences as well as reading and writing. The plays in the theatre dealt with real men and women rather than with the old gods, and the poems, paintings, and sculptures were more human.

The Whole of the Civilized World Falls Under the Sway of Rome

The world of the Hellenistic Age was growing more and more civilized, and that civilization might have lasted much longer if it really had filled the whole world. But these cultivated Grecian empires were surrounded by cruel and barbarous peoples who were destined to overwhelm them.

Great hordes of those barbarians had already swept over Europe even to the gates of Athens, and had flowed over into Asia. In Italy the power of Rome had grown apace. By 168 B.C. Roman armies had conquered all the kingdoms into which Alexander's empire had been divided. And soon the whole civilized world was Roman.

Now, the Romans did not by any means put an end to Greek culture. They adopted as much of it as they could understand, and with various changes made it their own. They carried it through the world. For that reason, at the height of the Roman empire most of the art and science in the world was such as had had its birth in Greece. We shall see later how this came about. But even proud Rome was in due time to go the way of all the ancient empires, and the fate of Greece naturally hung on the fate of her conqueror, Rome.

How the Land of Beautiful Things became a Battle-ground for Nations

It was an unhappy fate for many a century, under many a master. Seven hundred years after the death of Alexander, when the Roman world was divided into an Eastern and a Western empire, Greece remained a part of the eastern half; but all through the Middle Ages and down into modern times she was a battle-ground of many rulers. Alexandria was taken by the Mohammedan Arabs in A.D. 640, and its great library was burned. Its glory rapidly declined. After 1453 the Turks swept into Greece and took it captive, laying waste nearly all that was left of "the glory that was Greece." For nearly four hundred years the land was under the heel of the Turk.

Long before the collapse of the Roman empire in the fifth century A.D., the Greeks had lost the great part of their ancient spirit. The people had declined in vigour and in military prowess, and for centuries they submitted meekly to almost any conqueror who came to rule them. The fighting which occurred was between one conqueror and another. Often the invaders would destroy each other, and then the power naturally returned to the Greeks themselves, though they were never able to retain it. For many a year the Greeks made no struggle for independence, though they were often cruelly oppressed, especially by the Turks in later centuries.

The Spirit of Ancient Greece Awakens and a Nation Gains Her Freedom

By 1800, however, the descendants of the men who fought at Marathon had wakened once more to a strong desire for freedom, and in 1821 there was a revolution against Turkish rule, a revolution which Great Britain encouraged and helped. At first, the Turks were able, by massacring many Greeks, to quell the revolt, but in 1832 they were forced to recognize the Greeks as an independent nation. Greece then became a kingdom with a German prince as sovereign, and in various struggles with the Turks the Greek territory was gradually increased.

In the World War of 1914-1918, Greece took the part of the Allies against Germany and Austria. As a result she gained a great deal of territory when the war was over. But she opened a new war against Turkey in 1921 and lost much of what she had gained, including the city of Smyrna, which was burned by the Turks.

In 1924, after a revolution which drove the king of Greece from the country, the nation became once more a republic, and the citizens of that republic, as they look back to the republics in the cities of ancient Greece, feel justly proud of their long history.

694

What MAKES the WIND BLOW?

How the Great Currents in the Air have Helped to Determine Our Climate and Our History

(CONTINUED FROM PAGE 650)

WHAT is the wind? Of course, we know well enough how it behaves. We have felt all kinds of winds, from a gentle breeze barely strong enough to flutter a thistledown to blasts that snatch away our hats and send us chasing down the road to retrieve them. There are even tornadoes strong enough to root up a house. But this boisterous, powerful fellow no one has ever seen, for he is made of nothing but air. He is the roving atmosphere. Winds are rivers of air that flow along over the earth at varying rates of speed; and they are very important, for they bring us nearly all our changes of weather. Spring rains, summer storms and winter blizzards are all brought by the winds.

And what is it makes the winds? The answer is quite surprising. It is the sun that makes the winds.

Perhaps the easiest way to understand it is to watch the smoke from

The poet who lives on the shore may sing " Whichever way the wind doth blow, my heart is glad to have it so." The poet who lives on the sea, however, cannot echo this sentiment, for to him a fair wind only is welcome—a wind that will blow him safely to port.

a lighted match. The smoke rises steadily upward, curving this way and that, but always mounting. It cannot do anything else, for the flame has heated the air, and air that is heated expands—or spreads out. This makes it lighter, because it is thinner than it was before it was heated. Now, lighter air with heavier air all round it is forced to rise. The heavier air squeezes it up by flowing under it from every side. Warm air can no more keep from rising if there is cooler air round it than a cork can keep from coming up to the top of a pail of water.

Such upward currents of air as those we see when a match is burned and the warm air carries the smoke up are known as "up-draughts." Most of the movements of the air all over the earth are caused in this way—by the rising of air that has been warmed by the sun and the flowing of cold air into the place where the warm air has been.

Have you ever watched water boil in a large pan? Wherever the flame touched the bottom of the pan, the water bubbled

You may at times have observed that when there was something strange about the climate of a country, the Gulf Stream was said to be responsible for it. Now the Gulf Stream cannot account for everything, but it does bring about some remarkable conditions. Above is a map with the arrows showing the course of the Gulf Stream through the Atlantic Ocean. At the right is a similar map showing the course of its twin, the Japan Current, which gives British Columbia its mild climate. Both currents begin in the warm waters near the Equator and end in the cold waters of the north.

up fast; but if there were places round the edge where the flame did not reach, the water there was fairly quiet. The air behaves in much the same way under the rays of the sun. All along the Equator, where the sun is straight overhead, the ground is highly heated, and in turn heats the air over it. But farther north and south on either side the sun's rays strike with less power and the air is a good deal cooler. So the hotter air along the Equator constantly "boils" upwards,

forced up by the cooler, heavier air that is crowding it from north and south. This cooler air in its turn is warmed by the burning sun, and is forced up by still more cool air; and so a current is kept constantly flowing from the cooler temperate zones towards the Equator.

The March of the Winds

The heated air that "boils" up flows away to north and south and finally sinks to earth again, when it has been thoroughly chilled. Then it once more begins its journey towards the Equator, joining the procession of winds that are steadily flowing there, drawn by the constant rising of the air where the sun is hottest. So it is the rising of overheated air that makes the wind.

But strangely enough, those winds that flow in from north and south, to rise in a fountain over the Equator, really flow from north-east above the Equator and south-east below it. If you were given time you might very well guess why this is. But we shall save you the effort. Their path swerves to

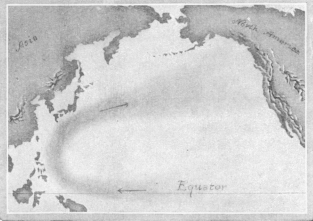

one side owing to the whirling of the earth. It is true that the earth as it turns carries its atmosphere round with it—as much a part of it as are the mountain ranges and the rivers; but it is also true that round the middle of the globe any given spot on the surface has to travel a good deal faster than a spot that is nearer the poles; it has farther to go on its way round the earth's axis.

Now, the winds that seek the Equator

These are the winds that sweep the oceans of the world in January.   Their direction is shown by the arrows.

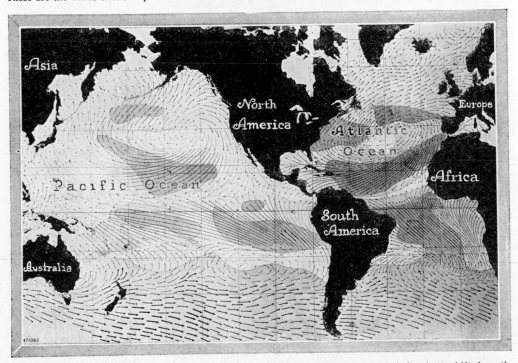

In July the sun is hottest north of the Equator, so the whole pattern of the winds has been shifted north.

start from regions where they do not have to travel very fast to keep up with the earth. Consequently, as they move northwards and southwards they are passing into new regions where the ground is wheeling faster and faster beneath them. The result you may clearly see for yourself. They cannot pick up speed fast enough to keep pace with the more rapid turn of the earth's surface, so the land has to rush by while they maintain their steady march towards the Equator. The result is that their path on the earth swerves from straight north and south towards the west, for the earth is spinning eastwards under them.

What We Mean When We Speak of the "Trade Winds" and the "Doldrums"

These winds blow steadily all the year round at an average of about twelve miles an hour; of old, in the days of sailing vessels, they used to be of great use to shipping. Because they kept such a steady course, they were called "trade winds"—for the old meaning of "trade" was "a straight path." They could always be relied upon to bring a ship to port. But they are of great importance even to-day, for the climate of the world depends mainly upon them to distribute the heat and cold.

Along the line where they meet at the Equator and rise in a kind of fountain, there is a broad belt of calm, where there are no steady breezes and the rain falls in torrents. Hardly a single day is without its shower. This zone is known as the "doldrums," and used to be a terror to sailing vessels, which might be caught there for weeks on end and remain "as idle as a painted ship upon a painted ocean." Though steam has freed our ships from such inconveniences, we still have the phrase "in the doldrums," meaning "in low spirits."

On either side of the trade winds there is a broad belt of winds which blow across the temperate zones from west to east. They are called the "prevailing westerlies," and in the southern half of the globe, where their path lies mostly across the ocean, they blow so steadily and swiftly that sailors in the olden days called them "the roaring

forties," since they swept along parallels of latitude between 40° and 50° S. A vessel coming back from the East Indies found it easier to round Cape Horn than to sail into the teeth of such a gale.

The winds that sweep from west to east in the north temperate zone are more or less broken up by the unevenness of the land they cover, and so are a good deal more variable. Yet in this country the breezes are commonly from the west, south-west, or north-west. And it is those business-like winds which, blowing steadily off the Atlantic and the warm Gulf Stream which crosses it there, give England and Western Europe their mild, moist climate. For though Great Britain is as far north as Labrador, snow rarely stays on the ground here more than a few days at a time. And though the northern coast of Spain is actually farther north than New York City, it has so mild a climate that roses bloom there at Christmas.

Between the trade winds and the great belt of wind in each of the temperate zones there are calm spaces, with little or no breeze and clear skies. It is here that the air which is always boiling up at the Equator settles to earth again. In the northern half of the globe this belt is called "the calms of Cancer," named after the tropic along which it lies; and in the south it is called "the calms of Capricorn," after the tropic of Capricorn.

Why the Men of the Sailing Ships Called the Calms of Cancer the "Horse Latitudes"

But the sturdy sailors did not bother with such learned names. They called those calms the "horse latitudes" because years ago when a sailing vessel carrying a cargo of horses was caught in the calms of Cancer on its way down to the West Indies, the horses often had to be thrown overboard when water began to run short. The old tars never lost a chance of coining a vivid phrase.

As the sun swings north and south in its yearly path, it carries the great up-draught along the Equator with it. So at different times of the year the doldrums are to be found at different places on the earth's surface, and the trade winds as well. They shift backwards and forwards with the sun.

(CONTINUED ON PAGE 723)

The WONDERFUL MEMORY of MACAULAY

He Could Remember the Contents of any Book that He Read, and Repeat Them Almost Word for Word

(CONTINUED FROM PAGE 645)

"I WISH I were as cocksure of any one thing as Tom Macaulay is of everything!" Those are the most famous words ever spoken about Thomas Babington Macaulay, and they tell us nearly all about him. First, he had a marvellous set of facts in his head; second, he was always just a little too certain that every one of those facts was right. We all know that kind of man, and Macaulay (1800–1859) was one of the greatest men of the kind who ever lived.

He had been like that from a child, for he was one of the most precocious boys on record. He talked like a book when he was four years old. At that age a lady had spilled some hot coffee on him and burned him rather badly. But he did not ask for any petting. A few minutes later, when the lady asked him how he felt, he answered, "Thank you, madam, the agony is abated."

From the time when he was three, he used to spend his happiest hours lying on a rug and reading, with a piece of bread and butter in one hand. He hated school because it kept him from reading all he wanted and made him study arithmetic; also because it made him keep his busy little tongue still. Yet he took all sorts of prizes. When he was eight he had written a long poem and a history of the world. And when he went to Cambridge he won many prizes.

He read an extraordinary number of books, and he remembered every single thing he read. He could read through a whole book and then repeat it almost word for word. This sounds almost unbelievable, but it is true. He was also a brilliant talker. Altogether a most charming man—except when he was a little too positive about all he knew.

He became a lawyer, but he never liked that profession very much. He wanted to be a writer instead. So he wrote an article on Milton for the "Edinburgh Review" and leaped immediately into fame at the age of twenty-five. From then on he was the most brilliant of the writers on that publication, and in it the majority of his "Essays" first appeared as articles.

Indeed, he was forced to make a living mainly with his pen. His father had been rich, but he failed in business when his son was a young man, and Macaulay had to support his sisters and himself.

At first he found the burden rather more than he could conveniently shoulder, and at one time he was reduced almost to poverty. But by means of his pen and various political offices to which he succeeded he was able to weather the storm and eventually to become possessed of considerable wealth.

Photo by National Portrait Gallery

Thomas Babington Macaulay, one of the most brilliant writers and speakers of the nineteenth century. It is said that he could read a book almost as fast as he could turn the pages—and yet would know all that was in it when he reached the end.

A Brilliant Orator Whose Speeches in Parliament Bristled with Facts

Macaulay sat many times in Parliament, and was one of the most brilliant orators of his day. No one in the House of Commons could marshal so many facts and put them into such eloquent speech. He was always a supporter of the Whigs, though he was never a strict party man; for he was too absolutely honest to vote except as he really believed, and no arguments could undermine his principles.

The most important thing he did for the government was to go to India as a member of the council appointed to undertake the difficult task of reforming British rule in that land. He was very just and very wise in all that he did, and India owed much to him. In 1857 he received the honour of a peerage for his public services.

But his deepest interest had always lain in writing, and he had never ceased from it. In his later years, with his financial position assured, he withdrew from politics and devoted himself wholly to his pen. He had already written those "Lays of Ancient Rome" which are still so much recited. And now he withdrew from the world and spent his time in writing the great history of England which he was afraid his frail health would never allow him to finish. But he managed to complete it before his death in 1859, and it is one of the most popular historical works ever written.

His WORDS Could ROAR Like THUNDER

And So the Mighty Mutterings of Thomas Carlyle Shook the Land Like a Great Storm

ONE dark, chilly morning in November, 1809, fourteen-year-old Thomas Carlyle and another boy set out for the university of Edinburgh, almost a hundred miles away. There was no money for a coach and the boys had to walk the whole way. Carlyle's father and mother went with them to the end of the village.

The father, a humble stonemason, had found out that his son Thomas was a bright lad, worth all the sacrifice that had to be made to give him a good education. He must be a preacher. The mother, a deeply religious woman, felt sure that God would watch over her favourite and eldest son and crown him with success. But, for all their dreams, neither the loving mother nor the father had the slightest idea of the honours and the fame that would be his.

Oatmeal and Potatoes for Dinner

Thomas Carlyle was born in a tiny whitewashed cottage in the small Scottish village of Ecclefechan on December 4, 1795. Life there was stern and hard, for his father found it difficult to obtain sufficient food for his wife and their nine children. There was money only for the bare necessities, and the family had to be content when there were oatmeal and potatoes for dinner. But Thomas was happy there, for he loved his

mother dearly. In all his life he knew no other person who was so patient and so understanding. Even when Thomas's violent temper got the better of him—and it often did —she talked to him in the kindliest way, and urged him to learn and to practise self-control.

At the village school Thomas showed such promise that he was sent on to the Annan Grammar School in a near-by town. He learned his lessons easily and well, but he did not understand the other boys and they did not understand him. He could find interest only in reading, and the bright boy devoured every book on which he could lay his hands. When he left the school at the age of thirteen he had acquired a good knowledge of both Latin and French and was deeply interested in mathematics.

When he had finished his studies at Edinburgh University, Carlyle taught at an Annan school for a time, but teaching did not allow him the independence of spirit that he felt he must have; so he returned to Edinburgh and began to write. In his early struggles, he still found happiness in his mother's encouraging letters. Very little money came from the translations he was making from the German and the critical essays he was writing for the magazines, but at least he was developing his skill with his pen. And when his "Life of Schiller" (shĭl'ẽr) appeared he gained a little recognition, although people did not yet truly value his ability.

In 1826 Carlyle married Jane Welsh, a brilliant and talented young woman. Shortly after they went to live in a small and humble cottage at Craigenputtock. In this quiet place, "the loneliest nook in Britain," Carlyle wrote some of his best works. But his poverty and his lifelong dyspepsia, coupled with the knowledge that his wife was unsuited to their lonely home, kept him miserable. Nevertheless, his beautiful essay on Burns and his peculiar but powerful "Sartor Resartus" (sär'tôr rĕ-sär'tŭs) slowly gained recognition for him. Here the young Emerson came to visit the man whose works he so admired. Carlyle had already had correspondence with the great Goethe (gēr'tĕ), who praised him for his fine essays on German literary men and for his translation of Goethe's novel, "Wilhelm Meister" (vĭl'hĕlm mīs'tĕr).

Eventually the Carlyles moved to London and took the house in Chelsea which stands to-day as a memorial to the great writer. Working incessantly, Carlyle finally finished writing the first volume of his "History of the

Photo by National Portrait Gallery

Thomas Carlyle, the rugged Scotsman, who spoke to his own generation with the voice of a prophet and is still speaking to the generation that is our own.

French Revolution." When the manuscript of this was burned by accident in the house of an acquaintance, John Stuart Mill, Carlyle was thrown into despair. But he rewrote the book from memory. It was published in 1837 and received a wonderful reception. Carlyle became one of the great prophetic voices of England, and no writer of his day had a stronger influence.

He had the highest reverence for the great men in history whom he could honestly call heroes—as shown in his book on "Heroes and Hero Worship"; and his two other chief works are the lives of two of his heroes—Cromwell and Frederick the Great. In addition to these he wrote much miscellaneous work.

His wife's death in 1866 so saddened him that he did not do a great deal more creative work, and he himself died on February 4, 1881. His great influence survived and still continues. His work has many of the qualities of the man himself—a certain ruggedness, an honesty that tolerates no sham or hypocrisy, a high idealism, and a fiery enthusiasm. His pages read like the mighty roars and rumblings of a majestic thunderstorm.

JOHN RUSKIN, ARTIST *and* PROPHET

Half His Life was Devoted to Explaining the Glories of Art, and the Other Half to Relieving the Miseries of Men

A SOLITARY little boy, with no one for a playmate and no toys but a bunch of keys or a box of bricks; a tiny, earnest figure bent over a Bible, which he had read through again and again, pronouncing every word, including all the hard names, aloud for his mother with the greatest care—this was the small John Ruskin, one day to become a great art critic and reformer.

He had a garden in which to wander, but he must not eat any of the fruit. There was nobody to whom to talk, for his mother and

father, though kind and well-loved, were stern and very grown-up. By the time he was seven, Ruskin tells us in his charming autobiography, "Praeterita" (prē-tĕr'ĭ-tȧ), he had begun "to lead a very small, perky, contented, conceited, Cock-Robinson-Crusoe sort of life" in the centre of his own tiny universe.

Ruskin was almost an old man before he overcame the habit of doing what his father and mother had told him to do. But in some ways he grew up very quickly. From his mother he learned to read before he was four, and the lovely rhythms of the Bible which he read to her were a delight to him all through his life.

His father was a man of culture and a lover of good books and fine art. From him Ruskin learned, before he was ten, to love the Iliad (ĭl'ĭ-ăd) and Sir Walter Scott. In his father's company the child saw most of the fine pictures in England, and learned to delight in the beauty of the English countryside; for the father used to go on long business trips every summer, and always took the family with him. It was his love of Nature, poetry and art that made him the able critic he was.

In 1833, when Ruskin was fourteen, he took his first trip to the Continent with his parents. They went to Switzerland, and the lad was enraptured by the Alps. He felt a sort of dedication—if he could only help other people to see and love beautiful things as he saw and loved them! He really spent his life trying to achieve this noble aim.

There were many other trips to the Continent, during which Ruskin became a great student of art. He once called Rouen, Geneva and Pisa "three centres of my life's thought," meaning that he had learned in them a great deal about art and its meaning in life. Meanwhile, he finally took his degree at Oxford University, although his course was sadly interrupted by ill-health after a disappointment in love.

It was in the year in which he entered Oxford that he read in "Blackwood's Magazine" an article which led directly to his fame; for it raised him, as he said long after, "to the height of black anger in which I have remained pretty nearly ever since." The

This wise and kindly face is that of John Ruskin, one of the masters of English prose in the past century, and one of the ardent reformers who tried to better the social conditions of the working man.

article was about the painter Turner, and the anger was at its foolish lack of understanding of Turner's art. Ruskin sat down to answer the article—not knowing that he was starting something which would take him half a lifetime to finish. For his ideas grew and grew, and lengthened into a series of books called "Modern Painters," which he did not finish until he was forty.

By the time the second volume appeared, Ruskin was a famous critic, as well as a notable writer of prose as gorgeous and musical as poetry. More of the volumes appeared, and his fame grew. His advice was eagerly sought, his writings were widely read, and his lectures were attended by thousands. Probably no one has ever done more to change people's ideas about art than did Ruskin. George Eliot, the famous novelist, said of him, "I venerate Ruskin as one of the great teachers of the age."

In 1848 Ruskin married. It was for his beautiful wife that he wrote the charming fairy tale, "The King of the Golden River," so much more light-hearted than most of his books; she had told him that he could not do it. The marriage was not a happy one, however, and after about two years it was annulled. Ruskin went back to live with his parents, and stayed under their roof until they died. He fell in love again, when he was more than forty; but his bad luck pursued him, for the girl sickened and died. He had many women friends and disciples, but never again a wife.

Meanwhile a great change had come over Ruskin's writings, a change which the people round about him never quite understood.

He had stopped writing about art and was writing about a subject which we should now call sociology (sō'shĭ-ŏl'ō-jĭ). Instead of telling his readers how beautiful Raphael's paintings were, he was crying out at the ugliness of English factories and the starved faces of the factory hands. He was writing a series of sermons on what ought to be done about poverty and ignorance and oppression.

They were beautifully written sermons, with very poetic names—"Unto This Last," "Ethics of the Dust," "Sesame and Lilies," "The Crown of Wild Olive"—and they were full of lofty sentiment, and of fine ideas which have since become fairly common, partly because of John Ruskin's influence. Why did the popular art critic change so suddenly into the unpopular social reformer?

It is not really very mysterious. Ruskin had always believed that beauty comes only from right living—and how, he asked, can people live rightly when they have no chance to learn, no chance to see beautiful things, not even enough to eat?

He worked very hard for the reforms that he preached, gave away most of his money, and founded a college at Oxford for working men. He started working men's clubs, produced a paper for working men, and even got himself laughed at by going out to break stones on the highway.

For a while Ruskin was professor of fine arts at Oxford. But his health was breaking, and finally he went to live quietly at his country estate at Brantwood, up in the Lake District. There, in 1900, he passed away.

The CLEAREST MIND of His CENTURY

John Stuart Mill's Gifts Matured in Boyhood, and He Never Lost His Lucid Power, No Matter What the Subject Upon Which He Set Out to Work

WHENEVER people talk or write about children who learn things at a much earlier age than the average child, they are almost certain sooner or later to mention John Stuart Mill. Born in London in 1806, he had for a father a well-known philosopher with very decided ideas about education, and the ideas were tried with astonishing success on his young son John.

The father himself took entire charge of his son's education. At three John was learning lists of Greek words with their meanings. At eight, he had read Aesop's Fables, and a large number of other books, in Greek. At that age he began to study Latin, and to teach the younger children what his father had taught him. By the time he was thirteen he had learned algebra and geometry and was starting on calculus, and had read numerous books on history and drama, besides most of the Latin classics.

He had started to write histories for himself before he was seven, though none of them ever came to much. At twelve he began logic, and at thirteen went through a "complete course in political economy." For years he and his father used to go on long walks, and John would tell his father what he had learned since the last time. Much of what he had learned would be from books that he had found and read

John Stuart Mill, who taught the Englishmen of Queen Victoria's day the wonderful beauty of clear, straight thinking.

for himself. When he was fourteen the young scholar went to France for a year or two of further study.

So it was a very learned young man who took a position in the India House and settled down in London shortly after he returned to England. He remained with the India House for nearly thirty-five years, gradually working up to a position of importance. The work did not take all his time, and hardly touched his tremendous store of energy.

The Fine Idea upon Which a Famous Society Was Founded

In one year, when he was only twenty, he edited a long and difficult book on political economy; it would have taken the full time of the average mature scholar for a much longer period. He wrote for and edited "The Westminster Review" and, later, another magazine. He thought and wrote on many thorny subjects, such as logic and economics and philosophy. During these years at India House, in fact, he became one of the most influential thinkers and writers in England.

In 1822, while he was still very young indeed, he founded a famous little society of brilliant and earnest young men, which came to be known as the Utilitarian (ū-tĭl'ĭ-târ'-ĭ-ăn) Society. Utilitarianism is the name given to the theory Mill worked out, building on ideas of his father and another well-known philosopher, Jeremy Bentham (bĕn'-tăm). Its main idea is that society should be organized for "the greatest good of the greatest number," that is, in such a way that, as far as possible, everyone shall have the chance to be as wise and happy as it is in his nature to be. These young men used to debate about such things and then put their thoughts into writing for the magazines. Later, Mill arranged his conclusions in a book called by the name of his system, "Utilitarianism."

In 1830 Mill met a charming and intelligent woman, a Mrs. Taylor, who later became his wife. Partly through her he became intensely interested in working for justice and equality for women: one of the most famous of his books is called "On the Subjection of Women," which was published in 1869. Indeed, he was one of the founders of the first women's suffrage society, which later developed into the National Union of Women's Suffrage Societies. It was Mill who presented the first petition to Parliament about women's suffrage, and his writings are still considered to be classic works on the subject.

Mrs. Taylor helped him, also, to write what is surely his masterpiece, his fine "Essay on Liberty." This essay is not even yet out of date, for the world still has much to learn about liberty.

In 1856 Mill attained a responsible position in the India House, a position which kept his time well occupied until 1858, when the company dissolved. He was offered a seat on the new council, but refused it and retired.

Unfortunately his dearly-loved wife did not long share in that retirement, for she died the same year, while they were on a trip to the Continent. She was buried at Avignon, in France, and ever after Mill spent half of each year there, that he might be near her grave. But he did not stop his study and writing. The "Essay on Liberty," with a dedication to his wife, was published the following year, and when his friends urged him to stand for Parliament in 1865 he consented to do so. He sat in Parliament for three years, and spoke boldly and well for many of the changes and reforms he believed in, whether they were popular or not. In the passage of the Reform Bill of 1867 he worked with the great Liberal minister Gladstone.

What John Stuart Mill Thought to Be the Most Beautiful Thing of All

Mill was a great walker, and loved the quiet beauty of the English countryside. Walking was indeed almost his only exercise and botany was his hobby. He kept up both until the very end. Three days before he died, in 1873, he had been on a fifteen-mile botanical excursion.

Mill is remembered most of all for his keen, clear intellect. Though he learned to read Wordsworth's poetry with joy and to love beautiful things in general, it was, after all, clear thinking that seemed to him most beautiful of all. He had learned it long before on those walks with his father, and he passed it on to his countless followers.

(CONTINUED ON PAGE 729)

Cirrus clouds are delicate feathery detached wisps, usually white, floating very high up in the sky.

A great ceiling of cloud across the sky is a stratus. The one shown above is made up of cumulus clouds.

The GUNPOWDER PLOT

How Guy Fawkes and His Fellow Conspirators Planned to Blow Up King James I and His Parliament

WHEN boys and girls all over England let off fire works and burn a "guy" on November 5, some of them probably know what event they are commemorating, although the small urchins who black their faces regularly during the first week of November, and run about the streets asking for pennies from passers-by, may never have heard of the Gunpowder Plot. But how many children know that on November 5 England remembers the failure of one of the bravest although most merciless conspiracies in history, and the capture and subsequent terrible death of a very gallant gentleman?

A Courageous Soldier of Fortune

Guy (or Guido) Fawkes was a Yorkshireman, and was born in 1570 in the city of York itself. Indeed, the register of his baptism on April 16 of that year may still be seen in the old church of St. Michael-le-Belfry, near the minster. He grew up to be a tall, athletic man, with brown hair and an auburn beard, and, although modest, proved as a soldier of fortune in the Netherlands that he did not lack courage. He was certainly well-read, and, apart from the fanaticism which was to bring him to such an untimely end, he seems to have possessed a self-controlled and probably attractive personality.

Unfulfilled Promises That Led to the Plot

At the time of the plot with which Fawkes's name will always be associated, King James I had sat on the throne of England for two years. Previous to his accession he had been James VI of Scotland, and when on the death of Elizabeth the two crowns became united, the Catholics looked to this son of Mary Queen of Scots to fulfil promises he had made in Scotland, and grant them the toleration which, since the Reformation, they had been denied. James, however, had no intention of keeping those promises, and discontent became widespread among the

THE GUNPOWDER PLOT CONSPIRATORS DISCUSSING THEIR PLANS

Robert Catesby, Guy Fawkes and Thomas Percy, the leading conspirators, are prominent in this group, which shows some of the chief members of the great Gun-powder Plot. One can see at a glance that these were no common murderers, but men who believed that they were striking a blow for their country and religion.

Catholics. This feeling was to reach its climax in the Gunpowder Plot.

The leader of the plot was one Robert Catesby, a man with a great power of influence over others. He came of a very old Catholic family, and his father had already suffered for his beliefs. When the younger Catesby also felt the weight of Protestant persecution, he conceived a bitter hatred against the government. The plot probably originated in a house in Lambeth at a meeting between Catesby, John Wright and Thomas Winter, and the last-named, being finally convinced of the justification of the plot, brought over from the Netherlands Guy Fawkes, an old companion in arms.

Robert Catesby Explains the Plot to His Fellow Conspirators

In the original conspiracy there was one other associated with them—Thomas Percy; but later these five were joined by the brothers of two—Christopher Wright and Robert Winter—together with Robert Keyes, Ambrose Rokewood, John Grant, Sir Everard Digby, Francis Tresham and Thomas Bates; all of them, with the exception of Bates, who was Catesby's serving man, being "gentlemen of name and bloode."

On May 1, 1604, each of the conspirators swore a solemn oath "never to disclose, directly or indirectly, by word or circumstance, the matter that shall be proposed to you, to keep secret nor desist from the execution thereof until the rest shall give you leave," after which Catesby explained the project, which was nothing less than to blow up the House of Lords, when the king went there to open Parliament. In short, the plotters proposed wholesale murder of the king and his ministers, afterwards intending to proclaim as king one of James's children, obtain the guardianship of him, and establish a Catholic rule.

To this end, as Fawkes said in his "Confession," "Thomas Percy hired a howse at Westminster . . . neare adjoyning the Parlt howse, and there wee beganne to make a myne about the XI of December, 1604." But the diggers soon encountered a high wall which they could not penetrate and so, when an opportunity occurred to hire a

cellar immediately beneath the old House of Lords, and belonging to a coal merchant named Bright, they eagerly seized it, and there stored a quantity of gunpowder in barrels, which Guy Fawkes was to explode by a train of powder on the appointed day.

Everything was now in readiness. The king and his court apparently suspected nothing, and it seemed certain that the plot would succeed, when there was delivered one of the most famous letters in history. Even to-day it is not clear which of the conspirators revealed the plot, but certain it is that on October 26, 1605, ten days before the intended opening of Parliament, Lord Mounteagle, one of the commissioners, received a warning which ran as follows:

My lord, out of the love I bear to some of your friends, I have a care of your preservation. Therefore I would advise you, as you tender your life, to devise some excuse to shift of your attendance at this Parliament, for God and man hath concurred to punish the wickedness of this time. And think not slightly of this advertisement, but retire your self into your country, where you may expect the event in safety, for though there be no appearance of any stir, yet I say they shall receive a terrible blow, this Parliament, and yet they shall not see who hurts them. This counsel is not to be condemned, because it may do you good and can do you no harm, for the danger is passed as soon as you have burnt the letter: and I hope God will give you the grace to make good use of it, to whose holy protection I commend you.

Contemporary Account of the Conspiracy Written by the King's Printer

It is interesting to read the description of the occurrence as given by King James's printer, in "A Discourse of the Late Intended Treason." Let it speak for itself:

The Lord Mounteagle, (he writes) son and heir to the Lord Morley, being in his own lodging ready to go to supper at seven of the clock at night, one of his footmen whom he had sent on an errand over the street was met by an unknown man of a reasonable tall personage who delivered him a Letter charging him to put it in my Lord his Master's hands, which my Lord no sooner received but that having broken it up and perceiving the same to be of an unknown and somewhat unlegible hand, and without either date or subscription, did call one of his men unto him for helping him to read it. But no sooner did he conceive the strange contents thereof, although he was somewhat perplexed what construction to make of it . . . yet did he as a most dutiful and loyal subject conclude not to conceal it, whatever might come of it. Whereupon notwithstanding the lateness and darkness of the night in that season of the year, he presently repaired to his Majesty's palace at Whitehall and there delivered the same to the earl of Salisbury, his majesty's principal secretary.

Now the member of Lord Mounteagle's household who read the letter to him was one Thomas Ward, who, being acquainted with Thomas Winter, went to him the next day and revealed the fact that Cecil, earl of Salisbury, knew of the existence of the plot. Winter hastened to White Webbs, a country house where Catesby and other of the conspirators lay concealed, and there attempted to warn Catesby, "assuring him withal that the matter was disclosed and wishing him in anywise to forsake his country." Catesby, however, refused to be warned, and accordingly Guy Fawkes visited the cellar, and there, finding his "private marks" undisturbed, returned to White Webbs confident that all was well.

But the unhappy Fawkes was mistaken. On the evening of November 4 Lord Mounteagle and the earl of Suffolk, the lord chamberlain, descended to the cellar and

Photo by Rischgitz

THE ARREST OF GUY FAWKES

When Guy Fawkes was seized by the soldiers he was discovered to be booted and spurred, ready for instant flight after he had set fire to the gunpowder train. Had his captors not acted immediately, he would have blown them and himself sky-high in a final reckless effort to fulfil his oath. Sir Thomas Knevett is seen on the right.

there discovered the thirty-six barrels of gunpowder and the preparations that had been made to explode it. There, too, they eventually "perceived a fellow standing in a corner, calling himself the said Percyes man and keeper of that house for him, but indeed was Guido Fawkes the owner of that hand which should have acted that monstrous tragedie."

The two noblemen departed and, although uneasy, Fawkes courageously waited to fire his train; but a little after midnight, having occasion to open the door of the cellar, found himself seized by Sir Thomas Knevett, a magistrate of Westminster, who with a band of soldiers had come to arrest him. He was forthwith taken before the king himself, who had but recently returned to London and been told of the plot, after which he was tortured abominably by order of the king to make him reveal the names of his accomplices, which he refused to do, maintaining steadfastly that his name was Johnson, and that he was alone in his attempt to blow up Parliament.

This treatment, which was gradually increased in severity, was carried on for three or four days, until, learning that the conspirators were discovered, he relaxed, scarcely able to sign his name to the "confession" his torturers had prepared for him. Finally, on January 31, 1606, he was hanged, courageous to the last. When he had been arrested he left behind in the cellar his dark lantern, which may still be seen in the Bodleian (bŏd-lē'ăn) Library at Oxford.

Meanwhile the other conspirators fled. They were pursued and finally run to earth at Holbeach House, the residence of Stephen Littleton, where most of them were killed. The rest were captured and brought to London, where they were executed, together with one of three Roman Catholic priests who were suspected of being implicated in the plot. So ended disastrously, but mercifully for the intended victims, the Gunpowder Plot.

The immediate result was an increased persecution of the Catholics, and on November 9, 1605, an act was passed by Parliament for the perpetual solemnization of the anniversary of the projected crime, and a Fifth of November service was inserted in the Common Prayer Book, the day itself being marked in the calendar as the "Papists' Conspiracy." It was not until 1859 that the special service was abolished by an Order in Council of Queen Victoria, together with others for the martyrdom of Charles I and the restoration of Charles II.

But the nation still commemorates the day, although the "guy" has not always represented the original Fawkes. Many people against whom there has been strong public feeling at times have furnished effigies as guys. At one time the burning of guys in London caused a riotous scene in Lincoln's Inn Fields, where all day long on November 5, fuel—often more than two hundred cartloads—arrived, and nearly forty different guys were burned before midnight.

Nowadays queer stuffed effigies of all descriptions are carried about the streets by children, who at night, after all the fireworks have been let off, set fire to them and dance round the flames singing "Guy, guy, guy, stick him up on high," with no idea of vengeance on a plotter of over three hundred years ago.

But the practice is not carried on by children only. Lewes, in Sussex, has six active bonfire societies, and you may see their notices posted up in the streets some time prior to the occasion. Bridgwater also boasts such societies. The commemoration of the discovery of the gunpowder Plot has also been employed to help charitable societies. For instance, on November 5, 1933, a chain of huge bonfires was organized in Essex, and a collection for the blind was taken from the crowds which gathered to watch the burning of them.

Old customs die hard in this land of ours. Even to this day the vaults of the Houses of Parliament are searched before the opening of Parliament! It seems that a long time must elapse before the name of the most famous participant in the Gunpowder Plot is forgotten by the British race.

"PLEASE REMEMBER THE GUY"

This twentieth century "guy" bears little resemblance to the original Guy Fawkes, but he serves the purpose of maintaining an old tradition as well as being the cause of excited cheers as the flames of the bonfire light up his weird figure to the noise of Chinese crackers and squibs.

ROMULUS AND REMUS WAITING FOR A SIGN FROM THE GODS

Romulus and Remus decided to build a city in that place of seven hills where they had been brought up. Since they were twins they could not decide which should give his name to the new city and govern it after it was built; so they left the decision to the gods, and each, with his followers, took his stand upon a hill-top, Romulus upon the Palatine Hill and Remus upon the Aventine. Then they waited for a sign from Heaven. This came in the shape of a flight of birds; but, as usual, the gods only made matters more difficult. For, although Romulus saw twice as many birds as Remus, Remus was first to see the birds. So after all, they had to settle the question by fighting. Romulus killed his brother and named the city Rome, after himself.

The BIRTH of a WORLD EMPIRE

How a Handful of People in a Narrow Strip of Land Gave Rise to the Proud Roman Race Who were Destined to Rule the World

THE ancient nations that lived and died before the rise of Rome had hardly any understanding of what is meant by law and order, or of obeying the law simply because it is the right thing to do, being the only way in which a community can live peacefully. The Egyptians and the Assyrians, and far too often the Greeks also were law-abiding only when they were compelled to be. A strong king or a strong general might force his people to obey him by sentencing to death all who failed to do as he said. And the subjects of such a king would tremble in fear of their lives. But such obedience rested only on the fear of one man. And there could be very little freedom, for there can be freedom only when people are willing to obey the law without any compulsion.

In tracing the story of mankind we find the people of Italy and the people of the city of Rome with minds very different from those of the Oriental peoples or even of the Greeks. The Romans, even when they were still barbarians, had respect for law. They liked to do things according to rule, in a proper and orderly manner. When a law was made they were ready and willing to obey it. They needed no whips or weapons to drive them to obedience. They stood together to uphold the law of the city of Rome, no matter what it cost them to do so.

In a world where every tribe was only too ready to fight its neighbours, a people who could co-operate peaceably was certain to prosper. At first the Latins—of whom the Romans formed a section—were few and weak in comparison with the Etruscans (ĕ-trŭs′kȧn), a people of Italy who had conquered them; and they simply did not count at all beside the Persians and the Egyptians. Yet, because they had learned to work together *pro bono publico*—that is, "for the public good"—they built up, little by little, an empire greater and stronger and more ably governed than any other empire the world had ever seen.

The real history of Rome begins shortly before 500 B.C., when the little city at last struggled free from the line of Etruscan kings who had ruled it for many years. It is true that some famous Roman stories place the founding of Rome more than two centuries earlier, in 753 B.C. For the Romans told many proud stories about the origin and early days of their great city. The most famous of them—we shall tell it a little later—related that the city had been founded by the twin brothers, Romulus and Remus, who had been saved from death in their babyhood by a wolf who nursed them and kept them alive.

But these stories are not historically accurate. What we do know is that the Latin tribe who were one day to found Rome came to Italy not long after 2000 B.C., as a part of the great migration of Indo-Europeans towards the west. It was another wave of the same great race that had penetrated into Greece.

We have little reliable information about the kings who had ruled Rome for some

THE CAPTURE OF THE SABINE MAIDENS

Romulus was soon joined by a large band of hardy men who came, in a pioneer spirit, from every part of the country. When the work of building was practically finished, Romulus realized that without wives to grace the houses and children to play in the streets, his city was not really a city at all, but merely a soldiers' camp. He sent out ambassadors to the neighbouring families to ask for their daughters' hands in marriage. These proposals were scornfully rejected—a bitter blow to the proud young Romans. So during a religious festival, the young men carried off all the maidens of a tribe called the Sabines. In this way they secured wives for themselves.

Photo by Rischgitz

THE FAMOUS TWINS ARE DISCOVERED BY THE SHEPHERD

It is said that at the time when wicked King Amulius gave orders that the twin babies, Romulus and Remus, should be put into a frail basket and set adrift in the waters of the Tiber, that river was in a state of flood. The servants of the king could not get near the deep waters of the stream, so they set the basket in the shallow, flooded area at the river's edge. When the Tiber returned to its normal channel, the little twins were left high and dry in the wild, deserted region that was later to become the centre of all the activity of the ancient world. And there they were found by a she-wolf who had come down to the water to drink. When one of the shepherds of the surrounding hills came upon the scene, he found the wolf feeding the babies with her warm milk and licking them affectionately, as though they were her own cubs. The shepherd took the twins home and placed them in the care of his wife, and there they grew up into strong, courageous youths, whose kingly bearing betrayed their noble blood. With the aid of a band of shepherds, Romulus slew Amulius and set Numitor, his own grandfather, on the throne. Then the twins set themselves to build a city.

time before the real history of the city begins. Some of the names of those kings seem to be merely legendary, and even about the famous Tarquins, who were Etruscans and the last of the kings in Rome, we know very little of which we can be sure. Certainly the kings built up the power of the city, and gave it a formidable army; and just as certainly they were such cruel tyrants that the people finally rose in hatred of them and drove them out of the city of Rome.

Dawn of the Republic

For many a century after that the Romans hated the very name of king. They made up their minds that they would have no such ruler ever to oppress them again. They would rule themselves. So every year the patricians, or noblemen, elected two officers called consuls to manage the affairs of the city. This plan made Rome a republic, although it was a long time before the common people had much voice in the government.

The powerful noblemen soon began to treat the populace very badly. They would often ensure that their own cattle got all the grass on the public lands, which were supposed to be free to all. They made it difficult for a poor man to obtain justice and easy for a rich man to obtain favour in lawsuits. And in many other ways the patrician nobles took advantage of the plebeians (plĕ-bē'yăn), or common people.

Early Roman Government

The common people of Rome, who did most of the work in the city, determined that they must have some voice in the government of the city, or else they would not support the rich nobles. Finally the patricians and the plebeians came to an agreement by which the plebeians were allowed to elect certain officers, called tribunes, to protect them. As time passed, the powers of the tribunes increased until they could set aside any law that they considered unjust, and could veto—cancel or alter—the orders of the consuls. They could even reprieve people who had been sentenced to death. And since the tribunes were themselves of the common people, they were usually ready

Photo by Archives Photographiques

The Romans were a stern race, to whom the honour of the family meant more even than life or death. It is said that Virginius, rather than allow his beautiful daughter Virginia to become the slave of a wicked Roman statesman, snatched up a dagger and stabbed her to the heart in the presence of a crowd of citizens of Rome.

THE BEAUTIFUL LUCRETIA BUSY AT HER HOMELY TASK

Lucretia was one of the most virtuous and industrious of the women of Rome. When other young matrons were banqueting or gossiping with their friends of an evening, Lucretia would stay at home and work far into the night. In the picture above you see her spinning wool while her maidens are sewing. As a matter of fact, her home could not have been nearly so magnificent as shown here, for the early Romans lived very simply.

Photo by Archives Photographiques   From the painting by J. Louis David

THE SABINE WOMEN PLAY THE PART OF PEACEMAKERS

While the fathers of the Sabine women were fighting the Romans to avenge the abduction of their daughters, Hersilia, wife of Romulus, and all the other captive women rushed into the midst of the fray and implored their husbands and fathers to cease fighting. They had grown to love their captors as much as their parents.

to help any commoner who found himself in trouble with the authorities.

At first the consuls took a prominent part in the government of Rome. They heard the lawsuits, led the armies into battle, and collected the taxes. In order to prevent either consul from becoming a tyrant, it was arranged that either one might veto any order of the other. When the two were in command of the same army, one of them gave orders one day and the other the next day, an arrangement that would appear to be far from satisfactory, one which could hardly have worked well for any other people but the Romans, with their genius for government and for law and order.

The Wise Old Men Who Made the Laws

In the course of time, as there was more work than the consuls could do, the people added more officers to the government. Among the new officers were the quaestors (kwĕs′tŏr), who took care of the public money; the censors, who made a voting list of the citizens and kept general watch over their behaviour; and the praetors (prē′tŏr),

who were appointed to act as judges in the various courts of law.

Behind all these officers there was yet another body of men, who made the laws. The Romans believed that old men were the wisest, and from *senex*, a word meaning "old man," they called the assembly of their elders the "senate." Only the nobles, or patricians, could sit in the senate; and a senator was a person of great importance. Often a senator was chosen consul, or a consul senator; so there was a close connection between the two offices.

Just as the common people did not like the consuls to have so much power, so, too, they objected to the great authority of the senate because they had no part in it. There was an assembly called the comitia centuriata (kŏ-mĭsh′ĭ-ȧ sĕn-tū′rĭ-ā′tȧ) in which the plebeians could vote, but their votes did not count for so much as those of the patricians. Another assembly, called the comitia tributa (trĭ-bū′tȧ), gave to each man an equal vote. In it the plebeians had their own way, and after many years this body gained the power of making laws also. Then

Photo by Archives Photographiques

Brutus was the liberator of his country, for he had expelled the tyrants. He was greatly honoured in Rome both for that and for his work in helping to establish a just government. While he was consul, a number of the noble youths of Rome turned traitor and plotted with the Tarquins against their own countrymen. Brutus's own two sons were among the traitors, and here you see him forced to sentence them to death.

From the painting by Henri Motte

THE SACRED GEESE BETRAY THE ENEMIES OF ROME

When the wild Gauls from the north came swarming down, they found the city of Rome undefended by walls. It was a simple matter for them to enter and do as much burning and plundering as they wished. Only the fort on the Capitoline Hill, with its steep walls and battlements, held out. Legend has it that when the Gauls attempted to climb the walls in the night, they awoke the sacred geese, whose fierce cackling soon warned the Romans.

they decreed that plebeians might sit in the senate and be quaestors or censors. Before the Roman republic came to an end, the common citizens had almost as many rights as the patricians.

The Centre of Power in Rome

The real centre of power in Rome was always the senate. There were three hundred senators, and they were men who had had a great deal of experience in the government or in the army. In time of war or rebellion they could meet and discuss the best policy to pursue, and then advise the consuls in the management of the affair. The Roman senate worked far better than the Greek assembly had ever done. It had its problems, and there were evil and corrupt senators; but, in the earlier days especially, the Roman senate consisted of wise and fearless men who guided the state with great skill.

All this goes to show what an orderly people the Romans were. They were not curious like the Greeks, nor were their main interests centred in poetry, in art, and in philosophy, but they had a genius for government and for building up an empire.

When the Romans extended their power over the neighbouring tribes in Italy, they did not oppress their victims as the Etruscans had done, and turn them into slaves and foes; they gave the conquered people a share in the Roman state, and protected them from other enemies. Gradually the city of Rome came to be looked upon as a guardian and a guide by the very nations that had been struggling against her.

Because the Romans were so business-like

Photo by Anderson

A BRAVE MAN LOOKS INTO THE FACE OF DEATH

All but the members of the senate fled from Rome after the victory of the Gauls. When the Gauls entered the senate house, they found the senators dressed in their purple-edged garments of state and seated like statues on their ivory chairs. The Gauls, stricken with awe, thought they must be gods. But one, consumed with curiosity, started to finger the beard of an aged senator who, incensed at the insult to his dignity, hit the Gaul over the head. In this way the spell was broken, and all the brave senators were immediately put to death.

HOW THE SACRED FIRE OF VESTA WAS KEPT BURNING

The vestals were the maiden priestesses of Vesta, goddess of the hearth of home and state. It was their privilege to tend the sacred fire of Rome to keep it burning. They were highly honoured by the people, for it was believed that if the fire of Vesta ever died out, some dreadful calamity would fall upon the city. Above, you see them fleeing from the attack of an enemy, but carrying away with them a brand from the sacred fire.

and careful, they often seem to us rather cold and heartless. Probably they were no worse than other people of their time, but they certainly lacked the fire and the imagination of the Greeks. When a Roman went to make a sacrifice he was not likely to see little piping gods peeping at him from the woodlands. He heard no laughter of nymphs in the forests. He missed the gaiety and charm and joyousness of a true lover of the pagan gods.

A Roman's sacrifice was a matter of business. When he presented a fine fat lamb to Juno he expected her in return to grant him what he wished. The Romans were religious; but their religion, like their lives and their thinking, was a matter-of-fact affair, almost devoid of imagination.

What Rome Borrowed from Greece

The Romans borrowed many of their gods from the Greeks, just as they adopted the Greek alphabet and the Greek method of shipbuilding. They changed the names of the gods, however. The Greek god Zeus became the Roman Jove or Jupiter; Hera became Juno; Hermes became Mercury. Practically every Greek god appears in Rome under another name.

Although the Romans had no such rich and beautiful myths, or stories of their gods, as did the Greeks, they had their own legends of the way their city was founded. They believed that a Trojan prince named Aeneas (ĕ-nē'ăs) had fled from the sack of Troy and had sailed to Italy, after many adventures. He and his followers lived with the Latins and built a city among them, so that many Romans held the belief that they were descended from the Trojans.

Romulus and Remus

The Romans believed that long after the days of Aeneas, one of the priestesses in the temple of the goddess Vesta had been beloved by the god Mars, and had borne him twin sons named Romulus (rŏm'ū-lŭs) and Remus (rē'-mŭs). The boys were hated by the king of the country, who set them adrift on the river Tiber. But they were rescued from death by a she-wolf, who nursed them until a shepherd found them and took care of them. When the twins were grown up, Romulus built the great city of Rome.

The story is only a myth, although it may have some tiny kernel of fact. The Romans had other legends, too, about ancient kings like Numa, the lawgiver, and heroes who lived in the early days of the city.

Rome Extends Her Boundaries

In the story of the Etruscans we have explained how the city of Rome grew up as a trading place where the Etruscan ships could come in from the sea and bargain with the Romans. But when the Romans began to feel their strength, and finally succeeded in throwing off the Etruscan yoke, they were not given time to enjoy their freedom. There were other enemies close at hand.

First they joined with their Latin cousins to fight the bandits of the hill country. The union gave the allies a territory of about 350 square miles. It does not appear to us a very extensive area for a country to cover, but it probably seemed quite spacious to them at that time. After expanding their boundaries in this way, they looked about and saw the Etruscan city of Veii (vē′yī), only a few miles distant.

The Etruscan power was crumbling, and the Romans did not feel that Veii was too strong to be attacked. They laid siege to the city and for ten years they struggled desperately to capture it. At last, in 396 B.C., Veii surrendered.

With this enemy removed from their gates the Romans were ready once more for peace; but almost immediately they met with a serious check, which almost ended the existence of the little state. Wild barbarians, called Gauls, had been sweeping down from the north of Italy, and in 390 B.C. they descended upon Rome, beat the Roman army, took the city, and burned it to the ground.

But they could not capture the fortress on the Capitoline (kăp′ĭ-tṓ-līn) Hill, and after a few weeks the Romans paid their

Photo by Alinari

From the painting by J. Louis David

THREE BROTHERS WHO WERE READY TO DIE FOR ROME

In the early days of Rome a great struggle arose between the Romans and the Albans, a neighbouring tribe. Each wanted to rule the other's land, but after many battles, which only served to weaken both parties, neither side emerged victorious. It chanced that in each of the armies there were triplet brothers who were well matched in age and strength, and it was decided that they should fight it out among themselves, each for his own country. Whichever side lost would come under the rule of the other. The Horatii (hŏ-rā′shi-ī), whom you see above taking an oath to fight to the death, belonged to the Roman side, and the Curiatii (kū-rĭ-ā′shĭ-ī) to the Alban. All the inhabitants of both cities congregated to watch the thrilling contest. At first it seemed that Alba would succeed, for two of the Horatii were killed and all three of the Curiatii fell upon the remaining brother, who then took to flight. But he was no coward; his flight was merely a clever plan to fight his enemies separately. He killed each of the Curiatii in turn, and so won the day for Rome.

enemies a heavy ransom and persuaded them to return to the north.

The reason the Gauls were able to take Rome so easily was that the city had no walls. The practical Romans therefore set to work at once and built good strong stone walls round their city. After that they felt safe, and again they hoped that law and order might were not remarkably daring as soldiers. They were able to triumph in the end because they were so steady and so patient. They possessed good and wise leadership, steadfastness, bravery, and coolness. The same qualities which made their government great made their armies great also.

When the Samnites, from southern Italy,

Photo by Anderson

BLIND APPIUS ABOUT TO MAKE HIS MIGHTY SPEECH

When Pyrrhus of Epirus sent ambassadors to Rome to make a peace pact, the blind old censor, Appius Claudius, persuaded the senate not to listen to any proposals of peace as long as the army of Pyrrhus remained on Italian soil. Appius is the earliest writer mentioned in Roman literature, for his brilliant speech was written down—the first time such a thing had been done in Rome. It established a form of prose composition. Above you see the blind old man being led in to make his impassioned appeal for his country's honour.

prevail. But many weak cities or tribes kept asking for help, and the Romans always went to their assistance. Each victory brought them a little more land.

The tribes living near grew fearful when they saw the power of Rome growing, and the Latins formed a league to resist the progress of the state. For ten years the Latin League fought Rome, country against city. But Rome finally emerged victorious in 338 B.C., and the Latin League was broken. Then Rome marched on to the conquest of all Italy.

Yet we must not think of the Romans as thirsting for empire in those days, as the Assyrians had thirsted for it a few centuries before. If Rome had not fought she would have been destroyed. It was a question of conquering or being conquered.

For all their bravery, the early Romans advanced upon Rome and attacked the Roman army again and again, in wars which lasted for many years, the Romans persistently fought them off. The Samnites had little discipline or leadership or organization. They were as wild as the Gauls, and as brutal and fierce. Finally the Samnites, combined with the Etruscans and the Gauls themselves, were beaten by the Romans in the terrific battle of Sentinum (sĕn-tī'nŭm) in 295 B.C.

After the battle of Sentinum there was no doubt that Rome was the strongest power in Italy. She had conquered the whole peninsula except the far north and the Greek cities in the south, and with high hopes the Romans set about completing their conquest.

But, here again, Rome met with defeat after defeat. The Greek cities united for a

719

time under Pyrrhus (pir'us), king of Epirus (ĕ-pī'-rŭs), from across the Adriatic Sea. And the united Greeks defeated the Romans at Heraclea (hĕr'ă-klē'ă) in 280 B.C. and again in the following year. But Pyrrhus lost so many of his own men defeating the Romans that he declared a few more such victories would ruin him; and from that day to this a victory that costs the winner too much has been called a "Pyrrhic" victory. Moreover, the Greeks fell to quarrelling among themselves, as usual; and Pyrrhus returned home in disgust, leaving the Romans to take one Greek city after another.

By 275 B.C. Rome was supreme in Italy. In the short space of sixty-five years she had grown from a struggling little city, fighting for bare existence, to a powerful state controlling the entire peninsula.

Never before had Italy been under one government. From the Greeks in the south to the Gauls in the north there were numerous tribes who spoke several different languages. These tribes had always fought

A PROPHETESS OF ANCIENT ROME

This strange, wind-swept figure is the sibyl of Cumae (kū'mē), the most famous of the prophetesses of Rome. Under her arm she clutches the three books of prophecies which she finally sold to Tarquin the Proud, one of the legendary kings of Rome. The story goes that there were originally nine books which the sibyl (sɪb'ɪl) offered to sell for a large sum. Tarquin tried to bargain with her, but the clever prophetess calmly destroyed three of the books and offered the king the remaining six at the same price. Tarquin again refused the offer—and the sibyl promptly destroyed three more books. Then she offered the remaining three, still for the same amount. Fearing that the volumes might all vanish, Tarquin bought the remaining three. The sibyl pronounced an opinion on many an ancient matter. It was her cave that Aeneas visited to discover the will of the gods; and the sibyl herself escorted him to the awful realms of Hades. Quite recently excavators have found the famous cave—the very one which Virgil describes. In the heart of Mount Cuma, in Southern Italy, are a number of rock-cut galleries which lead to a large subterranean chamber carefully hewn from the living rock. This is the spot where the sibyl, intoxicated by the fumes that rose from the sacred tripods, spoke the prophecies which people came from all over the ancient world to hear. The excavators have discovered many of the wise woman's secrets. A clever arrangement of sounding boards and rock-cut speaking tubes made a voice issue mysteriously from the centre of the earth and appear to come from every side—as Virgil and many another visitor testified. As for the three famous books, known as the Sibylline (sɪb'ɪ-lɪn) Books, they were for many years kept in the temple of Jupiter in Rome, under the care of specially appointed officials, and were consulted in times of great crisis.

one another except when occasionally they combined for the purpose of fighting someone else. Now they were to know the *Pax Romana*, "Roman Peace." They were to become loyal members of the Roman state, and to live peacefully with one another.

How did the Romans manage to control so many foreign and unruly peoples? What genius enabled them to win over the turbulent and self-willed tribes? The answer is that they were wise enough not to oppress but to encourage the people they conquered.

Instead of treating their defeated enemies like slaves, as the Greeks had done after their conquests, the Romans raised some of their former enemies to equality with themselves, while to others they held out the promise of a like equality. At the same time the Romans warned them that if they did not behave themselves they would lose their equal rights. The better class of people were made citizens of Rome. They could then trade freely in any Roman colony; they could use the Roman law courts; and they could marry with Romans.

Besides all these privileges, the Romans allowed each city or tribe to continue to govern itself in its own way, except that it could maintain no army. The army of Rome would protect it; and in return for this protection the conquered state would send soldiers to serve with the Roman army

Why the Romans Were Prevented from Leaving Their Native Shores

The population of Rome itself was increasing so fast that the citizens frequently sent out colonists to settle in some captured territory. This helped to strengthen the bond between Rome and her subjects.

The Romans began as a race of farmers, and even in 275 B.C. they were mostly tillers of the soil. When the poorer Romans went wandering about Italy they usually took to farming. They also reared large families, with many boys who could fight in the army. Thus Rome was always looking for more land for its citizens to farm.

If the Romans had all been farmers, perhaps the conquest of Italy would have satisfied them; but the richer people had become merchants and traders. Like the Phoenicians and the Greeks, they enjoyed travelling about, buying and selling goods. They travelled all over Italy, and they would have liked to sail to other lands as well.

But there were two disadvantages which prevented the Romans from leaving their native shores. First of all, they had few ships, for they were still very poor sailors. And secondly, the seas were ruled by a foreign and unfriendly power.

A city far richer and more powerful than Rome was ruling the western Mediterranean with a jealous hand. Proud Carthage (kär'-thảj) was queen of the seas. Carthage was situated in Northern Africa, just across from Sicily. Founded by the Phoenicians, it had grown to great wealth under the influence of its merchant princes.

The power of Carthage extended along the coast of Africa. Half of Sicily was under its domination. The Strait of Gibraltar and the tin mines of the British Isles were closed to all but Carthaginian ships. Many coast towns were held for trade by Carthage only.

The galleys of Carthage swept the seas, and their captains turned a scornful eye upon the puny sea power of Rome. The ships of Carthage would brook no interference with their trade, and to this the Romans had agreed in treaties arranged long before.

Rome Looks On While Carthage Rules the Sea-roads of the World

But could Rome, fresh from the conquest of all Italy, endure this state of things? Not while the Tiber flowed to the sea. With Roman arms and Roman persistence, a path for trade could be made to encircle the world if need be.

But, however indignant the Roman senate and the Roman citizens might be, they could not at once plunge into war with Carthage. True, they had a wonderful army three hundred thousand strong, but it was not within fighting distance of Africa. There was no Roman navy to carry troops and ram the Carthaginian battleships. Rome could not fight Carthage without ships.

For ten or eleven years after conquering Italy, the Romans rested sullenly on their arms, while the graceful galleys of Carthage plied their trade across the seas. Carthage was old and experienced in the ways of the world. She felt that she had nothing whatever to fear from her enemy in the north.

(CONTINUED ON PAGE 749)

This benevolent old man is Father Tiber. The Greeks and Romans thought of their rivers as people— and very kindly people too, for they knew that the streams brought trade and fertile fields, and consequently wealth into their coffers.

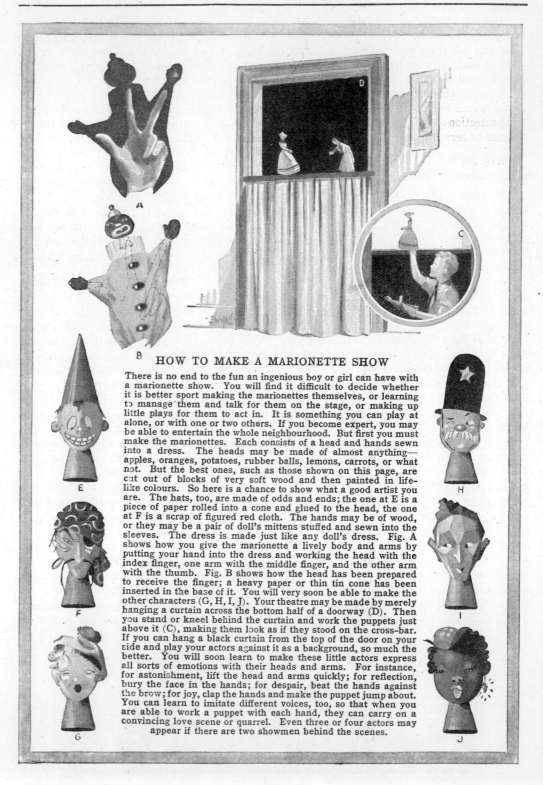

HOW TO MAKE A MARIONETTE SHOW

There is no end to the fun an ingenious boy or girl can have with a marionette show. You will find it difficult to decide whether it is better sport making the marionettes themselves, or learning to manage them and talk for them on the stage, or making up little plays for them to act in. It is something you can play at alone, or with one or two others. If you become expert, you may be able to entertain the whole neighbourhood. But first you must make the marionettes. Each consists of a head and hands sewn into a dress. The heads may be made of almost anything—apples, oranges, potatoes, rubber balls, lemons, carrots, or what not. But the best ones, such as those shown on this page, are cut out of blocks of very soft wood and then painted in life-like colours. So here is a chance to show what a good artist you are. The hats, too, are made of odds and ends; the one at E is a piece of paper rolled into a cone and glued to the head, the one at F is a scrap of figured red cloth. The hands may be of wood, or they may be a pair of doll's mittens stuffed and sewn into the sleeves. The dress is made just like any doll's dress. Fig. A shows how you give the marionette a lively body and arms by putting your hand into the dress and working the head with the index finger, one arm with the middle finger, and the other arm with the thumb. Fig. B shows how the head has been prepared to receive the finger; a heavy paper or thin tin cone has been inserted in the base of it. You will very soon be able to make the other characters (G, H, I, J). Your theatre may be made by merely hanging a curtain across the bottom half of a doorway (D). Then you stand or kneel behind the curtain and work the puppets just above it (C), making them look as if they stood on the cross-bar. If you can hang a black curtain from the top of the door on your side and play your actors against it as a background, so much the better. You will soon learn to make these little actors express all sorts of emotions with their heads and arms. For instance, for astonishment, lift the head and arms quickly; for reflection, bury the face in the hands; for despair, beat the hands against the brow; for joy, clap the hands and make the puppet jump about. You can learn to imitate different voices, too, so that when you are able to work a puppet with each hand, they can carry on a convincing love scene or quarrel. Even three or four actors may appear if there are two showmen behind the scenes.

BLOW, WINDS, BLOW!

The Breezes that Fan Our Farms and Cities are Just as Useful as Those that Bring the Sailors Home from Sea

(CONTINUED FROM PAGE 698)

WHAT a monotonous place the world would be if we had no winds! No gentle breeze would ever come to comfort us on a stifling day. No boisterous blast would ever rumple our clothes, and tease us by snatching our hats away or blowing umbrellas inside out in the midst of pouring rain. And no gigantic friend, with powerful, tireless arms, would turn our windmills for us, or help us fly our kites.

Sometimes the winds have an uncertain temper. They are all the time veering about, and the weather vane seems to be the busiest thing for miles around. But the gusty, changeable fellows that whistle round our chimneys are caused by the very same force as are the great winds of the earth—the romantic "trade winds" and the "roaring forties."

All winds, whether they work on the

Photo by the Tourist Information Office, The Hague

In Holland the wind is put to work driving picturesque mills, which are to be seen in every part of the country. As the great arms whirl round they grind the farmer's wheat and perform many other useful jobs.

farm or sail the ships at sea, are caused by the ceaseless exchange of the heated air towards the Equator for the colder air of the latitudes farther north and south, including the poles. It is the never-ending contrast of temperatures, all the way from the Equator to the poles, that starts the air sweeping and swirling along the ground.

As you know, the winds in the north temperate zone blow generally from west to east, but instead of roaring along at forty miles an hour they are so broken by mountains and forests that it is only at a height of some three miles that they run smoothly. Near the ground they are twisted and whirled so madly that there is no telling from whence they will be coming next.

The winds that bring us most of our weather form themselves into vast wheels, which the meteorologist (mē′tē-ŏ-rŏl′ŏ-jĭst) calls "cyclones." These must not be confused with tornadoes—those terrors of the Central United States—that can destroy a town in a few minutes. The real cyclone is a whirl so vast and so majestic that no one over whom it passes would know the wind was turning at all. It may be a thousand miles or more across, and wherever it passes it distributes the weather that it always carries wrapped up in its circling folds. Slowly it moves along from west to east with such a regular motion that the meteorologist can tell, as a rule, just where it will go and just about how long it will take to get there. In this way he can foretell what weather may be expected at any given place.

How the Cyclones Whirl

In the northern half of the globe such cyclones always whirl in the same direction —in the way opposite to that in which the hands of a clock go, or, as we say, "anticlockwise." That means that on its eastern edge the wind is blowing north and on its western edge it is blowing south. The wind at the north of the cyclone blows from the east and at the south from the west. Such are the great whirls that you see on any map of the weather. At their centre is the word "Low"—there and to the east it is usually raining.

The March of the Cyclones

One after another they appear from the Pacific, sweep across North America and out over the Atlantic. Constantly changing, growing, joining up and dividing, they reach the west of Europe, usually passing to the north of the British Isles, and finally dying out into the waste of the Arctic Ocean or the great deserts of Asia. In their wake comes the weather, hot, cold, moist or dry, whatever it may be. Between them are masses of cooler

This great cloud is a sandstorm. As the wind passes over a dry country it gathers up many tons of sand that it often carries for several hundreds of miles. That is also the cause of the simooms experienced in the desert.

THE TERRIBLE WIND THAT LEAVES DESTRUCTION IN ITS PATH

This is the whirling funnel that sucks up houses and trees and men. In some parts of America tornadoes have caused such loss of life that people have taken to building dug-outs, like the one above, in which to take refuge. Whenever they see a " twister " coming in the south-west and there is no dug-out near, they run as fast as they can towards the north or north-west. A tornado's path usually lies from south-west to north-east, and is rarely as much as a quarter of a mile wide. When the storm strikes, it is best to lie face downwards, in a depression if possible, with the arms stretched out ahead. In the inset is a picture of a pine board, 10 feet by 3 inches by 1 inch, which a tornado has driven right through a palm tree trunk without breaking the board.

air—known as "anti-cyclones" and marked "High"—where the weather is fine; in winter, the anti-cyclones bring us our cold weather.

The southern half of the globe has its own procession of great whirls, but as there is hardly any land to break them up, they march in a much more orderly and regular procession.

Typhoons and Hurricanes

But winds that begin whirling are not always so well-behaved as the ones that deal out the weather over Europe and the United States. When vast whirls of that kind form over tropical seas, they can work up a terrific speed and bring destruction to many a gallant ship. Such are the storms that are known as "hurricanes" on the Atlantic Ocean; and such are the dreaded "typhoons" (tī-foon') of the China Sea.

Hurricanes forming over the West Indies often travel in a great curve, first north-west across the islands, flooding the towns and destroying the crops, and then north-east along the Atlantic coast of the United States, where they sometimes wreck whole cities. Fortunately, their progress can be foretold, and people and ships in the zone of danger can be warned in good time.

The Terror of the Prairie

The most terrible whirlwind of all is the "tornado." It may start in much the same way as the little eddies of dust that spring

When a tornado is formed at sea its funnel sucks up great quantities of water, as shown above. If such a waterspout hits a small vessel, it may be the end of the gallant little craft.

up in the street on a windy summer's day when two opposing breezes collide and start spinning, just as you spin round when you collide with a playmate. But a tornado forms in the clouds of a thunderstorm where the air begins to whirl so fast that it forms a gigantic black funnel, the narrow end of which finally comes down to earth. The top is not often more than half a mile wide, and the whirling base that levels forest and town is usually only a few hundred yards across.

But the speed at which the whirl travels is tremendous—so fast that the meteorologist's instruments cannot measure it, though he knows that it must sometimes be more than three hundred miles an hour. No wonder it can snatch up trees by the roots, pick up a house and spin it, and crush a steel bridge as if it were made of matches!

It may drive a stiff blade of grass into soft wood or the bark of a tree, and has been known to leave chickens completely plucked. Sucking up dust and wreckage into its tube, the whirling funnel sweeps along and leaves a path of death and destruction behind it—sometimes for as many as two hundred miles. Settlers in the West often construct a "dug-out" in which they can take refuge when a "twister" looms up on the horizon.

If a tornado passes over a river or a lake its tube sucks up large quantities of water. At sea this is called a waterspout, and it is sometimes powerful enough to destroy any small vessels lying in its path.

In various parts of the world there are winds that have developed little habits of their own, and have even grown as famous as the gallant "trade winds" or the blustering "roaring forties." The "mistral" (mĭs'trăl) in Southern France is drawn down from the north-west by the rising of warm air over the Mediterranean. It is a wind sung by poets and woven into the lives of the people. From a gentle little breeze that cools the weary peasants in summer it can rise to a winter's gale that will bowl a horse over. It is dry and bracing, and brings a sparkling sky.

Southern Asia has its famous "monsoons" (mŏn-sōon') which, for six months of the year, blow from the land out over the sea, and in the opposite direction for the other six months. In fact, the word "monsoon" means "season," and the name has been given to these winds because they blow with the seasons. During the winter, when the land is cold, the air above it is drawn seaward by the rising of warmer air over the Indian Ocean. This makes a cold, dry wind. But when the sun is high enough to heat the land till it is warmer than the sea, the wind turns about and begins blowing inland. It is a dramatic moment—this turning of the monsoon—for all the people in these hot lands. For the sea wind brings them rain to grow their crops, and so carries in its bosom life or death for India's crowding millions.

The same thing happens on a small scale every day along nearly all sea-coasts. Under the rays of the sun the air above the land is warmed until the cooler sea air pushes it up and rushes inland for a few miles. For the land is always heated more rapidly than the sea; but it cools more rapidly, too. So during the night there comes a time when the sea air is warmer, and is forced to rise by the pressure of colder and heavier land air. Then the breeze wheels about and steals gently out to sea. So the sea breeze is a day breeze, and the land breeze a night breeze.

Out in the Rocky Mountains there is a west wind known as the "chinook" (chĭ-

The sea-breeze that springs up in the daytime on almost any coast is caused by the rising of hot air over the heated land, and the consequent flowing in of cooler air from the sea, which does not get hot so fast under the sun's rays. The arrows in the picture below show the direction of the sea-breeze.

As soon as the land cools off at night, a land-breeze springs up at sea. For the water is much slower to change its temperature than is the land, and so keeps the air above it warm long after the land and its air have cooled. As the night advances and the air over the land gets colder and colder, the warm sea air is forced up by the heavier cold air beside it. This sets up a current of air flowing out over the surface of the sea.

nōok'), supposedly named from an Indian word meaning "snow eater." When it starts to climb the western mountains it is loaded with moisture. Then it cools on top of the heights, and drops its vapour in the form of rain or snow. When it comes down the eastern slopes it is a warm, dry wind that heats the earth and turns broad acres that would otherwise be too cold to bear crops into the rich farm and grazing lands of Alberta, Montana and Idaho. A wind of much the same kind, called the "föhn" (fōn), climbs over the Alps in Europe and warms the lands situated upon the northern side.

There is another dry, warm breeze less welcome to the people who feel it. This is the famous "sirocco" that blows from off the Sahara, carrying a fine red dust sometimes as far north as Sicily. When chilled it gives up its moisture, and sometimes drops blood-red rain—so heavily has it been loaded with ruddy desert sands.

All deserts have fierce dust storms—or "simooms" (sĭ-mōōm′)—before which men and animals must crouch and turn their backs until the fury is past. On the Colorado Desert they blow sometimes as hard as seventy-five miles an hour. A large part of China has been turned into a flowering garden by terrible winds from off the Gobi Desert that have made up for their violence by scattering fertile desert soil wherever they blow.

In England a west wind usually brings us mild and genial weather, with a little rain to freshen things up. An east wind is disagreeable—dry and dusty, bitingly cold in winter and hot in summer. A south-east wind shifting or "veering" towards south-west usually foretells rain, but if in winter a south-east wind "backs" towards north-east, look out for snow.

The winds can blow at all strengths from the lightest air to a roaring gale, and we have learnt to tell their speed from their effects. A breeze just strong enough to rustle the leaves of the trees is blowing at four or five miles an hour. At thirteen miles an hour it raises dust and loose paper, and at nineteen rocks small trees in leaf. Only a strong man can walk in the teeth of a gale of forty miles an hour, and a wind with twice this speed is four times as powerful, so you can easily imagine the effect of a wind of a hundred miles an hour such as has blown occasionally over our own island.

(CONTINUED ON PAGE 759)

Photo by Ollivier

THE DREADED SAND-STORM OF THE DESERT

A sand-storm in the desert brings terror to man and beast. At its approach the camels are made to kneel, and beside them their masters take shelter, with faces covered to keep out the smothering dust. We who live near the green fields or in the paved streets of a city have not any idea how blinding such a storm can be.

A GIANT *Among the* NOVELISTS

Failing as an Artist, William Makepeace Thackeray Eventually Succeeded in Becoming One of the Great Masters of Fiction

(CONTINUED FROM PAGE 704)

AT THE age of twenty-five the great novelist Thackeray felt sure he was a complete failure. He had tried the law, as his mother wanted him to do, and found it altogether too dull. He had also failed at the one thing he himself wanted to do. He cherished a great desire to become an artist, but when he had his drawings for the "Pickwick Papers" of Charles Dickens rejected by the author of the book, he realized it was no use trying to make a living at painting. He had actually practised drawing ever since he had been a very small boy, and had later spent long years in Paris sketching and studying art.

But his work was not very popular, and he had to find some other way of making money to support himself and his young wife. The money he had inherited from his father had all been lost through the failure of a bank and his own bad investments. In real need, he turned at last to writing; and so his early failures turned out to be a piece of good fortune for Thackeray and also for all the world.

From the drawing by Fred Barnard

Above you may see one of the immortal characters in English literature—Becky Sharp. She trips through the pages of Thackeray's "Vanity Fair" with a daintiness and cleverness that forces us to admire her, even though we know that at heart she is thoroughly selfish. We can say with truth that her name is well suited to her character.

William Makepeace Thackeray was born in Calcutta, India, on July 18, 1811, the son of an agent of the East India Company, who died when the boy was still very young. At five the little fellow was brought to England to be educated, first at two private schools and later at Charterhouse School in London, where he spent a great deal too much time in general reading, drawing, and acting to become a very good scholar.

After six years there he was sent to Cambridge, but before long he decided that travel and study on the Continent would be better for him than a university education. So he went off to Italy, France and Germany, studying a little but devoting most of his time to sketching and to talking with his interesting friends. Then came all the troubles of which we have mentioned, followed by his work as an author of fiction.

Even then it took him some time to win real fame. The first of his writings were witty and humorous little stories for the magazines, some of them for the newly-founded "Punch." These were fairly popular, but were not published under his own name; so it was not until his first novels appeared that his success was assured. "Vanity Fair," published under his own name and illustrated with his own drawings, took its place at once as one of the great novels of the day.

In this book, as in "Henry Esmond," "The Newcomes," and "Pendennis," he probably gives us as perfect a picture of life among the upper classes in England as any other writer has ever drawn. And the people in his books are just as real as the men and women round us. There is the fascinating Becky Sharp, in "Vanity Fair," and the admirable Colonel Newcome, in the novel that bears his family name; these and many others stand out in the books like living men and women, who can never be forgotten.

In writing about them Thackeray felt so deeply that they were his friends that he used to laugh at their follies and cry over their misfortunes. One day, when he was writing "The Newcomes," he ran out of his study sobbing. "I have just killed Colonel Newcome!" he said. And when Helen Pendennis died, he wept again.

In the midst of all his success and fame, Thackeray's life was saddened by the long

Arthur Pendennis, the hero of Thackeray's novel "The History of Arthur Pendennis," while studying for the Bar shared a room with George Warrington, who, in the picture, is seen wiping a gridiron. Warrington is one of the most kindly and lovable of Thackeray's immortal characters.

illness of his wife, which finally led to her becoming insane. Left to take care of his young daughters and to struggle against poverty, he had a life that was far from easy, but he always remained cheerful and lovable in spite of his troubles. Although he has often been said to be a little cruel in his books, he was always gracious and kindly in his life. He once told Dickens that he could "never see a boy without wanting to give him a sovereign"; and one of his great desires was "to write something really good for children."

In 1851 Thackeray gave a series of lectures on the "English Humorists of the Eighteenth Century," which he had written that year, and the following year he repeated the lectures in America. Two years later he published that charming burlesque "The Rose and the Ring." He edited the celebrated "Cornhill Magazine" from 1859 to 1862, and continued to contribute to it until his sudden death on December 24, 1863.

Thackeray is known everywhere as one of the world's greatest novelists. His "Henry Esmond" has been proclaimed by some critics as the finest historical novel in the English language, and his "Vanity Fair" as one of the greatest of social satires, for in it Thackeray makes fun of the vanities and failings of men and women.

Which AUTHOR GAVE US *the* MOST FAMOUS CHARACTERS?

Next to Shakespeare, It was Charles Dickens; and Here You Will Read How He Came to Create Them

HAVE you ever met Mr. Micawber? If you have not yet had this pleasure, you can meet him in the great novel of "David Copperfield." You will find him a genteel humbug, always just a step from the debtor's jail, always waiting for "something to turn up" and save him. Some of Micawber's characteristics were suggested by the father of the man who wrote the novel, the immortal Charles Dickens (1812–1870).

No boy with a Micawber for a father would be expected to grow up into a great novelist, and the way in which Dickens did it is a moving and exciting story.

He was born in Landport, near Portsea, and at the age of two was taken to live in London; two years later the family went to Chatham, where the boy began to grow up. As soon as he had learned his letters he started reading all the great novels for which he found time, but often there was not very much time. At the age of eleven he was back in London again, living in one of the poorest suburbs, where the people were huddled in rows of houses in dingy streets, and where a good meal was an unusual event. The poor around him lived in constant terror of the workhouse, and the young children had to go out to work for next to nothing.

Young Charles Dickens Finds Employment in a Blacking Factory

Charles Dickens went to work like many of the others. His father had been im-

Photo by National Portrait Gallery

Charles Dickens was also a gifted actor; this portrait of him shows the fine eyes and expressive countenance which helped to make his readings from his novels so great a delight to the audiences of his day.

prisoned for debt, a fate that he was to meet many more times. The mother tried to set up a school, and the little boy went round leaving circulars at doors to advertise it, but the school was a failure. Then Charles went to work in a factory, pasting labels on the pots of blacking that were made there. It was an evil place, and the other boys were very rough indeed, but here Dickens had to work for long hours to earn a few shillings a week.

Yet he never would have been anything like the man he was, never would have written the kind of novels with which he charmed the world, if he had not worked in the blacking factory and lived the miserable life of the slums, with a father often in jail. He knew more about these slums, and all the kinds of people in them, than anybody else in his day. He put hundreds of those people into his novels, and so gave the world its greatest picture gallery of rogues and cheats, of rascals and eccentrics, of wretches and saints and heroes from the slums.

A little stroke of luck in the form of some money which came to his father enabled the boy to leave the blacking factory and go back to school again for a short time. Then he became an office boy to a lawyer, and began to learn all about the sharpers of the law whom he put into so many of his novels. He already longed to be a writer, and the best way he knew of starting was to get work as a reporter for a paper. Long into the night he would sit up learning shorthand; and at length he became a reporter for the papers in the press gallery of the House of Commons, where he could take down the speeches in shorthand faster than anyone else.

Then a paper published one of his original little stories, and he was so full of joy that he could hardly see his way along the street. After that he began a series of sketches that he signed with the name of Boz. He had playfully called his younger brother "Moses,"

Magazine." They drew from a publisher a request for other sketches, just to go with some humorous drawings by one of the great artists of the day. So Dickens started his famous "Pickwick Papers." But it was soon realized that these were so much better than the pictures as to eclipse them; and the "Pickwick Papers," with their wealth of humour and their queer but lovable characters, first showed the world what Charles Dickens could do. They were received with the greatest enthusiasm, and proved to be the foundation of the author's literary career.

Dickens could portray comedy and drama, farce and melodrama, and we see them all separately or combined in characters like Mr. Pickwick and his friends, Mr. Winkle and Mr. Snodgrass, with his marvellous servant Sam Weller and the almost equally marvellous father of that servant; with the rascally Jingle, the scoundrelly lawyers Dodson and Fogg, the brow-beating Serjeant Buzfuz, and all the other immortal people in this one book. In giving us characters like these Dickens outclassed anybody who had ever written stories before him. In giving us such characters he became and remained a master of his craft. And in a whole series of novels, during the rest of his life, he continued to portray the queer characters that we come to know as if we had lived with them.

From the drawing by Fred Barnard

MR. PICKWICK AT PEACE WITH THE WORLD

This is the immortal Mr. Pickwick, who never really walked the earth but who is nevertheless much better known to-day than he would be if he had lived in the flesh. For he is one of the great creations of the novelist Charles Dickens, and has been the intimate friend of thousands upon thousands of people.

and had pronounced it "Bozes," as if he had a cold in the head; and this he had shortened to "Boz."

These "Sketches by Boz," caricatures of the ordinary people of the street and market-square, appeared chiefly in "The Old Monthly

If someone could line up the hundreds of men and women from Dickens's novels in a long row, dressed just as he dressed them

Gathered round this portrait of Dickens are some of the creations of his gifted mind, all old friends, many of whom you will probably be able to name from their queer clothes or from the situation in which you see them.

and talking just as he made them talk—if someone could only do this, we should not have the least difficulty in passing along the line and picking out every one of them. "You are Peggotty, of course," we should be saying; "you are Barkis, you are Bill Sikes, you are Dick Swiveller, you are Scrooge, you are Little Nell, you are Fagin" —and so on.

There is hardly any other author except Shakespeare of whom we could say that.

And that is the glory of Charles Dickens, creator of character. On this his great fame chiefly rests.

After "Pickwick," Dickens gave us "Oliver Twist," with its vivid impressions of paupers and of criminals, of the workhouse and the debtor's prison. Then he wrote "Nicholas Nickleby" to expose some of the stupid and brutal schools of his day. "Barnaby Rudge" followed, and "The Old Curiosity Shop." Then came "Martin Chuzzlewit," which gave offence to many in America by its description of American ways.

A little later came "Dombey and Son," and then "David Copperfield"—the author's favourite work and largely the story of his own life. Next the magnificent series was continued in "Bleak House," "Hard Times," "Little Dorrit," "Great Expectations," and "Our Mutual Friend." Besides these there is "The Tale of Two Cities," a very popular story which always stands by itself because it is the author's

From the drawing by Fred Barnard

This will introduce you to Sam Weller, the incomparable servant to Pickwick in the book we know as "Pickwick Papers." The portly person at the right is Weller's father, another amusing Dickens character.

(CONTINUED ON PAGE 782)

one historical novel; and finally "The Mystery of Edwin Drood," a great story that was left unfinished at the author's death. Many have tried to guess what the end of "Edwin Drood" would have been, but that will for ever remain a mystery.

To-day, when the name of Charles Dickens is mentioned, we are apt to remember him merely as a novelist—but he was more than that. He was a great reformer —for his pen exposed many of the social evils of his day.

THE TYPE OF SCHOOL EXPOSED BY DICKENS IN "NICHOLAS NICKLEBY"

The bleak-looking building above is believed by many people to be the original of Dotheboys Hall, in "Nicholas Nickleby," in reality an example held up by Dickens of the many disgracefully managed schools in Yorkshire at this period. As the author himself states in his preface to the book, "Mr. Squeers and his school are faint and feeble pictures of an existing reality, purposely subdued and kept down lest they should be deemed impossible."

The craftsman hard at work in the picture above has received an order to make a stained-glass window for a country church. His patrons wanted to be sure that what he was planning to do would please them, so they asked him to submit the small sketch which now stands upright on the table. The worker is standing in front of a large outline drawing, or "cartoon," which you can dimly see upon the wall. It is from this that he got his pattern for each piece of glass that went into the window—shown nearly completed on the left.

The Most GLORIOUS WINDOWS in the WORLD

Here is the Story of Stained Glass, an Art Which was Long Lost to the World, and Which has Never Been Fully Mastered Again

WHEN we enter a great church, particularly if it is one of the fine old cathedrals built long ago in the Middle Ages, what is it that makes us feel at once an atmosphere of restful and solemn beauty? It is partly the Gothic columns and partly the sense of spaciousness from the lofty roof. But, perhaps more than anything else, it is the light—the soft and lovely light which comes through the tall, coloured windows of stained glass.

> Storied windows richly dight,
> Casting a dim, religious light,

as Milton wrote in "Il Penseroso." "Storied windows"—scenes from the Gospels and the lives of the saints, many stories in glass: "richly dight"—clothed in rich colour, glowing with the light that shines through them: "casting a dim religious light"—surely it is largely this rich half-light which gave us that first wonderful feeling of awe!

How is it done? How can men make those glowing pictures in glass? It is an art which the ancients did not know. It was developed during the Middle Ages, and from the first was used mostly to make the churches more solemn and beautiful. The nearest thing to it in earlier times was glass mosaic (mō-zā'ĭk), which consisted of fragments of coloured and gilt glass set into plaster so as to make designs or pictures. These mosaics, the story of which you may read elsewhere in this work, were used in pavements or on walls.

In Asia Minor some of the Mohammedan craftsmen learned to use mosaic panels as windows; such windows were not transparent, any more than were those in the cathedrals, but they let in a little light. Perhaps merchants from the rich trading city of Venice brought the secret of these brightly-coloured windows home with them. At least we know that by about A.D. 1000 they were being made in Italy, in France, and in Germany.

But true stained-glass windows, as we know them, did not attain their final perfection until the thirteenth century, about seven hundred years ago. The art flourished and grew and changed for three or four hundred years after that, and then fell into decay, not to be revived until almost our own time. During that time the methods of working underwent changes, but always the beauty of the design or picture was produced partly by means of pieces of coloured glass fitted together and partly by painting on top of the glass. So "stained glass" is really both stained and painted.

The older windows, dating from the thirteenth century, are mostly stained. The colour is *in* them, not *on* them, for the glass was coloured when it was still "pot-metal"—that is, when it was melted in the pot. Glass-makers, or glaziers, of that day did not know how to make large pieces of glass, nor how to make their glass clear and smooth as it is to-day. Their "white" glass was really a sort of sea-green, and could not be seen through very perfectly. All their glass was full of bubbles and had an uneven surface. But these imperfections only made the coloured glass more beautiful. And the

A SIXTEENTH CENTURY WINDOW

With soft lights streaming through his golden halo and monk's garments, Saint Bruno sits in state upon his throne. This stained glass was made in Flanders or Northern France in the sixteenth century. And how different it is from the mosaic-like windows of the earlier centuries! Large pieces of glass have taken the place of the tiny pieces which, in the twelfth and thirteenth centuries, were often not more than half an inch in width and only from one to two inches in length.

makers produced some very lovely colours for their pot-metal—yellow, olive, and emerald green, light and dark blue, a dark brownish-purple, a lighter brownish-purple, a dark ruby red.

The ruby red was so dark that it looked nearly black and did not let enough light through. So the makers worked out a process called "flashing," by which they made it lighter. The glass-maker took a mass of molten white glass on the end of his blow-pipe, and dipped the blow-pipe into the red pot-metal, too. Then he blew out a huge bubble composed of both red and white—white inside and ruby red all over. He blew and blew until the bubble was so thin that the red had attained the correct shade, then deftly he slit the bubble and laid it out in a flat sheet—white on one side, ruby red on the other. This same process was afterwards used for all sorts of pot-metals, so that the glazier could obtain any shade he desired.

Let us imagine that our thirteenth century worker in glass is making a window containing a figure of a saint. The holy man stands pointing to heaven, the great scarlet cloak which is his garment falling away from his lifted arm. The picture has first been sketched out on a whitewashed board supported on trestles. The glass-worker now lays a piece of stained glass over the saint's face, and roughly cuts the glass to the required shape with a red-hot iron, afterwards

There are no short cuts to the making of stained-glass windows. Each step in the process must be taken with care and precision. First the artist must make a painting or "cartoon." This is shown in the picture above. In the oval you see the artist tracing the cartoon on transparent paper. In the top right-hand corner he is cutting out pieces of cardboard which he will use as patterns for cutting the glass. In the pictures at the bottom of the page he is assembling the pieces of glass that have been cut from the cardboard patterns, and is binding them together with strips of lead. In the centre are two windows that are practically finished. All they need now is a little retouching and a final careful inspection to see that they have been made strong and perfect in every detail.

For more than thirteen hundred years stained glass has been used for church windows. This kind of glass was fitted by St. Gregory into the windows of the church of St. Martin at Tours in France. Originally, stained-glass windows were made by cutting coloured glass into small pieces of varying shapes and fitting them together with strips of lead which formed the outlined pattern. This method provided a mosaic effect, which in the course of time gave place to the more familiar pictorial style. The different styles of architecture had an important bearing on the designs in stained-glass work, and with the passing of the Gothic style round about the fifteenth century, the mediaeval style of stained glass passed with it. It was revived in the nineteenth century.

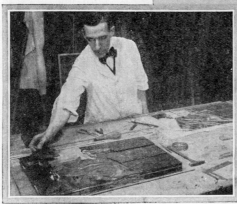

finishing it off more exactly with a "grozing iron," that is, an iron tool having a notch at one end, something like a spanner. This iron served him as a glass-cutter, for there were no diamond glass-cutters until about A.D. 1500.

So he goes on, cutting the arms, the red robe, the background, of glass of different colours. But he has to be careful about the size of his pieces, because they all have to be fitted together afterwards between strips of lead, and the glass-worker wants the finished window to be as strong and beautiful as possible. So he never cuts pieces that are too small, not only because they are difficult to cut with his red-hot iron, but also because the lead strips between them will occupy too much space and spoil the effect. Besides, the leading round tiny pieces has a way of collecting dust—which is a serious matter when your window is to be placed high up in the church and out of reach. And lastly and most important, our glazier knows that a window with too many little panes will be so pliable that it will bend and sway with every gust of wind. On the other hand, he cannot make very large pieces, and would not use them in any case, because that, too, would make the window weak. Moreover, the leading is a part of his design, and a few very large pieces of glass would be out of proportion to the rest.

So he cuts one piece for the upper arm of his saint and another for the lower arm, and makes the red cloak in several parts. But he cuts the whole hand out of one piece, instead of making a separate piece for each finger. In every piece he cuts he will remember not only the size but the shape too, since odd-shaped pieces are hard to cut and to lead together; and he never forgets to picture to himself how the dark lines of the strips of lead between the pieces of glass are going to fit into his design.

But he is not yet ready to fit his window together. The saint's face is still a featureless blur of glass; all his fingers are run together; and the background pieces are mere staring white patches that will let in too much light and spoil the picture by showing scraps of outdoor landscape. This is where the *painting* part of making stained glass first comes in.

The flesh colour has been obtained by staining what may be called the white glass—although pure white glass was not made until the fifteenth century—with a solution of chloride (klōr'ĭd) of silver. But the outlines of the saint's features and fingers, the folds in his crimson cloak, and any other sharp lines in the picture have to be put in with a dark brown enamel. Now enamel, as you can read elsewhere in this work, is really a sort of glass. So what our glass-worker does is to paint on glass with glass. When, with his enamel paint, he has put into the picture of

A COAT OF ARMS IN STAINED GLASS

The stained-glass windows of the Renaissance were not so beautiful as those that had preceded them, for the artists were using too much enamel. In Switzerland, however, the artists put enamel to good service. They used larger pieces of glass and, consequently, less leading. Dark brown enamel was used for the drawing, and a golden effect was obtained with silver stain. Above is a sixteenth century coat of arms which was made, not for a church, but for the home of some important person in Switzerland.

Photos by Ollivier and Alinari

BEAUTIFUL EXAMPLES OF PICTURES IN COLOURED GLASS

Some of the loveliest twelfth and thirteenth century stained-glass windows are in the cathedral of Poitiers in France. Nos. 1 and 3 show you two of them, but, of course, you cannot see their beautiful colours. Like all early windows, they are made of many tiny pieces. No. 2 is a German early sixteenth century panel made from a design by Dürer. It represents the Descent from the Cross. Nos. 4 and 7 are windows of the early sixteenth century showing scenes from the life of Christ. Nos. 5 and 6 are from the cathedral of Arezzo, Italy, and portray the conversion of St. Matthew. Above he is shown "sitting at the receipt of custom."

the saint all the details he thinks necessary, he places the painted pieces in an oven. The heat causes the powdered glass in the enamel to fuse with the surface of the stained glass and become a part of it.

Our glass-worker also uses this brown enamel on his background. Perhaps he includes a mass of foliage behind the pointing saint, perhaps a lovely arrangement of scrolls. Then he fills in the space surrounding this design with fine criss-cross lines called "cross-hatching." Or perhaps he coats the glass all over with enamel, and when it is partly dry pounds it lightly with a stiff-bristled brush. This "stippling" breaks up the enamel into tiny specks and gives it a powdery appearance; it is called "grisaille" (grĭ-zāl'), which means "greyish." This is one of the most beautiful backgrounds of all. How brilliantly the red robe and upraised pointing finger of our saint stand out against it! Now at last our glass-worker is ready to assemble his window. He lays out all the pieces in order, as though he were fitting together a puzzle. Then he places between them little bars of lead, shaped to hold the glass. Where these "leads" meet, he solders them together, and, to make the window firm and strong, rubs putty or cement into the crevices between the lead and the glass. He also solders in at its middle point

a piece of copper wire, here and there. Finally, the whole picture, now leaded together, is ready to be inserted in the window opening. That done, the workmen twist the copper wires round the "saddle-bars" that are to support the glass. These are iron bars that span the window opening every few feet; they are sometimes shaped to follow the main lines of the leading so as not to spoil the effect of the window.

And now our red-robed saint stands in the cathedral in all his glory, pointing the kneeling worshippers to Heaven. The sunshine streams softly through and about his figure, glowing with the reds and greens and blues and golds of the glass, and making it seem as though the pictured holy man himself gave forth a holy light.

This window, and all the others, would be fitted carefully into the general scheme of decoration of the church. It was a part of the beautiful Gothic architecture. At first the windows were tall, narrow, and pointed at the top. For these "lancet" windows the glass-worker usually prepared several round medallions, and placed them one above another, with small panes, or "quarries," in between. Later the lancet windows were often set close together to give the effect of a single window, with only narrow columns of stone called "mullions" between; then the glass-worker could plan a picture or design,

STAINED GLASS OF TO-DAY

This great window shows you what modern stained glass can look like. Notice how the scenes have been made to suit the shape of the window. The angel with his spreading wings fits into the circle, and the tall saints below fit into their tall arches. The artists of stained-glass windows have always had to face this problem of making their designs to fit a certain space. And that is one of the reasons why stained glass is often spoken of as the "handmaid of architecture."

THE QUIET BEAUTY OF THE COUNTRYSIDE PORTRAYED IN GLASS

It would be useless to try to compare this modern stained-glass window with the early windows of the Middle Ages. The artist's aims and methods have changed. This beautiful landscape is like a painting, and has no need for any particular setting. The early windows, on the other hand, were meant to look like clusters of gems; their setting was the Gothic church, and they told worshippers the stories of the Bible.

that would fill the whole opening. At the top of these great windows would be a rounded space, which the glass-worker filled with scroll-work or other designs.

As time passed, the makers of stained glass came to depend more and more on painting their pictures and less on piecing pot-metal colours together. They wanted to tell stories in their pictures, and it was extremely difficult to include details of the story when everything had to be pieced together.

The Windows of the Churches Enrich the World with Glowing Beauty

Thus the Early Gothic of the thirteenth century became the Middle Gothic of the fourteenth and then the Late Gothic of the fifteenth. By that time nearly every cathedral and chapel and minster in Europe was enriched with stained and painted glass. The windows at Cologne and Nuremberg and Augsburg, in Germany, were famous everywhere. In France there was the glory of Rouen and Chartres and Rheims, Bourges and Amiens and Paris. Spain, Italy, Austria, Switzerland, and the Netherlands could also boast of marvels in glass. Magnificent, too, were the windows of the English churches. Pilgrims to the shrine of St. Thomas Becket, at Canterbury, saw windows made by the most skilled glass-workers of Europe. At York the minster contained the largest and finest grisaille windows ever made. Westminster Abbey, the cathedrals at Winchester, Salisbury, Wells, and Lincoln—all these and countless smaller churches had gloriously beautiful glass.

A good deal of this splendour is lost to us now—destroyed in riots and wars. During the time of the religious troubles in the sixteenth and seventeenth centuries many people were breaking away from the older Church, and mobs of rioters or of angry soldiers often broke into the cathedrals, smashing and breaking down the symbols of the religion they had learned to hate. And glass windows, unless they are too high up, are temptingly easy to break. At Canterbury, they say, a madly excited rioter named "Blue Dick" armed himself with a ladder and a long pole, and systematically punched out piece by piece all the glass he

could reach. Nor have the guns of modern heavy artillery had more respect for beautiful things than had those mobs of past days.

Yet much remains. And many of the windows that were broken have been restored, although the new glass cannot be quite so beautiful as the old. The reason for this sad fact is not that the secret of staining glass is lost—though it is true that most modern glaziers depend too much on painting the glass—but the uneven surfaces and bubbly inequalities of the old glass made it soften and "mellow" with time.

The art of making stained-glass windows was by no means forgotten when the Middle Ages passed. At the time of intellectual awakening which we call the Renaissance (rĕ-nā'săns), fine stained glass continued to be made, especially in Germany and Switzerland. Much of it was used in private houses instead of churches, and so the craftsmen had an opportunity to depict other things besides bishops and saints. But the period of its greatest glory was past, and during the seventeenth and eighteenth centuries the art was at a very low ebb.

How New Ideas of Beauty are Being Expressed in Coloured Glass

It has been revived in our own day, and that, surely, is a fact to make us glad. At first the men who revived it—William Morris and Edward Burne-Jones and other English artists of the nineteenth century—tried simply to copy the designs of the Middle Ages. But it is never satisfactory merely to try to do things as others have done them, for men must express their own thoughts and feelings in art, not those of anyone else, however beautiful they may be. So more recent artists in glass have attempted to express their own ideas of what is beautiful, and especially to see if all the fresh knowledge we have gained about making glass cannot be applied in producing better stained glass.

These attempts have not been observed as much in England as on the Continent, and especially in Germany, where the workers in stained glass have introduced original thought into their craft, and have executed some excellent designs in keeping with the progress that has taken place in other branches of art.

Our friend the wolf has gone supperless to bed many and many a night, and when the winter comes on he has no warm hearth beside which to curl up for a nap. So what do you think he will do when he sees a chance to make a home with human beings and have comfortable quarters and plenty of good food?

TANSY and BOBBLES on FABLE ISLAND

How Pride Had a Fall, and What Became of the Wolf Who was Too Clever

(CONTINUED FROM PAGE 632)

THE big fir tree was in a boasting mood one morning. Tansy and Bobbles came along searching for cones, and when they smiled up at him, he waved his elegant branches in response.

"Look at me," he was saying to the bramble, who was modestly crouching below, "am I not strong? Doesn't my top nearly reach the sky? Can't I be seen for miles around? Don't the travellers guide themselves by me? When the storm comes, doesn't every creature take shelter beneath me? Don't the artists say to one another, 'Let us go and paint the big fir tree standing out against the sunset'?"

"True, true," admitted the bramble.

"As for you, you poor bramble," said the big fir tree, with kindly pity, "you are but a torment to man and to beast, as you tear them with your thorns."

"Ah, but you have forgotten," pleaded the bramble, "that the children deck themselves in my autumn leaves and laugh into my ears as they gather my fruit."

"Children! What do children matter?" replied the big fir tree in scornful pride.

"Pride ought to have a terrible fall," whispered Bobbles to Tansy, "and I believe it will." For both the fairies saw that a party of woodcutters were arriving with axes and ropes.

The fairies went up to the woodcutters, whom they knew quite well, and Tansy asked if they had come to cut down the bramble.

"Dear me, no," said the woodcutter scratching his head and wondering if he had heard aright. "We've come for the big fir tree."

The big fir heard his doom, and a shiver shot through him. But in spite of his pride he had a noble heart, and he straightened himself bravely for the coming torture.

Even when the first blow fell he made no protest.

"He's a wonderful tree," said Bobbles.

"That is why we want him," said the woodcutter. "He has been sent for by the king, for a great ship he is building."

"Good-bye, you fine old tree!" said Tansy, as she flew up and kissed the topmost twig. "Cheer up You are wanted by the king, and you will sail all over the wide world."

But the big fir tree couldn't speak. He was afraid his voice might break and disgrace him. Besides, he wanted every moment of the time to look and look at the island which he would never see from the wood again.

"The great are in more danger than the little," said Bobbles, as he pointed to the bramble, whom no one wanted to disturb.

"Come away," cried Tansy. "I can't bear to see the big fir tree fall down."

The Fat Dog and the Lean Wolf

That evening the fairies had been having great times with the glow-worms and the

He doubtless does his duty by the family, but he hardly seems happy about it. Perhaps if he could take life just a little more sweetly, he would never need to be tied up.

fire-flies. On returning towards the bower they noticed a gaunt and starved-looking wolf talking to a well-fed mastiff.

"Why is it that you look so fat and prosperous?" asked the wolf. "What do you do for your living?"

"I keep away robbers," said the mastiff, "and I follow my master; I am civil to his children, and allow no one to hurt them."

"I could do all these things," said the wolf. "But what is that strange mark about your neck? The hairs seem rubbed away."

"Oh," said the mastiff, lightly, "that is nothing. It's only where my collar rubs, when they chain me up for the night."

"Collar! Chain!" exclaimed the wolf. "Farewell! Half a meal and liberty is better than a whole one on a chain." And off he galloped.

"It's easy to discover the meaning of that," said Tansy, as she urged Bobbles on.

The Boasting Rushlight

But again they stopped as they noticed a rushlight set in its stand on the window-sill of a cottage.

The rushlight was boasting that it gave more light than the sun, the moon, and the stars.

But just then Tansy mischievously pinched it out, and the rushlight sighed, thinking it was his enemy, the wind.

"Stop that boasting," mocked Bobbles. "The lights of heaven can't be put out!"

Bobbles and Tansy were astonished one morning to find a shepherd hanging up a dead wolf which was clothed in a sheep's skin.

"Why do you do that?" asked Tansy.

"Why did the wolf do what he did?" asked the shepherd, wrathfully. "One of my sheep died by accident, and I left the skin lying. This wretch picked up the skin, dressed himself in it, and lured the sheep's lamb away to devour him. Then he had the audacity to get himself locked up with the other sheep in the fold.

"Luckily, I needed some mutton for my master, and going to the fold, I killed the first sheep upon which I laid hands. Instead of a sheep, he was a wolf—and now he hangs there. Sly tricks always bring their own punishment."

"He's a pretty good warning to all who pass by," said Bobbles.

The Buried Treasure

Now the fairies had determined to give their mother a present of the finest bunch of grapes on the island, and they knew exactly where to go.

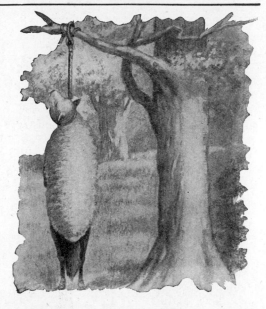

When they reached the vineyard, which belonged to three young men, Bobbles couldn't help asking one of them how it came about that this vineyard was more splendidly kept than any other.

"You must know," said the man, "that when our father was on his deathbed, he explained that he had left us this vineyard, and that within it there was a hidden treasure which we should find if we worked diligently.

"For quite a long time we worked hard with spade and hoe turning over the soil and seeking for the treasure. But after a while we noticed that the vines were im- proving, the growth was getting stronger, the leaves more healthy, and the fruit more luscious; and at last we guessed what our father had meant From that time onwards

A crafty old wolf once dressed himself up in sheep's clothing in order to raid the flock. It was not long, however, before he was discovered and the sheep could look out at his hide swinging to and fro as a warning.

we have been more and more diligent in our care of the vines, and have tried to make them as perfect as you now see them."

"I understand," cried Tansy. "The grapes are the buried treasure in the vine-yard?"

"Yes," said the young man; "and we now remember our father's words that 'industry itself is a treasure.'"

The fairies carried the grapes away with the greatest of care, meaning to take them straight to their mother.

But on the journey they were obliged to stop, as they noticed a weasel shaking his sides with laughter.

"What is the joke?" asked Bobbles.

"Oh, dear, dear!" exclaimed the weasel, pointing to a basket of grain. "See! No! Stoop down and listen."

So stooping down they heard a melancholy squeaking.

"It's a mouse," chuckled the weasel. "He's got through that hole, and now he's eaten so much grain that he's too fat to get back again."

"You'll have to wait until you've grown thin," called Bobbles.

But whether he ever did get thin enough to escape, Tansy and Bobbles never knew, for just then the woman who had left the basket returned for it and carried it away.

As for the weasel, he laughed until he was quite doubled up. But the fairies went off with the grapes, and when they reached the bower they cried in one breath, "Mother! Mother! Look! We've brought you a buried treasure."

An eagle was anxious to find a meal for her brood; and having left her nest high up on the rocks, she remained poised in the air, looking about her for a juicy morsel.

Presently she spied a young lamb, and

We hope that the weasel will profit by the sad example of this little mouse and learn not to eat too much, for greediness is a vice that, sooner or later, brings its own punishment.

with a swoop she seized it in her talons and carried it up to her nest.

Now a jackdaw, watching the eagle, decided that he could be just as clever; and as he was fond of chattering, he was delighted to see Bobbles and Tansy coming along.

They hadn't noticed the eagle, for they were racing up an oak tree. But now the jackdaw cried out, "Pray look at me!"

"We're busy," called Bobbles, and he and Tansy went on racing. Bobbles won the race up the oak; and then they raced down, and Tansy won. "Now can you listen to me?" cried the jackdaw as Bobbles sprang to the ground.

"Well, what is it?" asked Bobbles, impatiently.

"Perhaps it is something of which we have to learn the meaning," whispered Tansy.

So they decided to listen.

"The eagle has just carried off a lamb in his talons," cried the jackdaw. "Now you watch me carry off that old ram."

"You're absolutely mad!" exclaimed Bobbles.

But the jackdaw was sure he wasn't mad, and flying aloft he swooped down on the ram to carry him off.

But, alas, he wasn't an eagle, and his claws caught in the ram's wool; and seeing him so entangled the shepherd strode up and captured him.

"Oh, father," cried the shepherd's children, as they came rushing up, "what have you caught?"

"Well," and the shepherd laughed, "I believe he thinks he is an eagle, but in truth he is only a jackdaw."

"May we have him?" asked the children.

"After I've clipped his wings so that he cannot fly away," said the shepherd.

These great beasts are telling each other how very foolish they were to fall to fighting, for artful Mr. Fox has stepped in and run off with the prize over which they were quarrelling. We, too, may learn a lesson from this.

So the shepherd clipped the jackdaw's wings, and the children carried him off home as a playmate.

"That's the end of the jackdaw," said the fairies, rather sadly.

While the Lion and the Bear Fight over a Meal the Fox Runs Away with It

They didn't wait any longer, for they were attracted by a noise of growling and roaring and trampling; and on rounding the corner they saw that a lion and a bear were having a terrific struggle to decide which of them was to take the carcass of a fawn that they had found lying on the ground.

But just as the great beasts fell back exhausted and bleeding, a fox darted in, and without a word carried off the carcass.

"Booh!" said the fairies; and the lion and the bear looked at them mournfully, guessing that they would get a lecture.

"Really!" cried Bobbles, "I'm ashamed to see you two great animals fighting, just to give the fox a good dinner."

"Indeed," said the lion, as he licked his wounds, "you are right."

"Indeed," said the bear, "I think you are right, too."

"We are learning to be right," said Tansy confidingly, "because we've been so busy lately discovering the meaning of things."

"You had better take a long day to look for the meaning of things," said Mother Fairy one delightful morning, as she handed Bobbles a basket packed with the most delicious things.

"Mother!" exclaimed Bobbles, 'why do you look so strange?"

"Do I look strange?" she asked with a smile. "Forget that I looked strange and —away you go!"

But Tansy and Bobbles couldn't forget that Mother Fairy had looked strange, and although they thought and thought about it, they couldn't guess what the reason might be.

Tansy and Bobbles Hear Sad News from a Terrified Pigeon

They were wandering along a lane that led them past a pigeon-cote when Tansy said, "That pigeon-cote seems to be empty. I wonder why?"

"Alas, I know why," said a melancholy voice, and looking down the fairies saw an old pigeon crouching behind a log, as though in terror.

"Tell us," said Bobbles, eagerly.

"Indeed, that pigeon-cote was once full, for we kept near its shelter so that the kite couldn't attack us. But, alas, one day the kite beguiled us into making him our king, promising to protect us from our enemies. We believed him; but as soon as he became our king he showed himself a tyrant, and he devoured one of us every day, until I alone am left." He sighed despondently.

"We're very sorry," said Tansy, pityingly.

"It was all our own fault," admitted the pigeon, "for we put ourselves under this tyrant of our own accord, so what else could we expect?"

"What, indeed!" said Bobbles.

But just then a bull began bellowing and raging and tearing up the ground, and looking wildly round as though for an enemy.

The Impudent Little Mouse

"What is all this about?" cried Bobbles, as he seized Tansy's hand and flew with her to the bull's back.

"Oh, it's you, is it?" roared the bull. "Some enemy has pinched my foot, and I cannot rest till I have found him!"

"Did it hurt?" asked Tansy.

"No," said the bull, in a milder tone, "but I won't have my foot pinched."

Just then a mouse popped out from the shelter of his hole.

"I pinched your foot, noble bull," he squeaked. "Though I am but a mouse I have gained a victory over four hoofs, a mighty body, and a pair of horns," and he darted back into his hole.

"Never mind the mouse," said Bobbles. "Take us for a ride."

So the bull, who was rather ashamed of himself, bent down his head and then lifted it, and thundered off with the fairies, for hours and hours, until at last his passengers had ridden far enough.

The fairies were enjoying their meal by the side of a stream, when they heard such exquisite music that Tansy's eyes filled with tears.

They rose and tiptoed off in the direction of the music. Presently they saw a stork standing beside a dying swan. It was the poor swan who was singing so exquisitely.

"Why do you sing when you are dying?" asked the stork.

"That is why I am singing," said the swan, as she raised her head. "I am singing because I am going far, far away up into the sky, where there will be no arrows and no snares and no hunger."

"Tell us! Tell us!" cried Tansy, kneeling down by the swan.

"I cannot tell you," said the swan. "I can only sing to you."

So the swan sang on and on, and the stork, growing tired of the music, went off on his own business, and only the fairies were left.

As Bobby and Tansy listened they tried and tried to think what it would be like in a place where there were no arrows, no snares, and no hunger.

They wanted to ask the swan once more, but just when Tansy had made up her mind to interrupt the song it stopped, for the swan was dead.

Bobbles and Tansy Are Tired

And when Tansy and Bobbles returned to the bower they burst in upon their father and mother in great excitement.

"Oh, mother!" cried Tansy, "such a strange thing has happened."

"What, my child?" she asked anxiously.

"I am tired—and Bobbles is tired. We are both tired of finding out the meaning of things."

"We want to follow the swan up into the sky," said Bobbles, "where there are no arrows and no snares, and no hunger."

"Oh, mother! Oh, father!" cried Tansy. "Why do you look at each other so strangely?"

But neither Father Fairy nor Mother Fairy would answer their eager question.

(CONTINUED ON PAGE 857)

Only sails and hard work with the oars propelled the graceful ships of Rome and Carthage, for in those days the use of steam was unheard of, and even the rudder for steering had not been invented. When a Roman ship came close enough to an enemy vessel, a huge grappling iron crashed down and locked the two together. Then the fight took place as though on land—to the advantage of the Romans, who were not good sailors.

From a LITTLE NATION to a GREAT EMPIRE

Having Conquered Italy the Romans Came to Grips with Carthage, Whose Power They Destroyed, and then Swept On to Dominion Over the Whole of the Known World

(CONTINUED FROM PAGE 721)

THE time for the first war between Rome and Carthage came when a quarrel broke out among the citizens of Messina, in Sicily. One group asked the Carthaginians for help, the other appealed to the Romans.

Upon this request the Roman senate dispatched an army to Sicily with all haste, managing to muster sufficient ships to ferry the men across the narrow sea between Italy and the island. But safe conduct of the army was not all that was necessary. An army needs enormous supplies and constant communication to and fro between camp and city. The Carthaginian (kär′thä-jĭn′ĭ-ăn) warships obstructed the passage of the enemy supply ships, and so the Roman army did not have an easy passage, even when it had reached Sicily.

But the Romans never entered into a war half-heartedly. Their policy was that of a steady forward march. They had never been sailors, but now they saw the necessity of being good fighters on the sea also. Since they must have a navy, they set to work to build it. For many and many a day the rasp of saws and the clang of hammers sounded in the harbours of Italy, until at last a fleet of 125 battleships, each with five banks of oars, came into being.

How the Invention of the "Crow" Helped the Romans to Victory

What the Romans wanted to do with their navy was to come to close grips with the Carthaginian ships. Then they could fight as if they were on land, using their thick, short swords to cut the Carthaginian troops to pieces. They invented an instrument called a "crow" for their ships, with which to grapple an enemy vessel and keep it from sailing away.

The crow was a long, heavy plank of wood, with huge iron hooks on the end. It was ordinarily held upright on the Roman ship, but when the ship sailed alongside a Carthaginian vessel the crow was brought down with a crash on the deck of the enemy vessel. Then the two ships could not break apart, and the Romans could board the enemy craft and hack their way to victory.

The Carthaginians were brave fighters, but many of their troops were "mercenaries," (mẽr′sĕ-nȧ-rĭ), or hired soldiers, and the mercenaries were very likely to give way before the relentless Roman attack. In the first sea fight (260 B.C.) the Carthaginians were badly beaten, and in the second (256 B.C.) they were again defeated.

Then the triumphant Roman senate decided to send a great army over to Africa to attack the city of Carthage itself. The invading army carried everything before it, until one of its leaders, a Roman consul, was recalled to Rome with part of the troops. The army that remained could not stand before the Carthaginian defenders, and to add to their misfortune, the Romans were now defeated at sea, and their fleet was lost in a storm.

The Fate of the Sacred Chickens at the Hands of Publius Claudius

This defeat was probably owing to the half-hearted manner of many of the soldiers, and also to mistaken tactics of some of the leaders. But the Romans themselves

A SCENE OF SPLENDOUR IN THE CITY OF THE MERCHANT PRINCES

Carthage was a city of merchant princes. Ever since the legendary times of Dido, the tragic and romantic queen, the Carthaginians had been famed for their wealth and luxury. At the time of the Punic Wars, the city was exporting gold and silver and other metals, ivory and precious stones, beautiful woven fabrics, and even black slaves from Central Africa; these were carried all over the Mediterranean. Small wonder that Carthage grew rich and prosperous and that her women, some of whom you see above, lived in such splendour.

HANNIBAL MARCHES ON ACROSS THE MIGHTY ALPS

To cross the Alps in winter through a steep and narrow pass, blinded by raging snowstorms, and at every point in danger of falling into an icy crevasse or of freezing to death—these were hardships to test the mettle of any leader. But what must it have been for Hannibal, who came from a sunny climate and a land of ease!

believed that destruction befell them because of lack of religious feeling on the part of their consul, Publius Claudius. Before the battle someone told him that the sacred chickens, which were carried with the army, would not eat, and he hastily exclaimed, "Let them drink, then," and ordered them to be thrown overboard. This form of humour, thought the Romans, was bound to bring down the wrath of the gods.

The First Blow at Carthage

Whatever the cause, the Romans found themselves fallen from the peak of victory to the valley of defeat. Carthaginian ships were sailing along the Italian coast doing all the damage they could, and the Romans, with an empty treasury, could offer no resistance. But the spirit of the Roman was the spirit of determination. The wealthy citizens gathered together, and from their private fortunes provided the money to build more ships. This time they constructed a great fleet of two hundred battleships, which was placed under the command of the consul Catullus (kå-tŭl'ŭs). They sailed out to meet the Carthaginian fleet and destroyed it utterly (241 B.C.).

This defeat was a bitter blow for Carthage. She had expended all her money in the war, just as Rome had done, and she no longer had any ships to defend her on the sea. All she could do was to make peace, and on very unfavourable terms. She was forced to give Rome the whole of Sicily and pay a tribute of 3,200 talents, or about £800,000, an enormous sum at that time. Thus ended the First Punic (pū'nĭk) War, which had lasted twenty-three years (264–241 B.C.). There were in all three wars between Rome and Carthage, called the First, Second and Third Punic Wars.

A Man Who Hated Rome

During the twenty years that passed before the Second Punic War, the forces of the two countries changed places. Rome was now mistress of the seas, and Carthage looked to her army for protection and for new conquests to take the place of lost Sicily. While the Romans were busy forming Sicily into a province and conquering the wild natives of Sardinia and Corsica, the Carthaginians were by no means idle.

Their general, Hamilcar (hă-mĭl′kär), went to Spain, where many coast towns were already in Carthaginian hands. He added so much of the interior to Carthage, and sent back so much wealth, that Rome began to fear him. We are told that Hamilcar's hatred of the Romans was such that he made his young son Hannibal swear upon an altar his eternal hatred of all that was Roman. It does not seem likely, however, that Hamilcar ever dreamed of attacking Rome except by the sea. But when the Romans began to interfere with Carthage in Spain, Hanni-

bal, who had by now become commander, was forced in self-defence to dream of attacking Rome on the land, and to try to make the dream come true.

Of the great generals of the world, Hannibal, Rome's bitter enemy, ranks among the foremost. For courage, for foresight, for leadership, no one of his time could equal him. When he was only twenty-four years old he was brought face to face with the greatest military machine of his age, and by his brilliant genius he made the Romans tremble for their country and their lives. His charging cavalry were the wings of destruction; his quick and desperate infantry the very engines of death.

Hannibal Crosses the Alps

But for all his genius, Hannibal is a pathetic figure. Victory after victory fell to his arms, and yet he could never achieve final success. He slaughtered the best and boldest of the Romans; he drove their generals to the shelter of the mountains and marshes; he swept Italy from end to end; and yet the city of Rome was never within his grasp. The one great victory eluded him.

When a petty quarrel in Spain opened the Second Punic War (218 B.C.), Hannibal led

Photo by Anderson

ATILIUS REGULUS RETURNS TO CARTHAGE TO OFFER UP HIS LIFE

Atilius Regulus was a Roman general who was captured by the Carthaginians in the First Punic War. It is said that after the Roman victory at Panormus, Regulus was sent back to Rome with the understanding that he was either to bring about a peace treaty or return to Carthage to be killed. When he reached Rome he urged his countrymen not to make peace. Above you see him returning to Carthage to be tortured to death.

THE TERRIBLE DOOM OF A PROUD CITY

After the complete conquest of Italy, the Romans turned their attention to Carthage, the mistress of the seas. There followed the three separate conflicts with the Carthaginians, known in history as the Punic Wars. At last the great city of Carthage was doomed to destruction. Hordes of Roman soldiers invaded the palaces, public buildings, and private houses, levelling them as they passed, like a huge machine. To-day if you dug down into the soil where Carthage once stood, you would discover nothing but a thick bed of cinders.

his army across the Alps to Italy. With his cavalry, his war elephants—animals which had never been used for such a purpose before—and his forty thousand soldiers, he pushed his way onward, avoiding the Roman army that had been sent to Spain. Finally, after heroically threading a path through the cold and desolate mountains, he emerged upon the plains of Italy.

Two Famous Battles

Here he could obtain no more help from Carthage. He might look to the Gauls of the north, who hated the Romans, but for the most part he must depend upon his own resources. His valour and skill were such that he kept his army for fifteen years in the heart of an enemy country, where hundreds of thousands of hostile troops were ready to meet him.

Hannibal's first big success came at the Battle of Trebia (trĕb'yȧ), which was fought on a cold December morning (218 B.C.), when the numbed Roman soldiers, ambushed from the rear and attacked from the front, were scattered by the Carthaginian cavalry. Then Hannibal marched southwards through

the peninsula, and in the spring surprised and cut to pieces another Roman army at the battle of Lake Trasimenus (trä'zĭ-mē'-nŭs). Few of the enemy escaped, and the consul Flaminius himself was slain.

Rome was now in fear of attack. But Hannibal had no proper machinery for besieging a city, and his army was too small. He was doing all he could to increase it by adding Gauls and other enemies of Rome to his own Carthaginian troops.

The next year (216 B.C.) saw the greatest battle of all. Eighty-five thousand Roman troops came out to meet Hannibal's fifty thousand at Cannae (kăn'ē). By a clever piece of strategy the great Carthaginian surrounded the army of Rome. His men slew seventy thousand Romans on the field, and Hannibal sent to Carthage a bushel of gold rings taken from the fingers of dead Roman nobles.

After this victory every enemy of Rome came to the support of the Carthaginian forces. The Greek cities revolted, some of the Italian states joined them, and the Gauls had long been up in arms. And yet during the remaining thirteen years of his stay in

Here the young Scipio, who had been taken prisoner by Antiochus, is being returned to his father. It was this boy who was destined by Fate to deal the blow that ended for ever the mighty power of Carthage.

THE MOST PRICELESS JEWELS IN ALL THE WORLD

Cornelia, daughter of Scipio Africanus the Elder, and mother of the Gracchi (grak´ī), was as intelligent as she was charming. One day a haughty damsel of her ac- quaintance proudly displayed her own jewels and then asked to see what ornaments Cornelia possessed. Cornelia called her two sons and said, "These are my jewels."

Italy, even with the combined efforts of all these hostile armies. Hannibal was unable to take Rome.

Why could not Hannibal succeed? There were many reasons. First, a great many cities remained loyal to Rome and did all they could to hinder her foes. Secondly, the sturdy Roman character never would admit that it was beaten. Thirdly, the Romans were wise enough to refuse to meet Hannibal in open battle again. They used what we call "Fabian" (fā´bǐ-ǎn) tactics, so called from the dictator whom they chose to meet the emergency. His name was Quintus Fabius Maximus, and he was later surnamed "Cunctator" or "the delayer," because of the tactics he employed against Hannibal. He and his men followed the Carthaginian army everywhere and harassed it as best they might without actually entering into battle. Gradually they dispelled the hopes of the Carthaginians, who forgot their first successes.

Then, too, in the course of ten years the Romans had found a capable general of their own. This was Scipio (sǐp´ǐ-ō), a brilliant soldier, who was selected to lead a Roman army into Spain. He succeeded in driving all the Carthaginians out of that country. Ten thousand of them, under Hannibal's brother, managed to reach Italy, only to be destroyed by the Romans. Then Scipio returned to Rome and persuaded the senate to let him go with his army to Africa.

Scipio's campaign in Africa (204–202 B.C.) was a great success. After he had won two battles, Carthage had to call Hannibal home to defend his city.

The Power of Carthage Destroyed

And now the stage was set for the decisive battle of the war (202 B.C.). The two great generals, Hannibal and Scipio, were face to face at Zama. But the two armies were unequally matched in fighting capacity. The legions under Scipio were veteran troops, while the soldiers of Hannibal were many of them untrained clerks and merchants, lacking in military experience. In the clash of this last conflict an empire was to suffer destruction.

Hannibal tried to hem in the Roman army, as he had done at the battle of Cannae. But Scipio anticipated his intention, and met the quick movements of the Carthaginian troops with decision. He extended his forces to face the enveloping enemy. And at this moment of crisis Hannibal saw his army faced with defeat. The Battle of Zama ended for ever the prestige and power of Carthage.

To prevent the destruction of their city the Carthaginians agreed to pay 10,000 talents, or about £2,500,000, within fifty years. They had to surrender all their warships and their independence of action.

But Rome was not satisfied even with such a victory. When twenty years later Carthage had to raise an army to protect herself against attacks from fierce African tribes, the Romans—already become jealous of her rapid commercial recovery—seized the excuse to begin the Third Punic War. The conflict lasted three years, and in the end Carthage was taken and completely destroyed (146 B.C.).

Rome, Like a Tyrant, Feels She Must Conquer or be Conquered

When Hannibal had been conquered, Rome was without a rival anywhere in the Western world. Her armies were the biggest and strongest; her fleet ruled the Mediterranean. But she felt she could not rest on her conquests. She was like a rich tyrant who has to make everybody afraid lest his wealth should be stolen.

Rome was indeed surrounded by enemies. In the north, beyond the Alps, lived hordes of barbarians. These might sweep down at any time and overrun Italy as the Gauls had done. And in the east the empires left by Alexander the Great were already joining together to put down the rising Romans if they could. At the end of the Second Punic War, therefore, instead of entering upon a period of peace, Rome found herself just at the beginning of even greater struggles. She felt she must conquer or be conquered. Roman armies accordingly set out at once to overthrow the Eastern world.

They began with Macedonia (măs'ĕ-dō'-nĭ-å). King Philip of Macedon (măs'ĕ-dŏn) had promised to help Hannibal in his struggle against the Roman power, and so the Romans determined to crush him. They had learned much about war since the days when they first battled with Hannibal on the River Trebia. When the Roman legions met the heavy Greek phalanx with its long spears,

they had no trouble in surrounding it, beating down the spears, and hacking the Greeks to pieces with their terrible swords. It was the sword—a Spanish type of sword—which won the victory, for the Macedonians had only spears and daggers.

Greece is Conquered by Rome, and Syria Becomes Alarmed

At close quarters the Macedonians could find no way of combating the Romans, and Philip was utterly defeated (197 B.C.). Macedonia became subject to Rome, and soon all the Greek states and cities became subject likewise.

This victory, and the appearance of Roman soldiers so near to Asia, instantly aroused the fears of Syria. You will remember that when Alexander died his Eastern empire passed to one of his generals named Seleucus (sĕ-lū'kŭs). The descendants of this ruler were called Seleucids (sĕ-lū'sĭd), and it was one of the Seleucid kings, Antiochus (ăn-tī'-ŏ-kŭs), called the Great, who now looked upon Rome's conquest of Greece with an angry eye. He felt that the best plan was to strike first, and so he invaded Greece as a liberator bent on freeing the Greek states.

But the Romans soon drove Antiochus back to Asia, and quickly followed after him. Their stern and orderly legions came up with a disorderly throng of Oriental troops at Magnesia (190 B.C.), and under the leadership of Scipio the Romans easily conquered.

Egypt, the Land of the Pharaohs, Accepts the Protection of Rome

It seems surprising that a single battle should have won the enormous empire of the East. The triumph of Magnesia extended the rule of Rome even to the boundaries of the old Assyrian territory. Rome inherited or won the Greek states of Asia Minor, the lands of the Fertile Crescent, and finally Egypt. Egypt had long been Rome's ally, and after a time she accepted the guidance and protection of Rome (168 B.C.). Thus, by the close of the Third Punic War, the Mediterranean had indeed become a Roman lake, for Rome ruled it along both sides.

When the Greek cities came under the sway of Rome, she freely gave them the

A ROMAN WAVES FAREWELL TO HIS BELOVED CITY

Here is a Roman exile being rowed across the Tiber, sorrowfully waving farewell to his native land. To the Romans their great city was not only the capital of the country—they regarded it as the very centre of the world.

liberty which was dearer than life itself to the turbulent Greek nature. The Romans might be barbarians in art and literature, but they had a wholesome respect for Greek culture and Greek learning. The Greeks were still the masters of all the fine arts. When a rich Roman wanted to make his house beautiful with paintings and statues, or to enlighten his mind, he turned to the Greeks.

How Greece Rebelled Against the Domination of Rome

The Romans did not wish to make the Greeks slaves or vassals; they desired to protect and encourage them. But it was no easy matter to protect and pacify a group of states that had so long been at strife with one another. The Greek cities were continually annoying the Roman senate with their quarrels. At last, when open warfare broke out among them and they rebelled against Roman restraint, Rome had to treat them severely. The Roman army burned Corinth, deprived all the Greek cities, except Athens, of their liberty, and reduced the inhabitants to a state of subjection.

And now we see the beginnings of a strange falling off in the Roman capacity for govern-

ing wisely. When Rome first began her conquests, she generously gave a great many rights to the conquered peoples; but as her power grew she became less generous, and only a very few of her subjects outside Italy could hope for Roman citizenship.

Roman citizens began to realize that there was money to be made out of their conquered provinces. They could go out to them as governors or judges and make enormous fortunes. These men, returning to Rome, aroused the envy of the other Romans. For all their boasted law and order, neither they nor the other Romans were now very honest. They loved wealth and power. Corruption soon appeared everywhere—in the senate, among the consuls, the tribunes, and the other officials.

How Dishonesty Spread Like a Vile Weed Throughout the Great Empire

While Roman officials serving in foreign lands were becoming richer and richer, the plebeians at home were growing poorer and poorer. The old simple days were gone. Rome now had a far larger population, and there was not land enough around the city to provide farms for all the farmers. The people grew more and more discontented. The corrupt senate was ruled by the rich and powerful. The public lands were given to the wealthy instead of being kept for the people. Dishonest tribunes and foreign governors were helping themselves to the public money. Slaves were doing almost all the work and many of the poorer people went hungry.

Two Famous Brothers Who Championed the Cause of the People

All this meant trouble ahead. Within forty or fifty years after Rome had conquered the known world, a struggle began between the plebeians of Rome and their senate, and two tribunes who dared to champion the cause of the people were killed. These were the famous Tiberius Gracchus (tī-bēr′ĭ-ŭs grăk′ŭs), in 132 B.C., and his brother Gaius Gracchus (gā′ŭs grăk′ŭs), in 121 B.C. The people rioted now and then, but the riots were put down.

The matter was finally brought to a head by the struggle between Marius (mā′rĭ-ŭs) and Sulla, during the wars that were always going on somewhere or other on the borders of the Roman empire. In 111 B.C. the African Jugurtha (joo-gŭr′thȧ) had won a military victory by bribing the Roman consul. At the same time, certain restless German tribes, the Cimbri (sĭm′brī) and the Teutons, had been defeating one Roman army after another. The senate did not seem to be able to handle the situation. So the common people, in their assembly, appointed their own general, a soldier named Marius, who had once been a plough-boy.

How Marius Encouraged the People to Fight for Their Rights

Marius was a bitter enemy of every rich man and noble in the city. He marched away to the wars, doing his duty like a soldier, but after he had captured Jugurtha and had overwhelmed the Germans (102 and 101 B.C.), he did not forget his foes in Rome. On his return he encouraged the people to fight for their rights.

Marius was so violent that the common people would not follow him. For ten or twelve years he had to live in retirement. His opportunity arrived when a war again broke out in the East. Then the senate elected a general named Sulla, while the people defiantly chose Marius.

Now, in certain campaigns Sulla had served under the leadership of Marius, and between the two there already existed a great rivalry.

But it so happened that Sulla actually had charge of the Roman army, which was wiping out revolts in the Italian states, and as Marius had no army at all, Sulla, after first coming to Rome and forcing the people to consent to the rule of the senate, marched away with his army into the East.

As soon as Sulla had gone, the Roman people fell upon the senate and massacred many of the senators. Marius urged them on. They elected him consul for the seventh time, and under his rule the rich and mighty inhabitants of Rome trembled for the safety of their possessions and their lives.

How an Army Which Had Conquered the World Brought Death to Liberty

But Sulla was yet to be reckoned with. In five years he came marching home again. Marius was dead—he had died during his consulship—and there was no great leader to champion the people's cause. Every army sent out to meet Sulla was defeated, and when he appeared before the gates of Rome there was none to prevent him from entering. He caused himself to be appointed dictator, and, as soon as he was established in this position, the streets ran red with the blood of his enemies and the blood of those he suspected of being his enemies. His reign of terror lasted until 79 B.C., in which year he resigned the dictatorship.

When Roman generals began, like Sulla, to assume the powers of a dictator, the end of Rome as a republic was already in sight. It did not come immediately. Fully forty years of struggle and fighting were to pass before one man could become powerful enough to call himself emperor. But the idea of rule by the people never triumphed again. The very army with which Rome had conquered the whole of the civilized world brought death to Roman liberty.

(CONTINUED ON PAGE 773)

If you will only learn to take it as a game, you can get as much fun as these two girls out of a rainy day.

WHERE *the* RAIN COMES FROM

No Matter How Clear the Air, It Always Contains Water, Which Sooner or Later Falls to Earth

(CONTINUED FROM PAGE 728)

HAVE you ever asked yourself where the rain comes from? The air on a given day seems like any other air, but all at once gallons and gallons of water will come tumbling out of it. People tell you it comes from the clouds, but that is a puzzling answer. How did it remain in the clouds with nothing to support it?

The truth of the matter is that there is always water vapour in the air. Whenever we are out-of-doors we are breathing a certain amount of it in and out of our lungs. It floats in very tiny particles, even above deserts, and extends upwards to a distance of certainly seven or eight miles. We never know it is there; though in heated rooms, where the air is too dry, we soon feel uncomfortable. Everything moist—oceans,

rivers, lakes, and all living things—is constantly giving off water vapour into the air.

When air is warm a good deal more water vapour can enter a given space than when it is cold—at summer temperature five or six times as much as when it is freezing. In a medium-sized living room comfortably heated there would probably be some five teacupfuls of water. But if the temperature should drop to freezing-point the space could hold only one teacupful.

Now, what would become of the other four teacupfuls of water? It would have to collect on the walls and windows and furniture—or, as we say, it would have to condense. That is what has happened in the cellar on a hot day in summer, when the stone walls are dripping with moisture. The moisture has condensed. It is what happens whenever you take a glass of ice-cold water into a room on a hot day, for the cold water cools the vapour around it so much that the moisture condenses and turns from a gas into beads of water on the outside of the glass.

The point at which this happens we call the "condensation point"—for it is then that the water vapour "condenses." When a given space contains as much vapour as it can hold without dropping it—so much that the slightest cooling would start condensation—we say that the air is "saturated" (săt′ū-rā′těd), or that the "humidity"—or moisture — is 100 per cent., or that the air is at the "dew point." We call it the dew point because it is then that dew forms with the slightest cooling of the air. The point at which it occurs depends on the amount of moisture in the air. The dew point in dry air is much lower than the dew point in damp air.

Rain and snow fall from the sky, but dew does not. It forms in exactly the same way as the beads on the glass of ice-cold water. But it is not for long that men have realized this. Until only a little more than a century ago they thought the dew fell from above, and accounted for it in various poetical ways. Its ancient names were "star water" and "star tears." Later people came to believe that it was the breath of goddesses—or of angels.

Now we know it is the breath of our own Mother Earth. For during the day the sun draws moisture out of the ground, and when night falls and the twigs and flowers and grasses become cool, they chill the vapour that touches them, sometimes to the point of condensation. Then the air gives up a part of its moisture in delicate beads on all the grass and flowers. In this way the moisture that Mother Earth breathed out in the heat of the sun is given back to her at night.

The sight of those sparkling jewels is the reward of all who rise early. No one who has seen the fairy-like wheel of a spider's web on a dewy morning in summer can fail to feel repaid for his hour or two of lost sleep. For sluggards arrive after the sun has already drunk up again all the tiny drops that the night distilled —water so delicately made that it is the purest

These pictures illustrate water condensing at what we call the "dew point," though, of course, it is only the lowest picture that shows us dew as it has formed out of doors on a blade of grass. The moisture (magnified) has gathered on the outside of the jug because the water inside it was cold enough to chill the air round the glass. The air in the room contained tiny particles of moisture, called water vapour, and when the air round the jug fell to the right temperature, these tiny particles condensed into drops of water (magnified) on the jug. That is what makes any jug of cold water "sweat" in a warm room; the moisture in the air has condensed upon it. It is for the same reason that moisture gathers on the inside of the window-pane on a wintry day, when the glass is cold enough to chill the air near it to the "dew point," at which the moisture in the air condenses. And it is the same thing that makes moisture gather on blades of grass at night, when the air near the earth grows so cold that its moisture condenses on all the foliage and forms dew. From all this you can see that real dew never actually "falls"; it just gathers.

WHEN THE CLOUDS IN THE SKY COME DOWN TO EARTH

Here is the top of a tall building rising out of an ocean of fog. It is easy to see that the fog is only a great cloud that has settled down to earth. Within it every-thing is wet with tiny drops of moisture. Even the spiders' webs look like the one that is shown in the oval —though that was strung with gems by the soft dew.

to be found in Nature. In dry weather, dew is of enormous value to plants; sometimes they are forced to rely entirely upon it.

If the surface on which water vapour condenses is below freezing-point, we have not dew, but frost.

Why There is Always More Illness in Winter Than in Summer

Two or three times a day the meteor-ologist measures the "humidity" (hū-mǐd'-ǐ-tǐ), or the "wetness," of the air. When he says, for instance, that the humidity is 50 per cent., he means that there is just half as much moisture present as there could be at the temperature at which the measurement was taken.

All outdoor air contains moisture. It is only in our houses in winter that the air gets nearly dry. And that is very unnatural and very bad for the health. It is one reason why there is so much more illness in winter than in summer. If everyone took care to see that there was always plenty of moisture in the air in their homes, they would spend much less time lying in bed suffering from troublesome colds and influenza.

But if the air is too damp we are un-comfortable, for then the perspiration from our bodies cannot evaporate.

No one will be surprised that the water vapour in the air has a great deal to do with the weather, but it is harder to believe that dust has just as much effect upon it. As we have already mentioned, the reason why dust is so important is that every tiny drop of water in dew or rain or fog must have a centre on which to condense before it can form. The tiny dust particles act as such centres, and so do still tinier electrified atoms known as "ions" (ī'ŏn). Without any of those useful little cores, we should neither have gentle rain, nor should we have mist nor fog nor cloud. Our rains would become terrific downpours, to the great discomfort of all growing things.

What Happens When Water Vapour Condenses on Particles of Dust

Though all water vapour must have dust or ions or some other surface on which to condense, it can take many different forms once condensation has started. It may turn into rain, hail, snow, mist, cloud, fog, frost or dew. Of all these, the one we probably see oftenest is cloud or fog—for they are very much alike, although there are certain differences. In general, a fog may be described as a cloud that rests on the ground. Its particles of vapour are very small—perhaps two ten-thousandths of an inch in diameter.

Indeed, it is amazing how little water is needed to make a fog. A single gallon can make a cubic mile of air so dense that all traffic is brought to a standstill. A few quarts of water spread through the air in tiny, invisible specks can paralyse London for several days and cause a loss of hundreds of thousands of pounds. Of course, a city fog is made worse by the smoke that gathers in the air. The thousands of chimneys that pour forth soot are furnishing millions of particles of dust on which the vapour can condense.

The Terrible Fogs that Hang like Thick Blankets over the Sea

Sometimes all that is needed is a slight fall of temperature for the moisture to weave a veil behind which buildings look like ghosts and the lights are misty blurs. If the temperature rises, the fog will often disappear again, turned back into water vapour. If the air gets colder, the fog may rain itself away. But the oily smoke coats every tiny water particle with a greasy film which makes it hard for the particles to unite and fall in the form of raindrops.

It is at sea that fog is most dangerous. There it is the one form of weather that man has never conquered. It may blanket hundreds of square miles—so densely that ships do not know of one another's presence until the very moment when they collide. Of course, a ship always blows its siren in a fog—for five seconds every minute. But even so, hundreds of lives are lost in fogs. The danger of hitting an iceberg is far greater in a fog.

To avoid such accidents a vessel sometimes takes soundings from time to time to find out the temperature of the water, for an iceberg cools the ocean round it for a short distance. Sometimes a very large iceberg will echo the sound of sharp blasts from a siren and in that way show its presence.

Why Many Ships Have Found Their Doom Off the Coast of Newfoundland

Aviators, too, dread a fog. They can soar above a low fog, but not above high ones. If they try to mount above them, the air may become so cold that particles of water freeze to the plane and form a coating of ice which adds weight and disturbs the airflow over the wings, and finally forces the plane down.

Fogs at sea are caused in a somewhat different way from those that form over cities. When warm moist air floats over currents of cold water it is chilled and its moisture condenses into fog. Over the Grand Banks of Newfoundland this is constantly going on, for moist air from the warm Gulf Stream drifts over the cold waters brought down by the Arctic currents and is rapidly cooled. As a result, all that part of the Atlantic Ocean is a perilous place for the ships that go there to fish, or pass by on their way between America and Northern Europe. Many a boat lies at the bottom of the sea off the Grand Banks.

Perhaps some day man will learn to conquer fog, but at present he is helpless before it.

(CONTINUED ON PAGE 787)

Although it is summer-time, in the cold air above this mountain summit, moisture has formed into snow.

"FATHER *of* MUSTACHIOS"

That was the Name Given by the Arabs to Sir Richard Burton, the Fearless Explorer, Who Risked Death in Visiting Mecca, the Sacred City of the Mohammedans

THE life of Richard Burton reads like a romance. It was almost as though he had stepped out of the days of Drake and Hawkins, bringing with him their abounding love of adventure and exploration, and not a little of their blunt and rough ways.

He possessed, too, abilities which were peculiarly adapted to the life he was to lead. Born on March 19, 1821, he spent most of his early life in France and Italy, receiving little organized education, but acquiring an acquaintance with languages, and a love of wandering which was to develop as he grew older until his whole life became devoted to this end.

Although Burton went to Oxford University, he derived little benefit from his residence there beyond a skill in fencing, and a knowledge of Arabic which he taught himself. He was, in fact, far too wild a spirit for the place, and finally his eccentric behaviour caused him to be expelled. He joined the army in June, 1842, and saw service in India, but regular army life, with its strict discipline, allowed him no scope, and he accepted with relief a position on the Sind survey.

It was while engaged on this work that Burton evolved the daring scheme which was destined to be his first great adventure—namely, to penetrate into the heart of Arabia where no white man's foot had ever trod. Always intensely interested in the Oriental mind and customs, Burton was by nature fitted for the task. In features he was dark and of Semitic appearance, while his great ability in learning languages enabled him to master fully several native dialects. This, coupled with his skill in disguising himself, gave him every appearance of an Arab when he walked in the bazaars; and in this way he was enabled to immerse himself in the native life and not only to act, but to live the part he was playing.

Thus equipped, he started in 1853 on his enterprise. Owing to tribal warfare, Burton, who was known to the Arabs as "Father of Mustachios," was unable to penetrate farther than Mecca, but he managed to make the pilgrimage to the Holy City of the Muslims as one of themselves, and actually to obtain access to the Ka'abah (kä′ā̇-bä), a feat which no white man had previously accomplished.

It must be remembered that, in order to remain unsuspected, it was necessary for Burton to be possessed of the most intimate knowledge of every detail of procedure and ritual necessary for the undertaking, since one slip meant certain death. It was, in fact, only his remarkable presence of mind that saved him on the return journey.

On his arrival back from this hazardous expedition, Burton wrote a book, "Pilgrimage to Al-Medinah and Meccah," which was the most important monument to his achievement, displaying as it did a profound knowledge of Arab customs and insight into the native mind.

But this one expedition by no means satisfied Burton's adventurous spirit, and in 1854 the Indian government was persuaded to allow him to undertake the exploration

Above you see Richard Burton as he appeared when making the pilgrimage to Mecca. It is not surprising that the Arabs believed him to be one of themselves, for few would recognize the daring English officer in the romantic figure in the portrait.

of the unknown Somali country, at that time a subject of official concern.

Burton accordingly set out, accompanied by Captain Speke and two others, whom he left to rejoin him at Berbera while he continued alone towards the native capital of Harar, in the heart of the country. He reached that city, spent ten perilous days there, and even talked with the king.

Burton Sets Out with Speke to Discover the Source of the Nile

The return journey was attended by the most terrible hardships and dangers, averted only by his presence of mind; but he eventually completed it, only to start out again in December, 1856, with the object of exploring the great lakes of Central Africa, and searching for the source of the Nile. He was again accompanied by Speke, and setting out from Zanzibar on June 27, 1857, they reached Lake Tanganyika in 1858 after overcoming many difficulties. Here unfortunately, Burton fell ill, and Speke pushed on alone to the discovery of the Victoria Nyanza, a lake which, on a later expedition, he proved to be the source of the Nile.

This latter episode had an unfortunate sequel in the subsequent quarrel between Burton and Speke, who seems unwittingly to have received most of the credit for the expedition. Burton returned to England temporarily broken in health, but he derived great consolation from his marriage, in 1861, to a woman whose devotion was to prove both deep and enduring.

He spent the rest of his life in the service of the Foreign Office, acting as consul first at Fernando Po in West Africa, later at Santos in Brazil, then at Damascus, and finally at Trieste, where he died on October 20, 1890, having received the honour of knighthood four years previously.

His famous Translation of the "Arabian Nights"

He continued to travel occasionally during this last period, but perhaps the greatest achievement of his later years was his translation of the "Arabian Nights." This work, although not a strictly accurate transcript, displays such a minute knowledge of the language and remarkable insight into the Arab mind that, in spite of its somewhat harsh style, it probably ranks as the most important and typical of his works.

ON THE ROAD TO MECCA, THE HOLY CITY OF THE MOHAMMEDANS

Although most of the pilgrims to Mecca made the journey on foot, the grandees, or those of high rank, rode in a litter which was known as a takhtrawan. This must have been rather uncomfortable as it bounced up and down with the movements of the camels, but no doubt its occupants preferred it to walking.

The DISCOVERER of LAKE ALBERT

"As the Insignificant Worm Slowly Bores Its Way into the Heart of the Oak, Even So Did I Hope to Reach the Heart of Africa," wrote Samuel Baker

IT SEEMED as though Nature had endowed Samuel Baker, who was born on June 8, 1821, with qualities fit for an intrepid explorer. A descendant of Elizabethan seamen, he was big, handsome, strong and fearless, and in his early years had many fights with boys who had challenged or quarrelled with him ; he spent a lot of time in making experiments with materials such as gunpowder. He was generous and honourable, and, although not a very studious boy, was interested in both geography and natural history, a knowledge of which was to stand him in good stead in the future.

When Samuel was old enough, his father took him into his city office, but this was no suitable life for the restless young man, and so, after his marriage in 1843, he went to Mauritius (maw-rĭsh'ŭs) for a time, to manage his father's estate. This, however, only increased in him an already strong desire to travel in the little known places of the world in search of adventure.

After a short residence in Ceylon, he founded a small but flourishing colony in Nuwara Eliya, whither he had been sent to regain his strength after an illness. There he lived for a time, and introduced various breeds of cattle, but was at length forced to return home, as the climate was unsuited to his health.

Baker had for some time felt a great interest in the exploration which was at that time being carried on in the interior of Central Africa. He was filled with a strong

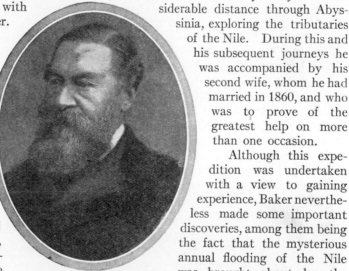

Sir Samuel Baker, who combined with his love of wandering and exploring activities the daring skill of a mighty hunter of big game.

desire to assist Speke and Grant who, in 1860 had gone into the heart of Africa in search of the source of the Nile, of whose geography little was known at that time.

But Baker realized that for an expedition of that kind he must have a knowledge of conditions of travel in Africa, and to this end he set out and journeyed a considerable distance through Abyssinia, exploring the tributaries of the Nile. During this and his subsequent journeys he was accompanied by his second wife, whom he had married in 1860, and who was to prove of the greatest help on more than one occasion.

Although this expedition was undertaken with a view to gaining experience, Baker nevertheless made some important discoveries, among them being the fact that the mysterious annual flooding of the Nile was brought about by the increased volume of its tributaries, the Blue Nile and the Atbara (ăt-bä'rä), which flow through Abyssinia, and not by the lakes of Central Africa, as had been previously supposed.

Baker also took part in much big game hunting, a sport to which he remained devoted all his life, and acquired not only a knowledge of Arabic and native customs, but a certain skill in medicine, which made him many friends among the natives, while his courage earned their respect.

On his return from what was for him a journey of preparation, Baker started to make arrangements for his attempt to travel up the Nile. He did not make his plans public, but set out quietly from Khartum (kär-tōom′) on December 18, 1862, with a party of nearly a hundred, financed by himself. In spite of mutinies, in which both he and his wife displayed great fearlessness and tact, the caravan eventually reached Gondokoro (gŏn′dŏ-kōr′ō), where Baker was met by the information that a party including two white men was expected from the south. He therefore decided to await their coming.

Speke and Grant Bring News of a Mysterious Lake

The new arrivals proved to be Speke and Grant, who informed Baker of the discovery of the source of the Nile at Victoria Nyanza (nī-än′zä). Baker felt that now there was nothing left for him to do, but he was reassured by the generous information given him by the two explorers, who explained their route and told him of a rumoured lake lying west of the Victoria Nyanza, which they believed to be a further source of supply for the Nile, and which they had been unable to reach because warfare had broken out among the tribes.

Baker accordingly continued on his way, following the route he had been given, and, in spite of mutinies and illness, was at last rewarded by standing, on March 14, 1864, on a great cliff fifteen hundred feet high and gazing over this western lake, which he called the Albert Nyanza. After a little further exploration of the lake, he discovered the Nile leaving it by means of a broad channel at the north-east end. He travelled down this river for some twenty-four miles until he arrived at a narrow gorge where the waters dashed over some magnificent falls. These he named the Murchison Falls, after Sir Roderick Murchison, the geologist.

Baker returned to Khartum in May of the next year. Honours were showered upon him and in 1866 he received a knighthood. Three years later he commanded a military expedition for the Khedive (kĕ-dēv′) of Egypt with the object of putting down the slave trade. Although not entirely successful, his efforts paved the way for the work of General Gordon.

Baker's love of wandering was to be satisfied once more when he made a tour of Cyprus in 1879, but after that he settled down in the beautiful country home he had purchased near Newton Abbot, in Devon, where he died in 1893, honoured by all.

A FIERCE FIGHT WITH AN OLD HIPPOPOTAMUS

Although hippopotami are generally harmless, sometimes the old bulls are very fierce, especially if they are in the water. Here you see one struggling hard with its captors, who are determined to kill it. The skull of one of these great creatures adorned Sir Samuel Baker's hall at his beautiful country home in Devon.

The MYSTERY of the NILE

How Speke and Grant Overcame the Many Obstacles which Beset Them in Their Partnership Expedition to Discover the Birthplace of Africa's Sacred and Greatest River

ON MAY 4, 1827, there was born at Jordans, in Somersetshire, the man who was at last to solve the riddle of the Nile, which, from the time of ancient Egypt, had baffled mankind. Where did the sacred river rise? No one had ever been able to discover, and it was left to John Hanning Speke to earn eternal fame by giving the knowledge to the world.

Speke was by profession a soldier, and had entered the Indian Army in 1844. There he served in the Sikh War under Sir Colin Campbell, spending his furloughs hunting and exploring the Himalaya (hǐ-mä′lā-à) Mountains, at one time crossing into Tibet. About this time Speke was seized with a desire to explore Equatorial Africa, but had to wait until he had completed ten years' service in India.

In September, 1854, however, he left for Aden, and there fell in with an expedition under Richard Burton, which had been formed for the purpose of exploring the Somali (sö-mä′lǐ) country. Speke was sent out to make observations to the south, but, owing to native deceit, was forced to return with his mission unaccomplished. Nevertheless, he made haste to join the main party at Berbera, and there found everything prepared for the main expedition which was to start on the return of Burton from Harar. But before they could set out, the camp was attacked by natives, Burton and Speke were both seriously wounded, and further exploration had to be abandoned.

Speke returned to England to recover, and later served in the Crimean War. At its

John Hanning Speke, who, of all the brave men who risked their lives in the attempt, can claim the distinction of being the first to solve the riddle of the source of the Nile.

conclusion he was delighted to receive from Burton an invitation to accompany him again on an exploration of the lakes of Equatorial Africa, and an attempt to discover the source of the River Nile. In June, 1857, the two set out from Zanzibar, and having heard from an Arab trader of three great lakes lying inland, they pressed on in spite of great hardships and reached Lake Tanganyika (tän-gän-yē′kä) in February, 1858. Soon after this, Burton was taken ill, and Speke, advancing alone, came upon the Victoria Nyanza, which he rightly conjectured to be the source of the Nile.

He arrived back in England in advance of Burton, and communicated his discoveries to the Royal Geographical Society. Unfortunately, and probably unintentionally, he was given the entire credit, which led to a permanent break with Burton, who not unnaturally was annoyed, and refused absolutely to believe in Speke's theories.

The Royal Geographical Society, however, believed his conjecture to be correct, and were satisfied that he had indeed discovered the Nile source; and when they fitted out an expedition for him to return and verify it, financial and other assistance was provided by the governments not only of Britain, but of India and the Cape. On this expedition the only white man to accompany Speke was James Augustus Grant, an old Indian army friend, who had taken part in the relief of Lucknow. About the same age as Speke, and united to him in a common love of all outdoor sport, he was to prove himself an ideal companion and a most loyal and unselfish colleague.

On April 27, 1860, the two friends left for Zanzibar, and by the end of September they were on their way to the interior. During the whole of their journey they were astonished by the overwhelming greed of the native chiefs, who would demand more and yet more cloth and beads before allowing them to proceed. This proved a great hindrance, but was not the worst of their troubles, as first Speke and then Grant fell ill with fever and suffered considerably.

At last they reached Uganda, and here Mtesa, the chief, entertained them hospitably, in spite of his extremely cruel character. Luckily Speke managed to gain some influence over his savage mind, and was able to check his fierce brutalities and the wholesale execution of his subjects.

Kamrasi, Speke continued his journey towards the east and the Nile source.

Unable to obtain any boats, Speke was forced to proceed on foot; but at length, on July 28, 1862, he reached the Victoria Nyanza, the scene of his former expedition, and with the finding of the Ripon Falls, proved beyond dispute that it was the birthplace of the Nile.

Speke, although desirous of penetrating to a further lake of which he had heard rumours, was prevented by the obstinacy of his native servants, and set sail down the Nile, although he was eventually forced to abandon that mode of travel owing to native hostility. At last, however, he succeeded in rejoining Grant, and the two finally found their way back to Gondokoro (gŏn'dŏ-kōr'ō).

At Gondokoro they met, to their surprise, Samuel Baker and his wife, who had come so far in the hopes of aiding the expedition. Speke, who was touched at the devotion of his friends, generously gave Baker information which led to the latter's discovery of the Albert Nyanza and finally returned to England, spending the rest of his life lecturing and writing on

In this little group of natives you see some of Speke's "faithfuls," as he nicknamed the eighteen of the ninety-six native servants who eventually struggled back to Gondokoro with him and Grant. The rest had deserted the expedition or died on the way.

After some considerable delay, Mtesa was persuaded by bribes into providing the two explorers with native servants and supplies, and while Grant turned north towards Unyoro to make friendly overtures to King

his discoveries. He died as the result of a shooting accident, on September 18, 1864.

Grant lived to take part in the Abyssinian campaign as an intelligence officer, and died at Nairn, on February 11, 1892.

The LORD MAYOR'S SHOW

How London's Chief Magistrate is Elected to Office, and the Story of the Gay and Glittering Pageant that Forms Part of the Ceremony

IT IS the ninth of November. How many are hoping that to-day the sun will shine, and they can line the pavements along the route to be taken by the Lord Mayor's Show with its gaily decorated cars, the soldiers, the various City officials, and, finally, my lord mayor of London himself in his great gilded coach.

From early in the morning the crowds will begin to gather to watch the show, and from early in the morning, too, the lord mayor himself will prepare for all that must be done on this busy day. He was elected on Michaelmas Day, September 29, and but yesterday he was "sworn in" at an impressive ceremony at the Guildhall. To-day there will be a breakfast at the Guildhall; later, the new lord mayor and sheriffs, all arrayed in scarlet and gold, will come in state from the Mansion House, the official residence of his lordship during his term of office. Parts of the procession are already waiting in the side streets near the Guildhall, and they will fall into their places under the direction of the City

THE LORD MAYOR PASSES BY

There is always an enthusiastic crowd assembled to greet the Lord Mayor on the day he rides in state through the City of London. Long before the first Lord Mayor's Show took place, the "ridings" were eagerly awaited by the apprentices as an excuse for a holiday.

marshal. Then amid cheers the lord mayor himself will take his place in his coach, and the procession will have begun.

Many of you may think that the Lord Mayor's Show is just a kindly gesture of the City of London to amuse the citizens, but this is not so. It is true that the pageantry part of the procession exists more or less for this purpose, but there is also the official part, the part which concerns the lord mayor and officials of the City. It is in the performance of their official duties that they make the journey, which takes them to the Law Courts. Here await them the judges of the King's Bench Division, and to these the lord mayor, accompanied by the sword-bearer carrying the sword point downwards, makes three reverences, taking off his hat each time.

The recorder then presents an address to the judges on behalf of the lord mayor, which is answered by the lord chief justice, the lord mayor keeping his head uncovered as he listens. After this ceremony the recorder proceeds to read a warrant from the mayor, commonalty and citizens of London, giving certain powers to their attorney, and ends by inviting the judges to dine with the lord mayor and sheriffs at the Guildhall that night.

The procession then returns by a different route to the Guildhall, and that night, after a reception in the library, there is held in the banqueting hall the lord mayor's magnificent banquet, at which the prime minister is always the last to arrive, and to which it is a great honour to be invited.

Chief Magistrate of the City

Does all this give you an impression of what an important personage the lord mayor is? For he is exceedingly important. Scarcely any civic function can be performed without him; he is the chief magistrate of the City; he summons and presides over several courts and meetings of the corporation; and during his year of office he takes precedence in the City of every subject of the crown, including princes of the blood royal.

He is the head of the City lieutenancy, an admiral of the Port of London and a trustee of St. Paul's Cathedral, to say nothing of being a chief commissioner of the Old Bailey. No troops may pass through the City without his leave, and within its precincts the lord mayor reigns supreme.

How the Lord Mayor is Chosen

With all these duties the lord mayor combines many others, and it is therefore not the least surprising that he is chosen very carefully. In fact, before any citizen of London can become lord mayor he must have been elected by a different body of electors on four separate occasions—by the citizens he desires to represent as an alderman; by the liverymen of the City guilds in Common Hall, on his election as sheriff; by the same liverymen, who nominate two aldermen for the office of lord mayor; and finally by the court of aldermen, who choose one out of the two whose names have been put forward.

But in order to understand the office of lord mayor and the Lord Mayor's Show let

Photo by Rischgitz

THE LORD MAYOR ARRIVES AT WESTMINSTER

At one time the Lord Mayor's Show was a water pageant, which proceeded up the River Thames on its way to West- minster. The last state barge, which was richly carved and gilt, was built in 1816, and sold by auction in 1850.

us go back and trace the origins of the office and the procession. We shall have to go back a very long way to find the first mayor of London, for the office is older than Parliament. Indeed, the first mention we have of a mayor is in 1189, when "Henry FitzEylwin, of Londenstane," was "made mayor of London and was the first mayor of the City, and continued to be such mayor to the end of his life." The mayor has always been chosen by the aldermen, and in 1215 King John granted a charter to the citizens of London, giving them the right to elect their mayor from among themselves annually, to be royally approved.

Now in those days every occasion for display was marked by public processions known as "ridings," and it is from the mayor's "riding" to Westminster, in 1215, to be approved by the king that the show originated. Later the lord mayor came to be presented to the barons of the Exchequer, but since 1881 he has made his reverences to the lord chief justice, although his name has previously been presented to the lord chancellor for approval by the sovereign.

Nobody knows exactly when the word "lord" came to be prefixed to "mayor" in connection with the chief magistrate of the City. It may have arisen from the custom of using the courtesy expression "my lord" mayor, which would be quite likely, especially as the mayor of London takes the rank of an earl during his year of office. The first mention in literature of a lord mayor occurs, so far as we know, in 1554, in Baler, who speaks of "Maister Harry, my lord mayor's fool,"

although it has been suggested that the title is traceable to 1378, in which year the mayor was classed with "the earls" when there was a general assessment for a war subsidy.

Although the lord mayor's "ridings" were first held in 1215, there was none of the pageantry attending them which we know to-day. That developed later, and it is not until 1566 that we have a really detailed account of a regular Lord Mayor's Show. But for the best account of the ordinary routine of ceremonies on lord mayor's day in the reign of Elizabeth we must turn to "A breffe description of the royall Citie of London, capitall citie of this realme of England," "wrytten by me Wyllyam Smythe citizen an haberdasher of London 1575."

"The day of Sts. Simon and Jude," he writes, "he (the mayor) entrethe into his estate and offyce: and the next daie following he goeth by water to Westmynster, in most triumphlyke manner." It must be noted that the lord mayor in olden times was chosen on October 28, the feast of St. Simon and St. Jude; from the fifteenth century until about the middle of the nineteenth century he went to Westminster by water. Sir John Norman, in 1453, is thought to be "the first lord mayor that was rowed in his barge to Westminster with silver oars at his own cost and charges." Whether this be quite true or not, he certainly established the fashion which was to continue for so long.

But to return to Wyllyam Smythe, who has left his haberdasher's shop to gaze in wonder at the show. He explains how the lord mayor went in his own barge, emblazoned

More than once elephants have taken part in the Lord Mayor's Show, and, although they have been known to break loose, on the whole they have been well-behaved and seemed thoroughly to enjoy the admiration of the crowd.

with the arms of the City, and after him a "shipboat of the Queen's Majestie," followed by the companies of London, all with the arms of their barges, "and so, passinge alonge the Thamise, landeth at Westmynster, wher he taketh his othe in Thexcheker, beffore the judge there (which is one of the chief judges of England), which done, he retorneth by water as afforsayd, and landeth at Powles wharfe, where he and the rest of the aldermen take their horses, and in great pompe passe throwgh the greate streete of the citie, called Cheapside."

First came two great standards, bearing the arms of the City of London and those of the mayor's company, then drums and flutes and "poore men," two and two together, "in blewe gownes, with redd sleeves and capps, everyone bearing a pyke and a target, whereon is paynted the armes of all them that have byn mayor of the same company that this new mayor is of." After them followed musicians, more officials of the City, then "a pageant of Tryumphe rychly decked," then more musicians and officials, the latter rising steadily in importance until there appeared the mayor himself, preceded by the swordbearer in gorgeous apparel. After him came the aldermen, past mayors and the sheriffs, and thus they passed through the City to the Guildhall.

The pageants that form part of the Lord Mayor's Show steadily increased in size and importance, and generally included speeches written by a City poet, of whom Thomas Jordan is the most famous. They suffered a set-back under the Puritans, who sternly forbade such vanities as the Show, but with the restoration of Charles II the City pageantry was restored to its old glory. In 1702 was held the last of the annual shows composed by a City poet and publicly performed, and after that the pageant proceeded without words. A little later another change was made, for in 1711 Sir Gilbert Heathcote was thrown from his horse, and it was decided that future lord mayors should ride in a coach. Then in 1757 a beautiful gilt coach, covered with all sorts of symbolical paintings and decorations, was introduced, of which the present-day coach, first used in 1896, is a replica.

The pageant itself, too, has undergone many changes. It has contained moral teachings, it has extolled the lord mayor, it has been mere political propaganda, it has even been arranged by "Lord" George Sanger, the king of showmen, and it has often contained circus elephants.

The whole of the arrangements for the Lord Mayor's Show, in which a strict order of official procession is observed, are in the hands of the remembrancer and sixteen other officials known as the "lord mayor and sheriffs' committee." The cost of the official show and banquet generally amounts to about £3,000 or £4,000, half of which is borne by the lord mayor and half by the sheriffs.

Although it is true that the lord mayor must be a rich man, you must remember that many lord mayors have started life as poor boys— Sir Richard ("Dick") Whittington was by no means the only one.

So when you next watch the Lord Mayor's Show as it passes on November 9, think what little London, with its quaint timbered houses and narrow streets, must have been like when the mayor rode to Westminster in 1215—the year of Magna Carta—and then remember all the stages through which it has passed since. Truly London is a city of memories and traditions.

PREPARING THE COACH FOR THE PROCESSION

The paintings which adorn the coach represent the virtues and attributes of the office of Lord Mayor. They are relics of the times when these were represented by living people. Here you see the coach having a wash and brush-up.

THE FORUM OF ROME IN ALL ITS MAJESTY OF LONG AGO

This is one of the most famous spots in the world. To-day it is a ruin, for the centuries have not been kind to it. But scholars have worked out how it must once have looked, and here you see a picture of what it may have been like two thousand years ago. On the hill—called the Palatine—is the palace of the Caesars.

Just below it is the house of the vestal virgins, who guarded the sacred flame in the little round temple of Vesta, seen in the centre of the picture. To the left of that temple is the temple of Julius Caesar, and on the other side is the temple of Castor and Pollux. At the extreme right is a corner of Julius Caesar's basilica.

The GRANDEUR That Was ROME

After Julius Caesar, the Mightiest Roman of All, There Came a Period of Great Glory and Profound Peace Under Augustus, the First Emperor

(CONTINUED FROM PAGE 758)

YOU HAVE often heard it said that history repeats itself. This was very true of the countries in early times. One nation after another conquered the world and grew rich on the tribute or taxes collected by her armies from the vanquished people; but as her riches grew, her character decayed, until finally it brought about her downfall.

Rome had started bravely as a republic, governed largely by the people. She had treated her defeated enemies fairly and kindly. Later, the lust for power and riches had seized her, and in a few years the world was at her feet. Her victories were her real defeat. She, too, was to grow rich and to decay, like the other conquerors.

If the Roman senate had been composed of honest and capable men; if the assembly of the people had been wise enough to make good laws instead of stirring up hatred and strife; if the army had not lent itself to the selfish aims of its generals, then the Roman state might have endured—as a free people governing themselves in a republic. But when the golden flood of wealth poured into the city from the conquered peoples, the ideals of fair play and patriotism that had inspired the early Romans were swept away. It was really rapacity that destroyed the republic, for when the people themselves no longer cared for law and order, some strong man inevitably seized the power of government, and compelled the citizens to bow to his rule.

Marius and Sulla had both discovered for themselves how power could be seized in Rome. Whoever controlled the army held Rome. Where was the patriotism of the Roman citizen who, if given a helmet and shield, could forget his duty to the republic and serve one man's will? What sort of soldier was he who would strike down defenceless citizens of Rome at the bidding of an ambitious general? Only one who had lost respect for the voice of his people and the free land of his fathers.

The Roman soldiers were now no longer sturdy citizens who came to serve for a short time in the army and hoped soon to return to their homes. The Roman trooper—or legionary—was now a professional fighter who spent his life in the army. He was carefully trained to do exactly as he was told, without thought or question. He was away from Rome most of the time, and regarded an ordinary citizen with all the scorn of a fighter for a man of peace. If he loved anyone, he loved his general, who paid him and gave him orders and decided everything for him. For this general he might lay down his life; for him he would certainly ravage the land of his fathers and kill the elected officers of his countrymen.

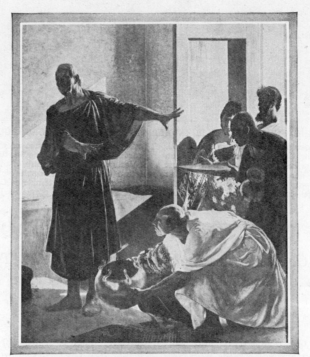

DENTATUS REFUSES A BRIBE

Romans always revered the memory of Manius Curius Dentatus, an early general and consul. And, long after they had lost the strength and virtue of the early Romans, they liked to tell the story of how the Samnites—an Italian tribe that Dentatus had conquered—came to try to bribe him when he was consul. They found the great man preparing his own meal, which consisted of roasted turnips. When they offered him rich gifts of gold and silver vessels, he refused them with scorn, saying that earthen dishes suited him quite well, and that he would rather rule over people who had gold than possess it himself.

It did not take the Roman people long to learn to fear their army, and the last days of the republic were wasted in a struggle between the assembly and the senate, with each one trying to appoint its own commander for the army. The story of the contests between the opposing generals is full of excitement and adventure. It is also full of great names—Pompey, Julius Caesar, Mark Antony, Octavian and others. These were the ambitious Romans who brought about the end of the republic and established the rule of an emperor. But we must not think of them as merely evil men who were bent on wrecking their country. They were sometimes trying to do their best for it, although they were often very self-seeking. But it is difficult to serve a country that has become corrupt, and most of whose leaders are selfishly ambitious.

After the death of Sulla, the people cast about for someone to oppose the senate. They found their champion in Pompey (pŏm'pĭ), an army officer. Pompey was eventually given command of the army. Immediately he set off to clear the Mediterranean Sea of the pirates who were making life hazardous for cities along the coast. When Pompey had vanquished the pirates he proceeded eastwards to Syria, where the kings who had succeeded Alexander the Great were becoming troublesome. Here,

THE ROMANS LAND ON THE SHORES OF KENT

The first landing of Julius Caesar and his army in Britain. His forces, consisting of two legions, were landed on the coast of Kent, but returned across the Channel on the approach of winter. The following year he came again with more than twice the number of foot soldiers and a strong force of cavalry. On this occasion he marched inland through Middlesex and across the Thames, but was compelled to return to Gaul once more. It was not until a century later that the Romans began the actual conquest of Britain.

also, he was victorious. He marched in triumph into Jerusalem, putting all Syria under Roman control.

While Pompey was away, a young man named Julius Caesar, who was a nephew of Marius, the people's champion, appeared before the people as a candidate for the consulship. Caesar was supported by a rich but corrupt man called Catiline (kăt'ĭ-lĭn), and was opposed by Cicero (sĭs'ĕr-ō), the greatest orator of Rome. Catiline and his evil followers—slaves and outlaws—raised a rebellion, and when it was over Caesar suffered a temporary eclipse.

Before very long Pompey returned and approached the senate with a request for land for his troops and approval of the peace settlements he had made with the eastern countries. Then Caesar came forward. He arranged with Pompey and a rich nobleman named Crassus that the three of them should rule the country jointly. This govern- ment by three was called a triumvirate (trī-ŭm'vĭ-rāt), and through its power Caesar was elected consul. At this he gave Pompey all the things he had sought from the senate.

But Caesar did not forget his own plans in gratifying Pompey's desires. The victories of Pompey in the East had made him popular and famous. Caesar turned to the free West in search of his own fame and power. As a first step he had himself appointed governor of Gaul—the land we now call France.

When Swords Ruled Rome

In 58 B.C. Caesar entered Gaul, determined to win a military leadership. Only a soldier could rule Rome, and Caesar meant to be that soldier. If votes were nothing and swords were everything, then he must gather behind him such swords as there had never been seen before.

Caesar was not only a wise governor but a military genius. He learned how to handle troops with a skill such as even Hannibal had never attained. In a battle he would handle the cohorts (cŏ'hôrt), or divisions of his legions, so rapidly that his enemies were dismayed and overwhelmed. He would march his armies hither and thither with such speed and skill that the barbarian hosts were often taken by surprise and overwhelmed.

In eight years Caesar had conquered all Gaul and had even visited the island of Britain. In the book telling of his wars, which boys and girls still read in school, Caesar told the people of Rome what he had done for the glory of his country. As his power in Gaul increased, his army increased too, until at last he felt ready to return to Rome, to obtain possession of it if he could.

Caesar had friends in Rome who were trying to secure his re-election as consul. But the senate were full of fears about Caesar's return. They knew too well his strength, his plans, and his ability. There was only Pompey to oppose him, and the senate disliked Pompey because he was the people's choice. At last, swallowing their pride, they gave the command of the army at Rome to Pompey, and sent Caesar an order to disband his troops.

It was Caesar's custom to act instantly in any crisis, and now, without a moment's hesitation, he took a step upon which his very life depended. Within an hour after he received the curt order of the Roman senate, Caesar crossed the little river Rubicon (rōō'bĭ-kŏn), the boundary between Italy and Gaul, and was marching towards Rome (49 B.C.). To this very day, when anybody makes an important decision from which there is no turning back, we say that he has "crossed the Rubicon."

Caesar's swift action took all Rome by surprise. It allowed Pompey no time to

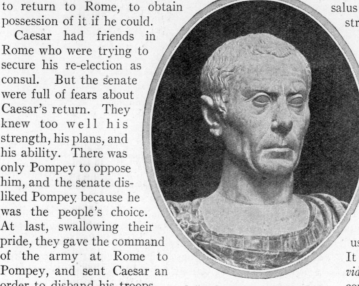

Julius Caesar, one of the world's greatest men—a conqueror, an author, and a statesman. Many heroes of the ancient world look strange and fierce and foreign to us, but we should notice nothing unusual about the face of Julius Caesar if it were possible to meet him to-day.

raise an army to meet the veterans from Gaul, and the senate and their general were forced to flee across the Adriatic Sea into Greece. Probably they did not really need to fly, for Caesar was neither a Marius nor a Sulla. When he entered Rome there was no butchering of enemies. He simply caused himself to be elected consul, and then announced that he would defend Rome against Pompey and the senate.

Caesar next marched into Spain, where a Roman army favourable to Pompey was stationed. He surrounded this army and made it surrender without bloodshed. Then, with his customary speed, he sailed to Greece and met Pompey on the field of Pharsalus (fär-sā'lŭs). By a clever stratagem Caesar cut Pompey's army to pieces (48 B.C.), and the beaten general fled to Egypt, where he was murdered. Caesar now set out to conquer every province that opposed him. He swept through Asia Minor, Egypt, Africa and Spain, and sent to Rome news of the triumphs of his arms. One of his brief but famous messages has come down to us through all the centuries. It was in three words, *"veni, vidi, vici"*—"I came, I saw, I conquered."

Julius Caesar was not only the greatest general of Rome, but also the greatest statesman. He was one of the few men in history who had the world at their feet. Had he chosen he might easily have proclaimed himself emperor. Many Romans believed that he intended to do so, and some were glad, hoping to see Rome the greatest of all empires under Caesar.

But there were also many men in Rome who believed that the republic was not yet dead, and that Caesar was trying to destroy it. They thought that if only Caesar were out of the way, the rule of the people might

Julius Caesar hearing complaints in Rome during his dictatorship. His desire for absolute power finally led him to set himself up as a god—at which the Romans became very resentful and eventually put him to death.

be restored. Several of these men, among them Brutus and Cassius, plotted against Caesar. When he returned to Rome and was planning another war in the East, they set upon him and assassinated him in the very senate house itself (March 15, 44 B.C.). It is this act that Shakespeare has made the climax of his great play.

The Men Who Divided the Empire

If Caesar's murderers had really hoped for a return of free government, they were greatly deceived. Although Caesar had never proclaimed himself emperor, he had enjoyed the power of an emperor in all the affairs of the Roman state. Senate and assembly had grown used to the rule of one man, and now it was merely a question of who would seize the reins that Caesar had dropped. There were several powerful men in Rome. There was Mark Antony, the fellow-consul of Caesar; Lepidus (lĕp'ĭ-dŭs), a brother general; and a young man of eighteen named Octavian, who was Caesar's great-nephew and his adopted heir. There were also Brutus and Cassius, with an army behind them, trying to rebuild the republic. Antony seized all Caesar's possessions and would have killed young Octavian if he had thought it worth the trouble. Octavian

himself, realizing that military force was the only real power in Rome, gained command of several legions within a short time. Then by skilful persuasion, although he was still only twenty, he caused himself to be elected consul.

As consul, Octavian joined with Antony and Lepidus in another triumvirate to make war on Brutus and Cassius, who were still hoping to restore republican government in Rome. The republican army was encamped at Philippi (fĭ-lĭp'ī) in Macedonia, and, in 42 B.C., Antony and Octavian met and defeated it. Then they divided all the Roman possessions between them. Octavian took Rome, Italy and the West, while Antony held sway in the East.

Mark Antony and Cleopatra

The next task of Octavian was to dispose of certain rebels to his rule, among them Lepidus and a son of Pompey. By the time Octavian was twenty-eight years old there was left in Rome no one to dispute his power. All this time Antony remained in Egypt. But rival rulers seldom agree well together, and Octavian soon came to feel that Antony was not using his power in the East to the best advantage. Accordingly he gathered his fleet and sailed out to meet Antony and the Egyptian queen, Cleopatra.

at the battle of Actium (ăk'shĭ-ŭm) off the coast of Greece (31 B.C.). In the midst of the battle Cleopatra fled and Antony followed her. The following year Octavian pursued them to Egypt, meeting with no resistance. When he gained control of the country, Antony and Cleopatra both took their lives. And Shakespeare has written another great play about Antony and his fatal Cleopatra, "for whom he lost the world, and was content to lose it."

The First Roman Emperor

Octavian was now the undisputed ruler of every inch of Roman territory. The Romans were so thankful to be at peace after nearly a hundred years of civil war and revolution that they welcomed him back to Rome with a magnificent celebration. When he wished to surrender his control of the army to the senate, they insisted on his keeping it. They made him tribune and governor of most of the Roman provinces, and gave him the title of Augustus, or "the honourable one." At the same time he was appointed imperator (ĭm'pě-rā'tŏr), or "commander"—or, as we should say, "emperor." He was to govern with the assistance of the senate.

Octavian, or Augustus Caesar, was the first Roman emperor who was actually recognized as such. To a war-worn world he brought a time of unbroken peace. His reign was marked by brilliant progress in every direction, in art and literature, in wealth and grandeur, so that we call it the "Augustan Age" after him. It was the most splendid age of the Roman state.

We have been following the fortunes of Rome in war without paying much attention to the Roman people—how they lived and what they did from day to day. Let us pay a visit to Rome during the Augustan Age and see what life there was like while this great emperor held sway.

The Centre of National Life

The centre of trade, politics, and of most other activities in Rome was the Forum. This was an open market, or square, in which the people used to meet to transact their

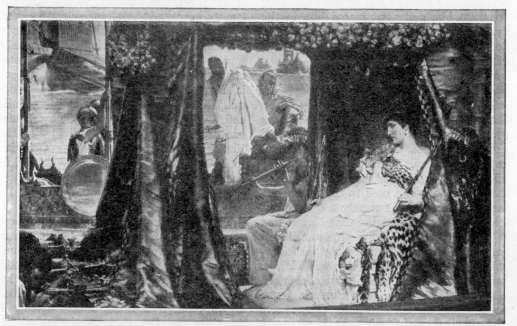

MARK ANTONY BEHOLDS THE BEAUTY OF CLEOPATRA

The charms of Cleopatra, the fascinating queen of Egypt, at one time helped to shape the destiny of Rome. Julius Caesar fell in love with her when he went as a conqueror to Egypt, and made her the sole ruler there. After Caesar's death Mark Antony became her victim, and largely on her account lost his power as ruler over the eastern part of the Roman empire. Here Antony is seen at his first meeting with Cleopatra, when, arrayed as the goddess Venus, she sailed out in a magnificent barge to offer him her royal welcome.

public and private business. Here they listened to speakers who were seeking office, to tribunes giving the latest news of the foreign wars, or to orators complaining about the conditions of the people. Around the Forum were the public buildings of senate and assembly, a few temples, and a basilica (bȧ-sĭl'ĭ-kȧ), or place of business, where merchants bought and sold shares in foreign ventures and transacted other affairs.

The old Forum was a small place with modest buildings. But Augustus immediately began the construction of a large and magnificent square with beautiful pillared walks about it and a fine house for the meetings of the senate. In addition to this new Forum, Augustus built many imposing public buildings, among them several temples and a library, besides his palace on the Palatine (pǎl'ȧ-tĭn) Hill. He once said that he found Rome a city of brick and left it a city of marble.

By the time Augustus had established

A TRIUMPH OF EMPEROR AUGUSTUS

When a Roman general had won honours in the field he often received a great public ovation, called a "triumph," upon his return to Rome. This was voted him by the senate, the general remaining outside the city until the act had been passed. Then, with a splendid procession, he entered the city and passed through garlanded streets filled with crowds of people who cried "Io triumphe!" Sometimes an emperor's heir rode with him and shared the honours. At the head of the procession were the magistrates and the senate. Next came the trumpeters, who were followed by chariots laden with spoils. Then white oxen with gilded horns and other victims for the sacrifice, and behind them marched the captives—often kings and queens in their own land. And finally came the general himself, arrayed like Jove in a costume of purple and gold, and riding in a laurel-crowned chariot drawn by four horses. In one hand he carried a laurel branch, and in the other usually an ivory sceptre surmounted by an eagle. A slave supported Jupiter's golden crown just above the general's head, and continually whispered into what must have been a deaf ear a reminder of the fact that the distinguished man must remember that he was only mortal. Behind the general's chariot followed his army, singing and shouting, "Io triumphe!" When the procession reached the temple of Jove, on the Capitoline Hill, the triumphant general placed his laurel branch on the knees of the god and offered his sacrifices. Then feasting and celebrations followed, lasting sometimes for several days. In the picture Emperor Augustus is being borne through the streets of Rome at one of the triumphs that were voted him.

his peaceful reign the Romans were living in fairly good houses, built after the Greek fashion, with a courtyard at the centre or at the rear, and a reception room, or atrium (ā'trĭ-ŭm), at the front of the house.

During the old days of the First Punic War the atrium had formed the whole house, with the kitchen in one corner and the bed in another. Since the only way for the smoke to escape was through a hole in the roof, the atrium of those days was rather sooty, and hence it derived its name from the Latin word *atreus*, meaning "black."

The simple houses of the Romans had long since disappeared when Augustus became emperor. After the Romans had seen the luxurious dwellings of Carthage and Alexandria, they soon introduced the same styles in Rome. The best houses had two floors, with bedrooms upstairs, and they might even boast of water and heating systems. In decorating and furnishing Rome could not compare with the other ancient cities.

The best the Romans could do was to carry away statues and mosaics from the cities they captured. And whenever a Roman wanted anything especially beautiful, he had to take it from Greece or employ a Greek to make it for him.

As in all ancient cities, the principal work was done by slaves. A rich man had hundreds of slaves, from his doorkeeper to the man who rubbed him down after his bath. The only servant in the house who was usually not a slave was the cook. A good cook in the Augustan Age could earn a large salary, because there was nothing the Romans liked better than good food.

How the Romans Came to Love the Magnificent Literature of Greece

In Rome, as in Greece, slaves frequently had charge of the schools where children were taught. The teachers were usually Greeks. Every educated Roman could speak Greek, and such men as Cicero and Caesar used it in daily conversation. Just as the Romans admired the Greek gods and adopted them as their own, so they admired the poetry of Homer and all the other great literature of Greece. In the fine houses they always kept a large library of Greek books; our own knowledge of Greek literature comes mainly through these Latin books and translations.

Some things which were very evident in Greece were noticeably absent in Rome. The Romans had little love for music, and took scarcely any interest in athletic games. On one occasion a Roman audience interrupted a musical performance and demanded a fight. Their sports were far more brutal than the sports of Greece. They never had anything like the Olympic games.

Although they lacked sculptors, painters and musicians, the Romans were great builders and great lovers of literature. The Augustan Age produced, on the one hand, many fine buildings and triumphal arches erected in honour of great heroes, and on the other hand a number of famous poets and writers.

One of these poets was Quintus Horatius Flaccus, whom we call simply Horace. He had been an enemy of Augustus and had fought under Brutus at Philippi. He wrote poetry that people still delight to read. But the greatest Latin poet was Virgil (vẽr'jĭl). He was a friend of Augustus, and desired to celebrate the rise of the new emperor to power, so he used the old story of Aeneas (ĕ-nē'ȧs) of Troy, and told it in Latin verse, tracing the fancied line of the Julians and the Caesars from the old Trojans to Augustus. He called this poem the Aeneid (ĕ-nē'ĭd). It became tremendously popular when it was published, and to this day is considered one of the greatest poems ever written.

In addition to Horace and Virgil there lived in the Augustan Age Strabo (strā'bō), who wrote a charming but inaccurate geography and book of travels. There was also Livy (lĭv'ĭ), who wrote a detailed history of Rome.

Rome produced no mathematicians, no astronomers, no natural scientists. The Romans could fight, write, and attend to business, but all Rome held nothing to equal the Lyceum or the Academy of Athens, or the Museum of Alexandria. In Rome there were no philosophers to walk about in groves or to speculate about the wonders of the great universe.

How Luxury and Power Began to Sap the Strength of a Great Nation

The Augustan Age was the high-water mark of Roman accomplishment and culture. After this time the wealth of the city increased and the luxury of her rich citizens rose beyond anything that had been known before in the ancient world; but the Roman vigour was never again equalled.

Augustus was a man of simple tastes, who wanted to lead the Romans back to simple things. He tried to curb divorce, to establish order and check extravagance, to bring back the reverence for the old gods. But the Romans had drunk too deeply of wealth and power. The old self-control was gone. They had entered upon a period of extravagant and riotous living which in the course of time brought about their downfall.

(CONTINUED ON PAGE 808)

SWEET MUSIC FOR TWO LADIES OF ANCIENT ROME

Roman ladies listening to a Greek musician. The Greeks had found music quite unformed and, with their skill in all things pertaining to beauty, had made it into a great art. But the Romans had few musical gifts. They liked to hear Greek performers or sometimes to perform themselves. The infamous emperor Nero, for instance, is known as a singer. But the teachers of music were almost without exception Greeks.

THE GREEK PICTURE-DEALER SHOWS HIS TREASURES

The Romans were not artists. Nearly all their beautiful things they learned from the Greeks, who were the artists of the ancient world. In the picture a Roman lady is seen paying a visit to a Greek art shop—much as ladies visit antique shops to-day—for it was fashionable in Rome to have the latest thing from Greece. To the end, in all matters of taste and culture, the Greeks, even as slaves, remained the masters of their conquerors.

The MASTER-POET of the VICTORIAN AGE

Although Alfred Tennyson was Told as a Boy that He Would Never Make Money by Writing Poetry, it was in This Sphere of the Arts that He Won Fame

(CONTINUED FROM PAGE 734)

ALL day long the rectory at Somersby, in Lincolnshire, rang with the voices and laughter of the twelve happy Tennyson children as they played at the games they had invented for themselves. The young Tennysons also loved animals, and spent a great deal of time tramping through the nearby woods and watching the birds and other creatures that lived there. Unable to bear the sight of an animal ensnared, they never failed to spring the gamekeepers' traps, a habit which led one of the keepers to remark, "If ever we catch that there young gentleman who is for ever springing the traps, we'll duck him in the pond."

By "that there young gentleman" they meant Alfred, the fourth child of the large Tennyson family; he had been born on August 6, 1809. Of all the children he was the most interested in Nature and spent the greater part of his time watching his pet owl and his mother's pet monkey, studying the flowers in the rectory garden, or lying flat on his back to gaze at the stars in the evening sky.

Of all their games none was more popular than the one they played at the family dinner table. During the day each child would write a story or a poem and hide it under a dish or plate. Then, when dinner was over, they would read them aloud —tales of adventure and daring, of knights and ladies, of goblins and dragons and Indians. And it was the stories by Alfred that delighted them most, for he seemed to have been born to be a writer.

Although his father understood him and felt sure that he would make a name for himself some day, his grandfather was not quite so sure. Once, when he had asked the boy to write a poem about his grandmother, who had recently died, the old gentleman did not find the poem to his liking. Handing the boy two shillings, he remarked:

"There! That is the first money you have

By permission of the Museum and Art Gallery Committee of the Corporation of Birmingham

Those who have read Tennyson's "Idylls of the King" will remember Morgan-le-Fay, the wicked half-sister of King Arthur. This picture, from the painting by Frederick Sandys, shows her standing at the loom on which she wove the magic mantle which was intended to consume King Arthur by fire.

ever earned by your poetry, and take my word for it, it will be the last."

But the grandfather was wrong, for Alfred Tennyson was destined to become one of the great English poets.

When he was seven the boy was asked whether he would rather go to school or go to sea, and at once he decided in favour of school. But his four years at the Louth Grammar School were so unpleasant that he may well have wondered whether he had chosen wisely. At last, however, he was brought home to be taught by his father, a learned man who was able to give the boy the educational training that he needed.

Surrounded by people who understood him, he found happiness in his refined home, where there was plenty of time for reading in his father's excellent library, for thinking, for enjoying and studying Nature, and for writing. By the time he was twelve he had written a poem of more than six thousand lines, and at fourteen he was the author of a whole drama in blank verse. Four years later, Alfred and his brother Charles published a volume of verse called "Poems by Two Brothers."

At Cambridge University, where he went to study in 1828, he took great pleasure in the friendship of the remarkable young men he met there, especially in that of Arthur Hallam, who became his dearest friend. When he won the Chancellor's Prize with his poem on "Timbuctoo," in competition with such a promising writer as the young William Makepeace Thackeray, his ability impressed both his instructors and his schoolfellows. A year later, when he published

Photo by Rischgitz

Alfred Lord Tennyson, the best-loved of the poets of the nineteenth century, whose poems we still read with the greatest pleasure.

a volume of "Poems, Chiefly Lyrical," he gained some notice from poets and critics out in the world, if not much attention from the public at large.

In 1831 he left Cambridge without taking a degree, for his father was ill and Alfred was needed at home. Upon his father's death a few weeks later, Alfred decided to remain at Somersby. There he finished the poems which were to be published in a volume printed in 1832. Many of these already showed remarkable gifts; but some of the critics of the day were heartless in their reviews of the little volume.

Stung by the harsh criticisms of his poems, and saddened by the sudden death of his great friend, Arthur Hallam, Tennyson let almost ten years pass without publishing a word of any consequence. He was busy all the time, reading and writing, and the work of those ten years came out in his "Poems" of 1842, and brought him real fame. From that time on he was always ranked as the greatest of the living poets.

Yet he was still to spend several more years of hardship and of worry over money matters. Next he published the narrative poem called "The Princess," and in 1850 the elegy of "In Memoriam," a great poem expressing the author's grief for his dead friend, Hallam, and the rebuilding of his own faith. His poems were now bringing in enough money for him to marry the girl who had waited for many years.

From then on life was easier. That same year he was made poet laureate; his fame was spreading very rapidly. It was greatly increased by his series of beautiful poems entitled "Idylls of the King." He also wrote a number of fine dramas in verse.

Hardly any other English poet received such honours during his lifetime, and hardly any other ever held such sway over the hearts and minds of the English-speaking world as did Tennyson. In 1884 he was given a peerage, and when he died, on October 6, 1892, he was honoured by being given a last resting-place within the hallowed Poets' Corner of Westminster Abbey.

The poems that flowed from his pen have a purity, a nobility, and an artistic beauty that is rare in any age and in any language.

A POET *Most* DIFFICULT *to* UNDERSTAND

Although Robert Browning Wrote Melodious Poetry, Some of It was so Obscure that People were Slow to Discover His Greatness

THE news that young Robert Browning had written another play was always likely to send a chill down the backs of the younger boys in the Reverend Mr. Ready's private school. They knew that the young writer would soon make them turn themselves into actors, and they did not enjoy the prospect. In fact, they did not like Browning quite so well as they might have done, for he was often showing them up in the class room; and Browning did not like them any more than they liked him. They seemed stupid, and so did his master. There was, indeed, little for the bright boy to like. The rules were annoying, and the older boys bullied him. Small wonder, then, that he always looked forward to the week-ends spent at his home in Camberwell, then a rural spot.

There he was perfectly happy listening to his mother's music, reading in his father's library, roaming out of doors, or watching the pets in his small menagerie. Few boys have ever had better parents. As soon as Robert could read, his father, a man of fine literary taste, encouraged him to spend as much time as he liked in his well-stocked library. His mother taught him to love music, art and the beauties of nature.

Long before he had learned to write, the little boy was composing verses and repeating them to her. Before he was eight he was trying to decide whether he would be an artist, a musician, or a writer. He really became all three; for though he is famous only as a poet, he was also a good musician and artist.

Robert Browning, one of the great English poets of the nineteenth century. He was also a gifted musician and an artist of considerable merit.

In 1824, at the age of twelve, Browning had written a "volume" of poems. His father was proud of the boy's work, and sought in vain for a publisher. But the failure did not discourage the young poet, and he kept on writing and studying the works of other poets. Although he went to a school in London for a time, most of his education came from the books he read at home. Travel on the Continent also widened his knowledge. Then, at the age of twenty-one, his first poem was published. From that time on his fame grew—though only very slowly, for reasons that follow.

When Elizabeth Barrett mentioned him in one of her poems, Browning called to thank her for the honour. That short visit was the beginning of one of the world's most famous love affairs. Almost at once he asked Miss Barrett to marry him. But her family were against the marriage because Elizabeth was so much of an invalid. Finally the lovers married against the wishes of the family.

They went to live in Italy, and there they remained for the rest of Mrs. Browning's life. The fifteen years they spent there were happy ones indeed. Praise of the poems which they wrote in their beloved Florence brought them ever greater joy. When a son was born, they probably felt the most radiantly happy people on earth.

Then, in 1861, Mrs. Browning died. Unwilling to remain in Italy without her, Browning returned to London to look after his son's education. He was greatly saddened by his loss, but he began to work harder than ever before. His interest in his son, in his own writing, and in his friends helped him to be brave and optimistic. Until his death in 1889, he retained the devoted friendship of all who knew him.

Much of Browning's great poetry is difficult to read. It is always deeply thoughtful, for one thing. For another, it probes into the inner recesses of the human soul, and so deals with obscure things. And sometimes Browning did not care to write so clearly as to make it easy for anybody to read and understand him. Because he was so hard to understand, people were slow to discover his greatness.

He began with a poem called "Pauline," and then wrote "Paracelsus" (păr'ȧ-sĕl'sŭs) and "Sordello." This last poem was so hard to understand that the witty Mrs. Carlyle said her husband could not tell whether Sordello was a man or a city or a book. Then Browning wrote a good many poetic plays, like "Pippa Passes," some of which were acted with success. He published several very great poems in the volumes

called "Men and Women" and "Dramatis Personae" (drămȧ'-tĭs pẽr-sō'nē). His masterpiece is the long poem called "The Ring and the Book." We have poetry that is more melodious, but none that is more thoughtful and searching.

It was always the minds and souls of human beings about which Browning thought and wrote. So he introduced what was practically a new method of writing poetry which was not meant to be part of a play. He would pick out some fascinating character, often an artist or a monk who lived in Italy five or six centuries ago in the days of the Renaissance. Then he would imagine

Photo by Rischgitz.

This picture, from the painting by James Elver Christie, portrays a scene from Robert Browning's famous poem called "The Pied Piper of Hamelin." The piper is seen playing a magic tune and the children of the city are following wherever he leads.

his character in some particular situation— and set him talking, either aloud or to himself.

He would have an Italian duke showing the portrait of his dead wife to a visitor and telling him about her, or a bad-tempered monk thinking about another monk whom he hates as he watches him stroll about the garden. "The Ring and the Book" is so long because in it Browning lets nine different people tell the same story—one of them twice—so that we may hear just what everybody concerned thought about it.

The QUEEN of ENGLISH POETRY

" Elizabeth Barrett Has Married Robert Browning; What Language Will they Speak? " Asked One of Their Friends

LITTLE Elizabeth Barrett never enjoyed very good health. Doubtless that is why she had such a quiet childhood. Born in Durham in 1806, her father soon moved to Hope End, in view of the Malvern Hills, and there the little girl early learned to love the beautiful out-of-doors. At other times, reading books that were much too difficult for most little girls, or grown-up people either, she learned many other things.

By the time she was twelve she had even written some poems. At fourteen she was reading Greek. Her first book of poems was published when she was twenty-seven, and it won her great praise. It was the beginning of the work that has made her so famous.

At twenty-nine she fell very ill. A year passed and she was little better; so her father sent her and her favourite brother to Torquay. In the warm air on the coast she seemed to be recovering. Then one day a terrible accident occurred. Her brother had gone out sailing with two of his friends, only to meet his death by drowning. Her grief was so great that it seemed for a time that she, too, would die.

For long years she lay on a couch in a darkened room, reading her favourite books, and seeing no one except her closest friends. When her doctor ordered her to read only "light" books, she deceived him by having a copy of Plato bound like a novel. For "light" books could not satisfy a mind like hers. Finally she took up writing again,

Photo by National Portrait Gallery

England's greatest woman poet, Elizabeth Barrett Browning, wife of the poet Robert Browning.

and then her health began to improve, but she was never really strong.

Her greatest happiness came to her in 1846, when she married Robert Browning. It was a famous marriage between two poets. Her husband was by far the greater poet, but at the time and for long afterwards her own poetry was much more popular than his, and she was thought to be the greater genius. Never would such a popular belief make either of the Brownings jealous.

Almost at once they went to live in Italy, where her new love and the bright Italian skies made her happier and healthier than she had ever been. When a little boy was born to her, the Italians called Mrs. Browning "the mother of the beautiful baby." For more than fifteen happy years the Brownings remained in Italy. Some of Mrs. Browning's finest poems were written there, but she is best remembered for the sonnets she wrote at the time of her engagement and in her early married years. These she called "Sonnets from the Portuguese," and they rank among the most beautiful love lyrics in our language. Mrs. Browning wrote a great many other poems, including "Aurora Leigh," a long story in verse. She died in Italy in 1861.

Elizabeth Barrett Browning is remembered for something better than her brilliant mind and her beautiful verses. She is remembered as one of the finest women of her day. But she was also one of the first English women to win true and lasting fame as a poet; and we still love to read her musical verse.

(CONTINUED ON PAGE 801)

CUMULUS CLOUDS AND A THUNDER CLOUD

These are the familiar cumulus clouds, great dense masses that take the shape of cauliflowers or anvils.

Above is the cumulo-nimbus, or thunder cloud, a gigantic mass of cloud from which rain has begun to fall.

We cannot all live in the midst of scenery like this, but everyone lives under the sky. The ever-shifting mountains of cloud are as beautiful as the most majestic Alps. It has been said that if everyone had to pay five shillings for a seat to see the sky, people would be standing in line for tickets all day long, and would not consider the price too high for the measure of enjoyment they received.

The FLEECY MOUNTAINS of the SKY

Clouds are so Light That They Float in the Air, and Yet They Send Down Tons of Water to Us

(CONTINUED FROM PAGE 762)

LUCKY is the man who has learned to study the clouds. Ever changing, always beautiful, they never fail to fascinate anyone who will take the pains to look skywards.

But we must know something about them if we are to appreciate how interesting they are. That is always the way with things that are really interesting—and that is the reason why people who are wide awake get so much more out of life than people with sleepy minds. They are not afraid to rummage about among the interesting things with which this world of ours is crammed so full. As a result, they are always meeting with some sort of adventure, even if they never journey more than twenty miles from home.

But clouds, you will say, are always practically the same—white things that float in the sky and sometimes send us rain!

There never was a greater mistake. There are so many kinds of clouds that more than a hundred varieties have been classified, and each one of them tells the weather-wise person something about the state of the weather.

That is where the interest comes in. For though the meteorologist may be very useful in forecasting the general conditions to cover a large territory, he does not attempt to tell what the weather will be in any particular spot.

How You May Foretell the Weather

That is where the person who has his eyes open and uses his wits can apply the information given by the meteorologist, and can often foretell just what is going to happen round him in the next ten or twelve hours. To be sure, this kind of skill is very much less common than it used to be, when people had no Meteorological Office and wireless, and were more dependent upon their own observations. But that merely means that people nowadays are always discussing the subject without really knowing much about it. How much more interesting life would be if, instead of always complaining and never finding anything out, we should set our wits to work and learn to be good weatherprophets! Let us suppose that we are all going to look upon the weather as a matter of intelligent interest— something always at hand to be watched, and something in which the humblest of us may become expert. One of the first things we must learn is to read the face of the sky.

That means that we must make friends with the clouds. For those fleecy white masses that sit lazily on the horizon, or scud along on the wind, are really gigantic reservoirs to hold the moisture that is going to fall as rain or snow at some time. As you already know, all outdoor air carries tiny particles of moisture that we call water vapour; and when the air is chilled, those particles of water gather together in larger drops—or, as we say, "condense." When water vapour has condensed, we can see it floating in the shape of clouds, sparkling on the earth as dew, or falling from the sky as rain or snow.

Any water that falls from the heavens has first floated in a cloud. Or, to put it another way, it has risen from the earth as invisible water vapour in some mass of warm air that has been pushed up by heavier cold air all round it. And when the warm air has risen far enough to be chilled in the cold upper atmosphere, its invisible water vapour has gathered itself together—or condensed—into cloud.

There are four great kinds of clouds, each of them easy to recognize and each of them telling a very clear story of what is happening up aloft. First of all there are the "cirrus" (sĭr'ŭs) clouds—those delicate, feathery wisps that are always gleaming white and always highest in the sky.

THE CLOUD ABOVE AN ACTIVE VOLCANO

When a volcano such as this one is in action, it belches forth great quantities of smoke and dust and steam that, rising into the air, form a cloud above the crater's mouth. Sometimes smoke ascends slowly for quite a long time before the actual eruption, and spreads out into the shape of a gigantic pine tree above the crater. And occasionally volcanic dust is blown long distances, and causes beautiful sunsets all the way round the world.

They are named from the Latin word for "curl" or "wisp." In extreme cases near the Equator they may be as far up as eleven miles. Their moisture has condensed into tiny ice crystals. Such clouds are very far from ready to send down rain. Indeed, they are too lacy to hold the gentlest summer shower. But from them we can foretell the

A SNOW-CLAD MOUNTAIN WREATHED WITH FLEECY CLOUDS

It is rather difficult to tell in this picture just which is the mountain, which the snow, and which cloud, for the moisture that will later fall as rain or snow often floats as a cloud around a mountain top. To the people living in such a district it is just a heavy mist, for to them even a dense cloud may appear to be thin.

weather, for they are the heralds of an approaching storm of wind and rain.

Next come the "cumulus" (kū′mū-lŭs) clouds—great white masses that look like cauliflowers or woolpacks—rounded at the top and always in motion. Their name is well taken from the Latin word for "heap."

How They are Formed

Like snow-capped mountains they often tower five miles up in the summer sky. Such glistening masses are formed by up-draughts of warm air that chill when they get to the colder upper levels and reach the condensation point. The moisture forms into tiny particles that gleam in the sun-light and grow denser and denser as more and more air mounts. When they rise four or five—and sometimes even eight—miles into the air, such clouds become "thunder-clouds" and often bring thunder-storms. You can recognize a thunder-cloud by a broad feathery crown, shaped something like an anvil, from which these clouds are called "anvil clouds." Finally they break up and drift away—they are scattered into thin air and their usefulness comes to a finish.

A third kind is the thin flat cloud that covers the sky like a ceiling. It is given the name of "stratus" (strā′tŭs), from a Latin word that means "a spreading out." Right across the sky it stretches, from horizon to horizon, and often shuts out the sun completely, though sometimes it is so thin that we can see its disk through it. Often, in breaking up, it is spread over only a part of the sky, and then we see it in great magnificence reflecting the light at sunset from its under side. For it is reflected sunlight that gives a cloud its silver lining.

The Rain-making Cloud

Stratus clouds are formed when a broad layer of air rises into the colder upper levels without being disturbed, and in cooling condenses its moisture into a blanket-like form that rests peacefully in the sky. Such clouds never send us rain unless they are chilled yet further.

It is the "nimbus" (nĭm′bŭs) cloud that is the rain maker. This is the dark, heavy cloud often seen at the base of a mass of white thunder-clouds. At other times it moves majestically up over the western horizon until it darkens the sky and lets fall the rain or snow. Like the cumulus cloud it is usually formed on the top of a rising column of air, but it has gone much farther in the brewing of rain than has the cumulus cloud. Indeed, "nimbus" is from a Latin word meaning "rain-storm," and rain is actually falling from a nimbus cloud, which is always very low. Sometimes wind comes with such clouds; but clouds never hold anything but moisture.

Perhaps you have already noticed that the blacker the cloud the more likely it is to bring rain. Clouds are light or dark according as the drops contained in them are large or small. The larger the drop the darker the cloud—and the nearer it is to raining. One weather-wise man has said, "A dark cloud is already raining; a white cloud, in the Indian's phrase, is 'rain—not yet.'"

There is another cloud form that we ought to know because of its beauty. It gives us what is commonly known as a "mackerel" sky—one in which little fleecy clouds four or five miles high are ranged along the heavens like flocks of sleeping sheep, all lying in even, quiet rows. The learned man calls them "cirro-cumulus" clouds, by which he means that they are cirrus clouds that have taken the shape of small cumulus clouds; that is, they have arranged themselves in little "heaps." They make one of the loveliest of all skies—and one which commonly brings rain before long. Cross currents of wind lay the cloudlets in such even rows.

Not only by bringing our rain and snow do the clouds serve us. They also help to regulate the heat. By protecting us, with their tiny drops, from the too-steady rays

These scenes show what a flood can do when it really sets to work on the business of destruction.

of the sun, they keep the earth from getting over-dry; and, by acting as a blanket at night, they keep the earth from giving off too much of its heat and getting unduly cold. All this is of great benefit to growing things.

It is the clear nights that are likely to be frosty, not the cloudy ones. There can be no frost or dew on a cloudy night, because the clouds do not let the heat escape, and so the temperature remains too high for frost or dew to form. But if the temperature at nightfall is below 40° F. and the air is clear and still, it is time to protect all the delicate things in the garden that you wish to keep unharmed.

The frost usually forms about two hours after midnight. Sometimes it is on grass but not on bushes or trees, for the air a few feet from the ground has not fallen below freezing point. On a very cold day we may see frost on the window-pane, even though the room is quite warm. It has formed because the outdoor air is so cold that the temperature of the glass falls below freezing-point and turns the moisture touching it into fairy-like designs in frost.

If it is the season of the year when fruit is hanging on the trees, the meteorologist sends out a warning to the fruit-growers on nights when frost is threatening. To save his valuable crop the grower then lights fires throughout his orchards. They burn during the night, and keep the air just warm enough for the fruit to survive in safety. Or he may make a "smudge" of smoke, for smoke acts like a cloud in retaining the earth's heat. But on cloudy nights this precaution is not necessary, as the clouds prevent the daytime heat from escaping.

(CONTINUED ON PAGE 833)

Round and round many times between the palms of his hands this Indian had to twirl his stick before the end of it in the hole began to smoulder. It was tedious work, but fire was necessary to the life of the tribe, and some-one had to kindle it if it was allowed to go out. Once alight, they took every precaution to keep it burning.

The MIGHTIEST SLAVE of MAN

How We Have Loaded Most of Our Work on the Shoulders of a Servant That was Discovered Long before History Began

MANY an animal will hover by a dying fire till the last glow has gone out of its ashes and left him shivering in the dark. But never has an animal dreamed of putting on another stick of wood to keep the fire burning.

It is hard to think there ever was a time when man could do no better. We are so used to fire that we may easily suppose our forefathers always had it; and we may even have a little shock when we first learn that fire was one of the things they had to discover.

Yet, for many a century, our ancestors had no sort of fire at all. They no more knew how to make a fire and keep it going, or what use to make of it, than did any of the animals.

If we only think a moment about what their lives must have been like without any fire, and if we remember all that fire has done for us since, we shall realize that it is one of the most important of all the discoveries of man.

There had been fires in the world before—from time to time. Once in a while the lightning would set a dead tree aflame, and the rain might be too slight to prevent a forest fire from following. Occasionally the red-hot lava from a volcano might start a blaze, or a meteor from the sky might do it. Such fires must have been so rare, however, that few men would ever see one. And any man who did so would have run for his life, like all the other creatures in the dark forests.

But one day a brave man did a thing that no other creature would have dreamt of doing. He picked up a burning branch to look at it. He was curious to see what it was really like, and what he could do with it.

Soon he must have found that he could do some remarkable and useful things with his burning branch. At the very least he could wave it round his head and so scare off the fiercest animals. He could put other branches on it—as he learned in due time—and so keep the fire going as long as he liked. He could place the fire at the mouth of his den and ward off the wild beasts while he and his family slept through the night. And as he lay near the glowing fire he came to know a comfort such as he had never thought to feel in the cold weather.

For these reasons he kept his fire going for some time before he ever

When a Kwakiute woman of British Columbia got dinner for the family, she cooked it over an open fire and used an invention like this instead of a frying pan. She probably believed that the smoke improved the flavour.

what a beneficial thing it was. And then if his own fire went out, he could relight it again from a neighbour's—if he were on good terms with the neighbour.

Before very long there may have occurred an accident that resulted in something being cooked. Perhaps some pieces of meat fell into the fire and tasted all the better for it. Possibly someone left a shoulder of deer too near the embers one night and woke up to a new kind of breakfast the next morning. However, by some means, all men came to like their meat better if it had been scorched. In due time came the clever person who simply set his meat right on the fire and let it burn. He was the first cook.

Even this clever man still had no way of starting a fire. If he or his neighbour already had one, he could light another from it; if not, he would be forced to go without for the

thought of cooking. It was not easy for him to keep a fire burning day and night in rainy weather, and to do his hunting at the same time. It was most important that his first fire should not go out, for in that case he would have to wait for a meteor or a volcano or a flash of lightning to make him another; and the chance of such a thing happening within the next few centuries would be very slight indeed.

But fairly soon many another fire must have been kindled from his first one. Everyone would want a fire when he found out

rest of his days. It was still many centuries before the next inventor found out how to make a fire where none had been before.

Possibly he merely noticed that his two hands grew hot when he rubbed them hard, and thought that two sticks might do the same thing. It may be that he saw two dry limbs of a tree rubbing together in the wind until they caught fire. At any rate, he finally succeeded in rubbing two sticks together so hard, or in pushing one stick to and fro in a groove so fast, that the dry wood began to scorch and to smoulder.

The cave man of the Early Stone Age knew how to twirl a soft stick back and forth in his hands until the point of it, which fitted into a hole, got so hot with the rubbing that it began to scorch and to smoulder. Suppose it took as long to light each one of the many millions of matches that civilized man uses every year!

In many parts of the world early men lighted their fires by striking sparks from flint with a mineral known as iron pyrites. The discovery must have come about naturally enough, for flint was their chief material for making arrowheads. When they came to use metals they struck the flint with iron or steel.

Inset photos by James's Press Agency

Anyone with a great deal of patience can light a fire by rubbing two sticks together rapidly until they get hot enough to burn. But you must have soft, inflammable wood, and not cease rubbing for an instant.

If you are very skilful and if your arms do not get too tired, you can kindle a fire by rubbing a soft stick back and forth in a groove, as this South Sea Islander is doing. The Indians used the dry root of a willow.

Such was the way in which man first made a fire. It was the way the Red Indians used to start a fire, and the way in which almost any savage will start one to-day; there are still a few savages, in some of the Pacific islands, who cannot make a fire, though none at all who do not have fires and know what use to make of them. Some of the savages who do know how to make fire will travel a long way to borrow it instead, if their own goes out; for it is not very easy to make a fire with two sticks unless you know just how to do it and have the best materials—as any Boy Scout who knows the trick will tell you.

Fire Made by Flint and Steel

For many centuries fires were made by means of two sticks, until at last men found other ways. Fire-making grew common with the use of steel. If we strike a sharp blow with a piece of steel upon a flint, we can make

HOW OUR ANCESTORS LIGHTED A FIRE

The curious collection below is what our forefathers used instead of a match—and glad enough they were to have these articles. There are three tinder boxes in the collection—one of them of wood—and the equipment of flint and steel and sulphur matches that went with them. Every tinder box contained a sharp piece of flint and a strip of steel curved round to form a handle, to be held in the left hand. When the sharp edge of the flint was struck against the steel, very tiny fragments of the metal were chipped off; and these, red-hot owing to the force of the blow, fell on the tinder in the box and set it on fire. The person lighting the fire then blew on the tinder—which was usually a piece of charred rag—until it flamed, and finally with much smoke and spluttering, lighted a sulphur match from the tinder. When the lid was put back on the box the fire in the tinder went out. You can judge how long it took to light a fire in this way when you know that people preferred to go half a mile to the nearest neighbour's to borrow a live coal. Sometimes a fire was made by means of the flint-lock off a gun. Powder was put in the pan of the gun, and as the flint in the hammer came down against the piece of metal above the pan, the spark it struck set fire to the powder, which in turn lighted the tinder held near it. One of these old flint-locks is shown at the top of the picture.

a spark; and if we have some tinder near by —some dry shavings or scorched linen—it may catch the spark and start to burn. So for centuries men used to make fire with flint and tinder, as is still the custom in some parts of the world to-day. Little more than a hundred years ago you would have found flint and tinder on every shelf where you now find matches.

The first matches fit to use were made in 1827, by an Englishman named John Walker. They were rather crude articles. They had to be scraped hard on sandpaper before they would strike, and it was dangerous for workmen to make them. The phosphorus (fŏs'-fŏr-ŭs) that was used to make their heads often gave the workers a serious disease. It is only recently that we have really had "safety" matches—safe for the men who make them, and safe also for those who use them, because they will strike readily only on a specially prepared box.

Let us now follow the fortunes of a box of matches from the time when it enters the factory in the form of a great log—usually of aspen poplar from the Baltic ports—until it lies in its packing-case, one of a gross of such boxes ready to be sent to the customer who has ordered them.

How Logs Become Matches

When the logs arrive at the match factory they are first cut up into convenient three-foot lengths by great circular saws, several feet in diameter. The short lengths are then taken away by means of implements

resembling billhooks, to have their bark shaved off by hand-knives. They are then ready to be made into matches.

For this purpose, they are turned on to a shaving machine, which cuts from them long strips of wood, rather like cloth. These are then pushed into another machine which must be one of the quickest workers in existence, for it cuts up the long rolls, or "veneers," into thousands of square sticks known as "splints," which fall out at the other end of the machine. Imagine 56,000 of these being turned out in a minute by one energetic machine!

The next process is achieved by means of continual vibration. You know how you shake down loose matches in a match-box—well, that is what is done to countless thousands of little sticks in a big factory. They are carried in metal drums, a million at a time, to great tanks for "impregnation" by a chemical solution, which ensures that no burning embers will be left when the match has been extinguished. Then for two hours they are dried and polished by being hurled about inside their drums.

The Matches on Parade

From these they are blown up large pipes on to screens, where they are sorted out. But how can it be possible to sort out the good from the bad among all these myriads of little sticks of wood? The answer is very simple—once more it is done by machinery, and again by means of vibration.

The "matches" are carried down a sloping screen, which is pierced with holes of just the right size. Through these holes fall the sticks which are too small, while the suitable ones pursue their course. But these must be marshalled into order, and so they fall eventually on to a shaking belt

which runs at right angles to the screen and which is partitioned into slots, into which the matches are jolted in place, side by side.

They are now taken up in large ducts, or cases, to the match room, where there are many slowly revolving wheels, on which run broad metal bands pierced with thousands of holes, each just large enough to take a match stem. The duct enters the machine, and each match is punched into a hole in the belt as this passes slowly by. They are now standing on end, and as the band

Photo by Bryant & May, Ltd.

There are millions of future matches lying hidden within these great logs, for it is in a forest that the life-story of a match begins. Below them you see a block from a tree trunk, which has been severed and then peeled ready for its entry into the match-manufacturing world.

moves on they first pass through a bath of melted paraffin wax, to make them burn readily. You have probably noticed how, when you light a match, a little stream of melted wax runs upwards to feed the flame.

The belt travels over another bath containing igniting composition. Through this pass the ends of the sticks, picking up their heads as they go. But by now they are wet and sticky, so for the next hour they must move very slowly over twenty-three large and small wheels, while whizzing fans blow air on to them, until at length, after a four-hundred-foot tour on the flexible metal belting, they are perfectly dry

Filling the Match Boxes

Moreover, they have returned, as complete matches, to the place where they entered the machine as little headless pieces of wood, and so they are now punched out of their holes into small steel slots or compartments, the size of match boxes, travelling across at a right angle. Here the boxes are fed to them by more machines, the cover and drawer—the part which holds the matches—being pushed apart, and each box receiving its correct supply of matches, which are shaken down by vibration. As the drawer moves along, the cover is gently pushed over, and our box of matches is all ready for packing.

But before we dispatch the cases we must first describe where the match boxes came

Photo by Bryant & May, Ltd.

The veneer has now assumed a very different shape. One end of the long strip entered this machine, and was transformed by rapid cutting into myriads of tiny sticks which you see lying at the right, ready to be made into matches. The machine can cut 56,000 in one minute.

from. They were made ready by other wonderful machines while their contents were being prepared for them. The wood for the boxes is first peeled, or "veneered," from the logs in very thin strips, and while being peeled it is "scored" with shallow cuts so as to bend easily where needed. A box consists of two parts, an "inner" and an "outer," and it takes not more than one second to make either of these portions.

The Finishing Touches

When the strips for the "outer" reach the machines, they are bent round pieces of steel shaped like a box; the label is pasted round, the superfluous paste is wiped off, and the finished cover is dropped on a conveyer and taken up a slope to the drying room.

On another machine the "inner" is being made. The rim is bent round a steel block, the bottom piece is fed to it, and the two are pasted together with paper supplied from a moving roll. These are also thrown on to a conveyer and taken to another drying room. Yet a third machine puts the "inner" and "outer" together, by bringing

Photo by Bryant & May, Ltd.

This is not cloth being unwound from an enormous bale, but veneer, which is peeled off the logs just as easily as if nothing but many yards of dampish, ribbon-like wood rolled round and round had gone to their making. From this veneer the "splints" are cut.

Photo by Bryant & May, Ltd.

Here is the match room, where the little sticks of wood are punched into the ever-moving conveyers, ready to be converted into real matches. It is here that they receive their preliminary bath of paraffin wax, before assuming their heads of pink, blue or any other colour.

them opposite each other in separate slots, and pushing them together.

Finally, the boxes are wrapped up in packets of a dozen by machinery which first places a paper wrapper in position, and then picks up the required number of boxes and deposits them neatly in the centre of the paper. Arms which seem almost human in their action fold the paper over, tuck down the edges and neatly tip them up. The packages then move along a runway to another machine which covers them with a label, and eventually the dozens are packed in grosses by girls who deposit them in packing-cases, which are even nailed down by machinery.

A World Without Fire

So when next you light a match, and throw it away after it has burnt, think of the marvellous and swift machines that are called into action to produce each one of the little matches which are used every day by the million. Each tiny stick has been treated carefully, and yet it has been calculated that in one big factory in England, if

a day's output of matches were put end to end, it would reach from London to Montreal and back again, and still leave five hundred miles to spare!

Without fire we should be savages to this very day. We should have no heat but that of the sun. We should have nothing but raw food. We could do next to nothing with the metals in the ground. We should have no iron, no steel, no tiles, no glass—we should have hardly any of the thousands of things without which we can scarcely consider life possible.

Guardians of the Fire

When in the past savages found anything as important as fire, it was only natural that they should fall down and worship it. It was so precious, and so perilous. That is why our early ancestors nearly always gave a place to fire in their religions, and often a very prominent place. They made fire a god, like the sun, and it is considered as such by many tribes to-day.

In some ancient countries fire was so precious that keeping it from going out was

Photo by Bryant & May, Ltd.

You will recognize these small boxes that are emerging from the machine which has neatly opened, filled, and shut them again. Now you know the life-story of a match—from its humble origin as a tiny part of a great tree down to the moment when it lies in its box.

a sacred honour. So in the days of ancient Rome, the sacred fire in the temple of the goddess Vesta was guarded by the holy Vestal Virgins, who were chosen for the office at the age of from six to ten years, and served for thirty years. And to this day the Parsees in Bombay guard and worship the sacred fire

Photo by Bryant & May, Ltd.

There is one more experience a box of matches must undergo before it can be sent to its destination in some great city or remote village. That is when, in company with eleven other boxes, it is neatly wrapped up in packets by this machine, whose skilful fingers work faster than human fingers, and seldom falter. Many people buy their household matches in packets of a dozen.

that they have kept burning ever since they took it with them when they were driven out of their home in Persia over twelve hundred years ago—where it is said to have been kindled by Zoroaster (zō′rō-ăs′tĕr) the founder of their faith, centuries earlier still.

Yet, although the ancients knew so much

about the value of fire, they had no idea of what fire would be doing for us to-day. It is only about a century and a half since fire was harnessed to make steam and so to turn thousands of wheels and do a great deal of the work in the world. Only then did it really perform its miracles—or its one great miracle of transforming life for us. It would be difficult to enumerate all the things it does; they would almost sum up our civilization. Every train and steamboat in the world, every motor-car and aeroplane, nearly every piece of the vast network of machinery on which we depend, would stop to-morrow if we lost the secret of fire that some unknown discoverer among our savage fore-fathers found out in the shadowy days of long ago.

What is Fire Itself?

Familiar as we are with fire, few of us know what it really is. There are many different kinds of fire. For instance, some coal is hard to light and then burns very slowly and with very little flame. But a camera film will catch alight the moment a flame touches it and will burn very rapidly and brilliantly. Because it flares up so readily it is said to be inflam-mable (ĭn-flăm′ă-b'l). Then there are substances like gunpowder and petrol vapour that burn much more rapidly still, for they flare up in a single flash. They are described as ex-plosive substances.

All these are different kinds of fire, and are used for different purposes. To heat a house all day long, or to keep up steam for a long railway journey, we require slow-burning coal. To blast through a rock we want instantly exploding dynamite. To drive a motor-car or an aeroplane a con-tinuous series of explosions of petrol vapour is necessary.

But if the fire in a lump of coal, a stick of dynamite and a drop of petrol is so very different, what is there in all of them that is the same ? In a word, what is fire itself ? The answer is, that a thing is on fire whenever

THE MIGHTY SLAVE BREAKS HIS BONDS AND BECOMES DESTRUCTIVE

Nowadays fires rarely wipe out whole cities, but a forest fire can trap all the little villages within a given area and reduce them to ruins, with appalling loss of life and money. For that reason an alarm in a thickly forested region during a season of drought brings out every able-bodied man to help in the difficult, tiring work. Here forest officers are fighting a fire in a national forest area in North America. Watchmen stationed in high towers on top of hills and mountains are constantly on the look-out to give the alarm at the first puff of smoke, when everyone within reach rushes to the spot. Fire lines—wide belts cleared of brush and débris—are often opened in the path of the advancing fire in order to prevent its spreading along the ground.

it starts combining rapidly with the oxygen in the air and giving out heat. It is that combination with oxygen that makes fire.

That is why a flame goes out under glass; all the oxygen is used up. It is also why a match goes out under your foot; you have shut off the air from it. It is the reason why the filament of an electric bulb is not really burning, for the bulb contains no air. It is the reason why the inside of the earth is not on fire, however hot it may be, for there is no air inside the earth. And it is why the sun is not alight, though it is hotter still than the interior of the earth· for there is no air on the sun either. We have fire only when a substance combines with oxygen.

Any power as strong as fire can always be a danger. Many a time it has got out of control and done enormous damage. It burned imperial Rome in the year 64, London in 1666, Chicago in 1871, Smyrna in 1922, Tokyo in 1923, and has destroyed many other towns and cities at other times. When a fire starts in a great forest it may sweep in mountainous walls of flame over hundreds of square miles, leaving black ruin in its path. No one who has never seen a forest fire can dream of the horror of its fury.

Many boys long to possess a pair of STILTS, and there are plenty of girls who like them, too. There is no reason why anybody should be without them, for all that is needed for making stilts is two blocks of wood 1" thick and 4" square, and two taller pieces for handles. The smaller pieces, which will be the foot rests, you should saw to fit the foot, as in Fig. 1, and then nail securely to the handles. The length and thickness of these handles depend entirely on the height and weight of whoever is going to use them, and on how high above the ground the young owner wants to walk. It is much the best plan to set the foot rests near the ground to begin with—say 6" above it— and move them up gradually as you become more expert in this new and exciting method of walking.

Fig. 1

Fig. 2

Fig. 3

Fig. 4

The size of your DOG-KENNEL depends on the size of your dog, and so we shall have to leave its dimensions entirely to you. You had best measure the lucky dog for his new house, remembering that he will not want to be cramped for space in his bed any more than you would. But though we leave this to you, we can give you some hints about making the kennel. The floor should be about 2" above the ground. There should be air-holes bored in the base-board (Fig. 6) and in the gable (Fig. 5). Felt makes an excellent roofing, and two coats of paint will work wonders in the appearance of your little friend's house.

These TOPS can be made from odds and ends. The stem of each is a dowel pointed at the end. Fig. 2 is a silk-thread spool. Fig. 3 is a cotton-thread spool sawn in half and shaped with a knife. Fig. 4 is the lid of a wooden pill-box with a hole bored through its centre.

Fig. 5

Fig. 6

A SEE-SAW is nothing but a long, strong board balanced on something. How long and strong the board should be, and how far from the ground it should be balanced, will depend on the size and weight of the people who are going to use it. The best sort of balance is a trestle such as that shown in Fig. 7. But you can have a very satisfying ride on a see-saw made by simply running a board through a fence, as in Fig. 8, or balancing it over a tree stump, as in Fig. 9. You will soon learn to manage the board: how to sit nearer the centre if you do not want to go so high, how to balance a heavier rider against a lighter by placing the lighter one nearer the end.

Fig. 7

Fig. 8

Fig. 9

A TEACHER of ALL ENGLAND

Not Only Could Matthew Arnold Tell the Subjects of Queen Victoria Just Where Their Worst Faults Lay, but He Could Also Delight Them with Some of the Finest Poetry Ever Composed

(CONTINUED FROM PAGE 786)

A GOOD many people seem to think that a person should not criticize what other people have written unless he can write very well himself. Yet you could count on the fingers of one hand the English writers who have been both great poets or novelists and great critics. One of those you would have to include is Matthew Arnold, the greatest critic of the Victorian Age and one of its finest poets, too.

Matthew Arnold was born at Laleham, near Staines, in 1822. His father was the famous Dr. Arnold of Rugby. So young Arnold came honestly by the interest he later showed in education. He went to Rugby himself, and won a prize with his first poem, written when he was eighteen. Three years later, at Oxford, he won another prize with a poem on Oliver Cromwell.

Matthew Arnold, the leading English critic of the nineteenth century, and one of its finest poets.

After graduating, he continued to mingle education and poetry. He was first a private secretary, then a master at Rugby, an administrator of public education, and later inspector of all the schools of England. From 1851 until a few years before his death, Arnold travelled through England, labouring hard at his inspectorship. He did a great deal to interest the English people in their schools, and managed to bring about some of the reforms in which he believed.

He travelled on the Continent, too, and studied schools in France and Germany, so that he could speak and write about whatever he saw that seemed to him good. Besides all this, he was for the ten years between 1857 and 1867 a professor of poetry at Oxford.

This honour had come to him because his own poetry was at last being read and appreciated. The first volume had appeared in 1849, and had made so little stir that the author soon withdrew it from circulation. Yet it contained two or three of his loveliest poems—for instance, the plaintive lament of "The Forsaken Merman":

Children dear, was it yesterday
We heard the sweet bells over the bay?
In the caverns where we lay,
Through the surf and through the swell
The far-off sound of a silver bell?

There was a second book in 1852, but that also had to be withdrawn. When the third appeared in 1853, voices at last were raised in its praise. It contained several of Arnold's best-known poems: the thoughtful musings of "The Scholar Gipsy," the richly beautiful lines on "Philomela," the nightingale, and the heroic story of "Sohrab and Rustum." Other volumes of verse followed. The best of the poems have a sober, stately beauty, all Arnold's own. There are exquisite pictures of the English countryside in some of them. In many of them Arnold expresses his own hopes and fears in strong and sombre phrases. He was the poet of people who love to think.

Arnold would have liked to have been able to write like the ancient Greeks, especially like Homer and Sophocles. By his criticism as well as by his poetry, he wished to bring into Victorian England something of the quiet and harmony of the Greek ideal. He thought people hurried too much, were too much interested in making money and in being comfortable, and too little interested in art and ideas. He called the busy trading classes "Philistines," and said that they went forth, as in the days of the Old Testament, to fight against the "children of light."

These children of light were the people who were truly educated; they were not merely learned, they were those who had studied "the best that has been thought and said in the world," and were therefore people of true culture. Arnold thought that if only more people would become interested in beautiful things and clear thoughts—"sweetness and light," he called them—everyone would be much happier. He was very fond of coining catch phrases like those just quoted, and you will not read much without coming across some of them, and you will hear them spoken—often by people who have no idea where they originated.

These ideas, and many more, Arnold incorporated in a long series of books, such as "Essays in Criticism," "Culture and Anarchy," and "Literature and Dogma." In them he criticizes books and authors, literature, religion, and life in general.

A great many people did not like what he wrote. People never like to be told that they are on the wrong tack. He was sometimes considered a snob because he had so little good to say of ordinary people. But there is so much solid sense in his criticism that he is still widely read and quoted. And his influence has been very great.

In spite of opposition, Arnold became a famous man, even in his own day. In 1883 he was granted a pension, and could at last give up his tiring school inspectorship—which he had never very much liked—and spend all his time writing and lecturing. He even went to America on a lecture tour. His death came suddenly in 1888.

He was one of the great Victorians—a critic of massive power and a poet of rare excellence. Some time, when you are feeling the sadness and difficulties of life, you should read his "Thyrsis," written on the death of his friend Arthur Hugh Clough, and one of the three or four finest elegies in our language; or perhaps his beautiful sonnet to Shakespeare; or his poem "Dover Beach," in which he describes the stupid affairs of men as taking place

here as on a darkling plain
Swept with confused alarms of struggle
   and flight,
Where ignorant armies clash by night.

ALL *the* FAMILY *Were* POETS

The Five Rossettis—Father and Four Children—Whose Poems and Prose Writings Helped to Enrich English Literature

THERE were greater writers in the nineteenth century, but there was no entire family so famous in literature and art as the Rossettis (rŏ-sĕt′ĭ). They were a father and four children. The father had been driven out of Italy in 1824, owing to his fight for freedom there, and had come to England. He was a poet of some note, and taught Italian at King's College in London, where he did a great deal to make the great poet Dante (dän′tĭ) known to the English-speaking world.

The oldest child was Maria Francesca (1827–1876). She wrote some excellent books on Dante and his work. Another child was William Michael, who lived to be ninety years old, dying in 1919. He was a fine critic of art and literature, an excellent biographer, and a good poet. But far more distinguished was his sister, Christina Rossetti, and especially his brother, Dante Gabriel Rossetti. The fame of all these children shows what it means to have a fine father and a good training.

Christina Rossetti, born in 1830, was a very precocious girl. At the age of twelve

Photo by Tate Gallery

Not only was Dante Gabriel Rossetti a great poet, he was also one of the finest painters of his century. His "Monna Vanna," which you see above, was painted in 1866, and now hangs in the Tate Gallery.

she wrote a poem for her mother's birthday, and at eighteen her verses were already appearing in several of the magazines. From that time on she continued to write beautiful poems, largely of a religious kind, till her death in 1894. With Elizabeth Barrett Browning for her only rival, she holds a high place among the women poets of her land and her century.

She was a beautiful woman, of a very quiet and retiring nature. Her fame was made by her book called "Goblin Market," in 1862, and was steadily increased by other poems, long and short. She is at her best in some of her shorter lyrics.

Dante Gabriel Rossetti, born in 1828, was the greatest poet of the family, and a noted artist. He was at once a leading painter and a leading poet of his age. After going to King's College School and to two art schools, he made up his mind to devote his life to painting. But he had been writing verses also since the age of five, and he continued as a poet all through his life. To-day he is more famous for his poetry than for his painting.

He was a leading spirit in the famous Pre-Raphaelite (prē-răf′ă-ĕl-īt) Movement inaugurated about 1850, which did so much for painting and also for poetry. The artists in this movement felt that all the art around them was far too artificial. They wished to return to the simpler and more natural art of earlier days, of the days before Raphael. With this aim they founded a magazine called "The Germ," still very famous though it was so short-lived; and for this Rossetti, Millais, Holman Hunt and other members of the Brotherhood painted some beautiful pictures and wrote some splendid poems.

Photo by National Portrait Gallery
Dante Gabriel Rossetti, poet and painter, whose work is full of a strange beauty which stamps it as his own.

There was a great tragedy in Rossetti's life. He married a young girl of great beauty—whom you can see in many of his paintings—and two years later she died. He was overcome by sorrow. In his picture, the "Beata Beatrix," and in his inspired poem of "The Blessed Damozel," we can see how much he idolized his young wife. At her death he placed all of his poems in her coffin and buried them with her. But they were later recovered and published, and he continued working till the end. His health gave way in middle life and he was the second of the Rossetti children to pass on into the unknown. He died in 1882.

Apart from "The Blessed Damozel"—his most famous work—he wrote some charming sonnets in "The House of Life," a good many ballads like "Rose Mary" "The King's Tragedy" and "The White Ship," and a number of longer poems, notably "Sister Helen" and "Jenny."

The MAN *Who* WROTE "*The* WATER-BABIES"

Clergyman, Poet, Novelist and Essayist, Charles Kingsley Throughout His Life was an Earnest Worker in the Interests of the Poor and Afflicted

EVERY boy and girl has heard about Charles Kingsley. He wrote the delightful fairy-tale "The Water-Babies," and also "The Heroes," a version of the old stories of ancient Greece. And, as boys and girls grow up, they find out that he did a great deal more: for he was also a poet, a lecturer, a famous novelist, and one of the great preachers of his day.

Kingsley was born in Devonshire, at Holne vicarage, Dartmoor, on June 12, 1819, and spent his youth in that glorious part of England. He did not care very much for the company of other children, but spent a great deal of his time in scribbling down the thoughts that came to him. Even before he was four he had tried to imitate his clergyman father by writing little sermons, and it is said that he was also composing poetry at that early age. He also liked to walk about the country, to go boating, and to collect shells, and in this way he acquired a great deal of the Nature lore that later proved useful when he was writing his scientific papers or was teaching botany and geology.

When Kingsley's parents took him to

London at the age of seventeen, he was by no means such a kindly spirit as one might expect in a young man who was later going to spend his time, his enthusiasm, and even his health trying to improve the conditions of the poor. As he himself said, he was a "thorough aristocrat," and he felt little but scorn for the poor working-men who came to the Kingsley home in search of help.

When he went to Cambridge the next year to study for the ministry, he was very restless and unhappy because of his religious doubts, and he often thought of running away to "become a wild prairie hunter" instead of a clergyman. But all his doubt and snobbishness soon passed, and upon leaving the university he became first, curate—and then rector—of Eversley, in Hampshire.

He found many of his parishioners in such a miserable state that he worked long hours to obtain better homes and higher wages for

Photo by National Portrait Gallery

Charles Kingsley, the author and clergyman who gave his life to working and writing on behalf of the poor and downtrodden. The young people of three generations have loved this gentle, kindly man for the stories he wrote for them.

them. Then at night he wrote lectures, sermons, pamphlets, and books, urging others to help the needy to a better living. In his first novel, "Alton Locke," he pictures the

miseries of a London tailor, while his "Yeast" shows the wretched conditions among the farm labourers of England.

In 1860 Kingsley became a professor of history at Cambridge University, but ill-health finally forced him to resign. During this time he travelled, lectured, taught geology and botany, gained several posts in the Church, was chaplain to Queen Victoria, and wrote on a variety of subjects, including sanitation, military life, science, politics, and religion. But it was his historical novels that brought him the highest fame. In our day these are still the books from his pen that are most widely read— "Hypatia," an Egyptian story; "Hereward the Wake," a tale of Norman times; and above all "Westward Ho!" a great story of old Devon and of exploration in America.

In 1874 Kingsley went to America to give a series of lectures, and was very warmly received as a faithful preacher and a famous writer. The next year, on January 23, he died and was buried at Eversley. But he still lives on in the affections of his many readers.

WHO *Was* "CURRER BELL"?

Three Sisters of the Yorkshire Moors Whose Wonderful Determination Has Given Us a Series of Novels of Surpassing Merit and Charm

IN THE long history of English literature there is no more tragic story than that associated with the Brontë (bron'tĕ) family. There were six children—Maria, Elizabeth, Charlotte (born 1816), Branwell (born 1817) the only son, Emily (born 1818), and Anne (born 1820). Their father was a clergyman, Patrick Brontë. Unhappily, their

Living their lonely life in their house on the Yorkshire moors, these three Brontë sisters nevertheless made for themselves an inner life so vivid and so real that their names are known wherever English is spoken.

mother died in 1821, and her elder sister came to look after the children at the parsonage at Haworth, on the bleak Yorkshire moors, where they all lived. Their father was strong-willed and eccentric, but a kind man, who drilled his children in politics and affairs, and their aunt seems also to have been good to them, giving the girls lessons and instructing them in household duties.

A Second Tragedy Occurs

A second tragedy in the family occurred in 1825, when the two elder sisters—Maria and Elizabeth—who had been sent to a school near Leeds, contracted consumption and died. The four remaining children clung together closely, making few friends and preferring long walks on the moors to taking part in the life of the district. Their existence was so isolated and uneventful that every small occurrence tended to become magnified, although Charlotte's natural common sense kept her imagination within bounds. They all wrote a good deal, and their other amusements consisted in reading and studying.

In 1831 Charlotte went to a school at Roe Head, Dewsbury, where she remained for a year as a pupil, returning in 1835 as a teacher. Emily accompanied her this time as a pupil, but the restricted life was not to her liking, so she returned to her home.

When Charlotte at length left Roe Head she received two proposals of marriage—one from the brother of her great friend Ellen Nussey, her letters to whom reveal a great part of her life. Both offers were rejected, and she then took a position as a private governess. Her experiences at this and a second similar place determined her to start a school of her own.

To that end she decided first to improve her knowledge of languages. In February, 1842, therefore, Charlotte and Emily entered M. and Mme. Héger's school in Brussels, where they worked diligently until recalled by the illness of their aunt, who died in October of that year, leaving her nieces sufficient money to carry out their plans.

Emily did not return to Brussels, but Charlotte, thinking she might still improve her French, accepted M. Héger's offer of a position as governess, and spent some time in reading French literature and generally acquiring a wider outlook. But without her sister she became so depressed that, when her father's eyesight began to fail, she returned home in January, 1844.

The Sad Fate of Branwell

Immediately the sisters planned to start their school at the parsonage, but the attempt was a failure. Their troubles were deepened by the fact that their brother Branwell, who had always been adored by the family, now became an habitual drunkard. He drifted from post to post, finally took drugs and died at the age of 31.

In 1845, however, a new interest was added to the sisters' life by Charlotte's discovery of some poems by Emily and Anne. Disappointed in their scheme for a school, the girls decided to turn their attention to literature, and in 1846 a little volume of poems by "Currer, Ellis and Acton Bell" appeared, the authors being in reality Charlotte, Emily and Anne, who from a desire to avoid publicity thus disguised their names.

Unfortunately, only two copies of the little book were sold, although we now know that Emily's "Old Stoic" and "Last Lines" are two of the finest things any woman has given to English literature. But the poems of the other two were quite trivial, and so they tried their hand at prose, in the realm of which they were to attain fame. Charlotte

wrote "The Professor," and, after many disappointments, received an encouraging letter from a publisher who offered to publish a longer novel if she would write one. She replied to this with "Jane Eyre," which attained immediate popularity.

Encouraged by its success, another publisher accepted Emily's "Wuthering Heights" and Anne's "Agnes Grey" and "The Tenant of Wildfell Hall," but tried to persuade the public that they were by the author of "Jane Eyre" (âr). This induced Emily and Anne to journey to London, where they interviewed Charlotte's publisher and put the matter straight, thereby proving that they were in reality women, and not men, as had been supposed.

Charlotte is Left Alone

Emily's and Anne's success was short-lived, for in December, 1848, Emily died of consumption, to be followed in the spring by Anne. Charlotte alone was left with her old father. She went up to London, and met many of the famous people she had for long wished to know. Matthew Arnold, Mrs. Gaskell and Thackeray were among her friends.

In October, 1849, "Shirley" appeared, and "Villette" followed in 1853. In June, 1854, she married her father's curate, Arthur Bell Nicholls. He had long been devoted to her, but old Mr. Brontë had opposed the match. But Charlotte, too, was doomed to a brief happiness and success, as she died not quite a year after her marriage, on March 31, 1855. Two years after she had passed away, "The Professor," her first novel, was published.

(CONTINUED ON PAGE 851)

ANSWERS TO PUZZLES ON PAGE 624

23—400 pounds

24—

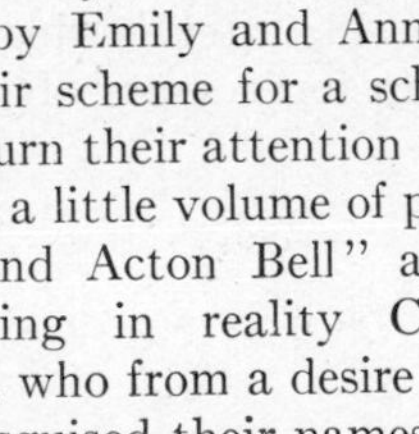

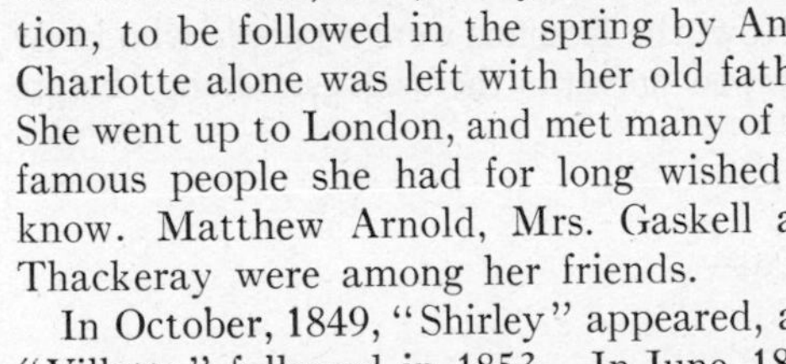

25—The first diagram shows how the servant arranged the bottles when there were 24 of them; and the second, when there were only 20.

Notice that there were, in both of the arrangements, nine bottles along each side.

26—30 inches.

When ALL ROADS LED to ROME

How the Stern Roman Empire Ruled the World for Several Centuries. Even After the Sturdy Roman Character Had Already Begun to Decay

(CONTINUED FROM PAGE 781)

NATIONS are very similar to individuals. It takes them a long time to form good habits, although when they begin to take to bad ones, they can go downhill very rapidly. We need never be surprised if a people who have for a long time been ground down and oppressed seem very slow in learning how to govern themselves, or if one that has grown loose in morals and defiant of law suddenly finds itself falling to pieces. Self-control is just as difficult for a nation to learn as it is for a person.

Now, the Romans were a people who knew how to govern themselves. Long before they became powerful they saw that everyone had to work together and abide by the laws if the state were to flourish. It was because they had seen this, and had put it into practice, that they became so great. But even the Romans, for all their ability, did not always know how to apply their knowledge to new conditions. They had always been used to a republic, and when they set up an empire they were a little clumsy at the start.

Augustus, their first emperor, died in the year A.D. 14, after having ruled Rome for more than forty years of peace and accom-

Photo by Chauffourier

WHERE ORATORS MADE SPEECHES TO THE CITIZENS OF ROME

This is a reconstruction of the great Forum of Rome. It was originally a simple market-place; but, as the city grew, more and more buildings and monuments were added to it, each more elaborate than the last. And when there was no more room, the emperors started to build other forums near it. To the left you see the Basilica Julia, and beside it the temple of Saturn. The building in the centre of the picture is the temple of Vespasian, and next to it, behind the arch of Septimius Severus, is the temple of Concord. The low platform in the centre is the famous rostrum from which the Roman orators made their speeches.

THE LUXURIOUS HOUSE-BOAT OF A ROMAN EMPEROR

This picture is called the "Ship of Tiberius." It shows one of the luxurious house-boats in which the emperors took pleasure trips on the beautiful lakes of Italy. Recently, a lake to the south of Rome was drained, and at the bottom were discovered a boat of this type and other valuable and interesting remains.

plishment. Even this long reign, however, had not accustomed the Romans to the rule of one man as an established thing. The senate had made Augustus emperor, but there was no arrangement as to his successor. The old political leaders hoped that he might have no successor; but the soldiers whom Augustus had led, and the people whom he had fed and for whom he had provided amusements, were of a different mind.

A Cold and Thrifty Emperor

Augustus, however, left no son. Even the sons of his daughter died before he did, and the only surviving male member of his family was his stepson Tiberius (tī-bēr′ĭ-ŭs). It was largely due to Livia, the mother of Tiberius, supported by the army and the people, that Tiberius was made imperator by the senate when Augustus died.

Tiberius turned out to be a cold and thrifty man. He hated to spend money on anything, and especially he hated to give entertainments to the people. The Roman citizens had been used to going freely to the circus, or public theatre, and enjoying the sight of men fighting wild beasts or fighting each other. When the emperor would not promote such sport, with his own money at any rate, he naturally became unpopular.

Tiberius did not care for private entertainments either. He made no attempt to please anybody, and he made many enemies among the nobles as well as among the people. He considered the assembly a farce, and so took the election of officials away from that body and gave it to the senate. This did not disturb the people, since the only men who could be voted for were those suggested by the emperor. What the masses disliked was the fact that Tiberius despised them. They could hope for nothing better, however, from the senate. That body was so weak that Tiberius despised it as well.

Tiberius Retires to Capri

In spite of his unpopularity, Tiberius was a strong ruler. He had a system of spies which kept him informed of what his enemies were doing, and he rid himself of the more dangerous as fast as they appeared. Indeed, he had to restrain the senate from killing too many people, because false informers were constantly appearing in the hope of making money by giving information.

Tiberius felt only contempt for the Romans, and after about twelve years in Rome he retired to the lovely island of Capri (kä′prē), where he spent the remainder of his life in peace and quiet. He left Sejanus (sě-jā'nŭs) in control at Rome, and although he had to have him removed and executed for treason after a time, nothing ever occurred to disturb Tiberius's power.

Caligula, the Mad Emperor

The next emperor ruled only four years (A.D. 37–41). He was a nephew of Tiberius, and was called Caligula (kă-lĭg'ū-lă), although that was only a nickname, given to him on account of the soldiers' boots caligae he was accustomed to wear. He was quite insane. He even made his horse a consul. For a time his excesses were allowed free scope while he spent the money that Tiberius had saved up, but at last even the Imperial Guard turned against him, and eventually he was murdered by them.

With the death of Caligula, the senate wanted to put an end to nominating imperators, but the Imperial, or Praetorian (prĕ-tōr'ĭ-ăn), Guard would not consent to this. They brought forward an uncle of Caligula, named Claudius, and insisted that he be nominated. Claudius was a man of fifty, weak and shaky in body, and generally thought to be rather weak-minded, but he proved to be a very capable emperor.

Claudius reigned from A.D. 41 to 54, and he greatly benefited the Roman state. He conferred citizenship again on conquered peoples, and he passed laws for the protection of slaves. He would never trust any noblemen or officials round him. He kept soldiers everywhere; even those who waited at his table were soldiers. The business of the state he carried on through Greek freedmen. In spite of all these precautions, he was assassinated, if report is true, after reigning for thirteen years.

The Cruel Emperor Nero

Then came Nero, Claudius's stepson (A.D. 54–68). Nero had been educated by a great and wise man named Seneca (sĕn'-ė-kă), whom he made his chief minister. As long as Seneca was in power Nero's reign was excellent, for Seneca taught that men should rise above passions and follow virtue. But within five years Nero dismissed his teacher and took control himself.

Photo by J. Laurent

THE TOILET OF THE VAIN POPPAEA

Poppaea (pǔ-pē'ă) was for a long time the power behind the throne of Nero. Her great beauty and evil schemes caused the emperor to murder both his wife and his mother; so she finally satisfied her ambition by marrying him and becoming empress. She was extravagant and luxury-loving—so much so, in fact, that it is said that wherever she travelled she was followed by a herd of asses, which furnished the milk for her beauty bath.

Photo by Chauffourier

A YOUNG MAN INCURS THE WRATH OF CALIGULA

One day as Caligula was entering Rome, a young man who was drinking wine toasted him, saying, "To the health of the goat!" The emperor was furious, and had the youth seized and immediately put to death.

Photo by Rischgitz

A HAPPY SCENE IN THE WOMEN'S QUARTERS

In the houses of all the well-to-do Romans, luxurious apartments were set aside for the especial use of the women of the family. Here we see a lady of ancient Rome watching her happy children at their play.

He soon began to lead such a life that even the Romans were amazed. The constant plottings that went on around the throne led him to have his mother put to death; then he had his wife assassinated; and finally he forced his old master to commit suicide.

Nero was very fond of music and art, and thought himself an accomplished artist. He would often go to different Greek cities and compete for prizes in music, dancing, or singing. The story goes that when the city of Rome caught fire and burned for a week, Nero sat in his palace giving a musical performance, and even played a violin while the fire raged.

The people believed that Nero himself had set fire to the city. But Nero blamed the Christians, and had a large number of them tortured and put to death in various ways.

weak and wicked emperor could do nothing to maintain his rule. The senate, seeing what was about to happen, sentenced him to death. But before they had a chance to execute him, he committed suicide. He had been reigning for fourteen years and was thirty-one years old when he died.

Nero was the last of the emperors related to Augustus. For a hundred years the family of the Julians had held power at Rome, and during all that time internal peace had been practically undisturbed. Whatever bloodshed and tumult had occurred, as the reign of each emperor had ended, was small indeed compared with the disaster of a great war. With all this peace the Roman empire had prospered. The government of the provinces had been regulated and established securely, the size and importance of Rome

Photo by Chauffourier

Chariot racing was one of the favourite sports of the Romans. People from miles around would gather to watch these most exciting races at the great stadiums, which were built in every part of the Roman empire

This was the first persecution of the Christians on any large scale (A.D. 64).

Nero's unpopularity was greatly increased by the heavy taxes he imposed on the people. When he had been reigning for about fourteen years, a revolt broke out in the Roman army in Spain, and soon the rebellious Roman legions marched on Rome. The

had steadily increased, and the wealth of its citizens had continued to grow.

The people had come to accept an emperor as the proper kind of ruler. Julius Caesar had been declared a god by the senate, and a temple had been erected to him. Augustus had permitted the Roman subjects to worship him even while he was alive, and both

Photos by Rischgitz

WHERE THOUSANDS SUFFERED TO MAKE A ROMAN HOLIDAY

Here are two views of the mighty Colosseum in Rome as it appears to-day. It was built by the Emperor Vespasian, and in it were staged some of the cruellest spectacles that have blackened the pages of History—fights between gladiators, fights between men and beasts, the martyrdom of Christians, and many other wanton cruelties conceived by the wicked minds of the emperors so that the mob might be kept in good humour. The building accommodated about 50,000 spectators.

Augustus and Claudius were also declared gods by the senate. Tiberius, Caligula and Nero were so hated that they were not deified. In general, we may say that if an emperor proved to be a leader he could be fairly certain of being made a god.

A Commoner Becomes Emperor

But there was another factor to be taken into consideration. The dead emperor needed the support of his successor, who made the nomination, and of the soldiers to demand that he be declared divine. The senate did in this case only what it did in all others, simply what it was told to do. After all, the man who could govern the Roman empire well was almost as powerful a being as any of the pagan gods of old. The only people who did not respect the emperors to any great extent were the soldiers and the generals. They were ever watchful to seize the power of a weakened ruler, and they did not stop at murder.

With the passing of Nero a year of strife among various officers followed, and Vespasian (vĕs-pā′zhĭ-ăn), a man of the common people, but a very able leader, emerged from the conflict as emperor. He set to work at once to restore law and order. He created many new nobles from among families that were loyal to him, bringing them from distant Italian cities and building up a court of friendly, helpful princes to replace the jealous, treacherous men who had surrounded the Julian emperors. Better still, these new families were people of simpler tastes and loftier morals than the old thriftless aristocrats of the Rome of the reign of Nero. The empire seemed to gather new life and to be ready to pass on to greater glories under Vespasian (A.D. 69–79) and his sons.

The most important event of Vespasian's reign was the destruction of Jerusalem (A.D. 70). The Jews, who had long been expecting a Messiah to save their nation, revolted, feeling certain that he would appear at the critical moment. The Romans besieged the city for five months, giving and receiving no quarter because the Jews would accept none. When Jerusalem fell, countless numbers of Jews were killed and less than a hundred thousand had surrendered. Those who survived were scattered far and wide over the earth.

At home, Vespasian began the building of the Colosseum (kŏl′ō-sē′ŭm), an enormous building, holding about 50,000 people, in which games and combats could be held.

Photo by Rischgitz   From the painting by Henri Motte

RIDERS IN THE CHARIOT WHO HELD THE POWER OF LIFE AND DEATH

When the vestals passed through the streets of Rome in their chariots drawn by milk-white horses, the crowd moved back respectfully and bowed low as a sign of respect for the maidens, for they were the most powerful women of the Roman empire. They had the best seats at the theatres and public games, and their residence was famous for its magnificence. It was a fortunate thing for criminals who, on the way to their execution, happened to meet a vestal, for the priestesses had the power to grant a pardon to any they chanced to observe.

Photo by Alinari

A SCENE FROM THE CARE-FREE LIFE OF A ROMAN LADY

To take a bath in Roman times was quite a complicated business. The Romans did not merely jump into a tub, scrub themselves all over, and jump out again. They went, instead, to one of the great public establishments, which were little cities in themselves. Besides various rooms for cold, lukewarm, and hot-water bathing, and halls where the bathers could rest while slaves massaged them with costly ointments and perfumes, there were also an outdoor swimming-pool, several gymnasiums, many shops, and in some cases libraries and even a theatre. So, you see, the ancient Romans did not go to a bathing establishment only to get clean; they went for amusement and recreation also. Statesmen and business men met in the elaborately decorated halls to discuss the affairs of the day; young men boasted of the charms of their lady-loves; and poets recited their latest masterpieces. And there were bath singers even in those days, for Seneca, who lived too near a public bath for his own peace of mind, complained that there was someone inside who loved to hear his own voice. The women's bath was smaller than the men's, but just as luxurious. The picture is a scene in the women's bath at Pompeii.

His son Titus, who ruled only three years (A.D. 79–81), completed the work. The magnificent ruins of the great amphitheatre may still be seen.

In the reign of Titus there occurred also a disaster which, strangely enough, has helped enormously to add to our knowledge of life in Rome under the emperors. A great eruption of the volcano Vesuvius (vĕ-sū'vĭ-ŭs) buried the Roman cities of Pompeii (pŏm-pā'ē) and Herculaneum (hĕr'kū-lā'nē-ŭm), covering them with ashes and lava and killing thousands of people.

After eighteen hundred years those two cities were excavated, and now we can see a Roman city almost exactly as it was in the time of Vespasian and Titus. The kitchens, the bedrooms, the streets and public places—all are perfectly preserved.

strengthening the boundaries of the empire. All along the north the barbarians were concentrating to invade the Roman provinces, and only a wall of soldiers held them back. As long as Rome had plenty of legions, plenty of hard and seasoned troops to meet the constant forays of the Germanic tribes, she had little to fear; but once her defences were weakened, the watchful barbarians would be ready to sweep over the empire.

The long period of peace had brought with it no great glory to Roman arms. The time was now ripe for some military leader to arise in Rome and show what the empire could do on the battlefield. Trajan (A.D. 98–117) was the emperor-general who was to shed a fresh lustre on the empire.

The Roman emperor Nerva, who ruled only two years (A.D. 96–98), adopted Trajan

Photo by Chaufourer

Hadrian was a good statesman as well as an able soldier. He made many journeys to the provinces to attend to their welfare and inspect the fortifications. Above you see him returning to Rome after one of these excursions.

Titus was the most beloved of all the Roman emperors. He felt that a day was wasted if he had not done some good work. But his brother Domitian (dŏ-mĭsh'ĭ-ăn), who succeeded him, was far less liked, even though he was much more energetic.

The fifteen years of Domitian's government (A.D. 81–96) were largely devoted to

(trā'jăn) as his son and heir. Trajan had great military ambitions. He led his army over the river Danube into the country now occupied by Bulgaria, Rumania, and the other Balkan states, but which was then called Dacia (dā'shĭ-á). He conquered it very rapidly. Then he penetrated the East, filled with ideas of spreading Roman rule

Photo by Clauffourier

The festival of spring was held regularly every year at Rome. On this most important day the temples were festooned with garlands, the people carried blossoming branches, and sacrifices were burned upon the altars.

even to the Indian Ocean, and bringing the ancient cities of Babylonia under his sway.

The people who had succeeded the Persians were called Parthians. They were fierce fighters, and the Romans had never managed to do more than defend the Roman boundary at the edge of the Fertile Crescent against them. Trajan, however, invaded their territory and, after defeating them, he marched on to Babylon and as far as the Persian Gulf. But he went farther than his supplies could follow, and was forced to withdraw. He died in Asia, while trying to make his way back to Rome.

Another general succeeded to Trajan's throne. This was Hadrian (117–138). He wisely turned his back on Trajan's ambitious schemes in the East; but, since the empire was not able to raise a bigger army, Hadrian did his best to make his troops the most efficient the world had ever seen. He made their work easier by building walls wherever the boundaries of the provinces were weak. We can still see the remains of Hadrian's Wall in the north of England. Along the German frontier he built a defence that was three hundred miles long.

The soldiers of Rome were no longer recruited from the streets of the city or from the neighbouring farms. They came from all parts of the empire. Legions raised in Egypt might serve in England, while cavalry composed of Gauls might sweep over the plains of Syria. The Roman army under Hadrian was disciplined and hardened by long marches and severe service. When the soldiers were not fighting, they were employed on public works.

There still stand in Rome two of Hadrian's magnificent structures. One is the Pantheon (păn′thē-ŏn), or "temple of all the gods," which was originally built by Agrippa in 27 b.c., but which Hadrian completely rebuilt. It is now used as a church. The other is Hadrian's tomb, an enormous building on the banks of the Tiber.

Last Great Days of Rome

These were the last great days of Rome. After Hadrian's reign there was only one more famous emperor. In many respects things were, it is true, better than they had been. There was still a great deal of coarseness and brutality, but the emperors had passed laws that had improved the conditions of the oppressed peoples.

One of the worst things that had gone on under the republic was the abuse in the collecting of taxes. These were gathered by the method known as "farming" the taxes, a system which was employed by the French up to the days of the French Revolution. For a certain sum of money a man could buy the right to tax the people of a certain district, and as the tax collector and his helpers were greedy and cruel the people suffered greatly. Under the emperors, however. taxes were no longer farmed out.

Then, too, when any Roman city, even one situated a long distance from Rome, suffered a great disaster from earthquake, fire, or the like, the government spent money freely to set things right again. The emperor looked upon all his dominion as his personal property, and he naturally wanted to keep it in the best condition possible.

The High Ideals of Marcus Aurelius, Author, Philosopher, and Emperor

The last great emperor before Rome began to totter was Marcus Aurelius (aw-rē′lĭ-ŭs), who reigned from 161 to 180. He was very fond of his adopted brother Lucius Verus, who he insisted should rule with him. But Verus was a man who enjoyed amusement more than anything else, and it was Marcus Aurelius who actually ruled.

He was a man of majestic character, upright and honest and blameless. Of all things, he would have liked most to study philosophy and read and write. But he looked upon his position as a sacred duty, which he carried out manfully because he thought it was right to do so.

Marcus Aurelius had no easy reign. At the very beginning he had to send an army to meet the Parthians in the East, and no sooner had he beaten them, after four years' fighting, than the barbarians at last broke through from the north-east and even advanced as far as the very soil of Italy (167). During the remainder of his reign, Marcus Aurelius had to struggle against these wild invaders from the north. He never did succeed in keeping them entirely out of Roman territory, and finally had to allow many of them to settle inside the frontier.

Marcus Aurelius has left us a little book of "Meditations" which he wrote in Greek, and which is one of the noblest books ever penned. When we think under what stress and turmoil of camp and battle he wrote down his thoughts, we can well appreciate the kind of man he was.

But Marcus Aurelius was not the only man of his age who loved literature. Somewhat before his time Pliny (plĭn′ĭ) the Younger had written a charming series of letters that we like to read to-day. Tacitus (tăs′ĭ-tŭs) was an historian who left us a book giving the most reliable information we now have about the German people of his time. Plutarch (plōō′tärk), a Greek, wrote some excellent biographies, which Shakespeare later used in writing his great plays; and Juvenal (jōō′vĕ-năl) wrote a series of witty essays called satires.

The Roman empire, just before it began to decline, was a powerfully organized and very successful state. There was a regular postal service from one end of it to the other. There were splendid roads, paved with stone, in all directions. There were banks in all the principal cities, so that money could be transferred from one town to another. There were regular lines of ships from Rome to the Mediterranean ports, and some of the grain boats bringing wheat from Egypt were quite as large as the freight steamships of to-day. Indeed, it was so easy to travel that many Roman tourists went to the East, or to Africa, Gaul, or Britain, just to see the world and its various peoples.

Scattered Monuments of Rome That Bear Witness to Her Greatness

In all the big cities of the empire—in Italy, in Africa, far out in what is now only desert, and in distant England or in Syria—we find Roman amphitheatres like the Colosseum, Roman aqueducts, Roman temples, schools, libraries, baths, and public buildings.

For two hundred years Roman civilization had flourished in such peace as the Mediterranean world had never known. But with the passing of Marcus Aurelius, the great organization began to rot at the core, although its weakness first became apparent in a breakdown at the frontiers. It was only a few hundred years before the glory and grandeur of Rome was to disappear under a wave of barbarian invasion.

(CONTINUED ON PAGE 861)

This is the famous Rospigliosi cup or salt-cellar. It received its name from the fact that it was once owned by the Rospigliosi family of Rome; but it is now in the Metropolitan Museum of Art in New York. This ornate and somehow beautiful jumble of tortoise, monsters, and sea-shell is made of enamelled gold, and is thought to be the work of Benvenuto Cellini, a famous sixteenth-century sculptor and metal-worker of Florence.

WITCHERY *in* PRECIOUS METALS

How the Expert Artist in Gold and Silver Can Rival the Painter with His Brush and Colours

YOU may read in Chapter xxxv of the Book of Exodus how the ancient Israelites wrought in gold and silver for the glory of the Lord. At the command of Moses, the people gathered together all sorts of precious and gorgeously coloured materials: "they came, both men and women, as many as were willing hearted, and brought bracelets, and ear-rings, and rings and tablets, all jewels of gold."

Beautifying a Holy Place

Then Moses appointed Bezaleel and Aholiab, men skilled "in all manner of workmanship," "to devise curious works, to work in gold, and in silver, and in brass, and in the cutting of stones to set them," and "to work all manner of work, of the engraver." They and their helpers built the tabernacle and all its furniture and fittings, the tables, the Ark of the Covenant, the seven-branched candlestick with its cups like almond flowers. The doors turned in sockets of brass; the walls were plated with beaten gold. Thus the goldsmiths and the silversmiths made beautiful the holy place.

Perhaps the Israelites had learned something of this skill in gold and silver while they were labouring as slaves in Egypt. For the Egyptians and the Sumerians were the first peoples, so far as we know, to attain skill as goldsmiths, even as they were the first to do so many other things. Five thousand years ago Egyptian goldsmiths were as skilled as any who have ever lived. We can tell this from the magnificent furnishings in the royal tombs which are from time to time discovered and opened.

Chariots Plated with Gold

In these tombs, what splendour do we find of silver and gold and bright enamel and precious stones! Chairs and bedsteads, tables, thrones, and even state chariots were plated with gold and silver. Toilet articles and jewellery of every kind were made of gold, set with precious stones, and highly decorated with something closely resembling modern enamel. The coffins were made of gold and silver, and covered with hammered and engraved designs. And the magnificence of crowns and sceptres, of diadems and breast-plates, is beyond description. The height reached by Egyptian civilization is exemplified by the work of the goldsmiths as fully as by that of the sculptors and architects.

To have worked in gold and silver at all, the ancient Egyptians must have been both rich and civilized. Savages sometimes wear nuggets of pure gold, picked up among the river sands, for gold is one of the few metals that can be found in a pure state instead of hidden away in ore. But when men hammer the gold and decorate it, they are beginning to work their way upwards out of savagery. Gold is too soft for weapons or tools, but for the more delightful and "useless" purpose of making ornaments its softness is all in its favour. It can be hammered into almost any shape. It can be beaten into sheets thinner than tissue paper, and this "gold leaf" can be used to cover baser metals such as iron, copper and brass. From the half-civilized gipsy to the most skilled goldsmith, every craftsman uses hammer and anvil, mallets and chisels and punches, for shaping and decorating his precious gold.

To the left is a silver mirror which once reflected the dark beauty of a lady of ancient Egypt. Below is a gold statuette of Amon, Egyptian god of the sun. It was found at his great temple at Karnak.

Silver usually grows very dilapidated with age, but this ancient vase, with its plant design and fragile handles, has withstood the ravages of Father Time.

The Many Ways of Working Gold

Sometimes goldsmiths and silversmiths hammer a design into the soft metal in very low relief; such work is called "chasing" or "repoussé" (rĕ-pōō'sā); sometimes they engrave the metal, carving delicate lines in it. Sometimes they fill the fine lines with a black substance that hardens when exposed to gentle heat; this black-outlined engraving is known as niello (nĭ-ĕl'ō) work. When they inlay the gold with silver or other metals of contrasting colour we call it damascene (dăm-á-sēn') work. When they draw the gold or silver out into fine wires, and then twist the wires together into beautifully interlaced designs, we call it filigree (fĭl'ĭ-grē) work. Often the gold or silver object, whether it be cup or dagger or ring, is beautifully decorated with different coloured enamels, or set with precious or semi-precious stones, with coral or amber on glass.

Because gold and silver are so often used with precious stones and made into jewellery of all sorts, the art of the goldsmith and the silversmith is very like that of the jeweller. They have to know how to do the same things. They have to be delicate and perfect craftsmen, and men of artistic talent and taste. Only an artist can conceive a still lovelier design for each successive brooch or ring; only a fine craftsman can fit the jewel into its setting perfectly. For centuries there was no distinction between the jeweller and the goldsmith, and even yet the maker of hand-made jewellery must have a knowledge of both crafts.

The real difference between the two lies in what they are most interested in undertaking. A jeweller is interested in setting off his jewel to the greatest advantage, and he uses his gold and silver in the way best suited to his purpose. A goldsmith or silversmith, on the other hand, is interested in making his gold or silver as beautiful as possible, and he uses precious stones and anything else that he needs merely to adorn his design. Then, too, a goldsmith or silversmith makes many other things besides jewellery—vases and flagons, salt-cellars and spoons, and all sorts of decorative objects.

A PRICELESS TREASURE OF GOLD AND LAPIS LAZULI FROM THE ROYAL GRAVES AT UR

This harp, one of the most beautiful of ancient works of art, was recently excavated on the site where Ur once stood. The bull's head is of gold and lapis lazuli, and the delicate inlay is of shell. Ur was an ancient city in the lower part of the plain of Mesopotamia, and was inhabited by the Sumerians, a people who were not only clever, hard-working farmers, but who were also highly skilled in other crafts, and noted for their love of learning. The harp is a specimen of their skill, and from this and other works of art found in the royal graves at Ur, we know that the Sumerians were excellent workers in gold and silver at a very early date. One prince was buried with a beautiful helmet of beaten gold upon his head. It was made in the form of a wig, with the hair shown in relief. It waves over the top, descends in curls over the forehead and cheeks, and is tied up behind in a very modern-looking knot. The same tomb contained many other objects of silver and gold.

Often he works in other metals besides gold and silver—in bronze, perhaps, or tin or pewter. His whole aim is to make beautiful things out of metal.

At about the same time as the Egyptian workmen were carrying on their craft, goldsmiths were labouring among the ancient Sumerians (sŭ-mēr'ĭ-ån) in the Tigris-Euphrates Valley. We discovered a few pieces of their work, and it shows that they well understood the art of moulding melted gold. They moulded little figures of men and animals, and then soldered the figures to vessels hammered out of gold. Sometimes they engraved precious stones, and decorated their gold and silver objects with them.

From Egypt and Sumeria the art of working in gold must have spread all over the Eastern world. There were skilful goldsmiths among the rich and adventurous race of searovers who dwelt in Crete for many centuries before the rise of Greece. In the ruins of their palaces and in their tombs we have found many beautiful articles made of gold. There are numerous vessels of beaten gold, and even some figures in the round that

The elaborate gold jewellery above was made by the Romans about a hundred years before the birth of Christ. The Etruscan powder-box to the right, which is of silver and decorated with gold, was made some three centuries earlier, and is a fine specimen of Roman workmanship.

have been beaten out with hammers. There are also many tiny figures, which have been cast, like those made by the Sumerians, and there is filigree work. One tomb contained as many as seven hundred small ornamented disks of gold, which may have been nailed on a coffin or may have been used to decorate some gorgeous garment. There are even masks of thin beaten gold, which seem to have had some connection with their funeral ceremonies, perhaps as portraits of the dead.

The Cretans—or Minoans (mĭ-nō'ån), as they are called—traded and colonized round the shores of the Aegean Sea, and the examples of gold and silver work dug up at Mycenae (mī-sē'nē) and other places in Greece show Minoan influence. At Mycenae also, a new kind of work in gold has been found—inlay, which does not seem to have been known to the Minoans. One dagger has an inlaid picture of some cats stalking ducks in the midst of clumps of papyrus by the side of a river in which fish are swimming; this is Egyptian scenery, but the workmanship is not at all like that of the Egyptians. There are two gold cups, found near Vaphio and hence called the Vaphio Cups, which are decorated with a hammered design showing wild bulls being captured with nets. Many of these designs from Mycenae are drawn with a free, bold stroke, and are most delicately modelled.

Mycenae and Vaphio are in Greece; yet the people who fashioned these articles were not of the race of Greeks who later built up the glorious Greek civilization. Those later Greeks, of the "classical" period, must have had fine goldsmiths among them, for they excelled in all the arts. But very little of their work remains to us. First one conqueror and then another came upon the scene, and each carried off many of the precious objects in gold and silver and melted them down for the metal they contained. So we have to depend on the glowing accounts that the ancient Greek writers have left

RARE EXAMPLES FROM THE HANDS OF CRAFTSMEN BEFORE THE BIRTH OF CHRIST

For many centuries before what is known as the "classical" period in the history of Greece, the people of that country and the neighbouring islands of Cyprus and Crete were producing magnificent specimens of the goldsmiths' art, many examples of which have been discovered during excavations among their ancient palaces, tombs, and other buildings. These treasures of the distant past disclose workmanship of amazing delicacy and skill, as may be gathered from the illustrations above. The helmet of gold (1) dates from 500 B.C.; the handle (2) belonged to a gold vase of great value; this gold bowl (3), which comes from Cyprus, and is decorated in an Egyptian style, was fashioned in 1200 B.C.; the fragment of gold plate (4) once adorned the sheath of a Scythian sword; the vase (5) is the work of a Cyprian artist of 700 B.C.; the bowl of silver-gilt (6) is of the second century B.C.; and the gold cup (7), one of a pair from Vaphio, Greece, dates from 1500 B.C.

us in order to understand what the gold-smiths' work was like in ancient Greece.

Some of it must have been very beautiful. Herodotus (hĕ-rŏd′ŏ-tŭs), the historian, tells us of the splendour of the work done by the goldsmiths for the temple at Delphi (dĕl′fī) at the command of Croesus (krē′sŭs), the Lydian king whose very name has come to stand for the possessor of great wealth. Then there was the statue of Athena (ă-thē′nȧ), which the sculptor Phidias (fīd′ĭ-ȧs) made for the Parthenon (pär′thĕ-nŏn), the magnificent temple at Athens. This statue was of gigantic size, and was fashioned of ivory and gold. The garments were strewn with flowers engraved in the metal and coloured with precious stones. Gorgeous indeed must have been this mighty shrine of the goddess of wisdom, patroness of the Athenians!

The Romans learned the art of the goldsmith, as they learned all the other arts very largely from the Greeks. Greek craftsmen went to Italy or sold their work to Romans and instructed some of the Italians in their art. The Etruscans (ĕ-trŭs′kȧn), a race of people living just north of Rome, seem to have been very apt pupils. They learned from the Greeks and from the Egyptians, and had a special dexterity of their own in goldsmiths' work, particularly in filigree. So, between the Greeks and the Etruscans, no wealthy Roman had any difficulty in finding gold-smiths and silversmiths to execute his orders.

And the Romans wanted splendid things, and gave orders for every kind of gorgeous ornament conceivable. They were especially fond of magnificent table services of gold and silver, for they liked to give great banquets and astound their guests with the gleam of their wealth and the perfection of their taste. Silver vessels ornamented with designs in relief were fashionable for many generations. At the time of Augustus the designs were very elaborate, and comprised pictures from history or legend, flowers and people and animals and birds. To own splendid silver pieces, to understand their styles and beauty and value, was at one time the fashion among the rich men of the Roman empire.

Even when they went on campaigns in Syria or Gaul, the Roman generals would carry their precious table services with them. Sometimes, fearing defeat or capture, they would bury them on the sites of their camps. Sometimes they could not return for their hidden treasure, and then it might lie in the earth for long centuries, to be dug up, perhaps, by some fortunate excavator of the present day. One such treasure, found near Hildes-heim, in Germany, may still be seen in a Berlin museum. But all too many of the masterpieces of Roman art were melted down by the barbarians who conquered Rome.

Yet when the Roman empire fell before these barbarians, in the fourth and fifth centuries, the art of the goldsmith did not disappear with it. During the next few centuries, known as the early Middle Ages, it

Copyright: Kouchakji Frères

A FAMOUS CHALICE OF SILVER

This is the famous Antioch Chalice. It is made of silver and decorated with figures of Christ, Peter, and Paul. Some people believe that the chalice was made not later than the middle of the first century A.D. and that the figures may, therefore, be real portraits. Others think that it is not so old, that it dates from the fourth or fifth century.

BEAUTY IN GOLD AND SILVER FASHIONED BY CRAFTSMEN OF ITALY

All these beautiful examples of metal work come from Italy. Nos. 1 and 3.—Fourteenth and fifteenth century copper chalices covered with silver, gold and engraving. No. 2.—Plate of silver. No. 4.—Silver chalice. No. 5.—Fifteenth century silver chalice. No. 6.—Beaked ewer of gilt silver done in the manner of Benvenuto Cellini. Nos. 7 and 9.—Byzantine chalices dating from the tenth and eleventh centuries, made of gilt silver. No. 8.—Gilt silver platter elaborately decorated with scenes from a legend of the sea nymph Amphitrite.

flourished in two main centres—in Gaul, or France, in the West, and in Byzantium (bĭ-zăn'tĭ-ŭm), or Constantinople, in the East.

There had been skilful metal-workers in Gaul even at the time of Julius Caesar's invasion. They knew how to make beautiful interlaced designs in bronze and silver, and how to decorate their work with coral and amber and enamels. From their Roman conquerors they learned how to use precious stones and coloured glass. After the decline of the Roman Empire, however, the northern people began to forget the more elegant tastes of the civilized south and to grow more and more like their half-barbarous neighbours of Germany and the Scandinavian countries.

Yet there was a large demand for the work of the goldsmith, for kings and princes and barbarian chieftains wanted numerous ornaments for themselves, their women, their weapons and their horses. Then, too, Christian bishops, leaders of the missions to those lands, wanted gold and silver and jewelled ornaments for their new churches. The Church, in fact, was the chief patroness of the goldsmith. Many of the best workshops were in the monasteries, and even some of the bishops were goldsmiths. One of them, Eligius (ē-lĭj'ĭ-ŭs), was canonized. Because he was so famous a goldsmith, and because he encouraged all the goldsmiths of

By courtesy of the British Museum

A CUP THAT ONCE BELONGED TO FRANCE

This is the "king's cup" which was made in France late in the fourteenth century and is now in the British Museum. The kings of France once drank from its shining bowl, but after the wars of Henry V and John, duke of Bedford, it came into the possession of the English crown. This lidded cup is made of gold and is decorated with scenes from the life of St. Agnes; they are done in the most exquisite of transparent enamels.

France with his enthusiasm and religious zeal, he has ever since been reverenced as the patron saint of those who work in fine metals.

Meanwhile, at the new seat of empire at Byzantium, in the East, the goldsmith's art was flourishing as it had never flourished before. The emperor and his court loved colour and pomp and lavish display. Christian patriarchs and bishops loved them too, and since there was no lack of wealth and skill, workers in precious metals and precious stones were inspired to do their best. The furnishings of the palaces and churches built by the emperors Constantine and Theodosius were magnificent beyond description. The emperor's chapel was as splendid as a jewel box. The decorations of the church of Santa Sophia and the church of the Holy Apostles were more gorgeous than those of any church today, perhaps than those of any other church before or since. The fame of Byzantine craftsmen spread far and wide. Semi-barbarous German rulers would buy jewelled swords from Constantinople, and tankards in enamel and gold. Even from distant France came a call for Byzantine (bĭ-zăn'tĭn) goldsmiths to come to Charlemagne's (shär'lĕ-mān) capital, where they were employed to decorate the churches throughout his vast empire.

During the following centuries more and more fine work in precious metals continued

ART IN GOLD AND SILVER

These brooches were made in England during the early Anglo-Saxon period—from about A.D. 500 to 600—at the time when Christianity was beginning to establish itself in Britain.

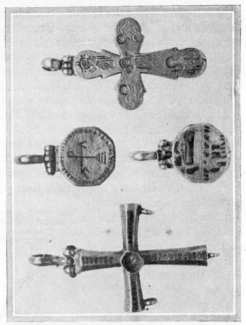

Here are two Byzantine crosses of gold. In the centre is a locket which once held a sacred relic. It was "a sure protection against all ills," according to the Greek inscription.

These articles were among a number of others that were buried with an English warrior about twelve hundred years ago. The centre buckle is of gold set with garnets. The vase is of silver.

All the above—except Nos. 3, 4, and 9, which are seal rings—are marriage or bethrothal rings. Nos. 1–4 were made before A.D. 500. The others are products of later centuries.

to be introduced into the Western lands from Constantinople and the East. Crusaders, returning from the long wars in the Holy Land, and frequently passing through Constantinople on the way, acquired and brought back with them a love of Oriental splendour. They wanted golden cups and silver spoons and gorgeous jewellery to brighten their huge and sombre castle halls. And then there were the holy relics they had brought from Palestine, and which they wished to have enshrined in some beautiful box or reliquary (rĕl′ĭ-kwā-rĭ). Or they might have brought ostrich-egg shells, coconut shells, horns of the water-buffalo, or horns—so they were assured—of the fabled unicorn; these they caused to be mounted with gold and silver and set with gems, to serve as drinking-cups at their banquets.

Often the things they brought had merely been taken as loot. Thus, in 1204, when Constantinople was pillaged, they carried off untold treasure. One of the finest pieces of work from this treasure, a gorgeous altar-cover, was taken to Venice and set up in the church of Saint Mark. There it may still be seen to-day, and from it we can get some idea of what Byzantium must have been like in the days of its glory.

In the fourteenth century there began to stir in Italy that great reawakening of appreciation for the art and thought of the ancients which is known as the Renaissance (rĕ-nā′-säns). The movement spread all over Europe, and ran its course for some three hundred years. To the goldsmiths and the silversmiths it meant new models and new styles, and a new inspiration. Gone were the massive designs of the Middle Ages, copied from the stone tracery of Gothic cathedrals; instead of these the Renaissance

The sword guards of Japan are often beautifully decorated with gold and silver work. The one below tells the story of Toddmoei, who mistook an old priest for a robber and rudely dragged him across the ground by his coat tails. The unfortunate man's rain hat and oil jar have fallen to the ground. To the left is a holy-water bucket from the Rhine Valley. It was made in the tenth century and is adorned with various scenes taken from the life of Christ.

goldsmiths sought designs that were elegant and graceful. They studied whatever Greek and Roman models they could obtain, and added all that they could learn from their own skill and genius, and from their study of Nature and of man. The results were magnificent. Never before nor since has such goldsmith's work been known as that which appeared during the Renaissance.

Master Craftsmen of the Renaissance

For the first two centuries or so most of the best work was produced for churches. It was often done by great artists. The names of these men are now famous for their painting or sculpture, but often in their own day they were equally renowned as goldsmiths. So great was the honour accorded to the worker in precious metals in those days! There was Lorenzo Ghiberti (lō-rĕn′zō gē-bĕr′tē), the illustrious architect; there was Donatello (dŏn′ä-tĕl′-lō), famous for his sculpture; there was Luca della Robbia (l′ōōkä dĕl′lä rŏb′byä), maker of beautiful pottery—all were masters of the goldsmith's art. About the middle of the fifteenth century, in which they all lived, Tomasso Finiguerra (tō-mäs′sō fē-nē-gwĕr′rä) was making the finest niello work ever produced.

The greatest of all goldsmiths lived in Italy in the sixteenth century. This was Benvenuto Cellini (bĕn′vĕ-noo′tō chĕl-lē′nē), of Florence. When we read his famous "Autobiography," we can imagine what a stormy temperament he possessed, and how many branches of art he mastered. Above

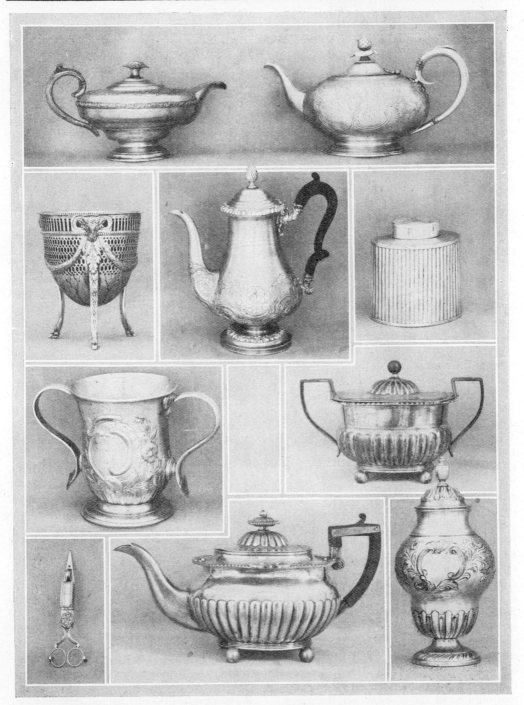

PIECES OF PLATE THAT HAVE BRIGHTENED MANY AN ENGLISH HOME

About 1742 an English craftsman, Thomas Boulsover, was mending a knife made of copper and silver, when he overheated it by mistake and found that the silver had fused with the copper. This discovery, later applied more widely by Joseph Hancock, led to the making of the old "Sheffield plate," which became so famous for its beauty and solidity. Above are examples of this plate made in the eighteenth and nineteenth centuries.

all else he was an exquisite goldsmith, famed throughout the world for his art

Only a few pieces of Cellini's work are still in existence, most of them in his native city of Florence. The reason for this is the same as the reason for the loss of so much Greek and Roman work—the ignorant rapacity of warring kings and princes, who wanted gold for hiring soldiers more than they wanted things of beauty to use or admire. If ever you chance to go to Vienna you may see the marvellous salt-cellar he made for Francis I of France. This piece alone is sufficient evidence that the world is right in calling him the prince of gold-smiths. Slowly, over the rest of Europe, the new Italian ideas blended with the native art developed in the Middle Ages. Each country—Holland, Germany, Spain, and France in particular— developed its own peculiar style. In the fourteenth and fifteenth centuries Denmark and Norway were famous for their silver-mounted drinking-horns. More and more silver forks and spoons were being made for domestic use. One spoon pattern, popular for two centuries, had figures of the apostles on the handle. These are called "apostle spoons." In Germany it was fashionable to have a combination fork, spoon, and toothpick made of silver. In the sixteenth century, Augsburg and Nuremberg produced immense quantities of spoons and drinking-cups; sometimes the drinking-cups were fitted with clockwork motors to propel them along the table. In England, during Queen Elizabeth's time, it was the fashion to have huge salt-cellars of elaborate design; one, for instance, is like a sturdy tower standing on four golden lions, with the cover of the cellar crowned by a tiny model of the human figure.

During a large part of the seventeenth century the centre of art in Europe was the court of the magnificent Louis XIV of France, who liked to hear himself called the "Sun King." But not many of Louis's artists worked in pure gold and silver. They generally preferred to execute their designs in tin or pewter, copper or bronze, and then gild them over. Although these men were very good workmen, they were not especially good designers. Their patterns, many of them devised by Charles Le Brun (lĕ brōōN'), Louis' artistic dictator, were for the most part composed of designs embodying interlaced scrolls, foliage, and shell-work.

The silversmiths of England, who had long been famous, did some exquisite work during the seventeenth and eighteenth centuries. The work of these craftsmen in the seventeenth century was influenced to a consider-

A VASE OF GOLD FROM THE NEW WORLD

While we may not, perhaps, admire the elaborate design of this gold vase, the work of an American craftsman, and may prefer the simplicity of earlier works, it is easy to see that it was made with great skill and required a complete mastery of the various methods of working in precious metals.

SIMPLE BUT STRIKING EXAMPLES OF THE SILVERSMITH'S SKILL

Most of these pieces are without exterior decoration, and even those pieces that have been given an ornamental finish present a plain and modest appearance in comparison with much of the silver ware of earlier periods. The teapots (1 and 3), the porringer (10) and the tankard (11) belong to the eighteenth century; the sugar-castoi (7) and the sugar-bowl (8) are earlier work of the same century; the tankard (6) was made about the middle and the sugar-bowl (5) and the coffee-pot (9) towards the end of the eighteenth century; the tea-caddy (2) is a product of the early nineteenth century. The spoons (4) were made by Paul Revere, who was a noted goldsmith and silversmith, but is better known for his activities in the War of American Independence.

able degree by the French Huguenots who sought refuge in England following the Edict of Nantes. A great deal of the eighteenth century work went into articles for the table —trays, cups and mugs, porringers, tureens, and decorative articles like vases and candlesticks. The work done during this time is notable for its simple elegance.

How "Sheffield Plate" Was Made

It was from England that the silversmiths in the American colonies learned their art. Most of the colonial silver, like that of England during the same period, is of simple, graceful design, and elegantly executed. In Canada the centre of the silversmith's art was Quebec, where it was introduced during the second half of the seventeenth century following the French conquest.

Much of the table silver we use to-day is not solid, or "sterling," but plated. A method of plating silver dishes was discovered by an English cutler in the middle of the eighteenth century. This "Sheffield plate," as it is called, was first made by laying a thin sheet of silver on one side only of the copper base. Later a method was discovered of plating both sides, and of covering the edges with little folds.

This kind of plate was popular for a long time, until, almost exactly a hundred years after it had been invented, it began to be displaced by the product of a process still in use to-day. This new kind of plating is done with electricity—the silver being deposited particle by particle on the metal base. It is so cheap and efficient that it allows nearly everyone to have spoons and knives, and even a vase or two, that are at least coated with silver.

But beautiful things are still being made of sterling silver, usually by machines but sometimes, even now, by hand. The hand work is naturally expensive, as it has always been, and so is comparatively rare. Relatively little work, either by machine or hand, is now done in gold. Even jewellery has of late years been wrought more and more of silver or platinum. Silver is less showy and more chastely elegant, and it is, of course, far less expensive, while platinum is more durable than gold. But goldsmith's work has by no means disappeared from the world.

Working for the Joy of Working

For here and there, in various countries, is a goldsmith or a silversmith of talent, patiently turning out beautiful creations for the joy of the work rather than for gain. Their work may be seen in great museums, along with that of the famous metal-workers of the past. And here and there in little villages, or in the midst of some great city, are many unknown craftsmen fashioning rings and necklaces of silver, or framing semi-precious stones in beautiful hand-wrought settings of gold.

We must not forget, either, that the designs, often very lovely indeed, which are produced by machines, must be conceived and worked out by artists. There seems little danger that the art of working in gold and silver will ever be forgotten while people continue to love beautiful things.

Photo by Presse-Photo

This Arab jeweller has set up shop in a street of Algiers and is busily at work on a golden chain. Although his tools are primitive, he may produce something very beautiful in design.

LITTLE BO-PEEP HAS LOST HER SHEEP

Little Bo-peep has lost her sheep,
And can't tell where to find them;
Leave them alone, and they'll come home,
And bring their tails behind them.

Little Bo-peep fell fast asleep,
And dreamt she heard them bleating;
And when she awoke she found it a joke,
For still they all were fleeting.

Then up she took her little crook,
Determined for to find them;
She found them, indeed, but it made her heart
bleed,
For they'd left all their tails behind them.

It happened one day, as Bo-peep did stray
Into a meadow hard by,
There she espied their tails side by side,
All hung on a tree to dry.

She heaved a sigh, and wiped her eye,
Then went o'er hill and dale, oh;
And tried what she could, as a shep-
herdess should,
To tack to each sheep its tail, oh.

There will be no fire alarm in this little village, for the house and the church are only toys, and that vivid lightning flash was produced in a laboratory. But the experiment gives a good impression of how real lightning behaves, and illustrates its habit of striking tall objects in the landscape—such as steeples and trees.

UP *in a* RAIN CLOUD

Where There are Forces That Will Polish a Hailstone or Hurl a Great Thunderbolt Through Space

(CONTINUED FROM PAGE 790)

MOTHER NATURE has a good many ways of watering her garden, for she is a thrifty old dame and never lets even a drop of moisture go to waste. Whatever water the warmth of the sun steals away from the earth has to be given back again whenever the air is chilled enough to make the moisture condense and fall.

As we have already seen, water vapour may condense into fog and cloud and yet remain floating in the air, though just how it manages to do so we cannot always tell. Often, of course, the particles are exceedingly small, and the updraughts that carried the vapour aloft continue to keep the cloud there. But clouds are heavy and lazy, and tend to drop their moisture whenever they get an opportunity. When this occurs we get rain and snow.

Any updraught of air is sure to be chilled, for as it climbs higher and higher there is much less air pressing down upon it and the mounting air has a chance to expand—or spread out. All gases that expand lose some of their heat; so as the mounting column of air gets thinner and thinner it gets colder and colder. Then, too, as it rises it enters levels of air that are much colder than those near the earth. When it reaches the condensation point its moisture gathers together into a cloud made up of tiny drops of moisture, each one having a speck of fine, invisible dust situated at its core.

But it is not until the tiny drops in a cloud have grown to raindrops or frozen into snow-flakes that they are heavy enough to fall to the earth. One small drop joins forces with others as it slowly sinks and finally becomes so heavy that even a strong updraught cannot stop it. Then it comes racing down. The large raindrops that usher in a storm may for a moment become a quarter of an inch across, though as a rule their own rapid motion breaks them in their long tumble earthwards. An ordinary raindrop is less than a tenth of an inch across. It is when millions upon millions of such drops fall helter-skelter to earth that we have a shower.

The Wind and the Rain

So rain is frequently caused by an up-draught of air which cools when it gets high above the earth and produces billowy clouds as it does so. Sometimes mountains force a wind to rise and cool; sometimes cool air pressing in at the sides sends a column of warmer air upwards. Always, in some way or other, before rain can begin, warm moist air must have risen and then cooled off.

All this explains why cold north winds are likely to bring, not rain, but clear weather. They are not cooling the warm air that lay over the earth before they came—they are driving it away. They would have to be yet more chilled themselves before they could shed their moisture. And it explains, too, why the windward side of mountains is usually well watered but the other side is much less moist.

In winter it is the great cyclonic whirls that distribute moisture over England; but in summer they have less effect. Rain then is more often brought about by the rising and chilling of columns of warm air that have been heated by the sun-baked earth—and these are what bring us our thunder-storms. When the rain falls, it chills the lower layers of air as it passes through them, so we say that a thunder-storm "cools the air."

Have you learned to enjoy thunder-storms? Many people are afraid of them all their lives long, and never know the thrill of delight that others feel at watching one of the most magnificent and dramatic sights

By courtesy of the Meteorological Office.

These remarkable branched flashes of lightning, which were seen from Herne Bay, are very unusual. Photographs of lightning flashes are of great interest, and are well worth the trouble of taking.

Here is the life history of a raindrop. Under the sun's rays the land and sea are always giving off moisture into the air, just as a boiling kettle does.

In some places the air grows very hot, and, like a cork in water, is compelled to rise by the cooler, heavier air that forces itself round it on all sides.

As the air mounts it is chilled, and its moisture begins to condense into drops round tiny particles of dust that are always present. This forms a cloud.

Finally these tiny drops join forces and get so heavy that they begin racing down to earth in the form of raindrops. Then we have a shower.

in Nature. Luckily, few of us will ever see the eruption of a volcano, or feel the terrible power that a tornado can let loose, but a thunderstorm is only a little less magnificent to see, and is really almost harmless. How many people have you ever known who were struck by lightning? For the most part, the crowded traffic in a city street daily puts many more lives in danger than all the storms that pass over a place during the course of a lifetime.

It is the lightning that does the damage and not the thunder— though it is the noise that makes many people afraid. Those enormous discharges of electricity that go zigzagging through the heavens are thought to be a result of the shattering of raindrops —all of which carry electricity — by the powerful updraught in a lofty cumulus (kū′mū-lŭs) cloud, or "thunder-cloud," in which rain is being formed. Certainly it is inside its mysterious folds that in some way or other great electricical power is set free.

Lightning often follows strange paths, and no one knows why it sometimes strikes where it does; but we have learned that there are certain reliable means of protection against it. If the building in the oval had been properly fitted with lightning rods, the flash that is striking it would have followed the rods into the ground instead of striking the building. The church was protected, so the discharge did it no harm.

The tremendous discharge that finally flashes towards the earth or towards another cloud may be compared with the spark you get when you stroke a cat on a cold, dry day in winter. And the splitting clap that follows the flash has the very same cause as has the gentle snap that accompanies the little spark in the cat's fur. But the great "spark" up in the sky has followed so long a path that the sound—which travels much more slowly than light—cannot reach you at once, as can the sight of the flash. It comes to you in a prolonged roar—and then is echoed and re-echoed by clouds and hills and buildings until it dies away in a murmur.

When the flash and the clap come at the same instant, the lightning is near at hand. And the length of time between them will tell you how far away the storm is. For, while you see the flash immediately, sound can travel at a rate of a little more than a mile in some five seconds. So if you can count slowly to five between the lightning and the thunder, you may take it that the flash was about a mile away —if you can count to ten, it was rather more than two miles away.

Now, electricity has a great preference for certain kinds of paths. For instance, it very much dislikes rubber and will not travel through it—so we say rubber is a "non-conductor." But it can make good progress through metal—such as a copper wire—so we say that copper is a good conductor.

Wherever electricity flows, it takes the easiest path. Thus, when great currents of it are darting about through the heavens, they will always flow in the direction that is easiest. If any tall object—a flagstaff.

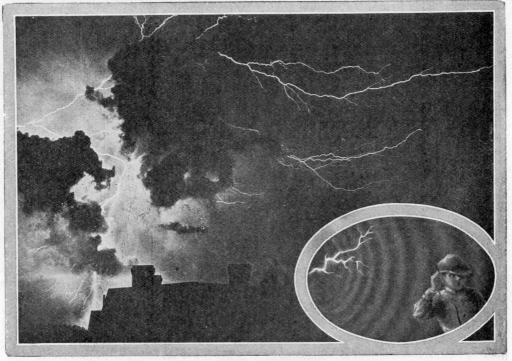

RIVERS OF FIRE FLASHING ACROSS A STORMY SKY

Lightning assumes many shapes, but often its path looks like the map of a great river system, as in the larger picture above; there the discharge is taking place behind a mass of clouds. The boy in the smaller picture is frightened. That last flash of lightning seemed right on top of him; but he is counting to see how long a time there is between the flash and the thunder. Then he will know how near the lightning is, for if he can count slowly to five—at one count a second —that will mean that the flash was about a mile away.

a church spire, or a tree—is reaching into the sky, the lightning will be apt to follow it to earth, since it is nearest at hand. Most of the people who have been killed by lightning have met their deaths because they ran to shelter under a tree—and the tree was struck, as trees are apt to be.

If you are caught out-of-doors in the open country during a severe thunderstorm, keep away from all trees and lie down flat on the ground. There you are practically out of danger. But if you are near shelter, the best thing to do is to go into the house, shut the windows and doors, and not go too near metal piping. Then no harm is likely to befall you.

Strangely enough, tall buildings that are massed together in cities seem to be in little danger of being struck. It is the building that stands alone—the church spire or the house on a lofty hill—that seems to attract the storm; but even this can be protected by

means of lightning conductors. Those long metal fingers, reaching into the sky, coax the electric current to follow them into the ground—or, at other times, discharge a current into the air that neutralizes the electricity above them.

Different Kinds of Lightning

An aviator, of course, can take none of these precautions. Since the cloud in which the lightning plays may reach seven or eight miles above the earth, he cannot mount above it. His best chance is to turn aside and try to avoid the centre of the storm.

Most lightning flashes follow a path a good deal like the course of a river on the map. The long, saw-toothed zigzags that illustrators like to draw have never been seen. The "sheet lightning"—common on warm summer evenings when no storm is anywhere at hand—probably comes from very distant flashes reflected by the clouds. Scientists are still greatly puzzled by "ball lightning," of which they have never been able to get a photograph. Anyone who sees one of those slow-moving globes of fire should watch it as carefully as possible, and send the Meteorological Office a painstaking description of its appearance, including all surrounding conditions down to the smallest detail. For it is only with the aid of all the facts that can possibly be obtained, that ball lightning may be explained by the scientists.

Thunderstorms probably do not occur at the poles, but nearly everywhere else in the world they discharge their batteries whenever an updraught occurs sufficiently powerful to break up raindrops and set their electricity free. They are most numerous in the tropics. Occasionally we even have them in winter, but usually they come in June, July and August. When a hot summer afternoon becomes oppressively still and "anvil" clouds mount high into the air, look out for lightning and thunder before long. But you need seldom expect them on a windy day, and rarely in the morning.

Often a thunderstorm pelts the earth with hail—little

In his right hand this man is holding a hen's egg, and in his left, a hailstone that fell during a storm in 1929. At the right is a diagram that portrays a hailstorm.

marbles made of snow and ice, sometimes no bigger than a pea and sometimes the size of a hen's egg, and occasionally very much larger still. When they come hurtling down from a height of half a mile or more, they can do terrific damage to crops. As a rule there are scarcely enough of them to cover the ground, but in Southern Europe they have been known to keep falling until they form a layer several inches deep.

They are altogether different from sleet, the little half-melted snowflakes that some-

times fall in winter. For hail is always made up of layers of ice or snow. When a raindrop on its way to earth is sent up again by the powerful updraught that is causing the storm, it meets a colder layer of air—very far up in the atmosphere—and is frozen. This may happen a number of times, and on each descent a layer of ice forms round the core, and the heavy little ball starts to fall to earth again—gathering another coat of water on the way. It reaches us as a small hailstone.

But if the updraught is powerful enough, the little marble may be juggled back and forth, each time adding a new layer of ice, until it attains a considerable size. When it finally reaches earth it consists of layer upon layer, rather like some of the sweets that you can buy at the confectioner's shop.

Hailstones usually fall near the beginning of a thunderstorm, when the up-draught is strongest. Luckily a hailstorm lasts only a few minutes and covers a very small territory; so the damage it causes is not wide-spread. And the hailstones never stay long on the ground. Like so many natural marvels, they must be examined quickly. For nature, as a rule, does not stage her effects for sleepy heads.

The hailstones we are more familiar with are those that come in summer time, as we have said, but there is another kind, a "soft" hailstone, which we see in colder weather. This is built up of snow particles and is in fact a kind of snow, though from its form we call it hail. It has not the hardness or bullet-like shape of the more familiar hailstones which we get with thunderstorms.

(CONTINUED ON PAGE 872)

A CITY LOST and FOUND

How a Seaside Resort of the Ancient Romans Was Buried and Came to Life Again after Nearly Seventeen Hundred Years

IT WAS a warm day in August. Peasants were working among the vines and olives on the green slopes of Mount Vesuvius (vĕ-soo'vĭ-ŭs), or piling their two-wheeled carts with fruit and vegetables to take to market in the city of Pompeii (pŏm-pā'ē). It was a good market, too, for in that year of A.D. 79 the little seaside town that nestled at the foot of the volcano was a fashionable resort for wealthy Romans, who fled to pleasant villas there to escape from the city's heat.

Up the steep street from the harbour came sailors just landed from their ships; and down the narrow highway flowed a steady stream of men with carts and donkeys laden with produce to be shipped away to other ports. The forum hummed with business. People were discussing the elections and laying wagers on the gladiators who were going to fight in the amphitheatre before ten thousand people; slaves were crowding the big meat shop to buy their masters' evening meal, and lovers were offering sacrifices at the temple of Venus, the finest in Pompeii.

There was no school on those hot summer days. The younger children played at blind-man's-buff and hide-and-seek, or rolled their hoops, or fondled their clay dolls and toy soldiers; but the older girls were learning to sew and spin and weave, while, from their fathers or well-educated slaves, the

Photo by Chauffourier

If we had lived in the days before the destruction of Pompeii we might have seen this charioteer driving his pair of spirited horses along the rough roadways. At one time this type of chariot was used in warfare, and later it appeared in processions and in races at the public games that were so popular among the Romans.

839

elder boys were taking lessons in swimming, riding and boxing, so that they might grow up to be strong and healthy.

The public baths were full. For the men would go to the baths as to a club, to stay long hours in the hot or cold or tepid water, to idle away their time in games or gossip, or to listen to a speech or poem. Old men played gravely at a game of "robbers," which was not unlike our draughts. It was just like any other day to the pleasure-loving people of Pompeii.

And then a shadow fell upon the city. People jumped up startled, and rushed into the streets. Out of the top of tall Vesuvius rose a great black cloud. At first it looked like a huge dark pine-tree against the clear blue sky, but swiftly it rose and spread. There were terrible rumbling noises. The earth shook; the sea rolled back in a towering wave; the sky grew darker and darker until it was black as night. Now and then it was slashed by streaks of vivid green or blue or red. Mighty explosions shook the houses. Ashes and cinders and small stones were showered from the great volcano, and people rushed frantically

about, trying to look for safety. Some went down into cellars, others ran to the sea and flung themselves into boats, rowing away as fast as they could from the terror that roared in the darkness. The heat was frightful. Suffocating gases poisoned the air. Many people searched for lost members of their families, and called to one another piteously. Gradually even those last sounds died away. The ashes piled deeper and deeper, and relentless night fell on the city.

Not until the end of three days did light dawn again. It found Vesuvius quiet, and nothing but silence where Pompeii had throbbed with life. Buried beneath the ashes that the majestic mountain had strewn around lay all that had so recently been a happy and wealthy city. The nearby towns of Herculaneum (hĕr′kū-lā′nē-ŭm)

The central court of almost every house in Pompeii had a beautiful pool and fountain like this. The roof was open to the skies, so that the rooms grouped around the court were full of light—in spite of the fact that they rarely had windows on the street side. The pool caught the raindrops which fell through the open space in the roof and held them until the maidens of the house gathered them into elegant vases for the household's use.

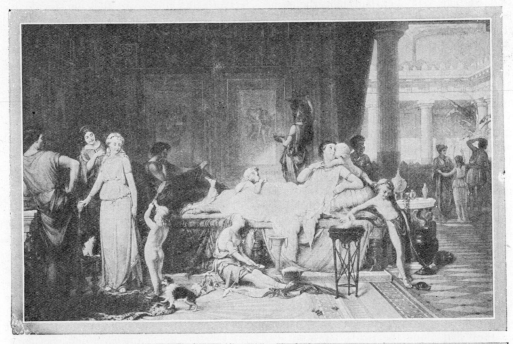

These pictures indicate how graceful and pleasant were the lives of the well-to-do people of ancient Pompeii.

and Stabiae (stā′bĭ-ē) had met the same sudden and tragic fate.

We have the story from an eye-witness. The Latin writer, Pliny (plĭn′ĭ) the Younger, happened to be staying with his mother and his uncle, Pliny the Elder, at a little town not far away. The younger Pliny saw the great eruption and described it to a friend in two letters that are often read to-day. His uncle, a great naturalist, was so deeply interested that he went too near to see what was happening and died of suffocation, caused by the terribly poisonous fumes.

Two thousand people, or one in every ten, are thought to have met death within the city, and many others perished as they fled along the roads. Fortunately, many more of them escaped. Some of them went back later and dug tunnels through the twelve or fourteen

Photo by Anderson

Soaked with moisture, the ashes which fell from Vesuvius hardened into moulds or shells around the bodies of the unfortunate human beings and animals trapped in Pompeii. And, to-day, if you pour plaster of Paris or wax into these moulds you can see what the original figure looked like. This is the cast of a dog that once ran through the streets of the city.

feet of ashes to recover their most valuable possessions from their homes. But it seemed quite useless to try to uncover the city, especially as the whole countryside had been desolated by the molten rock, or lava (lä′vȧ), that had flowed from the erupting volcano.

Years passed, and people forgot the exact site of the ill-fated towns. Fields sprang up on the fertile lava soil, the mountain was graciously clad in green again, and peasants began to tend their vines and olives on her slopes. At the end of the 16th century some labourers one day dug up two stones that bore inscriptions showing that the men had come upon the site of one of the buried cities. But nearly two hundred years went by before anything was done. At last some archaeologists (är′kē-ŏl′ō-jĭst) began to dig, and more than half Pompeii is now uncovered. A part of

Photo by Rischgitz

These refugees have finally reached a place of safety where they may rest awhile and look back upon all that remains of their once beautiful city, now transformed by volcanic eruption into a mass of shapeless ruins.

Photo by Anderson

THE DEAD CITY IN THE SHADOW OF VESUVIUS

Here is the unhappy city of Pompeii as we may see it to-day. And looming behind it is the fire-breathing mountain that sent it to its doom. The shape of the volcano has changed a good deal with every new eruption during the passing centuries, but smoke still gathers above its cone, and its crater is still full of steam and poisonous gas and seething lava. Many of the treasures from the city are in the museum at Naples.

Herculaneum has been laid bare, too, but digging there is much more difficult.

So to-day we can wander through the ancient streets and get some idea of the life that the Romans used to lead so long ago. In the paved roadways are deep ruts made by the wheels of ancient carts, and one can imagine boys and girls skipping home from school along the raised pathways on either side, or crossing over on the stepping-stones.

In the old kitchens are bronze frying-pans and cooking pots and spoons shaped much like ours; and in a surgeon's house were found forty bronze instruments a good deal like the steel ones used in modern surgery. In one of the many baker's shops were eighty-one of the thin round loaves the Romans ate, still in the big oven of masonry with its bee-hive top. The iron door was closed. And in the store-rooms of a rich man's house at

This is the figure of a man trapped in Pompeii on that eventful day over eighteen centuries ago. The wet ashes hardened into a mould round his body, and from that mould this cast was taken.

Herculaneum were found dates, chestnuts, walnuts, prunes, figs, pies and hams—all stored away for the winter nearly nineteen hundred years ago.

"Beware of the Dog"

Most of the houses of Pompeii were one or two stories high. Facing the street were blank, windowless walls, but sometimes the larger houses had in them little shops that were open all day long to passers-by and at night were closed by doors or sliding wooden shutters. Opening the front door of a house, one entered a vestibule where, in the homes of the well-to-do, there used to be a watchman or a dog. But if a family had neither of these, they sometimes had the picture of a dog, with the words "Cave Canem"—"Beware of the Dog." One such figure and inscription is a mosaic of tiny pieces of brightly coloured stone.

Two of the finest homes have been carefully restored to show as far as possible what they looked like when life stopped for their owners on that August day. One house belonged to a rich merchant; in the other— called the House of Menander—lived a man of higher class and more artistic tastes. The latter was thrown open to the public in October, 1933.

Let us pay a visit to the merchant's house. We open the front door and enter the vestibule. On either side are niches for the little statues of household gods, and in the hall that opens from the vestibule are two great bronze money chests with heavy fastenings. In the courtyard beyond, roofed only by the sky, there are bright flowers in bloom and statuettes that hold vases from which water is trickling.

All the rooms open on the courtyard— bedrooms only six or eight feet wide, with niches for bronze beds, and the big dining-room, where family and guests used to recline on sofas as they ate from the citron-wood table. Beautiful wall paintings, all fresh reds and yellows just as they were found, show Cupids busily baking or weaving or making wine. The floors are paved with fine mosaics.

A Laundry Bill of Long Ago

Here and there about the ancient city are scribblings done on walls with a pointed instrument of some sort, or with charcoal or red chalk. They show how much alike are people in all ages. Here is a note saying how many tunics have been sent to the wash. In a wine shop an advertisement promises a reward for the return of a stolen wine-jar.

Some envious boy left for us to see, all these centuries after, his opinion of "sheep-faced Lycurgus strutting about like a pea-cock and giving himself airs on the strength of his good looks," and a lovelorn youth has written, "Farewell, my Sava, try to love me." There are pleas to vote for such and such a candidate for office; and there are names of gladiators followed by inscriptions.

And so, after all those hundreds of years, Pompeii has come to life again. Its people have been dust for nearly nineteen hundred years, but up and down its streets walk crowds of tourists trying to imagine what life in the city was like so many years ago.

Photo by Anderson

Behind the bright blue waters of the Bay of Naples, one of the most beautiful spots in the world, Vesuvius still towers, a grim threat to all the countryside. At its foot you may see the white ruins of ill-starred Pompeii.

An EXPLORER of the DARK CONTINENT

The Workhouse Boy Who Became an Explorer, Found Livingstone, Traced the Course of the Mighty Congo, and Opened Up a Vast Expanse of Unknown Central Africa

HAD THE man who became known as Henry Morton Stanley not been possessed of extraordinary strength of will and courage in the face of adversity he surely could never have achieved what he did. For his youth was one of frustration and unhappiness, entirely lacking in affection and full of bodily and mental hardships which would have crushed a lesser spirit.

According to his own account, John Rowlands— for that was his real name —was born in 1841 at Denbigh (dĕn'bĭ), Wales. His father dying a few weeks after his birth, he was left in the care of his maternal grandfather, with whom he seems to have been fairly happy. Unfortunately, however, his guardian died suddenly, and, after living for a short time with uncles and then neighbours, the unwanted orphan was taken to the workhouse of St. Asaph.

There he met with the sort of treatment that so roused the indignation of Charles Dickens. Although a good scholar, being especially proficient in geography and draw-

Henry Morton Stanley as he appeared shortly after his discovery of Livingstone. The face is that of a visionary, who yet would never be turned aside from the goal towards which his footsteps were directed.

ing, both of which were to prove of use to him later, the brutal schoolmaster at the workhouse treated him, as he did all the unfortunate little boys in his charge, with the utmost cruelty. His tyranny over young Rowlands came to an end when the lad finally retaliated by giving the master a sound thrashing, and subsequently escaped from the workhouse.

But his troubles were not yet over, and the outside world, which had seemed so beautiful from the windows of St. Asaph, proved less hospitable than he had anticipated. After a time, he was given employment by a cousin as pupil teacher at a parish school; but, tiring of this occupation, he tried his fortunes in Liverpool, only to discover that no success awaited him there.

Finally he shipped as cabin-boy on a boat bound for America, and on arrival at New Orleans in 1859, escaped from the hard treatment he had received on board, and by great good fortune fell in with a kindly merchant broker, one Henry Morton Stanley, who first found him employment with a friend, and later adopted him as his son, the boy taking his name.

For some time young Stanley, as he was now called, was exceedingly happy with this good man, but fate had another blow in store for him. His adopted father died, and the lad was again cast adrift. Soon after this, civil war broke out in America, and Stanley, always courageous and eager for adventure, joined the army of the South. In April of 1862 he was taken prisoner at the battle of Shiloh (shī'lō), but became very ill and was allowed to return to Wales.

He reached his native land with high hopes, eager to see the family who had treated him so badly, and full of desire to pour out his heart to them. But he was met with absolute coldness and lack of affection. "I was told," he writes, "that I was a disgrace to them in the eyes of their neighbours, and they desired me to leave as speedily as possible."

The manner of his reception at what should have been his home, sank deep into his heart, and all through his life, right up to his marriage in 1890, he was oppressed with the thought of the lack of that affection for which he craved.

Disappointed and embittered, he returned to America, where the war still continued, and entered the United States navy

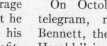

You may be surprised at the novel form of hairdressing adopted by this native. He came from Rua, and was visiting Ujiji at the time when Stanley arrived there in 1876.

in 1864, where he displayed great courage and resource. It was at this period that he began writing for the newspapers, and his articles were extremely successful and profitable. He was therefore enabled to indulge his love of travel, and accordingly visited the Far East, journeying to Tiflis and Tibet by way of Constantinople.

Back in America, he accompanied General Hancock's expedition against the Red Indians as correspondent for the "Missouri Demo-crat," and on his return to New York he obtained the post of special correspondent of the "New York Herald" on the British expedition to Abyssinia.

Stanley proved himself an excellent man at his job, and at the close of the Abyssinian campaign was sent by the "Herald" to Europe to report any important happenings. When he reached London, he was met by a representative of that paper with instructions to go to Egypt and get into touch with Livingstone, who was reported as returning home from Africa after years of silence, and to obtain the first news of him. But this proved a wild goose chase. No news could be received of the missing man, and Stanley accordingly abandoned the task and proceeded to Spain, where he spent six months under orders during the stirring times of the republican rising.

Stanley was the possessor of immense self-reliance and strength of purpose. An early experience had caused him to vow temperance in all things, and it was at this period in his life that he wrote "I mean by attention to my business, by self-denial, by indefatigable energy, to become, by this very business, my own master, and that of others." He indignantly repudiated all suggestions that he should take a well-earned holiday, remarking, "My body carries Stanley and his fortunes. With God's help I shall succeed."

On October 16, 1869, he received a telegram, requesting him to meet Mr. Bennett, the proprietor of the "New York Herald," in Paris. On his arrival there he was given instructions that were as astonishing to him as they were definite. He was to proceed to Africa and there search for Livingstone in earnest, and, if necessary, render him every assistance.

To Stanley this was a wonderful opportunity; but, before he started on his great

While Stanley was staying at Zanzibar in 1874, previous to setting out on his journey to the great lakes of the interior, he took a photograph, on the roof of the house where he was staying, of some of those who were to be his companions on the arduous expedition. The picture shown above is taken from his photograph.

attempt, he made several preliminary expeditions for the "Herald," including visits to the Suez for the opening of the canal, Constantinople, Jerusalem, Russia and Persia —journeys which were in themselves feats of endurance, but which Stanley regarded merely as preparations for the great work that lay ahead of him.

Preparing for the Great Attempt

In 1871 he arrived at Zanzibar, full of enthusiasm for his mission, and nothing daunted by the fact that no news of Livingstone had been received for a considerable time, and that he had no funds at his disposal, although allowed a free hand in all arrangements. The American consul at Zanzibar, however, came to his help with a generous loan, and on March 21 he started off on his quest.

His path carried him through country infested by dangerous savages, among them one Mirambo, who was a terror to all that part of Africa, and Stanley was forced to endure months of struggle with this black despot. Not only that, but he had to contend for some time with frequent mutiny in his own ranks, together with the ever-recurring fear of starvation; while, as he penetrated farther, his progress was hampered by constant halts when he was forced to pay forfeits to native tribes in order to proceed. Stanley himself suffered greatly through illness, but his weakness and solitude led him to turn more and more to his Bible, and from it he derived great consolation.

Meeting with Livingstone

At the Malagarazi (măl′ä-gä-rä′zĭ) River, however, he had received news of a white man's presence at Ujiji (oō-jē′jē), and the hope of succeeding in his mission buoyed him up. At last Ujiji was reached, and the Arab settlers, finding that the approaching force did not come from the dreaded Mirambo, accorded Stanley a hearty welcome. But his only concern was—would he find Livingstone here?

Suddenly a native rushed up to him and addressed him in good English. It was

Livingstone's faithful servant, Susi, and he assured Stanley definitely that the doctor was there. Even when Stanley stood face to face with the white-haired Scotsman he still felt doubts as to whether it really was Livingstone alive and in the flesh.

"Under all these circumstances I could do no more than exercise some restraint and reserve," he wrote; "so I walked up to him, and, doffing my helmet, bowed and said in an inquiring tone: 'Dr. Livingstone, I presume?'

"Smiling cordially, he lifted his cap, and answered briefly, 'Yes.'"

Stanley then cried, "I thank God, Doctor. that I have been permitted to see you," to which Livingstone replied, "I feel most thankful that I am here to welcome you."

This eventful meeting occurred on November 10, 1871, and from it there sprang up a very close friendship between Livingstone and Stanley. The latter, having handed Livingstone letters he had brought for him, tried earnestly to persuade him to return home, but he refused, being determined to complete certain explorations. Finally, Stanley persuaded Livingstone to return to Unyanyembe with him and there await a relief force which should be sent out.

The proud owner of this plaited beard twenty inches long is Kiteté, the chief of Mpungu, which Stanley also visited on his march. Notice, too, how his hair is trussed up on his head. His symbol of royalty was a huge blackened truncheon.

On March 14 of the following year the two friends parted, never to meet again. They had spent the intervening months together, hunting and travelling, including a joint exploration of Lake Tanganyika (tän-gän-yē′kä), and now felt the parting keenly, although Livingstone's determination was not to be shaken. The farewell took place with expressions of regard on both sides.

"I will say this to you," said Livingstone, "you have done what few men could do. And for what you have done for me, I am most grateful. God guide you safe home and bless you, my friend."

"And may God bring you safe back to us, my dear friend," answered the younger man. "Farewell."

They separated, and Livingstone awaited Stanley's relief force, with which he shortly after set out on an expedition from which he never returned.

When Stanley reached England he was met by disbelief and suspicion. It was affirmed that he had never found Livingstone, and that he had told a trumped-up story; and, although many did believe in him, the rumours received widespread publicity. Livingstone's own family, however, eventually declared the validity of the letters which Stanley had brought back with him, and expressed their gratitude for what he had accomplished. But the whole experience caused Stanley great suffering, and for a time he became very embittered.

He was not long to remain inactive, however. The "Herald" sent him out to report on the British campaign against the Ashanti in 1873–74, when he displayed his usual cool courage. On his way home from this expedition he was met with the news of Livingstone's death while engaged on an attempt to solve the problem of the Lualaba (lōo′ä-lä′bä) River. "May I be selected," cried Stanley, "to succeed him in opening up Africa to the shining light of Christianity."

Undeterred by his previous hardships and the death roll of the Dark Continent, Stanley made up his mind to circumnavigate Lake Tanganyika and clear up the problems surrounding that lake and its neighbour, the Albert Nyanza. If he could perform this task, perhaps the world would believe at last that he had found Livingstone.

Accordingly he walked into the London offices of the "Daily Telegraph" one day and offered his services. His offer was cabled to Gordon Bennett, and an answer having been received containing the single word "Yes," Stanley was financed jointly by the two newspapers and sailed to Zanzibar. There mutual pledges were exchanged between him and 356 chosen followers, and the journey began on November 17, 1874.

"By the time we had gone through Ugogo (ōō-gō′gō)," he wrote, "we were rich in experience of African troubles, native arrogance and unbridled temper." When the party reached the Victoria Nyanza, illness, famine and native hostility had taken their toll. Nevertheless, Stanley was bent on sailing right round the great lake, and to this end had brought out a boat from England in sections, which he now proceeded to put together. Eventually eleven of his black companions were induced to accompany him and the boat was launched.

Many dangers were encountered on the water, principally from hostile and savage natives, but Stanley found a good friend in Mtesa, the emperor of Uganda (ōō-gän′dä),

whose hospitality was bounteous, and with whom he "talked of many things, principally about Europe and Heaven." The emperor was keenly interested in Western civilization, and Stanley seized the opportunity to do missionary work. It is a great tribute to his character and treatment of the natives, that Mtesa became converted from Mohammedanism to Christianity by reason of "the difference of conduct he had observed between the Arabs and the whites." Stanley left a young missionary with the king and his subjects, and later a mission-station was established.

Apart from this good work, Stanley made a great contribution to geography in clearing up the mystery surrounding the great lakes and their supposed relation to the Nile system. He discovered that Lake Tanganyika had only a periodical outlet, and no connection with the Albert Nyanza, and that the Victoria Nyanza was one lake and not a series, as had previously been suggested. But there yet remained Livingstone's work to be completed, and that was to solve the

MEMBERS OF THE EXPEDITION TALK THINGS OVER

The courtyard of Stanley's house at Ujiji, where a council is being held as to their future movements. At Ujiji the expedition suffered a great deal through smallpox, while Stanley himself was attacked by fever.

mystery of the Lualaba River. Was it the Nile, the Niger (nī′jẽr) or the Congo? Stanley determined to find the answer to this riddle.

Accordingly he started out for the north and the Lualaba River, and at length reached the junction of that river with the Ruiki (rōō-ē′kĭ). In spite of dangers and suffering, he sailed on in his little boat to Stanley Falls, and after experiencing great difficulties in getting the boat past the Seven Cataracts, he discovered that the river, which had previously been flowing towards the Nile, curved north-west. "Ha! it is the Niger, or the Congo," cried Stanley, but he had "not much time to specu-late. Every hour was replete with incidents." A little lower down, the river was joined by another great stream, and thenceforth the explorer floated for hundreds of miles on a stretch of water four miles wide, until it curved west, then south-

Above you see the audience hall of Mtesa's palace in Uganda, which Stanley visited in 1875. It was made of straw, and was about twenty-five feet high, sixty feet long, and eighteen feet in breadth. Here Mtesa sat in state to hear petitions.

west, straight for the mouth of the Congo. "I knew then," wrote Stanley, "beyond dispute of the most captious critic, that the Lualaba, whose mystery had wooed Living-stone to his death, was no other than the . . . mighty Congo."

Worn out, ill and exhausted, the party at last reached Boma on August 9, 1877, where a warm welcome by European merchants awaited them. But Stanley refused to take the rest that he deserved until he had seen all his faithful companions, or those of them who had survived, to their homes; and his tribute to their constant loyalty and devotion is very fine.

From that time on Stanley's one thought was to civilize. He saw to what uses the great Congo could be put, but urged his schemes in England in vain. Finally, King Leopold of Belgium became interested, and it was while acting under orders from Bel-gium, instead of his own country, that

Stanley established the Congo Free State and governed it himself for a time.

Once again he was to visit the Dark Continent, when in 1885, after the fall of Khartum (kär-tōōm′), he went to the relief of Emin Pasha (ĕm′ĭn pȧ-shä′) and succeeded in his quest, after enduring hardships which would have broken the strength of many a younger man. On his return journey he made a most important discovery—that of the Albert Edward Nyanza and the Ruwen-zori (rōō′wĕn-zōr′ĭ) Mountains—Ptolemy's (tŏl′ĕ-mĭ) long lost "Mountains of the Moon." The Dark Continent was dark no longer.

In 1890 he married, and, after lecture tours in America, Australia and New Zealand, entered Parliament in 1895. In 1897 he paid his last visit to the land to which he had given the best years of his life. In 1899 he was made a Knight of the Grand Cross of the Bath, but he was not long to enjoy this tardy recognition of his great services in the cause of exploration.

Completely worn out by a life of hard-ship and devotion to service, he died on May 10, 1904, happy at last in the society of his wife and child, and the affection for which he had longed in his childhood and lonely years in Africa. After a service in Westminster Abbey he was buried in the village churchyard at Pirbright, in Surrey, where a great monument fashioned out of a single stone from Dartmoor marks his last resting place. On the monument the follow-ing simple words are engraved:

HENRY MORTON STANLEY
BULA MATARI
1841-1904
Africa

"Bula Matari" was the name by which Stanley was known to the natives of Africa.

The MOST MUSICAL of POETS

We Can Probably Award that Title to Swinburne for His Majestic and Graceful Melodies and Harmonies in Words

(CONTINUED FROM PAGE 807)

THE SCHOOL librarian at Eton used to be immensely amused to see the odd-looking youngster sitting in a sunny bay window, day after day, cross-legged like a little tailor, with a great book on his lap. The boy had a slim body, frail hands and feet, and a huge head, made to appear even bigger by its unruly mop of red-gold hair. The librarian would point him out to all the visitors as one of the curiosities of the school.

All his life Algernon Charles Swinburne was being pointed to as a curiosity. Sometimes, later, he was disliked for his new ideas; usually he was admired for his learning and his melodious poetry; but always he was considered an oddity. A whole legend about him grew up while he was still alive.

He was regarded as unusual even before he went to Eton. Born in London, in 1837, his early years were spent by the sea, in

Photo by National Portrait Gallery

These three charming children are the little Swinburnes, Algernon Charles and his two sisters. The boy was destined to write some of the most musical verse in the English tongue, and also excellent prose.

the Isle of Wight. He had been a very sickly baby, but as a child he lived such an active life out of doors—riding, swimming, and climbing cliffs—that he was in fairly good health by the time he was sent to school, though still nervous and slight of body. By that time, too, he had acquired a knowledge of French and Italian and could read and write good English—though he had never been allowed to read a novel. He arrived at the school carrying under his arm a copy of Shakespeare.

The Young Poet's School Days

While at Eton he read a great deal in Italian, French, and Greek. He had plunged into the novels previously forbidden him, and had rapidly devoured the old English dramatists and all the poetry upon which he could lay his hands. A friend reports that it is hard to say what Swinburne did not know and appreciate by the time he was sixteen. When he was not reading in the sunny window, he would be wandering through the woods—"he could swim and walk for ever," another friend reports—almost dancing along, and reciting page after page from his favourite books.

He had a desire to become a soldier, but he was too weak and small. Instead, he went up to Oxford. Here he developed such strong ideas about religion and politics that his friends feared he might be expelled, just as Shelley, one of his favourite poets, had been expelled before him. He used to recite fiery verses in front of a portrait of the Italian patriot, Mazzini (mät-sē'nē), and when he visited France with his parents in 1858, he nearly got himself and them into trouble by expressing his views of the French emperor. Years later (1871), at the urging of his hero, Mazzini, he put his enthusiasm for freedom and democracy into some of the most stirring poetry in our language—his "Songs before Sunrise."

Youthful Literary Lion

All this time he had been experimenting in verse, but he did not publish anything important until 1865. At that time he was living in London, in the intimate circle of George Meredith, the novelist-poet, and the Rossettis, a family of poets and painters. In Paris he had made a friend of the painter, Whistler, and had visited the poet Landor in Italy. Already he was a familiar and much-talked-of figure at literary parties—with his top-heavy figure, his flaming hair, his restless hands, his incredible memory, his flow of brilliant talk, and his habit of declaiming his own verses in an impressive chant. At length, with the appearance of "Atalanta in Calydon," in 1865, he leaped into full fame with the public at large.

"Atalanta in Calydon" appeared in cream-coloured bindings, with strange but lovely illustrations by Swinburne's dearest friend, Dante Gabriel Rossetti (rŏ-sĕt'ĭ). It was an immediate success. And no wonder! Who could resist the interwoven melodies of lines like these:

When the hounds of spring are on winter's
    traces,
  The mother of months in meadow or
    plain
Fills the shadows and windy places
  With lisp of leaves and ripple of rain . . .

It is like soft and lovely music, with its easy rhythms and its playing with the m's and l's and r's.

Famous and Hated

But the very next year, after winning fame with this book, Swinburne incurred the wrath of some people who were shocked by certain views expressed in his next book, "Poems and Ballads." Yet whether they praised or condemned the poems, people all over England, and America too, were talking about the works and what many imagined to be their eccentric author.

Meanwhile, Swinburne continued to write, turning out an immense number of poems, poetic dramas, and criticisms in prose. But life in London affected his health, and he was often compelled to go into the country for long periods of rest. Finally his health became so bad that he went to stay with his great friend, Theodore Watts-Dunton, at his house, The Pines, at Putney. There he spent the last thirty years of his life very quietly indeed, scarcely ever going into the heart of London even when his health improved; and there, in 1909, he passed away.

AS GEORGE ELIOT SAW THE COUNTRYSIDE OF ENGLAND

Here is a typical example of the country and the period of which George Eliot wrote in many of her novels. She describes in a vividly refreshing style the fields and the lanes of the countryside, and the simple people, presenting a true picture of the romance of their family affections and the pathos and humour of their lives.

The WOMAN Who WROTE "ADAM BEDE"

She Published it Under the Name of George Eliot because in Her Day a Woman was Scarcely Expected to Write Novels

A HUNDRED years ago a girl was scarcely expected to be clever or to read many books—far less to want to write them. It was quite enough if she could cook and sew and help in the home. Any further interests than these were considered unladylike by many people.

But Mary Ann Evans loved her books, and she also loved to romp with her elder brothers. So there were some people who did not think very well of her. How her old-fashioned mother would have been astounded to know that one day the little girl would grow to be a great novelist, and would make the lovely scenes and the simple folk of her childhood so famous in her stories!

She was born in 1819, on a large farm in Warwickshire of which her father was the bailiff, or manager. Her father petted her and allowed her to do much as she pleased. Among other things, he let her ride over the countryside with him and learn all about the cottage people from whom he used to collect the rents. And she would also trot around with a favourite brother, joining in his games and fishing with him, and even peeping into the books he read and studied.

At her own school she could surprise the teachers with the clever compositions that she wrote; but as she grew older she learned mostly for herself—music and languages especially. She was passionately fond of reading; and, even after she took entire charge of her father's house at sixteen, when her mother died, she still found a good deal of time for her books.

Then she became acquainted with some thoughtful people named Bray, who lived near her home. They told her she ought to write, and encouraged her to translate Strauss's "Life of Jesus" (1846). With them she travelled on the Continent after her father's death, and through them she later met a good many interesting people in the literary world. In this way she became one of the editors of the well-known "Westminster Review," and she met the man for whom she acquired a great affection—George Henry Lewes (lū′ĭs).

It was Lewes who discovered the value of her writing. Under his guidance she published her first stories in the book called "Scenes from Clerical Life" (1858); they had appeared originally in "Blackwood's Magazine." With "Adam Bede" (1859) she came into great fame, increased in the following year by "The Mill on the Floss." Her fine inspiration was derived from her own belief in the noble purpose of life.

Photo by National Portrait Gallery

George Eliot, possibly the greatest woman novelist in the English language, who wrote of country life and simple, homely people.

But it was the books rather than Mary Ann Evans that were so well known at first. It was still so unusual for a woman to be writing novels that she had taken the name of George Eliot, just as a little earlier another woman novelist, in France, had called herself George Sand. And to this day there are people who do not know the real name of George Eliot.

After she became famous she wrote many other novels. The simplest and sweetest of them all is "Silas Marner" (1861), that story of the poor miser who is so deeply changed by his love for the little girl he adopts. "Romola" (1863) is a longer work with a background of Italian history, and "Felix Holt" (1866) treats of English political life. "Middlemarch" (1872) is one of her masterpieces, while "Daniel Deronda" (1876) is a novel of lesser merit.

Towards the end George Eliot's life was saddened by the death of Lewes, and her writing ceased. In May, 1880, she married John Cross, but in December of that year she died in London.

POET *or* NOVELIST—WHICH?

George Meredith Had to Wait Till He Was Sixty Years Old Before Fame Came to Him, but after That He was Acclaimed as One of the Great Writers of His Day

IF YOU should ask a book lover about George Meredith you might be told that he was a poet, or you might be informed that he was a novelist. It is exceedingly difficult to say whether he was greater in his poems or in his novels. But the person you asked would be sure to know that Meredith was one of the great English

Towards the close of his long and brilliant life, George Meredith was unable to walk far without assistance, and whenever he went out it was in this little donkey-carriage. This photograph was taken outside his home at Mickleham, near Dorking, Surrey, where he died.

writers of the latter half of the nineteenth century. Yet if you had put the same question to such a person any time before Meredith was sixty years old, you would very probably not have found out anything at all. For Meredith was one of those unlucky writers to whom few listen until they are nearly too old to enjoy their fame.

The Orphan and His Favourite Book

Meredith was born at Portsmouth in 1828. His father, who was a tailor and a naval outfitter, lost his money and went away when his wife died, leaving little three-year-old George to be brought up by his aunts. George was sent from place to place and school to school in and around Portsmouth; and later on, practically all he could remember enjoying during these years was his reading of the "Arabian Nights."

When he was sixteen, he went for a time to a school on the Rhine, in Germany, and there he began to study in earnest. But he really had to teach himself most of what he learned; and one can easily tell from reading his novels and poetry that he did it well.

He was only seventeen when he settled in London. He became an articled clerk to a solicitor, but his tastes did not lie in the direction of law, and so it was not long before he took leave of it and set about the task of becoming a writer. This period of his life was one of considerable hardship, and often there were occasions when he would have done any odd job that would have been rewarded with a substantial meal. He managed to get some verses published, in a paper edited by Charles Dickens, the famous novelist; and he earned a little money acting as "writing master," or critic, for other young beginners in the art.

Famous Father-in-Law

When he was about twenty, this handsome, brilliant, but almost penniless young poet was taken into the delightful circle of an older novelist and poet, Thomas Love Peacock. Within a year he had married Peacock's daughter, and shortly afterwards, Peacock gave them a little cottage not far from his own home at Halliford. Meredith dedicated his first volume of poems (1851) to his distinguished father-in-law.

But the marriage, as Meredith said later,

had been a "blunder," and in 1858 they separated. Meredith has told us a little about the tragedy in a thoughtful and beautiful poem called "Modern Love." His wife died in 1861 and three years later he remarried, this time more happily.

His Struggle for a Living

Meanwhile he had tried his hand at novels. One of the very first he wrote—"The Ordeal of Richard Feverel," published in 1859—is one of his masterpieces. But it did not seem to strike people's fancy at the time, and only after nineteen years was a second edition printed. Meredith now felt that he must earn his living in some other way. He had always been desperately poor, and since his break with his father-in-law he had been living, with his small son, on no one quite knows what. He took up regular journalistic work, and read and judged manuscripts for a publishing house, work he continued to do for about thirty years.

For some years he lived in a charming cottage at Copsham, in Surrey, a lovely place with a breezy meadow, a pine wood, and a pond with a heron on it. He travelled sometimes; once he acted as war correspondent when Italy and Austria were at war. For a time he lived with the poets Rossetti and Swinburne in London. In 1867 he moved to another charming cottage in Surrey, where he could wander in the fields and villages, with his sharp eyes taking in every mood of Nature and every type of man, woman, or child, to be included later in his novels and poems.

He built a retreat at the end of his garden, where he could write undisturbed. Sometimes people could hear him there, carrying on lively conversations with the characters in his books, just as if they had come to life and were really talking to him. At other times he would ask his friends to come there, and would read them in rich and measured tones some new chapter or poem.

George Meredith, a novelist for people who like to think as well as to be amused.

In one or another of these places he wrote his other masterpieces: "Evan Harrington," which has a good deal in it about his own grandfather and his aunts, "Beauchamp's Career," "The Egoist," "Diana of the Crossways," and many of his fine and thoughtful poems. Both the prose and the verse are so packed with ideas that some people find them hard to fathom. But there is brave philosophy and true poetry in such poems as "The Lark Ascending" and "The Woods of Westermain." And in the novels he makes us see and remember his people, especially his women, and marvel at the poetry and wit of his style. Meredith himself said that what he wanted to put into his books and his life was the Comic Spirit, which he described as "thoughtful laughter."

It was "Diana of the Crossways," published in 1885, which finally caught the public's attention. For a long time men of letters had realized Meredith's genius, and now at last a wider recognition came. The honours so long overdue were heaped upon him. When Tennyson died in 1892, Meredith was chosen to fill his place as president of the Society of Authors. In 1905 King Edward VII bestowed upon him the Order of Merit.

What Meredith said about literature was regarded as a sort of oracle. Though his splendid health broke towards the last, his wit and his interest in life remained keen down to his death in 1909. A petition was raised pleading that he should be buried in Westminster Abbey, but the proposal not being successful he was laid to rest near the grave of his second wife at Dorking. To-day we regard him as one of the masters of the novel.

(CONTINUED ON PAGE 907)

News! News! And a stately herald to tell it. Exciting things are about to happen on Fable Island. This little inhabitant is carrying the news to his friends as fast as his legs can take him.

TANSY *and* BOBBLES *on* FABLE ISLAND

Their Beautiful Island Leaves the Sea and Sails Away into the Golden Sunset

(CONTINUED FROM PAGE 748)

A THRILL of excitement had struck Fable Island, as though all Jupiter's lightning had run through it.

Curiously, Tansy and Bobbles had not felt it; and they were sitting idly by the great green, counting how many times an old cow chewed the cud before swallowing it, when the boy, Jack, came rushing up to them.

"How can you sit there so quietly!" he cried. "Haven't you heard the news?"

"Another wolf, I suppose, after your sheep," mocked Bobbles.

"It's nothing like that," said Jack, impatiently. "The king's father has died in Faraway Land; and our king and queen are leaving the island to reign across the sea."

"That certainly is news," admitted Bobbles, thoughtfully. "It may make a lot of difference."

"Of course it does!" cried Jack. "See— through those trees! The king's herald is coming this instant to the great green to make a proclamation; and afterwards he is going on to the town."

"Hark! The trumpeters!" exclaimed Tansy. "Bobbles, let us fly to the bower."

When they reached the bower they found that their father and mother had gone; but the old dog said that they were at the king's palace.

"We'll just hear the proclamation and then we'll fly off to the palace," said Bobbles, full of excitement.

Now the people had all crowded together on the green, and there was a great buzz of talk. But when the herald lifted his hand, the talking ceased.

"Be it known to all the folk on this island," cried the herald, "that their Majesties have decided to reign in Faraway Land. But inasmuch as they are filled with affection for all their island subjects, we make royal proclamation that any of you who wish to follow the king to Faraway Land will receive homes and land and comfort in double measure of what you have enjoyed here. It is his Majesty's pleasure that you give him your answer to-night, just before the king's ship sails."

Tansy and Bobbles Fly to the Palace and Receive a Royal Welcome

The herald and his trumpeters departed to make the same proclamation in the town, and the people broke up into groups, talking earnestly.

"But we don't want to leave the island!" burst out Tansy, passionately. "Oh, Bobbles, we must find out what Father and Mother think. Perhaps this is why they have been looking so strange."

"Come," said Bobbles. He was thinking too hard for words.

So they flew to the palace and walked up the marble steps, and were surprised at the respect of the bowing servants.

"You might be a prince, and I might be a princess," whispered Tansy.

They were ushered into a dainty little parlour, decorated with roses and white and golden lilies; and they found the king and queen talking to their father and mother.

"Ah, here are your children," exclaimed the queen, as Tansy stood curtseying, and Bobbles bowed his very best. "Do not be afraid, my children. See, I am wearing the jewel which a fairy child once gave me."

And, indeed, the jewel shone radiantly in the queen's dark hair.

"As your Majesty has suggested," said Father Fairy, "it might be well for our children to have a word in this decision."

So the king and queen and Father Fairy and Mother Fairy sat down, and Tansy and Bobbles stood waiting respectfully as the king asked their father to explain.

"It appears, children, that their Majesties are leaving the island, as their duty takes them to Faraway Land; and if to-night the people agree to follow them, then everyone will leave the island."

Tansy and Bobbles knew that part, and they waited anxiously for the rest.

"Many years ago," Father Fairy continued, "this island belonged to the fairies, and now there are none left, except ourselves. It is his Majesty's desire to hand over the island to your mother and to me, that we may be its king and queen, and rule over the creatures and bring them all to peace and happiness. But we have our choice, and we also may follow the king and queen to Faraway Land."

"Oh—and leave all the creatures?" broke in Tansy. "They love us so!" Then she blushed, ashamed at having interrupted.

"Indeed, the creatures will be miserable unless we are there to say 'Booh!' to them," Bobbles laughed.

"It seems clear what your children wish," said the queen. "But tell them the rest."

"Is there some more?" gasped Tansy.

"The island will no longer remain in the sea," continued Father Fairy, speaking slowly, so that his children could understand. "It will rise up towards heaven and become a sky island."

Father Fairy Explains His Plans for His New Home Up in the Sky

"But when?" asked Bobbles.

"To-night," said Father Fairy. "As soon as the king's ship has sailed beyond the sunset. As for the people, I have looked into their hearts, and I know that all will wish to follow the king, save one. I shall put them to sleep, and they will wake in Faraway Land."

"And then?" asked Tansy.

"Then," said Father Fairy, "the island will ascend into the sky and the sky will be our home."

"With all the creatures?" asked Bobbles. "The creatures who have taught us the meaning of things?"

"The creatures will go with us," said Father Fairy. "They will learn many new and strange things in the sky."

"And sometimes," said the queen, "when I hold out this jewel, you will fly down to Faraway Land and tell us all the news?"

"Oh, yes, beautiful queen!" cried Tansy. "And if your Majesty will sometimes look up into the sky, you will see Bobbles and me waving."

That evening, all the islanders from the country and the town came down to the shore to give their answer and to watch the king's beautiful ship set sail to Faraway Land.

TANSY AND BOBBLES ON FABLE ISLAND

THE ANIMALS ON FABLE ISLAND ASSEMBLE TO BID YOU GOOD-BYE

Here are some of our good friends, gathered together to say good-bye to us—for they are going to live on a fairy island against the setting sun. And if they look a little sad, it is not because their life is going to be unhappy. It is because, as we have seen, they have had to go through painful things in order to learn wisdom. But they have tried hard to learn their lessons, and, let us hope, will never be vain or selfish or cruel or greedy any more; for in that case they will live happily through all the years to come in their new island home in the sky.

The music was playing, and the king and queen had never looked so happy as when they passed through the crowd, with the people on each side bowing low.

As Father Fairy had known, they had all decided to follow the king except one, and he was a boy.

So the oldest man on the island delivered the message to the king; and the king smiled and shook him by the hand, and then told his subjects that he wished them all long life and happiness in Faraway Land.

"May it please your Majesty," said Jack the shepherd boy, coming forward and bowing respectfully, "I will remain on the island, because I cannot endure to leave Fairy Bobbles and Fairy Tansy, for I wish to be their faithful servant for evermore."

The king and queen smiled, and gladly agreed that Jack should remain. And then the procession started for the ship.

"And when do we go to Faraway Land?" asked the people eagerly of Father Fairy.

"You go to-night," he said with a smile.

"But where are the ships to take us?" they said. "We cannot go without ships."

"Beware," said the fairy, with mock sternness, "if you dare to say 'cannot' to a fairy!"

The king's ship was weighing anchor, but there was no breath of air to spread her sails.

"Winds! Winds!" cried Father Fairy, "blow the good ship safely over the sea."

So the winds came and filled the sails, and the ship sped over the dancing waters as though she had been a bird.

The islanders cheered, and Bobbles and Tansy flew off, following the ship and kissing their hands to the queen. As for the beasts, the birds, and the insects, they found it difficult to understand all that was going on and stood round very much puzzled.

The people watched until the ship was like a speck against the sunset, and then, strangely enough, they all sank down on the shore, while a few of the house dogs, who loved them, snuggled beside them.

"They are all asleep!" cried Tansy, as she came flying back, with Bobbles after her.

"No! They are gone!" said Bobbles.

And so they were, for Father Fairy had wafted them over to Faraway Land by one stroke of his magic wand.

"Oh! Look! Look!" cried Jack. "All the sky is full of fairies."

Tansy and Bobbles rose and threw up their arms and cried. "We are coming! We are coming!"

"Be ready!" called Father Fairy.

Suddenly there was a strange, soft sigh from the sea, as she loosened her clinging

fairies still beckoned, and the moon and the stars came out; and the sky animals, the Great Bear, the Little Bear, the Scorpion, the Crab, the Lion, the Bull, and all the rest of them, gave forth thundering welcomes.

Jack was so thrilled that at first he could not speak; though presently he waved his cap and shouted, "Hurrah! Hurrah for the sky!"

At last the island came to rest on a wonderful mountain of cloud, all silver with moonshine; and Father Fairy spoke.

"On Fable Island, when she rested on the

This is a fairy ship that never sails upon a real sea. It carries a cargo of longings and hopes and building stone for castles in Spain. And the strange part of it is that no matter how safely it comes to port in the harbour of Faraway Land, it must always start out at once upon its voyage again. For people have never learned to be satisfied with just one cruise and the riches it may bring, but must always be faring forth in search of some still greater treasure to make them happy on some far-off day that they may never see.

arms and set the island free, so that it might rise up into the sky like some living cloud.

"I'm not sure that I care for this!" roared the lion.

"Where are we going?" faltered the sheep.

"With me!" said the wolf, with a strange smile.

"Peace!" cried Father Fairy.

"Booh!" mocked Tansy and Bobbles. "You'll soon know all about it."

Higher and higher they went: and the

sea, we learned the meaning of many things. Some of the meanings we have liked, and some we have disliked. But now that we have all reached the sky, we have left behind all the passions, the anger, the hunger, the pain, the greed, the meanness—and indeed—indeed——"

"We are all going to live happy ever after!" cried Bobbles and Tansy in one breath. And because they had learned the Meaning of Things, their prophecy came true.

Photo by Anderson

Here is a group of Roman clients paying a morning call upon their noble patron. In the early days of Rome, the duties of a patron to his clients were similar to those of a father to his adopted children. Later, clients merely went to their patrons for advice; and still later, they became a fawning mob of worthless parasites who lavished attention on some wealthy man. He, flattered by their fulsome compliments, fed and clothed them.

The FALL of the CIVILIZED WORLD

Stormed from Without and Rotting from Within, the Mighty Empire of Rome Tottered at Last; and with it Passed Nearly All the Culture of its Day

(CONTINUED FROM PAGE 818)

ROME had been the greatest city the ancient world had ever seen. The farmer - soldier - citizens of the republic had made her powerful, and the emperors from Augustus to Marcus Aurelius had made her beautiful. In population she was larger than Babylon had ever been, for at one time there were over a million people living on her seven hills. Her emperors and her nobles were immensely wealthy. In the display of riches, in fine houses, costly gold and silver dishes, multitudes of servants, and magnificent feasts and entertainments, neither Babylon, Athens, Alexandria, nor Carthage ever equalled the city by the Tiber.

The Romans loved magnificent display. Nothing pleased a wealthy noble more than to hear people marvelling at the way he spent money. Small fortunes were sometimes spent on a single dinner. Dishes of peacocks' tongues were served, and other strange food was brought to the table, not because it was good to eat, or because people specially liked it, but just because it was costly.

Signs of Trouble Ahead

In spite of all this wealth and display, there were many indications of trouble ahead. The emperors, especially the more thoughtful, read the signs and tried their best to guard against trouble; but they could neither stop the machine nor change its direction. No one knows to-day whether any one circumstance caused the failure, but we do know a number of causes which may have produced it, and which certainly helped to break up the great world empire of Rome.

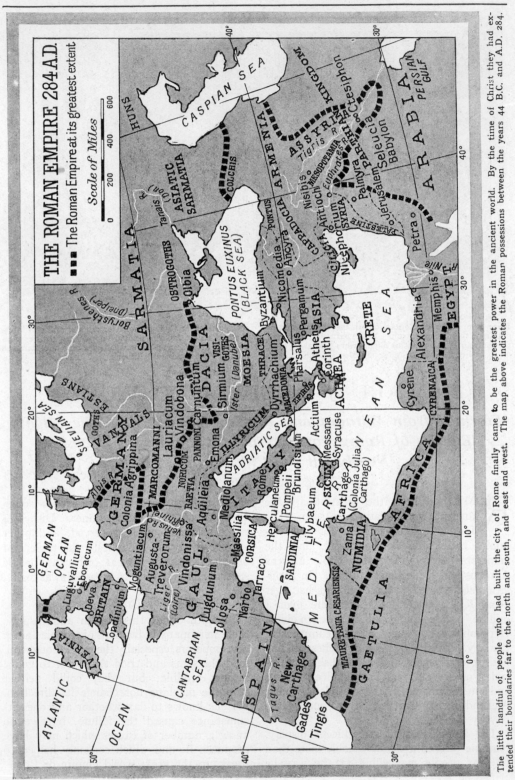

THE ROMAN EMPIRE 284 A.D.

The Roman Empire at its greatest extent

Scale of Miles

The little handful of people who had built the city of Rome finally came to be the greatest power in the ancient world. By the time of Christ they had extended their boundaries far to the north and south, and east and west. The map above indicates the Roman possessions between the years 44 B.C. and A.D. 284.

Some of the weak points began to appear even in republican times. We cannot blame the emperors for these. In the early days, for example, the Roman citizens were almost all farmers. They would leave the plough to fight for Rome, and return to the plough when the war was over. But when wars were waged in Sicily, or in Spain, the soldiers had to be absent from their farms for a long time. And when they came back, what did they find? The farm was deserted, or so badly deteriorated that it seemed hopeless to begin work on it again. It would be better to sell the farm, or give it away to a thrifty neighbour, and go back to Rome to wait until the next war was started.

Then came Hannibal, who spent fifteen years burning farmhouses in Italy. After that there were more wars in the East, then civil wars. Finally, when Augustus brought

By courtesy of the British Museum

This is a bust of Septimius Severus. It is a good example of the only art in which the Romans excelled the Greeks—the art of making lifelike portraits.

peace, there were few small farms left in Italy. The rich men of Rome had annexed most of the land, and were employing slave labour. They turned their attention to stock-breeding because that was easy, and to olive orchards and vineyards, because from them they received a large profit. Very little wheat was raised in Italy.

This did not worry the Romans greatly, for each year Sicily sent about a million bushels of wheat to Rome as a part of her tax. The real question was this: where were soldiers to be found? Out on the farms of Italy there were only slaves. In the cities the families were small. Even Augustus was concerned about that, and when the Germans defeated one of his generals and destroyed a Roman army, we are told that Augustus cried out to the dead general, "Give me back my legions!"

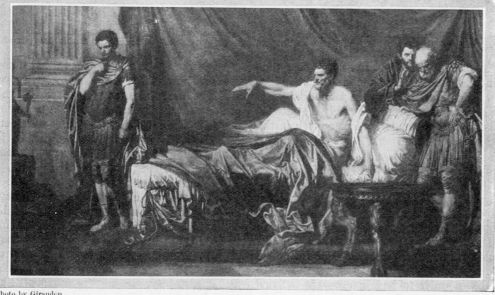

Photo by Giraudon

Here you see Septimius Severus reproaching his evil son Caracalla for having wished to assassinate him. Had he banished him or punished him with death, it might have been better for the future welfare of Rome.

That cry, however, did not bring any soldiers back to life. Augustus and his successors had to turn to the provinces for men, just as they had turned to them for food. For a long time the plan worked very well.

living. There were large cities, beautiful homes, games, races, travel, excitement, and entertainment of all kinds. Each city had its poor and destitute; but who cared about them until he, too, was compelled to swell

Here is a reconstruction of the Meta Sudans, a fountain built by Domitian. The fountains and public baths of Rome were fed by huge aqueducts which extended many miles into the country to supply pure water.

Spaniards, Gauls, Africans, and other provincials guarded the frontiers and fed the people of Italy. But after a hundred years the provinces began to feel the strain. There were not enough men to work in the fields and in the army.

The Scarcity of Money

Then came other troubles. Money began to be scarce. The Spanish mines could not supply the demand for gold and always more gold. That was one reason why Trajan added Dacia to the empire, for there was gold in the mountains of that country. But money still continued to flow steadily to India in order to buy luxuries for the rich and extravagant Roman nobles.

On the surface, life seemed well worth

their numbers! We may be sure that many people were leading an unhappy existence, and that there were many bullies, cheats, and corrupters among the populace. But no one has ever thought that the Romans were perfect. Possibly more people lived happily in the years between about 27 B.C. and about A.D. 180, than ever before or since.

Into this peaceful and prosperous life—with its steady hum of business and pleasure—there came a new and terrifying noise, the clamour made by barbarians knocking for admission at the doors of the empire. They pounded away at the doors for a number of reasons. They were hungry; they wanted an opportunity to be "prosperous" like the Roman subjects, and they were afraid of other and fiercer barbarians

Masterpieces of Man The Builder

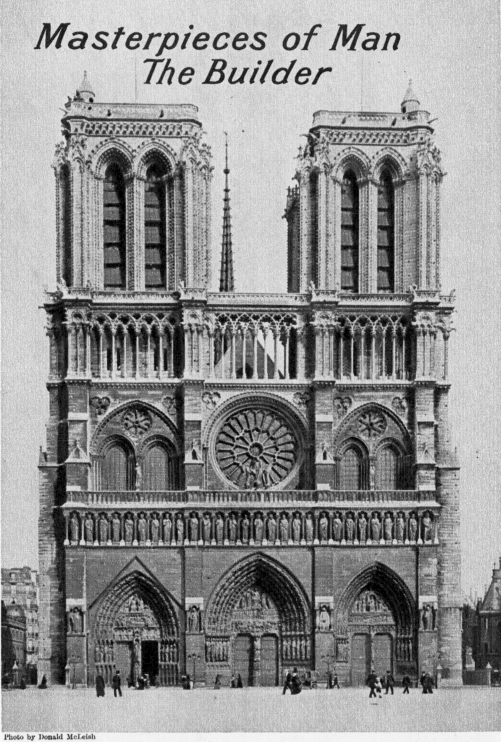

A view of the façade, or front, of Notre Dame de Paris, a glorious example of decorated Gothic architecture which, with its beautiful rose window thirty-one feet in diameter, and its massive towers bearing numerous stone gargoyles, or rain-water spouts, was completed in 1240. It has served as a model for many churches.

BUILDINGS OF WORLD-WIDE FAME

The building at the top left is the restored temple of Bodh Gaya, in India; it is 170 feet high. On the right is the famous Leaning Tower of Pisa; it was begun in 1174 and completed in 1350. Although fourteen feet out of the upright, it is perfectly safe. At the bottom is the fine cathedral of Milan, the third largest in Europe.

The Eiffel Tower, on the left, is one of the best-known landmarks of Paris. Designed by Gustave Eiffel for the Exhibition of 1889, it is made of iron, and reaches a height of 984 feet. Visitors may ascend to the summit by means of lifts. The Chrysler Building, on the right, is the second tallest building in the United States.

Photo of Taj Mahal by Indian Railways Bureau

The Taj Mahal, the "gem of buildings," at Agra, India, is one of the loveliest examples of architecture in all the world. Designed in the Persian style, it was set up by Shah Jehan as a tomb for his wife. The lower picture shows the dome-crowned mosque of Santa Sophia, at Istanbul, a glorious example of Byzantine art.

STRANGE and CURIOUS THINGS

It may be the fashion of the country to which these people belong to wear neck-bands of coiled iron, and leg ornaments of a similar kind, but it would appear to be one that is decidedly uncomfortable. Years ago it was fashionable for men and women in England to wear very high collars, and they looked almost as painful.

The curiosities on this page show a tree growing out of the trunk of another; the remains of a tree that bears some resemblance to a man; and a "motor-car" of very unusual design. The proud owner of this "sports model" can feel quite secure against the law of the road so far as exceeding the speed limit is concerned!

WHEN JUMBO HAS A MANICURE

The African native in the top left picture has adopted a curious style in head-dresses of which he is probably very proud. The two natives of New Guinea on the right are wearing highly coloured dancing-masks of red, blue and purple. In the bottom picture you see an elephant having his periodical manicure, or toe trim.

Is it an elephant or an ant-eater? No; it is just a common swede which has taken the form of one or other, or a mixture of both, of those animals. The two young "birds" on the right will never be able to fly—they are actually curiously-shaped potatoes. The giant vessel is an ice-cream stall built in the shape of a tub.

A MESSAGE OF PEACE AND LOVE DELIVERED IN THE CRUEL ARENA

Criminals and slaves composed the company of gladiators who fought and died in the arena for the entertainment of a bloodthirsty people in the early days of Rome. In later times these brutal games became so popular that scarcely a town from Britain to Asia Minor was without its arena; and prisoners of war, tattooed giants from the north, and black men from Africa were forced to become gladiators. What a change had come over the world since the days of the beauty-loving Greeks who gathered at Olympia and Delphi to watch their graceful athletes! No wonder the Christian Fathers stepped in to stop such cruelty.

who were continually pressing down on them from the rear.

The Romans did not want these barbarians, and tried hard to keep them out. But first in one place and then in another they broke through the lines, burning and destroying because they had been denied admission. It took the Romans a full century and more to turn them out and to build up the broken frontiers again. And when at last the fighting was over, the Romans settled down to a different kind of life.

An Emperor Who Died in Britain

A few names stand out in the long list of emperors from 180 to 284. Septimius Severus (sĕp-tĭm'ĭ-ŭs sĕ-vēr'ŭs), who ruled from 193 to 211, was made emperor by his soldiers after a year of revolution. He fought the Parthians and drove them out of Mesopotamia, the land between the Rivers Tigris and Euphrates. Then he returned to Rome, where he made many changes. The senators who had not supported him in the revolution he put to death. He depended altogether on his soldiers, and gave them more pay, higher honours, and many of the offices which used to be filled by senators. Then he went on to Britain, where he died, leaving a weakened empire to be ruled by two worthless sons.

All this time the number of young men who would enlist in the army and take over the farms from their parents had been declining. There were less food, less money, and more barbarians. The Roman armies would destroy one tribe to-day, and the following day another tribe would appear demanding land.

The emperors were all generals—it was necessary that they should be; and the generals were all emperors—or tried to be. One of the bravest and most successful of them all—there were eighty altogether in ninety years—was Aurelian (aw-rē'lĭ-ăn), who ruled from 270 to 275. He began his

CONSTANTINE THE GREAT SEES THE FLAMING CROSS OF CHRISTIANITY

Legend has it that Constantine was led by a miracle from Heaven to champion the cause of Christianity. One day, just at noon, a flaming cross appeared to him, on the eve of a battle. He accepted this cross as a sign from God, and, marvelling at the miracle, determined to establish Christianity as a lawful religion.

WITH A COURAGE BORN OF FAITH THE CHRISTIANS AWAIT THE END

A great hush comes over the vast audience of the Colosseum as the ferocious lions enter the arena. In that hush the last prayer of the Christians can be heard, as they bravely prepare themselves for death.

THE MEN OF DEATH PAY A VISIT TO THE SILENT CATACOMBS

In the dark and musty underground passage-ways called catacombs, where the Romans buried their dead, the persecuted Christians sought refuge and a place for worship. But even there cruel men hunted them down.

reign with little more than Italy, Greece, and the northern part of Africa under Roman control. One great campaign won back the whole of the East, which had been left to itself while the Romans were fighting one another. Another set of victories recovered Spain, France, and Britain for the empire. Then some officers, jealous of their leader, killed Aurelian, and a new civil war broke out. After nine years, another general fought his way to power, this time a man who was a statesman as well as a warrior.

How Diocletian Attempted to Instil New Life into a Dying Empire

Diocletian (dī′ō-klē′shǎn), for that was his name, made many mistakes. Some of the changes he introduced were foolish, and many of his acts were brutal; but he restored law and order, and patched up the Roman machine so that it ran for another two centuries. When we consider the state of the empire at that time—the war-torn country, the war-weary people and the vast number of enemies—we should accord him the great credit he deserves. Let us examine a few of his many problems and see how he dealt with them.

In the first place, he had to obtain food and pay for his soldiers. Taxes were increased until it seemed as though farmers and merchants were living and working only to pay these taxes. No man was allowed to leave his farm, or his shop, to try his fortune in some other place, or in some other business. By this plan, Diocletian hoped to prevent tax evasion, not only for one year, but for all successive years.

In the second place, he increased the size of his army, employing as many barbarians as he could trust. But the enemies were advancing so rapidly, and attacking in so many different places, that he could not meet them all in person; and so he divided the empire into four military districts. He took charge of one and put three other generals in command of the three other districts.

In theory everything promised well. There were more soldiers, more tax money, and a steady income. Even Diocletian's plan to prevent profiteering, an order which fixed the maximum price for every article and every kind of labour, looked well. But in practice nothing worked smoothly. The armies certainly drove back their enemies and restored a certain degree of peace. But they were restless, and their generals were jealous of one another. The taxes did not yield the amount that Diocletian had expected, and many people paid no attention to his list of prices, although the penalty for breaking this law was death.

The failure of these two plans of Diocletian was really due to the failure of his third plan. This was an attempt to induce his subjects to obey him, and yet show some spirit, some willingness to work for their country. In order to make them obedient, he dressed like an Oriental king, wearing a diadem and gorgeous robes. He lived in a magnificent palace and made it very difficult for visitors to see him. When they were granted an audience, men were compelled to kneel before him and to humble themselves by bowing their heads to the floor.

How Diocletian Failed to Break the Spirit of the Christians

All this, however, did not give the Romans much spirit. Many felt so discouraged, forlorn and hopeless that it seemed useless to try for any happiness in this world. Diocletian learned that a great number of these hopeless men and women had become Christians. He learned, too, that Christians refused to be soldiers, refused to worship him as a god, refused to take part in any holiday—for the holidays were all in honour of one or other of the old gods—and even refused to make bricks if they were to be used in building a pagan temple. He ordered a general persecution of all Christians, but it was soon discovered that every martyr was replaced by two new converts. Finally, he gave up his plans and his position. We are told that he spent his last years happily, growing cabbages.

In the years which followed the abdication of Diocletian, it seemed that all his work would prove to have been useless. Jealousy and unrest led to civil war, which ended with one man as ruler of the entire state, the emperor Constantine (kŏn′stǎn-tīn). If we

THE FORUM OF ROME AS IT MAY HAVE APPEARED IN ANCIENT TIMES

This is the Forum as it may have looked in ancient times. Romulus is said to have prophesied that his Rome would become the capital of the world. He would have been greatly surprised to find that the heart of Roman rule and religion could be so magnificent as this—and then, centuries later, become a mere ruin.

Photo by Anderson

THE FORUM OF ROME AS IT APPEARS TO-DAY

Here is all that remains to-day of the once magnificent Forum. Time and Nature have both taken a part in bringing those great buildings to ruin, but man has been the greatest vandal of all. In the Middle Ages and later, the amphitheatres, the baths, and the basilicas were used as stone quarries by people too lazy to quarry their own stone. Costly marbles, sometimes beautifully sculptured, were thrown into the fire to make lime for building.

examine carefully, however, we find that the government had not changed greatly. The four districts of the empire were still in existence, each one ruled by a lieutenant of Constantine. There were the same heavy taxes, an army just as large, enemies just as numerous, and life just as hard to bear. Even the new capital, a second Rome built in the East, which was named Constantinople after the emperor, did little more than increase the expenditure.

The Triumph of Christianity

There was one important change. Constantine made Christianity a lawful religion. It was no longer a crime to be a Christian. But the change came too late to save the Empire. The people of the country districts did not care who governed them. Many of them really preferred barbarian rulers because these rough soldiers were not so skilled in extorting tax money from them.

The story of the West may be summed up in the story of one group of these barbarians, the Visigoths (vĭz′ĭ-gŏth). They first appeared on the southern shore of the Baltic Sea. Driven from that region by lack of food, they gradually worked their way down the corridor between the Roman wall on their right and the Slavic tribes on their left. At the end of that long trail, on the northern shore of the Black Sea, they turned to the west. The Romans allowed them to come beyond the wall, so that they might be protected from the Huns. But the Romans did not give them enough to eat.

Photo by Rischgitz

Rome fell a victim to the Goths in A.D. 410. This wild, uncivilized tribe had no more respect for the beautiful things they found than for the inhabitants; they plundered and sacked and burned as the spirit moved them.

were not converted, for the Christian missionaries and preachers carried on their work for the most part in the cities. Even there the converts were taught to look for happiness only in the next world.

No wonder, then, that most of the soldiers of this period were barbarians. And it is not surprising that the bulk of the people

So the Visigoths fought and defeated a Roman army, killed the emperor who was in command, and journeyed on to Greece, seeking land. Not liking the farms there, the Visigoths turned to Italy, where they finally defeated another Roman army and captured Rome in 410. Italy did not satisfy them, and so they marched on once more, this time through Southern France to Spain, where they finally settled.

Rome had now become a second-rate city. No emperor wanted to live there. The city was captured and sacked once more in 455 and, by 476, Rome and the whole western part of the empire was given up to the barbarians.

Constantinople and the eastern part of the old empire survived for another thousand years. Students have puzzled over that for a long time. The reason, perhaps, was that

narrow corner of Italy beside the River Tiber, and moved them to spread their power and dominion from one end of the Mediterranean Sea to the other. Other Italic tribes were much like them—the Etruscans were a bold and warlike people—but the crown of victory now settled on those peoples. It fell to Rome, and there it remained in splendour for centuries.

Frequently beaten in their fights with the other tribes in Italy, the Romans neverthe-

In this detail of a Roman fresco a marriage ceremony is being performed. Early Roman weddings were usually quite simple, and were accompanied by less display than is often associated with similar ceremonies to-day.

the East possessed more money, more food, and more men than the West. In any case it was really a Greek empire. Its rulers and citizens disliked the half-Roman, half-barbarian Westerners, and were cordially hated in return.

Thus we have seen unfolded the story of the rise to grandeur of the great city of Rome, from its small beginnings as a trading post between the Latins and the Etruscans to the height of its glory under Augustus and Vespasian. Then we have seen its power slowly die until the emperors departed and the wild tribes of the north came down to slaughter the inhabitants and ransack the palaces and temples.

The whole history of the rise and fall of Rome occupies about nine hundred years. In some way that we can never explain, the habit of conquest entered into the hardy and determined Latin tribes that occupied a

less spread their power over the peninsula within the short space of sixty-five years. Then, after a ten years' rest, they chose to open war on Carthage, the greatest sea power of the time, in order to establish their liberty to trade when and where they would. It took them a hundred and eighteen years and three wars to destroy Carthage, but when that was finally accomplished the Romans found themselves without a rival worthy of the name.

Our world to-day would be very different if it were not for Rome. The Roman system of government was the model for most of our modern governments, and our law is borrowed in many ways from Roman law. The great works of Latin writers still delight and inspire us. Moreover, much of Greek art and literature comes to us by way of Rome. The best of the Roman state still lives in the modern world.

WHAT *we* OWE *to* SNOW *and* RAIN

Without Them the World Would Have Been a Desert Waste and Mankind Could Never Have Existed

(CONTINUED FROM PAGE 838)

THERE are millions of people who have never seen a snow-flake. They have never dashed down a hillside on a smooth-running sled. They have never skimmed along over the frozen surface of a pond and listened to the ringing of their skates at each long stride. For them it is always summer time. Although at certain seasons of the year clouds may swim across their skies every day and bring them rain, those clouds can never send down snow, except to high mountain tops. The ex-

quisite, feathery stuff that gives us such a thrill whenever it starts to fall and clothe the world with beauty can usually be seen only in regions some distance north or south of the Equator.

This is because snow is formed when the moisture in the air condenses at a stage below freezing-point and falls through layers of air that are too cold to melt it. If rain freezes as it falls, we have an "ice storm" or "glazed frost." Then pavements, buildings and trees are sheathed in ice that

Learn to take cold weather as a game and then you will not fear it. If you walk briskly and take deep breaths you will love winter's frosty tingle, and his tweaks at your ears and nose will seem to be only in play. And if you want a hobby, try photographing the delicate flowers of the frost, like the one in the inset.

MILLIONS OF SPARKLING JEWELS HIDDEN IN A FIELD OF SNOW

It is difficult to believe that the whole of this immense blanket of snow consists of countless tiny flakes as delicate as the half-dozen shown above, and very much smaller. No jeweller ever designed anything more exquisite than these little crystals. Each one of them is different from all the rest, though they are all made on the same six-pointed plan. If you will only try to design a few, you will very soon realize how ingenious Nature is. It is safe to say that in all these millions of years she has never made two snow-flakes exactly alike.

sparkles in the sun like countless jewels. The world is turned into Fairyland, but great is the damage that may result. A twig has been known to carry a hundred times its own weight of ice, and trees are broken down by the weight they carry.

There is nothing in Nature more beautiful than snow-flakes—those flowers of winter that perish so quickly under a breath of warm air. Most of those that we see have had their delicate crystals tangled and broken in the long journey to earth. But when the air is still and the temperature is not above 25° F., one may have the good luck to gather a whole bouquet of the exquisite, glistening blossoms.

There is literally no end to their variety. Each one of the countless millions that fall is different from all the rest—

This is what Goat Island, at Niagara Falls, looks like when it is transformed by a fall of snow into a glorious fairyland.

and all are alike beautiful. Under a microscope—which must be thoroughly chilled if a flake is to be examined for any length of time—they show still more amazing loveliness. But no matter how great their variety, any given flake is always six-sided or six-pointed and perfectly regular in form. It is the countless millions of such delicate crystals that make up a snowstorm, which poets and painters have often tried to portray.

It is hard to believe that the tender flakes falling so softly on a hushed winter's day can turn into the sharp, stinging weapons with which a snowstorm assails us. The gale drives them, like so many needles, into our tingling faces. It whips them up from the ground like powder and smothers us in the whirl. It heaps them in treacherous drifts across railways and streets, and sifts them

through every cranny and chink into which it can squeeze its way. Buffeted by its smothering blows and blinded in the cloud of swirling atoms, people may lose their way and freeze to death when only a short distance from home.

Snowstorms occur fairly often in very cold countries such as parts of Russia, Siberia, the United States and Canada, where they are known as "blizzards." Luckily, in England we do not have many of them to bury our lanes in snow, tie up our city streets, and imprison railway trains for two or three days at a time.

And yet even the blizzard may be a godsend and in the long run help the crops. In countries like Russia, which have a very severe winter, the feathery blanket of snow preserves the earth's heat and prevents the cold from penetrating deeply into the soil. Then in spring, when the snow melts, its water is able to sink into the ground and make a good seed-bed. In other parts of the world, where fertile plains are partly surrounded by high mountains, as in China and the western United States, the snow which falls on the mountains in winter melts in spring and summer, filling the rivers and keeping up a good supply of water for irrigation throughout the growing season. Without this supply of melted snow, some of these plains would be too dry for crops to grow.

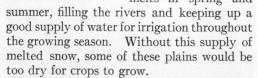

In fact, if it were not for rain and snow— what the meteorologist calls "precipitation" (prĕ-sĭp′ĭ-tā′shŭn)—all the land in the world would be a desert, and mankind could never have been born. For it is from the great oceans—that cover nearly four-fifths of the globe—that all our moisture comes in the beginning. The winds are merely the carriers—and the clouds merely the reservoir in which the rain is temporarily stored.

In all parts of England enough moisture falls to raise crops. Of course the amount varies, and not all crops are equally thirsty —though every crop must have water at certain times when it needs it most. Some

It seems a long way from those snow-clad mountain tops to the thriving field in the bottom picture. And yet it is the snows that make the fields possible in many parts of the world. For during the winter, moisture is "kept in cold storage" in the form of ice and snow on the tops of mountains. Then as the snows melt during the spring and summer, their water is drained into great reservoirs, like the one in the centre, and carried by a network of canals through the neighbouring deserts, which soon begin to "blossom as the rose."

plants have an enormous appetite for moisture. The roots of a single corn plant will draw several pounds of water from the soil during a warm day. Some of it goes towards building the plant, and some evaporates from the leaves and is taken into the air as water vapour. A skilful farmer is careful to put in only such crops as are certain to have enough water for their needs.

In south-east England about twenty-five inches of water fall in a year, and in Lancashire about forty inches. For rainfall is measured by the depth of the water it leaves. There is a container for measuring it in every meteorological station. A heavy summer shower may leave an inch of water behind it. A single inch of water means that more than 27,154 gallons will have fallen on one acre, and 16,500,000 gallons— or 72,320 tons—on a square mile. Imagine the extra weight on the earth after a day of heavy rain. But this is nothing in comparison with the weight of rain that may fall in a year in parts of India and the Hawaiian Islands. About a hundred miles from Calcutta is one of the wettest places in the world. It is deluged with more than four hundred inches of water a year—and sometimes as much as forty inches in a day.

Contrast this with the great deserts, where there is not enough rainfall to keep crops alive. In the Sudan, which is part of the great desert of the Sahara, it rains so seldom that the meteorological stations do not find it necessary to keep rain-gauges.

Yet the Sudan is very fertile; but instead of rain the crops are supplied by a network of canals and ditches bringing water from the River Nile, which rises in the mountains farther south. We call the process irrigation (ĭr'ĭ-gā'shŭn). In this way the desert of the Sudan, as well as Egypt and many

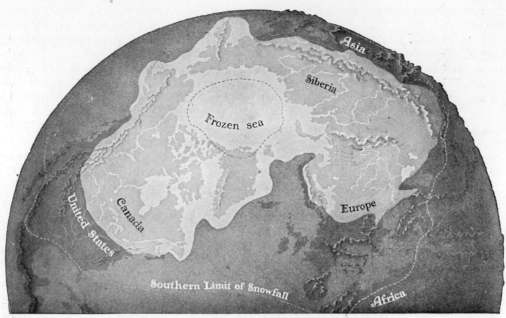

SNOWFALL MAP OF THE NORTHERN HEMISPHERE

When we speak of the "rainfall" of a region we refer to rain and snow and hail and sleet and any other form that moisture may take as it comes to us out of the air. But when we speak of "snowfall," we mean snow only. The map above will show you how far south snow falls in the Northern Hemisphere. The lighter the shading of an area, the heavier is its snowfall. The snowfall in Britain is comparatively light.

HOW THE RAINFALL IS DISTRIBUTED THROUGHOUT THE WORLD

This map shows the distribution of rainfall over the whole of the world—the lighter the shading, the lighter the rainfall. In general, the countries whose civilization is well advanced have a good supply of rain. They are backward only if their climate is too hot. Notice that along the Equator the rainfall is particularly heavy, but that in general it is light farther north except where the winds bring the rain in from the ocean.

other desert regions, has been changed to a fertile garden.

In the tropics rain falls only in certain seasons of the year. The rest of the time the thirsty earth has to live on water stored up in rivers or springs and in the soil. The season that brings the rains is the one in which the sun in its march north and south carries with it the strong updraught that always lies directly under it— the "doldrums" of the sailors. Along that belt rain falls every day, but north and south of it the skies are usually fair, for the trade winds have little to chill them in their trip towards the Equator. The calms of Cancer and Capricorn, north and south of the trade winds, are always sparklingly clear, for they are the result of a downdraught of the winds that rose over the Equator and lost their moisture in rising.

A glance at the map will show you that all the great desert regions, where the soil is parched for water, lie in those belts on the earth's surface that are too far from the Equator to be reached by the "doldrums" in their yearly journey north and south, and too far from the poles to get any of the rain distributed by the prevailing westerlies. The bright sun of the "horse latitudes" and of the edge of the trade winds always shines upon the great deserts of the world.

Often, too, a desert lies behind a range of mountains that **dries** out the prevailing winds. When a moist wind climbs a moun-

tain, it is chilled by being forced up and drops its moisture on the windward side. So when it sweeps down the other side it is warm and dry and cannot bring rain. That is what happens to winds coming in from

ANNUAL RAINFALL IN INCHES

Reproduced from the "Journal," 1923, by kind permission of the Royal Meteorological Society

The map above shows the distribution of rainfall over the British Isles. Very dark patches indicate that a given region has an extremely heavy rainfall, and light patches show a light rainfall. The west coast is very moist, for the prevailing westerly winds blow off the ocean laden with moisture and are forced to climb the hills. So they drop their moisture at once, with the result that they have little left to deposit on the districts situated farther inland.

the Pacific and striking the Rocky Mountains. They drop their precious water on the western slopes, and many of the lands on the other side have to remain parched. Most deserts have a very slight rainfall.

About a third of the moisture that falls from the skies sinks into the earth; another third is taken up into the air again as water vapour ; and the rest runs off into the rivers.

(CONTINUED ON PAGE 903)

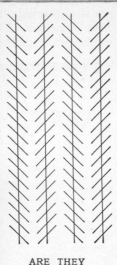

(THE SOLUTIONS TO THESE PUZZLES WILL BE FOUND IN VOLUME III ON PAGE 1062)

ELEVEN FINGERS

Count all the fingers of the two hands. Then begin to count backward on one hand, saying, "10, 9, 8, 7, 6" (with emphasis on the 6), and hold up the other hand saying, "and 5 makes 11." This simple deception has often puzzled many.

THE MYSTERIOUS PORTRAIT

No. 27

For a long time the gentleman in the picture looked at the portrait he is holding in his hand. Then he was heard to mutter:

Brothers and sisters have I none,
But that man's father was my father's son.

Can you guess whose portrait it was?

ARE THEY PARALLEL?

The figure above is another example of the tricks our eyes can play on us. The vertical lines seem to slant, and look as if they would meet if they were continued far enough. But in reality they are parallel.

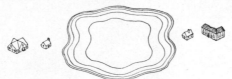

THE GREEDY RICH MEN

No. 28

Four poor men built their houses near the shore of a small lake. Later, four rich men bought the land and built houses away from the lake, as shown at the left. Then they put up a fence in such a manner that the poor men were quite shut out from the lake. How did the fence run?

TRICKY LINES

Which of the two lines below is longer, AB or CD? You will need to measure them to prove that you are right, and when you have done so, if you think hard you will be able to guess at the principle governing a good many of these optical illusions. And when you arrive at that principle, you will understand just why it is that fat people should not wear very broad hats, or clothes having horizontal stripes.

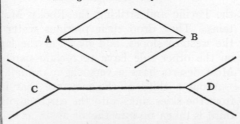

THE TWISTING ARCHES

At first glance you will probably take the above arches to be leading from left to right; but if you look at them intently, they will suddenly shift and will seem to be leading downward from right to left. Can you work out what it is that seems to change?

Here is the merry company of pilgrims who are about to leave the Tabard Inn at Southwark near London and, with its jolly host, set out on the long journey to Canter-bury. To while away the time, each of the pilgrims will tell a story—and, of course, there will be gossip and jesting, and the miller will play tunes on his bagpipes.

The MERRY TALES of CHAUCER

Wittiest and Shrewdest of All Our Poets, He Left Us, in His "Canterbury Tales," a Picture Gallery of the Motley Life and Characters of the Later Middle Ages

IN THE great cathedral at Canterbury, in the old days, stood the shrine of the holy St. Thomas Becket, who had been martyred at the very altar by four over-zealous courtiers of King Henry II. From all over England came a stream of pilgrims to pay homage at his tomb, and many were the miracles of healing which were wrought by the relics of the saintly man. Sometimes, too, the good people would call upon his name when far away, and, when their sickness had left them, would arise and journey to Canterbury in token of their gratitude.

Now, in the latter half of the fourteenth century there lived and wrote, as you may know if you have read his story, a very great English poet—Geoffrey Chaucer. It is probable enough that Chaucer once made the pilgrimage to Canterbury, splashing on horseback along the muddy roads with some gay company bent on the same errand. At all events, when he came to write his greatest work, he called it "The Canterbury Tales"; it is the record of an imaginary pilgrimage to Canterbury and of all the heroic and merry tales the pilgrims told each other to pass away the long hours of the journey.

They had gathered together quite by chance, he tells us, "full nine-and-twenty in a company," at the Tabard Inn in South-wark (sŭth'ĕrk), on the outskirts of London. Harry Bailey, the host, was a jolly man, and he bade the company a pleasant welcome. Seeing them so numerous and so merry, he suggested that they all go on to Canterbury together, and that each one tell two tales for the amusement of the others on the way to the shrine, and two more on the homeward journey. Then they would all gather at the Tabard Inn again and toast the one who had related the best story.

A Glimpse of Merrie England

Chaucer did not live to write all the tales that such an immense plan demanded, but he wrote twenty-four of them; and no better stories in verse were ever told. He gives us, too, a vivid picture of that motley company who gossiped and quarrelled and jested as they rode down to Canterbury. We see the grave and noble knight, pattern of chivalry, and the gallant young squire, his son, who sang serenades all night to his lady and slept "no more than does the nightingale."

We see the happy and gentle-hearted prioress, the rollicking friar, the magnificent monk, who loved fine clothes and hunting better than a good monk should. We see the princely

Photo by Risengitz

This is the type of knight and esquire, described by Chaucer in the Canterbury Tales, who, in the latter half of the fourteenth century, set forth on pilgrimage to visit the shrine of "the holy blissful martyr," Thomas Becket.

merchant, the physician, the tradesman and the distinguished man of law. We see rascals from the lower ranks, too—a drunken miller, a knavish seller of false pardons which he claims have "come from Rome all hot," a quarrelsome steward from some big estate, and many others.

There is a sturdy farmer and a poor country parson, a really good man, though possibly a little too fond of preaching. There is a gay and talkative woman called the Wife of Bath, who knows the world and is willing to talk about it. Last of all,

there is Chaucer himself—but he remains very quiet except when he is telling his own interesting tale.

We can relate only a few of the stories here. The story about the cock and the fox is told by one of the priests in the party; the tale of the patient Constance is told by the lawyer; the story of the two noble kinsmen comes most appropriately from the knight. These are good tales, and worth retelling. But we shall never really know Chaucer and love him as he deserves unless we read his own words.

With very little trouble we can learn how to pronounce his English; and then we can enjoy his sly humour and make friends with his sprightly characters, and marvel at his witty poetry as we never can in any other way. To many a reader Chaucer is the most amusing poet who ever wrote in the English tongue. And here are some of his tales.

There was once a poor widow who lived on a tiny farm. She was very happy, for her food was so simple that she never suffered from gout or any other complaint, and she was very proud in the possession of two daughters, three large sows, three cows, a sheep named Malle (mäl′ĕ), a cock, and seven hens.

Now, curious as it may seem, the birds and beasts could talk to one another at sunrise. So we must not be surprised to hear Chauntecleer (chawn′tĕ-klēr), the widow's fine cock, in conversation one morning with his favourite hen, Pertelote (pĕr′tĕ-lōt), as they sit side by side on the roost. He began by groaning in his throat as though he were suffering the most dreadful pain.

"Heart's dearest," cried Pertelote, aghast, "what ails you? Why do you groan thus?"

Scarcely had Chauntecleer opened his beak to crow when the wily fox seized him in his mouth, and hurried off. Wild confusion reigned over the farmyard, and the poor cock thought that his last hour had arrived.

Chauntecleer only groaned the more as he told his loyal spouse that he had had a fearful dream. In this dream he had seen a beast rather like a hound, of a colour between yellow and red, and with ears and tail tipped with black. His snout was small, said Chauntecleer, "And oh, my dear," he concluded, "his eyes looked at me until I feared that I should die."

Chauntecleer and the Fox

"Nonsense!" scoffed Pertelote. "Away with you! How can I love a coward?"

Then she gave Chauntecleer a lecture, telling him that he ought to be ashamed of himself to confess that anything made him afraid. Besides, she said, it was absurd to take any notice of dreams. Chauntecleer had a long argument with her about this last remark, and told him many marvellous stories of dreams that had come all too true. But he could make no impression on her. And in the end she persuaded him to get down from the roost and go out into the yard as usual.

Proudly he strutted about with his seven hens, little knowing that a sly fox had broken through the fence and was crouching in a bed of weeds awaiting his opportunity. Pertelote and the other hens were scratching in the sand, and Chauntecleer, who was a famous singer, lifted his voice "merrier than a mermaid in the sea."

Presently he let his eye follow a butterfly that was fluttering among the weeds. Then all at once his dream returned to him in its full horror—for there, half hidden in the weeds, lay the beast with glaring eyes.

"Cok! cok!" cried Chauntecleer in terror. But the sly fox spoke to him politely.

The Great Cunning of the Fox

"Nay, gentle sir," he said, "surely you are not afraid of me, who am your friend?"

Chauntecleer stared at him, too stupefied with terror to reply or even to move. If only he had been guided by the dream!

"I came only to hear you sing," the smooth-tongued fox continued; "your voice is as lovely as an angel's. How well I remember the matchless singing of your father! I had both your father and your mother in my house, and greatly enjoyed their company. How your father used to stand on his toes and blink his eyes and stretch his neck, so as to be able to voice his glorious song! I wonder whether you can sing like your father?"

Chauntecleer, who was very vain of his singing, felt so flattered that he lost sight of the danger that he was in. He stood on his toes and began to crow, to show how splendidly he could do it. But, alas, at that very instant the false fox sprang at him, seized him in his mouth, and dashed away as fast as his legs could carry him.

What a terrible commotion was set up in the farmyard.

The widow ran, her daughters ran, the maidservant, the hired man, and the dog ran. The dog barked so loudly that the cow, the calf, the sows, and the ducks ran. The geese flew over the trees, and the bees swarmed out of the hives.

"Ah," said Chauntecleer to the fox, "if I were you, I should despise all this noise, and say, 'I will wait here and eat him, and that at once!'"

"It shall be done!" cried the fox. But alas for him that he should let Chaun-

Unhappy Constance! Set adrift in an open boat without sail or rudder, it seemed that she must surely perish.

tecleer flatter him exactly as he had flattered Chauntecleer! No sooner had he opened his mouth than the wily cock escaped and flew safely out of reach to the branch of a tree.

"Come down! come down!" cried the fox. "I did not mean to frighten you by carrying you off from the farmyard. Let me explain that I meant no harm."

"No, no, I can do very well without your fine explanations," answered Chauntecleer.

Then off he flew to tell the story to Pertelote and the other hens. And there was nothing for the angry fox to do but to trot mournfully home.

The Tale of Princess Constance

The princess Constance, daughter of the Roman emperor, had sailed away to Syria to become the sultan's bride. She loved the young sultan, and rejoiced that he and all his court had been baptized as Christians when he sought her hand. So both she and her bridegroom believed that all was well.

Alas, they had reckoned without the sultan's mother. The news that her son had been baptized and was bringing home a Christian bride was more than her fierce spirit could bear. So as her son and his company sat peacefully at supper, she basely sent ruffians to murder them all. Then she bade her henchmen stock a vessel with food and clothes and set Constance adrift in it without sail or rudder.

Now Constance was brave and steadfast, and she made no complaint, only praying that God might keep her as He had helped Daniel in the den of the hungry lions. And in answer to her faith there was performed a mighty miracle. For although the lonely vessel drifted on for a whole year and more, she never wanted for water or for food. At last the winds drove her to the distant shore of Britain, and she was found and cared for by good folk who served the king of Northumbria.

When the king, whose name was Alla, returned from the wars and saw the forlorn Constance, he was so enchanted by her

THE REUNION OF KING ALLA AND HIS BELOVED WIFE

When the banquet was over, King Alla accompanied the senator to his home, and there he found his beloved wife employed as a waiting-woman. This is the scene of their reunion. Constance is so overcome at seeing her husband after all the cruel years of separation, that she has let her dishes fall to the ground unheeded.

beauty and modest bearing that he married her, and became, for her sake, a Christian.

The King's Cruel Mother

But once again neither bride nor groom had reckoned on the bridegroom's mother. King Alla's mother hated Constance no less than the sultan's mother had hated her— not so much because she was a Christian, perhaps, as because she was a strange girl cast up out of nowhere by the sea and had been set in authority over the queen-mother herself. For Constance had never told any-one that her father was emperor of Rome.

The queen-mother hid her hatred deep in her heart, and the king went off to the wars without suspecting it. Then his mother wrote him a letter, accusing Constance of monstrous crimes; but the king bade them

be kind to his wife until he could return and investigate the trouble. That did not please the queen-mother at all; so she altered the letter, making it read that the king had commanded his followers to set Queen Constance and her little babe once more adrift upon the sea, in a boat with neither rudder nor sail.

Constance is Set Adrift Again

Constance could not understand this supposed order of the king, for she believed he had loved her dearly and she knew that she had done no wrong. The people loved her and wept bitterly at her plight. But there was nothing for it but to obey the king.

The poor queen knelt humbly in the sand before she entered the ship, and prayed so that all the people of that heathen land might hear. "God can keep me from harm and shame," she said, "even on the cruel salt sea. My trust in Him shall be like a rudder and a sail on my journey." Then she bent over her babe, who was crying piteously. "Peace, little son," she said, soothingly; "I will not harm you."

Then she removed the kerchief that was round her head and placed it over the baby's eyes; and as the ship floated away, she lulled the tiny prince to sleep and cast up her eyes to Heaven.

For five years that strange boat drifted on the waters, through storm and sunshine, cold and heat; and the mother and her child lacked for nothing. Then one day they came in sight of the shores of Italy, Constance's native land.

A Roman senator, walking on the shore, saw with amazement the beautiful woman and the lovely little boy adrift in the boat. He took pity on them and brought them to his house.

This is the fair Emelye, Duke Theseus's daughter, whose appearance in the castle garden disturbed the lifelong friendship of Palamon and Arcite. In the tower the two young knights are imprisoned, and they are eating out their hearts for love of the beautiful maiden, who as yet is quite unaware of their existence.

There Constance, being ashamed after all that had happened to tell anyone who she was, served contentedly as a waiting-woman. She was happy enough, and everyone loved her and Maurice, her son.

But in far-off Britain she was not forgotten. When King Alla came home from the wars and learned what his mother had done, he was half mad with grief and rage, and in his passion slew his mother. Then when his anger cooled he repented of his deed, and set out on a pilgrimage to Rome to beg forgiveness from the Pope. In Rome he was received most graciously, and many notable people were bidden to a feast in his honour.

Now Constance, living at the senator's house, could not fail to hear of these things that took place in Rome. Great was her distress to know that her husband was so near, for she still supposed that it was his mysterious displeasure that had sent her wandering over the sea. But she said nothing although the senator took her handsome young son with him to the feast.

At the banquet little Maurice looked with curiosity at the British king, and the king noticed the boy's eager gaze.

"Whose fair child is that standing yonder?" he asked the senator.

"I cannot tell," was the reply. And the senator told Alla that the boy had a mother, but no father, and that his mother was the truest and noblest woman he had ever known.

But what was King Alla's amazement when, accompanying the senator to his house after the banquet, he saw his wife serving as a waiting-woman! He recognized her at once, and greeted her joyfully, although Constance stood dumb as a tree, her heart bursting with distress at the thought of the great injustice and cruelty of her husband.

But all was soon explained, and Constance knew the truth at last. She and her husband kissed each other a hundred times, and displayed the greatest happiness at their wonderful reunion.

So Constance's troubles were over at last, and her patient faith rewarded. As for little

morning Palamon (păl'a̤-mŏn), looking out of the grated window into the castle garden, saw walking there fair Emelye, Theseus's daughter. Her yellow hair fell down her back a yard in length, and she was very beautiful. Poor Palamon fell deeply in love at that first sight of her, and groaned in an

When Duke Theseus had stopped the fight in the wood and had discovered that the two knights were his enemies, he doomed them both to die. In the picture Emelye is shown interceding for her unfortunate suitors.

Maurice, he had found his father at last, and grew up to be a great prince in Britain.

The Tale of the Theban Princes

The two noble kinsmen, Palamon and Arcite, princes of Thebes, had sworn everlasting love and loyalty to each other. Each held the other very dear, and they were loyal friends until jealous love parted them for a time, as you shall hear.

A day came when there was fighting between Athens and Thebes, and when the battle was over the two noble cousins found themselves prisoners of Theseus (thē'sūs), duke of Athens. He shut them up in a strong tower of his castle and, refusing all ransom, doomed them both to imprisonment for life.

For a long time they comforted each other to the best of their ability. Then one fatal

agony of despair to think that he was but a luckless prisoner and could not hope to win her hand.

He poured out his grief to Arcite (är'sīt), certain of his cousin's sympathy. But even as he spoke, Arcite too had looked on Emelye, and knew that he must see her every day or he would die.

In grief and amazement Palamon reminded Arcite what they had sworn together: that "never for death nor pain, till life departed" would either of them hinder the other in love. But Arcite could not see why Palamon should have any more right to love the lady of his choice than he. High words arose, and a tragic bitterness sprang up between the cousins, to make their captivity even more unbearable.

Then one day Arcite was told that through

the pleadings of a friend the duke had been persuaded to set him free—but only on condition that he leave Athens, never to return on pain of death.

You would think that Arcite might rejoice at this news. But it only made his grief more bitter, for release from captivity meant that he must go away and never see fair Emelye again.

"Now would that I might die!" he groaned. "Farewell, sweet life, and all its joys!"

Indeed, when one thinks of it, it is difficult to say which lover was in more piteous plight. For one might see his lady every day, but must live for ever in prison, and the other might ride forth at will, but must see his lady nevermore.

Arcite Pines for His Lady and, Braving Death, Returns to Athens

So Arcite left Palamon a prisoner, and rode forth into banishment. But so sorely did he pine for the sight of his lady that he grew thin and pale, for in truth he desired greatly to die. At last he could bear it no longer and, braving death, returned to Athens in disguise. Calling himself Philostrate, he ventured even into the castle of the duke, whom he completely deceived, and managed to become fair Emelye's page.

This was too much for Palamon. When he heard of it, as he shortly afterwards did, he was beside himself with misery and rage. So desperate was he that he actually managed to escape from prison, and reach a wood in which he hid till morning.

Here he met Arcite—the very man against whom his jealous fury raged. Nothing would do but that they should fight it out. But Palamon had no arms; so Arcite brought him some and chivalrously waited until he was ready for the fray. Then they set upon each other with such a will that you would never have thought the two had once sworn lasting friendship and loyalty.

What might have happened no one can say. But fortunately—as it turned out—Theseus with his wife and daughter, and many knights and ladies of the court, chanced to come riding through the wood on their way to the hunt.

Instantly the duke stopped the duel and demanded to know the whole story. Great was his wrath when he discovered that one of the combatants was a prisoner escaped from his castle and the other a banished knight who had been living at his court in disguise—and that it was his daughter over whom they were fighting. Sternly he doomed both Palamon and Arcite to die.

But the lovely Emelye and her gentle mother could not bear to see two fair and gallant youths thus die for love. They and all the ladies of the court fell upon their knees before the duke, crying out their pity and begging him to be merciful. Finally he relented, and even consented that Emelye should marry one or the other of her rash young suitors; and in order to decide which it should be, commanded that a tournament be held at which the matter could be decided.

From far and near the knights assembled for the tournament, and all Athens became wild with excitement. Desperate were the combats, with men and horses going down all over the field. How Emelye's heart must have trembled for both her lovers, how anxious she must have been to know who was destined to be her plighted lord!

How Arcite Won a Great Victory but Lost the Treasured Prize

In the end Arcite was proclaimed the victor. But all this time, you must know, the gods had been taking sides in the quarrel between the two kinsmen, and had finally decided that Arcite might never enjoy his reward. So Pluto, at Saturn's request, shot up through the ground a flame of fire which so frightened Arcite's horse that the knight was thrown violently to earth. And although all the other combatants who had been wounded in the tournament recovered of their hurts, it was fated that Arcite should die.

On his death-bed he remembered his old love for Palamon, his friend and kinsman. And he begged his bride to marry his rival when he should be dead, saying that there was no nobler knight or one more worthy to be loved.

So Arcite won the victory, and Palamon won fair Emelye. And before Arcite died, the bond of loyal friendship between him and his noble cousin Palamon, was renewed.

The GIRL GUIDE MOVEMENT

A Companion Organization of the Boy Scouts That Owes Its Foundation to a Casual Request to be Inspected by Lord Baden-Powell

THE Girl Guide movement, like that of the Boy Scouts, was a spontaneous growth and not an educational system drawn up by grown-up people and imposed upon children for their good. The Guides founded themselves—and the organization followed when the necessity for it arose.

When General Baden-Powell was inspecting the Boy Scouts at their first big Rally at the Crystal Palace in 1909, a small company of girls came up and, through their leader, requested him to inspect them. They were dressed in a uniform which was as nearly as possible an imitation of that of the Boy Scout, complete with cowboy hat and staff.

Up to that time the Chief Scout had not contemplated any scheme for girls, but he felt that it was a pity to damp their obvious enthusiasm, and that, after all, in dealing with boys only he was leaving the greater and more important part of the nation untouched; so with the help of his sister, Miss Agnes Baden-Powell, he adapted the handbook "Scouting for Boys" for the use of girls, substituting such subjects as nursing, homecraft, and the care of children for some of the more boyish activities.

It took some little persuasion to induce the numbers of girls who had started life as "Scouts" to reorganize themselves as "Guides"—a title taken from that of a

Lady Baden-Powell, Chief Guide of the World, with her husband Lord Robert Baden-Powell, Chief Scout of the World.

famous Indian regiment whose loyalty and courage won renown for it throughout the British Empire—but when they found that they could not be registered as Scouts and that, as Guides, most of the Scout training would still be open to them, with all the joys of tracking and stalking, camping and swimming, as well as the more womanly arts and crafts, they agreed and formed their own body independently of the Scouts, and with their distinctive title, uniform and badges.

During the first few years of its existence, up to the time of the World War, the Guide movement had literally to struggle to maintain itself. The children were keen enough, but parents feared it as a movement which countenanced many things that they had hitherto regarded as dangerous or unsuitable for girls, and the general public criticized it as tending to take girls out of their proper sphere and teach them to imitate boys. Only a few far-sighted people recognized that times were changing, and that the training of girls must be adapted to meet them.

The World War, coming when it did, gave the Girl Guides their first real chance, and those at the head of the movement did not fail to seize it. A girl or woman in uniform was no longer out of place; it became the ambition of every girl to do some service for her country; and those who were too young for the nursing services or for work in the Women's Army

Auxiliary Corps, the Women's Royal Naval Service and the Women's Royal Air Force, as these various bodies came into existence, gladly joined the Girl Guides, finding therein an opportunity to do useful work.

Much good public service was done during the four years of war, including messenger and orderly work in public offices, the formation of hostels for the wounded in case of air-raids, the growing of food for the Navy, the collection of every sort of commodity required—from garments to horse-chestnuts—and the provision of a soldiers' recreation hut and several motor-ambulances for use at the front.

It was certainly very largely due to the war, and the consequent change of outlook regarding women's work, that the Girl Guide movement became so firmly established. But there was also another very important cause which must not be overlooked.

In 1912 the Chief Scout had married Miss Olave Soames, and in marrying her he had secured not only a wife for himself, but one who would take in hand his vast and growing family of Girl Guides, and organize that movement side by side with his Boy Scouts.

For the first few years after their marriage her own home-making and the care of her family had occupied Lady Baden-Powell, but in 1916 she took up work as a county commissioner for the Guides in Sussex, her home county; in the autumn of the same year she was elected chief commissioner of the Guides, and in 1918 she won, by sheer devotion to the work of the movement and the force of her own personality, the title of Chief Guide, which put her on a parallel footing with her husband, the Chief Scout.

In 1930 this title was enlarged still further to "Chief Guide of the World," in recognition of the great work which she had done for the Guides, not only in her home country but throughout the empire and the world. This work was further recognized in a more public manner by the award of the honour of "Dame Grand Cross of the Order of the British Empire" in the king's birthday honours of 1932.

The title had not been lightly earned. The Chief Guide's energy and enthusiasm in directing the movement at home, coupled with constant travelling throughout the empire and in foreign countries, had deprived her of leisure for more ordinary recreation; but the knowledge that the time so gladly given was not thrown away, that the movement was increasing in numbers and developing in enthusiasm and efficiency every year, was a reward greater than any honour or distinction could have been.

At the end of the war a large body of trained and efficient workers took their places in the organization of the movement, and from that day the movement has continued to grow and expand in all directions until it has become one of the most popular movements of our times.

The first Guide Conference was held in February, 1911, when it was decided to register the name as "The Baden-Powell Girl Guides," and in September, 1915, a charter of incorporation was granted by the Board of Trade. Her Royal Highness the Princess Royal is the president. There is a headquarters council, with an executive

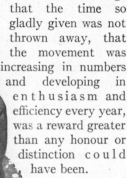

These three Guides are acting as the colour party while at camp.

Photo by Speaight, Ltd.

THE PRESIDENT OF THE GIRL GUIDE MOVEMENT

The Princess Royal, who is president of the Girl Guides, takes a great interest in the activities of the movement. When Foxlease, the beautiful estate in Hampshire was presented to the Association as a training centre for "Guiders", the Princess Royal endowed it with £6,000 from the sum subscribed as a wedding present to her from the Marys of the empire, and a further £4,000 from the proceeds of the exhibition of her presents.

committee consisting of the heads of various branches of Guide training. Each county is placed under the direction of a county commissioner, with division and district commissioners responsible to her.

The girls themselves are divided into three grades for purposes of training, according to age: Brownies, from eight to eleven years of age; Guides, from twelve to sixteen years; and Rangers, over sixteen.

Photo by V. J. Riches

The camp at Foxlease, the home and training centre of "Guiders" not only of the British Isles but of the whole world. The house, which can be seen in the background, is situated at Lyndhurst, in Hampshire, and was the gift of Mrs. Archbold.

The companies of Rangers and Guides and the "packs" of Brownies are in charge of captains and lieutenants and "Brown Owls" and "Tawny Owls" known under the general name of "Guiders."

The Brownies, whose training is carried out almost entirely through fairy tales and "make believe" games, have a simplified Promise and Law suited to their age and understanding. The Promise is as follows:

I promise to do my best;
To do my duty to God and the king;
And to help other people every day, especially those at home.

The Law of the Brownies is:

The Brownie gives in to the older folk.
The Brownie does not give in to herself.

The Brownie's uniform consists of brown overall and belt, brown straw hat, brown socks and shoes. Their totem is a toadstool, their Guider is a "Brown Owl," with a "Tawny Owl" to help her.

They work to pass simple tests for badges, and their ambition is to win their first-class badge and so obtain their "wings." When they reach the age of 11, with these wings they "fly up" to join their older sisters, the Guides proper.

The Guides, like the Scouts, work on the patrol system, six or eight girls forming a patrol under a leader specially chosen for the position. Two, three, or four patrols form a company, under a captain, who may have a lieutenant to help her in her work.

The Guides make the following Promise on joining the movement:

On my honour I promise that I will do my best:
To do my duty to God and the king.
To help other people at all times.
To obey the Guide Law.

The Guide Law is:

A Guide's honour is to be trusted.
A Guide is loyal.
A Guide's duty is to be useful and to help others.
A Guide is a friend to all, and a sister to every other Guide, no matter to what creed, country or class the other belongs.
A Guide is courteous.

A Guide is a friend to animals.

A Guide obeys orders.

A Guide smiles and sings under all difficulties.

A Guide is thrifty.

A Guide keeps herself pure in thought, word and deed.

The Guide's uniform is navy blue, with black shoes and stockings, and a broad-brimmed navy blue hat. The training is carried out largely through games and camping, country dancing, swimming, singing, and other such health-giving recreations; but the girls have also to work for badges in a variety of subjects, such as child-nursing, domestic service, sewing and knitting, cooking, and many others which train them to be useful and happy home-makers.

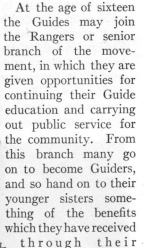

Looking forward to a thoroughly enjoyable time, these smiling Guides are just setting out for camp.

At the age of sixteen the Guides may join the Rangers or senior branch of the movement, in which they are given opportunities for continuing their Guide education and carrying out public service for the community. From this branch many go on to become Guiders, and so hand on to their younger sisters something of the benefits which they have received through their Guide training.

Those, then, are the three main branches of the Guide movement, but there are many other "off-shoots" of the training. Girls in boarding-schools are formed into cadet companies of Guides, preparing themselves for the management of companies later on.

Many of the rooms at Foxlease have been furnished by the subscriptions of Girl Guides of different countries and counties, and they have been named after them. The furniture in this room was supplied by Guides of Wiltshire, so the room is called by that county's name. The smaller picture shows a front view of Foxlease.

At Foxlease Park, in Hampshire, where a world camp attended by 1,100 Guides from many countries was held in 1924, and at Waddow, in Lancashire, "Guiders" undergo courses of training such as will enable them more efficiently to carry out their work of training the children.

In many hospitals and institutions for cripples, deaf-mutes, and mental defectives,

"We are the Brownies, here we stand, play the game and lend a hand." That is what these happy little people sing as they form a Brownie ring.

children who are debarred from most of the pleasures of life are carrying out Guide training, and feeling themselves to be members of a big and happy sisterhood although they may never be able to take part in a camp or rally.

The Guide movement, like that of the Scouts, includes members of every class, creed, and country; and this brings us to its international side.

The movement was introduced into the United States in March, 1912, and three years later the name of the American organization was changed to Girl Scouts. By 1929 there were about two hundred thousand members in the United States and its possessions.

From the national headquarters in New York City, work is now directed in every state and every colony of the Union. An international council also keeps the organizations of all countries in touch with one another, and gives the girls of every nation a chance to know their sisters in other lands. In this way a broad understanding of other peoples and a kindly feeling for the whole world is instilled into the girls who are fortunate enough to belong to the movement.

Out of the million Guides in the world some six hundred thousand belong to the British Empire. The others are Guides in foreign countries where the spirit of the movement has caught on, and where, under the same Promise and Law, the girls are training themselves through Guide methods towards good citizenship. The uniform varies slightly according to the climatic conditions of the country; but the spirit is the same whether in Poland or Norway, France or Czechoslovakia, America or Japan.

A world bureau with headquarters in London keeps these organizations of the different countries in touch one with the other, and an international committee holds meetings from time to time in different countries of the world.

At Adelboden, in Switzerland, the Guides of the world have their international châlet where they can meet and take part in outdoor sports, and at the same time exchange ideas and methods of carrying out their system of Guiding.

In the friendships thus established between young people of different countries there would seem to be a practical step towards the end which all thoughtful people are seeking—a time of peace in the world.

HEALTHY AND HAPPY GIRL GUIDES AT THEIR VARIOUS CAMP DUTIES

The patrol in the top left corner are cheerfully washing-up after a meal. The cook on the right belongs to an overseas party which came to a camp in England along with Guiders from all over the world. In the lower picture is an industrious patrol about to enjoy an open-air repast. They are wearing their camp attire, and have all the necessary appliances for the work in hand. Note the camp-made plate-rack in the background!

WHY *are They* CALLED *the* "MIDDLE AGES"?

The Story of the Races Who Inhabited Europe All Through the Centuries from the Fall of Rome until the Rise of the Modern Nations

WHEN we first look through the magic window of history at the people of very long ago, we see only two tiny bright spots on the globe—Egypt and Sumeria. Outside these two bright areas many people were living, but because they were not civilized, and did not know how to read and write, we know little of their history.

Little by little the ancient world expanded to embrace Babylonia, Assyria, Palestine, Phoenicia, Syria, Persia, India, Greece, and Rome. By the time of the decay of the ancient world and the beginning of what we call the Middle Ages, history begins to deal with most of the countries bordering on the Mediterranean Sea, the Black Sea, the Persian Gulf, and large parts of the Indian Ocean. China and the Far East had long been civilized, while Central America from Mexico to Peru was surprisingly far advanced. In short, civilization was slowly spreading over the whole earth.

What had really happened was that several barbarous peoples had little by little learned the ways of civilization. In the four thousand years covered by the period of ancient history, one people after another emerged into the light of day by learning to read and write and so fit themselves to leave us a record of their doings. All this happened

ARMINIUS AFTER HIS VICTORY OVER THE ROMAN LEGIONS

When the Middle Ages came into being after the collapse of the Roman empire, it was the tall, fair-haired Germanic peoples who took over from the Romans the rulership of Europe. For generations before Rome fell they had been stirring restlessly in their northern forests, and had resisted strongly every attempt of the Roman legions to subdue them. They were hardy people—as many a Roman knew to his cost. Here you see the German patriot Hermann, or Arminius—as the Romans called him—greeted by his people as he returned from his famous victory over the legions of Varus in the Teutoberg Forest. The Roman army was practically exterminated, and the defeated emperor cried, "O Varus, Varus, give me back my legions!"

Photo by Flaudrin

Wherever we travel in Europe we shall be met by ghosts of the Middle Ages. Suddenly we may come upon the crumbling walls of some once-fortified town, and follow the crooked and narrow streets crowded with them.

very slowly, for it takes a long time to build up a civilization; but gradually the light spread from one land to another, and the world of history grew larger.

As that light of civilization grows clearer, we begin to see amazing things taking place. All Europe is in a ferment. It is like a mighty cauldron in which the various tribes and races are all boiling up together—seething, crowding, pushing, always driven along by forces we cannot see.

Europe's Era of Migration

The historians tell us it is an "era of migration." And if we could visualize the past we should see whole races picking up stakes, gathering their few humble tools and cooking utensils, packing their babies on their backs or into ox-carts, and gallantly marching through forests and over brimming rivers in search of new homes.

There goes a tribe of clear-eyed Franks pushing steadily westwards into the smiling plains of the country that now bears their name. Those shaggy men and weary, unkempt women are going to help found a highly intellectual and artistic nation: they are going to mingle their blood with that of the Romanized Celts to make up what will one day become the French nation.

Here are a handful of earnest Germans—Angles and Saxons and Jutes—who launch their boats and drive them over the sea to an island that promises not only plunder but better pasture and richer soil for their crops. They will help to form the British nation.

Everywhere they sweep on, those relentless floods of human beings, all of them seeking a home where their children may grow up stronger, where there shall be a brighter hope of peace, where the tribe shall prosper. Babies are born on the march and the feeble die of hardship, but the strong ones of the tribe must push onwards. They will murder and rob and enslave all who block their way. But they will settle down peaceably in the end, and their children and their children's children will forget that they are of a different race from the people who originally lived on the soil. They will intermarry and have children, and the new and old peoples will become one.

The March to Civilization

In this way men were marching on to become the nations that we know to-day. It was between A.D. 300 and 1300 that most of this migration took place. Nearly all Europe was drawn into the magic circle of civilization during those ten centuries, including the thousands of barbarians who were inhabiting the lands that lay between Italy and Sweden and between Russia and Ireland. These new peoples, belonging mostly to the great Slavonic and Germanic groups, swept down from the north upon the older countries, overwhelming and almost burying the arts and culture of those lands beneath a mass of barbarism.

At one time the five or six centuries after the fall of the Roman empire were known as the Dark Ages, because ignorance and superstition were then so general that it seemed as though the glory of Greece and the grandeur of Rome had been lost for ever. The free, restless spirit of Greece, the magnificent organization which was Rome, were hidden beneath a mass of fighting barbarians. No wonder that these times were known as the Dark Ages!

But let us view these times as one of the barbarous tribes then living might have done. We see these more backward races slowly learning to lay aside their crude ways, to adopt the graces of civilization. We see them mingling with one another and producing the great peoples of to-day, the British, the French, the Germans. We see the light of history dawning over the whole of Europe.

It might possibly be better indeed to call this period the Dawning Ages rather than the Dark Ages, for they saw the rise of a new and vigorous type of culture in Western Europe. It was a time when civilization was widening its boundaries, and it seemed sometimes that the task of civilization might be too great, and that the majority of men might never be much better than they were.

Photo by the Autotype Fine Art Co., Ltd.
"The Viking's Farewell" is the title of this picture. It helps us to remember that the bold Norse vikings were not legendary figures, but living men, and that when, in their winged helmets, they set out on perilous journeys to strange shores, they left women behind to pray for their safe return.

But men went forward with the great task, and they are continuing to do so to-day.

The great task of the vigorous northern barbarians in the early Middle Ages was to learn all they could from the tradition that had been handed down from the great days of Greece and Rome, and to form a new composite civilization by combining Teutonic and Romanized peoples and ideas. But before we go on to describe the new civilization they founded, we may well ask who those barbarians were that first wrecked so much of the old culture and then combined to build up a new one.

There are three main racial types among men — the black, the yellow, and the white. All the peoples of Europe have been white. But within the great white division there are a number of groups.

In Europe there seem to be three principal groups, called the Mediterranean, the Alpine, and the Nordic. The Mediterraneans are slighter in build and not very tall; they are brunette in complexion, with brown eyes and black hair, and their heads are rather long from front to back, in proportion to the breadth from side to side. The Alpines are taller and heavier, usually with brown or dark hair, greyish or hazel eyes, and distinctly rounder heads. The Nordics are still taller and heavier, with blond complexion and hair, and blue eyes. Their heads are long in shape, like those of the Mediterraneans.

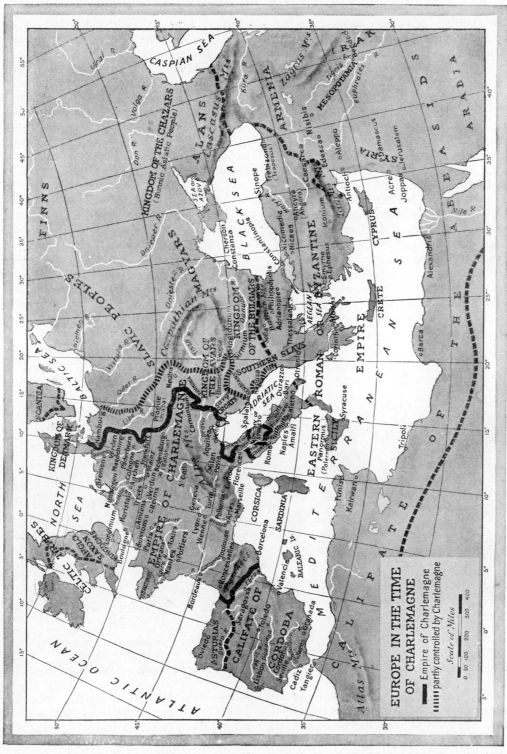

Here you see a map of the continent of Europe in about A.D. 800, showing the empire of Charlemagne, the Anglo-Saxon kingdom and other political divisions.

For a long time there has been a constant intermingling of these peoples, and no national group that we have ever known has been composed of a single type. Whether the races vary in temperament and ability is a question that has been very much debated.

Most of the people in Southern Europe have been Mediterraneans. There is a central belt from east to west where they are mainly Alpines, while around the North and Baltic seas they are mostly Nordics.

We do not know the exact racial class of the barbarian invaders of the Roman empire, but they seem to have included both Nordics and Alpines. We know more about the languages they used, and when we speak of Celts, Teutons, and Slavs, we are talking about language groups and not about races.

The Gauls, a Celtic people, were the first of the barbarians to be influenced by civilization. Coming originally from the plains of Southern Russia, some of them had was known as Gaul. The people there were civilized long before the Roman empire ended. Under the Roman rule they had made their country a fruitful land.

Other Celts, coming perhaps by way of the mountains of Central Europe, had crossed over to the British Isles, settling in England, Wales, and Ireland, and driving back into Scotland a more primitive people they called the Picts. These British Celts, called Britons, had also come under the rule of Rome, and had learned much from their conquerors.

The Goths and the Vandals

The Germanic tribes lived in the marshes and forests of Central Europe. Into the east, on the great plains, or "steppes," of Russia, pushed the Germanic tribes called the Goths (gŏth) and the Vandals, each of which was in turn to overrun Rome, the capital of the world. The Goths invaded Italy in 402 and 403, and in 410 they took

This is Pope Leo I entreating Attila not to march on Rome. The Hun leader had conquered Venetia, and the emperor had asked the Pope to meet this terrible enemy in Northern Italy (452), and to see what could be accomplished by peaceful eloquence. Marvellous to relate, the barbarian chieftain listened—and was persuaded. This was only one of the many famous deeds of Leo I which earned him his title of " the Great."

entered Greece and Italy as early as five hundred years before the dawn of the Middle Ages, but most of them had penetrated the western part of Europe, especially what is now the land of France. In those days it Rome. The Vandals sacked Rome in 455. In 476 Odoacer (ō'dō-ā'sẽr), a Gothic general, made himself master of Italy.

Some long time before the break-up of the Roman empire, the Germanic peoples

THE FIERCE VANDALS CAPTURE THE MIGHTY CITY OF ROME

Under their leader Gaiseric the Vandals descended upon Rome by boat. They captured the city in the year 455, and spent two weeks sacking it. Not a vestige of its precious treasure did they leave behind them.

had begun their mighty westward movement, which was to cover all Northern Europe as far west as England. These Germanic peoples were composed of various groups, sometimes in conflict, sometimes in confederation, but all speaking the same general language. Among these invading peoples, besides the Goths and Vandals already mentioned, the most important were the Suevi (swē'vī), the Alemanni (ăl'ē-măn'ī), the Franks, the Saxons, the Burgundians (bûr-gŭn'dĭ-ăn), and the Lombards (lŏm'bärd). These peoples had overrun the countries we now call Germany and Austria, and in the fourth and fifth centuries after Christ they were still sweeping like a flood over the western Baltic countries, Scandinavia, England, and France.

The Northmen, or Normans, represent a still later expansion of these restless barbarians, some of whom were much later to travel south into the north of France and then cross over to England with William the Conqueror. From these Northmen were descended the vikings, those hardy sea-rovers of Norway and Sweden and Denmark who were later to be the first people to sight America. The Saxons, Angles, and Jutes settled in England, and other tribes spread through Germany and France.

How a Mighty Nation Was Scattered Over the Face of the Earth

Now, you will remember that of the nations who made history before the Christian era many were Semitic (sē-mĭt'ĭk) peoples. What has become of them? When did they make their exit from the stage of history? There were the Hebrews, the Phoenicians, the Babylonians, Assyrians, Chaldeans, Syrians, and Arameans, all mighty races.

Of these the Hebrews, now the Jews, were gradually scattered throughout the known world. When in the year A.D. 135 they were forbidden to enter their holy city of Jerusalem on pain of death, their existence as a nation, that is, a people living in the same country and under the same government, was over. The Phoenicians (fē-nĭsh'ăn) had survived for a time in their great colony of Carthage, but by now it was broken and destroyed. The Babylonians, Chaldeans, and Assyrians

had vanished long before, and the other Semitic peoples were finally swallowed up by the Arabs, the last great wave of the Semitic race to appear in Western Asia.

The Arabs were a mixed group, largely Semitic. By the people of the Middle Ages they were called Saracens (săr'ă-sĕn), and when they rose to great power about 700, it really seemed that they might conquer the world, as Alexander and Caesar had done. Together with other kindred peoples, they overran all Northern Africa and crossed into Spain, where the Berbers, or Moors, formed a part of their advancing army. But we shall speak later of all this.

How the Barbarous Mongolians Brought Terror into Europe

Besides the Indo-European and the Semitic peoples, both belonging to the white race, the other great race which plays a part in the moving picture of the Middle Ages is the Mongolian (mŏng-gō'lĭ-ăn), or yellow, race. The Chinese, Japanese, and many of the other peoples of Asia are partly Mongolian. The first advance of Mongolians into Europe occurred about 400, when a wandering tribe known as the Huns, a branch of the Mongolian race, swept into Russia in the form of troops of wild horsemen, killing and burning wherever they went. They were extremely cruel, and so rapacious that the Germans who had to fight them had a saying that if you put a coin on a Hun's grave a hand would reach out of the earth to snatch it.

In 452 the Huns were at the gates of Rome. But they never entered the city, and the next year saw the death of their greatest chief, Attila (ăt'ĭ-lă). Without Attila to lead them, the Huns broke up into small bands and completely disappeared from the pages of history, leaving only a vivid memory of the terror they had inspired.

Once again a horde of western Mongols swept into Europe under Genghis Khan (jĕn'gĭz kän) towards the end of the Middle Ages, about the year 1200. This time it was a tribe we call Tatars (tä'tär), and they penetrated little farther than Russia. There they set up a "Kingdom of the Golden Horde," which lasted for three centuries. But it, too, finally disappeared, and the

Photo by Levy et Neurdein

THE MAN OF PEACE LOOKS DOWN ON A SCENE OF STRIFE

This picture is an allegory—an imaginary story with a meaning. The artist must have been mournfully turning the blood-soaked pages of history, wondering how the followers of Christ could have gone on for centuries torturing and killing one another. Then he must have wondered whether there ever came to kings and warriors and fighting priests a vision of their Master reproaching them for such deeds. One can only hope that as men begin to understand Christ's teaching better, they will grow less cruel, and peace will at length come on earth.

Mongol had no more power in Europe until the coming of the Turk.

The Turks are not pure Mongols, although they are largely descended from the Tatars. The Turks were opposed to both Saracens and Christians. About the year 1000 they came westwards and established a great empire in Western Asia and eventually in South-eastern Europe. Jerusalem fell to them, and the Christians, when they came to win it back, had to fight Turks as well as Arabs. The Turks have never been entirely driven from Europe, but still maintain a foothold on the south-eastern fringe.

It would be very difficult to draw lines on a map of Europe and say, "This race or this people lived here and that one there." Ex-cept for the Roman empire itself, there were no kingdoms with fixed lines dividing them from one another. A German tribe might settle in one locality for a few years and then move on to another place.

How could such shifting pieces be fitted together to form great and enlightened nations? The first strong civilizing influence was Rome. As early as a century before the Christian era began German tribes called the "Cimbri" and "Teutones" threatened Italy, and between 58 B.C. and 51 B.C. Julius Caesar checked their attempted invasion of Gaul and drove them back into their northern lands. Later the Romans subdued and ruled a large part of Germany, as well as all France and almost the whole of England.

This Roman rule taught the uncivilized peoples methods of organization and government. The Celtic people of France even adopted the Latin language in place of their own, and this northern Latin speech was the mother of French, just as a western Latin was the mother of Spanish, and the Latin of Italy itself was the mother of Italian. The people of England and Ireland still spoke their original Celtic tongues, and the Germanic tribes east of the Rhine clung to their native Germanic speech. Nevertheless, Rome, its government and its language, tended to knit the Western European world together and make it more closely united.

The strongest force working to civilize the European peoples and to make them one in thought was the Christian religion. When men pray to the same God they tend to become brothers in many ways When the Goths, the Huns, and the Vandals, with other uneducated peoples, had overrun the Roman empire, and when the Arabs had occupied Alexandria in Egypt, that vast storehouse of Greek culture, the Christian Church was the only force left that was capable of handing on and spreading education among the invaders.

How the Monks Handed Down Learning from Generation to Generation

It is true that the Christian Church was often only too much like the world around it—full of ignorance and superstition—and indeed, its members both feared and hated the heathen learning of the Greeks and Romans. But the Christian Church did much to keep learning alive, and without its efforts nearly all the store of knowledge in the world might have been lost.

In monasteries all over the known world in the Middle Ages, from Ireland to Syria, monks handed down what knowledge they possessed. Outside the monasteries, the religion that teaches us all to be brothers began its slow work of exalting men above their cruelty and greed.

By the close of the Middle Ages the peoples had distributed themselves much as they are to-day. In Ireland, Scotland and Wales, as well as in North-west France, the Celtic

folk still lingered, mixed with the Germanic. The Celts we know as Britons had been driven into Wales by other peoples who had liked their beautiful little island only too well. As a result, the English had now become a mixture of Celts, Norman-French and Danes, with an admixture of those three other Germanic tribes, Angles, Jutes, and Saxons, who had begun migrating to Britain about the year 450.

A Powerful New Empire on the Southern Shore of the Mediterranean

Except for Russia, Northern Europe was Germanic. The north Germans in Norway, Sweden, Denmark, and Iceland were now Scandinavians. In France there was a mixture of Germanic peoples like the Franks with the Romanized Celtic peoples who had been there before them. All the various tribes of Germans east of France retained their German language and character.

South of this band of northern, or Germanic peoples lay the southern, or Mediterranean, peoples who had survived from the days of the Roman empire and had mingled with each invading wave that swept down from the north. Out of this intermingling arose the Spaniards, Italians, Greeks, and other peoples along the Mediterranean Sea. But in Spain and Asia Minor, they were bounded by a strange new religion, that of the followers of Islam (ĭz'lăm)—the Mohammedans (mō-hăm'ĕ-dăn) — whose empire stretched along the southern shore of the Mediterranean.

The modern ages, the six or seven centuries since 1300, have seen no great migrations in Europe. But they have seen the greatest movement of all history in the settling of new lands by the northern and southern European peoples. North and South America, Southern Africa, Australia, New Zealand, and countless smaller countries have adopted the culture and civilization of Europe, a civilization which, for the first time in history, covers a large part of the whole habitable globe. There is nothing more important in the story of mankind than this spread of European culture. The Middle Ages were the dawn of this process.

(CONTINUED ON PAGE 927)

HOW WE FIND OUT WHAT THINGS ARE LIKE IN THE UPPER REGIONS OF THE AIR

These balloons are about to carry instruments high up into the air to find out for the meteorological officials of Canada what conditions are like in regions man has never yet been able to visit. Such balloons have ascended as high as twenty-three miles. They are made of india-rubber, as a rule, and are partially filled with a very light gas—hydrogen—when they leave the earth. As they rise into the thinner upper atmosphere, where the air pressure grows lighter and lighter, they gradually expand until at last they burst. Then the torn rubber acts as a parachute and carries the instruments down to earth again. No one has the faintest idea where they will land; but attached to them is a tag informing the finder what they are for and offering a reward for their safe return. Instructions as to packing and shipping are also given. It is pleasant to be able to say that sooner or later most of those instruments find their way back to their owners—sometimes after a long, long time, and from places as many as two hundred miles away from the starting-point. The scientific instruments in such "sounding balloons" usually register temperature and air pressure, and sometimes humidity.

HOW MUCH DOES *the* AIR WEIGH?

Here We Shall See that a Thing which Appears to Have No Weight at All is Yet Quite Heavy

(CONTINUED FROM PAGE 877)

THE soft blanket of air into which the earth is so snugly tucked weighs 5,600,000,000,000,000 tons. Perhaps you cannot even read so vast a figure. It is five thousand six hundred million million tons. And yet the air seems to weigh nothing at all!

Now this great ocean of atmosphere is not distributed evenly. Winds are constantly pushing through it, piling it up in one place and thinning it out in another. Every storm wind that blows moves millions of tons of air from one part of the earth to another. Such a heaping up makes the air press more heavily in certain places upon the earth beneath. It is easy to see that changes in the weight of the air must always go with stormy weather.

In order to help him estimate what kind of weather is coming, the meteorologist weighs the air two or three times a day. If you had to do so, how do you think you would set about it? It would take you a long, long time to work out a way! Certainly it could never be done with the kind of scales the grocer uses for tea and sugar. The meteorologist uses an instrument called a barometer (bả-rŏm′ĕ-tẽr). With it he weighs the air that rests on one square inch of earth. But what a tall column it is! It reaches up into space at least two hundred miles. And although its weight is always changing, it averages fifteen pounds. So the air that rests on a square foot—one hundred and forty-four square inches—of ground at sea-level weighs more than two thousand pounds. Think of all the tons your body is supporting!

The barometer is very easy to understand. It was invented by Evangelista Torricelli (tŏr-ĭ-chĕl′ĭ), an Italian, about 1643. The simplest kind is made from a glass tube about thirty-three inches long, closed at one end and filled with mercury, or quicksilver. The tube is turned upside down, so that the open end is inserted in a small cup partly filled with mercury. Of course, some of the mercury runs out of the tube into the cup; perhaps three inches of tube at the top is empty. But it cannot all run out, because the weight of the air pressing down on the mercury in the cup

will not allow it to do so. It holds the column of mercury in the tube as securely as if the tube were corked.

You must remember that a weight of fifteen pounds is bearing down on every square inch of the surface of the mercury in the cup—and there is no air inside the tube to press down on the top of the column of mercury, for the mercury in falling two or three inches left a vacuum above it. Now, as you may perhaps know, mercury is a very heavy liquid, and weighs 13·6 times as much as water. So if the mercury in the cup has a surface exposed to the air, the weight of the air upon it will just balance the weight of the thirty inches or so of mercury in the tube.

If the air should get heavier it will press down harder in the cup and push the mercury up in the tube. Sometimes, when the air is heaped up in a great billow, it can force the mercury up a whole inch—as measured on the scale marked alongside the glass tube. We then say that the barometer reads thirty-one inches. At such a time the weather is likely to be fair. Then, if the air flows away and so does not press down so hard, a little mercury will run out of the tube, sometimes more than an inch. The column of mercury will then reach less than twenty-nine inches in height—and less than twenty-nine inches is a very low barometric (bǎr′-ŏ-mĕt′rĭk) pressure. It denotes stormy weather. So, strange as it may seem, we measure the weight of the air by inches instead of pounds. Of course we could weigh the air by means of a column of water, but it would need to be 36 feet long!

If we could do the air up in tight bundles, we should find that every one of us carries a weight like this on his head—for every square inch of surface has to support a weight of fifteen pounds of air. So on his whole body each one of us has to stand a pressure of over thirteen tons of air. How can it be that we are not crushed to jelly beneath such an enormous weight? It is be-

cause our bodies are so made that there is an equal pressure inside, to support them. A fish that swims in the depths of the sea has to support still more enormous pressures from the water above it. A mile down in the ocean the weight is more than a ton to the square inch. The fish can

support it because the water in its body is at the same pressure; but as soon as such a fish is brought to the surface the pressure on it is released and it bursts. In the same way we should burst if taken suddenly from Earth into outer space.

WHY WATER BOILS MORE QUICKLY ON A MOUNTAIN PEAK

Here are two barometers—the left-hand one situated on a lofty mountain top and the other placed at sea-level. If we could see the air, we should realize that on every square inch of surface it is bearing down with a surprising weight, like a shaft reaching up to the top of the atmosphere. In the pictures above, the two columns of air are coloured black, so that you may understand how it is that the air on a mountain peak has less weight. The air there is "thinner" or less dense than at sea-level, and water boils more quickly in it.

A mercury barometer is the most reliable, but it is expensive and bulky to carry about; so for all ordinary purposes the aneroid (ăn'ĕr-oid) barometer is used—named from two Greek words meaning "not wet." It has no liquid of any kind, but comprises a small metal box with a thin, elastic corrugated cover. Most of the air has been drawn out from the inside of the box, so that when the pressure of air is increased on the cover, there is nothing but a light spring to keep the thin sheet of metal from being pushed inwards under the weight. When the pressure is lighter the cover comes back into its first position again. The slightest movement of the cover to and fro is registered by a pointer on a dial, and the figures are so gauged as to read the same as the scale in inches on a mercury barometer.

Another highly important use of the aneroid is for measuring height ascended. Thus for every 120 metres we ascend—in a balloon, say—the barometer registers a fall of 1 centimetre.

Because the pressure of the air can change so quickly, most stations of the Meteorological Office have an instrument by which the barometer can record all its changes. A strip of ruled paper is fastened round a drum that slowly revolves by clockwork. As it turns, a pen connected with an aneroid barometer draws a line upon the paper and records all the changes that take place in the pressure of the air.

Why Our Climate is Mild

Air pressure varies greatly over different parts of the earth. Wherever the air is turning in a cyclone, the pressure is low at the centre of the whirl. In some places the pressure is nearly always low—as near Ice-

Evangelista Torricelli, the famous scientist, is here shown experimenting with his barometer.

land and in the great updraught along the Equator. In other places it is high. The low-pressure area near Iceland is very important for the weather of England. The air travels round it in a great whirl more than a thousand miles across, and part of this whirl crosses our islands as a south-west wind. That is why our winds so often blow from south-west, and one reason why our climate is so mild. Sometimes the "Icelandic low," as it is termed, shifts its position nearer to us, and then we have very stormy weather.

The area of high pressure which most often affects us lies to the south-west, over the Azores Islands, and is called the "Azores high." Sometimes it moves nearer to us, or even right across England, and if this happens in summer we have very fine weather indeed. There is another area of high pressure in winter over Siberia; this forms because the air is so cold, and cold air, as we have seen, is heavy. It sometimes sends out a stream of cold air across Europe, and then we shiver in a bitter east wind.

So you see there probably is a good reason why on a crisp, clear day one should feel like conquering the world. Many physicians say that a high air pressure forces more blood into the interior of the body, so that the brain and all the vital organs are well supplied.

But a moist, still day, when the air pressure is light and a storm is not far off, robs us of ambition. We say that the air is "heavy," meaning that it is damp and hard to breathe. But what we ought to say is that the air is light, for it is then that it weighs the least, if the barometer tells the truth. And it is in quite a different electrical condition from air that is riding in on a keen blast from the north. The change is easy to see among hospital patients.

(CONTINUED ON PAGE 959)

The GREATEST TRAGIC NOVELIST

Why Thomas Hardy Would Not Let His Heroes and Heroines *"Live Happily Ever After"*

(CONTINUED FROM PAGE 856)

OCCASIONALLY there appears a novelist who feels that the world is not such a very happy place, and that the good people do not always get their reward, while the wrongdoers sometimes prosper only too well. Some of these novelists have the courage to say so in their stories, and then the stories end unhappily. The greatest English novelist of the past half-century felt this to be the case, and most of his novels have a gloomy ending. This novelist was Thomas Hardy (1840–1928).

In his native Dorsetshire, Hardy lived among all those sombre beauties of Nature that form the background of his stories. The nearest town, Dorchester, was some miles away, and as a boy he had few playmates. He used to wander through the beech groves, over the broad and desolate waste lands of the heath, and by the river-side, until he knew all the region which he was later to make so famous in his books under the name of "Wessex." And he used to talk with the simple country people until he knew their thoughts and feelings and their speech so well that he could reveal them to all the world in his novels.

He was educated at the local schools, and when his school days were over his father, who was a builder, placed him in the office of an architect at Dorchester. There he remained for six years, and then, in 1862, went to London, to continue in that profession. Working all day, and going to evening classes at King's College, he still managed to find time for writing verse—for he had begun to do that before he went to London.

Then, although he seemed to have a bright future as an architect, and had already taken several prizes for essays on architecture, he began to wonder whether he had chosen the right calling. He thought he might do better as a writer. So he continued writing poetry, and when he could not get it published, he turned to fiction.

In 1867 he went to Weymouth, where he continued as an architect and also as a writer. His first novels met with very little favour, and it was not until 1872 that he made a real success. "Under the Greenwood Tree" laid the foundation of his fame in that year, and soon after it was followed by "Far from the Madding Crowd."

He now saw that he could give all his time to his pen, and he moved back to Dorchester, where he spent the rest of his life among the scenes and people of his childhood. There he wrote the rest of his great novels—"The Woodlanders," "The Mayor of Casterbridge," "Tess of the d'Urbervilles," "Jude the Obscure," "The Return of the Native," and several others. The tragic story of Tess has always been his most popular book, but "The Return of the Native" is probably his greatest.

As a novelist he is a master-craftsman. There are, in fact, many people who think of him as the greatest of all English novelists, but that, perhaps, is a matter of individual taste and opinion.

All through his life he continued to write poetry. And perhaps even to-day his poetry is not appreciated at its true worth. His shorter pieces, as well as his longer poems—such as "The Dynasts," which describes the rise and fall of Napoleon—show great tragic power and give him a high place in the history of English literature, apart from his novels.

Photo by National Portrait Gallery

Thomas Hardy, the greatest English novelist of the later nineteenth century, and, in the opinion of some, the greatest of all English novelists.

The AUTHOR of "TREASURE ISLAND"

Besides Thrilling Adventure Stories, Robert Louis Stevenson Gave Us Many Delicate Poems and Delightful Essays

ROBERT LOUIS STEVENSON was always plucky, even as a sickly child when he marched his tin soldiers up and down "the land of counterpane" on his bed. The courageous spirit of his father and grandfather, both civil engineers, who worked on the construction of lighthouses, made him love exciting games and books of adventure. While he bravely fought his own battles in the sick-room his nurse, "Cummy," fired his imagination by reading to him books like "Three - Fingered Jack, the Terror of Jamaica"!

Almost from birth, in 1850, he suffered from delicate health, and when he was eight years old he was attacked by a fever which nearly proved fatal, and left his constitution impaired. It was intended that he should either adopt his father's profession of engineering or study law, both of which he attempted, but he chose instead a literary career, possibly from reasons of health, for a brave man like Stevenson could write amusingly even though flushed with fever, or racked by terrible fits of coughing.

Stevenson tells us that he idled his way through college and took trips abroad where he wandered about on foot or, as described in "An Inland Voyage" (1878), made journeys by canoe. In "Travels with a Donkey" (1879), he tells of a walking trip with a stubborn little beast named Modestine.

About this time Stevenson met the woman who later became his wife. Soon afterwards she returned to America, and he threw common sense to the winds and followed her, first across the Atlantic, then on to San Francisco, travelling like the poorest immigrant because his parents disapproved of the

Photo by National Portrait Gallery

The natives of Upolu gave Robert Louis Stevenson the name of "Tusitala," which means "Teller of Tales." It was a fitting name.

adventure. His health suffered greatly from the hardships, but he won a wife, who proved to be also an excellent nurse and an ideal companion.

Some of Stevenson's admirers love him best for his thoughtful and amusing essays. But most people—and all boys and girls—know him as a spinner of delightful yarns, a magical story - teller. "Treasure Island" (1883) is a breath-taking pirate story; "Dr. Jekyll and Mr. Hyde" (1886) is a gruesome tale of a man who led a double life; "Kidnapped" (1886) tells of a courageous boy's adventures in Scotland; and children never tire of "A Child's Garden of Verses" (1885), wherein the author tells in charming rhymes the thoughts of his own childhood. Stevenson always loved children.

For years he lived in America —at Saranac Lake, a famous health resort in the Adirondacks, and in sunny California. Then he and his family cruised the Pacific Ocean and finally settled near Apia, on Upolu, one of the beautiful Samoan Islands, where they lived until his death in 1894. Stevenson ruled almost like a king over the natives, who loved and served him. At his death they cut a path up the steep slope of a mountain top where his body was laid to rest. On the stone at his head they carved his beautiful lines:

Under the wide and starry sky,
Dig the grave and let me lie.
Glad did I live and gladly die,
  And I laid me down with a will.
This be the verse you grave for me:
" Here he lies where he longed to be;
Home is the sailor, home from the sea,
And the hunter home from the hill."

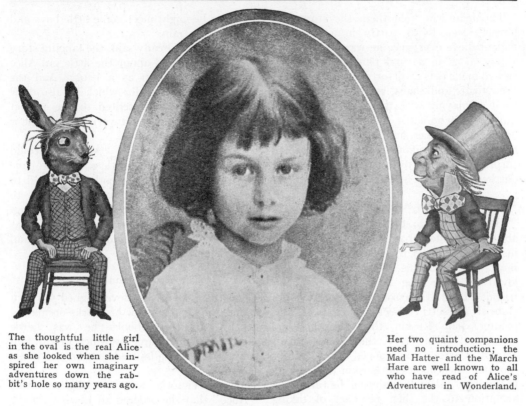

The thoughtful little girl in the oval is the real Alice as she looked when she inspired her own imaginary adventures down the rabbit's hole so many years ago.

Her two quaint companions need no introduction; the Mad Hatter and the March Hare are well known to all who have read of Alice's Adventures in Wonderland.

The CHILDREN'S STORY-WRITER

He was a Professor of Mathematics, but We Know Him Best as the Author of " Alice in Wonderland" and " Through the Looking-Glass "

ONE summer afternoon a good many years ago a man started to tell a story to three little girls. He had no notion that it was going to make him famous. How could he have? He was always telling stories to little children. They were resting by the cool bank of a stream near Oxford, when the girls begged for the story, and he just started as usual to make one up for them. He invented some adventures about one of the three—her name was Alice—in a land of make-believe.

The story grew longer and longer, but whenever the man became tired and said he would tell the rest next time, the little girls cried out, "But this is next time!" and he had to go on. Now and again he would make out that he had gone to sleep, like a dormouse, much to the children's dismay. But he had to wake up and keep on.

In the end he wrote down the story, and it made one of the most famous books in the world. For the man was Lewis Carroll (1832–1898), and the story he was telling came to be known as "Alice's Adventures in Wonderland."

Not that the little girls ever called him Lewis Carroll. To them he was Mr. Dodgson—Charles Lutwidge Dodgson—for that was his real name, and he taught mathematics in one of the colleges of Oxford University. He even wrote important books on mathematics. But the little girls were not thinking about all that—only about the story, which was so much better than any other they had ever heard or read.

The man who told them the story had himself been living partly in a world of make-believe ever since he was a child. As a boy, born in a rural parsonage in 1832, he had made pets of all sorts of queer animals, even toads and snails, and had never been tired of playing with them. When he was quite young he had a talent for mimicking, for making rhymes, and for telling tales, but he was also a studious boy, and he used to surprise his father by his eagerness to work out hard problems in mathematics.

Carroll's Artistic Friends

He was sent to Christ Church, Oxford, and there he stayed as a tutor for the rest of his life. He loved the place, as everybody must. He loved his science. And he also loved to have long talks with his good friends—Lord Tennyson, the poet, Dante Gabriel Rossetti (rō-sĕt′ĭ), the poet and painter, John Ruskin, the writer and art critic, and Ellen Terry, the Shakespearean actress. Carroll always longed to be a painter too, but when his friend Ruskin told him he had no real talent for painting, he turned his attention to the then new art of taking photographs.

He never had any real adventure. He did not need one. Above all things he loved children, and he would do anything to give them pleasure. Whenever he was going on a train journey he would fill his pockets with toys, for he might meet some little boys and girls on the train.

As we have already said, the fanciful story Lewis Carroll told about the little girl Alice came to be written as a book. And the original manuscript, for which he also drew the pictures, was presented to the subject of the story. And that very manuscript is still in existence.

When he had finished "Alice," he could not stop writing. The little girls would have seen to that, even if he had not wanted to go on himself. So he wrote a sequel to "Alice" called "Through the Looking-Glass," and several other stories of a similar kind, like "The Hunting of the Snark" and "Sylvie and Bruno."

Queen Victoria and "Alice"

To these books he never signed his own name—he kept that for his works on mathematics. In these books he was Lewis Carroll, the only name by which we call him now. He never admitted that he was Lewis Carroll.

Queen Victoria was so delighted with "Alice" that she ordered all Lewis Carroll's works to be sent to her. When the parcel arrived containing such titles as: "A Syllabus of Plane Algebraical Geometry," "The Formulae of Plane Trigonometry" and "Euclid and His Modern Rivals" you can imagine how great was her surprise.

Do You BELIEVE in FAIRIES?

Little Wendy Did and So Did Her Brothers, and Sir James Barrie's " Peter Pan " Converts Us to a Similar Belief

IF YOU ever go to see Sir James Barrie's fairy play "Peter Pan" you will at one stage be asked a question which, whatever age you may be, will compel an answer. There is a moment in the play when Peter Pan makes the members of the audience cry out that they believe in fairies. Little Tinker Bell is lost, and unless the children will believe in fairies she can never come back. So Peter comes to the front of the stage and stretches out his arms to the audience. "O, *don't* you believe in fairies?" he cries. And he has never cried in vain. Not only the children, but often the grown-ups, too, cry out their belief in the existence of fairies in response to Peter's plaintive inquiry. They cannot help it.

Any man who can make a whole host of people act like that cannot help being loved, and Sir James Barrie is certainly loved by all who have seen "Peter Pan," the creation of a lovable and sympathetic mind.

James Matthew Barrie was born at Kirriemuir, in Scotland, in 1860. It was natural to him to tell stories—as a boy he used to tell them to his mother when she was ill. Before he was twelve he used to write tales of adventure in the attic of his home. When he was old enough he was sent to an academy at Dumfries and then to the University of Edinburgh; and after a time he found his way to Nottingham, and became a journalist, removing to London about eighteen months later.

In a short time his stories about the simple life in his native Scottish village began to bring him fame. These were the delightful "Auld Licht Idylls" and "A Window in Thrums." Then came his first novel, "The Little Minister," which was dramatized a few years after. This was followed by "Sentimental Tommy" and "Tommy and Grizel"; and by the fine story of his early life with his mother in "Margaret Ogilvy," a beautiful and affecting tribute to the woman to whom he owed so much.

THE AUTHOR OF "PETER PAN"

If Sir James Barrie had given us nothing more than the deathless "Peter Pan" his name would be known for many years to come. Instead of that, we have from him some half-dozen works that, taken together, ensure for him a lasting fame in English literature.

In "The Little White Bird" Barrie gives a foretaste of what he has in store for us in "Peter Pan"—for in it he first introduces Peter, the "boy who would not grow up."

He has written many other delightful plays—among them "Quality Street," "What Every Woman Knows," "The Legend of Leonora," "A Kiss for Cinderella," "Alice-Sit-by-the-Fire," "Dear Brutus," "The Admirable Crichton," and "Mary Rose." These have all delighted thousands of audiences in every English-speaking country of the world. In pure fantasy, that is to say fanciful thoughts, no English dramatist has been so successful. And it is a very difficult thing to convey fantastic ideas in a stage play.

Barrie has had many honours. He was made a baronet in 1913, and the Order of Merit—which is awarded only to Britain's greatest sons—was conferred on him in 1922. For the past few years he has written nothing to gladden our dull, everyday lives. How much we have missed!

The POET of MAN and MUSCLE

Rudyard Kipling Sang the Praises of the Empire in Stirring Ballads and Inspiring Stories that were Original in Both Theme and Method

ONE DAY in 1889 a young man from India arrived in San Francisco. He was almost unknown in America, but he felt sure the manuscripts he carried in his bag would make the name of Rudyard Kipling a familiar one to the American people. The publishers. however, were not so certain that his work would interest their readers. They declined to take his writings even when he offered them at a ridiculously low price. Yet, just a little more than a year later, he found himself as famous in England and America as he had been in India, for an English publisher had at last been persuaded to bring out some of his short stories and ballads. And soon some of the very pages of the manuscript he had offered for next to nothing were bringing him in hundreds of pounds.

Kipling was born at Bombay, in India, on December 30, 1865. His father was a well-known artist in charge of a museum at Lahore and an art school at Bombay. His mother was said to be "the wittiest woman in all India." At the age of five the boy was sent to England to be educated. After seven years at school he entered the United Service College, a government school in Devonshire. The discipline here was very strict, and Kipling himself has said that it was no place for "a milksop, a boy without spirit and a rigorous constitution." His stories in "Stalky and Co.," published years later, tell of the adventures and pranks of his days at the college.

At seventeen Kipling went back to India to take a place on the editorial staff of a paper at Lahore. Impressed by the novelty and mystery of India, he began to write verse and short stories of Anglo-Indian life. When these found their way into print they brought him an offer of a position as assistant editor on the "Allahabad Pioneer." In this paper appeared some of his best stories, among them the now famous "Soldiers Three" and "Wee Willie Winkie." It was the success of these stories in India, dashed off between the hours of his work, that led him to seek out a publisher in England.

His Second Visit to America

In 1892 Kipling paid a second visit to America. During this visit he met and married Miss Caroline Starr Balestier, and after three years he moved to Brattleboro, Ver-

mont, where he lived for a few years. Then he returned to England, where he has lived ever since—with the exception of another short visit to America and a highly successful tour of Canada in 1907.

Before he was thirty, Kipling was known all over the world as a story-teller, a novelist, and a poet. His "Plain Tales from the Hills" had shown his power to amuse and interest all sorts of readers in the life of the East. His "Barrack Room Ballads," in the racy language of the soldier, had shown his gifts in verse. But it was poems like his "Recessional," written for the Diamond Jubilee of Queen Victoria, that brought him into highest favour as a poet. And some of his later stories and novels are even more powerful than his early "Plain Tales."

Photo by Elliott and Fry

Rudyard Kipling, beloved by thousands of children because of his "Jungle Books," and by thousands of grown-ups for his stirring poems and matchless tales.

His two "Jungle Books" and his "Just-So Stories" are wonderful tales for boys and girls everywhere, and for grown-ups as well. His "Captains Courageous" is a great adventure story of the deep sea. "The Light That Failed," his first long novel, is less successful, but the great story of "Kim," probably his best work, has a peculiar power to enthral the reader. These are only some of his best-known books.

What He Did for English Literature

Kipling came into English literature when it was at a rather low ebb, and put fresh life into it. For he is a man of tremendous force and energy. No one has surpassed him as a poet of the strenuous life, of the great work of the world. The abounding vigour that he brought to English letters was exactly what it needed most at the time of his coming. For that reason his influence has been enormous. He has had many imitators, but he remains in a class by himself.

(CONTINUED ON PAGE 955)

SCOTLAND   WALES   IRELAND (NORTH)   IRELAND (FREE STATE)

ST GEORGE   ST ANDREW

THE UNION JACK

QUEEN ANNE   ST PATRICK

CANADA

AUSTRALIA   SOUTH AFRICA   NEW ZEALAND   INDIA

The Union Jack and other flags of the British Empire are shown here.   Flags of foreign countries will be found in the colour plates facing pages 609 and 961.

WHAT *the* FLAGS MEAN

How Their Designs and Colours Tell Tales of Heroic Things That Happened Centuries Ago

THERE is perfect quiet in the assembly. The children stand facing a flag. All at once their right arms are lifted towards the emblem—they are saluting the Union Jack, for it is May 24, Empire Day, the day on which the school-children throughout the British Empire salute the flag.

Every year, since as far back as 1902, British schoolboys and schoolgirls have saluted their flag on this day. May 24 is the anniversary of the birthday of Queen Victoria, and so was chosen as a particularly appropriate day for a British imperial celebration.

In the very early days of the world, before men lived in communities, it is reasonable to suppose that there were no such things as flags. It would be when men began to combine together that the need for flags was felt. To look upon the emblem would be to remind the men of the tribe of brave deeds performed in the past, and to spur them on to emulate such valour themselves.

These early flags must have been very different from the flags we have to-day. In such countries as Assyria and Egypt the

The flag flying from the stern of this battleship is the White Ensign. It consists of the cross of St. George on a white background, and the Union Jack in the upper quarter nearest the flagstaff. It is flown only by ships of the British navy and by the vessels of certain yacht clubs.

men rallied and fought under standards, or tall staffs, with perhaps a figure of a king or a great hero or a sacred animal on top of them; but in very early times the Persians had something that might be called the germ of the kind of flag we know. For hundreds of years their soldiers used to go into battle led by the leather apron of a blacksmith. The story of that emblem is lost in the mists of time, but it is not so very difficult to imagine how the custom may have come about. May we not suppose that on some occasion the Persians were getting the worst of a fight, when suddenly some leader, bolder than the rest, snatched up a blacksmith's apron and, waving it above his head, rallied the failing troops to victory?

And there must surely have been some such story to account for the equally strange fighting symbols used in the early days of the Roman Republic, when bundles of hay were carried on poles in front of the soldiers—long before it became the law that every Roman legion should have only the imperial eagle on its standard. The emblem of the early Greeks was simply a piece of body armour borne aloft on a spear. Later, when the various city-states were formed, each city had its appropriate emblem. Thus the Athenians showed an owl, the bird of Athena; the Thebans, a sphinx, in remembrance of Oedipus, who guessed the riddle of the Sph'nx, and so on.

For us a star and crescent mean the flag of Turkey, but such objects on national flags are often steeped in ancient history and tradition. Centuries before the star and crescent were adopted by the Turks they had appeared on the standards and banners of Byzantium (the old name of Constantinople, which we are now learning to call Istanbul), since they were the symbols of the moon goddess Diana, the city's patroness. Earlier still, it seems, Philip of Macedon, the father of Alexander the Great, had laid siege to the city and tried to take it by a surprise attack at night; but the beams of the crescent moon had revealed his plans, and so the Byzantines raised a statue to Diana and adopted the emblems of the moon goddess out of gratitude to her.

Nearly eighteen hundred years later, in 1453, when the great Moslem leader, Mohammed II, captured Constantinople, he found the flag still there and took it for his own; and to this day the Turkish flag has a white star and crescent on a red field.

A Flag That Has Been Flying for More Than Seven Hundred Years

Religion has played an important part in the origin of flags, and many of the early ones started as sacred banners. This is true, for instance, of the oldest of all national flags, that of Denmark, which has been flying for more than seven hundred years. In 1219, as the story tells, King Waldemar II, when the battle seemed to be going against him, lifted his eyes to Heaven and beheld a cross in the sky. This was taken as a sign of divine aid, and the cross was placed on the national flag.

It was under the Chape de St. Martin— the hood that the saint divided with Christ in the guise of a beggar—that the kings of France fought of old. The Chape de St. Martin in its turn gave place to the famous oriflamme (ŏr'ĭ-flăm), which was the banner of the abbey of St. Denis, and which made its last appearance on the field of battle at Agincourt, to be superseded first by the lilies of France, and later—at the time of the Revolution—by the tricolour.

A cross is seen on the Swiss flag, which is about six hundred years old. Its white Greek cross on a red field is all the better known because the Red Cross, when it started in Switzerland, adopted the Swiss flag with the colours reversed. And the Red Cross flag is now the best known of all flags, for it flies in every country of the civilized world as the peaceful emblem of aid to suffering humanity.

How the Union Jack, National Flag of Britain, Came Into Being

The British national flag is a blend of the crosses of St. George, St. Andrew and St. Patrick, the patron saints respectively of England, Scotland and Ireland. When the crowns of England and Scotland were united in 1603 the cross of St. Andrew was added to that of St. George. This cross is in the shape of an **X**.

For a short time after 1649 the Union Jack ceased to be used, its place being taken by the old flag showing the red cross of St. George only. This was after Charles I's death, when the union with Scotland was temporarily dissolved. Cromwell, when he became Protector, soon altered this, and the Union Jack once more came into being, this time with a new feature added, namely, the Irish harp, which was placed over the centre of the cross. This innovation did not last long, for at the Restoration Charles II took the harp off the flag, thus restoring the original union flag. Later still, at the time of the union with Ireland in 1801, the cross of St. Patrick, also in the form of an **X**, was added. And thus the familiar Union Jack came into being, with its three crosses, red and white, on a blue field.

But first an important question had to be decided: how were the three crosses to be arranged on the flag? How this was done can be seen if we examine the Union Jack carefully. Across the middle the red cross of St. George is conspicuous, with its white border representing the white field, while the

The birth of Old Glory, the first flag of the United States. Under the skilful fingers of Betsy Ross and her helpers the thirteen stars and thirteen stripes were fashioned into a flag that is now dear to some 120,000,000 people.

two other crosses are clearly seen, the one with its blue field and the other with its white border, or fimbriation (fĭm′brĭ-ā′shŭn) as the heralds call it. To make everything fair, the white cross occupies the upper position in the first and third quarters, and the red cross has the corresponding place of honour in the second and fourth quarters.

The Flag of the Vikings

The first flag to be planted in the New World may well have been the black raven on a white field, the emblem of the vikings. Columbus carried with him a quartered flag of red and silver and gold that bore a lion and a castle, the emblems of his patrons Ferdinand and Isabella of Spain. Five years later John Cabot planted somewhere in Nova Scotia the flag of Henry VII of England—a white flag bearing the red cross of St. George. But it was the flag of a united England and Scotland that accompanied the first permanent English settlers to Virginia in 1607.

The stars and stripes of the United States flag tell a whole story about the country's valiant fight for freedom under Washington.

In the beginning, every colony—and even every body of militia—had a flag of its own in addition to the common flag of the country to which they all belonged. Among these may be mentioned the pine-tree flag of Massachusetts and the silver crescent on a blue ground of South Carolina. Various flags bearing the image of a rattlesnake were flown among the colonists when trouble began to brew with England, and one of them carried the warning "Don't tread on me." Surely it was no accident that some of the crude serpents on these flags had thirteen rattles on their tails, one for each of the colonies.

The Birth of Old Glory

It was only when Washington went to take command of the army at Boston, in 1775, that the thirteen stripes appeared. These were combined with thirteen stars to represent the union.

The honour of sewing the first flag together fell to Mrs. Elizabeth Griscom Ross of Philadelphia, who was noted for her skill with the needle.

Old Glory, as the flag is affectionately known to Americans, remains to-day just as it was, except that forty-eight stars have taken the place of the original thirteen, as one state after another has entered the union.

With the creation of new countries and the amalgamation of existing ones after the World War several new flags came into being. Some were quite new; others were variations on the old flags. The colours on the old flag of Serbia and Montenegro, for instance, were red, blue and white, and the same colours have been used for the flag of the new state of Yugoslavia, which embraces these two kingdoms. The only difference is the order in which the colours are arranged. The old tricolour of Serbia and Montenegro had the top stripe red, the middle one blue, and the lowest white. In the Yugoslavian flag the blue stripe comes at the top, the red at the bottom, and the white in between.

The Flags of Austria and Hungary

Again, in the case of Austria, the change has been very slight. The old flag of Austria had three horizontal stripes of red, white and red, and that of Hungary three horizontal stripes of red, white and green, while in the flag of the Dual Monarchy the green of Hungary appeared in the lowest stripe halved with the red. The only change in the present Austrian flag is the omission of the green; the bottom stripe is now entirely red, the flag thus assuming its original appearance.

Very similar to the Austrian flag is that of the new Baltic state of Latvia. The colours are similar, and they are shown in the same order, but the red stripes are much darker and twice as wide as the white. Another of the new Baltic states, Estonia, has a horizontal tricolour of blue, black and white.

The flag of the amalgam of states known as Czechoslovakia has two horizontal stripes —white above and red below—with a triangle of blue extending from the staff to the middle of the field. A similarly disposed triangle, red in colour, appears in the flag of the new Arabian kingdom of Hejaz, in which the stripes are black, green and white placed horizontally. The flag of the Union of Socialist Soviet Republics has a red ground and displays in the left-hand upper corner a golden sickle and hammer surmounted by a five-pointed red star with a gold border.

If you will turn to the colour plates, you will there find the flags of most of the nations of the world, and you will be able to obtain a far better idea of their actual appearance than by merely reading a description of them.

From early times armies carried flags and banners into the field with them. Regiments still have their special flags, or colours, although they are not now taken on active service, but are deposited in churches or public buildings until the return of the regiments. Here is a parade of regimental colours during a military tattoo.

THE FIRST MAN TO REACH THE NORTH POLE

Here is a portrait of Robert Edwin Peary, the first man to reach the North Pole. On the right is his little ship, the '' Roosevelt,'' which carried him through icy waters on the first lap of his hazardous journey. Below are two of his sleds, drawn by hardy Eskimo dogs, which hauled his supplies on the dangerous dash to the Pole.

How the NORTH POLE was DISCOVERED

The Enduring Story of the Fearless and Hardy Explorers who Braved the Unknown Dangers of the Arctic Wastes

"STARS and Stripes nailed to the Pole." These were the words of the historic telegram that reached the White House, the residence of the president of the United States, on September 6, 1909, from Indian Harbour, in Labrador. It was signed by Robert Edwin Peary. This man had at last reached the North Pole, exactly five months earlier, and he had just returned to the first place from which he could let the world know about it.

Explorers had been searching through the frozen north for many a century before this, and had even been trying to reach the Pole for a long time. Nothing that they had ever attempted had been more daring or more perilous. The long account of their heroic efforts is full of bravery and tragedy.

Many centuries ago the people living around the Mediterranean thought the world was a flat disk surrounded by the great river Oceanus. They knew little about any region far away, but they liked to imagine such places—for instance, the places that must lie to the north beyond the Alps and the mountains of the Balkans. From those regions came some of the tin for making bronze, and the amber that was worn as ornaments.

But there was no reliable account of the north, so the poets used to invent marvellous tales about it. Homer tells us of the Cimmerians (sĭ-mēr′ĭ-ǎn) who lived far to the

917

north in a land of perpetual darkness, and about a race of giants who lived in a place where the nights were so short that one shepherd driving out his flock for the day might meet another bringing in his sheep for the night. And there were many other tales. They show that those who told them knew *something* about the north—for example, the fact of the shortness of the nights in summer—but only very, very little, and nearly all of which was wrong.

First True Story of the North

Bit by bit, little by little, people learned more. About 500 B.C., a man from Carthage named Himlico made a great voyage north, apparently as far as Ireland, and wrote the story of his trip. It is the first true story of the north we know. Nearly two hundred years later, about 325 B.C., a Greek named Pytheas (pĭth'ē-ȧs), living in the town that was then Massalia and is now called Marseilles, sailed to Britain and saw the tin mines of Cornwall. Later he skirted the eastern coast of Britain to its northernmost point; and there he heard about the land of Thule (thū'lē), on the edge of the frozen ocean, where half of the year was day and half of it night. This was probably the northern part of Norway, and it is possible Pytheas may have visited it. So Pytheas was the first man to discover a little of the real truth about the Arctic, and indeed approached very near to the Arctic Circle.

It was still more than a thousand years before any reliable account was written of the Arctic. During that long time many people, especially the Romans, found out a great deal about the northern coasts of Europe. Many years later, King Alfred

Photo by W. S. Berridge

This little inhabitant of the Arctic has just taken an invigorating plunge into his icy bath, and is poking his head above the ice to see if anyone would like to join him. He is one of the few creatures that dwell in the far-off polar regions.

had a very interesting visitor named Ohthere (ō'thĕr-ĕ) who recounted how he had, in about A.D. 870, sailed north along the coast of Norway and then east as far as what we now call the White Sea. We still have the story as King Alfred wrote it down. So the first man to bring back a story from the Arctic that has come down to us in writing was a Scandinavian, and the man who put the story into writing was an Anglo-Saxon. And from that day to this, most of the polar expeditions have been made by men of Scandinavian or Saxon blood. These races have always produced many sailors, and have always been extremely hardy.

King Alfred wrote his story about the year 890. But long before that other men from Scandinavia had been sailing the icy northern seas. They had found Iceland and settled in it. From that island and from their own mainland they had set out boldly year after year to search for land and treasure. Just about a hundred years after Ohthere's voyage, the famous Eric the Red, an Icelander, set out to the west across the waters and landed on the coast of Greenland. So men had sailed already far beyond the farthest land that any Roman ever dreamed of seeing.

For three years Eric sailed up and down the shores of Greenland in search of suitable places to settle. He found several of these. Then he returned home, and in a few years revisited Greenland with twenty shiploads of colonists. Just try to imagine what it was like to settle down in Greenland nearly a thousand years ago!

From the time of Eric to that of Columbus there was no great interest in exploring the frozen north. But once Columbus had claimed the New World for Spain, various

Photo by Rischgitz

IMPRISONED IN A WORLD OF CRUEL ICE

Nature did not intend that any but the most hardy and experienced should conquer this forbidding country, where the desert wastes of snow are swept by gales and fearful blizzards, and the harbours are locked with great ice floes.

other nations began to send out men to see what they could discover. Many of them went north, especially if they already lived in the northern part of Europe. As early as 1497 England sent out John Cabot and his son Sebastian. They reached the great island of Newfoundland, and sailed many miles along the coast of America, which they thought was Asia.

What Cabot Was Looking For

Cabot never dreamed of looking for the North Pole, any more than did Eric the Red. That dream was to be born in men's minds many years later. When Cabot and the men who followed him went far north, they were all looking for something very different. They wanted to find a way to China.

That was what had sent Columbus across the ocean. He had set out hoping he could reach Asia by going west across the water. Even when it was found that America was not Asia, the explorers continued their efforts to find a way *through* America to Asia. And they tried many routes, north and south; one of them, Henry Hudson, thought he might get through by way of the Hudson River, which is named after him. But as time passed, explorers realized that the way to Asia, if there was one, must be along the northern coast of North America—it must be the North-west Passage. And the North-west Passage was what many brave explorers in the Arctic toiled in vain to find.

The Lure of the Mysterious North

As time went on, however, they discovered more and more about the Arctic Zone, and penetrated farther and farther north. Finally the imagination of some of them was fired to attempt to reach the Pole, mainly for the sake of daring and curiosity.

Before we come to the men who were trying to get to the Pole, we must say something about those who were attempting to reach Asia.

One of the first was Martin Frobisher (frō'bĭsh-ĕr), an Englishman who made three voyages, beginning in 1576. On his last trip he took with him some colonists, but they decided that the country around Labrador was no place in which to settle. Frobisher's name was given to the bay that he discovered. Then came a skilled sea captain named John Davis, who also made three voyages, in 1585 and the two following years. On one of these he penetrated as far north as 72° 41'—seventy-two degrees and forty-one minutes of latitude, or about twelve hundred miles from the Pole. He gave his name to the great Davis Strait.

In 1616 William Baffin followed in the path of Davis and discovered the great body of water known as Baffin Bay. He journeyed about 350 miles farther north than Davis, to 77° 45'; that was the farthest north that any man had ever gone, and the farthest anyone was to go for the next two hundred years.

The End of Henry Hudson

A little before Baffin, Henry Hudson had sailed up the Hudson River in 1609, and in the following year had gone north and discovered the vast bay that bears his name. Somewhere in its frozen reaches he met his end; for his mutinous crew set him and his young son and some sick men adrift in a small boat and they were never heard of again.

All of these explorers had but a vague idea of the size and shape of the world, or they would never have tried to discover a route to China by sailing up the Hudson. But they were slowly finding out the truth, and after Davis and Baffin the

idea of a North-west Passage to China or India was more or less abandoned. So there was little exploration in the Arctic for the next two hundred years.

Then an English captain, William Scoresby, came back from one of his whaling trips and wrote a fine book called "Account of the Arctic Regions," which helped to arouse a great new interest in the region. In 1806 Scoresby got as far north as 81° 12'. In 1818 two exploring parties went out, one of them under Captain David Buchan (bŭk'ăn) and a young lieutenant named John Franklin, and the other under Captain John Ross and Lieutenant William Parry.

What William Parry Learned

They were still looking for a North-west Passage; and although in these and other trips they failed to find it, they brought back a good deal of information. Parry, in particular, learned that no explorer must expect to remain on board his ship in the farthest north, but must be ready to make his way over the ice in sleds and on foot. In this way he managed to penetrate as far as 82° 45'—the farthest north that had yet been reached, only seven and a half degrees from the Pole.

These men taught the world a great deal about the conditions and dangers of the far north, and also the best way in which to travel in those terrible regions. Travellers there had, first of all, to contend with the intense cold—it froze the mercury in the thermometers as hard as ice. Then there was the lack of food. When the men had to fight their way over miles and miles of snow-field and ice crags, it was very difficult to carry

Inhabitants of the northernmost countries sometimes keep their supplies in houses built on stilts; the taller the house, the less likelihood there is of its being snowed in.

sufficient food. There was also the scurvy, a terrible disease that often attacks those who cannot get green food to eat. And among many other troubles, there were the mosquitoes—for strange as it may seem, the swarms of these pests in the Arctic make

his goal at last—the mouth of the Coppermine River, far out west in northern Canada. He did not find the North-west Passage, but he was able to furnish some valuable information for later explorers.

Some of his ideas were adopted by Sir

HARDY INHABITANTS OF THE FROZEN NORTH

These are not explorers, but real Eskimos, who are quite at home in a temperature below zero. In the winter they live in huts built of stone and earth, or any material upon which they can lay their hands. There is practically no ventilation, and the heat from the blubber lamps is often unbearable. Sometimes, when they are not going to remain in one place for a very long period, they build neat little round houses of snow bricks.

the mosquitoes of other lands seem comparatively harmless creatures. To bear up under all these conditions one has to be a man of steel who knows no fear.

Samuel Hearne Sets Out

So far we have been dealing with sailors only, but there was also many a gallant man who tried to cross the Arctic region of America on land. The great Hudson Bay Company had a noble list of these bold spirits in their employ. In 1771 Samuel Hearne, a servant of that company, set out with four others from the western side of Hudson Bay. They had a single sled-load of supplies to provide for their wants on a journey across the Arctic wastes to the west.

The party met with terrible trials, and twice the men threatened to turn back and leave Hearne to his fate. They finally did so; but Hearne went on, without a firearm or a scrap of food. Each winter he managed to struggle into some Indian camp or some Hudson Bay post; each summer he pushed on west. After four years of this he reached

John Franklin—the same John Franklin we mentioned a moment ago—who became the greatest Arctic explorer of his day. In 1819 he set out across Hearne's country and travelled under heart-breaking conditions to the Coppermine River and back—a distance of nearly six thousand miles across the lonely wastes. This was followed by still further explorations and by other services to his country. And then, more than twenty-five years after his first trip, he set out upon his fatal voyage to the north.

The Vain Search for Franklin

He had two ships, and took supplies for three years. When two full years had passed without a word from him, the world began to grow anxious, and exploring parties started out from France and from America as well as from England, in the hope of finding him and his hundred or more men. No trace of him could be discovered, although the search parties learned a good deal that was new about the Arctic. The story of the various expeditions sent out from England in a vain effort to rescue Franklin has been told elsewhere in this work. Although unsuccessful in their primary objective, the leaders of these expeditions were able to explore much hitherto unknown country, and succeeded also in charting more than six thousand miles of coast-line. It was discovered later that Franklin had died.

Among others who went to search for Franklin was Dr. Elisha Kane, an American. In 1853 he went north again, and this time he was attempting to reach the Pole; but his ship was locked in the ice for nearly two years. The food ran short, and scurvy broke out. After great suffering Kane and his party abandoned the ship and made their way on foot for thirteen hundred miles to a town in Greenland. All but one arrived there safely.

The search for the unfortunate Franklin had fired the American nation with an eagerness to be first to achieve the honour of reaching the Pole, and soon one party after another set out on the seemingly impossible task, each one meeting with extreme hardship but little real success. But although they failed to gratify their fondest hopes, they did succeed in adding considerably to our knowledge of the Arctic regions.

In 1860 Dr. Isaac Hayes made the perilous attempt. In 1871 Charles Francis Hal' sailed north, only to die in the Arctic snow, though his men returned. In 1879 Lieutenant George Washington De Long essayed the task, but he and all his men lost their lives. In 1881 Lieutenant Adolphus W. Greely set out on a voyage lasting three years. Nearly every one of these pushed a little farther north than man had ever gone before, and Greely reached a latitude of 83° 24'.

The English and Americans were by no means the only people trying to get to the Pole. Among the others there was Dr.

SPRING SETS FREE THE PRISONER OF THE ICE

In the spring the great ice sheets begin to break up, leaving channels, or "leads," through which boats may pass. What a welcome sight it must be for the men who have been frozen in during the long, dark winter!

Fridtjof Nansen (frēt'yŏf nän'sĕn), who nearly succeeded in 1895. He reached as far north as 86° 5'—only about two hundred miles from the Pole.

Nansen had long been in training for the feat. Seven years earlier he had crossed the ice plateau in Greenland and lived among the Eskimos through the winter, learning a great deal about life in the land of snows. Then in 1893 he started for the Pole with twelve other gallant men on the "Fram," a boat that he had built to withstand the crushing ice. He sailed from the north of Russia and then floated with the

Dr. Fridtjof Nansen, the famous Norwegian explorer, never reached the Pole, but he and his companion, Lieutenant Hjalmar Johansen spent a long year in the desolate Arctic. They were attacked by bears and walruses, were nearly frozen to death, and barely managed to return to civilization.

Arctic ice drift as near to the Pole as it would carry him. Then with dog sleds and provisions for a hundred days, and with only one companion, Nansen made the dash for the Pole. He pushed on until there was food left for only two weeks—and then he had to turn sadly back. But he had made a successful exploration, and justified his own surmises and plans.

And now we must leave the explorers of the Polar regions and turn for a moment to those who were still making valiant efforts to find the famous North-west Passage. They were convinced of its existence, though it was still amazingly hard to discover. But at last, more than four hundred years after the first man had set out to search for it, it was discovered. The man who found it

was a Norwegian named Roald Amundsen (ä'mŭn-sĕn). He set out in 1903 and remained icebound for three long winters; but in 1906 he finally reached Alaska. He had navigated the North-west Passage—but no one will ever use it as a route to China.

It should be added, however, that all this time there had been other navigators searching for a North-east Passage—a way to China through the icy seas north of Russia and Siberia. In 1553 Sir Hugh Willoughby had tried it, and had perished from starvation and exposure. Three years later Stephen Burrough had gone as far as the islands of Novaya Zemlya. During the next three centuries explorers kept on pushing farther eastward through the region. In 1873–4 an Austrian lieutenant, Julius Payer, discovered a new country there and named it Franz Josef Land, in honour of his emperor. Four years later the route west to east—the North-east Passage

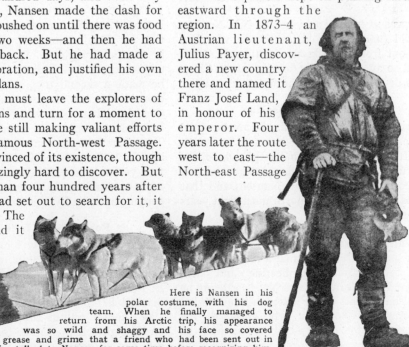

Here is Nansen in his polar costume, with his dog team. When he finally managed to return from his Arctic trip, his appearance was so wild and shaggy and his face so covered with grease and grime that a friend who had been sent out in search of him talked to Nansen for some time before recognizing him.

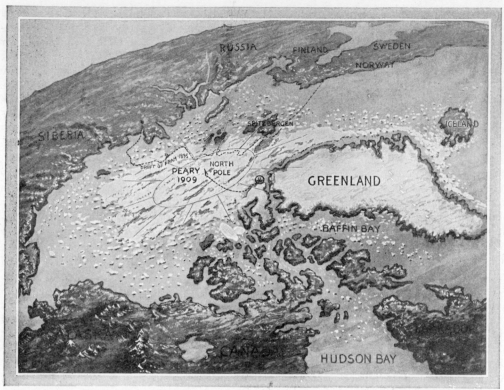

This is a map of the polar region showing the drift of the "Fram," Nansen's ship, and Peary's route to the Pole, which he reached in 1909 and found to be in an ocean of ice, miles from the nearest point of land.

—was successfully achieved by Nils Nordenskiöld (nŏr'dĕn-skyōld), a Swede, who had set out from Karlskrona on June 22, 1878. And so an easterly Arctic sea-route to China was discovered before the westerly route.

An Italian Expedition

And now we return to the discovery of the Pole. Six years after Nansen's attempt, an Italian expedition, under the duke of the Abruzzi (ä-brōōt'sē), managed to get eighteen miles farther north than Nansen; and that remained the farthest north until eight years later.

Robert Edwin Peary was destined to be the first man to reach the North Pole. He was born in Pennsylvania, U.S.A., in 1856. He studied civil engineering and then entered the United States Navy. Before he was thirty years old he was greatly interested in Arctic exploration. He knew all the dangers that explorers had to face and the disasters they so often met, and he thought

he could best fit himself for Arctic exploration by first learning all about conditions in the polar regions. In 1886 he made a trip to northern Greenland. Five years later he made a second trip, studied the people, crossed the ice plateau, and proved that Greenland has a northern shore line and so is an island—one of the largest in the world. Two years later he went again to Greenland, and in 1896 to Melville Bay. He made a four-year trip in 1898, during which time he made several long sled-journeys in the winter, coming back badly frost-bitten.

Robert Peary Tries Again

Peary now felt ready for a dash for the Pole. He set out in 1902, reached 84° 17' north latitude, and then had to turn back. In 1905 he made another trip, and this time reached 87° 6' north latitude. Finally, in 1908, he set out in the ship "Roosevelt" on his eighth trip, the one that was to bring him a well-earned reward. The ship made its way north as far as it could go, and then a sled party left it and made for the Pole. From time to time a few members of the party dropped out and set up a camp or station. With a chain of these behind him, Peary made sure that he would find help and food on the return journey. Then, with one negro servant and four Eskimos, and with supplies for forty days, Peary bade good-bye to those he left behind at the last station, and set out on the final dash to the

On July 11, 1897, he and two companions left Spitsbergen in a balloon. There was no way of steering it; their intention was simply to drift with the air currents across the Pole. A few hours after it left, a carrier pigeon came back with a message saying all was well. That was the last that was heard of the party. But thirty-three years later, in 1930, a group of Norwegian fishermen found the bodies of Andrée and his companions, with their equipment and their records, on White Island, not far from Spitsbergen. The balloon had remained aloft three days. When it landed, its passengers had started southwards on foot. The last entry in their diary was dated October 6, 1897.

Here is Peary's expedition on the march. They walked in Indian file, for as each sled or each man passed over the snow and trod it down, the path became a little easier for the man walking behind.

This monument at Cape Columbia marks the point from which Peary set out on his successful dash to the Pole.

Pole. He reached it on April 6, 1909. At last he stood on the "top of the world."

A few days before Peary sent his telegram announcing his success, another American, Dr. Frederick A. Cook, cabled from the Shetland Islands

This is Peary at the Pole calculating his position with instruments. As a matter of fact, he passed over the Pole twice in his march before he managed to determine its exact position.

that he had reached the Pole about a year before. When Dr. Cook's claims were examined, the scientists decided that he had never reached the Pole at all. They did, however, give him credit for notable explorations in the Arctic regions.

Even before the aeroplane was perfected, attempts had been made to reach the North Pole by air. The first was undertaken by Salomon A. Andrée, a Swedish scientist.

The next attempts to reach the North Pole by balloon were made by an American journalist, Walter Wellman. Having already tried several times to reach the Pole by sled, he attempted to get there in a balloon in 1906, 1907, and 1909, but failed on each occasion.

With the coming of the aeroplane and the dirigible airship, various flyers tried to reach the Pole by air. The first was Roald Amundsen, the hardy Norwegian who had discovered the North-west Passage. He and

Lincoln Ellsworth set out by aeroplane from Spitsbergen on May 21, 1925, but they were unsuccessful, and were compelled to make their way back to Spitsbergen on foot, and reached there on June 15.

The next year the North Pole was first crossed by aircraft. On May 9, 1926, Lieutenant-Commander Richard E. Byrd and pilot Floyd Bennett, of the United States Navy, flew in an aeroplane from Spitsbergen to the Pole and back in a single day. They were favoured with excellent weather, and made the trip of more than fifteen hundred miles in about sixteen hours. Two days later, a dirigible, named the "Norge," carrying its Italian designer, General Umberto Nobile (nŏ-bē'lĕ), Roald Amundsen, Lincoln Ellsworth and several other men, left Spitsbergen and flew over the Pole to Teller, in Alaska. The flight of more than 2,700 miles was made in seventy-one hours despite high winds and heavy fog.

Once aviators had learned that flying is possible in Arctic regions, and once the North Pole had been passed over by air, other daring airmen were eager for the flight. Some were successful, others met with failure. On April 15, 1928, Captain Hubert Wilkins flew from Point Barrow, in Alaska, across the Pole, and after a delay of several days he continued his flight to Spitsbergen. The distance of 2,200 miles across the snowy wastes was accomplished in twenty and a half hours of actual flying. Captain Wilkins was knighted on his return.

That same year a further tragedy of Arctic exploration occurred. In May, General Nobile, the Italian who had reached the Pole in the "Norge" in 1926, started from Spitsbergen in that airship, which had been renamed "Italia." In the near-polar regions the airship became disabled and crashed, and later floated away with some members of the crew, leaving the others stranded on the ice. The survivors sent a wireless message for help, and at once explorers from various countries set out to the rescue. Aften ten weeks a Russian rescue ship found the party and brought them home.

Nobile and all but one of his crew were saved, but the famous Norwegian explorer, Roald Amundsen, who had gone in an aeroplane to search for the party, was never heard of again. His five companions were also numbered among the missing.

In 1931 Sir Hubert Wilkins made another journey to the Arctic regions. This time he went in a submarine, the "Nautilus," but his plan of crossing under the Pole had to be abandoned as the submarine was damaged by ice.

The silent north is still far from safe, even for those who know it best. Yet all its dangers fail to keep men at home. For until the spirit of adventure dies in the human race, there will always be brave souls to whom the threat of death is only a challenge. Our earth, even to its most forbidding corners, is nearly all conquered, but the spirit of its conquerors still lives on.

The ill-fated "Italia," veteran of the successful expedition of 1926 when, as the "Norge," it passed over the North Pole, is shown here moored near its hangar before starting out on its last journey in May, 1928.

IN THE DARK DAYS WHEN MIGHT WAS RIGHT

Never was there such a time of contrasts as the Middle Ages. No task was too arduous for the saint to perform in the service of his religion; nothing was too cruel for the strong to do to the weak. Nearly everybody was either immensely rich or miserably poor. Our picture hints at some of these things. Here are strong men, well mounted and armed, forcing the weak and the old to racking labour far too heavy for their feeble strength.

EVERYDAY LIFE *in the* MIDDLE AGES

Conditions in Europe During the Thousand Years of Government Under the Feudal System

(CONTINUED FROM PAGE 902)

LET US pretend that someone has invented a time machine in which we can fly back a thousand years and see how people were living in what we call the Middle Ages. We shall begin, not with the palace of the king or the stone castle of the great baron, but at the other end of the social scale, in the hut of the poorest man of all—the villein (vĭl'ĕn) or serf.

This hut may be in a tiny clearing in a great forest, it may be beneath the frowning walls of a castle, or on the broad lands of a monastery. But, wherever it is, it is almost certain to be one of a little group of huts that belong to the serfs who work their lord's land, and to be poorer than we of the present day can realize.

The peasant of the Middle Ages is practically a barbarian. He can talk, but he knows nothing of reading and writing. His home is the meanest kind of hut—many a boy could build a better one. There are no windows and no chimney. A few farm animals, nothing like our plump cattle of to-day, wander about, in and out of the house. Rain drips through the roof, and the wind howls through the wide cracks in the wall.

The hut is as dirty as it is poor. There is no floor, except the hard packed earth, and that is covered with scraps and refuse of all kinds. The floor probably serves also for a bed. The fireplace, at one side, is of dried mud.

If we talk to the peasant, and ask him why he or his son does not leave this wretched hovel and go to live elsewhere, he will look at us in surprise and tell us that it would be against the law. He, his family, and all that he possesses, belong to the land—and the land belongs to his lord, to the owner of his hut. If the land changes hands, the serfs attached to it change hands with it, just as if they were barns or cattle. He may not even marry without his lord's permission. He must work his lord's land, as well as the little scattered strips he calls his own, and of the animals and grain he raises a certain proportion must go to his lord. More than that, at any time his own little fields may be overrun by soldiers—either his lord's or another's — who will rob him of what little he has and leave him destitute; for there is no law to protect his rights.

Thus he lives, with his fellow serfs, huddled together in a little village along a single street, just outside his lord's great gate. There is a church, a mill, and a smithy, and a plot of "common" land where everyone may let his pigs and chickens run. From his lord's woodland he will get his firewood, and from the flocks of sheep that roam the pastures will come the wool that his womenfolk will weave into rough homespun and dye with colours made from garden herbs. He tans his own leather, and his bees supply him with a little honey and the wax to make candles for the church.

It is easy to see that his little village is a small world in itself. His lord's domain—which is known as the "manor"—provides him and his fellows with everything they need. Even justice is dealt out to them by the lord at the court he holds in his great hall. All they have to obtain from the world outside are salt and iron, occasionally a millstone, tar to use when the sheep get the scab, and a few drugs like camphor and laudanum. This simple list will be bought at the annual fair, which is held in the neighbouring town. That fair is the poor serf's one opportunity to see a little of the world— the great yearly event in his monotonous round of labour.

By good fortune we have a record of what one Hugh Miller and seventeen other serfs owed every year to their lord, the abbot of Peterborough. Different lords made different demands, but this is probably a fair example of what every serf had to pay.

Hugh had twenty-five acres of the monastery land on which to support himself and his family; and though its yield was poor according to our modern standards, and though a third of his allotment always had to lie fallow, Hugh was nevertheless glad to know that when he died it would not go out of his family. But for the right to hold his little plot Hugh had to work for the abbot three days out of every week, except for a week at Christmas, one at Easter, and one at Whitsuntide, in May or June. The other three days he could work for himself.

He must provide the abbot with a bushel of wheat, eighteen sheaves of oats, three hens, and one cock every year—and five eggs at Easter. If he sold a brood mare for ten shillings or more, he must give the abbot fourpence—about three per cent, and if his daughter married he must make a payment to the abbot. Besides all this he had to

Photo by German National Rlys.

In days when robbers swarmed through woods and highways and one's nearest powerful neighbour might any day become one's enemy in war, the mediaeval baron made his house of thick, strong stone and often set it high up on a hill. This castle has been added to in modern times, but parts of the old walls stand.

THE LITTLE WORLD OVER WHICH A LORD RULED IN THE MIDDLE AGES

In some such way as this a mediaeval lord's domain was laid out. Each part has been labelled so that we may understand its special use in the life of the people. In the midst stands the castle, a fortress for defence and a home for the lord's family and his many servants and retainers. Beyond its walls are the huts of the serfs, and the church. There is a pasture for grazing, a woodland to furnish fuel, and a pond for fish. Each serf has his little square of land to till, but he must work on his lord's land as well; and a third of the land has to lie fallow each year. Somewhere on the domain there is probably a blacksmith's shop and a mill.

cart goods to the neighbouring towns whenever the abbot told him to do so. Of course none of this included the heavy church tax Hugh had to pay in his own parish. The Millers could scarcely have lived lavishly.

Yet it was on this hard-worked peasant that the whole structure of society in the Middle Ages rested. On the food that he laboured so hard to produce, monasteries and castles and the courts of kings depended for their rich incomes. But in return for all his grinding toil he was, it is true, protected by the strong arm of his lord; and that was a very great advantage in those times.

It is pleasant to be able to say that before the Middle Ages were over, conditions had changed a good deal. Hugh Miller's descendants were no longer bound to the land, and the law would protect them more directly. They could marry when and whom they pleased, and could even go to live in the town and learn a trade if they wished to do so.

But let us take a closer look at Hugh Miller's hut. Practically the only cooking utensil his wife possesses is a huge iron pot. Into it she puts whatever there is to eat—a rabbit, a little pig, or perhaps a chicken or dove—and all are boiled to make the meal. Potatoes, beetroots and tomatoes are all unknown to the good folk of the Middle Ages, and, of course, the boiling takes the flavour out of the most delicious meat. But no one can help that. With long wooden spoons the stew is ladled out on to wooden plates, or "trenchers," and the meat is picked off the bone with the teeth. There are no forks in the Middle Ages. King and peasant alike must gnaw the bones of the "sodden," or boiled, meat that is put before them.

In the richer homes we shall find this sodden meat flavoured with spices. Spices are precious, because the boiled meat is so tasteless, and they are the most important commodities that come over the long trade routes from Asia into Europe.

In the great castle, which we shall next visit, perfumes as well as spices are a necessary luxury. And the perfumes are not delicate like those which ladies use to-day. They are strong perfumes, because people in the Middle Ages seldom or never take baths. The ladies of the castle use musk or ambergris (ăm'bẽr-grēs), and the banquet hall is often sprinkled with pleasant odours, in order to mask unpleasant ones.

Let us ride up to the great "hall," the stone castle in which the knight and his lady live. This castle may cover a good deal of ground, and if it is not built on a rocky crag, it is surrounded by water—by a river which forms a defence against enemies, or by a moat which has been dug and filled with water.

We clatter over the drawbridge and under the heavy iron portcullis (pōrt-kŭl'ĭs)—a hanging door which is drawn up to allow us to pass through, but which may be lowered at any time on the approach of an enemy. We are now in the castle yard.

It is a broad open space, filled with life. Pages hurry hither and thither on errands, or perhaps gather in little groups to gossip and play. Armourers are busy mending or making armour or harness for the knight and his men-at-arms. The men-at-arms themselves idle about, playing at dice or bowls, and teasing the serving-maids who manage to find business out of doors on such a pleasant day.

Inside, in the kitchen, a bright fire is burning, and a cook's boy is turning before the fire a pig fastened on a spit—a slender, pointed rod run through the animal. The floor is strewn with rushes, which are replaced now and then with fresh ones. This is a very necessary proceeding, for all sorts of mess and refuse fall to the floor. Dogs wander in and out, hoping for scraps or bones. No one is very careful about keeping things neat and shining, but the wives and daughters of the serfs are busy, baking and brewing and making cheese to set forth the stupendous meals that the lord and his men are able to eat. For eating is one of their chief diversions, and their capacity is almost unbelievable to us to-day.

For table service there are the same wooden trenchers, with knives for cutting up the meat, and an enormous cup for the drink. We may see this cup go from hand to hand round the long table in the great hall. No one expects to have a cup to himself.

The great hall is dining-room, council

THE BOWMEN OF ENGLAND

It was not only Robin Hood and his Merry Men who were skilled at archery in the Middle Ages. The bow was, in many armies, the most important weapon of the common soldier; and since that was so, rulers naturally encouraged their people to practise archery as a sport. In the later part of the 14th century there was a law in force in England that prohibited any sport other than archery to be practised on a Sunday.

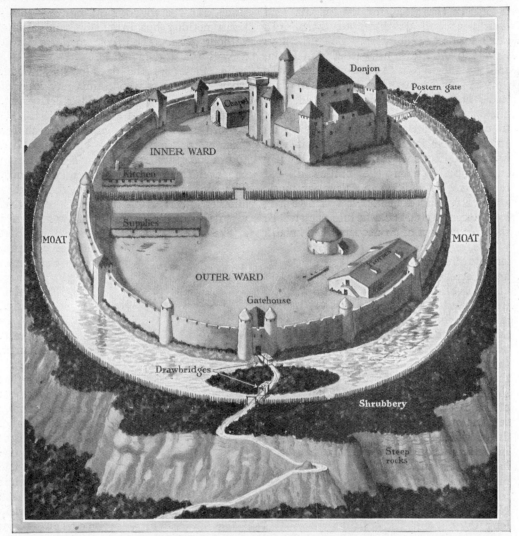

INNER WARD

Donjon

Postern gate

Chapel

Kitchen

MOAT

Supplies

OUTER WARD

MOAT

Gatehouse

Drawbridges

Shrubbery

Steep rocks

WHAT A MEDIAEVAL CASTLE LOOKED LIKE

The next time you read a mediaeval romance like "Ivanhoe," you need not be puzzled by its talk of "postern-gates" and "moats" and "donjon keeps." For here is a typical castle drawn in the form of a diagram which shows every part clearly. A postern-gate, by the way, is merely a private entrance—a back door. The main gate is heavily guarded and can be approached only by way of the drawbridge. The donjon is the central fortification, and the castle yard around it is divided into two parts, the inner and the outer wards.

chamber, living-room, and for most of the people in the castle even a bedroom. It is an immense, draughty place. The stone walls are hung with tapestries to make them less dreary, and hangings in front of the doors keep out the wind. All about are deer antlers, fox-brushes, and other trophies of the chase; and if you know just the correct whistle, a falcon will come and perch on your arm.

The tapestries have been made by the lord's lady and her women, working in their "bower," a smaller room, perhaps in the great tower beside the hall. Sometimes it is just a little closet cut in the thick wall. In this bower the little girls are taught needlework, and the tapestries are wrought with quaint pictures of landscapes and of famous deeds of war and peace. When everyone gathers in the hall, to listen to the tales of travellers or hear the minstrels sing, the fingers of the lady and her maidens are never idle.

There are always plenty of people about

to enliven the place, for the knights send their sons and daughters to their lord's castle for proper education. There the boys serve as pages, learn a smattering of Latin, and, as they grow up, become the lord's squires. As squires they must clean their lord's horses, make their lord's bed, help him to dress and undress, learn to dance, to carve a joint or a fowl, to cut up an animal killed in the chase, to hunt with hawk and hounds, and to fight bravely and skilfully upon the battlefield. If they have, in addition, a talent for music and poetry, and can compose verses to sing to an accompaniment on the lute, they will be the very pattern of an accomplished knight.

The maidens learn to direct the housekeeping in the castle, to weave and sew and embroider, and to doctor and nurse the sick. In these early times their life is very simple. The lady of the castle herself has only one dress, which she inherited from her mother and may hand down to her daughter. Neighbours are a long way off, and castle life is dull and dreary.

As the centuries pass, life grows more and more elegant; the great hall, with its vast fireplace, its gorgeous hangings, and its gallery of minstrels, sees more and more mirth and magnificent entertainment. Women, too, are more and more respected.

Below the castle floor are the store-rooms; and here, too, are the dungeons, underground cells where miserable prisoners fret their lives away. The walls are massively built of stone, and the windows are narrow—sometimes nothing but little slits, and always without glass. The whole castle is a fort as well as a dwelling-place.

For these are the days of knighthood, when every man who claims any kind of social position is either a soldier or a priest. We call it the age of chivalry (shĭv'ăl-rĭ)— a word that comes from the French for "knight" or "horseman." Every knight had to win his spurs by some brave deed; for no one, even the king, was born to knighthood. The honour was received from the hand of another knight, often on the field of battle, when the candidate knelt and was given a stroke on the side of the neck with the flat side of a sword, while the person knighting him said, "I dub thee knight," "Arise, Sir Knight," or some such phrase.

But the Church, aided by the romantic tales that people loved in those days, finally made the ideal of the perfect knight a very noble one indeed for the Church did her utmost to teach the cruel, lawless nobles that knighthood was almost like priesthood in its duty of service. In the later Middle Ages the ceremony of knighting a man always took place in a church, after the candidate had fasted and "watched his arms" all night alone before the altar. His arms were blessed by the priest, who told him solemnly that it was now his duty to be pure, honest, and true, to protect the Church, revere womanhood, and rescue all who were oppressed.

These qualities of a perfect knight were

A KNIGHT PUTS ON HIS SUIT OF MAIL

It was no simple matter to arm a knight for battle or tourney, for his armour was elaborate and heavy. It was usually the part of the ladies of the household to perform this task. The Knight shown in the picture is about to buckle on his sword.

summed up in the sorrowful tribute paid to Sir Lancelot after his death at the hand of one of the other knights of King Arthur's Round Table:

"Thou wert the courtliest knight that ever bare shield, and thou wert the truest friend

travelled on horseback from castle to castle, for sometimes a single lord owned many castles and manors, and when the supplies had been exhausted for the time being on one domain, his household moved on to another. It was easier than bringing the

Photo by Rischgitz

A PASTIME OF THE MIDDLE AGES

War was not only the business of life to the mediaeval knight, it was his sport besides. Young knights would joust at a festival, and huge glittering tournaments were often arranged at which many a knightly reputation was won or lost. The king himself might be a spectator; and unlucky was the combatant who could not steal a glance before the combat from the eye of the fair lady whose favour he wore. Sometimes the knights fought in single combat, or on occasion there would be two or three or even fifty or more on each side.

. . . that ever bestrode horse, and thou wert the truest lover . . . that ever loved woman, and thou wert the kindest man that ever struck with sword, and thou wert the goodliest person that ever came among the press of knights, and thou wert the meekest man and the gentlest that ever ate in hall among the ladies, and thou wert the sternest knight to thy mortal foe that ever put spear in breast."

In the muddy path which served as a road to lead away from the castle, a crowd of people was always going to and fro about their business. The lords and their families

produce many weary miles over the bad roads, and cheaper too.

There were also pilgrims going to some far-off holy place and seeing the world on the way. There were humble serfs, like our friend Hugh Miller, carrying their produce to the monastery, sometimes many miles away. For the monks could not move their household from place to place, as the nobles could.

We can imagine a body of professional soldiers galloping along, their horses' hoofs striking sparks from the loose stones of the ill-kept road. If we talk to one of these soldiers he may tell us of the many battles he has seen, now on this side, now on that. He has hardly any real home; fighting is his life, and he will hire himself out to the man who will pay him best.

Next we may see a soberly-clad monk jogging along on his plump horse. Perhaps he is thinking of the learned book his tired hand has been so many days in copying, or of the remedy he will give an ailing peasant woman when next she calls; or it may be he is thinking only of the hot meal that awaits him within the abbey walls.

If we turn aside to see the monastery where our monk lives, we may find it less a fort than the knight's castle, but nevertheless provided with ample means of defence against attack. For in these times no house is safe, not even the house of God, and often the bishops and abbots are able warriors, who know how to lead their forces into battle.

Within the monastery is a schoolroom where the young monks on probation—they are called novices (nŏv′ĭs)—learn to read and write in Latin. There is a library, too; a cold, stone-walled room furnished with high benches, where monks are busy copying manuscripts. Sometimes the precious book from which the copies are made is chained to the heavy table. In the sheltered cloister, which is open on the side facing the garden around which it is built, other monks are busy copying and adding those delicate "illuminations," or coloured decorations, which make their manuscripts so beautiful to our eyes.

In the refectory, or dining-hall, of the monastery we may chance to see a pilgrim recently returned from one of the holy places sacred to some saint or martyr; perhaps he has even been to far-off Jerusalem. He will

Most of the books in the Middle Ages were in the monasteries, and in those days before printing monks did nearly all the copying of old books and most of the writing of new ones.

tell strange stories of his pilgrimages and of the news he has heard in other lands, and if he has been to the Holy Land his hat will be trimmed with scallop shells. All listen intently to his words, and all long to follow him to interesting countries, where men's heads are said to grow beneath their shoulders, or where that marvellous bird called the phoenix (fē′nĭks) rises out of its own ashes once in every five hundred years. No story is too amazing to be believed by these simple-minded folk.

Thus far we have been wandering in the country, where the majority of men, except the monks, are either very rich or very poor, and where the rich live in a different world from that of the poor peasant. The monks stand, in a sense, between rich and poor, but even so there is no great middle class in the Middle Ages, such as we have to-day. Men are at the top or at the bottom of the ladder, and there are hardly any rungs on which to climb. If you are born near the bottom, you remain where you are—unless you become a priest or monk. In that case, you may climb as high as your talents and fortune will take you.

Let us look next at a town of feudal Europe, with its narrow streets, sometimes only five feet wide, and its crowded, top-heavy houses. Often the houses are built with the second story jutting out over the street. For the first floor may well be devoted to a little shop that in the day-time lets down its wooden shutters and is open to the street, under the shelter of the upper story.

You must be careful as you walk along, for out of any window may come flying a mass of rubbish, or a pail of dirty water, or some even less savoury refuse. The dogs

Photo by J. Laurent

Some towns present to-day a picture which does not differ greatly from their appearance long ago in the Middle Ages. This panoramic view of Avila, in Spain, shows it still surrounded by its mediaeval wall and towers.

Photo by German National Rlys.

This is the delightful little city of Nuremberg, in Germany, where one may still see the crowded, steeprooted mediaeval houses, and the great mediaeval citadel of the Kaiserschloss, or "Imperial Castle," looking down as of old from the hill on the north side of the town. Parts of the old walls and the moat still remain to be seen.

act as dustmen, and clean away all the edible rubbish; but even then the street is very filthy. Pigs come and go as they please, and here the stench is unrelieved by spice or perfume.

Small wonder that pestilences attack the people now and again! In 1348 the Black Death—perhaps the bubonic plague or typhus fever—swept into Europe from Asia, and in England alone carried off about a third of the population. The crops rotted in the fields; everywhere life stagnated; and the very wheels of government stood still.

But town life has its lighter side, just the same, with cock-fighting, bear-baiting, wrestling, dancing, and hawking and hunting outside the city walls. It is a noisy place, for the town-criers go about shouting important news, and at dawn the various pedlars begin to cry their wares—meat, fish, cheese, onions, honey, pepper, charcoal, old clothes, flowers—almost everything but soap. On holidays there are sure to be religious processions, with perhaps a play produced by the weavers or candle makers or some other group of skilled workmen. And there is a steady coming and going of knights and nobles and churchmen to and from the castle or monastery near at hand.

Crowded inside the city walls we shall find rich and poor, high and low, just as we did in the country. Many of our townspeople make a living by serving in the great houses of knight, abbot, duke, or king. Many follow the trades of baker, armourer, carpenter, blacksmith, barber, and the like. And many are skilled labourers working with their fellows in a sort of union known as a craft guild.

A craft guild is simply an association of all the workers in one particular trade. Let us pause in the street and question that busy fellow in the leather apron. Perhaps we can find out about his guild, the guild of the silversmiths. These men in the Middle Ages always have time to talk. It is one of their chief pastimes. He tells us that the city we are in needs the services of some forty silversmiths, who all live here in this street and receive for their work a fair wage —perhaps a penny a day. These forty silversmiths have banded together to control conditions in their trade. They have agreed that they will not teach the secrets of working in silver to more than a certain number of apprentices each year.

How the Apprentice Took a Place in the Family of His Master

The apprentices will work for their keep during a given number of years—three years in most trades, but as much as ten if they are to be goldsmiths. Their duties and rights are all regulated. It is understood that their master must treat them as sons, and in return they are to perform errands for him, attend to opening and closing the shop, and work faithfully at their trade. In some ways they are better off than the master's sons, for they are not to be made to wash dishes or tend the baby, and the master's wife may not beat them.

At the end of their apprenticeship they become members of the guild and are called "journeymen," for they often work for wages by the day—or "journée." If they have sufficient money, and can execute a fine piece of work to show their skill, they may become "masters," and take other apprentices and journeymen to work for them. It is interesting to know that the final piece of work, which is like an examination, is called the "masterpiece." That is how this now familiar word came into our language.

The silversmiths' guild has also decided upon other conditions under which they will work. They take care of disabled members and their families, and they meet at certain times in the year to make sure that their rules are being carried out. Nor do these forty silversmiths consider only the trade conditions in their own towns. They are connected with other silversmiths in other cities; they hold meetings and elect officers and maintain a treasury. Their members, like the members of other guilds, are all enrolled as masters and workmen—or the heads of shops and the journeymen.

The Most Famous of All the Mediaeval Craft Guilds

In Italy, in the beautiful city of Florence, towards the close of the Middle Ages there arose perhaps the most famous guild of all —the Calimala (kä′lĭ-mä′lä), or Clothmakers' Guild. From all over the world cloth in bales came to the Calimala, to be dressed and dyed. The clothmakers of Florence had secret processes by which the dirty grey fabrics sent to them emerged soft and shining in beautiful colours. No one outside the guild itself could learn those processes.

The heads of the Calimala were powerful men, and they and the other members of the guild became enormously rich through their trade. They had representatives in every great city of Europe to protect the rights of their merchants and to see that nothing went wrong with their trade. They were soon able to lend money to kings, who treated them as equals.

How the Merchants of the World became More Powerful Than Kings

Now, the power of money is very great, greater than the power of war itself. To make war, a king must have money, and to get money he must often borrow. As long as the kings could obtain enough money for war by taxing their people, they were supreme. But as soon as merchants grew richer than kings, trade became king.

Thus it is in the towns of the Middle Ages that we can see most clearly the seeds which are to grow into our modern life. Here are men of a single trade banded together for the good of all the members. Here, too, are all the merchants banded together into powerful and prosperous "merchant guilds," in order to foster trade. They enjoy special privileges, and administer the rights of trade monopoly granted by the king to their borough.

On the Continent these merchant guilds were known as "Hanses," and many North German towns banded together to form the Hanseatic League; the first charter for foreign trade granted in England was given to branches of this League.

The origin of the English merchant guilds is to be found in the Merchants of the Staple, who enjoyed a monopoly in staple products, largely wool, the trade in which was regulated and protected by a statute of Edward III.

In the towns, therefore, are large groups of people becoming rich from something besides agriculture. Here at last we see a change from the eternal fighting and robbery which marked the early Middle Ages. We have the beginning of a great "middle class."

By courtesy of the British Museum

A page of manuscript in English as it was written in the thirteenth century. It is taken from the first of the romances after Beowulf, which was the earliest sign of a revival in English literature after the Norman Conquest.

The towns have had a difficult time winning the right to wealth and independence. There has been some hard bargaining between them and the lords on whose land they are built, and their taxes are still very heavy. But they are persevering. They have built a high wall round their huddled houses, and they fight valiantly when the lords attack them.

And, more than that, when he is in difficulties and needs money badly, they refuse to provide it for him unless he grants them a charter allowing them certain rights. That brings him to terms. He ceases from interfering with their trade and, if he is wise, he does what he can to encourage it.

For instance, a charter from the king himself, granted to the good people of Wallingford in England, states that "wheresoever they shall go on their journeys as merchants through my whole land of England and Normandy, Aquitaine and Anjou, by water and by strand, by wood and by land, they shall be free from toll and passage fees and from all customs and exactions." We may imagine what that meant at a time when every lord charged for the use of his muddy highroad, his bridge, his ford. One might not even sail a vessel up a river without paying the lord whose land ran beside the stream. No wonder the men who were building up the nation's wealth by trade grew tired of such petty annoyances. It was their constant effort towards attaining something more large-minded and more reasonable that helped to make the cities the centres of progress and culture which they are to-day.

Our visit to the Middle Ages, the Dawning Ages, the Ages of Faith rather than of Reason, is over. We shall find little in the old times to make us love our own times the less. They contain, it is true, the seeds of modern progress, but the growth is choked by the weeds of unfriendly forces. Therefore we shall return to our own twentieth century more contented with what life has to offer us, and truly thankful that mankind has made so much progress in cleanliness and kindliness, in liberty and enlightenment, during the past five hundred years.

(CONTINUED ON PAGE 941)

Before starting on any of the things illustrated here, practise making the joints explained on another page. Plan carefully, measure accurately, work neatly, and finish thoroughly with sand-paper. The GARDEN BENCH (Fig. 3) is 40″ wide, and 18″ from top surface to ground. The seat board is 1½″ or 2″ thick. The mouldings are made with drawing-knife and plane from odds and ends.

A useful CORNER SHELF (Fig. 1) may be cut out with a hack-saw from boards 18″ long, 6″ wide, and ⅜″ thick. Fig. 2 shows the shape to which to cut them. Make the shelves the same thickness as the side-pieces; for the other shelf dimensions, measure after you have fitted the side-pieces to the corner.

The HANGING BAS-KET (Fig. 4) is made of ½″ branches, ranging in length from 8″ at the top to 6″ at the bottom. They are held together by wires passed through holes ¾″ from their ends; these wires are fastened to the wood bottom.

Here is a fine DESK AND BENCH SET (Figs. 5, 6) made of 1″ timber. The other dimensions will depend entirely upon the height of the person who is going to use the set; so make actual tests to see what height is most comfortable. On another page you will find directions for decorating your set with stencils. This bunny would delight a little sister; but there are plenty of designs to suit every taste.

To make this FLOW-ER-POT HOLDER (Fig. 7) you will need 4 pieces of board 8″ x 5½″ x ½″ for the sides, and another piece ½″ thick and 5″ square for the bottom. Fit the sides together with a mitre-joint. Then tack strips of sheet brass over the joints with brass-headed upholster-ing tacks. Stencil or paint a flower design on each panel.

The MAGAZINE RACK (Fig. 9) is 24″ high and 18″ long; it is made from boards ½″ thick. The side boards are 12″ x 18″. They should be assembled in a V shape— joining at the bottom and 10″ apart at the top. The picture will give you a general idea of the shape of the end boards. The design may be varied to match the rest of the furniture.

A WINDOW BOX (Fig. 8) should be made of boards about ¾″ thick. Make it the right length to fit the window. The best depth is 6″. Saw the end pieces to taper from 4″ to 6″ in width, so that the completed box will be 4″ at the bottom and 6″ at the top. Bore holes in the bottom for drainage.

Here you see a wagon laden with a few of the things necessary for the "shooting" of an outdoor scene.

PICTURES *That* MOVE *and* TALK

There are Few Towns To-day Without a Cinema, Yet at the Beginning of the Present Century the Moving-Picture was No More than a Possibility of the Future

IF YOU had been living in New York in 1894, you could have gone to a certain house on Broadway and seen the first real moving-picture show. The house was not a theatre, of course, and you would not have sat down in a comfortable seat to look at a screen. You would have had to peep through the eyepiece of a little machine while you turned a crank to make the picture move inside it. The machine was a kinetoscope (kĭ-nĕt′ŏ-skōp), and it was the humble parent of all our many moving-pictures of to-day.

Even earlier there had been a good many people in different countries trying to make pictures of things in motion. Before man even found out how to make a photograph, he began to wonder whether he could manage to make a picture move—to make it show a man walking across a room or running down the street—and in 1824 Peter Roget read before the Royal Society a paper bearing on the subject.

All over Europe people began experiment-ing. It was not long before Dr. Joseph Plateau, of the university of Ghent, and an Austrian named Dr. Simon von Stampfer had discovered, at about the same time, a way to present a rapid series of pictures of an object in motion. They achieved it by mounting a series of pictures in order round the rim of a disk and then whirling the disk, which had slits cut in it through which to view the pictures. By 1853 another Austrian, Baron Franz von Uchatius, had discovered a way to combine the disc with the magic lantern. He arranged a light behind the disk, and in that way the pictures could be thrown on a screen.

It was Coleman Sellers, a Philadelphia engineer, who seems to have first used photographs instead of drawings to show his moving object. In 1860 he took a number of pictures of his son driving a nail in a box with a hammer. In the first picture the hammer was raised in the air, in the second it was posed a little lower, in the next a little lower still, and so on until it was striking the nail.

Then Sellers made a paddle wheel with many blades, and mounted one picture on each blade. When he spun the wheel round, one picture rapidly followed another and showed his son hammering. It was an interesting device, but nothing came of it.

In California, about twelve years later, Leland Stanford, railway director and sportsman, wished to obtain a picture of a racehorse in action. He entrusted the problem to John D. Isaacs and to Eadweard Muybridge, an Englishman, who worked out a scheme for arranging a great many separate cameras along the course, under electric control, and so snapping the horse in various positions as it passed. But there were still large gaps between the views.

Of course it was not possible to arrange enough cameras to make a reel of a few thousand pictures, so a way had to be found to make one camera take them all, and very rapidly. But this could not be done until George Eastman produced a celluloid film to take the place of the old glass plates on which separate pictures had been made before.

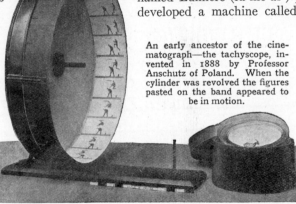

An early ancestor of the cinematograph—the tachyscope, invented in 1888 by Professor Anschutz of Poland. When the cylinder was revolved the figures pasted on the band appeared to be in motion.

Photo by Will Day

In 1889 an Englishman named William Friese-Greene took out a patent for the first moving-picture machine using a celluloid film. About the same time Thomas Edison wound a strip of film on a reel and managed to snap a rapid series of pictures in a special kind of camera as the film unrolled. The camera he made was very much like those in use to-day. The narrow strip of film unrolled behind a shutter that opened and closed forty-eight times a second. When it opened, the film remained still and took a picture; when it closed, the film moved on into place for the next picture.

So the moving-picture is a long series of photographs taken so rapidly that the eye will not notice the gaps between them, and will therefore appear to see the things in motion. Now for a sixteenth of a second the eye will hold any image it has just seen; and in that brief moment one picture may go off and another come on, without our realizing it. All we seem to see is something moving on the screen, though what is really moving is a strip in the projecting machine.

When we have once taken a photograph and developed it, we can make any number of copies. And, since the film is transparent, we can flash a light through it and throw it on a screen for all to see. But, curiously enough, that is something that never occurred to the great Edison. He made only the little kinetoscope, with a peep-hole for a single person at a time to watch the performance inside.

Many other men, however, began to work on the invention. Two French brothers named Lumière (lü-mē-âr') perfected it and developed a machine called a projector to throw the image on the screen — magnified some thirty-five thousand times. The Lumières used to take sixteen pictures in a second and for each foot of film. For the talking picture of to-day we take twenty-four a second.

The early pictures seem very jumpy and unsatisfactory to us now. In the very short time since their invention we have brought the camera and the projector to a high state of perfection, and we can even show pictures in colours now. And, finally, we have made the screen talk! Until 1928 the "pictures" were always silent: they used to be called the "silent drama." Now there is as much talking as there is on the stage.

The machinery for talking was not invented by any one man. Sound was first recorded in 1857, by Léon Scott, on an instrument which he called the phonautograph, and its reproduction and development to

This strange affair, affectionately called the "Black Maria," is often spoken of as the world's first moving-picture studio. It was here that Thomas Edison carried on experiments with moving pictures.

present-day perfection is due to the inventive genius of various people, as we have related elsewhere in the story of the gramophone.

In combining sound with motion-pictures two general methods have been developed. One of these, which was first demonstrated successfully in 1926, embraces the features of the gramophone and wireless.

The Delicate Microphone

When the actors speak the sound is taken up by a microphone. A microphone will catch every sound round about it, and if we want to capture nothing but the actor's voice, we must keep out every other sound. So, from being a very noisy place indeed, the moving-picture studio has become one of the quietest on earth. It is hung with heavy curtains to deaden every echo, and the cameras are placed in padded booths. No one must go in or out while the work is in hand.

As the player speaks, the little instrument picks up his voice, and electricity carries it to a sound record that is being made along with the pictures. With the help of vacuum tubes the sound may be increased or reduced to secure the best effect.

The camera and the sound record have to run at precisely the same speed, otherwise the picture will not match the voice. It will not "synchronize" (sĭng′krō-nīz); and then we might hear the voice before we saw the lips move. So the electric motors that operate the cameras and the sound records must always work together in perfect harmony.

The other way of recording the sound is on the film itself instead of on a sound record. It is only in the past few years that this method has been adopted. By a remarkable invention, the sound is simply changed into light and then photographed on the film. The electric current from the microphone is made to work upon a glowing lamp. When the sound is loud, the lamp is bright, and when softer the lamp is dimmer. And then the light is photographed either in a narrow streak down the edge of the film, by the side of the pictures, or on a separate film, in which case the two are photographed on to a third film.

Light Becomes Sound Again

When the picture is flashed on the screen the light is changed back into sound again. A ray of light shining through the narrow streak gives the same glow as the original lamp; and when this is taken up by the photo-electric cell an electric current is developed that operates a loud speaker on the stage of the theatre.

But now we are far ahead of our story. We have explained how all the machines were perfected, but we have not mentioned what was being done with them. So we must go back again and explain what sort of plays were made.

In the beginning there was no play at all. The moving-picture was merely a toy, and not a very popular toy at that. It was shown as an item in a variety performance, and was accepted by the audience as a curiosity rather than as a desirable contribution to the programme. For the moving-picture of that day had little to present apart from a few stale tricks and oddities. It reached its very peak when it showed half the people of a village chasing a comical fellow through the streets. Nearly every picture closed in some such way, and the people in the theatre were generally relieved rather than sorry when the end arrived.

The First Cowboy Films

But in 1903 a real story was told in a picture called "The Life of an American Fireman," and this was followed by "The Great Train Robbery." These little plays were packed with thrills, and for a long time afterwards the moving pictures presented very little except feats of daring and danger—Wild West scenes and cowboy adventures. But these were at least plays, however poor.

The early plays were one reel long—a thousand feet of film—and for some time this was the standard length of moving pictures. It was a great event, therefore, when Adolph Zukor, a pioneer in the industry, began to produce plays in two and three reels. And to such directors as Zukor and D. W. Griffith the amazing growth of the photo-play of our times is chiefly due.

Wonderful Films of the Past

In 1907 "Ben Hur" was shown on the screen, and by 1913 "Quo Vadis," a film eight reels in length. These were magnificent spectacles in their time. In 1912 Zukor scored a great triumph by persuading the famous French actress Sarah Bernhardt to play in a moving-picture—for at that time the well-known actors were very scornful of the "pictures."

In 1914 D. W. Griffith, one of the most enterprising and enthusiastic of picture-play producers, presented "The Birth of a Nation," a spectacular film in fourteen reels, which may well be said to have set the hall-mark of perfection on silent pictures. It met with a remarkable reception, and attracted to the cinema many thousands of people who had never before seen a picture-play.

From that time the picture-play progressed steadily and surely to the perfection it enjoys to-day. It has told stories that are longer and very much better. It has shown more and more marvellous scenes and

A SHIP THAT NEVER SAILED UPON THE OCEAN

This is not a view of the harbour of a great seaport; nor has the majestic "ocean liner" ever put to sea, for it is just a dummy that was built for the purpose of producing a moving-picture scene. You would never suspect that the "ship" was merely riding on sand, or that the storm was caused by pumps that splash huge waves of water over decks that are made to roll by machinery. Nevertheless, the effect is vivid and realistic.

In the oval is shown the inside of a moving-picture camera. The person taking a picture looks through the hole at B and sees in the "finder," A, the object to be photographed. Then he presses a button and sets the mechanism working. The round shutter at G begins to revolve, like an electric fan, and every time the hole in it comes into position behind the lens F, light passing through the lens strikes a little square of exposed film at the bright spot marked H, and a picture is taken. As the shutter revolves the light is shut out again, and while it is shut out the two little claws at I seize the film through a pair of small holes in its edges, and pull the film down just far enough to bring a fresh, unexposed square of film—or "frame," as it is called—into position behind the lens. Then, when the shutter has revolved far enough to bring the hole in it behind the lens once more, another picture is taken on the fresh frame. And so the process goes on. The unexposed film is wound, to start with, on a reel which is invisible (being inside, behind a hinged door) and passes over the guide-reel at E to the little cog-wheel at C, in the centre of the camera, which pulls it off the reel by fitting its cogs into the pairs of holes along the edges of the film. At the same time this little wheel passes the film that has been exposed at H to the reel at D, where the exposed film is wound up. The pieces J and K serve to hold the film against the cog-wheel, so that the cogs may fit into the holes. The claws at I have to work by jerks, for they must pull the film past H by stops and starts. They give the film twenty-four jerks a second; that is, twenty-four pictures a second are taken on the film.

At the right is a projector which sends a powerful ray of light through the pictures on a moving-picture film, and focuses the ray on a screen in such a way that the shadows cast by the film may be clear and sharp. The machine is run by electricity, which furnishes the light and operates a motor—out of sight in this picture—to drive the mechanism for passing the film in front of the light. The oblong wire cage at the left contains the "lamp house," in which is an electric lamp to furnish the light and a lens for condensing the rays. These are concentrated on the projecting lens, which is in the little cylinder at the right. Between the lens and the lamp is a curved strip of metal, D, with a hole in it just in front of the lens. This strip of metal is known as the "gate." As the long strip of film, with its series of pictures, is passed over the gate, each picture stops for a brief instant in front of the hole. This allows the light to pass through it and fall upon the lens. Then, as the film passes down over the gate, another picture comes between the lens and the light, and another set of images is cast on the screen. And so they follow, in swift succession. In order that the shadows on the screen may not be blurred as the film passes rapidly in front of the light, there is a revolving shutter, E, which consists of a disk with holes in it. Whenever the film is being moved, this shutter, which passes between the lens and the film, shuts off the light from the lens; but as soon as a picture on the film comes squarely in front of the lens, the hole in the shutter has come into a position to let the light through for just an instant.

A neat mechanism keeps the film passing at even intervals over the gate. It consists, first, of two little cog-wheels at A and B. The cogs in A fit into the holes along the edges of the film, and as the wheel turns, it slowly unwinds the film that is wound on the upper reel. This film passes down over the gate, and then is fed to the lower reel in the same way by the wheel at B. A little pronged lever, operated by the wheels F and G, fits into the holes in the sides of the film and jerks the film, a picture at a time, down past the hole in the gate. This little lever must work very quickly. It has to seize the film twenty-four times a second, jerk it down, let go, and then seize it again.

settings. It has absorbed some of the greatest actors and actresses in the world—many from the regular stage, and many who have never acted anywhere except before a camera.

It has achieved wonders in a new style of acting—for never before had actors known how to express so much with their faces and their gestures, with the curl of a lip, the shrug of a shoulder, the glance of an eye. The industry has spent enormous sums of

to act for the films, and many others nurse the fond hope that one day they may succeed in writing a play that will bring them fame in screen history; but few of them have the vaguest idea how to proceed about it. It is one thing to write a story for a book or magazine, and a very different thing to write one for the films—so different that few men can do both.

First it is necessary to divide the story up into various scenes. In the regular theatre there would usually be three or four scenes, for the properties on the stage cannot be constantly changed. But in a photo-play there may be hundreds of scenes, for we may alter them as often as we like. So in this way the moving-picture can accomplish far more than the regular stage could ever dream of doing. And the first thing to do is to com-

It is not always easy for a moving-picture actor to get just the right expression. The greatest actor may fail in this. So producers have invented ways of helping the performer by action just out of range of the camera. Above, you see a man looking quite as startled at the thought of being hit in the eye with a pea-shooter as he would look if he had just been informed that the police were hot on his trail. And at the right a number of men in threatening attitude are helping the hero to find the expression that he should wear when waiting for the appearance of the villain.

money; for in these few years the photo-play has grown into a vast business enterprise. It is now providing entertainment for hundreds of times as many people as were ever entertained by any one thing in the history of the world.

It is the ambition of a great many people

pile a list of scenes and of the action in each one. That is the "scenario."

But the scenes may be in very different places—some in Devonshire and some in London: some on an ocean liner and some in Bagdad, with many more in various other places. Clearly, we must take all the pictures

BUILDING A RAILWAY STATION IN A STUDIO

It is fortunate that when we visit a picture theatre we cannot see all that has been taking place just outside the range of the camera. It is, however, most interesting and instructive to watch the actual making of a moving-picture, on which months of careful thought and intensive labour have often to be spent. In the filming of "Rome Express," which was produced by the Gaumont-British Picture Corporation Limited, not the least of many remarkable achievements was the construction of a full-size model of a train and station of the Paris, Lyons and Mediterranean Railway. In the picture above, you can see the locomotive and tender nearing completion, the low railway platform and the roof pillar supports, and the train departure notices.

for each place—or "location"—at one time. We do not start the first scene in Devonshire, go to Bagdad for the second and return to London for the third. Instead, we take all the Devonshire scenes at one time, wherever they may finally come in the picture; then all the Bagdad scenes, the London scenes, and so on with the remainder. Our scenario must therefore be cut up into various sets of scenes for the various locations. It is then a "continuity."

At this point it goes to the director. He is a most important man. You may not see him in the picture, but his hand is in it everywhere. He plans the whole play, and by heroic effort sees that every person in it does exactly the right thing at the right time. He alone knows the composition of the whole picture; and in any given part he may be forcing an actor through a special piece of a scene —of sorrow for the death of a sweetheart or of joy in the discovery of a gold-mine—when the actor has no idea what it is all about or what the finished play will be like.

Before the actors begin, the scenery must be ready. In many plays the most extraordinary scenes must be shown—courts and palaces, deserts and dungeons, ice-huts and mediaeval castles and Roman arenas. So every big studio must have its architects and artists as well as its costumiers, and they are often called upon for the most wonderful feats of art. Sometimes a whole city has to be built for a single film. A big studio may keep ten thousand costumes in stock, and then have many made to order as required for the play that is being prepared. The cost is frequently enormous, and may run into a hundred thousand pounds or more.

While the scenery is being made, the actors will be chosen. There are stars in every studio, of course, but often hundreds and even thousands of extra people have to be engaged—soldiers, Indians, cowboys, and crowds. A play like "The Covered Wagon" needs some three thousand "extras." The extras are not among the highly paid, but the "stars" receive large salaries.

When all is ready the filming begins, and this brings into action a number of other experts. A large studio may employ as many as forty camera-men, twenty or more property men, a few dozen chauffeurs and scenery men, and a hundred or more electricians; and all of these may be engaged at the same time when the "shooting" begins. The lighting of the scenes is an art in itself.

Over the vast army of workers the director reigns supreme. The players in particular obey his every word and gesture. They must be very highly skilled in make-up, for the camera plays strange tricks with colours. Anything red will look black on the screen, and anything yellow will be white. So if you want your cheeks pink in the picture and your hair yellow, you must have them some other colour when you stand in front of the camera. In the studios actors and actresses are often seen with their faces greenish and purple in colour, but they will look quite natural on the screen.

The players must be even more highly skilled in acting. It is no easy thing to keep in the right position before the camera, no matter how much you have to move round, and to have your photograph taken thousands of times without ever looking at the camera or appearing conscious of its presence. And it is far more difficult to make your features express the intense emotions you are supposed to feel as the story of the play proceeds.

If you cut off the top of this picture there is nothing to suggest that it was not a snapshot taken by some ranchman. But well above the heads is a microphone, so placed as to catch all the sounds and yet be out of range of the moving-picture camera. It betrays the scene as one enacted for the "pictures."

That would be hard enough in the quiet of the studio; but often it must be done in a burning desert or on an icy mountain peak, in the midst of a howling mob or in a blazing building. Even in the studio the glare of the powerful lights will ruin the looks of anybody but an actor of long experience.

For these and other reasons, the very best actors often have to go through a scene time and time again before it is perfect enough for the camera. Even then it is likely to be too long, and so when the completed film is examined by the editorial department of the studio it often has to be cut and pieced together again in many places before it is ready for exhibition.

In one sense the camera always tells the truth—it reproduces exactly what it sees. But we can still make it do a thousand and one tricks that will look like anything but the truth.

In the early days of the moving-picture, it was a favourite trick to show a man diving off a spring-board into the water, and then coming up out of the water feet first, floating in a graceful curve through the air and landing on the spring-board from which he had dived. This curious effect was produced simply by running the picture through the projector backwards.

But suppose we wish to show a great train plunging over a bridge into a river. No railway is going to lend us a bridge and a train to wreck, and it will be very costly to build one for ourselves. So we just make a tiny bridge and train modelled exactly like the big ones. Then we wreck it in the studio and take the picture; and when we magnify

THE CINEMATOGRAPH

A COMPANY OF FILM ACTORS "ON LOCATION" IN THE DESERT

Here is an impression of what happened every day at noon in a desert city specially constructed to house a moving-picture company. They were acting in a production photographed near Zion National Park, in Utah, U.S.A. Often "mountains" and "deserts" can be set up in the studio, but if a whole drama with a great deal of scattered action, such as a "Wild West" play, is to be filmed, it is necessary to convey the company and the equipment to some suitable spot. There they work very hard until the photographs have all been taken.

THE WONDERFUL MODEL OF A CITY OF TO-MORROW

When a really spectacular production is to be filmed, no expense is spared. Those are not cheap costumes you see in a good film, nor is the antique furniture made in the studio. Everything is genuine. Talented artists and interior decorators design the settings, and the greatest pains are taken to have the smallest details perfect.

The scene above is a photograph of a model made in the studio for use in a film called "Just Imagine." It is supposed to be a picture of the New York of 1980. Of course, the New York of 1980 could hardly be shown "true to life," but many months were spent in making this model as perfect architecturally as was possible.

this on the screen, nobody will ever know the difference. In the same way we can wreck a steamboat on a table in the studio. Then we can take some photographs of the ocean, and put the two sets of pictures together to show the ship sinking in the sea.

Sometimes a single actor appears as two different persons in the same picture—one on the right of the screen, the other on the left. To achieve this two pictures have had

In one picture twenty lions were turned loose on a group of Christian martyrs; but the front rank of the martyrs were all lion-tamers, though they kept their whips and revolvers out of sight. As the lions sprang at them, the cameras ceased to operate and the lion-tamers drove the beasts back to their dens. Then some dummy bodies were suitably arranged, and the cameras were started again to show the lions mauling them.

We have all seen a man on the screen run over by a steam-roller, only to get up and walk merrily away. Of course, the camera stopped just before the roller struck him, and a dummy was placed in position to be run over. The camera took the picture, and was then stopped again while the man took the dummy's place. When it started once more, the man was getting up and running away.

By courtesy of the Western Electric Co. Ltd.

A typical sound projector, which can reproduce sounds either, as at (B), from a record, or from photographic marks on a film (A). The latter operation is performed through the agency of rays of light, which are directed on to the film and thence to the photo-electric cell, a device which is capable of producing electricity when light falls on it. The marks on the film vary the strength of the rays, and thus the energy produced varies accordingly. Loud-speakers transform this into sound, and in this way we can listen to our wonderful talking pictures. A switch (C) controls the two methods of sound reproduction.

Moreover, the camera can show us a great many things that we could never see without it. In many ways it is by far the best teacher that we can have.

It is the only instrument that can show us the wonders of motion. There is a special camera to take pictures as fast as fifteen hundred a second. When these are put on the screen at twenty-four a second, we see an extraordinary slow motion that shows, to the smallest detail, how everything was done. So we can see exactly what a graceful diver does as we watch him floating slowly through the air. In the same way, we can watch an expert tennis-player or a galloping horse or even a bullet in flight.

to be taken and pieced together. If you have ever seen, on the screen, an angry lion springing at a frightened heroine, you may be fairly certain that, actually, he was only jumping to seize a piece of raw meat.

For things that move very slowly we can do just the opposite. We can make a snail

Here you see the sound-recording machine, which stands in the studio and records sounds by photographing them on to a film in a series of thin horizontal lines, at exactly the same speed as that at which the pictures are taken.

Above you see the mixing room. Here the mixing man sits in his sound-proof booth overlooking the stage and by means of the panel in front of him controls the volume and quality of the sound which is being picked up by the delicate microphone for recording.

This "bomb" is really a very harmless object. It is the latest type of microphone used for talking pictures. To the left is a strip of sound film: the arrow indicates the horizontal lines of the sound track. These variations in shading produce the sound.

By courtesy of the Western Electric Co., Ltd.

By courtesy of the Western Electric Co. Ltd.

You will recognize these projectors, which are waiting to perform their duties in an operating-box. The reason why a cinema possesses two is that each one can carry only 2,000 feet of film, and most big films consist of 7,000 or 8,000 feet. The projectors, therefore, have to share the task of amusement, one swiftly following on the other. In the background you see the big amplifier, a wonderful device employed for magnifying the sound.

dart about like a lizard. We can take pictures of a growing plant, one every few hours. When we run these off rapidly on the screen, we may see the whole plant sprouting, growing, budding, flowering, and dying, all in a few minutes. There is a wealth of education in the screen.

Originally the moving-picture industry was mainly an American monopoly, but in recent years rapid development has taken place in Great Britain and on the Continent. Whereas, at one time, we were almost solely dependent on the United States for the films shown in our cinemas, we now not only produce a large proportion of them in England, but also send a great number into the original homes of the industry.

Formerly British artists who wished to act for the films were compelled to go to Hollywood under contract with American companies: but, to-day, there are numerous film studios in our own country, where first-class films are produced.

During 1932 the British Board of Film Censors, which was established in 1912, viewed 5,613,476 feet of film, embracing 1,884 subjects, and passed all except twenty-two subjects amounting to 88,560 feet. Only eighteen of the films were of the silent type. The total number of feet showed a decline on the previous year of 160,990 feet, which was almost entirely due to the decreased production from America. British-produced films were largely in excess of the number for any other year.

All of this vast industry has resulted from the success that attended the efforts of Léon Scott to record the human voice and the later experiments of other scientists who devised a means of reproducing sound and invented mechanism for obtaining a series of photographs with the utmost rapidity.

This picture shows a charming scene from the British film "Dick Turpin," the dramatized version of Harrison Ainsworth's well-known novel—"Rookwood." The part of the highwayman is played by Victor McLaglen.

Photos by courtesy of Gaumont-British Distributors, Ltd.

Eleanor Mowbray, the heroine, is carried off by Luke Rookwood to his house at York, and Dick Turpin follows on his bonny Black Bess, but the gallant mare dies on the outskirts of the city. Turpin arrives at Rookwood Manor, and defeats Rookwood in a duel, but is then forced to take flight to escape the Bow Street runners.

WHY *Is the* SKY BLUE?

It is Just a Trick of the Air that Sifts the Sun's Rays and Scatters Them into Space

(CONTINUED FROM PAGE 906)

HOW would you describe the clear blue sky to a man who had never seen it? You would find it a difficult task; a poet describes it as "that inverted bowl we call the sky," but this would not mean much to a man who had never seen it at all.

The truth is that there is nothing else in Nature that looks just like the heavens on a clear summer's day—and that is because there is no other place where we can look on and on into vast oceans of space.

Yet it is certainly not empty, for if it were, even in daylight we should see nothing but inky blackness. And if the air were transparent, the blackness of the sky would appear to be stabbed with bright points of light, the sun and moon and little twinkling stars. What we are really looking at is countless particles of moisture and dust, and

still tinier atoms of gas. Those are what make up the atmosphere—and it is the atmosphere that looks blue. For all those tiny particles sift and hold blue rays out of the sunlight and scatter the sunbeams about until, no matter where we look, the world seems bathed in light. And when, at sunset, the rays of light have to pass through a still greater thickness of air, the orange and red and yellow rays are caught by the tiny particles and pinned to the western sky.

Weather Signs in the West

It is the air, then, that we can thank for our beautiful blue heavens and our gorgeous skies at sunset; and since this is true, you can readily see that the weather will have a great deal to do with the colour of the sky. No one can mistake the promise

JACK FROST PLAYS A TRICK ON THE MIGHTY NIAGARA FALLS

Winter has a fine gift for scenic effects. Even an ugly city street is imposing under a blanket of snow; but when Niagara Falls are partly sheathed in ice, the sight is stupendous. Up in the corner is a view of the falls before the fingers of Jack Frost got to work and fashioned those towers and hanging colonnades.

of a clear blue sky; and the colour of the west at evening often tells us quite plainly what the weather will be next day. A practised eye can read all such signs.

The air gives us a great many beautiful effects besides sunsets and blue skies. Do you remember the joy of Noah when, after the long, dark weeks of rain and the terrors of the Flood, he saw a rainbow in the sky, and learned that it was a token that mankind would never be destroyed in that way again? Something of Noah's thrill of delight we feel, even to-day, at sight of the exquisite bow that comes after the rain.

But conditions must be right if we are to see it. The sun must be shining in one part of the sky while the rain is still falling in another; and we must stand with our backs to the sun and have the rain in front of us. Then, if everything is right, we shall see a great arc of colour in the sky above us. Now and then a second bow will show faintly outside the first, and sometimes, but very rarely, even a third—this last between us and the sun. Red is the outside colour in the brightest —or primary (prī'mă-rĭ)—bow, and the inside colour in the secondary bow. The rainbow is best seen when the sun is about halfway down the sky to the horizon.

You can make your own rainbow. By standing with your back to the sun and throwing a fine spray of water into the air from a garden hose, you can sometimes create a full circle of colour. This little rainbow is as real as the big one up in the sky, for it is made in just the same way.

When a ray of light passes obliquely from one substance into another, it is bent out of its course. That bending we call "re-

The pencil is not really broken. It is only that the water has bent the rays of light passing through it, and so the part of the pencil that is under water seems to be out of place. Glass, too, will bend a ray of light. And since sunlight is made up of rays of many colours, all those colours may be separated by passing them through a glass prism, like the one in the centre, which spreads them out like a rainbow. The reason for the separation is that each colour is bent at a different angle from all the other colours. A drop of water acts in just the same way as a prism. It divides a ray of light into the colours that make it up and spreads them out like a rainbow. So when there are millions of drops of water in the sky, all working at once sorting out the colours in the sunlight, we have, as the result, a beautiful rainbow.

fraction" (rĕ-frăk'shŭn)—from the Latin word for "break up." It is refraction that makes a stick look bent when you thrust it slantingly into water. The light rays are bent as they enter the water.

Now a beam of sunlight, you may remember, is made up of all the colours of the rainbow; and when it passes at an angle from one substance to another, as from air to water or glass, the rays of different colour are bent at different angles. If the piece of glass is a flat slab with parallel sides, the rays when they leave it are bent back to their original direction and merge again, giving a white light. But if the glass is a prism, with sides making a sharp angle, the rays leaving it are dispersed or spread out and can be seen as separate colours. In a raindrop the rays enter at one angle, are both reflected and refracted, and leave the raindrop at another angle, as you see in the picture. The second rainbow is formed by rays which are reflected and refracted twice inside the raindrop. The rainbow, then, is caused by refraction.

Where the Rainbow Ends

But as for the crock of gold that the old story says is at the foot of the rainbow— it is as far away as all other bright things that seem beautiful because they are just out of reach. For it is in the nature of things that the foot of the rainbow can never be reached. It is always just a little way in front of you, and moves away just as fast as you walk towards it. So there are really as many different rainbows as there are persons looking at them, and whenever you move you see a different

The broad whitish disk or ring that you sometimes see surrounding the sun or moon is called a corona (kŏ-rō′nă)—or "crown." It is caused by thin, misty lower clouds made up of very tiny water drops, which scatter the light and so cause the "crown." Now these are the commonest tricks the air

No accident has happened to our old friends the sun and moon in these two pictures. It is only that we are looking at them through thin clouds that bend the rays of light. The result is that, as befits the king and queen of the heavens, both sun and moon seem to be wearing a crown, or "corona."

rainbow —which only means that a different set of raindrops is refracting the light that you see. The rainbow is only as thick as the little drops that are causing it—and no matter how near it may be, it is always just out of reach.

Once in a while you may see a ring of light round the sun or the moon. It happens when you look through very high, thin clouds—cirrus (sĭr′ŭs) clouds—containing icy crystals that bend the rays of light. This small, faint ring round the sun or moon, but at some distance from it, is called a halo (hā′lō). Its inner border is brownish red. There is a very old saying—of no real value—that the number of stars you can see inside the ring tells you the number of days that will pass before rain will fall; but one can be sure that the meteorologist never wastes any time counting them. Sometimes several haloes round the sun cross each other, with brighter spots at the points at which they meet. Such spots are often called "mock suns."

Photos by the Tourist Information Office, The Hague

can play, but there are others seen occasionally. There are, for example, the strange mirages (mĭ-räzh′) that appear at sea or over deserts, and deceive weary sailors and travellers with what seem to be castles and ships and trees. They are caused by the bending of light rays that pass through layers of air heated to widely differing temperatures; the rays are "refracted" just as they are in passing through water. You may see much the same sort of thing taking place in the air just above a paved road on a hot summer's day; the road will often seem to be covered with a sheet of shimmering water, or even with growing grass.

(CONTINUED ON PAGE 983)

From SAILOR BOY *to* POET LAUREATE

John Masefield Gained Experience on the Sea and in Many Other Places—Even in a New York Bar-parlour

(CONTINUED FROM PAGE 912)

AT FOURTEEN he went off to sea. His father and mother had both died long before, and he had been brought up by an aunt. He had not had much schooling, though he had read many books and had been very good at telling stories to the other boys at school. Then for three years he lived just like any other sailor boy, and that is no easy life.

But he learned all about the beauty and the cruelty of the sea; all about the ships and the men who sail them; all about the sailor's speech, the sailor's ideas, and the sailor's dreams.

Then he gave up the sea, much as he still loved it. In 1895 he landed in New York with a scanty wardrobe and a few shillings in his pocket. He worked at any odd jobs he could find—in a livery-stable, in a bakery, as a beach-comber, and even as a porter in a bar-parlour. But he had left the sea because he wanted to read and study and now he was spending his free nights, in the garret bedroom that he shared with two other men, in reading and writing stories. About this time he discovered for himself the wit and wisdom of the great poet Chaucer; and from then on he felt within him the power to be a poet himself.

John Masefield, a man who has seen life from angles very far apart: first as a sailor boy before the mast, then as a youth in many humble tasks, even as porter in a bar-room in old New York, and also as poet laureate of Britain.

What is a Poet Laureate?

In 1930 he was made poet laureate, which means that the king appointed him to celebrate important national events in verse. But most of his poetry is about the sea or about the plain but heroic people that he came to know so well during his wanderings among them in various parts of the world.

This man is John Masefield. He was born at Ledbury, in Herefordshire, in 1878. He returned home from his wanderings in 1897.

"Salt Water Ballads"

When he first came back to his native land he had rather a hard time in making a start as a writer. But his first book of poems, the "Salt Water Ballads," was published in 1902, and he began to be known. Then followed some short stories of the sea, some books for boys, and several novels and plays. In 1911 his poem "The Everlasting Mercy" told the world that a new great poet had arisen. This was followed quickly by "The Widow in the Bye Street," and "Dauber," narrative poems of extraordinary strength and pathos. In 1919 his "Reynard the Fox" gave us a brilliant picture of the English countryside. Besides these, he has written a good deal in prose and verse, and in dramatic form. Of his dramatic works we may mention "A King's Daughter" (1923), a fine verse tragedy; and of his novels "Sard Harker" (1924) and "Odtaa" (1926). He is one of the most powerful and most moving of our realists in verse, but he is a realist with a lofty ideal.

But perhaps what we most love about his work is his way of making us feel the spirit of the sea, as when he says in his fine ballad called "Sea Fever":

I must go down to the seas again, to the lonely
    sea and the sky,
And all I ask is a tall ship and a star to steer
    her by,
And the wheel's kick and the wind's song
    and the white sail's shaking,
And a grey mist on the sea's face and a grey
    dawn breaking.

The WITTIEST MAN of OUR TIME

How George Bernard Shaw has Dazzled and Provoked Millions of Readers and Theatre-goers

BERNARD SHAW is possibly the wittiest man of our time. By his satire and ridicule he has kept the world laughing for a good many years; and he has made it do a great deal of thinking as well. When Shaw begins to poke fun at you or at anything you like, you will laugh first and think afterwards—which is just what he wants you to do. And sooner or later he pokes fun at most of us and at most of the things we like or respect.

Once he said, "My method is to take the utmost trouble to find the right thing to say, and then say it with the utmost levity. And all the time the real joke is that I am in earnest." That exactly describes Shaw. And that is why people flock to his plays and come away laughing and thinking, and wondering what he really means, and arguing about it.

"G. B. S."—as he is known everywhere—was born in Dublin on July 26, 1856. He had very little regular education, for he had to start earning his own living at fifteen. In true Shavian fashion—"Shavian" (shā'vǐ-ăn) is a word coined from his surname—he tells us, "I am an educated man because I escaped from school at fourteen." At the age of twenty he went to London and did various kinds of office work.

George Bernard Shaw, the most distinguished English playwright of recent times.

A Socialist From the First

All the time the unknown lad from Dublin was giving a good deal of his leisure to reading and writing, and especially to debating. From the first he was a Socialist, of a fairly moderate kind, and he soon won fame as a formidable man to meet in a debate on Socialism. At first he used to speak at the street corners of London. Soon he was talking before larger audiences indoors. Socialism had no more brilliant or provoking defender in the world. He became one of the first and a leading member of the well-known Fabian Society of moderate Socialists, and did a great deal of writing and speaking for them and for the cause of social justice.

His first five novels have a good deal to do with Socialism. They were not very popular, and Shaw continued to be better known and more feared for his spoken words than for his written ones. But then, after various kinds of miscellaneous literary work—essays, book reviews, dramatic criticisms, and musical criticisms—he started to write plays. The result has been a series of the wittiest plays of our time—a series of the most amusing and the most tantalizing plays of any time. There are a good many people who seldom ever attend the theatre unless the play is one written by George Bernard Shaw.

He has provoked nearly everybody in the world, and he has captivated nearly everybody. When you go to a Shavian play you very often do not know whether you ought to laugh or frown. Nearly everybody ends by laughing.

His first play, "Widowers' Houses," was presented in 1892. Since then there has followed one brilliant success after another, and it is hard to say whether it has been more fun to see the plays acted in the theatre or to read them when they were published. "Candida" (kăn′dĭd-å) is one of the most popular, and "Man and Super-man" had a splendid reception. But there are many other successes, among them being "Arms and the Man," "The Doctor's Dilemma," "Major Barbara," "The Man of Destiny," "Fanny's First Play," "Androcles (ăn′drŏ-klēz) and the Lion," "Heartbreak House," "Back to Methuselah," "The Apple Cart," "Too True to be Good," "Saint Joan" and "On the Rocks". At many times, and by many people, Shaw has been vehemently criticized for things he has said in most of his plays. But it is impossible not to appreciate highly a man who makes you laugh so heartily, especially when you see how fearless and original he is. He has entertained and stimulated a whole generation, and his very caprices and oddities have set it thinking in its own defence. He is a riddle, and he knows he is a riddle. He loves it—and so does his public.

"Terrible Child" of the Theatre

When Shaw was a young man many people were amazed with this enigma. They used to call him the "enfant terrible" (ôN-fôN-tĕr-rē′bl′)—terrible child—of the theatre. That was because he went about upsetting people's pet prejudices like a mischievous little boy. Did people think that soldiers were always bold and patriotic? He would show them one who stuffed his gun with chocolate drops instead of bullets. Did they

suppose it was really the man who decided whether he was going to marry a certain girl? He would show them how deftly the girl made him do it. And in the give-and-take of conversation—to quote the title of another of his plays—"You Never Can Tell" what surprising idea a character is going to put forward next.

But the joke was on the people who thought Shaw's ideas absurd or alarming. For now that Shaw has grown old he finds that the world has caught up with him. Though we still delight in his wit, we no longer find it so alarming. Since Shaw loves to shock people, perhaps this annoys him!

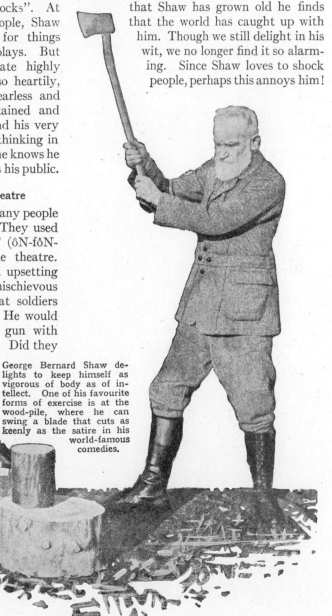

George Bernard Shaw delights to keep himself as vigorous of body as of intellect. One of his favourite forms of exercise is at the wood-pile, where he can swing a blade that cuts as keenly as the satire in his world-famous comedies.

A TELLER *of* GREAT SEA TALES

Born in Poland, Joseph Conrad went to Sea and became One of the Few Great Writers in a Language Not Their Own

HAVE you ever wanted to run away to sea? When he was fifteen, Joseph Conrad began to feel a great desire to be a sailor. He did not want to run away, and so he told his family. They took little notice of his wishes, but their obstinacy only goaded Joseph to a stronger desire to become a sailor. The family were naturally scornful, for he lived in Poland, out of sight of the ocean. He had been born there in 1857, and his real name was Joseph Konrad Korzeniowski (kôr-zĕn′ĭ-ŏf′skĭ). His ancestors h a d n e v e r been sailors; they had been soldiers, fighting for the freedom of their land, or poets and authors adding to its literature. Why should one of them be so set now on turning sailor?

But finally his parents had to let Joseph go. He said good-bye to the family, some of whom he was never to see again, and made his way to the French seaport of Marseilles. There, in his own words, "the puppy first opened his eyes"—for the boy obtained a berth on a sailing ship, at the age of seventeen.

Twenty Years a Sailor

For the next twenty years or more Joseph Conrad roved the seas, and went to many far-away places—to the Malay Archipelago, to Burma, to the wilds of Africa, and back to London. In the British service he worked his way up from an ordinary seaman to a captain in the merchant marine.

It seemed a strange thing to have a Pole as master of a British vessel. But it was never strange to him, for he had come to love England and he only wanted to serve her as best he could. In his twenty years of roving about the world, he saw

Photo by National Portrait Gallery

Joseph Conrad was a dreamer as well as a sailor, as you can imagine from this fine portrait of him.

many strange things and met with many exciting adventures. And he stored up all his memories without any fixed idea of what he was going to do with them. He remembered all the colours and smells and flavours of the Indian seas and of the ports and cities that he visited. He learned all about the sailors and adventurers, and about the brown, sun-baked natives whom he loved.

At the same time he read books, for there was plenty of time on a sailing vessel in those days, and more time between trips. He read stories in French and in Polish and in English, but he liked the ones in English best because he had grown to love and admire the language, of which he knew scarcely a word on his first visit to England.

One bright autumn day when he was ashore in London, he happened to be looking out of a window and thinking about the first time he had seen the man Almayer, far off in the Malay islands. For some reason that he did not know, he sat down at the table and began writing the story that turned out to be "Almayer's Folly." It was a strange thing for him to do. He was thirty-two, and not many authors begin to write so late in life. He was writing in a language which was not his own by birth, and that is a still rarer thing.

But neither of these things bothered him that sunny morning. His story began to write itself, as stories sometimes will for some authors. And soon there was a whole group of characters crowding around Almayer—a wife and daughter and a whole band of Malays Arabs, and half-castes. These people began to follow Conrad wherever he went, insisting on being included in the story, until Conrad felt almost like a haunted man.

So for several years he carried the growing manuscript of his story round the world with him—from London to the Malay Archipelago, to France, to Poland, to many other places. At last, in 1895, the book was finished and printed, and Conrad had started on the road to literary fame.

For a little while he felt free again, but soon many other characters began to crowd into his mind and beg him to put them into a book. The result was that down to his death in 1924 Conrad was as busy with his pen as he had ever been on the sea. He was a slow writer, because he wrote so carefully; but a score of his novels came from the press. Soon after "Almayer" there followed "The Nigger of the Narcissus." This was succeeded, among others, by "Lord Jim," by "Youth," and by "Typhoon," all powerful stories. He published his "Victory" in 1915, and his last book, "The Rover," which was left unfinished at his death, appeared in 1925. In 1926 his "Last Essays" were printed and given to the world.

Down to the Sea with Conrad

Although it was not his native language, Conrad's use of English is excellent, and he is loved and admired for his mastery of words. Because he knew so well the men, the places, and the things about which he wrote, his stories are wonderfully vivid. He took it as his task "by the power of the written word to make you hear, to make you feel, before all to make you see." And in that he has shown a fine skill and achieved an equally fine success.

He has taken us to places we should never see without him, and made us feel that we must have spent years there in his company. He has brought before us all the terrors of the deep, the beauty of the ships, the bravery of men that sail them to strange, far-distant lands. He loved to write about man's struggle with the elements, and of man's courage in the face of danger.

(CONTINUED ON PAGE 1057)

A lonely sea, a hidden reef, and a good ship going to her grave upon it—this is the kind of picture that Conrad painted in words so vivid that the memory of it lingers in our minds long after the tale is done.

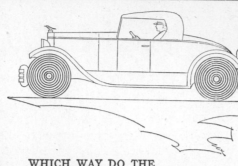

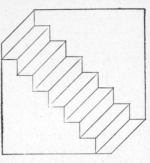

COULD YOU CLIMB THESE STAIRS?

At first glance these steps look quite as they should, but look at them a moment and they will seem to turn upside down.

WHICH WAY DO THE WHEELS TURN?

Look steadily at the centre of either wheel. Both wheels will begin to turn, especially if you give the page a quick circular motion.

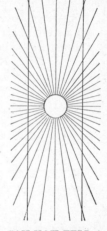

CAN YOU TELL A STRAIGHT LINE?

Are the two vertical lines above straight or curved? Be sure to test them with a ruler.

HOW WIDE ARE THESE STRIPES?

If you will fix your eyes on the two white spaces above, the space at the left will seem to grow narrower at the ends and the one at the right wider at the ends. They are really the same width throughout.

WHO IS THE TALLEST?

Guess which of the men above is tallest. Then measure them and see.

BLACK OR WHITE?

Which circle of the two below is larger, the black one or the white one? You may have to measure them to believe that they are the same

You perhaps will need to measure them to convince yourself that the two sets of lines at the left are each perfectly square.

FLAGS OF FOREIGN COUNTRIES

Flags of thirty foreign countries.   Other flags appear in the colour plates facing pages 609 and 913.

THE LAST JOURNEY OF A CHRISTIAN MARTYR

Down into the tombs of the catacombs sorrowing friends are carrying an early Christian martyr. The hunted Christians of Rome had built these secret tombs, some of them as much as seventy feet below the ground, as safe places in which to bring their dead; and sometimes, when the hunt was fiercest, they themselves sought refuge, too, in those underground galleries, which are still among the sights of Rome.

When the CHRISTIAN FAITH Saved EUROPE

For about a Thousand Years after the Fall of Rome There was Scarcely Anything Except the Church to Hold the Western World Together and to Tend the Lamp of Learning

(CONTINUED FROM PAGE 937)

WHEN the Christian religion was born into the world, it found a good many pagan religions there already—and by "pagan" (pā'găn) we mean religions that did not teach their followers to worship the God of the Bible. Now, there had been some good features in many of the pagan religions, and one of these was their willingness to allow a man to worship any god he chose. This respect for the beliefs of others we call "toleration." In Rome or in Athens there were numerous temples dedicated not only to the state gods but to the gods of other states as well.

If you lived in Athens you might spend a pleasant hour in the temple of Zeus (zūs), admiring the magnificent statues and paying your respects to the father of the gods. The next day you might attend a feast or celebration in honour of Mithras (mĭth'răs), a Persian deity. You might also learn something of the worship of other strange gods—

Isis (ī'sĭs) and Osiris (ȯ-sī'rĭs) of Egypt, Baal (bā'ăl) of Phoenicia, and Astarte (ăs-tär'tē) of Babylon. Worshipping at one of their shrines would no more prevent your visiting another than having one friend would mean that you must not have any more—although of course, there might be some among the gods whom you preferred above the others.

The Worship of Jehovah, the God of the Hebrews, the One True God

Among the many gods of the old world there was only one whose worship could not be shared with the worship of any other god. This was the Jehovah of the Hebrews. The worshippers of Jehovah believed that He alone was God. Certain kings, among them Nebuchadnezzar of Babylon, had tried to reconcile the Hebrew faith and the worship of other gods, but this was impossible. Either you believed in this one God, or in many gods. You could not worship both.

The Romans realized that there was a real difference between the one God of the Jews and the many gods of their own religions, and it was a rule in Rome that a Jew should not be forced to take part in general public religious feasts or ceremonies. The Romans were always tolerant of the Jews.

The Strange People called "Christians"

But towards the strange new people who followed Jesus of Nazareth, and to whom the name of Christians was first given in scorn, the attitude was different. These people claimed the same one God as the Jews, and indeed they numbered some Jews in their own ranks. But most of the Jews would have nothing to do with the Christians. They hated them even more than they hated the easy-going pagans, and the Christians could obtain no protection or help in that quarter.

Even so, this new sect might have won the friendship of the Roman government if they had not been so silent, humble, and secret. The hearty Romans could not understand them. These strange people claimed to work marvels in healing and saving men, but they would not drop a pinch of grain on Apollo's altar or pour out a little wine in honour of Bacchus (băk'ŭs), even though

they were torn to pieces by wild beasts for their disobedience. They would not even strike back when they were injured, and to the Romans this was simply cowardice.

Soldiers who became Christians often threw down their weapons and refused to serve. And the regular Christian meetings which were held for the purpose of worship led the emperors to fear a political conspiracy. In fact, these people took their religion so seriously that the pagans could not understand them at all. The Romans decided that the Christians were very immoral and superstitious. One writer spoke of them as "men of a new and vicious superstition"; another spoke of their "hatred of the human race," and branded them as "criminals who deserved the most severe punishment."

Persecuted for Their Faith

During the first few centuries after Christ there were terrible persecutions of the Christians, and their strong faith was severely tested by bloodshed. But through all the storms of hatred the Christian Church grew, because it gave to common men and women for the first time a faith great enough to comfort them for all the evils in the world, even for being thrown to the lions. The Christians preached love, patience, goodness,

Photo by Anderson

A NOBLE CHRISTIAN SUFFERS FOR HIS FAITH

It takes a fierce flame of faith and courage in any human creature to overcome the fear of pain and death. Yet through the long years men and women have died bravely for many great causes—religion, country, friends, their own honour. Perhaps no cause has had more heroic martyrs than those who died for their faith, like the one shown in this picture, in the early days of Christianity. He is being stoned to death.

humility of mind, gentleness and charity; and in the end their gospel of peace conquered the heathen worship the world had known before.

From the very early days of the Christian Church each little flock or congregation had a "presbyter," or priest, chosen from their

Galerius (gȧ-lēr'ĭ-ŭs) published a decree that Christians were no longer to be persecuted for their faith, because persecuting them was of no use. In 324 the emperor Constantine (kŏn'stăn-tīn) himself embraced Christianity.

By this time there were only two lead-

GENTLE ST. FRANCIS GIVES HIS LAST BLESSING

As St. Francis of Assisi lay dying, he bade the friars carry him to the church of St. Mary of the Angels, near Assisi, for he longed to die in the dearly-loved oratory there, where he had first dedicated himself to God. As the sad procession wound its way slowly out of Assisi, Francis asked the brothers to set down his litter a moment. Then he once more solemnly blessed the city which his blind eyes could no longer see.

own number to guide and help them. Later, groups of congregations began to meet, and higher officers, called "episcopi," or bishops, were chosen. By A.D. 300 there were several large groups of Christians in Italy, Syria, Africa and Greece.

Triumph of Christianity

These groups did not always agree. For example, in Greece and Syria it became a rule that no images were to be allowed, and that the priests must marry and wear beards. In Italy the priests were to be unmarried and clean-shaven and images were permitted. Many disputes were later to arise over questions such as these. One such question which convulsed nations was the correct way in which to calculate the date of Easter Sunday.

All this time the Christians were growing stronger and stronger. In A.D. 311, just after the terrific persecution under the emperor Diocletian (dī'ŏ-klē'shǎn), the Roman emperor

ing Christian branches—a Western Church at Rome, and an Eastern Church at Constantinople, the city which Constantine founded in 330 as his new capital. These two branches have both survived through the centuries, but with curiously different histories. In the East the Church came almost entirely under the control of the emperor, while in the West it was often to a large extent independent of civil control, and sometimes, indeed, far more powerful than kings or emperors.

The Greek Orthodox Church

The Eastern Church used chiefly the Greek language, and is usually called the Greek Orthodox Church. It differs from the Western or Latin Church not so much in its beliefs as in its refusal to accept the Pope as the head of all Christendom. The patriarch at Constantinople has always held the leadership in the Eastern Church, but as various states have grown up in Eastern

Europe they have formed national churches which govern themselves. Thus we have seen Russian, Bulgarian, Rumanian, Serbian, and Greek divisions of the Eastern Church.

From the time of Peter the Great until the Russian Revolution in 1917, the tsar of Russia was the head of the Russian Church, although he was tsar first and churchman afterwards. With the Russian Revolution the power of the Eastern Church was seriously crippled, although not destroyed.

The story of Christianity in the Middle Ages is for us mainly the story of the Church at Rome. When Constantine established his capital in his new city on the Bosporus (bŏs'pô-rŭs), the city that was named Constantinople after its founder, the Pope became the chief power remaining in the old capital of Rome. During the years when the Goths, the Huns, and the Vandals were sweeping down upon Rome, the Pope—whose name came from the Latin "papa," or "father"—quietly took up the task of maintaining what order he could and holding back Rome's enemies as firmly as possible. Undoubtedly, without the Pope Rome would have suffered even more ruin than she did suffer at this time.

Quarrels Between Popes and Kings

Leo the Great, who was Pope from 440 to 461, declared that the Pope, as the governor of men's souls, was higher in authority than the emperor, who only governed their bodies. Later in the century this doctrine was again preached by another Pope. But naturally the idea did not please the emperors themselves, who were still calling themselves rulers

of Rome, even though they had moved to an eastern capital.

The final split between East and West came towards the middle of the eighth century. Then began the great quarrel over images, beards, and the marriage of priests. The quarrel over Easter occurred between the Roman and the Irish Churches, but here there was no split, for the Popes triumphed, and Ireland and England entered the great Roman fold (664). It was very important that they should not be cut off from that powerful civilizing force.

In the Western world the Popes at Rome maintained the Christian doctrines with fairly little dissent for five hundred years, from 700 to 1200 and after. Strong Popes might well dictate to emperors, as we shall see, while weaker Popes could live quietly amid the magnificence of the papal court, influencing the affairs of kingdoms in many ways, great and small.

So long as the Christians were poor and persecuted, they remained simple and humble in their tastes. But when everyone was compelled by law to be a Christian—as later became the case—many people who cared nothing for religion, and who often were very wicked, became members of the Church. It is easy to see that the Church might suffer from this in many ways. It was becoming very wealthy and powerful, and sometimes selfish and dishonest men were eager to seize the wealth and power for themselves. We shall not be surprised, then, to find that many greedy, domineering men were tempted by the prospect of acquiring power, and of making themselves and their families rich out of the Church coffers.

The Church suffered from these bishops

Photo by Alinari

This is the church of Santa Maria in Aracoeli, one of the oldest Christian buildings in Rome. It was built originally in about A.D. 600.

and priests and Popes who used it for their own selfish ends. It grew rich and powerful, but its people were heavily taxed, and its more saintly priests were filled with grief to see those who were in authority over them caring more for the good things of this life than for the teachings of Jesus.

They saw their fellow clergymen committing simony (sī'mŏ-nǐ), the crime of buying an office or appointment in order to obtain the money or power that accompanied it. They sometimes saw men who had gone into religious houses to lead a holy life ignoring the vows they had taken. They sometimes saw people who had been summoned before the Church courts paying bribes to the Church officials in order to be let off.

But there are always people who, seeing that men have gone astray, are willing to devote their lives to trying to lead them back. One of these was a gentle soul known as Francis of Assisi (ä-sē'zǐ), as sympathetic and lovable a figure as we can find in all history, a man with the soul of a saint and the mind of a poet. He was born to ease and a gay life in the beautiful Italian town of Assisi, but when he was twenty he could no longer bear living in luxury while people were suffering in poverty all around him. He put on simple clothes, and after two or three years spent in ministering to lepers and outcasts, started out (1209), with neither food nor money, to devote his life to preaching,

and helping the poor. Other young men joined him and called themselves "frati"—brothers. We call them "friars," a shortened form of the word.

The Franciscans (frăn-sĭs'kăn), or followers of St. Francis, spread all over Europe. They called themselves "God's troubadours," and followed the rule that Jesus gave to His disciples when He said, "And as ye go, preach, saying, The kingdom of heaven is at hand . . . Provide neither gold, nor silver, nor brass in your purses, nor scrip for your journey, neither two coats, neither shoes, nor yet staves; for the workman is worthy of his meat" (Matthew x, 7–10). The Pope gave these "mendicant" (mĕn'dǐ-kănt) friars his protection, and by the time St. Francis died (1226) they had become very influential.

Photo by Anderson

ST. DOMINIC PERFORMS A MIRACLE

Many are the beautiful legends which are told of the mediaeval saints, and of the miracles of healing wrought by them in life or by the believer's faith in their holy relics. In this picture the artist has shown us St. Dominic raising a man from the dead.

St. Dominic (dŏm'ǐ-nǐk), a Spanish priest, founded another mendicant order (1214) known as the Dominicans (dŏ-mǐn'ǐ-kăn). They were "preaching friars" and had a powerful influence over the universities, where their vows of poverty and their many learned men won them more respect than they received in the wealthy life of courts. They, too, grew numerous and influential, for people everywhere were glad that the teachings of Jesus should be preached and applied to the everyday lives of men.

Now, while it is true that there were some wicked men in the Church in the Middle Ages, we must not imagine that it was mainly bad. Into it was gathered all the life of the mind and the spirit during those troubled times. In the first place, it was the centre of all the education and learning there was in Europe. All the schools and colleges were organized by the Church; there were no others. The learning of the time may sometimes seem strange to us now, in some ways, but it was very profound and very subtle.

Most of it centred round the monasteries (mŏn'ăs-tĕr-ĭ). Those were places, scattered all over Europe, where men and women could escape from the turmoil around them and lead lives of prayer and usefulness. Other religions in the East had had such retreats for a long time, and the custom began in the Christian Church in Egypt as early as the third century, when St. Anthony, at the age of twenty, gave all his property to the poor and for the next fifteen years led a life of the strictest self-denial, and then went off into the desert to live the life of a hermit until his death about sixty-five years later. Others came to live near him, and he spent many years in leading them in the quiet ways of holiness.

Other leaders had other flocks, and large organizations, or "orders," sprang up, with houses in many lands. The Augustinians (aw'gŭs-tĭn'ĭ-ăn) were followers of St. Augustine (354–430), the Benedictines (bĕn'ĕ-dĭk'-tĭn) of St. Benedict (480–543), and there were many other orders, both for men and women. Monasteries—or abbeys, as they are called in England—grew rich and afforded a safer and more pleasant life to many people than could be found anywhere

else. And if a man or woman was intellectual, to be a monk or a nun was practically the only opportunity the Middle Ages afforded of leading the life of the mind.

Thus it was in the monasteries that the flowers of learning grew. There books were copied in the pillared cloister around the central garden; and there were trained the great teachers who later went out to lecture at the universities.

But there were plenty of things a monk had to do besides study. All who were able were assigned some kind of manual labour, usually for about seven hours a day. The monastery carried on all sorts of work—farming, milling, baking, brewing, carpentering, tailoring, the raising of stock, and even the manufacturing of certain articles. For it was just like a village—a "model village," where the poor people in the neighbourhood could come to learn how things ought to be done. The monasteries and nunneries served as hospitals, too, and as inns for travellers—for the Benedictine rule laid it down that "All guests who come shall be received as though they were Christ."

The monks, then, were kept busy, for the most part. Moreover, their way of life was very strict. When they joined a monastery it was for their whole life, and they had to give up all their money and take solemn vows of poverty, chastity, and obedience. The Benedictines went to church seven times a day, with the first service before sunrise. In some very strict orders the monks or nuns might not even talk. But they were happy, for the most part, and

Photo by Anderson

ST. ANTHONY IN THE DESERT

One part of the ideal which the monks held before themselves was asceticism (ă-sĕt'ĭ-sĭz'm): the belief that the best way to perfect the soul is to neglect or torture the body. St. Anthony, who is portrayed in the picture above, went into the desert, as did many others, putting aside all the pleasures and comforts of ordinary men to spend his days in prayer and fasting.

THE HEAVENLY POWERS INSPIRE THE GENIUS OF FRA ANGELICO

Many of the great painters who arose in Italy at the close of the Middle Ages were monks. One of the most saintly of them was that "angelic brother," Fra Giovanni Angelico, who painted in an ecstasy of adoration, never taking up his brush without prayer. Have you ever seen, even in a good book-illustration, any of his lovely angels and haloed saints set against a background of clearest gold? If you have, you will understand why in this picture Fra Angelico is shown with angels playing and singing to him and guiding his hand.

those old-established orders of monks and nuns have lasted right down to our own day.

There were many other good works that the Church accomplished. For instance, it established an international language. This was Latin—for that had been the language of the early Roman Church. Latin was taught in all the church schools, and consequently no matter in what country an educated man had been born, he could always speak it. This helped greatly in the spread of learning. As late as 1600 Sir Francis Bacon wrote some of his great works in Latin because he thought Latin would be known longer than English.

The Church also kept the love of beauty alive. Almost all the art of the Middle Ages was religious. Architecture meant the building of vast cathedrals; painting and sculpture meant decorating their walls. The music was for the most part sacred, and most of the literature that has come down to us from this time was written by learned sons of the Church.

But, above all, the Church kept civilization from decay at a time when it would certainly have been swept away if there had not been some strong power to preserve it. The Roman empire had done this for hundreds of years past; and when it was overwhelmed by the hordes of barbarians, the Church was the only organization in the world that could take its place. The Church was like a great cosmopolitan state watching over the welfare of men, teaching them,

PETER THE HERMIT

Peter the Hermit, who emerged from his retirement to urge Christians to recover The Holy City from the infidel.

disciplining them, and passing on the torch of civilization from one century to the next.

The Christian faith and the Christian Church were at all times dearer to the great number of the common people than to anybody else. The message of Jesus spoke straight to the heart, as it will always speak, and the life of a true Christian was still the good life, to be led in a world full of evil and strife. The hold that faith had on men is shown in one of the most remarkable movements in the history of the world—in the Crusades (krōō-sād').

But in order to understand them we must go back a little in our story.

Three of the world's great religions have the same God; these are the religions of the Jews, of the Christians, and of the Mohammedans (mȯ-hăm'ė-dăn). Both the Christians and the Mohammedans adopted the Jewish conception of one God, and both regarded the Jewish Scriptures as revelations from God.

Mohammedanism is the youngest of these three religions. Its prophet, Mohammed (mȯ-hăm'ĕd), or Mahound (mȧ-hound'), as he was called in the Middle Ages, began to preach in Arabia in about 610. The Arabs heard him and were converted. As their ranks became stronger, Mohammedanism spread far and wide in Western Asia. It spread into Palestine, even into the holy city of Jerusalem.

To the Christian as well as the Jew, Jerusalem was a sacred city, and Christian and Jew loved to make pilgrimages to its ruined

Photo by Rischgitz

A WARRIOR RETURNS FROM THE FIRST CRUSADE

There were many such scenes as this witnessed during the time of the Crusades, either when the people sent off the Crusaders in high enthusiasm, or when they welcomed the warriors back again after some victory. The picture above portrays Leopold VI, duke of Austria, returning to Vienna in 1219 during the Fifth Crusade.

places, where Jesus and the prophets had lived and suffered. The pilgrims came in caravans overland, and each pilgrim had to pay the Arab Mohammedans a fee for permission to visit the holy places. This arrangement satisfied everyone. The Arabs were glad of the fees, and since they also regarded Jesus as a prophet, they had no religious reason for quarrelling with the Christians.

The Turks Capture Jerusalem

This plan continued until about the year 1000, when the Seljuk (sĕl-jōok′) Turks, a Mongolian race, began to move westwards from Asia, driving the Arabs themselves west and south. The Turks quickly became converted to Mohammedanism, but not to human kindness. They had not had time to advance very far out of their native barbarism. They were soon attacking the Christian caravans, and robbing and killing the pilgrims. After 1071, when Jerusalem fell into the hands of the Mohammedan Turks, no pilgrim was safe in the sacred city.

The Eastern Christian Church was helpless to prevent these outrages—indeed, in less than four hundred years (1453) Constantinople itself was to fall before the conquering Turk. But long before that, Mohammedanism had been spreading south and west throughout Northern Africa. It seemed that the new religion might be strong enough one day to overwhelm Christianity itself. The Saracens (săr′å-sĕn), as men of the Middle Ages called the Mohammedans, were growing in power, and the Christian world was beginning to suffer in consequence.

The Clever Plan of a Pope

Now, the Pope at this time was Urban II. He realized the danger that was threatening, he saw the restless spirit that had seized upon men all over Europe, he saw the violence and the bloodshed—to which the Church appeared unable to put an end, no matter how hard it tried. He decided to play off one of these forces against the other—to set the unruly warriors of Europe to fight the Mohammedans instead of one another, and so, by this means, to spread Christianity and strengthen the power of the Church.

The First Crusade

In 1095 he called a council at Clermont, (klĕr-mŏN′), in France, where, under the sky, he made a stirring appeal to the great throng who had gathered. "It is the will of God" were the words that burst like thunder from the multitude when he had finished; and thousands rushed forward to "take the cross." All who went on the Crusades were to wear a cross—on their breasts when they were going towards the Holy Land and on their backs when they were journeying home.

The movement spread like a flame. A monk named Peter the Hermit did a great deal to raise people by his preaching. From one place to another he rode barefoot through France on his mule and called men to repentance. So great was his influence and so saintly his reputation that "even the hairs were snatched from his mule to be preserved as relics." Thousands of people went with him, and started out, months before the date of departure set by the Pope, to follow him to Palestine.

They were little more than a mob—a lowly gathering of peasants and labourers and even women and children, untrained and unorganized. Under the leadership of Peter the Hermit, Walter the Penniless, and a few others who knew just as little of the art of war, they started to march those two thousand weary miles to crush the Mohammedans. They were themselves completely defeated by the Turks and the natives of the countries through which they passed, and thus never reached Jerusalem.

An Army of the High and Low

The main army, better organized and trained, set out somewhat later, various bodies taking different routes in order not to exhaust the food supplies along the way. This great army contained many representatives of the feudal nobility as well as

Photo by Rischgitz

Even the end of the Crusades did not bring to a close the long warfare between Christian and Moslem. The harbour of Malta, shown above, was the scene of a fierce fight between the Knights of St. John and the Turks in 1565.

BRAVE MARTIN LUTHER REFUSES TO DENY HIS BELIEFS

There had been heretics and reformers in the Church from early times, but it was Martin Luther, in the 16th century, who opened what we call the Protestant Reformation. Here he is refusing to recant his heresies.

common people, for the fever of the Crusade attacked high as well as low, although William Rufus of England, Philip I of France, and Henry IV of Germany were all out of favour with the Pope at the time and accordingly did not take part in the Crusade. Early in 1097 Constantinople was reached.

Jerusalem is Taken

Although hundreds of thousands of Christians perished on this first Crusade, it attained its main object, which was the capture of Jerusalem (1099). But, unhappily, the Christians showed no more mercy than the Turks had shown. All Jerusalem was put to the sword. The streets, it is said, ran ankle-deep in blood, and after a few days the decaying, unburied bodies caused a pestilence.

The Crusaders set up Godfrey of Bouillon (bōō-yŏN′) as king of Jerusalem, and vowed that nevermore should the Holy Land hold the followers of Mohammed. When Godfrey died, his brother Baldwin succeeded him.

Thus was begun the great series of conflicts that we know as the Crusades. Every generation saw a mighty wave of warriors moving eastwards to win titles or fame, money or lands, power or the forgiveness of their sins by going to fight in the holy cause. Fresh Crusades were continually being organized to the Holy Land.

Even children started out (1212), some twenty thousand strong, to conquer the Saracens. They were led by a boy named Nicholas, and took as their motto the Bible text, "Out of the mouths of babes and sucklings hast thou ordained strength, O Lord." From Germany they crossed the Alps and braved the heat on the plains of Northern Italy. People thought that the Lord would dry up the Mediterranean and let the host cross on dry land, and that then they would take back the Holy Land without having to fight at all. But many died by the wayside, others were sold into slavery, and some fell into the hands of evil men. Very few succeeded in returning home.

In 1187 the great Saracen leader, Sultan Saladin (săl'ȧ-dĭn), recaptured Jerusalem. Already Antioch had fallen before the Eastern hosts. Various Crusades were organized to recapture the sacred cities. The Third Crusade (1190) had for its leaders Richard the Lion-hearted of England and King Philip II of France. But the royal leaders fell to quarrelling, and the Holy City remained in the hands of the Saracens. By 1291 the Christians were completely dislodged from the Holy Land, and those amazing and exciting wars were over.

Why We must not Regard the Crusades as Being Only a Waste of Lives

The Crusades were thus a failure. But they accomplished things more valuable than the capture of the Holy Land. They welded men together in a common cause, at a time when people were devoting their energies to cutting one another's throats. The travel and contact with other men was an educating and civilizing force which turned the whole current of people's minds. The trade that was set in motion to furnish forth the knightly warriors and to bring back from the East things they had learned to use there, was one of the main forces that helped to make the world into the sort of place we inhabit to-day. All these things would probably have taken place sooner or later; but the Crusades hastened them, and therefore, though very costly reckoned in terms of bloodshed and money, they must not be counted as a total loss.

By the beginning of the fourteenth century the power of the Pope in Rome had ceased to be supreme. It was weakened in two ways. First, the turbulent kings would not always recognize a power superior to theirs, and in 1309, after much conflict, a Pope found it advisable to move to Avignon (ä-vē-nyŏN'), in France, where he might live under the protection of the French monarch. For nearly seventy years (1309–76) the Popes continued to live in France. Thus in the struggle between political and religious authority the religious power could hardly triumph.

How the Great Fear of Heresy Brought a New Terror into the World

The power of the Church was weakened in another way. During the thirteenth century a number of new beliefs as to the teaching of the Bible began to spring up. These were called heresies (hĕr'ē-sĭ) and believers in them were severely punished. But the punishments did not always have the effect of putting an end to the beliefs.

Later, a court known as the Inquisition was set up for trying heretics. Accused people were tortured to make them confess, and then were put to death in terrible ways, such as by being burned alive or boiled in oil. In this the governments were as much concerned as the Church, for nearly all people at that time had a horror of heresy. It was not just a religious matter. It was felt that the Church was the sole guardian of civilization in a world of great violence, and that to attack it was to attack the very foundation of order and security.

How the Desire for Greater Freedom of Thought Gave Birth to New Churches

But as fast as one band of heretics was suppressed another would appear. From this time, one group after another had to be suppressed, right up to the time of the Protestant movement, which began in Germany and spread over North-western Europe. It grew too strong to be stamped out, and a large section of the Christian people broke away from Rome to form various other Churches. For good or for evil, men's minds were not to be held longer in the mould of a single institution. They wanted greater freedom for thought, and this freedom was slowly won, through the centuries of the Modern Age which was to follow the Middle Ages.

(CONTINUED ON PAGE 1063)

How the SOUTH POLE Was DISCOVERED

Nearly Three Thousand Years Ago People Began to Say There was Land There; About a Hundred Years Ago We Discovered There was a Continent Larger than Europe

IT WOULD sound rather strange if we heard somebody talking about the Bear Zone and the Bear Pole. Yet that is what we are really saying when we talk about the Arctic Zone and Arctic Pole. For centuries ago, when the ancient Greeks noticed some stars that never seemed to move from their position due north, they called the constellation "Arctos," or "The Bear"; so our Arctic Circle and our Arctic Pole really mean Bear Circle and Bear Pole.

Now the ancient Greeks knew there must be another pole on the other side of the earth, opposite the Arctic one. They could not see any stars down there, because they lived too far north for that; so they had no name like "Bear" for the other pole. They just called it "Anti-Arctic," "Antarctic," which means merely "opposite the Arctic"; and that is the name by which we know it to-day.

The Greeks knew nothing about this region, but they imagined there must be some land down there, to balance all the land on the northern side of the world. And the legend of the land around the South Pole survived through the centuries from their time. Many centuries later, when explorers were going to most other parts of the world, some of them were seized with the idea of going towards the South Pole and finding out whether the fabled land really existed there.

Many years were to pass and many attempts were to be made before it was finally discovered, about a century ago. It is a great icy continent, bigger than Europe or Australia. And still we have no real name for this seventh continent — we just call it the Antarctic, or Antarctica.

This is the story of the way in which we found the South Pole and the vast continent that surrounds it.

Although the Greeks had believed in the existence of a southern land, it was not until 1418 that the southern hemisphere began to be explored. This was when Prince Henry

Photo by Herbert G. Ponting from "The Great White South"

This ship in its icy harbour is the "Terra Nova," which carried Captain Robert Falcon Scott to a gallant death in the Antarctic.

the Navigator of Portugal started sending expeditions on attempts to reach India by sailing round Africa, and to this end studied every possible scientific way of aiding such exploration. He it was who started the great explorations of the fifteenth centuries, and to him is due much credit for subsequent discoveries.

In the beginning the explorers were not looking for a South Pole, but for something else. They were all searching for a way across the water to India and China; one of them struck America merely on the way to India. Then they continued to search for the route to India, but they had to go far south, round the tip of Africa or the tip of South America; and little by little they approached nearer to the South Pole—though they were not looking for it—and learned more and more about the waters and the islands down in that part of the world.

That is what Diaz (dē'äzh) was engaged on when he rounded the Cape in 1488, as was Ferdinand Magellan (mă-jĕl'ăn) when he rounded South America in 1520. Magellan even saw some land to the south, and thought it was part of the continent that people had so long believed to be there. He named the land Tierra del Fuego (tyĕr'rä dĕl fwā'gō), or the "Land of Fire"—not because it was hot there, but on account of the many fires he saw.

During the next century a good many bold captains, mainly from Portugal and Spain, sailed through the Straits of Magellan and out into the Pacific. They discovered various islands, but they never went far south, for they were all bound for Asia; so New Zealand and Australia remained undiscovered, as did also the fringes of Antarctica.

Drake Makes a Discovery

By 1578 Sir Francis Drake was sailing round South America. Then a storm blew his ship southwards about as far as fifty-six degrees south latitude—the farthest south that any sailor had ever gone; he discovered that Tierra del Fuego was a group of islands, and not part of the Antarctic continent, as Magellan had taken it to be.

In the next century and a half there was plenty of travel round Africa and round South America, but little effort to go far south or to find the fabled continent down there. Nobody went far south unless he were blown there by high winds. Although Australia and New Zealand were soon dis-

By courtesy of Lady Shackleton

Brave men of several countries have explored the Antarctic; but of them all it is the British who have endured the greatest hardships. The pillars of snow seen in the picture above were built to guide Sir Ernest Shackleton's party back to the ship in the event of a blizzard destroying all their other guiding landmarks.

Landscapes and seascapes are familiar, but few of us have seen a view so completely made up of snow that it can be called a snowscape, like this photograph of Ross Island, with Mount Erebus in the background.

Photos by Herbert G. Ponting from "The Great White South"

The penguins are not interested in the iceberg seen in the distance. They are possibly wondering if their enemy the killer-whale has gone off far enough for them to take a swim in safety. They may stand here for some time debating the point until one of them goes a little too near the edge and gets pushed in. Then the rest will watch eagerly to see if he is eaten up, and if he is not, they will all flop in after him and sport joyously in the water.

covered, and many a little island was added to the map, and although the southern oceans were full of ships from many lands, very little search was made for the great southern continent, and nobody dreamed of going to the South Pole. They had other things to occupy their attention.

Practically the only man to try to reach the southern continent was the French aptain Pierre Bouvet (pyâr boo-vā′). His was the first trip made solely for the sake of science. In 1739, on New Year's Day, he sighted a new land about fourteen hundred miles south of Africa. He skirted it along the edge of an ice pack for some four hundred miles, nd then had to give up. He could not find out whether it was an island or a continent. We now know it was only an island—Bouvet Island—and that he was not within a thousand miles of the Antarctic continent, although he helped to find the way to it.

All this time there had been many people who still believed in the existence of the continent, and many maps showed some indication of it. One of the men who still had faith in the belief was Alexander Dalrymple of the East India Company; and he managed to persuade the British government to send out an explorer to search for it. The man they chose to go was James Cook, who had run away to sea when only a boy and had slowly worked his way up till he was a lieutenant in the navy. He became one of the greatest explorers of all time.

Captain Cook made three voyages to the South. In 1768–71 he charted the coasts of New Zealand and Australia, and gave final proof that these lands were separate islands and not part of the great southern continent. In 1772 he tried to find Bouvet Island and make a map of it. But he missed it and sailed on southwards, crossing the Antarctic Circle in 1773—the first man who is definitely known to have done so.

In spite of cold and ice, he eventually got as far as 71° 10′ south, the farthest any man had then gone. He discovered the mountainous island that we now know as South Georgia. But he found no southern continent, and came back convinced that none existed. Nearly everybody accepted his belief, and for a good while there was very little faith in the existence of any land round the South Pole.

But explorers continued to go south, and discovered island after island in the icy region. One of the greatest of these men was Bellingshausen, who was sent out by the tsar of Russia in 1819. He made two long cruises round the Antarctic Circle, and discovered Alexander Land

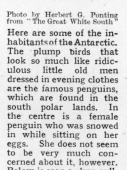

Here are some of the inhabitants of the Antarctic. The plump birds that look so much like ridiculous little old men dressed in evening clothes are the famous penguins, which are found in the south polar lands. In the centre is a female penguin who was snowed in while sitting on her eggs. She does not seem to be very much concerned about it, however. Below is seen a skua gull.

and Peter Island in 1821. Two years later Captain James Weddell created a new record by sailing about two hundred miles farther south than Captain Cook had gone. In 1831 a whaling captain named John Biscoe reached a point of land which he called Cape Ann. This, at last, was a part of the long-sought continent, for the point which he named Cape Ann juts out from the land that covers the South Pole.

Soon after this there were various other

By courtesy of Lady Shackleton

In spite of tremendous hardships and bitter disappointments, Sir Ernest Shackleton returned again and again to the Antarctic in search of scientific knowledge.

Below his portrait you see his ship the "Endurance," which was caught and crushed between two enormous ice floes, and sank when the ice at length released it.

voyagers from different nations. An American, Charles Wilkes, set out in 1839 on the first of two expeditions. He reached the coast of the southern continent and reported that he saw mountains there—and we now know that there are very high ones. A year or two earlier the Frenchman Jules d'Urville (jül dür-vēl′) had sighted the continent. In the same year as Wilkes, Captain Ross of the British Navy made the first of three trips to this land, on the second of which he got as far as 78° 10′—or about eight hundred miles from the South Pole. No one voyaged farther south until the present century.

It was not until then, either, that anyone attempted to spend a winter in the far south. But in 1898 a Norwegian, Carstens Borchgrevink, sailed with a party of scientists to stay for the six months of night that is the polar winter. On their sleds these men managed to penetrate about forty miles farther south than Ross had gone.

And now the stage was set for a great dash over the frozen continent to the Pole itself. Thousands of years after the Greeks had declared their belief in a southern continent, its actual existence had been verified. But what was it like? Although many men

THE NORWEGIAN FLAG FLIES AT THE SOUTH POLE

Some simple people think that Nature, in a thoughtful mood, placed a post at a spot at the southernmost part of the world with a sign marked "South Pole." But it was only after careful calculations with instruments that Roald Amundsen discovered the spot—exactly like any other on the vast polar plateau—that really was the South Pole. Here he planted the Norwegian flag and photographed one of the party with the dog team.

Here are some of the pictures taken by the ill-fated Scott expedition, showing how they lived in a land that would be too cold even for Eskimos.

A. Fish for dinner! Yes, but what a lot of work to get it! Often they had to cut a hole in the ice before the iron fish trap could be lowered into the water. And how would you like to eat fish for months on end—if you were lucky enough to catch any?

B. Here are the members of Scott's party at the Pole. C. The motor crew seem to think that life can be amusing even in this forbidding land.

How disappointed Scott must have been when, as is shown at F, he found Amundsen's tent and knew that he was not the first to reach the Pole!

At D is a portrait of Captain Scott and at E you see him in his tiny shack writing the famous journal which was later found on his body. It contained valuable scientific records and that last brave passage: "We took risks. We knew we took them. Things have come out against us, and therefore we have no cause for complaining; but bow to the will of Providence, determined still to do our best to the last." H. On the march with a heavy sled of supplies.

G. Under this rough mound lies the body of one of the bravest of Englishmen, Robert Scott.

Photos by Herbert G. Ponting from "The Great White South"

had sailed round it and mapped out its coasts, they had not travelled over it and explored its icy and craggy wastes. If they made the venture for the Pole, they would find out a great deal about the continent they had to cross to reach it.

In the past thirty years explorers of many countries have undertaken expeditions to the southern continent, and made several dashes for the Pole itself. The men of Norway, England, and America have led in all polar exploration, and the greatest names are those of Amundsen, Scott, Shackleton, Mawson, and Byrd.

Heroic Roald Amundsen, the First Man to Reach the South Pole

Roald Amundsen was the first to reach the South Pole, on December 14, 1911—two years and a half after Peary had discovered the North Pole. Amundsen had made the final dash with four companions and a pack of dogs. This was the same heroic Amundsen who first sailed through the North-west Passage five years earlier, who was to fly over the North Pole fifteen years later, and who was later to perish while searching in an aeroplane for the lost Italian flyers in the Arctic in 1928.

Sir Douglas Mawson never attempted to reach the Pole, but he spent about three years in the Antarctic, beginning in 1911, and with his party made very valuable discoveries for science.

Names That are Famous in the History of Antarctic Exploration

The names of Robert Falcon Scott and Ernest Shackleton are justly famous. No explorers of the Antarctic have been more heroic, and few have done more than they for the cause of science.

They began together in 1901, when they sailed for the far south in the "Discovery." They spent the winter in the ice and made many observations of the land. It was at this time that Scott made the first balloon ascent in the south polar region, though he had no intention of reaching the Pole by balloon.

But Scott and Shackleton, with one other man, did start on sleds towards the Pole.

They were forced to give up at about 82° because Shackleton fell ill; but they found out a great deal about the glaciers, the mountains, and the vast plateaux they would have to cross whenever they made another attempt. Shackleton had to return to England on a relief ship, but Scott remained for another winter.

Captain Scott is Beaten by Amundsen in the Race to the Pole

In 1910 Scott started on his second and last trip. This time he reached the Pole —on January 18, 1912—only to find that Amundsen had arrived there one month ahead of him. But neither Scott nor any of the four men with him were destined to return. They met with furious blizzards and endured heart-breaking sufferings as they tried to struggle home over the ice mountains.

One of them, Petty Officer Evans, fell from exhaustion and died from the effects of concussion. The others soon realized that their end was near. Captain Oates was the next to fall. His feet were so frozen that it was impossible for him to drag himself along further. He was too courageous to jeopardize what little chance of safety remained for the others. He hoped that by sacrificing his own life he might save theirs.

Why the Name of Captain Oates Will Live in Our Memory for Ever

When he woke in the tent one morning it was blowing a blizzard. He said: "I am just going outside, and I may be some time," and he staggered out into the storm. The others knew that Oates was walking to his death, and though they tried to dissuade him they knew it was the act of a brave man. Captain Scott kept a diary as long as his fingers could move, as a record of their journey, and nearly a year later the bodies of Captain Scott and his two companions, Dr. Wilson and Lieutenant Bowers, together with the diary, were discovered by a search party.

Shackleton did more than any other man before him to discover the secrets of the frozen south. In 1908 he made a heroic voyage and came within a hundred miles of the Pole. He climbed Mount Erebus, an icy, smoking volcano about thirteen thousand feet high.

These photographs were taken during Commander Byrd's expedition to the Antarctic. Modern science has at last produced ships which can plough through ice-filled waters, aeroplanes which can fly over the great ice barriers, and safe, almost luxurious, equipment of other kinds; so while the men of "Little America" suffered many hardships, they all returned alive.

Byrd's geological party found this heap of stones eighteen years after Amundsen left it there to mark his trip. Buried inside in a tin can was a page from the Norwegian explorer's note-book. On it he had written a short account of his discovery of the Pole.

The queer-looking specimen of humanity above is the man who drove the "snowmobile". He had to wear dark glasses because the sun on the endless expanse of white snow was so blinding.

The furry lump you see above is an Eskimo dog, which can sleep out in the snow in the coldest weather, kept warm by his thick coat.

Here is Commander Byrd with Igloo, his faithful little companion who went with him on his trips to both the North and South Poles.

Because of those tall broadcasting towers this settlement of Byrd's in "Little America" was in constant touch with the greater America at home.

With his comrades he fought his way through incredible blizzards, over the ice peaks, and along the great unknown glaciers.

Six years later he returned to the far south. This time his ship broke up in the ice, and he and his men drifted on an ice-floe for nearly a year and a half. Then they made a trip of nearly eight hundred miles through icy seas in a tiny boat. A man who has lived through that sort of thing has something to remember. He might surely be excused if he stayed at home for the rest of his life. But that was not Shackleton's way. The south called him once again, in 1921, and the next year he gave up his life there.

In more recent years explorers in the far south have been trying to learn more and more about the great continent there. One after another they have added to our knowledge, and enabled us to correct our maps of that inhospitable part of the world. In this work the aeroplane has been of great help, in spite of the terrific winds around the Pole and the lack of good landing places.

In 1928 Commander Richard Evelyn Byrd, of the American Navy, set out for two years in the Antarctic. Among other things, he intended to fly to the South Pole, just as he had flown over the North Pole two years earlier. There had never been an expedition so well fitted out. It included a special boat, built to resist the ice. There were also sleds run by tractors, several aeroplanes, an electric plant, and a wireless apparatus, so that he could keep in touch with the outside world. And every morning one could read in the paper about what he was doing in his icy camp—even about the puppies that were born down there, puppies that never saw the light until the six-months' night was over.

Byrd discovered a great deal. He charted an enormous stretch of land, and found a great range of mountains, with peaks reaching fifteen thousand feet. He and his companions made many flights in their aeroplanes. At last the day came when the winds were favourable for an attempt on the Pole. On November 28, 1929, he made the flight of sixteen hundred miles in nineteen hours, and thus was the first man to fly over both the Poles.

Photo by Herbert G. Ponting from "The Great White South"

A VERY GALLANT GENTLEMAN

This is Captain Oates, who laid down his life for his friends. When the survivors of the Pole party of Captain Scott's expedition lay in their small tent, hoping against hope that the blizzard which prevented their pushing on would end, Captain Oates, already badly frost-bitten, walked deliberately to his death outside the tent, so that his companions might share the few supplies that remained, and thus have a chance of surviving. Remarking that he was just going outside for a minute, this best of comrades made the supreme sacrifice without a thought of self-pity.

So men have gradually penetrated the most out-of-the-way corners of the world. Only a small field is left for the explorers of the future; but of course, there are areas of snow and ice that still remain to be charted.

The pioneers whose means of transport was a covered wagon could not set up wireless sets in the little cabins they built, and no newspapers were left at their doors every morning. They had, therefore, to be their own weather prophets, and take their readings from the winds and clouds and other natural objects around them.

Is It GOING to RAIN TO-MORROW?

How, with a Little Careful Attention, We May Become Fairly Successful Weather Prophets

(CONTINUED FROM PAGE 954)

IN OUR grandparents' time the ordinary person was far more expert in foretelling the weather than he is to-day. They had no meteorologist who pored over charts and tables and kept in constant touch by telegraph with the weather all over the country. So they learned to use their mother wit, and they were much more dependent on the weather than we are at the present time.

Consider the contrast—driving in an open carriage on a pitch-black night with a heavy rain falling and a rough country road ahead —and gliding along in a closed car with bright headlights and a smooth road in front.

So our ancestors, for thousands of years, kept a practised eye on clouds and noted changes in the wind. And ever since the earliest man decided that he did not like the heavy stillness of a hot summer afternoon, and drove the children into the cave before the storm broke, his descendants have been storing up observations on the weather and passing on their experience to their children. This is what we call folklore. Much of it was sheer nonsense; some of it was true only for the place and time when the rule was made; but a little of it is true for us to-day.

It is unfortunate that we do not know more about why and when the weather will change round our homes—especially since we must always be talking about it. Many of the forecasts from the Meteorological Office have to cover a large territory, and so cannot give much attention to any particular spot. But the new forecasts and advices now being given for air travel, go into the greatest detail for short periods. Before taking off, pilots and passengers of aircraft now know—with a good deal of certainty—the kind of weather they are going to meet.

How to Find Out From Which Direction the Wind is Blowing

Anyone who would know the meaning of the sky and its signs must own and study a good cloud atlas, which classifies, names, and explains clouds. The clouds are most important weather signs, for they change in accordance with variations in the upper atmosphere. A wet forefinger held up in the breeze is a rough and ready device, centuries old, for finding out from which direction the wind is blowing. But any boy or girl can make a weather-vane out of a very thin piece of wood and mount it on a pin, so that it will work quite as well as the one the meteorologist uses—and very much better than some of the rusty affairs that are continually telling untruths from the tops of towers. It is even possible to make a thermometer, a barometer, and a rain-gauge; you will find directions for them all elsewhere in this work.

None of these instruments is necessary; but if you want to be really scientific you will set them up and take readings from them regularly, as often as three or four times a day. And the record of those readings, jotted down in a book, will not only furnish matter for a great deal of interesting discussion and settle many an argument as to what the weather has been and when the first frost came, but it will soon teach you amazingly interesting things about how temperature and air pressure affect the weather in your particular locality. For every place has its own weather rules, resulting from the effect of neighbouring seas or mountains or lakes or plains or deserts. It is a fascinating game to try to discover them, and one which a group of friends can well carry on together, each one making and watching a different instrument and recording his observations.

But first of all let us see how much we can learn from our forefathers. They had a way of weaving their weather lore into homespun rhymes that were often better science than poetry. Here is one:

> Evening red and morning grey
> Sends the traveller on his way,
> Evening grey and morning red
> Brings the rain upon his head.

The same fact had been noticed long ago, for in the Bible we read, "When it is evening, ye say, It will be fair weather: for the sky is red. And in the morning, It will be foul weather to-day: for the sky is red and lowering." This is true now as often as it was twenty centuries ago. For in England, as in Palestine, the weather mostly comes from the west. A red sky in the evening means that the clouds have broken to the westward and are passing over; a red sky in the morning means that the clouds are still to the westward and have still to pass overhead. The rule does not always hold, but when it fails there is always a reason why.

Why We Know that Rain is About When Salt Suddenly Becomes Damp

Increasing moisture in the air, especially in the middle of the day, is likely to bring rain. We now know that this is because, if an updraught is started, the slight chilling will cause condensation of the damp air. Early observers did not know all this, but they had noticed that certain signs of increasing moisture were likely to precede rain. So the learned Roman Pliny (plĭn'ĭ) said that when metal "sweats" it is a sign of bad weather; and the North American Indians made the gruesome observation that "when the hair grows damp in the scalp house, we surely shall have rain." The early New Englanders had the homely saying that "a red sun has water in his eye"; and people in many parts of the world have noticed that when the salt grows suddenly damp, or walls gather moisture, rain is probable.

So an elaborate apparatus has never been necessary to tell men when the air was nearing the condensation point and would soon drop rain. Outdoor workers could see the signs all around them. The gar-

Photo by Swiss Federal Rlys.

A WISE WEATHER PROPHET OF THE ALPS

The shepherds who tend their flocks in the Alps have inherited many curious weather proverbs from their forefathers; and many of those old sayings are as useful in forecasting the weather as they were centuries ago.

dener noticed that the sunflower raised its head when the air grew damp and that all flowers seemed to give off a stronger perfume. He thought, too, that when spiders strengthened their webs rain was to be expected, and he observed that the pretty convolvulus always closed its trumpet at the approach of a shower.

How the Shepherds Prophesy

The shepherd, anxious to save his tender lambs from the chill of a downpour, had a wealth of "signs" at his command. His sheep frisked about before rain, for they were glad of the change from dry air to a comfortable moisture. Horses and cattle grew restless. Fowls oiled their feathers and were unusually noisy. And so sure were the bees to stay close to the hive that this gave rise to the saying, "A bee was never caught in a shower." If he looked skywards the watchful shepherd saw that the rooks were flying oddly, gliding like kites, and the distant hills appeared near if wet weather was on the way.

One of the most famous of all the weather prophecies for shepherds is the old rhyme:

> Rainbow in the morning,
> Shepherds take warning:
> Rainbow at night,
> Shepherds delight.

And it may often prove true, for the same reason that a red sky at night or in the morning often foretells the weather. Since most storms come from the west and since, in order to see a rainbow, you must be looking into raindrops with the sun behind you, it naturally follows that if it is the morning light that is being reflected by the rain, the storm must be coming up in the west. But if you are seeing your rainbow in the evening, with the sun behind you, the shower must be vanishing eastwards.

Sailors, whose very lives depended upon their skill in forecasting weather, used to watch the sky with great anxiety. They, too, would notice all the signs of increasing moisture. So they learned that a whitish-yellow western sky meant rain, and that a white, yellow, or greenish-yellow sunset meant a storm. A purple sky overhead they believed to be a forecast of hot, dry weather; but unusual colours set as a background to clear-cut masses of cloud were thought to bring rain and wind.

A hazy sunset was a sign of coming storm, and a hazy horizon a sign of unsettled weather; but a rosy sunset and a grey dawn were signs of fine weather. For haze in the air is always caused by moisture or dust. If it is moisture, the haze is white; and if it is dust, the haze is blue. A circle round the sun warned them of storm, and a mock sun or a moon rising red among broken clouds meant rain. There was also a saying that "the moon with a circle brings water in her beak" — and the larger the moon's halo, the sooner the rain was expected.

Pliny left us the observation that before a rising wind the fainter stars cannot be seen, even on a clear night. We know to-day that this is because churning air currents up above disturb the light rays. A few stars twinkling brightly against a very dark sky also mean rain—for moisture dims the fainter stars.

Of course, clouds are one of the best weather prophets, even for the scientist. The Bible says, "When ye see a cloud rise out of the west, straightway ye say: There cometh a shower; and so it is." And some would-be poet left a rhyme, that we may well remember, when he said:

"A mackerel sky—
Twelve hours dry."

No sailor in the olden days liked the look of this kind of sun. That ring meant that a storm was near.

Scientific prophets say that masses of greenish cloud gathering in the southeast mean heavy rains, and that clouds that are growing may perhaps reach a size when they will drop their moisture; but that rain from very high or thin clouds cannot last long. Rapidly growing cumulus clouds turn into thunder-clouds, but if they are still or move very slowly, the weather will probably remain fair. If a layer of cloud against the side of a mountain range rises, the air pressure is rising also; if it drops, the air pressure is falling.

An ice storm like this one, which occurred in America in 1921, can be very destructive. It lasted for three days and sheathed everything in ice, in some places to a depth of two inches. The damage it did to trees and telegraph wires amounted to hundreds of thousands of pounds.

Wisps of cloud in a white sky show the approach of an area of low pressure with rains—though sometimes the centre of the storm may be as much as a hundred miles away. After the storm centre has passed, the clouds are harder, and appear in a blue sky. If high clouds cover the sky there will be no rain unless they sink to lower levels. If they do, look out for a storm.

The Great Weather Carriers

The direction of the wind is one of the first things that a weather prophet notices, for the great cyclones that distribute weather always carry a variety of breezes. A wind blowing from the south-east means, as a rule, that the centre of the disturbance will pass near or to the southward. Rain then is almost certain. In general, winds that blow from the west, north-west, or south-west are loaded with moisture from their long journey across the ocean, and bring heavy rain on the hills in the west of England and Scotland, but they do not always bring rain to the lowlands in the east.

Over most of Britain the driest weather comes with steady winds from north, north-east and east. North and north-east winds are too cold to hold much moisture, and steady east winds have travelled for a long distance over dry land. In our unstable climate, however, there are no certain rules about wind and weather.

Veering winds should be watched with interest, but after a long spell of wet weather a change of wind to the north-west or north will probably blow the clouds away. The reason for all this will not be hard to understand if you will look at a diagram of one of those great cyclones and notice the direction in which the wind blows on its various sides, as it makes its counter-clockwise revolutions. You will see then why a north or north-west wind means that the storm has passed and ushers in clear, cold weather. Whenever clouds high in the heavens are moving in a direction opposite to those near the earth, you may know that a storm centre is on its way or else is taking its departure.

All along we have told you the signs that are more or less reliable. Most of them were based on the fact that, a rapid increase in the air's moisture or the passing of a storm centre was apt to bring rain. But there are many false "signs"—age-old superstitions—that are still passed on faithfully from one generation to another by people who ought to know better. One of them is the saying that if Candlemas, or February 2, be sunny, there will be much snow before May; and another is the superstition regarding St. Swithin's Day (July 15), which runs thus:

> St. Swithin's Day, if thou be fair
> For forty days 'twill rain nae mair.
> St. Swithin's Day, if thou dost rain
> For forty days it will remain.

The story, which has no historical foundation, goes that when St. Swithin died he laid a curse upon anyone who should disturb his grave. In spite of this, his remains were moved, and by chance on that very day a frightful storm swept the land. From this coincidence the superstition sprang.

If you are interested in learning more weather proverbs, you will find many of them in Richard Inwards's "Weather Lore."

It is common knowledge that everyone complains of the weather; and certainly it is true that people are perhaps a little sillier in their discussion of that eternal subject than they are about anything else. If it rains, they grumble because it is not fair; if it is fair, they grumble because it is too cold; if it is warm, they grumble because it is too damp; and if it is dry, they grumble because the wind blows.

One reason why it is so silly to be always complaining of the weather lies in the fact that no human power can change it. So to complain about it is just about as foolish as crying because you cannot go to live on the moon. The wise man makes the best of things as they

WHO CARES IF IT RAINS?

It is not particularly good weather in which to make a voyage, but this little fellow does not seem to mind it in the least. Well clad in his mariner's oilskins and Wellington boots, he laughs at the rain as he sets off for the pond with his precious new boat tucked safely under his arm.

are, and in doing so he conquers both the uncomfortable conditions and his own foolishness.

We should not be happy even if we were able to order from the meteorologist the kind of day we should like to have. For if we could do that, people would always be fighting about who was to have his own way. When one wanted rain to water his garden, another would want sunshine to go for a picnic; and when one wanted it warm because he liked to go swimming, another would want it cold because he liked to skate. On the whole the kind of weather we get is the kind that is most likely to make our lives run smoothly. If by chance there are floods or a very long dry spell, the event is so unusual that the papers are full of it.

So people would do well to stop worrying about the weather and to take it as it comes. By watching the clouds and the winds and the weather reports, we can learn to forecast it for some twenty-four hours, and so keep reasonably comfortable. And sensible people never complain of what they cannot help!

(CONTINUED ON PAGE 1042)

DOWN *Where the* MERMAIDS LIVE

In the Depths of the Mighty Ocean and Along the Vast Extent of Its Shores Live Creatures as Strange as Any of Those in Fairy-Land and as Beautiful as the Loveliest Flowers

FAR out in the sea the water is as blue as the petals of the most beautiful cornflower, and as clear as the purest glass. But it is very deep, deeper than any cable can sound; many steeples would have to be placed one above the other to reach from the bottom to the surface of the water. And down below live the sea-people.

The sea-people in Hans Andersen's delightful tale, "The Little Sea-Maid," were mermaids and mermen, sea-kings and sea-queens, who lived in castles of rosy coral and pale golden amber, played on golden sands, and floated hand in hand through groves of tall sea-plants, where rainbow-clad fishes glided through the waving branches, just as birds flit about among the trees in our own everyday world.

There were fascinating caves and grottos in which the little mer-children played hide-and-seek; and the sea-floor blossomed with wonderful gardens of sea-flowers for them to tend. But there were fearful forests of dark, writhing polyps—"half animals, half plants"—that clutched at them with long, snaky arms if they were bold enough to venture near; and there were terrible sea-witches, hundreds of years old, ugly enough to make one shudder.

Now, if we could plunge down, down to

The largest playground in the world! Twice a day, when the tide goes out, it leaves tons of fresh sand with which to build moated castles, and a brand-new set of trinkets of all kinds—seaweed and bright shells and many quaint and curious little creatures of the ocean— that anyone can play with until another tide comes in the bottom of the sea and wander as we pleased under the blue water, it is almost certain that we would look in vain to-day for the curious sea-people of the old fairy-tales. It is hardly likely that we should disturb a mermaid combing her hair in a coral grotto, or be startled by an old sea-witch peering out at us from a gloomy cavern. But we should have no time to feel disappointed at this, for we should find ourselves surrounded by so many strange and bewildering sights that we might well imagine we had somehow strayed into an enchanted kingdom.

Here in a dim, blue, mysterious light, a magic city of coral castles and fairy palaces rises from a floor of finest silver sand and rainbow-tinted shells. Domes and spires, towers and pagodas, that might have come straight out of the "Arabian Nights," are round about us on every side.

sponges and sea-anemones of every hue, where dainty jewelled fishes, gay as humming-birds, dart here and there, light as air bubbles, or poise themselves in the water, gently waving their little fins.

Shoals of mild-eyed fishes, for ever nibbling and nibbling like a flock of grazing sheep, move slowly together over wide-stretching meadows—blue, green, red and brown. Others chase each other in and out of the rocks in a never-ending game of follow-my-leader.

Queer little fishes, for all the world like gnomes and hob-goblins, peer from holes and sheltered nooks. Numbers of small, oddly-shaped creatures creep and glide about the rocks and slip hastily away out of sight when the shadow of some big fish passing overhead causes a sudden panic. In the deeper, darker waters, mysterious lights shine out here and there from

One could almost imagine that the makers of certain motor-cars had studied the eyes of this jewfish before designing their head-lights. If we were to study him we would find him a marvel of efficiency. Like all other fish, the jewfish has eyes with lenses almost as round as a marble, for that helps him to see under water. The two little holes not far from either eye are his nostrils. But he does not use them for breathing—

they only serve him for smelling, for they are nothing but little pits lined with a sensitive membrane. The jewfish is a formidable fellow. He is seven feet in length, and weighs at least five hundred pounds. He inhabits the waters along the coast of California, and his equally big cousin, the black jewfish, is found off the coast of Brazil. And yet this mighty creature is no more strange to look at than countless other beings that share his watery home.

We may discover a real Aladdin's Cave stocked with treasures of precious coral, glistening mother-of-pearl, and sparkling crystals; or we may wander into a wondrous rock-garden, gorgeous with coloured

the rocks on the sea-floor, or pass swiftly overhead, leaving gleaming trails behind them.

All sorts of thrilling adventures, too, may befall us in this wonderful kingdom of the sea. We may meet alarming-looking creatures, clad like knights of old in complete suits of armour and carrying weapons of fearsome spines and spikes. Or we may encounter a terrifying sea-monster with gaping jaws that will make us wish we were safely on dry land again.

Then there are those bewildering sea-people who have a startling habit of altering in shape and turning themselves into something else as you look at them. A weed-covered stone at your feet—or what looks like one—will suddenly come to life and calmly move away; a lovely flower-like thing will shrink up and transform itself into a dull-looking lump of jelly if you touch it; a slight hump in the sand will suddenly heave itself up and swim away as a large, flat fish with head and tail and fins complete.

There are, indeed, so many astonishing creatures living under the salt sea waves, and their ways and manners are so extraordinary, that the story of the real sea-people is as thrilling as any fairy-tale that was ever told.

The scenery of the under-water world is often as strange and picturesque as the wonderful little creatures that dart about in it so gracefully and rapidly.

But before we make the acquaintance of the interesting inhabitants of old Father Neptune's kingdom, it is just as well to know something of this wonderful water-world of theirs. There are vast multitudes of creatures living in the sea—many, many more than there are land creatures living on firm dry ground.

For the waters of the earth occupy considerably more than twice as much space on the surface of the globe as the land. To be more exact, if the earth's surface were divided into seven equal parts the sea would cover nearly five of them. In some parts of the ocean the water is several miles deep,

much too deep for any diver to go down to explore the sea-bottom. Yet we know that in these dark depths countless delicate sea-people live out their strange lives, moving about under an enormous weight of water that would crush a human being as flat as would a steam-roller.

But these dainty creatures live here as comfortably as their relatives who make their homes in the shallow sunlit pools of the sea-shore. No matter whether the water be deep or shallow, warm or cold, clear or muddy, it is sure to be inhabited by a vast multitude of strange and interesting animals of all sorts and conditions. Some live in the surface waters; some swim about at different depths; and others pass the whole of their lives deep down at the bottom of the sea.

There are hills and valleys under the sea, just as there are on dry land. There are vast plains and gentle slopes covered with sands and gravels of different colours. Here and there are raised terraces and steep cliffs, and far out in mid-ocean are deep, dark abysses where the sun's rays can never penetrate.

The surface of the sea, as we well know, is often lashed to frenzy by fierce gales. The angry waters swirl and gather into mountainous waves strong enough to batter and sometimes even to sink the largest ocean liner. Yet, only a short distance below the wild tumult, the water is hardly agitated. The lower you go the calmer it grows; and the sea-folk living at or near the bottom of the sea are not at all disturbed by the storms raging over their heads.

Everyone knows that the sea is salt, but not everyone, perhaps, could tell us why this is so. In olden days, before people had learned very much about this wonderful world of ours, many quaint tales were invented to account for the strange saltness of the "briny ocean." Here is one of the best of them.

A Wonderful Mill which Ground Out Anything that was Required of It

A certain miller possessed a couple of mill-stones which had the delightful power of grinding out of nothing at all whatever their owner desired. Did he wish for gold, food, clothing, or any pleasure or luxury, he had only to say,

> "Mill, mill, grind away;
> Grind me silver and gold, I pray—"

or anything else he needed at the moment. So the lucky miller lived in great contentment, doing no work, yet having everything he wanted without the slightest trouble. But his neighbours grew envious, and were always trying to discover the secret of his wealth. This he prudently kept to himself.

At last one day a seafaring man hid behind the door of the mill and overheard the miller repeat the magic rhyme. Then, fearing he might be discovered, he ran off as fast as he could. In the dead of night, he came back with some companions, and together they stole the millstones and carried them away to their ship.

When they were far out to sea the men began to prepare a meal; but they found they had no salt on the ship. Thereupon, the thief who had learned the magic rhyme ordered the stones to grind salt for him. Immediately the stones began to grind, and a stream of salt poured forth upon the deck. "That's enough," cried the man. But the stones paid no attention to him. Too late he realized that, although he knew how to start the stones grinding, he did not know how to stop them!

The Mill Refuses to Stop Grinding and the Ship Sinks Under Its Load

He tried everything he could think of, crying "stop," "cease grinding," "we don't need any more salt." But it was no use; the millstones went on grinding until the ship sank beneath the weight of the salt and went down, down to the bottom of the sea. The men, of course, were drowned; but the stones went on grinding. As no one knows where they are, or how to stop them if they could be found, the magic millstones go on steadily grinding out a stream of salt to this day.

The idea of the old millstones grinding away for ever and ever at the bottom of the sea is very fascinating, but the real, sober truth is that the salt is carried down to the sea by all the rivers of the world that flow into it. That fresh water should make sea

The boat is surely going to sink unless someone has the sense to throw the machine overboard. But you see they are all stupid—as greedy people are likely to be—and so instead of thinking hard they just await events.

water salty seems to be impossible; but so it is. All rivers really contain salt, though in such small quantities that if we taste the water we do not notice it. The average amount of salt in river water is only about twelve grains to the gallon—sometimes more, sometimes less.

How the Salt from the Earth Finds its Way Down to the Sea

The salt in the river comes, in the first place, from the earth's surface. The rain descends upon all the continents and islands of the world and dissolves small quantities of mineral salts out of the rocks upon which it falls. The dissolved salts are washed away by the streams and rivers as they wander through the land on their way to the sea.

For millions of years the rivers, like the magic millstones, have been pouring salt into the sea—and leaving it there. So the sea becomes ever saltier and saltier. How-

volcanoes, are always being washed or blown into the sea, while the waves are for ever pounding upon the rocks near the shore and breaking off fragments, which are ground into powder and washed away by the tides.

Dame Nature is always at work, hewing and carrying, and altering the face of the earth. Her tools are the wind and the frost and the rain, the little springs and the waves, and her grindstone is the seashore, where the pieces of rock that are split from the cliffs by her chisels and hammers are beaten and pounded into pebbles and finally ground into sand.

How the Carpet that Covers the Floor of the Sea Has Been Formed

But it is not only from rocks ground up by the waves, dust blown by the winds, and earth carried by the rivers, that the thick carpet of sand and mud and ooze covering

LACE-LIKE DESIGNS FORMED BY THE SKELETONS OF TINY SEA CREATURES

On the left is a picture showing what a tiny piece of sea-bottom is like when magnified fifty thousand times. The little tower in the centre and the piece of lace on the right are really the lime-encrusted skeletons of tiny creatures too small to be seen with the naked eye. They are called "Radiolaria," which comes from the Latin for "little rays." Large tracts of the floor of tropical seas are covered with these skeletons.

ever, the change is taking place so slowly that it will take millions of years to make any appreciable difference.

For untold ages the rivers, the winds, and masses of floating ice have been carrying all sorts of material to the sea to help to form a carpet for the great rocky floor of the ocean. Particles of earth, dust from the deserts and

the floor of the oceans has been formed. Sea creatures themselves have played an important part in its manufacture. Deep layers of crushed and broken shells, mixed with the brittle skeletons of numberless sea-folk that have lived and died in the sea, extend for many miles at the bottom of the Atlantic, Pacific, and Indian Oceans.

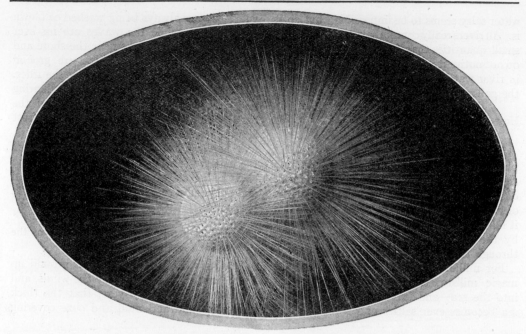

You can imagine how fine are the threads on these little Globigerina when you know that in real life the whole animal is the merest speck. Yet it was millions of these tiny creatures that ages ago gave their skeletons to make the limestone in our buildings. Note the tiny holes through which the long "feelers" are extended.

It is not so much the monsters of the deep, the whales and giant fishes, that have contributed chiefly to the making of these layers—though their bones are of course constantly being added to the piles accumulating below. They are formed principally of the shells and bones of the little sea creatures, the millions upon millions of tiny animals, many no larger than specks of fine sand or dust, that swarm in the oceans.

Beauty in Specks of Living Jelly

Little things often have long names. Some of these living atoms of the sea are called "Foraminifera" (fō-rȧ-mĭ-nĭf′ĕr-ȧ); but as that is really much too long a name for everyday use, we will call them "Forams" for short. These Forams belong to the simplest forms of animal life. They are, in fact, nothing more than specks of living jelly. You would hardly think that such tiny things as these could be either interesting or beautiful, but indeed they are; if you once saw some of them under the magic eye of the microscope, you would quickly change your opinion.

In reality they are most beautiful creatures: for their shapeless, jelly-like bodies are enclosed in dainty shells, which make the most charming little dwelling-houses imaginable. Some are like crystal globes pierced all over with hundreds of tiny holes, through which hundreds of fine, glistening threads stream out, surrounding the ball with a cobwebby rainbow cloud as it whirls and twirls in the water. Some are pearly, fluted shells, with cloudy streamers issuing from a single opening to guide the tiny craft on their way. Others are shaped like vases, goblets, bottles, or spiral shells; but as there are some two thousand different kinds of Forams, it would be hopeless to attempt to describe them all.

The sea, the Atlantic Ocean especially, is so stocked with these tiny, shell-like things that it is useless even to try to calculate how many there may be living there at the present moment—you might just as well try to count the grains of sand on the seashore. They swarm at every depth of the ocean, from the very surface to the floor of the sea. We do not notice them, for they are much too minute for the naked eye to see.

The Forams start life as mere blobs of

jelly, with nothing at all to protect their little bodies. Each one has to build its tiny house—or "test," as it is called—for itself. They have their own ideas on the subject, and each little Foram constructs its home according to the plan approved and always followed by its own particular family, or species (spē'shēz), with never a tool to work with and nothing in the shape of a hand, a claw, or a mouth to aid it.

One little creature will pick up the finest grains of sand and fashion a flask-shaped residence with a short neck and a single door, or opening. Another will take the coarser quartz grains from the same patch of sand and build them into the shape of a spiral shell, fixing each grain in position with a kind of natural cement that comes from the body of the strange little animal. Some use both fine and coarse grains of sand in their building operations; others mix the tips of sponge needles with the sand; and still other houses are decorated with chips of coloured quartz, red and green, orange and amber, which flash like jewels.

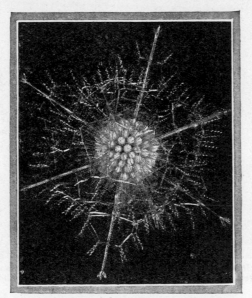

This little Radiolarian seems to be imitating a snow-flake, which is just as exquisite in its own way. But when you remember that you must have a microscope to see this beautiful lace, it makes a snow-flake appear rather coarse beside the tiny animal.

These little "sand-masons" live at the bottom of the sea. Those animals that spend their days floating about in the water must needs choose some other material with which to form their tiny dwellings. So, instead of sand, the floating Forams use carbonate (kär'bŏn-āt) of lime, which they extract from the sea itself. For sea water contains several kinds of salts in solution; and these microscopic, headless, brainless, limbless creatures are able in a wonderful way to select from it exactly the right materials for their work.

The tests of floating Forams are of two kinds. Some are smooth and white, and look as if they were made of the finest porcelain; others are clear as glass, and often covered with long, delicate, tapering spines.

The porcelain shells have only one opening; but most of the glassy ones are covered with minute holes or pores. Through these pores, or through the single opening, as the case may be, the little inmate pushes forth long, slender threads of jelly which stream out all round it as it moves through the water. These streamers are called "false feet," for by shooting them out on one side and drawing them in on the other the strange little animal can journey in any direction it pleases.

But they have another and even more important mission in life, for the Forams use these waving threads as fishing tackle wherewith to fish for their dinner. When a microscopic speck of anything eatable floats within reach of these streaming threads, it is surrounded and entangled in a living net. The threads then fuse together, enveloping the tempting morsel in a blob of jelly; and then and there all the goodness is sucked out of it. Having finished its meal, the Foram allows the indigestible portions of the food to float away and draws its streamers inside its shell, in order that the nourishment may be distributed all through its body.

A strange way indeed to eat one's dinner! But then, these peculiar little animals have no head, mouth or stomach. They simply take in food and digest it at any part of their elastic bodies that comes in contact with it!

Now, year in and year out, unthinkable numbers of these wonderful little sea-dwellers are starting life as invisible atoms in the deep blue sea. They build their tiny houses,

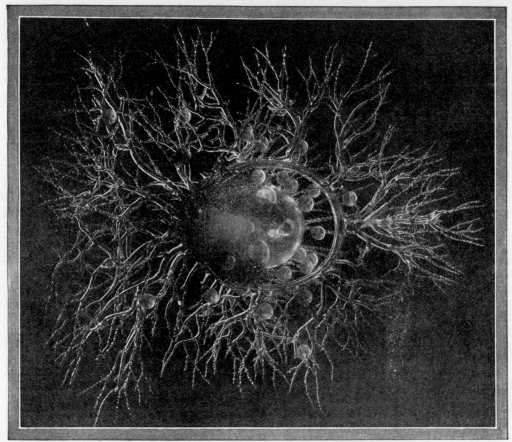

This, also, is a Radiolarian. It is one of the great tribe of the Foraminifera. Could you imagine a more beauti- ful basket of flowers than it appears to be if you turn the picture sideways, with the top of the page to the left?

live their little day; then, dying, their frail bodies are dissolved by the salt water. But their indestructible shells sink lightly, gently, down to the bottom of the ocean, and are added to the ever-increasing pile below.

A constant rain of these tiny shells is for ever falling, falling through the deep waters to the dark depths at the bottom of the Atlantic, especially the shells of one little Foram with the imposing name of "Globigerina" (glō-bĭj'ĕr-ī'nȧ). This species is so abundant that great beds of "Globigerina ooze," extending for thousands of miles under the sea, are composed almost entirely of these beautiful glassy tests.

This rain of microscopic shells has been falling for ages and ages. For the Foraminifera are a very, very old race of tiny beings. Their family history goes back to the earliest ages, and their ancestors were floating about in the ocean long before any of the upstart fishes—who act as if the sea belonged to them —were even thought of.

Rocks and Cliffs That Consist Largely of Crushed Shells

The story of these little creatures is written for all to read in the records of the rocks, the cliffs, and the hills. Their shells, called fossils (fŏs'ĭl), are found in some of the oldest rocks of Canada; while the white chalk cliffs and downs of England and the masses of limestone rock in many of the mountain ranges of Southern Europe are largely composed of the crushed shells of these remarkable little animals.

At the first this may seem rather astonishing, that the cliffs and the hills and the downs, which are on dry land, should have been formed at the bottom of the sea, but the reason is this: In the long, long ages that have passed away, great changes have taken place in this old world of ours. Much of the earth's surface that to-day is high and dry was at one time, long ago, completely covered by the deep, rolling waters.

There rolls the deep where grew the tree.
O earth, what changes hast thou seen!
There, where the long street roars, hath been
The stillness of the central sea.

The shells of yet another race of tiny sea animals are found in vast numbers in the old rocks of Bermuda and Barbados and other islands of the West Indies, and in many other parts of the world. These "Radiolaria" (rā′dĭ-ŏ-lâr′ĭ-ȧ), as they are called, are most abundant in the tropic seas, where great tracts of the ocean floor are covered with deep layers of their tiny, flinty skeletons, all blended together into

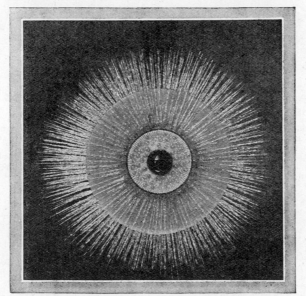

Here is another of the beautiful and varied Radiolaria.

a soft, oozy mud which is known to the Scientists as "Radiolarian ooze".

They are quite as interesting as the Foraminifera and, perhaps, even more beautiful. Their tiny transparent bodies glow with rich tints of crimson, yellow, or blue, and their little skeletons are like exquisitely carved stars, spiked helmets, bells, and coiled shells, all beset with the long, delicate, radiating spines which have given these tiny creatures the name of Radiolaria.

In comparison with the Forams and the ray animals, the Noctiluca (nŏk′tĭ-lū′kȧ), another quaint little sea-dweller, is a positive giant. although actually it is scarcely larger than a full stop on this page. It is a funny-looking little thing, like a minute blown-out bladder or an air bubble, with a dent in one side which gives it somewhat the shape of a peach. In this dent is the creature's mouth, through which it sucks in its food, consisting of fragments of water plants so small that they are quite invisible to our eyes. A short lasher, like a funny little tail, projects from one side of the mouth; with this the Noctiluca vigorously thrashes round in the water, and so jerks itself along.

In warm weather millions of these odd little animals crowd together at the surface of the sea, not far from the shore. They are sometimes so abundant that they colour the water, giving it the appearance of tomato soup. A still summer night is the best time to see these small wandering sea-folk. Then every little Noctiluca is transformed from a bag of dull reddish jelly into a fairy lamp glowing with a soft blue or greenish light that comes and goes as they jostle and bump against one another in the water. They cause the gently rippling waves that break upon the shore to flash and sparkle as with fire.

This strange power of illumination that Nature gives to certain of her children we know as phosphorescence (fŏs′fŏ-rĕs′ĕns). Such light is without heat. Not one of the creatures that flaunt their bluish fire ever gets tail or toes burned by it. The glow-worms, the fire-flies, and the many other luminous creatures that live in the sea light up their lamps as safely as any of us may press an electric button. And, considering their size, what a wonderfully vivid light it is!

(CONTINUED ON PAGE 1127)

OUTDOOR GAMES

ORANGES AND LEMONS

This is a very old game, which has been played by many generations of children. Two players, generally the tallest, stand face to face and clasp each other's hands high above their heads, in this way making an arch. A single file is then made and the rest of the players pass under the arch, singing:

Oranges and lemons,
Say the bells of St. Clement's;
You owe me five farthings,
Say the bells of St. Martin's;
When will you pay me?
Say the bells of Old Bailey;
When I grow rich,
Say the bells of Shoreditch;
When will that be?
Say the bells of Stepney;
I'm sure I don't know,
Says the Great Bell of Bow.
Here comes a light to light you to bed;
Here comes a chopper to chop off your head.

When the singers come to the words, " chop off your head," the bridge falls over the head of the person who happens to be beneath it. Now, before the singing began, the two players who form the bridge decided that one of them should represent "Oranges," and the other, "Lemons," but the rest of the players are not allowed to know which is which. As soon as the bridge has fallen the person caught is asked in a whisper whether he will be an orange or a lemon. When he has chosen, he is sent to stand behind the player who represents the fruit he has selected.

The song and march begin again, and as each one is caught and chooses, he or she lines up behind "Oranges" or "Lemons." When all have been caught, and have taken their places, a mark is made between the two players forming the arch, and a tug-of-war takes place between "oranges" and "lemons." The side that succeeds in pulling the leader of the other side over the mark wins the game. New leaders are then chosen.

CHINESE TAG

The game of tag is similar the world over except in China. There the player who is " it " must put his hand over that spot on his body on which he has been tagged, and must keep it there until he has tagged someone else. Since a player may be tagged on the heel, between the shoulders, or in some other place that is inconvenient for him to reach, the game may be very amusing.

CROSS TAG

This game is another version of the familiar game of tag. Let us say that Joe, who is " it," is chasing Ann. Now if Ted should run between them, Joe must give up chasing Ann and follow Ted. Then if John should run between Joe and Ted, Joe must follow after John—and so on until Joe succeeds in tagging the last person to cross his path.

WOOD TAG

This, too, is a form of tag. It will be the duty of the player who is " it " to tag one of the other players. But no one may be tagged who is standing on wood, clinging to a tree, or holding on to a wooden fence.

MIMIC TAG

The person who is " it " starts out after one of the other players, whereupon the person being chased begins to perform various antics. He jumps over an obstacle, lies down and rolls over, or does anything else he can think of. The player chasing him must mimic each action; if he fails to carry out this rule his tag will not count.

SHADOW TAG

In this form of tag the person who is " it " must step on the shadow of the person he tags, or else his tag does not count. You can have a great deal of fun playing this game in the moonlight, or on a day when the sun comes and goes behind the banks of clouds.

Buildings **are dreams**, dreams that have come true in wood and stone. But the dream must be lived with and pondered, sometimes for many years, before the man who cherishes it can take the solid blocks and pile them into a pyramid or tower.

The FIRST HOMES BUILT by MAN

The Primitive Architects were Trying only to Keep Out the Wind and Rain, but Their Crude Efforts Led to the Building of Magnificent Temples and Palaces

WE ARE all builders. We have all piled up wooden bricks into a towering castle on the floor, and called to everyone to come and see. For we were as proud as if we had built St. Paul's Cathedral.

And we have all built sand castles or breathlessly set up a house of cards. What if they should collapse! We did not know, then, that our little towers and domes had to obey just the same laws as a cathedral spire or a skyscraper—for every builder has to overcome certain great forces of Nature. We went ahead and did our best with our castles and our houses because it is in the nature of all mankind to love to build and to create. As soon as we can build something that is beautiful as well as strong and useful, we are happy indeed. And it is then that we may be said to be architects.

When men first began to build, they did not have much time to worry about how their houses looked. What they needed was a shelter to keep out the wind and rain and to ward off prowling animals at night. So their early homes were not very different from the tents or huts you can make with some pieces of wood and an old tablecloth— except, of course, that early man had no boards or nails.

Houses Built of Trees and Mud

The first houses probably resembled tents. Young trees or saplings would be stuck in the ground in a circle, their tops tied together with a piece of raw hide or strong creeper. Thin branches would be woven between the saplings until the contraption looked like a basket, and then the whole thing would be plastered over with mud or covered with turf and a hole left for the door. A flat stone in the middle of the floor would form the hearth, but as the chimney was not thought of until very much later, the smoke had to find its way out through a hole in the roof.

You can see at once that the first huts had to be very small, and that, no matter how carefully they might be built, a strong wind would lay them flat. Many an early family must have wakened during a thunderstorm to find their tiny but very precious house tumbling in confusion about their ears.

The men who lived in caves looked something like this. Their homes could not have been very comfortable, but at least they afforded shelter from the wind and the rain and the unwelcome attentions of hungry beasts.

Time has played strange tricks in preserving for us certain things from the long ago. Countless vast stone structures have crumbled away; but scholars digging recently in the soft earth in Southern Mesopotamia (Iraq) near Ur, the city of Abraham's birth, came upon some of the little ancient homes. Here women worked and children played six or eight thousand years ago, and here the tiny tots built houses in the soft, warm mud that lay about them everywhere in that marshy land, just as children do to-day.

Man, however, lived on the earth a long, long time before he learned to make a house for himself. At first he roamed about without a home. Then he dwelt in caves that he found or dug in the side of a cliff. He was a savage in those days, and lived on the animals he killed and the fish he caught—and it did not take away his appetite to eat them raw. But, even then, he had a desire for beautiful things, and sometimes he decorated the walls of his dark, smoky den with drawings that amaze us—they are so skilful in design and lively in colour and action!

As long as man was a savage, the cave served him very well for a home; but after a good many thousands of years he began to tame some of the wild animals—the cows and goats and sheep—and drive his flocks wherever he could find grass. He could not carry his cave with him, nor yet the materials to set up a hut, so he invented tents, made out of skins from his flocks. Such were the dwellings of Abraham, of Isaac, and of Jacob, and such are the only homes the Bedouin Arabs know to-day. But what do caves

A house like the one above is not by any means perfect, but it is quite convenient if its owners must keep travelling about. But it is not to be recommended for those who dislike a draught of chilly air.

At the right is the very simple affair that serves to shelter certain natives of the tropics. Luckily, in their climate, a free circulation of air is desirable, and a leafy covering keeps off the sun better than a tiled roof.

and tents and huts have to do with architecture? Now the answer to that question is very interesting and important, and when you know about it you will understand a great law that governs all our history—a law which in architecture has helped to produce all the different

Here are some of the strange houses that men have built: A—Swiss lake dwellings of six or eight thousand years ago, the first wooden houses in Europe. B—Tree house in the Philippine Islands. C—Native mansion in West Africa. D—Wigwam of the North American Indian. E—Laplander's cottage, for the winter weather. F—The first flats, homes of the picturesque cliff dwellers in the south-western United States.

A—Primitive people always build their houses of materials provided by Nature. So we need not be surprised to find the African Zulus building their "kraals" of reeds and grass, as shown here. Those thatched domes serve very well to shed the rain and ward off the sun's rays. And in that climate the last thing anyone wants to do is to keep out the cold! We might find the interior, with its mud floor, a trifle bare, but the Zulu has not yet reached the stage of feeling a need for any other kind.

B—This hut shows how clever the natives of the Tonga Islands are at building with grass and reeds.

C—Some of the natives of South Africa like to perch their little huts on stilts.

D—The Laplanders need a sturdier house than one of straw and reeds. So they build it of poles and mud.

Here are Eskimos hard at work building their igloos, temporary residences which they construct out of blocks of snow and ice, the only building material available in many parts of the desolate, frozen North.

kinds of buildings we have to-day. It is the Law of Growth and Change.

Nothing in this world comes into being just of its own accord. Everything has undergone a long process of development, with centuries of growth and change behind it—the rocks, the trees, the animals, and you and I. Houses are no exception to the rule, for by the Law of Growth and Change men can make the new only out of what has gone before. Just as the ocean liner has evolved from some primitive canoe of long ago, so a modern hotel with its great restaurants and ballrooms and story upon story of bedrooms had its far-off beginning in that little hut in Mesopotamia. Everything that we shall have to say will be by way of tracing the growth that has led to such an amazing climax.

Until quite recently, the greatest builders in the world have all been busy, in the main, in doing just what you and I did with our bricks on the floor. That is, they have been finding new or safer or more beautiful ways

In some parts of Russia the nomadic tribesmen cover the frames of their houses with leather. The strange home above has been built in this way. The Eskimos, too, build cone-shaped skin tents for summer residences.

of putting one brick on top of another and seeing that it stayed there. Sometimes their bricks were made of wood, sometimes of tile or stone, and sometimes even of ice, as in the frozen north. But they were always bricks of some kind or other—and they always had a stubborn way of falling down again almost as soon as they were built up.

If people had lost heart as easily as you and I did, we should still all be living in caves! But luckily there are always men who will not let themselves be beaten—no matter how long and hard the task may be. We have those men to thank that we can live in beautiful, warm homes to-day, without worrying as to whether the roof will tumble in.

When men first began to feel the need of buildings that should be more lasting and more beautiful, they had at hand the three types of dwelling we have mentioned upon which they could experiment and improve—the cave, the hut, and the tent. You will hardly be surprised to learn that the growths resulting from those three seeds are quite startling in variety—as different, for example as a pagoda, a rock-hewn temple, and a house.

The cave was of course much safer than the hut or the tent, though a good deal less comfortable; so when men no longer lived in caves they still used them for the burial of their dead and as temples for their gods. Do you remember how Abraham, when Sarah died, bought—for what was then a large sum—a cave in which to bury her and all the other

To find the buildings that sprang from the early herdsman's tent we must go very far from home—to India and China and Japan. We are by no means sure that they came about in this way; but if you will look at a picture of a pagoda you will have no trouble in seeing why certain writers, at least, have believed that the dainty storied tower is nothing but a series of tents, piled one upon another. The pagodas that are

THE TENT STILL REMAINS THE HOME OF THE WANDERING ARAB

Wandering over the desert, the Arab pitches his tent wherever he happens to be, and rolls it up again when he is ready to continue on his journey. Castles and palaces, villas and bungalows may house the rest of mankind, but he still lives in a structure that is similar in appearance to the first one his forefathers took shelter in.

members of his family when they should die? For hundreds of years men used caves as tombs and temples, and they often excavated a room as big as a church out of the solid rock.

An Egyptian Temple that was Hewn out of a Hill of Granite

So we find that at Abu Simbel (ä′boo sĭm′bĕl), in Egypt, Rameses the Great, who had so many slaves that he did not care if he worked them to death, ordered a temple ninety feet long to be carved out of a great granite hill-side. There were two large pillared halls, a sanctuary—or "holy of holies"—and eleven smaller rooms. Outside, against the front wall, four enormous figures, seventy-five feet high, were carved in the side of the cliff. All of them were portraits of the king himself. For thirty-two hundred years those images have looked out upon the mighty Nile, which in life the king had worshipped as a god.

standing to-day are none of them very old, but we may be sure that they are just like the ones of long ago, for until lately nothing changed very much in China. Her people were absorbed in the worship of their ancestors, and so they were always looking backward over their shoulders into the past instead of forward into the future.

They did not worry very much about the generations that were to come, and seldom tried to put up houses that would last. There are very few ancient buildings in China, the oldest dating only from the sixth century after the birth of Christ. But the Chinese are a people of exquisite taste, and whatever they make, even if strange to our Western eyes, is generally beautiful. Many consider Chinese art the most perfect in the world.

Though the pagodas may seem monotonous in shape, their ornament is nearly

When one looks at the little tent at the right, it hardly seems strange that certain scholars have believed that the pagoda was nothing more than one tent-like shape piled on top of another, until the builder had erected a tower like the one below.

On the right is the donjon of Osaka Castle, Japan. It is built on the pagoda principle, with a projecting roof at every floor, and each story of the structure occupying a smaller area than the one immediately below it.

At the left is a model of the Great Pagoda at Suchow, in the province of Kiangsu. It is 250 feet high, and one of the finest in China. Pagodas are built in Japan and India, as well as in China, but the most famous of all was the beautiful Porcelain Pagoda at Nanking, destroyed in 1854. It was covered with tiles of bright-coloured porcelain, and from its many angles swung hundreds of little bells that made a silvery music whenever the breeze sprang up.

Beautiful memorial gateways, like the one standing knee-deep in the water above, are common in China and Japan. Often they lead to a shrine, as does this one in Japan, and they are always full of dignity and beauty. As a rule Chinese and Japanese structures are picturesque but not imposing.

Photo, top right, by Nippon Yuson Kaisha Line

always beautiful. Often they are decorated with porcelain tiles of brilliant colour and clever workmanship; and the interiors are magnificent with carving. The building always has an odd number of stories, usually thirteen; for the Chinese believed that odd numbers were masculine and even numbers feminine, and felt that the powerful odd numbers would be more successful in keeping evil spirits away.

A Chinese Building that Seldom has More Than One Story

The "t'ing" looks still more like a tent than does the pagoda, and is the common type of building in China. It has only one story as a rule, with an elaborate roof, like an awning, supported on short columns, or piers, which are usually wooden. It is the roof that is the important thing about the building. It may be double or triple, made of brilliant tiles, decorated under its up-curved eaves with carving and brightly coloured woodwork, or along the ridges with images of dragons or other quaint animals.

Caves, tents, and huts—those were the homes of men thousands of years ago. And they are the homes of many men to-day. Their forms may vary to suit the corner of the earth where their builders live; and they may be made of anything from mud to ice —for simple men have to build with whatever lies at hand. But in many parts of the world those crudely constructed homes are still the only ones men know. For example, certain primitive people who inhabit parts of Central Africa live in caves all the year round, while others, in northern Mexico, use them only as winter dwellings; the Arab finds the tent well-suited to his needs—for he is a wanderer, and he carries his house with him; and Kaffir huts, or kraals, are still a familiar feature of the South African landscape. Even in regions where men learned to erect fine temples for worship, they still put up with mean dwellings for themselves. Still, knowledge and craftsmanship spread, and you and I are warm and comfortable to-day because of that which our forefathers worked so hard to learn many long centuries ago.

(CONTINUED ON PAGE 1089)

Through this fine gate one enters Peiping (formerly known as Peking), the capital of China. No matter where you saw it you would recognize it as Chinese. The elaborate "roof," the strange shape of the tiles, and the wealth of ornament, all show that it comes from a country where the people are fine decorators as well as good architects.

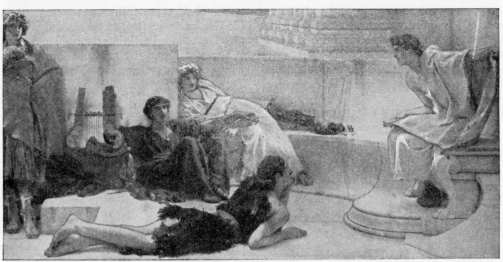

From the painting by Sir L. Alma-Tadema, R.A.

This famous painting is called "A Reading from Homer." The artist, Alma-Tadema, has shown us what it must have meant to the ancient Greeks to read their greatest poet. The reader scarcely needs to look at his scroll, and the listeners hang breathless on the living and glorious tale as it is unfolded to them.

WHICH *is the* GREATEST *of* ALL POEMS?

Long Ago Lovers of Poetry Decided That It was the "Iliad" of Homer, Most Ancient of the Epic Poets That We Know

LONG centuries ago, the legends tell us, there wandered from city to city among the Greeks of Asia Minor a minstrel, mighty in song, but poor and old and blind. His name was Homer. Some said that his name came from the Greek word meaning "hostage," and was given him because in his youth he had been a hostage among enemies; others thought the name meant "blind." At all events, he wandered from place to place, playing on his harp and chanting to the music marvellous tales of the brave days of old; and after his death he became so famous that seven different cities claimed the honour of being his birthplace.

For Homer was the greatest poet who ever recounted the lives of heroes in song, and even to-day, nearly three thousand years after his death, we still read and admire his great poems, "The Iliad" (ĭl′ĭ-ăd) and "The Odyssey" (ŏd′ĭ-sĭ).

Now, as a matter of fact, we know nothing about the author of "The Iliad" and "The Odyssey" but what we can infer from these writings, and the stories of the wandering, blind minstrel are only legends. Yet, however the great poems came to be written, they are still in existence for us to read—and that is what matters, after all.

The Siege of Troy in Song

In all probability, this is what happened. About the year 1194 B.C. invaders from Greece conquered and sacked the rich and prosperous city of Troy, in Asia Minor. The siege must have been a mighty one, for many a legend and story gathered round it, and minstrels soon began to weave them into song. There were probably a large number of these songs and stories in existence—not written down, but passed from mouth to mouth and sung by the bards around the camp fire or at the banquet. Then—we are not certain of the date—the figure we know as Homer made his appearance to make great epics out of these "lays."

An epic is a long narrative poem dealing with the feats of some great hero. Some scholars say that all Homer did to build up each of his epics was to link together the different lays or story-poems into one long story; in fact, they say it is possible that there never was such a man as Homer at all, and that the epics developed out of the lays. But others say that the style of the epics is so similar from end to end—and so magnificent—that Homer must have rewritten most of the stories in his own way.

Even so, we do not know how long a time elapsed before the poems were written down —for how long they were repeated from tongue to tongue, of course with alterations, as time went on. The first authentic written text we know of comes from about 150 B.C., when Aristarchus of Samothrace,

From city to city, if legend be true, blind Homer wandered singing for his bread. Here the artist has portrayed him with his staff in his hand and his harp strapped on his back, in the care of a youthful guide.

a poet and critic who was head of the library at Alexandria, published his editions of the text of Homer, more than a thousand years after the fall of Troy. During those long years poets might well have imagined brave heroes and lovely women, and marvels and miracles enough to alter the original story entirely.

What a story they have built up, and how marvellously Homer has told it! "The Iliad," which really has two heroes, tells of the wrath of Achilles (å-kĭl'ēz) and of the

death of Hector. When the poem opens, the Greeks are encamped before Troy, which they have been besieging for ten long years.

The war began, we are told, because the young Trojan prince, Paris, carried off to Troy the most beautiful woman in the world, Helen, wife of Menelaus (mĕn'ĕ-lā'ŭs), king of Sparta. The Greek kings came to the aid of Menelaus, determined to recapture Helen and to conquer Troy. But now Achilles, mightiest of the Greek warriors, had quarrelled violently with Agamemnon (ă g'å-mĕm'-nŏn), leader of the Greeks, over the division of the spoils of war. And Achilles sulked in his tent and would not fight.

With the mighty Achilles out of the way, the Trojans took heart, and drove the Greeks before them. Then Achilles, entreated to save the day, compromised by lending his armour and his war chariot to his friend Patroclus (på-trō'klŭs). The Trojans were deceived by the stratagem, and, thinking it was Achilles himself, fled before him. At least, all of them fled but Hector, the bravest of the princes of Troy and the most glorious of all Homer's heroes. Hector withstood the fierce onslaught of the Greek champion, and Patroclus fell.

Photo by Braun and Co.

In the Louvre, at Paris, hangs this famous picture by the painter Ingres. It is called "The Apotheosis of Homer," which means the raising of that mighty poet to receive the honours of a god. The picture is a product of the artist's imagination, but it shows clearly how highly lovers of poetry and art have ranked Homer.

Then was Achilles wroth indeed, for he had loved Patroclus dearly. He rushed forth to battle. And once more all the Trojans —except Hector—fled. But even Hector could not stand before Achilles in the fury of his vengeance, and, in the hand-to-hand struggle that followed, Hector was slain. Achilles shamefully dragged his courageous opponent's body round the walls of Troy behind his chariot. He would not even surrender it to the sorrowing Trojans to be buried until the aged King Priam himself, the father of Hector, came to his tent to plead for his dead son. Then Achilles relented, and the poem closes with a vivid account of the none

Photo by Alinari
Homer is generally depicted in his old age, when wisdom and his poetry had set the seal of greatness on him.

funeral of Hector, and of the celebrations in his honour. We are not told in "The Iliad" how the City of Troy actually fell.

"The Odyssey" is a romantic tale of what befell Odysseus (ŏ-dĭs′ūs), or Ulysses (ū-lĭs′-ēz), one of the Greek heroes, on his way home when the war was over. For ten years he wandered, while at home in the island of Ithaca his son Telemachus (tĕ-lĕm′-ā-kŭs) ruled in his stead until he at last set out in search of Odysseus. The hero's faithful wife, Penelope (pĕ-nĕl′ŏ-pē), warded off the many suitors who were sure that Odysseus must be dead. This she did by declaring that she would wed until she had finished her weaving, and by unravelling the web every night she progressed no further.

But Odysseus was by no means dead. Many marvellous adventures befell him during his ten years of wandering. He was driven by a storm to the land of the Lotophagi (lŏ-tŏf'ă-jī), or "lotus eaters"; and there his men ate of the fatal lotus and, forgetting their homes and even their very names, longed only to dream away the rest of their lives in that indolent land. Odysseus had to drag them back to the ships by force, and tie them there until he had set sail.

How Odysseus Escaped from the Land of the One-eyed Giants

On another occasion he was driven to the land of the Cyclopes (sī-klō'pēz), huge one-eyed giants who lived in caves. He and his men were captured by one of these monsters, named Polyphemus (pŏl'ĭ-fē'mŭs), and had to overcome many perils before they escaped. Finally Odysseus managed to put out the giant's single eye. Then he and his men clung to the undersides of a flock of sheep kept in the cave, and thus passed safely out, though Polyphemus felt every sheep—luckily only on their backs—to see that all was well.

Then at Circe's (sẽr'sē) island, Odysseus' comrades were turned into swine, and he narrowly escaped; and at another time it was only by lashing himself to the mast that he prevented himself from leaping into the sea, lured by the fatal singing of the Sirens (sī'rĕn). But at last the wrath of the sea god Poseidon (pŏ-sī'dŏn), whom Odysseus had offended, was appeased, and Odysseus came safely home. At first the only one who recognized him was his faithful dog, which died of joy at the coming of his master. With the slaying of the suitors of Penelope, Odysseus became again the master of his own home.

Both these long tales are told in a powerful style, vivid, straightforward and noble, which has received the admiration of the world ever since Homer's day. In the greatest period of Greece, Homer was styled simply "the poet," and his works were regarded with the utmost veneration and respect. Moralists quoted texts from them; scholars spent their lives discussing the exact words and phrases; and at a great festival held every four years both the epics were recited aloud in the open air to enthusiastic multitudes.

We have learned a great deal about the early Greeks from Homer's descriptions, and we reckon the stories of his heroes as the greatest tales in all the world. Only some of us can read the poems in the original Greek, and that is a great pity, for there is no reading that is more fascinating. But we can all read them in translation, and picture to ourselves their many beautiful scenes.

The SUPREME POETESS of the WORLD

Even if Only a Few Lines of Her Verses are Left to Us, We Can Realize that Sappho Must Have Been the Most Brilliant of All the Women Who Have Ever Written

JUST as the ancient Greeks spoke of Homer as "the poet," so they spoke of Sappho (săf'ō) as "the poetess." Even to-day, some twenty-five hundred years after her death, Sappho occupies the foremost place among the women poets of the world, and has even been regarded as the greatest poet, man or woman, who ever lived. The poet Swinburne, who translated many of the fragments of her poetry into English, said that, judging from the fragments—which are all that has come down to us from her pen—he agreed with the Greeks "in thinking Sappho to be beyond all question and comparison the very greatest poet that ever lived."

Who was this writer of wondrous poetry, and when and where did she live? Alas, for centuries people have been asking similar questions, and no one has been able to answer

Her draperies and her dark hair blowing in the wind, Sappho sits brooding on the Leucadian Rock, in the Ionian Isles. And from her musings will be born poems of matchless beauty which will entrance the world for all time. There is an old and romantic legend that it was from this rock that the famous poetess hurled herself when Phaon scorned her love; but there is only the evidence of tradition that she ever was in love with Phaon or died in this way. Her life remains a mystery and will probably do so for ever.

Photo by Berlin Photographic Co.

From the painting by Sir L. Alma-Tadema, R.A.

At Lesbos, it is said, Sappho established a school where women might learn to write songs and to sing them. In this picture the artist has imagined the poetess singing to her pupils one of her own matchless songs. How the listeners hang upon those golden sounds, which they know they can never emulate, try as they may!

them with any degree of certainty. We know scarcely anything about the "female Homer," but there are certain traditions that help to make up a picture.

Sappho was born long ago, in the dawn of Greek civilization, about 600 B.C. She probably came of a noble family. Tradition says she was born in the Isle of Lesbos (lĕz′bŏs), at either Mytilene (mĭt′ĭ-lē′nē), the chief city of Lesbos, or Eresus.

Her father, probably a wealthy wine-merchant, is supposed to have died when Sappho was very young. Of her mother we know little more than that her name was probably the same as that of Sappho's only daughter, Cleïs (klā′ĕs). Of her brothers we have a little more information, but even that is scanty, and we do not know whether there were two or three of them. One is said to have been a cupbearer to the high officials of Mytilene.

Sappho's Love for Phaon

Many and varied are the tales that have grown up about the illustrious Lesbian herself. Her friends, her lovers, her marriage, her husband, her children—of these we know practically nothing definite, but are told a great deal. The most famous of all these stories is the one that tells of the beautiful youth Phaon (fā′ŏn), whom Sappho is said to have loved in vain. He is supposed to have spurned her love. His neglect broke her heart, so she leaped to her death from the Leucadian (lū-kā′dĭ-ǎn) Rock, which overhangs the sea. This story is probably quite imaginary, but countless lovers have believed it, and many poets have celebrated it in verse.

Even Sappho's poems we know only by broken fragments. Until 1898, indeed, we possessed only the extracts quoted in odd passages by other writers, or inscribed on vases. In that year several more fragments were unearthed from the sands of Egypt, but they remain merely fragments, and there are less than two hundred of them in all. Sappho is supposed to have written many volumes—songs of love and friendship, odes and marriage songs, drinking songs, epigrams, elegies, even puzzles and riddles in verse. How tragic that the fragments which remain are so brief and rare!

Yet "though few, they are roses." Poets who have learned to read them with understanding in their original Greek have despaired of recapturing their intensity and exquisite simplicity in any other language.

The MOST MAJESTIC of All DRAMATISTS

That Title Must be Accorded to Aeschylus, Earliest of the Supreme Trio of Greek Tragic Authors

ONCE, when Aeschylus (ēs'kĭ-lŭs) was a boy—so the legend goes—he was sent into the vineyard to see that no one should steal any of the ripening grapes. He fell asleep and, while he slept, Dionysus (dī'ō-nī'sŭs), god of wine and merriment, appeared to him in a dream and bade him write a tragedy. He did so, and then wrote another, and another, until he had composed about ninety tragedies, and had become one of the greatest dramatists who ever lived.

It was naturally Dionysus, rather than any of the other gods, about whom the young Greek dreamed. For this occurred at his birthplace, Eleusis (ė-lū'sĭs), near Athens, where ceremonies in honour of the god were held yearly. At this time, not so many years after 525 B.C., when Aeschylus was born, Greek plays were still only an item of the ceremonies connected with the worship of Dionysus, as they had been from the first. They were really more like what we call pageants than like plays, being composed of solemn dances, a chorus intoning chants, and included no acting at all as we, to-day, understand the term.

The artist here shows us the youthful Aeschylus reading aloud from one of his earlier plays. Little could he or his listener dream that people living in undiscovered lands and speaking unknown tongues would still be enthralled by the noble grandeur and beauty of those plays twenty-four centuries after his death!

Aeschylus has been called the "father of Greek drama," as well as the greatest Greek dramatist or writer of plays, because he did so much towards making these religious pageants like real plays. But we must not suppose that they were anything like the plays of Shakespeare or Bernard Shaw. Imagine yourself in a great outdoor theatre, rather like a modern athletic stadium. There is no curtain, no changing scenery, on the stage. There is a chorus, of old men or maidens or peasants, perhaps, who chant and move rhythmically to and fro across the stage. The actors are masked, and wear long flowing robes to give them height and dignity. If the play is a tragedy —as were all of Aeschylus's plays—there is an air of religious solemnity about it. It is almost as much like modern opera as it is like a play.

The story deals with some familiar legend, which all the thousands in the audience know by heart. Of the seven plays by Aeschylus which we now possess entire, the most famous deals with Prometheus (prŏ-mē'thūs) and Orestes (ŏ-rĕs'tēz), son of the great Agamemnon (ăg'ȧ-mĕm'nŏn), who had led the Greeks against Troy. The story of Orestes is told in a series of three plays, called a "trilogy" (trĭl'ŏ-jĭ). Aeschylus also wrote a trilogy on the subject of Prometheus, although we possess only the second play, "Prometheus Bound."

Prometheus was the friend of man, and stole fire from heaven to give it to mankind. As a punishment for that act Zeus (zūs), the father of the gods, chained him to a rock and sent a vulture to devour his liver. In the third play, "Prometheus Unbound," the great rebel was freed from his punishment. This story of Prometheus, with his splendid courage and defiance, has been a favourite ever since Aeschylus's day, and many modern poets, among them Shelley, in his "Prometheus Unbound," have adopted this ancient story as their theme.

So interested were the Athenians in tragedy that it was their custom to hold each year, at the festival of Dionysus, a contest in which each poet would enter a group of tragedies. Aeschylus presented his first play when he was twenty-five, and he was more than forty when he won the first prize. After that he must have competed at least every other year; he won the first prize about twelve times.

There is a story that when, in 468 B.C., the younger dramatist, Sophocles (sŏf'ŏ-klēz), supplanted him in the first position, Aeschylus left Athens in disgust and went to live in Syracuse. He certainly did leave for Sicily, where he spent the rest of his life at the court of a friendly ruler; but he seems to have entered the Athenian contests subsequent to his departure from Athens, and it is very unlikely that he grudged Sophocles

Photo by Anderson

This sculptured head of Aeschylus portrays well the noble dignity which characterized his life and is manifested in all his plays.

his prize to the extent that ancient literary gossip would imply.

Although he spent his last years in Syracuse, no one could have been a better Athenian than Aeschylus. As if it were not enough to make his city glorious by his splendid poetry, he moved as well in the midst of her public life. He came of the old nobility of Athens, a fact in which he took great pride.

He was proud of his own record as a soldier. He fought at the great Battle of Marathon, when the Greeks saved Europe from the Persians, and both he and his brother were counted among the heroes of that day. He fought at the Battle of Salamis (săl'ȧ-mĭs), too, and told the story of it in a magnificent burst of patriotic poetry, which occurs in his drama, "The Persians." Indeed, when he died the epitaph he had written for himself mentioned nothing of his plays, but only spoke of his "noble prowess," of which "the grove of Marathon can speak, or the long-haired Persian who knows it well."

Perhaps he was too modest to mention the plays. Yet it is for them that we remember him. Even in translation we can feel their noble poetry, and those who can read them in the original Greek enjoy an experience of the sublime. They are sad plays, for we always know from the first that the heroes and heroines are doomed.

Aeschylus died in 456 B.C. According to an old story, he was sitting in the field one day when an eagle, flying overhead, mistook his bald head for a stone and dropped on it a tortoise it was carrying. The eagle wanted to crack the tortoise's shell in order to secure the meat inside, and its error brought death to the most majestic of all dramatists.

(CONTINUED ON PAGE 1145)

Our FINGERS and Our FIGURES

This is the Story of the Ways of Counting, and of the Marvellous Machines that Add, Divide, Multiply and Subtract, Sort the Different Coins, and Total Up the Day's Takings

NUMBERS are alike all over the world —even more alike than the fingers on which so many people count them. If you were in China and wanted half a dozen eggs, you might not know how to ask for them; but you could point to the eggs and hold up five fingers of one hand and one finger of the other. You would get your six eggs. And the same thing would happen in Mexico or Madagascar or anywhere else. The names of the numbers would all be different, but the numbers for which they stand are the same all over the world. So by using your fingers you could usually make yourself understood.

The early people learned to count on their fingers just as children often do to-day. Even now we may see the natives in Africa counting first on one hand and then on the other. Of course, they do not go very high, but they can count as far as is necessary. They have little to buy or sell, no rent to pay and no money to bank; so they are not in need of higher mathematics. If they want

Late again! But lateness would not appear to matter very much, as the teaching at this school could not have been of a high standard. Most of the pupils would probably have found it well beyond their intelligence to understand what is described in this story of figures and their uses, and in their efforts to add, subtract and multiply would most likely have made free use of their fingers for counting, and even then not been correct.

to remember numbers they make a few notches on a stick or scratches on a stone. That is all the book-keeping they do.

When people had learned how to write, they soon found a way of putting down numbers. At first they just made some kind of simple mark—/// for three and ///// for five. But they could not write any very large numbers in that fashion. So the earliest writers that we know, the Egyptians, invented a special mark for ten —it was like a U turned upside down. They could make plain marks up to nine, but then they would start all over again. ∩ was ten, /∩ was eleven, //∩ was twelve, ///∩∩∩ was thirty-three, and ////∩∩∩ (was fifty-///∩∩) seven.

These were all such simple signs that any Egyptian could read them and keep his accounts, even though he could not read and write the language that he spoke.

But not all the old peoples used such an easy method. The Babylonians had a more difficult way of writing numbers. Here is a number in Babylonian style:

▼▼ ⪦ ▼▼

Can you tell what number this represents?

It looks like six arrow-heads pointing different ways, because the Babylonians wrote by making wedge-shaped marks in soft clay. The number here is 142, and this is how to count it: 60 + 60 (the first two big arrow-heads) + 10 + 10 (the two little arrow-

heads) + 1 + 1 (the last two big arrow-heads) = 142. The same big arrow-heads stand for sixty or for one, according to their position at the beginning or end of the number.

The Babylonians used to count by sixties instead of by hundreds, just as we count our minutes and seconds on the clock. In fact, we got our sixty seconds and our sixty minutes from their way of counting.

Apart from Babylonian sixties and Egyptian hundreds there have been—and still are—many other ways of counting. Some tribes have counted by fives, because we have five fingers on each hand; some by twos, because we have two hands and two feet, two eyes and two ears; and some, like the Eskimos, by twenties, because we have ten fingers and the same number of toes. But most Europeans have always counted by tens, like the Egyptians, because of the ten fingers on the two hands.

Thus the Greeks, who learned from the Egyptians and Phoenicians, took ten for their basic number; but instead of mere marks for one, two, three, and other numbers, they used letters from their alphabet. The Greek word for "five" began with the letter p, or π, and the letter stood for "five." The word for "ten" began with d, or δ, and that sign stood for "ten." And so on for all the other numbers, with combinations as they grew larger. This was rather a clumsy method,

A PICTURE THAT MEANS "MILLIONS OF YEARS"

Men have always felt that numbers held something of the world's mystery. Pythagoras, the Greek philosopher, made a religion out of them. Plato and many other thinkers have spoken of God and creation as the One and the Many. There have always been sacred numbers, such as three and seven. Even more mystery lies in "infinity," which is vastness beyond numbers. Something of this sacred mystery is expressed in the beautiful hieroglyph above, which comes from an Egyptian tomb dating from about 500 B.C. The meaning of the picture is "millions of years."

and it was exceedingly difficult to do arithmetic in Greek.

The Romans used a few plain marks together with a few letters, and made up a system that was a good deal easier. For one, two, and three they used plain marks. For five they used a V, which seems at first to have been the picture of a hand, and for ten they used two of these, one of them upside down below the other, like this:

V

Λ

In time this sign became an X. For fifty they employed L, for a hundred C, for five hundred D, and for a thousand M. With these few signs they could write their numbers.

They never used more than three straight marks together—I, II, III for one, two, and three. Four was IV, or one from five, and nine was IX, or one from ten. So XC was ninety, or ten from a hundred. The Romans wrote "ten from a hundred" for ninety just as we say "a quarter to twelve" for "forty - five minutes after eleven."

Did you ever try to add and subtract in Roman numerals? It looks hard until you try it, but it is not nearly as hard as it looks. This is probably the way in which a Roman schoolboy would have done it:

X	VII	=	17
XX	IV	=	24
LXXX	VIII	=	88
XXX	III	=	33

| C | LX | II | = | 162 |

(Carry C) (Carry XX)

The boy separated the units from the tens just as we do. Then he added up—maybe

on his fingers—and "carried over" just in our way. In this sum he carried XX (twenty) over from the units, and C (a hundred) from the tens. He could do this very quickly.

Counting by Roman numerals was better than the older ways of counting, and the method remained in use for nearly two thousand years. As late as the end of the Middle Ages most scholars still added and subtracted in the signs that had come down from ancient Rome.

Yet long before that time there were far better numerals—those we are still using to-day. And these came from the Arabs. But the Arabic numerals did not by any means replace the Roman ones all at once. In fact, they took several centuries to do so, and meanwhile the two systems lived on side by side, with one slowly dying out and the other slowly gaining ground. For when men have learned to count in one way, it is hard to get them to use any other. If we suddenly discovered now that the Chinese had a better system of counting than we have, do you suppose we should adopt it to-morrow? By no means. In fact, we are still refusing to adopt the French method of measuring and weighing—the "metric system"—though everybody knows it is better than our own.

HIEROGLYPHIC HIERATIC		PHOENICIAN SYRIAC		ENGLISH
I	?.?.l.)	I	/	1
II	4.4	II	ſ′	2
III	44	III	Π	3
IIII	ᴄ⁴ᵞᵞ	\III	ſſ	4
IIIII	₃.ꞁ	IIIII	≥	5
∩	ƅᴧᴧ	↗	ʒ	10
I∩	ıᴧ	ſ⁻ʃ	ʒ	11
∩∩	ᴈ	⊙ȝ.ᴈ.ᴈ	⊙	20
ꝯ	ꝯ	ᴈ.Pl.)o|ɴ	ᴛ|	100

This table gives some of the ingenious ways in which men have written numbers. Of the two systems at the left, both Egyptian, the hieratic gave many hints to the Phoenicians and Syrians. But none of them looks much like the English system—or rather the Arabic, if we are to give the credit to the people who introduced it into Europe.

The Arabs' Gift to Europe

So, although the first manuscript in Europe with Arabic numerals dates from the year 976, the teachers of arithmetic were still explaining the Arabic system very carefully as late as 1500, because for so long people had been used to Roman figures. But finally the Europeans took to the counting system

1017

which the Arabs, or Moors, had brought with them when they came over from Africa and conquered Spain. And once their numerals were fully adopted, the Roman numerals were completely abandoned—although they still appear on the faces of many clocks and watches, in inscriptions on some churches, in the chapter numbers of certain books, and in a few other places.

These numerals were not really invented by the Arabs. They came from the Hindus in India, who were skilled in mathematics as long ago as the year 200. The numerals as the Hindus wrote them look a good deal like those we write to-day. They taught these numerals to the Arabs, and the Arabs passed them on to us.

We are all so used to the decimal system that we often feel it is the only natural way of counting—by tens. But in the older days of Europe there were other ways. For instance, the old Franks liked to count by twenties. Whenever they passed twenty they made a mark, or a score, and that is why we still call twenty a "score." So "three score years and ten" are three twenties plus ten, or seventy. And the French to-day say "four twenties" instead of "eighty," and "four twenties ten" for "ninety."

But twenty is too many to be convenient, and ten is very much better. It is by no means the best unit, however; and in fact our decimal system, good as it is, remains inconvenient. For twelve would be the best unit to use, and a duodecimal (dū′ō-děs′ĭ-măl) system — reckoning by twelves—would be a great improvement on the decimal one. The reason is that ten can be divided only by two numbers, two and five, while twelve can be divided by four—two, three, four, and six. So we could count and keep books

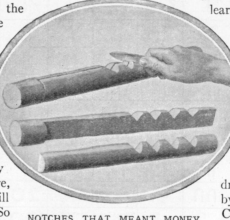

NOTCHES THAT MEANT MONEY.
Tallies like this were much used during the Middle Ages to record debts. Every notch meant a certain amount of money. When the notches had been made, debtor and creditor would split the stick into two parts, each taking one. If they disagreed over the amount of the debt, they could put the two parts together and see if they "tallied."

a good deal better if we reckoned by twelves instead of tens.

The mathematicians have known this for a long time, but what chance is there of persuading people to change? It would be ten times harder than it was to get them to adopt the Arabic numerals. And yet we all use the system to a certain extent. Eggs are reckoned in dozens; and nearly all commercial stocks are counted by the dozen or by the gross—which is twelve dozen.

When people have once learned how to count, they soon require to know more. They need to add and subtract, multiply and divide, and do still other things with numbers. In this way arithmetic was born, and it is not surprising to learn that it is a very old science. Of course people used arithmetic a great deal before any book was ever written about it. But a book of arithmetic was written in Greece by the famous mathematician Euclid (ū′klĭd), about twenty-three hundred years ago, and another by the great astronomer Claudius Ptolemy (tŏl′ē-mĭ) in the second century after Christ. By this time scholars could do very difficult problems in arithmetic.

And by then they had also advanced much farther than arithmetic. The whole science of mathematics is based on simple counting, but as man progresses he finds out a great many kinds of things to count and a great many different ways of counting them. For instance, he learns to count angles, triangles, squares, cubes, and other figures—because he must be able to do these things if he is going to survey his land, to build pyramids, and to do many other things. And, as soon as he begins counting and measuring such things, he is beginning the study of the science known as geometry.

The ancient Egyptians learned much geometry. It is often said that they had to do so; for the Nile overflowed every year and washed out all their boundaries, so in order to mark the boundaries off again they had to know something about angles and other figures. However that may be, we know

that the great Euclid in Greece learned all he could from the Egyptians and with what he added himself became the most famous man of all time in geometry. He placed on record nearly all there is to know about the subject; and to this day boys and girls who are studying geometry often say that they are learning "Euclid."

On the left is a set of "Napier's bones," in handy cylindrical form. In the lower corner to the right is a set in the original form, arranged for multiplying 765,479—the number across the top—by 6.

Children often learn to do simple sums with the help of an arrangement of sliding beads like that above. Did you know that the contrivance had a dignified name, "abacus" (ăb'á-kŭs), and was really the first adding machine? It is still in everyday use in many Eastern countries.

What is Algebra?

As the science of counting progressed, in due time algebra was invented. It was a very important invention. We have seen how convenient it is to write down figures, instead of letters of the alphabet, for our numbers. But in algebra we have found a short cut in counting by reversing the process—and we actually use letters in the place of figures. Sometimes, when a large number has to be repeated many times, we just call it a for short; and if there are several

such numbers, we call them a, b, c, and so on. Sometimes when we do not know what a number is, we simply call it x until we can find out. Until then it is an "unknown quantity"; and if we have several of these, we can call them x, y, z, and so on. The business of algebra is to find out what x is; and the answer can then be translated into simple figures.

For instance, suppose you had 81 pennies and wanted to divide them with your brother so that you would have twice as many as he has. Let x be the number of pennies that he will receive; then $2x$, or twice that number, will be the number you keep. So $x + 2x = 81$, which is to say that $3x = 81$. Now divide 81 by 3, and you find that $x = 27$. Then $2x = 54$. So you would hand over to your brother 27 pennies and keep 54 for yourself.

The expression "$x + 2x = 81$" is an equation, with 81 for the known quantity and x for the unknown one. The whole of algebra is based on the system of equations. This one is very simple, but sometimes they are long enough to cover a whole blackboard, and hard enough to take days or weeks to solve.

Algebra was studied for centuries by the Egyptians, Greeks, Romans, Arabs, and other peoples, but it was not really perfected in its present form until the time of Descartes (dā-kärt´), a Frenchman who died in 1650. We take its name from a treatise on it written in Arabic about eleven hundred years ago, and called *Al-jebr*, which means "the reunion of parts."

If you are good at algebra, you might test your ability at the following problem: A column of soldiers one mile long advances one mile. Just as the column starts, a courier leaves the rear, goes to the front, and returns to the rear, arriving there just as the column stops. How far has the courier walked?

There are still higher ways of counting than by algebra. There is trigonometry (trĭg´ŏ-nŏm´ĕ-trĭ), which also has come down to us from the Egyptians, and which goes beyond the ordinary diagrams of geometry into complicated formulas. It is useful to men in steering boats and making maps, and for numerous other purposes. There is analytical geometry, which is the study of complicated curves — useful to engineers and scientific workers. And there is the calculus, or the study of quantities that are always varying. B e s i d e s these there are many other great

branches of mathematics—so many that the most brilliant man, working on them all his life, can hardly master them all. And that is what has arisen from the earliest methods of counting.

All of these ingenious inventions we owe to the thousands of men who have worked at them, both before the days of Euclid and Ptolemy and ever since that time. One of them was the great Descartes, who gave us analytical geometry in 1637. Others were Leibnitz (līb´nĭts) and Sir Isaac Newton, who both invented the calculus about the same time—around 1686. Then there were Johann Kepler, Blaise Pascal and John Napier, in the same century. Among the great mathematicians of our own day is Albert Einstein (īn´stīn). For after all these centuries it has been left to Einstein to make some new discoveries of great importance in mathematics. No one but a highly trained mathematician can possibly understand them, but for him they seem to be as important as the law of gravitation. We had always thought the law of gravitation one of our most definite pieces of knowledge, but Einstein appears to have found a little fault in it to

Once Darius the Great had to leave some of his Ionian allies to guard a floating bridge in his absence; and this is what he said to them: "Men of Ionia, keep this thong and do as I shall say: so soon as ye shall have seen me go forward against the Scythians, from that time begin and untie a knot each day; and if within this time I am not here, and ye find that the days marked by knots have passed by, then sail away to your own land."

be corrected. For this and other mathematical discoveries he is one of the most famous men in the world to-day. He is our greatest "counter"—what a difference from the Eskimo, doing sums by the aid of his toes and fingers!

A Machine That Does Our Counting

Machines have been invented to do many remarkable things, so it is not surprising that there is one for counting. We can add and subtract, multiply and divide, by pressing keys and pulling levers— and we can do it faster than by our own calculation, with less chance of error.

It was Blaise Pascal who made an adding machine as long ago as 1642. Since that time the machine has been greatly improved and its scope increased, but the principle remains the same. For it is founded on solid numbers, and these do not change.

How an Adding Machine is Made

If we take a little wheel and divide it into ten parts, we shall have the beginning of an adding machine. Suppose we start with number 1 at the top of the wheel. Now if we turn the wheel three parts round we shall have number 4 on top, $1+3=4$. If we turn it three parts more, we shall have 7. So we can get up to ten with one wheel.

If we have a larger number, we need only put several other wheels alongside the first wheel. When the first wheel turns all the way round—up to ten—it will make the second wheel turn one part, or one-tenth. It "carries over" one to the next wheel, just as we carry over one from the units column to the tens column in adding. In the same way the second wheel can "carry over" into the third, which represents the hundreds column; the third into the fourth, or thou-

Photo by Remington Typewriter Co. Ltd.
This remarkable accounting machine can do the entire work of a book-keeper at a much greater speed and with perfect accuracy.

sands column, and so on. Some of the machines write it all down, with the sum, just like a typewriter. There are big machines to-day that are worked by electricity and add as many as seventeen columns.

Of course, if they can add they can multiply too, for multiplying is only repeated adding. So 7×4 is only $7+7+7+7$, or 28. And 472×3 is only $2+2+2$ and $70+70+70$ and $400+400+400$, or 1416.

Any adding machine will show that this is so, as it is the method in which it does its work. It can subtract, too, and also divide.

In 1617 a Scotsman, Napier, invented his multiplying rods. The different multiplication tables were printed on sticks of wood in such a way as to show the product of any numbers at a glance. But the numbers had to be written down by hand, and therefore "Napier's bones," as his wooden sticks were called, were less useful and accurate than Pascal's machine.

Since that day there have been many varieties of adding machines, though they are built upon the same idea. Only since 1892 have they been printing the figures and their total. Such machines are found in every bank and every big office, where they save the book-keepers a great deal of time and trouble.

A Machine With a Wonderful Brain

The modern adding machine is a development of the typewriter. The type-printed letter was so superior to the hand-written letter and effected such a great saving of labour that it was only natural inventors should seek to apply the principle of typing letters to the task of writing up ledgers. What had to be discovered was a means whereby typed figures could be made to add themselves within the mechanism of the machine at the actual time of typewriting.

This difficulty was solved when a totalizer first made its appearance. This totalizer is simply a mechanism, enclosed in a metal case, which adds or subtracts according to the will of the operator of the machine. By means of this adding mechanism the typewriter could now be used, not only to print the details of figure work, but to add or subtract the resulting figures as required without any further operation being necessary. An invoice could be typewritten and the total of its money column would be added and credits subtracted at the same time.

Further improvements followed quickly. Not only could several columns be added vertically, but the totals of each of these columns could be added together in a cross or horizontal totalizer, which would be totalling the amounts in the different vertical columns, thus:

1	3	6	1	2	6	8	4	9 = 10 10 9
1	4	6	2	3	6	2	3	3 = 5 11 3
2	2	6	1	3	6	1	1	6 = 4 7 6

4 10 6   4 9 6   11 9 6 = 20 9 6

Still further, by the addition of a clever device known as "front feeding," it is now possible to print these figures on several documents in one operation. Front feeding means the placing of all the documents that are to be typed into the machine from the front of the typewriter cylinder instead of the usual method of inserting such papers or documents from the back. Thus a ledger can be typed, added and proved, and the customer's statement of his account and an auditor's copy can be produced at the same time. In fact, this wonderful machine accomplishes in one operation five important functions necessary in accounting. It will:

Post a customer's ledger, keeping it in balance.

Write up a customer's statement of account, keeping it in balance ready to send out at the end of the month, or at any time desired.

Provide a day-book in condensed form of all entries posted to the various ledger accounts. This day-book is also used for auditing purposes.

Prove with machine accuracy all debit and credit postings.

Furnish a daily trial balance.

In short, not only can the machine carry out any form of accounting originally done by pen and ink, but it can do it with far greater speed, with mechanical accuracy, and with machine neatness.

Another wonderful machine is the cash register, which is designed to give shopkeepers every possible protection for their money and vital information about their businesses, which they could not obtain otherwise. Even though the owner of a shop is absent part or all of the time, by using this machine he can know every detail of every transaction that occurs there. This is because, before the cash-drawer of this machine will open, the person operating it must, by pressing certain keys, make a complete record of the transaction he or she is carrying out.

When the necessary keys have been pressed, the register will display the record on both sides. In the illustration it will be seen that Assistant "A" has made a cash sale for 3/5. This double announcement of the details makes the customer—and anyone else in sight of the register—an inspector of the transaction. At the same moment as the amount, etc., appears, the cash drawer is thrown open and the register prints two complete records of the transaction; one on a roll

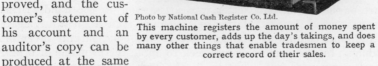

Photo by National Cash Register Co. Ltd.
This machine registers the amount of money spent by every customer, adds up the day's takings, and does many other things that enable tradesmen to keep a correct record of their sales.

of paper inside the machine, and the other either on a ticket, which it immediately ejects from the upper slot, or on a sales bill which must be placed in the lower slot for that purpose.

By this means both the shopkeeper and the customer are supplied with a printed record of the transaction, and at the end of the day or week, on pressing a few keys, the shop-keeper or someone authorized by him can get a detailed, printed account of all business done, that is, the amount of cash business, credit business, accounts paid and money paid out.

By referring to the paper roll inside the register he can find out who was responsible for any individual trans-action. The register will also tell the number of each class of transaction, including those which did not concern an actual sale (if coins or notes are changed as favours, for instance), the totals of purchases of more than one item being given separately. When sales of more than one item are made, the register will add the prices of the items and print them, with their total, on the ticket which it then issues.

It is obvious that human weaknesses such as forgetfulness, carelessness, mistakes and temptation can have little scope in a shop where the cash register is in use.

In no class of work has greater necessity arisen for economy of time and labour than in the actual handling of large sums of money. The very nature of the work calls for the exercise of the utmost accuracy, which means

that it can be given only to responsible people, and the time of such people, in practically every instance, could be much better and more profitably occupied than in

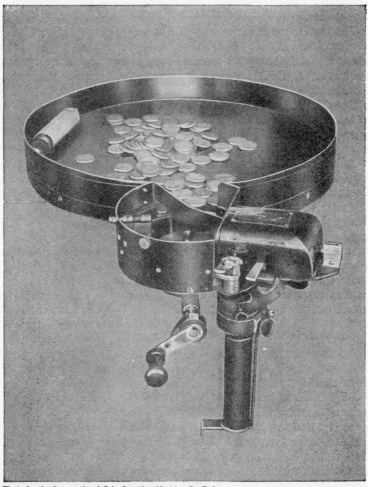

Photo by the International Coin Counting Machine Co. Ltd.

Coins can be sorted and counted by this machine in very quick time. This model is worked by hand, but there are other types that are operated by electricity.

sorting and counting money, which of course is only routine, although responsible, work.

This problem has been satisfactorily solved by the invention of a remarkable coin counting machine which counts and sorts coins in the minimum time, with absolute accuracy, and without any fear whatever of mistakes occurring. Several different models of this ingenious machine have been produced. In one of the power models, which is mounted on a mahogany cabinet fitted with an electric motor, the coins to be counted are carried from the table by a travelling belt into a container from which they are picked up by a disk, one at a time, and passed through the registering mechanism.

The total value of the coins passed through the machine is recorded on a dial in pounds and fractions of pounds. A small control lever, which, when moved, instantly arrests the action of the machine, enables the operator to stop the machine for each £5 counted, while a bell indicator can be set to give notice to the operator enabling him to work the control lever on the exact amount.

This machine counts and records the totals of coins of the four denominations, 6d., 1/-, 2/- and 2/6. It also automatically separates the coins, and puts them into bags if required. It can also be used for counting and separating pennies and halfpennies. No thought or attention is required in connection with the counting. Five pounds of mixed silver can be counted and bagged up by the machine in less than twenty seconds, and a single count can always be relied upon.

Another Machine That Counts Coins

Another interesting and very efficient machine, which is made in models for operation by electric motor, treadle, or hand, totals the number of coins or tokens passing through, but only one denomination of coins or kind of token can be counted at a time. The machine is designed to deal with coins of two or more denominations, the coins being previously sorted in a box sorter and separate counts made for each denomination.

The coins to be counted are carried under the counting mechanism; openings in a horizontal rotating disk receive the coins, one at a time, of the denomination to be counted. An indicator which is provided shows the total number of coins which have passed, and a simple device automatically stops the machine when the required number of coins has been counted. For example, when set the machine will count 60 pennies (5/-) and stop automatically after each 60 has passed through the mechanism.

If required, coins can be piled up automatically in paper tubes by using the coin packeting attachment. The packets are made by rolling paper round a wooden spindle, a carton being formed by folding down the projecting end. This packet is then automatically filled with the number of coins required. An experienced operator can fill five packets of 60 pennies or halfpennies each in one minute, as the machine will give a continuous count of 60,000 coins per hour. Bags can be substituted for the coin packeting attachment if desired.

The Marvellous Slide Rule

The most remarkable of all the devices for calculating is not a machine, but just a simple rule. It is called the "slide rule." It has several different scales printed on it, and a little wooden bar that slides to and fro in it. With this we can not only multiply and divide, but we can calculate compound interest and do problems in arithmetical progression.

The first slide rule was built by Robert Bissaker in 1654, although attempts had been made as early as 1620 to build a workable rule on the same principles. Since then it has been improved in various ways and adapted to many uses, and is now of considerable help to engineers, scientists and accountants.

Why We Must Learn Arithmetic

If we have machines to do all these things for us, why do we work so hard to learn arithmetic? Why not let the machines do it all? Well, because we could never work the machines unless we understood figures ourselves. But, above all, it is far more important to have a good head than to have the best machine ever known. Once we use our brains we can set the machine to work when we like, but without man's brains there would never have been any machines at all. The study of mathematics has not yet been completed, for there are still all kinds of discoveries to be made—by the Euclids and the Einsteins of the future. There is still plenty to be learnt about the great science of "counting."